WORLD WAR II SITES
IN THE UNITED STATES
A Tour Guide & Directory

WORLD WAR II SITES IN THE UNITED STATES
A Tour Guide & Directory

by Richard E. Osborne

Riebel-Roque Publishing Co.

Library of Congress Catalog Number 91-68129

ISBN 0-9628324-1-3

Date of Publication: April 1996
Third Printing: 2007
Pulished and printed in the U S A

Book design and production by **SM**Design.

ORDERING ADDITIONAL COPIES OF THIS BOOK
Additional copies of this book may be ordered from:

Riebel-Roque Publishing Co.
6027 Castlebar Circle
Indianapolis, IN 46220

Price per book	$19.95
Postage & Handling (1 book only)	2.25
Postage & Handling (Ea. Addl. book)	1.00
Indiana residents please add $1.00 sales tax.	

Riebel-Roque Publishing Co.
6027 Castlebar Circle
Indianapolis, Indiana 46220

CONTENTS BY STATES

SPECIAL NOTE

Museums, memorials, monuments, homes, warships and other sites that are open to the public and welcome visitors are highlighted by a tint bar behind the first line of text.

ALABAMA

Alabama was a part of the "Old South" when WW II started. It had strict racial segregation, areas of severe poverty, lingering popular resentment against "Yankees", 43 "dry" counties out of 67 and a one-party political system based on the conservative wing of the Democrat Party. Alabama politics had produced a clique of long-serving Senators and Representatives in Congress who had become well-entrenched and held several important Congressional positions.

The state produced lumber, paper, cotton seed oil and meal, grain, potatoes, peanuts, hay, tobacco, livestock, sugar cane, pipes and fittings, coke-oven products, cement, chemicals and electric power. A large aluminum plant was built at Mobile just before the war and in 1940 a second large aluminum plant was built at Sheffield. These plants made the state a major supplier of that metal. In 1944 oil was discovered at Gilbertown.

Alabama emerged from the war with renewed prosperity and with a strong economy that lasted well into the postwar years.

ALICEVILLE is in the west-central part of state near Mississippi border.

ALICEVILLE PRISONER OF WAR CAMP was a main prisoner of war camp built near Aliceville in late 1942 and held approximately 6000 Axis prisoners. This was one of the largest prisoner of war camps in the SE part of the U.S. The POWs, most of them from Rommel's Afrika Korps, were held in 6 separate enclosures. After the war the camp's buildings and land were sold at auction to the city and private individuals.

ANNISTON is about 60 miles east of Birmingham off I-20. Kilby Steel Co. at Anniston produced 90 mm and 105 mm shells.

ANNISTON ARMY DEPOT was one of the nation's largest depots. Opened in Oct. 1941, the depot received and stored Army ordnance materials in numerous igloos and issued the material to 7 southeastern states and several overseas locations. The Anniston site was chosen because it was considered relatively safe from enemy attacks. Peak employment during the war was 7780 people. The depot remained active for decades. Location; 9 mile west of Anniston on Hwy 202.

COOSA RIVER ORDNANCE PLANT, near Anniston, was built in 1940-41 as one of several bag-loading plants being built in the country at that time. The plant loaded gun powder into bags used by the Army's and Navy's largest guns.

FORT McCLELLAN, 6 mi. north on US 431 and SR 21, was established by the Army as Camp McClellan in July 1917. As World War II approached the 27th Infantry Division (the former New York State National Guard) was in training here. The base was expanded rapidly by the Army to train additional soldiers in large numbers. McClellan had several artillery ranges and its own airfield, the Henry J. Reilly Field, 2.5 miles NE of the base. During the war some half a million U.S. soldiers trained here including a company of Japanese-Americans.

In 1943 a 3000-man prisoner of war camp was built on the Fort's property and operated until 1946. The fort had a German War Memorial Cemetery with an impressive iron cross monument marking the graves of German POWs who died here while in captivity. A bi-lingual ceremony is held at the monument each year in November, sponsored by the German Consulate in New Orleans, LA and the local German Club in Anniston. In the postwar years the fort became a center for basic training and the permanent headquarters of the Military Police.

U.S. Army Chemical Museum: This

One of many displays at the Women's Army Corps (WAC) Museum, Ft. McClellan, AL.

museum is on the grounds of Ft. McClellan and houses some 4000 artifacts tracing the history of chemical and flame warfare in the U.S. Army since the establishment of the first gas and flame regiment during World War I. Address: Ft. McClellan, AL 36205-5000. Phone: 205/848-3355. Hours: M-F 9-3, Sat. & Sun. by appointment. Free.

U.S. Army Military Police Corps Museum: This museum, on the grounds of Fort McClellan, surveys the role and history of the Army's "MP's" since their inception during WW II. Address: Ft. McClellan, AL 36205-5000. Phone: 205/848-3522/3050. Hours: M-F 8-4, Sat. & Sun. by appointment; closed major holidays. Free.

Women's Army Corps (WAC) Museum: This is the third museum on the grounds of Ft. McClellan. It tells the story of women in the U.S. Army since the creation of the Women's Army Auxiliary Corps (WAAC's) in 1942 until it was discontinued in 1978. The Pallas Athene Garden is a part of the museum. Pallas Athene is the insignia of the Women's Army Corps. Address: Ft. McClellan, AL 36205-5000. Phone: 205/848-3512. Hours: M-F 8-4, Sat. & Sun. by appointment. Free. Location: To see the museum, enter at the Galloway Gate, the fourth gate northbound on SR 21.

AUBURN/OPELIKA AREA: These are twin cities 55 miles NE of Montgomery on I-85.

OPELIKA PRISONER OF WAR CAMP: This was a large main POW camp holding about 3000 prisoners on the outskirts of Opelika.

BIRMINGHAM is in the north-central part of state and was Alabama's largest city. The Pullman Standard Car Mfg. Co., in nearby Bessemer, produced 500 lb bombs, Conners Steel Co. made 75 mm high explosive shells, Stockham Pipe Fittings Co. made 75 mm high explosive shells and a variety of bombs and grenades, U.S. Pipe and Foundry Co. manufactured 105 mm high explosive shells and forgings for 155 mm shells and National Iron & Pipe Co. made 155mm high explosive shells.

BIRMINGHAM ARMY AIR BASE was, before the war, Birmingham Municipal Airport. When the U.S. went to war the War Department leased the airport for $1.00 a year and it became Birmingham Army Air Base. The Air Services Technical Command and Air Transport Command used the airport throughout the war. There was an air freight terminal here and a large aircraft modification facility. In 1948 the airport was returned to the city.

SOUTHERN MUSEUM OF FLIGHT, just east of the Birmingham Municipal Airport, displays aircraft and memorabilia from the earliest days of aviation to the present. There are WW II airplanes, uniforms, photos, models and other artifacts on display. Address: 4343 73rd St. North, Birmingham, AL 35206. Phone: 205/833-8226. Hours: Tues.-Sat. 9:30-5, Sun. 1-5, closed Mon. Admission charged.

COURTLAND is 20 miles west of Decatur.

COURTLAND ARMY AIR FIELD, 1.5 miles SW of town, was occupied by the AAF's Eastern Flying Training Command, and used as a pilot training field for the 70,000 Pilot Training Program. When the program ended, the AAF departed. Courtland AAF had one auxiliary field, Anniston Aux. Airfield 15 miles SW of Estaboga.

DOTHAN is in the SE corner of the state.

NAPIER FIELD, 7.5 miles NW of town, was established in mid-1941 by the Eastern Flying Training Command for the 30,000 Pilot Training Program. It eventually had four auxiliary fields and offered advanced and specialized pilot training in single engine aircraft. Later in the war pilots of the Mexican Air Force and other Latin American countries were trained here in P-40 fighter planes. Napier Field's auxiliary air fields were:

- Aux. #1 Wicksburg Airport, 2 miles NW of Wicksburg
- Aux. #2 Dothan Municipal Airport, 2.5 miles NW of Dothan
- Aux. #3 Headland Airport, 2 miles NE of Headland
- Aux. #6 Ozark Army Air Field, Ozark (See below).

FLORENCE/SHEFFIELD AREA is in the NW corner of the state on the Tennessee River along a portion of the river known as Muscle Shoals. There were several chemical and metal refining companies here. When the German saboteurs, who landed by submarine in Florida and New York in June 1942, were apprehended, they had plans in their possession to sabotage some of these installations.

FOLEY is 30 miles SE of Mobile on US 98.

U.S. NAVAL AUXILIARY AIR STATION, FOLEY, three miles ENE of Foley, was a local pre-war airport. It was taken over by the Navy early in the war and used as an auxiliary air field to NAS, Chevalier at Pensacola, FL. After the war the air field was returned to its civilian owners.

GADSDEN is 60 miles NE of Birmingham. The Lansdowne Steel and Iron Co. here produced 105 mm artillery.

CAMP SIBERT, 7 miles west of Gadsden near the town of Attalla, was built in 1943 to be a replacement training center for soldiers of the Army's Chemical Corps. At its height, Camp Sibert had about 1500 buildings, a large POW camp and housed thousands of people.

HUNTSVILLE is in the north-central part of the state. Much of America's early postwar space program was developed in Huntsville and the community became known as the birthplace of the American space program. NASA's space program was headed by Dr. Wernher von Braun who had been in charge of Nazi Germany's rocket program during World War II. In downtown Huntsville a large civic center is named after Dr. von Braun.

REDSTONE ARSENAL/HUNTSVILLE ARSENAL were two large plants built in Huntsville by the Federal Government in 1941 across the road from each other. Huntsville Arsenal manufactured poison gas, mortar and howitzer shells and the Redstone Ordnance Plant, as it was first known, assembled those shells to an explosive charge making them into a completed artillery round. In 1943 Redstone Ordnance Plant was redesignated Redstone Arsenal. When the war ended chemical weapons from other locations around the country were transferred here. In 1949 Huntsville Arsenal was deactivated and its assets turned over to Redstone Arsenal. In 1950 Dr. Wernher von Braun and his team of 100 European and American scientist moved here from Ft. Bliss, TX to head America's rapidly expanding rocket program. Other government agencies followed, including NASA and for several decades the Arsenal and NASA's George C. Marshall Space Flight Center were among America's most important space facilities.

THE SPACE & ROCKET CENTER: This is an indoor/outdoor museum displaying one of the world's largest collection of rockets and space hardware. Included in the displays are models of the German V-1 "Buzzbomb" rocket and V-2 high-altitude rocket, both of which were used against British and western European cities in the closing months of World War II. Address: One Tranquility Base, Huntsville, AL 35807. Phone: 205/837-3400, 800/633-7280, 800/572-7234 (inside Alabama). Hours: Memorial Day-Labor Day daily 8-7; rest of year 9-6, closed Dec. 25. Admission charged. Location: West of Huntsville just off I-565.

MOBILE is in the SW part of state on Mobile Bay. Mobile's shipyards built, modified and repaired hundreds of ships. Two of the larger shipyards at the time were McPhillips Manufacturing Co. which built tankers; Alabama Dry Dock & Shipbuilding Co. which built cargo ships and tankers and Gralf Shipbuilding Co. at Chickesaw, a northern suburb of Mobile, which built cargo ships, destroyers and mine sweepers.

BATES FIELD, 10 miles west of the city, was a small sub-base of Brookley Field.

BROOKLEY FIELD was an AAF air field just south of the city built around a small municipal airport that had been donated to the Army Air Corps. Construction of the base began in late 1939 and proceeded slowly, but after the US entered the war the base was rushed to completion in Jan. 1942. Brookley had the Mobile Air Depot (also called the Southeast Air Depot), which was a control depot, and a maintenance center operated by the Air Technical Services Command. The Depot served the needs of the AAF in the SE US and the Caribbean. The Air Transport Command also operated from the field.

USS ALABAMA BATTLESHIP MEMORIAL PARK: This is a 100-acre waterfront open-air park displaying several permanently-anchored warships of WW II. The main attraction is the battleship "USS Alabama" which is preserved as it was when in service during WW II. Other warships on display are the cruiser "USS Mobile", the destroyer "USS Evans" and the submarine "USS Drum". All are veterans of World War II and are open to the public. Address: Battleship Parkway, Mobile AL 36601. Phone: 334/433-2703. Hours: daily 8 am to sunset, closed Dec. 25. Admission charged to tour ships. Location: 1.5 miles east of downtown Mobile on I-10 at Battleship Parkway exit.

FORT MORGAN, at the entrance to Mobile Bay on Mobile Point, was built in 1840. In 1927 the fort was converted into a park, but in 1941 it was reactivated as a military installation. The Army, Navy and Coast Guard made various uses of the fort. Army artillery pieces were put in place to protect the harbor entrance, and Coast Guard patrols operated out of the fort using Jeeps and horses to cover the area's beaches. After the war the fort was again made into a park. There is a gift shop and a small museum in the fort. Address: Rt. 1, Box 3540 Hwy. 180, Gulf Shores, AL 36542. Phone: 334/540-7125. Hours: Fort is open 8-dusk and museum is open daily 9-5, closed Thanksgiving, Dec. 25 and Jan. 1. Admission charged.

MONTGOMERY, the capital of Alabama, is in the south-central part of the state. During World War II the AAF established an air depot at 1420 N. Court St. near downtown.

ALABAMA WAR MEMORIAL, located at the corner of Jackson and Monroe Sts., commemorates citizens of Alabama who have served in America's wars. A Hall of Honor recognizes citizens of the state who have won the Congressional Medal of Honor. Phone: 334/262-6638. Hours: M-F 8-4:30, closed holidays. Free.

GUNTER FIELD, five miles NE of Montgomery, was originally Montgomery Municipal Airport. In Oct. 1940 the Army Air Corps opened a training facility here called the Army Air Corps Basic Flying School. In early 1941 the Air Corps took over the field completely and named it Gunter Field in honor of William A. Gunter, a former mayor of Montgomery.

The big guns of the Battleship "Alabama".

For the duration of the war the base was used to train U.S. and Allied pilots in basic flight training. In Sept. 1945 flying activity stopped and the field experienced a period of limited activity. In 1948 the US Air Force acquired the field and named it Gunter Air Force Base. In 1957 flying resumed at the base and Gunter became a part of the Cold War's NORAD operations. By 1971 flying activity had again diminished and the Air Force relinquished the air field and much of the acreage to the city of Montgomery. Gunter AFB remained a relatively small base doing primarily administrative work. During WW II Gunter Field's auxiliary air fields were:

- Aux. #1 McLemore Auxiliary Field (Taylor), 10 miles east of Montgomery
- Aux. #2 Elmore Airport, 10 miles north of Montgomery at Elmore
- Aux. #4 Mt. Meigs Airport, 5 miles SE of Mt. Meigs
- Aux. #5 Taylor Auxiliary Field, 10 miles SE of Montgomery
- Aux. #6 Dannelly Airport, 7 miles SW of Montgomery
- Aux. #7 Deatsville Airport, 9 miles west of Deatsville

US Air Force Enlisted Heritage Hall: This is a small museum on the grounds of Maxwell AFB annex paying tribute to the enlisted men and women of U.S. military aviation. There are displays on enlisted men's uniforms and artifacts, a WW II Sperry Ball Turret and a rare B-32 top turret. Address: Building 1210, Gunter AFB, AL 36114. Phone: 334/416-3202. Hours: M-F 8 to 4, closed holidays. Free.

MAXWELL FIELD, just west of downtown Montgomery, was located on the site of a flying school established in 1910 by Orville Wright. In 1922 it was named Maxwell Field and in 1931 the Air Corps moved its prestigious post-graduate school, The Tactical School, here from Langley Field, VA. This was a school for selected officers who were taught the latest in air tactics and other subjects, including Air Corps doctrine, in preparation for staff work. During the 1920s and 1930s Maxwell became a showplace for the Air Corps and headquarters for the Eastern Flying Training Command. In 1940 the Tactical School moved to Orlando, FL. but Maxwell remained the headquarters for the Air Corps' heavier-than-air flying schools and a basic training field for pilots. In 1941 Maxwell became an AAF Reception Center and during the war thousands of U.S. pilots trained here as did airmen from several Allied nations. The field also had a large regional AAF hospital. In late 1944, because of its long runways, the base was chosen as one of the few air fields in the country to train B-29 crews. In late 1945 the AAF established its own finance school here and in 1946 the several academic units were combined and designated Air University. All major flying activities ended. In 1948 the US Air Force took over the base, renamed it Maxwell Air Force Base and made into one of the Air Force's principle centers for professional military education. Maxwell Field had one auxiliary air field, Troy Municipal Airport, 4.5 miles north of Troy, AL.

Maxwell Air Force Base Museum: This museum is on the grounds of Maxwell AFB, and has aircraft, artifacts and other displays for public viewing as well as for the interests of the students attending the Air University. Address: Chennault Circle, Maxwell AFB, AL 36112. Phone: 334/293-2017. Hours: daily 7-6. Free.

OZARK is in the SE corner of the state.

OZARK ARMY AIR FIELD, 12 miles SW of town, was Ozark's local airport. It was taken over by the AAF and operated as a sub-base for Key Field, Meridian, MS and as auxiliary field #6 for Napier Field. It served as an operational and a replacement training field. After the war it was returned to the community.

FORT RUCKER was an Army infantry training center built in 1942. Four infantry divisions trained here during the war; the 81st, 35th, 98th and 66th. The Fort had a major prisoner of war compound holding about 1700 POWs. Fort Rucker was closed in 1946, but reactivated during the Korean War and eventually became the center for the U.S. Army's

Aviation School and the "home" of Army aviation.

U.S. Army Aviation Museum: This museum is on the grounds of Fort Rucker at the corner of Andrews Av. and Novosel St. The museum traces the history of Army aviation, especially light planes and helicopters, from their beginnings to the present. The museum has one of the largest collections of helicopters in the world including a rare R4-B, the first U.S. military production helicopter. "Piper Cub" airplanes are also a main attractions at the museum. Address: PO Box 610, Ft. Rucker, AL 36362. Phone: 334/255-4507. Hours: daily 9-4, close Jan. 1, Thanksgiving, Dec. 24-25 & 31. Free.

SELMA is 40 miles west of Montgomery.

CRAIG FIELD five miles SE of Selma, was built in 1941 for the AAF. Its mission was that of pre-flight, specialized and advanced pilot training for fighter pilots. Several French units were trained here. The facility survived for several years after the war as Craig Air Force Base but was eventually closed. Craig Field's auxiliary fields were:

- Aux. #1 Selfield Airport, 4 miles east of Selma
- Aux. #2 Furniss Auxiliary Field, 10 miles SW of Selma
- Aux. #3 Henderson Aux. Field, 1.5 miles north of Miller's Ferry
- Aux. #4 Mollette Auxiliary Field, 10 miles SE of Orrville
- Aux. #5 Autaugaville Airport, 20 miles east of Selma

SYLACAUG is 40 miles SE of Birmingham.

ALABAMA ORDNANCE WORKS was built in 1941-42 and run by E. I. DuPont de Nemours Co. to make TNT, DNT, Tetryl, Oleum, Diphenylamine and cannon powder. In 1943 the plant had extra steam capacity so it was one of three plants in the country selected to make heavy water as a back-up supplier to the Manhattan (atomic bomb) Project. The plant remained active throughout the Cold War and came to be known as the Alabama Ammunition Plant. It closed in the 1990s

TUSCALOOSA is 50 miles SW of Birmingham. In May 1939 a civilian-owned flying school at

Tuscaloosa's city airport became one of the first in the country contracted by the Air Crops to give Army cadets primary pilot training under civilian instructors.

NORTHINGTON GENERAL HOSPITAL was built by the Federal Government in Tuscaloosa in 1943 to treat Army war wounded. It specialized in neurology, plastic surgery, ophthalmologic surgery, neurosurgery and psychiatry. In Apr. 1946 the 2100-bed facility was turned over to the city of Tuscaloosa.

TUSKEGEE is 40 miles east of Montgomery.

TUSKEGEE ARMY AIR FIELD: In 1939 Congress, as part of the 30,000 Pilot Training Program, authorized the Civil Aeronautics Administration (CAA) to designate one or more air fields in the U.S. for the training of negro pilots for the military. The Tuskegee Municipal Airport, 7 miles NW of town, was chosen due to its proximity to Tuskegee Institute and because a civilian flying school already existed at there. The airport was taken over by the CAA and the Army contracted with the flying school to train the pilots. Tuskegee Army Airfield trained negro pilots in single and twin engine aircraft, and remained the principal training field for negro pilots throughout the war.

The pilots who trained here have become known as the "Tuskegee Airmen" of WW II. Several books have been written about these unique pilots and displays on the "Tuskegee Airmen" can be found in several museums across the country. Tuskegee Army Air Field's auxiliary fields were:

- Aux. #1 Griel Auxiliary Field, 3 miles SW of Tallassee
- Aux. #2 Shorter Airport, 2 miles NE of Shorter

TUSKEGEE INSTITUTE FIELD #2, four miles SE of town, was Tuskegee Institute's own air field. A civilian flying school existed here before the war and it was contracted by the U.S. Government to give primary flight training to Army pilots.

ARIZONA

Arizona had been a state for only 29 years when the United States entered World War II. She came into the Union in 1912 as the 48th state. Her nickname, "The Apache State", reflected her recent past as a true part of the old west. Memories of frontier days were still vivid in the minds of many old timers.

The 1940 census counted 499,261 people in the state of which 57,000 were Indians and 37,000 Mexicans.

With its sparse population, wide open spaces and mild and dry climate, Arizona was vacuum waiting to be filled … and the U.S. Government filled it generously during the war. Military installations, war plants, internment camps, bombing ranges, airfields, people and money poured into Arizona in a brief span of 5 years.

Arizona's mineral wealth had already been tapped. She produced half of the country's copper ore and significant amounts of other ores; gold, lead, molybdenum, silver and zinc. And, soon after the ware ended Arizona began producing uranium ore.

In Dec. 1941 and early 1942 the scare of a Japanese invasion of the west coast spilled over into Arizona. Arizonans and the military, saw the possibility of the Japanese invading northern Mexico, driving inland and then north into southern Arizona. Because of this, the southern half of the state was declared a part of the west coast security zone from which a handful of ethnic Japanese were required to relocate.

Arizona emerged from the war with an increase in industry, agriculture and population that would have otherwise taken decades to achieve.

CALIFORNIA/ARIZONA MANEUVER AREA (CAMA) (DESERT TRAINING CENTER): See description of this huge military area under the same heading in the California section. The following camps and airfields were a part of CAMA in western Arizona.

CAMP BOUSE, about 100 miles west of Phoenix, was located in Butler Valley 20 miles east of the small town of Bouse. The site was selected for its remote location to train the 9th Tank Group (Medium) (Special). Tanks of this unit, which were out-of-date M-3 Grants, were equipped with a top secret device called "Canal Defense Light" (CDL). It was a British-designed light system which produced a very brilliant beam of light that flashed 6 times per second in different colors. When used in a night attack and shined on the enemy, the light disrupted the vision of the enemy soldiers sufficiently so that they couldn't see anything but the light itself, thereby making it virtually impossible for them to fire their weapons with any accuracy. In combat about 15 CDL-equipped tanks, lined abreast, would attack with infantrymen following close behind.

Operations at Camp Bouse began in Aug. 1943. There were several homesteaders in Butler Valley who were asked to move away temporarily but refused. When training began, all of it at night, they had second thoughts and

moved.

British officers worked with the 9th Tank Group because the Americans and British planned to introduce this secret device onto the battlefield at the same time.

The 9th Tank Group trained here until April 1944 and eventually went to Europe. The CDL tactic was used in combat for the first time in late Dec. 1944 during the Battle of the Bulge with good results. It was used several times thereafter and was found to be especially useful for river crossings.

After the 9th Tank Group left Camp Bouse, it was closed. Concrete foundations, old streets, sidewalks and the camp's dump, which has been well-gleaned by souvenir hunters, remain.

CAMP HORN was 45 miles west of Gila Bend at the Horn water stop on the Southern Pacific Railroad. Horn was not a town, just a water tank and a sign saying "Horn". There were two area residents, both old men who lived as hermits guarding inactive gold mines. Here at Horn was built one of the six division-sized camps of CAMA. During June & July 1943 the 81st Infantry Division moved in from Ft. Rucker, AL where they had undergone basic training. The day the trains arrived with the majority of the division it was 126 degrees F. The 81st trained here until Nov. 1943, but by that time there was no more need for desert-trained Infantry units so the division was shipped to California and Hawaii and retrained in amphibious landing operations and later served in the Pacific.

Today there is a stone pyramidal monument at the former main gate of the camp commemorating 7 men who died here during training.

CAMP HYDER, 35 miles west of Gila Bend, just SW of the small town of Hyder, was another of the division-sized tent camps of CAMA. The 77th and 104th Infantry Divisions trained here, one after the other from April 1943 to Feb. 1944.

The 77th Division was used as somewhat of a "guinea pig" unit for the testing of desert clothing and the physiological stress limits of soldiers operating in a desert.

Most of the camp area is now farm land, but several foundations remain and some of the streets can be made out. At Agua Caliente, a nearby ghost town and the site of some natural hot springs, there is a hot water swimming pool built by engineers of the 77th.

CAMP LAGUNA in the SW corner of Arizona is 20 miles NE of Yuma on the site of the Army's Yuma Proving Ground. During the war the 3rd, 6th and 9th Armored Divisions trained here as well as the 79th Infantry Div. The Colorado River was used by engineers to test newly designed river-related equipment such as pontoon bridges.

Italian POWs worked in the area and built a small but elaborate structure shaped like a castle in which they stored paint. The paint castle remained for many years.

COOLIDGE, 45 miles SE of Phoenix, was a very small town.

COOLIDGE ARMY AIR FIELD, 6 miles SE of town, was established by the Air Transport

Command as an air ferrying station. The Navy also used the field for ferrying under its Naval Air Ferry Command.

DATELAN, 60 miles east of Yuma, was a very small farming community.

DATELAN ARMY AIR FIELD, four miles west of the community of Aztec, was used to train B-25 bomber crews. The field was a subbase of Yuma AAF and after the war was acquired by the US Air Force and used well into the 1950s as a training facility. I-8 runs thru the old camp site, and at the Datelan Exit, numerous foundations can be viewed on either side of the road.

DOUGLAS is a border town in the SE corner of the state.

DOUGLAS ARMY AIR FIELD, 8.5 miles NW of Douglas, was the town's local airport. It was taken over by the AAF for use as a training field for the 70,000 Pilot Training Program. The field offered specialized night-training in B-25 and B-26 bombers. Chinese pilots and crews also trained here in single and twin engine aircraft. The air field was returned to the community after the war. Douglas AAF's auxiliary fields were:

- Aux. #1, McNeal Airport, 6.5 miles SW of McNeal
- Aux. #2, Forrest Airport, 2 miles SE of Douglas
- Aux. #3, Webb Airport, 4 miles NE of Webb
- Aux. #5, Hereford Airport, 1.5 miles NW of Hereford

FLAGSTAFF is the largest city in northern Arizona.

NAVAJO ORDNANCE DEPOT was built on Navajo Indian land 12 miles west of Flagstaff and south of highways 66 and 89. The facility was activated on July 1, 1942. Many Navajos worked on the construction of the plant and in its operation during the war. The depot received, stored and shipped ammunition and general supplies. In 1943 the Army built a hospital on the grounds of the plant primarily for its civilian workers. There was a small prisoner of war camp here and the POWs worked at the depot and locally.

The depot functioned well into the postwar years and eventually came under the control of the Arizona National Guard. In the 1990s the facility was closed.

FLORENCE, 45 miles SE of Phoenix, was a very small community.

FLORENCE PRISONER OF WAR CAMP was located just north of Florence and held over 9000 prisoners, mostly Germans and Italians. Many of the POWs worked in local agriculture picking cotton and maintaining irrigation ditches. In their spare time they built a swimming pool for themselves. Later in the war the camp was used to house ardent and troublesome Nazis removed from other POW camps. After Italy's surrender in Sept. 1943 the camp became a refuge for Italian POWs also transferred from other camps to get them away from the angry German POWs. No trace of the camp remains. The site, which is on the west side of U.S. 80/89 north, was occupied by a

Troops of the 1st all-negro infantry division, the 93rd, in training at Ft. Huachuca.

water treatment plant, an Immigration and Naturalization Service Processing Center for illegal aliens, an Army National Guard post and a mobile home park.

GILA BEND/AJO AREA: Gila Bend is 50 miles SW of Phoenix, and Ajo is 35 miles south of Gila Bend. Between these two small ranching communities lay a huge wasteland that the Army's Western Flying Training Command took to create one of the largest bombing and gunnery ranges in the country.

AJO ARMY AIR FIELD, 6 miles north of Ajo, served the Ajo-Gila Bend B. & G. Range. It was a subbase to Luke Field and some advanced pilot training was done here in single engine aircraft. Auxiliary fields were:
- Luke Landing Field #1, 12 miles NW of Ajo
- Luke Landing Field #2, 16 miles north of Ajo
- Luke Landing Field #3, 20.5 miles north of Ajo

AJO-GILA BEND BOMBING AND GUNNERY RANGE, later know as Luke Air Force Bombing and Gunnery Range, was created during the war as a huge practice range for air crews in training at Luke and Williams Fields. The range remained in use throughout the Cold War and stretched for 125 mile along the south side of I-8 from a point 25 miles east of Gila Bend to the outskirts of Yuma.

GILA BEND ARMY AIR FIELD, four miles south of Gila Bend, was built during the war as a subbase to Luke Field and was used throughout the Cold War. WW II Auxiliary fields were:
- Luke Landing Field #4, 13 miles SW of Gila Bend
- Luke Landing Field #5, 15.5 miles SW of Gila Bend
- Luke Landing Field #6, 8 miles SW of Gila Bend

HEREFORD, 20 miles SE of Ft. Huachuca, had a sizeable prisoner of war camp just west of town holding mostly Italian POWs.

FORT HUACHUCA, 23 miles SW of Tombstone in the SE corner of Arizona, is an old Army fort with a long history associated with the early days of Arizona. In 1942 the newly formed 93rd Infantry Division, the 1st all-Negro combat unit, trained here, and soon afterwards the 92nd Infantry Division, also all-Negro, staged here before departing for Europe.

In 1947 part of Fort Huachuca was turned

over to the Arizona National Guard and the remainder became a wildlife sanctuary. In 1950, during the Korean War, the U.S. Army returned and used the fort to train Army engineers. After the Korean War Fort Huachuca was closed, but reopened again in 1954 to become the U.S. Army's Electronic Proving Ground. In the postwar years the fort became the home of several Army commands and a National Historic Site.

Charleston, AZ: This was a ghost town 12 miles NE of Fort Huachuca on the San Pedro River at the time of WW II. The Army used it to train infantrymen from Ft. Huachuca in house-to-house fighting. In the process most of the remaining buildings, which were made of adobe, were reduced to rubble. The ruins remain and can be visited. Park at the San Petro River bridge on the Fort Huachuca-Tombstone road and walk 1.5 miles north along the river. Watch for rattlesnakes.

Fort Huachuca Museum: This fine museum is on the grounds of Fort Huachuca and tells the history of the fort including its role in WW II. Address: PO Box 766, Fort Huachuca, AZ 85613-6000. Phone: 602/533-5736. Hours: 9-4 M-F, 1-4 weekends. Location: A two-building complex on the corner of Boyd and Grierson Sts. Free.

KINGMAN is in the NW corner of the state and was unincorporated.

KINGMAN ARMY AIR FIELD, 8.5 miles NE of Kingman (on SR 66, formerly US 66), was built as a training fields for the 70,000 Pilot Training Program. The air field had a gunnery school and a bombing and gunnery range 20 miles to the south. The field was retained after the war and used to store and dispose of surplus aircraft. After that the air field became Kingman's local airport and an industrial park. The old control tower and several of the WW II hangars remained in use. Kingman's auxiliary fields were:
- Aux. #1 Cyclopic Airport, 9 miles SE of Cyclopic
- Aux. #3 Hackberry Airport, 7 miles NW of Hackberry
- Aux. #5 Topock Airport, 3 miles east of Topock
- Aux. #6 Lake Havasu Aux. Field, 19.5 miles south of Powell in present-day Lake Havasu City.
- Aux. #7 Signal Airport, 19 miles SW of Signal

LEUPP, 30 miles east of Flagstaff, was one of two locations in the west chosen in 1942 as sites to receive troublemakers from the Japanese Relocation Camps. The other location was Moab, Utah. Soon after the ethnic Japanese entered the relocation camps it became obvious that every camp had a number of troublemakers. The War Relocation Authority (WRA) saw the need to isolate these people from those who were cooperative. Working with the U.S. Justice Department, the two sites were chosen as "Citizens' Isolation Camps", and it was agreed that the Justice Department would run the camps. The Leupp site was chosen because it was an abandoned CCC camp which could be made quickly into a detention center with the addition of fences and guard posts.

This camp and the one at Moab soon filled to capacity, so the WRA decided to convert one entire relocation camp into an isolation camp and chose the Tule Lake camp in California. Dissidents were then moved to Tule Lake and the Leupp and Moab camps closed.

LUKEVILLE/SONOITA, MEXICO: In March 1945, near these border towns 115 miles SE of Yuma, an American fighter shot down a drifting Japanese bombing balloon. It came down on the Mexican side of the border near Sonoita. Arrangements were made with the Mexican Government and an American team went into Mexico to recover the balloon. This was the first bombing balloon discovered in Mexico.

MARANA is a small community 25 miles NW of Tucson on I-10.

MARANA ARMY AIR FIELD, 6 miles NW of Marana, was built as part of the 50,000 Pilot Training Program for basic flight training and the training of transport pilots in instrument flying and navigation. Later in the war Chinese pilots were trained here. The air field survived the war and was used into the 1990s. Marana's auxiliary fields were:
- Aux. #1 Picacho Airport, 14.5 miles NW of Marana
- Aux. #2 Rillito Airport, 7.5 miles SE of Marana
- Aux. #3 Coronado Airport, 12.5 miles north of Marana
- Aux. #4 Avra Airport, 5 miles south of Marana
- Aux. #5 Sahuaro Airport, 7 miles SW of Marana

MAYER was a very small town 50 miles north of Phoenix on SR 69.

MAYER ASSEMBLY CENTER, just NW of town, was a former CCC camp. This was the smallest of the 14 such centers established on the west coast and the only one in Arizona. It operated for less than a month, from May 7 to June 2, 1942 and never had more than 245 residents at any one time. After the ethnic Japanese had been processed the center was taken over by the Forestry Service.

OATMAN, in NW Arizona 22 miles SW of Kingman on old Highway 66, is one of many Arizona ghost towns. Oatman became a ghost town during, and mostly because of, the war. In 1942 the Federal Government declared gold mining a nonessential industry for the duration of the war and the local mines closed down. With the drafting of young men and the availability of high-paying defense jobs all over the country, the citizens of Oatman simply abandoned their town.

PHOENIX, the capital of Arizona, had 65,000 people and was the largest city in the state. The war would propel its population to over 100,000, a phenomenon typical of many cities in the west.

One of the big plants to move into the Phoenix area during the war was the Goodyear Aircraft Co. which made nonrigid airship flight decks and did aircraft modifications. The Southwest Cotton Co., another big war plant, made aircraft flight decks.

ARIZONA MILITARY MUSEUM: This museum is east of downtown Phoenix at Papago Park

Military Reservation, a facility of the Arizona National Guard. Exhibits trace the military history of Arizona from the time of the Spanish to the present, and the roles of Arizona citizens in all of our nation's armed conflicts. Address: 5636 E. McDowell Rd., Phoenix, AZ 85008-3495. Phone: 602/267-2676. Hours: 9:30-2 Tues. and Thurs., 1-4 weekends. Free.

CHAMPLIN FIGHTER MUSEUM at Falcon Field in Mesa, a SE suburb of Phoenix, is housed in two former WW II hangers and has an outstanding collection of fighter planes from WW I, WW II and the Korean War. On display are over 30 originals or authentic reproductions of the world's most famous fighter planes. All are flyable. Planes of WW II include "Pappy" Boyington's Corsair, a Supermarine Spitfire and its arch rival, the Messerschmitt Me-109, a P-40, P-47, Focke Wulf FW-190, F6F Hellcat, FM-2 Wildcat, F8F Bearcat, North American SNJ-5 and others. The museum has a large collection of memorabilia from air "Aces" of various nations including some 700 signed photographs of "Aces" from 15 countries. Many personal artifacts from well-known American "Aces" are on display. Headquartered at the museum is the American Fighter Aces Association. Address: 4636 Fighter Aces Dr., Mesa, AZ 85215. Phone: 602/830-4540. Hours: daily 10-5. Admission charged.

FALCON FIELD, 7 miles NE of Mesa, a SE suburb of Phoenix, was used during the war to train British pilots by the Southwest Airways Co., a civilian flying school, under contract with the AAF. The field became a local commercial airport, and retained the name Falcon Field.

LUKE FIELD was 11 miles west of Glendale, a western suburb of Phoenix. It was built in 1941 under the name Phoenix Air Corps Advanced Flying School, for use as a training base offering advanced flight training in P-38s for Army Air Corps pilots. In June 1941 the field was renamed Luke Field. It was enlarged several times during the war and by war's end was the largest single-engine advanced training base in the world. Later in the war Chinese pilots were trained here in P-40s. When the war ended training operations were cut back and much of the base was used to store fighter planes. It was also used as a facility where experienced fighter pilots came for additional training and updating to maintain their skills and proficiency. The U.S. Air Force took over the field in 1949 and renaming it Luke Air Force Base. In 1951, during the Korean conflict, the base was fully activated again, enlarged and made serviceable for jets. It remained an active Air Force base throughout the Cold War. Luke's WW II auxiliary fields were:

- Aux. #1 Whitman Airport, 5 miles south of Whitman
- Aux. #2 Beardsley Airport, 4 miles NW of Beardsley
- Aux. #3 Fighter Airport, 3 miles NW of Agua Fria
- Aux. #4 Wickenburg, Airport, 8 miles SW of Whitman
- Aux. #5 Buckeye Airport, 6 miles east of Palo Verde
- Aux. #6 Goodyear Airport, 5 miles north of Liberty

- Aux. #7 Hassayampa Airport, 4 miles north of Arlington

CAMP PAPAGO was a prisoner of war camp at Papago Park 8 miles east of downtown Phoenix. Before the war the park had been the site of an Arizona National Guard post and a CCC camp. In Sept. 1943 the park's facilities were converted into a prisoner of war camp for German naval personnel; one of four such camps in the country[1]. In 1944 twenty five German submariners tunneled out of the camp and escaped. This was one of the largest POW escapes in the U.S. The pictures of the escapees were published in the local Phoenix with a $25.00 reward posted for each of them. Eventually all were recaptured and returned to camp.

The POW camp was closed in April 1946 after all of the POWs had been repatriated. The grounds of the former camp were eventually used for the Phoenix Zoo, the headquarters of the Arizona National Guard and a variety of nonmilitary purposes.

THUNDERBIRD AIRPORT #1, four miles north of Glendale, a western suburb of Phoenix, was taken over by the AAF and used to train Chinese pilots. All Chinese pilots went through primary training here and were then sent on to other air fields for further training. Thunderbird Airport #1 was returned to the local community after the war. Thunderbird Airport #2, 15 miles NE of Phoenix, was not used by the military.

U.S. NAVAL AUXILIARY AIR STATION, LITCHFIELD PARK was five miles south of Litchfield Park, a western suburb of Phoenix. It was established in 1944 as an auxiliary field to NAS, Terminal Island, San Pedro, CA to accommodate naval aircraft being modified by the Goodyear Modification plant which was adjacent to the field. When the plant closed at the end of the war the air station became a long-term storage center for naval aircraft. The aircraft were stored in the open and given regular maintenance to keep them in flying condition. Some of the aircraft from here were used in the Korean War and the Berlin Airlift. In 1967 the facility closed and the remaining planes in storage shipped to Davis-Monthan AFB near Tucson.

WILLIAMS FIELD was located 25 miles SE of Phoenix sandwiched in between the Salt River Indian Reservation to the north and the Gila River Reservation to the south. The field was built by the AAF in the summer of 1941 as a part of the 30,000 Pilot Training Program to train U.S. and foreign airmen. It was first

[1]The others were Camp Beale, CA, Camp Blanding, FL and Camp McCain, MS.

named Mesa Military Airport but a few months later was renamed Higley Field and in Feb. 1942 renamed again as Williams Field. From then on it was affectionately called "Willie". Its first mission during the war was to train twin-engine bomber crews and bombardiers. This was changed in late 1943 and training in single-engine planes began. In 1944-45 its mission changed again and four-engine bomber crews were trained. In late 1945 single-engine fighter pilots were again being trained here as well as radar observers. In 1948 the base was taken over by the US Air Force and named Williams Air Force Base. Throughout the Cold War the base operated as a training facility and was closed in the 1990s. Williams' WW II auxiliary fields were:

- Aux. #1 Gilbert Airport, 5 miles NW of Chandler
- Aux. #2 Rittenhouse Airport, 3 miles SE of Chandler
- Aux. #3 Coolidge Airport, 7 miles SW of Florence.
- Aux. #4 Casa Grande Airport, 6 miles NW of Casa Grande
- Aux. #5 Goodyear Airport, 5 miles east of Goodyear

POSTON was a very small town 12 miles SW of Parker.

COLORADO RIVER RELOCATION CAMP, three miles south of Poston, opened Mar. 8, 1942. This camp and the Manzanar camp in California were the first two camps built and were intended to be transient camps for the voluntary relocation program. The plan was that the two camps would receive the ethnic Japanese being evacuated from the west coast and provide them with shelter, food and assistance until they could find work and living accommodations in communities further to the east. When the voluntary program proved to be a failure, the camps was converted into more permanent facilities to house the ethnic Japanese for the duration of the war. Because of its location on an Indian reservation, this camp was administered by the Bureau of Indian Affairs (BIA) and not the War Relocation Authority (WRA) which managed all the other camps. The BIA worked closely with the WRA,

Aircraft in storage at Davis-Monthan Air Force Base. The stored aircraft can be seen easily from the public streets and roads around the perimeter of the base. The base also offers tours.

although the BIA's first interest was that of the Indians. The camp consisted of three separate compounds a few miles from each other and designed to hold 10,000, 5,000 and 5,000 evacuees respectively. This made it the largest relocation camp in the system. The complex never reached full capacity and housed 17,814 residents at its maximum residency. Most of the residents came from the Los Angeles and Stockton, CA areas. The camp operated throughout the war and closed on Nov. 8, 1945.

SACATON, about 30 miles SE of Phoenix, was a very small town.

GILA RIVER RELOCATION CAMP was located three miles west of Sacaton on land belonging to the Gila River Indian Reservation. The camp was comprised of two compounds a few miles apart and was designed to hold 15,000 people. It opened in July 1942 and operated until Nov. 1945. At its peak it held 13,348 residents.

TUCSON was the state's second largest city during the war with a population of 35,800 and grew tremendously during the war.

CORTARO, a small community 10 miles NW of Tucson, had a 900-man prisoner of war camp which was a subcamp of the Florence POW camp.

DAVIS-MONTHAN FIELD was SE of, and adjacent to, the city of Tucson. It was founded in 1925 as Davis-Monthan Landing Field, and in 1927 became Tucson Municipal Airport serving both commercial and military aircraft. By the late 1930s military traffic at the airport became so heavy that the city of Tucson built a second airport, primarily for commercial traffic, about two miles SW of Davis-Monthan. The Army Air Corps then took over the airport and renamed it Davis-Monthan Field on Dec. 3, 1941 (four days before the attack on Pearl Harbor). Soon after America's entry into the war Davis-Monthan became a training center for crews of B-24 bombers and underwent a major expansion which was completed by Jan. 1943. The base acquired a regional AAF hospital and three bombing ranges. In Dec. 1944 Davis-Monthan's runways and other facilities were expanded again and the training of B-29 bomber crews began.

After the war many B-29s and C-47s were brought to the base for storage and Davis-Monthan soon had the largest collection of these two planes in the country.

In 1948 the US Air Force acquired the base and renamed it Davis-Monthan Air Force Base. During the Korean War many of the base's B-29s and C-47s were used again. When peace returned, so did the B-29s, C-47s and many other planes, and Davis-Monthan again became a major aircraft storage center. For most of the Cold War years Davis-Monthan was one of the AAF's largest storage and maintenance facilities. The stored planes can easily be seen from the roads and streets around the perimeter of the base. The base also offers tours upon request.

PIMA AIR MUSEUM, just south of Davis-Monthan AFB, has the largest collection of vintage aircraft in the west. Many of the planes on display are from WW II and from both Allied and Axis nations. A 20,000 square foot indoor museum, called "Hanger Number One"

The Pima Air Museum, Tucson, AZ has the largest collection of vintage aircraft in the west.

holds the more fragile items such as fabric-covered aircraft. A restored two-story army barracks is on the grounds and it too houses exhibits. The Arizona Aviation Hall of Fame is in yet another building and pays tribute to famous Arizona citizens associated with aviation. Among those honored is the late Senator Barry Goldwater who was a pilot during the war in the China-Burma-India theater. The Hall of Fame has a sizeable research library.

The 390th Memorial Museum, a museum within a museum, is also on the grounds and commemorates the activities of the 390th Bombardment Group of WW II. Inside this museum is a restored B-17 and many items relating to the personnel and activities of the Group. Address of the Pima Air Museum: 6000 E. Valencia, Tucson, AZ 85706. Phone: 602/574-0462. Hours: daily 9-5, doors close at 4 pm. Admission charged. Location: From I-10 eastbound exit at Valencia. From I-10 westbound exit at Wilmot Rd. Follow signs to the museum.

TUCSON MUNICIPAL AIRPORT, now Tucson International Airport 6 miles south of town, was built in 1940 to be a commercial airport after military activities at the city's original airport, Davis-Monthan Field, increased substantially and forced the need for a separate commercial airport. The Tucson Municipal Airport was no sooner built when the war started and military operations began here too. The brand-new airport was expanded and improved for military needs. The Consolidated-Vultee Aircraft Corp. built three large hangers here in which they modified B-24 bombers, and the AAF's Air Transport Command operated an air terminal here. The field was also used in the AAF's ferrying system. Commercial airlines continued to use the field throughout the war, and after the war the military operations pulled out and the airport reverted to commercial use.

WILLCOX BOMBING RANGE: Driving along I-10 just west of the town of Willcox one will see a broad expanse of alkali flats on the south side of the road. This is the Willcox Bombing Range established during WW II for the use of bomber crews and fighter pilots in training at Davis-Monthan Field.

WINDSLOW, is 50 miles east of Flagstaff on I-40.

WINDSLOW MUNICIPAL AIRPORT, two miles SW of town, was used by the AAF's Air Transport Command for ferrying aircraft and for the servicing and maintenance of aircraft. There was also an AAF freight terminal here. The Navy used the field for ferrying also under the Naval Air Ferry Command.

YUCCA, 18 miles south of Kingman on I-40, was a very small town.

YUCCA ARMY AIR FIELD, 1.5 miles NE of town, was a subbase of Kingman AAF and was used by both the Army and the Navy for training purposes. Yucca AAF had a 555,000-acre bombing and gunnery range which was also used by Kingman AAF. The bombing range, Yucca Bombing & Gunnery Range, had four runways, three of which served as auxiliary fields #5, #6 and #7 to Yucca AAF.

YUMA is in the SE corner of the state on the Colorado River.

YUMA ARMY AIR FIELD, 4.5 miles SE of Yuma, was built in 1928 by the Army Air Corps and known then as Fly Field. During WW II it was used as one of the training fields for the 70,000 Pilot Training Program and later as a training field for bomber crews and radar observers. In 1946 Yuma AAF was closed, but then reopened again by the US Air Force in 1951 and named Vincent Air Force Base. At various times in the postwar years the field became U.S. Marine Corps Air Station, Yuma and Yuma International Airport. Yuma AAF's auxiliary fields during WW II were:

- Yuma Aux. Field #1, 12 miles SE of Yuma
- Yuma Aux. Field #2, 15 miles SE of Yuma
- Yuma Aux. Field #3, 12 miles south of Yuma
- Yuma Aux. Field #4, 15 miles SW of Yuma
- Landing Field #1, Wellton Ground Gunnery Range, 5 miles east of Wellton
- Landing Field #2, Colfred Ground Gunnery Range, 57 miles north of Yuma
- Landing Field #3, Stoval Ground Gunnery Range, 6 miles SE of Stoval

YUMA TEST STATION, NE of town, was established by the U.S. Army in Jan. 1943 as Yuma Test Branch, a temporary test facility for research and development projects. The facility operated in that capacity throughout WW II and eventually absorbed Camp Laguna, one of the desert warfare training camps of CAMA. After the war the facility became known as Yuma Proving Ground.

ARKANSAS

At the beginning of the war Arkansas was a sparsely settled, rural, racially segregated southern state and one of the poorest in the nation. Like other southern states, Arkansas had a virtual one-party political system based on the conservative wing of the Democrat Party. This had resulted in the state's senators and representatives being returned time and again to Washington to gain powerful positions in Congress due to seniority. During the World War II the state had one young Congressman who would, in the post-war years, serve for decades and become one of the most powerful men in Washington … Wilbur Mills. The state's two wartime senators, J. William Fulbright and John L. McClellan would also have long and distinguished careers in Washington.

Arkansas produced cotton, corn, rice, potatoes, fruits, nuts, lead, coal, zinc and manganese. In the late 1930s the state was "discovered" by industry because it had cheap labor, cheap land, a central location and an anti-union atmosphere. By 1939 about 100 new factories had come to the state. A few years earlier oil had been discovered in the state and several new refineries were built. These activities gave new life to the state's economy. When the war started in Europe the importation of bauxite (aluminum ore) and cinnabar (mercury ore) diminished or were cut off altogether. Cinnabar was the most critical. Its price double almost over night. Arkansas's deposits of these two ores suddenly became very important to the U.S. economy and round-the-clock mining operations were soon underway. Because of the presents of the bauxite and natural gas a large aluminum plant was built in 1941 near Hot Springs. Later in the war a second aluminum plant was built in the state.

When the war ended Arkansas's economy suffered badly when military activity scaled down and the cheaper foreign sources of bauxite and cinnabar became available again. Other facets of the state's economy survived, however, to keep the state more prosperous than it had been before the war.

BLYTHEVILLE is in the extreme NE corner of Arkansas.

BLYTHEVILLE ARMY AIR FIELD, three miles NW of town, was activate in June 1942 as a training base for the 50,000 Pilot Training Program. Several levels of training were carried out here; basic training, advanced training, training of women transport pilots and training of troop carrier crews under the I Troop Carrier Command. In 1948, when the U.S. Air Force took it over, the name was changed to Blytheville Air Force Base. The base operated throughout the Cold War and in May 1988 the base was renamed Eaker Air Force Base after General Ira C. Eaker, the first commander of the U.S. 8th Air Force during WW II. Eaker AFB closed in 1992. Blytheville AAF had the following auxiliary air fields during WW II:

- Aux. #1 Steele Airport, 2 miles NW of Steele, MO.
- Aux. #2 Manila Airport, 1.5 miles NE of Manila
- Aux. #3 Hornersville Airport, 1.5 miles west

of Hornersville, MO.
- Aux. #4 Cooter Airport, 2 mile SE of Cooter, MO.

DERMOTT, in the SE corner of Arkansas, was the site of a 5400-man prisoner of war camp. When the camp closed, its buildings and land were sold at auction.

ELDORADO is in south-central Arkansas near the state line.

OZARK ORDNANCE WORKS, near Eldorado, was built early in the war to make ammonium nitrate, a necessary ingredient in the manufacture of munitions, especially smokeless powder. The ammonium nitrate was made from local deposits of natural gas.

FAYETTEVILLE is a county seat in the NW corner of Arkansas.

DRAKE FIELD was built by the Government during the war and used by the military services. After the war it was turned over to the local community and retained the name Drake Field.

Arkansas Air Museum: This museum, located on Drake Field, is housed in a restored all-wood WW II hanger. The museum documents the history of flying in northwestern Arkansas. Several of the planes, all of which are flyable, are from the WW II era. The museum has its own restoration shop. Address: PO Box 1911, Fayetteville, AR 72702. Phone: 501/521-4947. Hours: Daily 9:30-4:30, closed major holidays. Donations requested. Location: 4 miles south of town on U.S. 71.

FORT SMITH is in west-central Arkansas on the state line. Cargo gliders were made here the Porterfield Aircraft Co.

CAMP CHAFFEE was SE of, and adjacent to, the city limits of Fort Smith. It was activated in March 1942 as a training camp for Army armored divisions. The 6th, 14th, and 16th Armored Divisions trained here from 1941 thru 1944. Chaffee also had a prisoner of war camp holding 3000 prisoners. From 1944 to 1946 Chaffee served as a personnel center and at the end of the war became a re-deployment and separation center. The camp was deactivated in 1946, but reactivated two years later to become the home of the 5th Armored Division. In 1956 it was renamed Fort Chaffee. In 1959 it was deactivated again, but was reactivated in 1961 during the Berlin crisis and remained an active Army post until the 1990s when it was closed.

THE DARBY HOUSE, near downtown Ft. Smith, was the boyhood home of General William O. Darby, the organizer and commander of the Army's 1st Ranger Battalion, better known as "Darby's Rangers". Two rooms in the house are

open to the public. The living room is restored to appear as it did in May 1945 when, in this room, Darby's parents were informed of his death. The second room contains memorabilia and tributes to General Darby. Darby is buried in the Fort Smith National Cemetery at 522 Garland and S. 6th Sts. Address of the Darby House: 311 General Darby St., Ft. Smith, AR. 72901 Phone: 501/782-3388. Hours: M-F 8-3, Sat.-Sun. by appointment. Free.

OLD FORT MUSEUM, in downtown Fort Smith, preserves the history of the area and the town from its earliest days as an army fort. There are a number of interesting displays concerning the WW II era. One entire room of the museum is given over to honor General William O. Darby, commander of the famous "Darby's Rangers". The museum has other exhibits on WW II and on Fort Chaffee. Address: 320 Rogers Ave., Fort Smith AR 72901. Phone: 501/783-7841 and 7848. Hours: June thru Aug. M-Sat. 9-5, Sun. noon-5, rest of year M-Sat. 10-5, Sun. 1-5. Closed Jan. 1, Thanksgiving, Dec. 24-25. Admission charged.

CAMP JESSE TURNER, at Van Buren, a NE suburb of Fort Smith, was activated in 1942 to train Army railroad crews. The soldiers in training learned their skills on the area's railroads and were sometimes given instructions by professional railroaders. Camp Jesse Turner was closed in 1945.

HOPE is in the SW corner of the state on I-30.

SOUTHWESTERN PROVING GROUNDS was built near Hope in 1940-41 to proof test ordnance components such as primers, fuzes, boosters, cartridge cases, propellants, and later in the war, rockets.

HOT SPRINGS, 45 miles SW of Little Rock, is a year-around health resort with many deluxe hotels and the government has had a military hospital here since 1884. In Sept. 1944 the Hot Springs area was one of five resort areas[1] in the U.S. where the Army Service Forces leased several of the largest hotels and converted them into redistribution centers for service personnel returning for overseas. They

The **Old Fort Museum**, *Fort Smith, AR.*

were given several weeks of morale-lifting rest and relaxation before being sent to new assignments.

ARMY AND NAVY GENERAL HOSPITAL, jointly run by the two services, accommodated many wounded servicemen during WW II. The hospital specialized in general medicine, arthritis, deep x-ray therapy, radium therapy and had a training school to train WAC's as medical technicians. The hospital's first building was built in 1884 and has continued in operation through the years. The hospital served military personnel and their dependents for decades after the war.

WHITE & YELLOW DUCKS LAND/WATER SIGHTSEEING TOURS: This company uses WW II DUWKs (ducks), amphibious vehicles, to take tourist on land and water tours in and around Hot Springs. The ducks have been modified for the comfort of the passengers and are safety-approved by the Coast Guard. Address: 406 Central Av., Hot Springs, AR 71901. Phone: 501/623-1111. Hours: daily with tours generally at 9, 11, 2 and 6.

JEROME and ROHWER are two small communities in the SE corner of Arkansas 28 miles apart. Near each of these communities the government established relocation camps for the ethnic Japanese evacuated from the west coast. These camps were the eastern-most camps in the system. Each camps had a capacity of 10,000 residents and was built on flat delta land that had recently been cleared by loggers and then abandoned to the state in lieu of taxes. State officials recommended the sites to the War Relocation Authority (WRA) in the hopes that the land would be revitalized and turned into productive farmland after the war. Also, it was expected that the ethnic Japanese would raise some of their own food.

The first ethnic Japanese arrived at Rohwer on Sept. 18, 1942, when the camp was still under construction. The camp was west of, and adjacent to Rohwer. Conditions were crude but improved and the camp reached a maximum residency of 9475. Many of the residents came from the Los Angeles and Stockton, CA areas.

The first ethnic Japanese arrived at Jerome, also partially completed, on Oct. 6, 1942. The Jerome camp was adjacent to the town of Jerome and reached a population of 8497, mostly small-scale farmers from the Fresno, CA area.

The ethnic Japanese were not welcome in Arkansas, a state with a long history of segregation. The camps' residents, when out in the local communities, were usually require to use facilities, such as rest rooms, drinking fountains, etc. reserved for negroes. Japanese of college age were not welcome in Arkansas's colleges and universities because it was feared that their presents would open the doors to negroes. Local doctors refused to treat the camp residents so doctors from outside Arkansas were employed in the camps. Various church groups became active in the camps easing the lives of the residents as much as they could and frequently scolding their fellow Arkansans for failing to "love they neighbor". Not surprisingly, the Japanese worked hard at finding jobs and schooling outside of Arkansas where they would be accepted. With time,

their efforts succeeded and a sizeable number of residents were able to leave the camps and go elsewhere.

Jerome, the last camp in the system to open, was the first to close on June 30, 1944. When it closed, its population was down to 2750. Surprisingly, these residents resisted moving. They had become relatively comfortable in their quarters and even appealed directly to the Secretary of the Interior, Harold Ickes, not to close the camp.

The birthplace of General Douglas MacArthur. At the time of his birth this building, called the Tower Building, was the headquarters of Little Rock Arsenal and the living quarters for married officers. Today it is the **Arkansas Museum of Science and History** *in MacArthur Park in downtown Little Rock.*

Ickes denied their request, the camp was closed and they were transferred to other camps.

After Jerome was vacated by the Japanese it became a prisoner of war camp for German POWs.

Rohwer remained operating as a relocation camp for a year and 5 months longer, closing on Nov. 30, 1945.

After the war, the camps were closed and their buildings were torn down or sold at auction and removed to other sites. Despite their ill-treatment, some of the ethnic Japanese decided to settle in Arkansas rather than return to the west coast.

At Rohwer the camp's water system remained in use by the local community and there are two monuments, built by the camp residents, that have been preserved over the years. The Rohwer camp site is on the National Register of Historic Places. To reach the Rohwer site, take SR 1 north from McGehee 12 miles and watch for a sign marking the turnoff on a gravel road leading to the site.

LITTLE ROCK, the capital of the state, was Arkansas' largest city during the war and had a diversified economy.

ADAMS AIRPORT, four miles east of town, was used by both the Air Technical Service Command and the Air Transport Command (ATC). The field was used in the ATC's ferrying system and for pilot transition training. The ATC also had a freight terminal here, and there was a specialized depot of the San Antonio (TX) Air Technical Service Command.

THE ARKANSAS MUSEUM OF SCIENCE AND HISTORY: This museum building is the birthplace of General Douglas MacArthur. It is known as the old Tower Building and is the central structure in MacArthur Park on E. 9th St. in downtown Little Rock. The Park is the site of the former Little Rock Arsenal built in 1836 when Arkansas became a state. On Jan. 26, 1880 the wife of the Arsenal's commander and civil war hero, Captain Arthur MacArthur, gave birth to their first son, Douglas. Young Douglas was christened at nearby Christ Episcopal Church. The MacArthurs left the

Arsenal a few months later and were never posted here again. In 1892 the property and buildings were deeded to the city of Little Rock and the arsenal became a park. Through the years all of the Arsenal's buildings were torn down except for the Tower Building. In 1942 the Tower Building became a museum, and in 1952 General Douglas MacArthur returned to his birthplace to give a speech.

One room in the museum is devoted to displays and exhibits of the MacArthur family.

There is also a monument in the park dedicated to the 206th Coast Artillery (Anti-aircraft) Regiment, a unit comprised mostly of local men, that was at Dutch Harbor, AK in June 1942 when the Japanese bombed that American city. Museum address: MacArthur Park, Little Rock, AR 72202. Phone 501/324-9231. Hours: M-Sat. 9-4:30, Sun. 1-4:30. Admission charged.

MAUMELLE ORDNANCE DEPOT, was built early in the war at Maumelle, a NW suburb of Little Rock. At first the depot stored ammunition for the Army, but in the fall of 1943 Maumelle was transferred to the AAF and stored their ordnance. The Army's ordnance was transferred to Red River Ordnance Depot. The Maumelle Ordnance Depot was abandoned after the war but many concrete and steel storage igloos remained in the woods around the town. One of the igloos has been converted into a band shell at Lake Willastein.

CAMP JOSEPH T. ROBINSON, 7 miles north of Little Rock on Camp Robinson/Remount Rd., was activated as a tent camp in 1941 on the site of Camp Pike, a World War I cantonment. Wooden barracks and other buildings were soon added. Robinson was one of the first new Army camps completed and served as a model for the construction of other camps. The camp was a reception center and a training center for Army infantry units. The first major unit trained here was the 35th Infantry Division comprised of the National Guard Units from Kansas, Missouri and Nebraska. Later, the camp was a training center for replacement infantry troops. Several units of Japanese-American, who had volunteered for service in the U.S. Army, were trained here. Camp

Robinson had a subpost at Little Rock Municipal Airport, Adams Field, and a prisoner of war camp holding 2290 POWs.

After the war the camp was turned over to the Arkansas National Guard and to Reserve units.

MONTICELLO, in the SE corner of Arkansas, was a county seat and in 1942 it acquired a prisoner of war camp. The POW camp, when fully occupied, held Italian 2706 POWs. Late in the war, after the Italian Service Units (ISU) had been formed, the camp was used to hold troublemakers that were expelled from the ISUs. Some of those sent here had violated regulations by marrying American women.

NEWPORT is a county seat 80 miles NE of Little Rock.

ERWIN AIR FORCE AUXILIARY FIELD, 6 miles NE of Newport, was Newport's local airport when it was taken over by the AAF as a training field for the 70,000 Pilot Training Program. The field was later relinquished to the Marine Corps as a training field for Marine pilots and renamed U.S. Marine Corps Air Station, Newport. MCAS, Newport had an auxiliary field,

Milltown Airport, five miles east of Tuckerman, AR. MCAS, Newport remained in military hands well into the 1980s and was known as Newport Air Base.

PINE BLUFF is 40 miles SE of Little Rock. During the war the town had a small prisoner of war camp holding 554 POWs.

GRIDER FIELD was built early in the war as an elementary pilot training facility. It performed that mission throughout the war and was turned over to the local community after the war to be used as a commercial airport and has retained its WW II name.

PINE BLUFF ARSENAL was built NW of the city during the war to make chemical weapons, mostly artillery shells and bombs containing some very lethal agents such as mustard gas, chlorine, sulphur monochloride, Lewisite, and arsenic trichloride. Operation of the Arsenal continued into the post war years.

STUTTGART is a county seat 42 miles SE of Little Rock.

STUTTGART ARMY AIR FIELD, 7 miles north of town, was the local airport before the war. The 3rd AF took it over and used it as a training

field for the 70,000 Pilot Training Program. The II Tactical Air Command operated the field and taught aerial maneuvers. The Army declared the field surplus after the war and it was returned to the community. Stuttgart AAF's auxiliary fields were:

- Aux. #1 Carlisle Airport, 4 miles west of Carlisle
- Aux. #2 Hazen Airport, 4 miles SW of Hazen
- Aux. Texarkana Airport, 4 miles NE of Texarkana
- Aux. #5 Prairieville Airport, 3 miles west of Almyra

WALNUT RIDGE is a county seat in NE Arkansas.

WALNUT RIDGE ARMY AIR FIELD, four miles NE of town, was a training field operated by the AAF as part of the 50,000 Pilot Training Program. It was later turned over to the Marines to train Marine pilots and renamed U.S. Marine Corps Air Station, Walnut Ridge. MCAS, Walnut Ridge had an outlying field, Biggers Airport, two miles SE of Biggers, AR.
[1]The other areas were Lake Placid, NY, Asheville, NC, Miami Beach, FL and Santa Barbara, CA.

CALIFORNIA

California was witness to some of the most traumatic events that happened during the war in the then 48 states. When Pearl Harbor, Hawaii was bombed on Dec. 7, 1941 California was racked from north to south with near panic conditions because tens of thousands of its citizens expected similar attacks, possibly by the same naval force that attacked Hawaii, at any time on California cities.

Within days of the attack on Hawaii, Japanese submarines were attacking merchant ships off California's coast reinforcing those fears. Wild rumors circulated of Japanese invasion fleets being seen in California water and of actual Japanese landings. There were rumors of air attacks, rumors that secret Japanese air bases existed in California's deserts or in Mexico, rumors of sabotage, of periscope sightings and of many other fearful things. Worst of all, there were wild and unfair rumors about the ethnic Japanese: Japanese fishermen were mining harbors; supplying food, fuel and secret information to submarines off the coast; Japanese farmers were poisoning fruits and vegetables they brought to market; the Japanese were secretly organized into military units to carry out attacks behind American lines if and when an invasion came. None of these things were true, but every such rumor was believed by someone.

These fears lead to a series of immediate and unusual events in California. Martial law was declared on Terminal Island in Los Angeles Harbor where a major U.S. Naval base, important oil facilities and a large ethnic Japanese community existed side-by-side. Soldiers from west coast Army posts, some of them only partially trained, were rushed to various points along the coast to prepare defenses against an invasion. California's beaches were strung

with miles upon miles of barbed wire. Coastal cites were blacked out and citizens sandbagged their homes and businesses. Radio stations went off the air, commercial airliners were grounded and ships were ordered to stay in port. These measures were seen as absolutely necessary by the west coast Army commanders because at the time of Pearl Harbor the AAF in California consisted of only 16 modern fighter planes available to defend the entire state.

Citizens of enemy countries (enemy aliens), most of them Germans and Japanese who were known to the FBI and thought to be dangerous, were taken into custody under international laws defined by the Geneva Conventions and shipped off to internment camps as far away as North Dakota. This represented only a small percentage of the 531,882 registered enemy aliens in the state[1].

In time, the wildest rumors faded away but others persisted, especially those about the ethnic Japanese. Fears turned into harassments and attacks on the ethnic Japanese many of whom began to fear for their safety and that of their families. Soon, a fantastic plan began to evolve to expel all people of Japanese ancestry from California, and within a few months that plan was put into effect.

In late Feb. 1942, as the evacuation of ethnic Japanese was just getting under way, Californian's war fears were rekindled when news came that an oil facility near Santa Barbara had been shelled by a Japanese submarine. Some saw it as a prelude to greater attacks or perhaps an invasion. The night following the shelling Los Angeles had a false
_____
[1] California had the second largest enemy alien population in the nation. New York had the most with 1,234,995.

air raid that looked and sounded like the real thing and went on for several hours. Anti-aircraft guns fired away at imaginary planes and search lights scanned the skies looking for them. It was weeks before everyone in the area was finally convinced that Los Angeles had not really been bombed.

While Californians were learning to live with war fears their aircraft and shipbuilding industries exploded with defense work. Unemployment virtually disappeared and everyone was called upon to do their share for the war effort. California's huge oil and mineral resources were cranked up to full production, new industries of all kinds sprang up, trainloads of people flocked to California looking for work, and her southern border was opened to Mexican workers. During the war California would receive 11.9% of all U.S. Government war contracts and her plants and workers would produce 17% of all war supplies made in the U.S. Military bases were built by the dozen, sometimes in little towns that people in the big cities didn't even know existed. California's deserts became bombing ranges, her harbors became naval bases, her airports became air bases and infantry and tanks rumbled across her farm lands, orchards and deserts. During the course of the war California would acquire more military installations, by far, than any other state.

During the long war years California's big cities became mega-cities and the automobile became the main means of transportation. Already, California lead the nation in the number of cars; one for every 2.3 persons in the state. The Los Angeles area, already large and growing rapidly before the war, experienced the greatest growth of any metropolitan area in the country. By the end of the war the Los

Angeles metropolitan area stretched 80 miles solid from the San Fernando Valley to San Bernardino, and a new phenomenon had occurred … smog.

War fears for most Californians never really went away and with good cause, for the Japanese had plans to carry out further attacks against the state, if and when the opportunities arose. During the winter of 1944/45 the state was attacked again . . . this time by Japanese bombing balloons. Many bombs were dropped on California by these curious weapons but no significant damage was done, and effective U.S. censorship kept news of individual incidents secret from most Californians.

As a direct result of the war, millions of Americans "discovered" California for the first time. Many stayed on after the war and others returned to settle in the state. In doing so, they started a trend of strong and steady growth that lasted for more than four decades.

ALTURAS: On Jan. 10, 1945, near this small community in NE California, two forest rangers spotted a Japanese bombing balloon drifting high over the nearby forests. They reported it to military authorities and an Army P-38 fighter plane was dispatched and shot it down. It descended slowly drifting over Tule Lake, CA in sight of the Japanese Relocation camp there, and came to earth in trees on a mountain slope 30 miles west of Alturas. It was recovered and found to be remarkably intact, still carrying four incendiary bombs and one high explosive bomb. It was sent to Moffett Field in Sunnyvale, CA where it was examined and test flown. Eventually the balloon was given to the Smithsonian Air & Space Museum in Washington DC.

AUBURN is 30 miles NE of Sacramento in the heart of gold country.

DEWITT GENERAL HOSPITAL was build in Auburn in 1943-44 to treat Army war wounded. The 1852-bed hospital specialized in general medicine, neurology, neurosurgery, vascular surgery and psychiatry. After the war the hospital's patient population declined and in Dec. 1945 Dewitt was turned over to the state.

BAKERSFIELD is a farming center 100 miles north of Los Angeles.

BAKERSFIELD MUNICIPAL AIRPORT: In late Dec. 1941 this field, 4.5 miles NW of town, was one of 7 in California to receive combat-ready AAF fighter units assigned to defend California against an enemy attack. After the threat of such attacks subsided the field was taken over by the 4th AF for use as a sub-base to Hammer Field, Fresno, CA and used for elementary pilot training. The Naval Air Transport Service (NATS) also operated here.

GARDNER FIELD was a small AAF training field built early in the war 9 miles SE of Taft, CA. The field was operated by the Air Technical Service Command. Auxiliary air fields serving Gardner Field were:

- Aux. #1, Parker Air Field, 15 miles SE of Taft
- Aux. #2, Taft-Kern County Air Field #2, 21 miles SE of Taft
- Aux. #3, Allen Airport, 25 miles SE of Taft
- Aux. #5, Taft-Kern Count Air Field #5, 7 miles SE of Taft

MINTER FIELD, an AAF training field near the town of Shafter, 13.5 miles NW of Bakersfield, was established in June 1941. For a while it was known as Bakersfield Air Corps Flying School and offered pre-flight and basic flight training. Late in the war Chinese pilots trained here. There was a prisoner of war camp here that held about 600 POWs. Minter Field was abandoned by the AAF soon after the war but continued in use as Shafter Airport, a private airfield. Some of the WW II buildings remained in use after the war including two hangers. Location: on the Lerdo Hwy., one mile west of Hwy. 99. Minter had the following auxiliary air fields:

- Aux. #1, Wasco Airport, 12 miles NW of Bakersfield
- Aux. #3, Famoso Air Field, 9 miles NW of Bakersfield
- Aux. #4, Dunlap Airport, 4 miles south of Richgrove, CA
- Aux. #5, Semitropic Airport, 17 miles NW of Bakersfield
- Aux. #6, Poso Field, 9 miles NE of Bakersfield
- Aux. #7, Lost Hills Airport, 1/4 mile NE of Lost Hills, CA

BARSTOW is 60 miles north of San Bernardino in the Mojave Desert.

BARSTOW MARINE CORPS LOGISTICS BASE, just east of Barstow, was activated in Jan. 1943 as a Marine supply depot to service the needs of the Marines in both the Los Angeles and San Francisco areas. After the war the base was expanded several times and eventually became the center for logistics for all Marine Corps activities west of the Mississippi and in the Pacific. The base played significant roles in Marine Corps activities in Korea and Viet Nam and remained fully active during the Cold War.

DAGGETT MUNICIPAL AIRPORT, 6 miles east of Daggett, CA, had a private flying school which was contracted by the 4th AF to give primary pilot training to AAF fighter pilots.

FORT IRWIN was a huge desert warfare training facility located 37 miles NE of Barstow. In the early 1930s the area was used for maneuvers by General George S. Patton and his fledgling armored units. In Aug. 1940, President Roosevelt establish, by executive order, a huge military reservation covering 1000 square miles of the Mojave Desert called the Armor and

²The others were near Boardman, OR, Wendover, UT and Tonapah, NV.

Desert Training Center. In Oct. 1940 the Army used a part of the Center to establish the Mojave Antiaircraft Range, one of four huge bombing and gunnery ranges established in the west in 1940². A year later the Range was renamed Fort Irwin, and during WW II various Army units trained here including the famous "Desert Commandos". Fort Irwin was closed in 1944 but then opened and closed again several times during the Cold War.

BISHOP, in the east-central part of the state east of the Sierra Nevada Mountains, had a small Army air field, Bishop Army Air Field 2.5 miles NE of town. The field was used for a short time and them turned over to the Air Technical Service Command.

BLYTHE (See California/Arizona Maneuver Area)

BYRON HOT SPRINGS, 20 miles west of Stockton, was a very small community and health spa at the time of the war. It was here, in a resort hotel, that the U.S. Army chose to put one of several secret interrogation centers for German naval prisoners of war. The U.S. Navy had asked for these centers to gain naval intelligence. Since it was a violation of the Geneva Convention to set up such centers and question prisoners of war in this manner, the centers were made to look like POW processing centers where POWs were brought for a brief period before being sent on to established POW camps. The Americans had learned from the British that such centers were effective and copied their methods. The POWs were made as comfortable as possible with good living quarters, good food and plenty of recreation. This, the British had learned, loosened tongues. Also, anti-Nazi Germans working for the Americans, were intermingled with the POWs to draw them out. The activities were kept secret from the local citizenry and from the Swiss Government representatives who visited the center from time-to-time.

CALIFORNIA/ARIZONA MANEUVER AREA (CAMA) (DESERT TRAINING CENTER): This was the largest Army base in the world covering some 18,000 square miles. It stretched from the outskirts of Pomona, CA eastward to within 50 miles of Phoenix, AZ, southward to the suburbs of Yuma, AZ and northward into the southern tip of Nevada. It existed primarily to train U.S. forces in desert

Maneuvers in the California/Arizona Maneuver Area.

The General Patton Memorial Museum at Chiriaco Summit, CA. This site is also the entrance to Camp Young, the tent camp that served as headquarters for the California/Arizona Maneuver Area (CAMA).

warfare for the North African campaign.

Major General George S. Patton, Jr., commander of the 1st Armored Corps, was responsible for selecting this site in early 1942. As a native of southern California he knew the area well from his youth and from having participated in Army maneuvers here and in the Mojave Desert in the 1930s. Patton chose the small town of Desert Center, population 19, as his headquarters. At that time the training base was called "Desert Training Center" and had not yet reached it maximum size. Six months later it was given the CAMA name, and by Nov. 1943 it had reached its maximum size after several expansions. Patton and his advanced team designated various locations within the area where tent camps would be built to house individual units. The camps were situated so that each unit could train individually without interfering with the other. Air fields, hospitals, supply depots and sites for other support services were selected as was a corps maneuvering area. The plan was that each division and/or major unit would train in its own area, and near the end of its training period would participate in a corps (two divisions or more) exercise in the corps maneuvering area at Palen Pass. Upon completion of the corps exercise, the trained units would leave CAMA and new units would arrive to begin their training and the process repeated.

Gen. Patton, who was independently wealthy, purchased some commercial radio broadcasting equipment with his own funds and set up his own radio station within CAMA. The station broadcasted music and news most of the time except when Patton wanted to address the troops. He kept a microphone at his desk and another by his bed and broke into the programming whenever it suited him.

Patton's 1st Armored Corps trained here from April to Aug. 1942 and then departed to participate in the invasion of North Africa which occurred in Nov. 1942.

As Patton and his troops moved out, the 2nd Armored Corps, under Maj. Gen. Alvan Gillem, Jr., moved in. They trained at CAMA

until Oct. and their place was taken by the 4th Armored Corps. They were followed in successive order by the 9th Army Corps, 15th Army Corps, 4th Army Corps and 10th Army Corps.

When the Allied victory came in North Africa, the need for desert-trained units faded and in May 1944 CAMA was closed.

Most of the sites can be visited, but some are difficult to reach. In most cases the only things that remain at the camp sites are streets, sidewalks, building foundations, patterns of hand-laid rocks for various purposes and trash dumps. Monuments have been erected at some of the camp sites and there are areas within CAMA that are fenced off with danger signs warning of unexploded ordnance.

For CAMA sites in Arizona, see this heading under that state. There were no CAMA camps in Nevada.

BLYTHE ARMY AIR FIELD, 7 mile west of town on I-10, was built for the I Troop Carrier Command but was given up by that command, without ever occupying it, to the 4th AF as a CAMA training field. The 46th Bomb Group and later the 34th Bomb Group occupied the field during the CAMA days and flew a variety of planes including B-17s, B-24s, A-31s and A-36s. Blythe AAF later became a sub-base of Muroc AAF and after the war it became Blythe's local airport.

There was another airfield in Blythe, Gary Field, near the present-day golf course, which had a private pilot training school known as the Morton Air Academy. The school was contracted by the Army

Air Corps early in the war to give primary training to Air Corps cadets.

CAMP CLIPPER, also known as Camp Essex, was 42 miles west of Needles and is adjacent to I-10 and NW of the town of Essex. There were actually two sites here, a temporary camp site used first by the 33rd Infantry Division and a second and more permanent camp used later by the 93rd Infantry Division.

CAMP COXCOMB was 15 miles north of Desert Center. It was home, at different times, to the 7th Armored Div., 93rd Infantry Div. and 95th Infantry Div. To reach the site take S.R. 177 NE out of Desert Center. After 177 makes a 45 degree turn to the left watch for a ranch house on the right, then a hard surface road soon afterwards on the left. Take that road westward to its end which is the southern perimeter of the old camp.

DESERT CENTER ARMY AIR FIELD, one mile NE of the town of Desert Center, is now the town's local airport. During the days of CAMA it was a sub-base of San Bernardino AAF and served several installations in the area including Camp Young, CAMA headquarters. To reach the air field, proceed NE out of Desert Center on S.R. 177 about five miles to an orchard on the right. Just past the orchard is a road to the SE. Take that road to the air field. There are numerous WW II foundations and several post-war buildings at the old air field.

GENERAL PATTON MEMORIAL MUSEUM, at the Chiriaco Summit exit on I-8, honors Gen. Patton and the men who served at the California/Arizona Maneuver Area (CAMA). The museum has a large display on the General as well as other displays showing how the soldiers trained and lived during their training here at CAMA. There are natural science displays on the area's minerals, plants, fossils, animals, etc., and a gift shop. The museum offers guided class tours, field trips and lectures. Address: Chiriaco Summit, CA 92201. Phone: 619/227-3227. Hours: 9-5 daily. Donations requested.

CAMP GRANITE and **CAMP IRON MOUNTAIN** were two camps across the road from each

The remains of an outdoor scale relief map of the area at Camp Iron Mountain. The map is inside the fence on the NE side of the post.

One of Camp Lockett's original buildings serving as the Campo, CA Post Office. Behind the Post Office is an original 2-story barracks building boarded up.

other on S.R. 62 just east of its junction with S.R. 177. Camp Granite was south of the road and Iron Mountain north. Camp Granite was first used by the 76th Field Artillery Brigade then the 90th Infantry Div. Camp Iron Mountain was used by the 3rd Armored Div. Both camps are visible from the highway. Much of Camp Iron Mountain has been fenced off by the Bureau of Land Management to keep out vehicles, but gates are open to visitors on foot.

CAMP IBIS was 15 miles NW of Needles. It was home to the 4th, 9th and 11th Armored Divisions in that order. To reach the site go north on U.S. 95 from its northern junction with I-10 to the first railroad crossing. The camp was to the east and was served by that rail line.

NEEDLES AIRPORT, 5.5 miles south of Needles, CA, was used by the Army during the CAMA days.

PALEN PASS, east of Camp Coxcomb, was the site of several corps maneuvers. Defensive fortifications were built at the Pass and still exist. During corps maneuvers one division would defend the Pass and the others would attack and try to take it. There is a dirt road leading to the Pass, but it is recommended that only 4-wheel drive vehicles be used. To reach the Pass, proceed to the Camp Coxcomb turnoff of S.R. 177 (See Camp Coxcomb above). The dirt road that heads eastward from 177 is the Palen Pass Rd. The Pass is 18 miles down that dirt road.

CAMP PILOT KNOB was at the southern end of CAMA just north of Yuma, AZ. The 6th and 85th Infantry Divisions trained here. To reach the site, go north one mile on Sidewinder Rd. from its junction with I-8 just NW of Yuma. The camp can be seen from Sidewinder Rd.

RICE, a small community on SR 62 and 19 miles west of Vital Jct., CA, was the site of a large Quartermaster depot. Remains of the depot can be seen on both sides of the road. In 1944 Dr. J. Robert Oppenheimer, Director of the "Manhattan (Atomic Bomb) Project" visited Rice and examined the nearby Tularosa Basin as a possible site for the testing of the first atomic devices. Oppenheimer subsequently chose the White Sands area of New Mexico.

RICE ARMY AIR FIELD, two miles SE of town,

was a small air field and a sub-base of San Bernardino AAF used to train pilots and crews of aircraft whose mission it was to support ground troops. This included a wide variety of aircraft from observation planes to bombers.

SHAVERS SUMMIT ARMY AIR FIELD, 29.5 miles SE of Indio, CA, was used by the Army during CAMA days.

THERMAL ARMY AIR FIELD, two miles SE of Thermal, CA, was used by the Army during the CAMA days, and later in the war the Navy used it. The air field is 119 feet below sea level.

CAMP YOUNG, the headquarters camp for CAMA, was several miles west of Desert Center. It was here that Patton and the other generals resided during their stay. They lived in tents just like their troops. The Gen. Patton Memorial Museum (see above) sits at the main entrance to Camp Young.

CAMPO is 50 miles SE of San Diego near the Mexican border.

CAMP LOCKETT was built at Campo in 1941 as a subpost for Fort Seeley at El Centro to house the 11th Cavalry (horse) Regiment that had been deployed along the California-Mexico border since Nov. 1940. At first a tent camp, it grew to have 138 buildings. In the summer of 1942 the War Department dismounted the 11th Cavalry Regiment and sent its personnel to Ft. Benning, GA for retraining. In their place the 10th Cavalry (horse) Regiment, an all-negro unit, moved in from Ft. Riley, KS. In Feb. 1944 the 10th Cavalry Regiment left Lockett for Ft. Clark, TX to become a part of the reactivated 2nd Cavalry (horse) Division. With no more troops at Lockett, the War Department decided to build a large convalescent hospital here for wounded personnel needing long term care. Using the original camp hospital as a base, a large hospital complex of 405 buildings emerged known as Mitchell Convalescent Hospital. There was a prisoner of war branch camp here with 200 Italian POWs working for the hospital. Near the end of the war the Italians were replaced by German POWs. In June 1946 the hospital was declared surplus and in 1950 was sold to private interests.

Many of the old camp buildings remain in the area and are being used by the citizens of Campo. The Italian POWs built a religious shrine in the hills outside of Campo and it is being maintained by the local citizens.

CARMEL was, before the war, a picturesque retreat of 2800 people catering to artists and writers. It was also the home of one of America's most colorful heros, General "Vinegar Joe" Stilwell. He retired here after his long military career, and when he died his ashes were scattered over the area from a plane. After the war General Jimmie Doolittle made

Carmel his home and lived here until he died in Sept. 1993 at the age of 96.

CHICO is a farming center 90 miles north of Sacramento.

CHICO ARMY AIR FIELD, five miles north of town, was Chico Municipal Airport, but when the U.S. went to war the 4th AAF leased the field for the duration and converted it into a training base for bomber crews and fighter pilots. It had a sub-base at Sacramento Municipal Airport and several bombing ranges. In June 1948 Chico AAF was returned to the city.

CRESCENT CITY: (See Eureka/Crescent City Area)

CROWS LANDING, 18 miles south of Modesto, was a general store, a gas station and a freight train stop in 1942.

U.S. NAVAL AUXILIARY AIR STATION, CROWS LANDING, 2.5 miles NW of town, began in late 1942 as an auxiliary air station to NAS, Alameda. It was used to train Navy fighter pilots. Pilots of F4F Wildcats, TBF and TBM Avengers trained here first in Link and Panoramic trainers then eventually in actual planes. Later, pilots in R4D Skytrains and R5D Skymasters trained here. After the war the station was placed in caretaker status.

DESERT TRAINING CENTER: (See California/Arizona Maneuver Area)

DOS PALOS or FIREBAUGH: Each of these two communities, about 25 to 30 miles respectively south of Merced, claim the WW II air base known as Eagle Field.

EAGLE FIELD, 6.5 miles SW of Dos Palos, was built in 1942 as an AAF training base. It was abandoned after the war, sold to private interests. Several of the old hangers and other buildings remained for decades, but eventually fell into disrepair. Location: From I-5, 35 miles SE of Merced, turn east on the Firebaugh Road (Nees). Proceed 17.5 miles to Russell, turn north on Russell and proceed 14.7 miles to Althea. Turn west on Althea and proceed 13.7 miles to Prince. Turn north on Prince which will take you to the Field.

EDWARDS: (See Mojave)

EL CENTRO is a large agricultural center in the south-central part of the state near the Mexican border.

CAMP SEELEY was a tent camp, 8 miles east of El Centro, established by the Army in Nov. 1940 to house elements of the 11th Cavalry (horse) Regiment that had recently moved in from the Presidio at Monterey. In Dec. 1941 these elements moved, on horseback, to Camp Lockett at Campo, CA to join the main body of the unit. Camp Seeley then became an ordnance proving ground.

U. S. MARINE CORPS AIR STATION, EL CENTRO is 7 miles west of El Centro and 52' below sea level. The CAA had already begun construction of a runway here when the Marines took it over in 1943 for use as a training field for Marine pilots. Marine Air Groups (MAGs) began training in Jan. 1943 and in 1944 the base was enlarged. The Naval Air Ferry Command also used the field.

After the war the base continued in use by the Marines and Navy in various ways. Surplus TD2 Devastators were stored here for a while and some commercial airlines used the runways. In the late 1940s the base became active again as a Marine training center and remained active throughout the Cold War.

U.S. NAVAL AUXILIARY AIR STATION, HOLTVILLE, 7.5 miles NE of Holtville, CA was an auxiliary field to NAS, San Diego.

U.S. NAVAL AUXILIARY AIR FIELD, SALTON SEA was 16 miles NW of Westmoreland, CA and 245 feet below sea level. The field was on the west shore of the Salton Sea and was used for seaplanes. It was an outlying field to NAS, San Diego and remained in use well into the post war years.

EUREKA/CRESCENT CITY:
These two towns are on the northern coast of California. In Crescent City's Beach Front park is a monument consisting of the anchor and parts of the hull of the U.S. freighter "Emidio" which was sunk off the coast in Dec. 1941 by the Japanese submarine I-17.

U.S. NAVAL AUXILIARY AIR FIELD (LTA), EUREKA was a small blimp base two miles west of Eureka and 1/2 mile inland from Humboldt Bay. It had two mooring circles, a landing field for small aircraft and was an auxiliary field to NAS Moffett Field (LTA).

U.S. NAVAL AIR AUXILIARY STATION, ARCATA was 7.5 miles NW of Arcata, CA. This station was an auxiliary field to NAS Alameda.

FAIRFIELD is 15 miles east of the north end of San Francisco Bay.

FAIRFIELD-SUISUN ARMY AIR BASE was five miles east of Fairfield and began operating in May 1943 under the Air Transport Command as a processing and ferrying base for planes, troops and cargo going to the Pacific theater of war. It became known as "The Gateway to the Pacific". The base underwent several expansions during the war including a very large expansion in early 1945 in preparation for the invasion of Japan. The US Air Force took over the base after the war and renamed it Fairfield-Suisun Air Force Base. In 1950 the base was renamed Travis Air Force Base after Brig. General Robert F. Travis who had commanded the 41st Combat Wing of the U.S. 8th AF in Europe during WW II. The base was fully active in air transport services throughout the Cold War and retained its slogan, "The Gateway to the Pacific".

Travis Air Force Museum: This museum is on the grounds of Travis AFB and has a generous indoor display of artifacts relating to the history of Travis AFB and the US Air Force in general. Outside the museum are about 30 planes on exhibit, many of them from WW II. Inside the museum is a replica of "Fat Man", the atomic bomb dropped on Nagasaki. The museum also has a gift shop with many interesting items for sale. Address: PO Box 1565, Travis AFB, CA 94535-5000. Phone: 707/424-5606. Hours: M-F 9-4, weekends 9-5. Free.

The bomb release mechanism of the Hayfork, CA balloon as it looked after falling from a dead fir tree after the gas bag had been ignited. Still aboard were four incendiary bombs and one high explosive bomb.

FONTANA: (See Los Angeles and the Los Angeles Metropolitan Area)

FRESNO is in the lower San Joachin Valley. There were many ethnic Japanese farmers in the area and during the short-lived voluntary evacuation program many ethnic Japanese from areas to the west came to Fresno County because it was just across the line from the restricted defense area. When the voluntary evacuation program proved to be a failure Fresno was chosen as the location for two assembly centers to which the ethnic Japanese were taken before being evacuated to the relocation camps.

FRESNO ASSEMBLY CENTER, PINDALE ASSEMBLY CENTER, CAMP PINEDALE AND FRESNO GROUND TRAINING CENTER: The Fresno Assembly Center was located at the Fresno Fairgrounds, two miles east of downtown Fresno, and the Pinedale Assembly Center was at Pinedale, a Fresno suburb, 7 miles north of downtown Fresno, in the former employee housing units of an abandoned mill. The Fresno Assembly Center (fairgrounds) was the larger of the two. At this center accommodations were crude tarpaper barracks with cots, outhouses and overhead water pipes with holes drilled in them to serve as showers. Accommodations at the Pinedale Center were somewhat better. The use of both centers was short-lived.

The Pinedale Assembly Center ceased functioning in Aug. 1942 and the Fresno Assembly Center in Nov. 1942 when the last group of ethnic Japanese departed. Most of those processed at the Fresno center went to Jerome, AR and those from Pinedale went to Tule Lake, CA. Both facilities were then turned over to the 4th AF which converted them into non-flying training facilities called Camp Pinedale and the Fresno Ground Training Center. Signalmen, camouflage specialists, chemical warfare specialists, ordnance technicians, clerks, truck drivers and cooks trained here. The camp continued in operation throughout the Cold War.

HAMMER FIELD, five miles NE of Fresno, was a training base of the 4th AF specializing in night fighters. It had three sub-bases and two gunnery ranges. Hammer also had an AAF regional hospital.

HAYFORK is a small community in northern California about 40 miles west of Redding. On Feb. 1, 1945 a Japanese bombing balloon was spotted by several local residents drifting over the Trinity National Forest area and slowly decending. No one knew what it was, but an alert forest ranger called the military authorities at the Presidio in San Francisco and reported it. Meanwhile the balloon came to rest atop a 60' dead fir tree in the forest near a local road. In the next few hours several people gathered in the area to gaze up at the strange object. Shortly after dark there was a tremendous blast. The balloon's gas bag disappeared in a fireball and the balloon's undercarriage came crashing to the ground. No one was hurt. Forest rangers kept the curious well back from the fallen debris until Army personnel arrived. Upon examination, it was found to be a Japanese bombing balloon with four incendiary bombs and one high explosive bomb still aboard and the bomb releasing mechanism still very much intact. It later proved to be one of the most intact bombing balloons yet to fall into

One of the displays inside the Travis Air Force Museum; a WW II Jeep and a Piper L-4 Grasshopper light observation/liaison aircraft of WW II.

American hands. As was usual in instances of this sort, the local people were told what it was and were asked to keep secret what they had seen.

HEMET is a small town about 25 miles SE of Riverside, CA. There was a private flying school here, the Ryan School of Aeronautics, at Ryan Airport, 2.5 miles SW of town. The School was contracted by the Army Air Corps to give elementary and advanced flight training to Army pilots. There was an auxiliary field, Ryan Air Field #1, 4.5 miles NW of Hemet.

HERLONG is a small community 60 miles north of Lake Tahoe near the Nevada border that came into being during WW II to serve a new Army Ordnance depot that was built on land surrounding the town.

SIERRA ARMY ORDNANCE DEPOT was built here in 1941-42 to receive, store and ship military supplies and to serve as a backup facility for other depots. The depot remained in service into the 1960s.

HOLLISTER is 30 miles SE of San Jose.

U.S. NAVAL AUXILIARY AIR STATION, HOLLISTER, three miles north of Hollister, was Hollister's local airport. It was taken over by the Navy early in the war and used as an auxiliary field for NAS, Alameda. The air station was returned to its owners after the war.

HUNTER LIGGETT MILITARY RESERVATION is 60 miles NW of San Luis Obispo. Much of the reservation was purchased from newspaper magnate, William Randolph Hearst in late 1940. Hunter Liggett MR was a subpost of Fort Ord and was used for training and maneuvers. It also had a bombing and gunnery range used by Salinas AAF.

The centerpiece of the Reservation was the elegant and rambling ranch house built by Hearst in 1929-30 called the "Hacienda". The ranch house was used as the Reservation's headquarters, bachelor officers' quarters, guest house and general all-around social center. The standardized wooden military buildings of the reservation paled in comparison to the "Hacienda".

Hunter Liggett was retained by the Army after the war and renamed Fort Hunter Liggett. In the 1990s it was closed.

INDIO: (See California/Arizona Maneuver Area)

INYOKERN was a small community about 50 miles NE of Mojave, CA.

U.S. NAVAL AIR FACILITY, INYOKERN was acquired by the Navy in Nov. 1943. It consisted of Inyokern's local airport, one mile NW of town, and a large desert area of several hundred square miles north of town. The facility was used to test rockets then being developed at the California Institute of Technology. U.S. NAF, Inyokern was retained after the war, expanded to cover 1800 square miles, renamed U.S. Naval Weapons Center, China Lake, and used to test various types of naval weapons including guided missiles. It was operational throughout the Cold War.

IRVINE: (See Los Angeles and the Los Angeles Metropolitan Area)

LANCASTER was an unincorporated town 40 miles north of Los Angeles.

WAR EAGLE AIRPORT, five miles west of Lancaster, was used by the AAF as a training field. There was an auxiliary field, Liberty Auxiliary Field #1, four miles south of Rosamond, CA.

LEMOORE is 25 miles west of Visalia and 30 miles south of Fresno.

LEMOORE ARMY AIR FIELD, 9 miles SW of town, was a dirt air field usable only in dry weather. It nevertheless was used by the 4th AF as a processing and training field. Lemoore had a sub-base, Porterville Army Air Field near Porterville, CA.

LOMPOC is midway between San Luis Obispo and Santa Barbara.

CAMP COOKE was built by the Army as a training base for armored units. Various units trained there during the war and there was an 800-man prisoner of war camp on the base. After the war Camp Cooke was partially inactivated and, for a while, became a branch of the Army's Disciplinary Barracks. In 1953 it was inactivated by the Army but in 1957 the base was acquired by the US Air Force to become its first missile base. It was renamed Vandenberg Air Force Base in honor of Gen. Hoyt S. Vandenberg who, during WW II, was commander of the 9th AF and helped plan the Normandy invasion. Vandenberg AFB remained active throughout the Cold War.

U.S. NAVAL AUXILIARY AIR FIELD (LTA), LOMPOC was a small blimp base 3/4 mile north of Lompoc. It was an auxiliary field to NAS, Santa Ana and had a landing strip for small planes.

LONG BEACH: (See Los Angeles and the Los Angeles Metropolitan Area)

LOS ANGELES and the LOS ANGELES METROPOLITAN AREA:

During World War II Los Angeles was the boom town of boom towns. The Los Angeles metropolitan area grew faster than any other major metropolitan area in the U.S. and experienced more of the traumas of war while doing so. By 1943 the population of metropolitan L.A. was larger than 37 states, and was home to one in every 40 U.S. citizens. By the end of the war, the L.A. area had produced 17% of all of America's war production.

Of the 120,000 ethnic Japanese eventually evacuated to the relocation camps, 80,000 came from the L.A. area.

The evacuation of the ethnic Japanese was just getting under way when, on Feb. 23, 1942 a Japanese submarine shelled an oil facility near Santa Barbara, just 80 miles up the coast form Los Angeles. Many saw this as a prelude of to a greater attack and tensions rose rapidly in L.A. Rumors started and spread. The next night, around midnight, a false report was sent out to anti-aircraft gunners on the heights overlooking L.A. that enemy planes had been spotted over Los Angeles. That was the spark that ignited "The Battle of Los Angeles". The gunners in one section of town opened fire on the unseen airplanes and their search lights scanned the sky. The frenzy spread and other

Headlines in the Los Angeles Times, Feb. 25, 1942.

gunners opened up. Some civilians rushed for shelter, while others rushed outside to see what was happening. Some thought they saw the planes, while others thought they saw parachutes and bombs falling. Spent anti-aircraft shells rained down on roof tops and cars. Santa Monica and Long Beach were hardest hit. Air raid wardens dashed about ordering people to extinguish lights and take cover. Rumors spread that section of the city were on fire and that a plane had crashed at 185th and Vermont Ave. There was a rash of auto accidents as drivers tried to maneuver in darkened streets with their headlight off, and several people• had heart attacks.

The "battle" went on for over two hours before the guns fell silent. The next morning headlines of the Los Angeles Times screamed "L.A. AREA RAIDED". It was not true, but the newspaper editors had succumbed to the rumors as had most other people.

The truth eventually became known that the city had not been bombed and life went on at its hectic pace for better or for worse. Experiencing an "air raid" was beneficial, in a way, for the people of Los Angeles because they gained experience in case the real thing ever came. And, the Japanese had plans to provide the real thing by bombing the city with giant seaplanes if and when conditions were favorable. Those raids never came about, but the Japanese had the planes and wherewithal to accomplish such a raid throughout the war.

The growth of L.A. didn't stop with the war. It went on at a healthy pace in the postwar years and lasted for decades.

Japanese American National Museum: This museum is in the Japantown section of Los Angeles. It is in an old Buddhist temple and has numerous displays and artifacts tracing the history of the Japanese people in America. One of the larger permanent displays in the museum relates the story of the relocation of the ethnic Japanese on the west coast during

World War II. Address: 1st and Central Sts. Los Angeles, CA 90012. Phone: 213-625-0414. Hours: Tues.-Thurs. and Sat.-Sun. 10-5, Fri. 11-8. Closed Jan. 1, Thanksgiving and Dec. 25. Admission charged.

Los Angeles Municipal Airport (Mines Field) which, after the war, became Los Angeles International Airport, was used extensively during the war by the AAF, Navy and local aircraft manufacturers, and continued to function as a commercial airport. The Air Transport Command and Air Technical Service Command had operations here and their was a large military air freight terminal.

Martyrs Memorial & Museum of the Holocaust: The Primary purpose of this Memorial & Museum is to educate: to bring the facts of the Holocaust to the attention of all people everywhere. On display are numerous photographs, paintings, drawings, maps and other artifacts related to the Holocaust. The museum provides tours, speakers and offers an extensive collection of archives and audio-visual materials. Address: 6505 Wilshire Blvd., Los Angeles, CA 90048. Phone: 213/651-3175. Hours: M-Thurs. 9-5, Fri. 9-3, Sun. 1-5. Free.

Museum of Tolerance: This 8-story museum has permanent and temporary exhibits on racism and prejudice in America. The permanent exhibits have two main themes, the history of racism and prejudice in America and the story of the Holocaust. There is an Interactive Learning Center, a theater, a library, an archives collection, a memorial plaza and a museum store. Tours, lasting three hours, depart every 15 minutes. Address: 9786 W. Pico Blvd., Los Angeles, CA 90035. Phone: 310/553-8403. Hours: M-Thurs. 10-5, Fri. 10-1, Sun. 11-6:30. Closed Thanksgiving, Dec. 25 and Jewish holidays. Admission charged. Underground parking available.

ARCADIA is 7 miles east of Los Angeles.

Santa Anita Assembly Center For Ethnic Japanese: This was the Santa Anita Racetrack. Between Mar. 27 and Oct. 27, 1942 it was used as an assembly center for ethnic Japanese prior to their being evacuated to the relocation camps. This was the largest assembly center in the system and at its peak held 18,719 people. There were existing living accommodations on the property, dozens of tarpaper barracks

P-38 fighter planes under construction at Lockheed Aircraft Co., Burbank, CA.

The Air Museum Planes of Fame in Chino, CA. An outstanding museum with numerous WW II aircraft. A "must see" museum for WW II buffs.

buildings were built to house the people and the horse stalls were converted into small apartments. While in the center some of those who volunteered to work were put on a project making camouflage nets for the Army. Eventually 22,000 nets were produced. Most of the people processed here were sent to the relocation camps at Heart Mountain, WY, Granada, CO and Rohwer, AR. After the ethnic Japanese departed the track was taken over by the Army Ordnance Corps as a training center and became known as Camp Santa Anita. Later still, it served as a Prisoner of war camp holding several thousand German soldiers from General Rommel's Afrika Korps.

BURBANK, north of L.A. in the San Fernando Valley, was home to the Lockheed Aircraft Corp., one of the primary aircraft builders of the war. Vega Aircraft Co. was also in Burbank.

Lockheed Air Terminal: This airport, in the NW corner of Burbank, was built in 1930. By 1934 the airport had become Los Angeles' primary airport known as Union Air Terminal. During the 1930a Lockheed Aircraft

Co., adjacent to the field, evolved into one the nation's largest aircraft manufacturers, and in 1940 Lockheed purchased the airport. It was then renamed Lockheed Air Terminal and used to test and delivery Lockheed aircraft. It also remained Los Angeles' primary civil airport and remained the area's only civil airport throughout the war. During the war Lockheed built P-38 fighters, Hudson and B-17 bombers. The AAF's Air Technical Services Command and Western Technical Training Command had operations at the field. The airport and the Lockheed plant were extensively camouflaged during the war. The main Lockheed plant and runways were made to appear as grain fields and houses, and the parking lot was covered over with netting to appear as alfalfa fields. In addition, an extensive smoke screen system was installed to hide the plant under smoke.

In 1947, when Mines Field was expanded to become Los Angeles' primary airport, this facility became a secondary airport. In 1978 the cities of Burbank, Glendale and Pasadena bought the airport and renamed it Burbank-Glendale-Pasadena Airport. Lockheed continued in operation at the field for many years.

CHINO is SE of and adjacent to Pomona.

The Air Museum Planes of Fame: This is one of two air museums at the Chino Airport. It has an outstanding collection of WW II aircraft and is a "must see" museum for WW II buffs. It was founded in 1957 making it the first

Making camouflage nets at Santa Anita Race Track. The nets were hung in the grandstands as they were worked on.

A P-38 fighter plane being restored by Fighter Rebuilders, Inc. on the grounds of the Air Museum Planes of Fame in Chino, CA. The wing in the foreground is that of a P-51 Mustang also under restoration.

Nose sections for A-20 bombers under construction at Douglas Aircraft Co., El Segundo.

permanent air museum west of the Rocky Mountains. The museum has several planes that are the last surviving models of their type including the world's only flyable P-26 "Pea Shooter" and the only totally authentic flyable Japanese "Zero" fighter plane. There are some 80 aircraft of which 30 are flyable. Many of the aircraft have appeared in air shows around the country, in movies and on television. There are four main buildings at the museum. Fighter Rebuilders, Inc., an independent company that specializes in the rebuilding of vintage aircraft, is on the grounds of the museum and museum visitors can visit their shop and watch rebuilding work in progress. Address: 7000 Merrill Ave., Chino, CA 91710. Phone: 909/597-3722. Hours: daily 9-5, closed Thanksgiving and Dec. 25. Admission charged. Location: SE of, and adjacent to, the town of Chino at the Chino Airport.

Cal Aero Academy was an independent flying school at Chino Airport when WW II started. The Army Air Corps contracted with the school to provide primary flight training for Army air cadets. The name Cal Aero is preserved at the Chino Airport and can be seen on several buildings.

The Yanks Air Museum: This is the second of the two air museums at Chino Airport and is also an outstanding museum. Actually, this is the restoration department of a much larger museum-to-be which will be built at Greenfield, CA in Monterey County. Until that comes about, this facility will display approximately 45 planes of the collection that have been restored and are flyable. The Yanks Air Museum specializes in piston-engine planes, mostly of U.S. make and mostly single-engine fighter planes. Address: 7000 Merrill Ave., Chino, CA 91710. Phone: 909/597-1734. Hours: M-F 8-3. Free. Location: This museum is on the west side of Chino Airport.

COSTA MESA, 13 miles SE of Long Beach, didn't exist during WW II. The city incorporated in 1953 and in 1955 annexed the former Santa Ana Army Air Base (SAAAB), which now comprises a major part of the town.

Santa Ana Army Air Base (SAAAB): This was an air base without planes, hangers or runways. It was a huge basic training camp where newly inducted soldiers, earmarked for the AAF, were given 9 weeks of basic training and then testing to determine if they were to be pilots, bombardiers, navigators, mechanics, etc. From SAAAB the cadets went on to other bases for training in their specialties. The base was dedicated in March 1942 and grew rapidly as the need for pilots and air crews sky-rocketed. Turnover was rapid so that by the end of the year 23,470 cadets had passed through SAAAB. By the end of 1943 that number jumped to 57,895. In the Fall of 1942 SAAAB became an Overseas Replacement Depot (ORD) housing AAF personnel awaiting transportation overseas. In Nov. 1943 members of the Women's Air Force Service Pilots (WASP) began training at the base, followed shortly by members of the Women's Army Corp (WAC). In 1945 SAAAB became one of six Redistribution Centers in the country for airmen returning from overseas who were to be assigned state-side duty.

Being close to Hollywood and with such a large turnover of service personnel, the base attracted a lot of Hollywood celebrities who put on shows at the base.

In late 1945 Japanese aliens from the alien internment camps being returned to Japan by the Immigrations and Naturalization Service (INS) were housed here while awaiting transportation to Japan.

SAAAB continued as a basic training camp after the war and in the 1950s training in Nike guided missiles was added. In 1958 the base was declared surplus and soon afterwards the land was divided for many uses. In the postwar years private homes, apartments, two colleges, the California National Guard and the Orange County Fairground shared the land. Many of the base's original buildings remained in use for years by the colleges and the fair grounds. At the fairgrounds is Memorial Garden whose centerpiece is a preserved WW II-era two-story barracks building that is destined to be a museum preserving the history of the air base.

DOWNEY, 7 miles SE of L.A., had a large Consolidated-Vultee Aircraft plant at Vultee Airport 1.5 miles SE of downtown Downey. Consolidated-Vultee built primary trainer aircraft. Vultee Airport no longer exists.

EL SEGUNDO, five miles south of L.A. on the coast, had a large North American Aviation Corp. plant that built P-51 fighters, A-36 bombers and B-25 Bombers. There was also a Douglas Aircraft Co. plant in El Segundo that made air frames and SBD-5 dive bombers for the Navy.

A restored WW II-era two-story barracks building, one of the original buildings of the Santa Ana Army Air Base, stands as the center piece in Memorial Garden at the Orange County Fairgrounds in Costa Mesa, CA. There are plans to make the barracks into a museum commemorating the base.

B-25 bombers under construction at North American Aviation Corp., Inglewood.

EL TORO: (For U.S. Marine Corps Air Station, El Toro, see Irvine)

FONTANA, west of, and adjacent to, San Bernardino, was the site of the Kaiser Steel Co., financed and built by the wartime government agency known as the Defense Plant Corp (DPC). It was run by Henry Kaiser and his industrial empire and sold most of its steel to the west coast shipbuilders. The building of steel plants west of the Mississippi had long been a pet project of President Roosevelt who wanted the American steel industry to diversify across the country. Roosevelt took advantage of the war to see that two new plants were built in the west, this one and another in Provo, Utah.

GLENDALE is north of, and adjacent to, Los Angeles.

Grand Central Air Terminal: This airport which, in the postwar years, became known a Glendale Airport, had a well-known flying school, The Grand Central Flying School. In May 1939 this school was one of 9 such schools in the country selected by the Army Air Corps to train Air Corps pilots. After a while, though, the Air Corps canceled its contract with this school because of mounting air congestion in the area. The airport continued to serve, though, as a sub-base to Van

The "Lane Victory" at her berth in San Pedro, CA.

Nuys Metropolitan Airport.

HAWTHORNE, five miles south of Los Angeles, had Northrop Aircraft Co., a large manufacturing complex at Northrop Field, which was originally the company's air field. The plant built B-17 bombers. Also at the airport was a company school contracted to the AAF's Western Technical Training Command. The airport later became Hawthorne Municipal Airport.

HUNTINGTON BEACH is a coastal community 7 miles SE of Long Beach and had many active oil wells close to the shore. At the corner of Bolsa Chica and Warner Avenues is the remains of a gigantic concrete pad which was one of the coastal defenses for the Los Angeles area. The beach area was heavily patrolled by Coastguardsmen on horses.

INGLEWOOD, south of, and adjacent to Los Angeles, had a large North American Aviation plant that made air frames.

IRVINE is a planned community 35 miles SE of Los Angeles that didn't exist during the war. When the town came into being after the war it became the post town for El Toro Marine Corps Air Station that had been built in the area during WW II.

U. S. Marine Corps Air Station, El Toro: This was one of several major Marine Corps facilities built in California during WW II to train Marine Corps pilots. The base was four miles NW of El Toro and was commissioned in March 1943. It had several satellite bases. Hundreds of Marine pilots trainer here during the war, and almost all of them served in the Pacific. After the war the base was was retained as a permanent Marine Corps training base, and as a home for several active Marine Corps air units. The base continued in those roles throughout the Cold War and worked closely with the Marine Corps base at Tustin, 7 miles north. In the 1990s MCAS, El Toro was closed.

During the war MCAS, El Toro had an outlying station, Oceanside Airport, 5.5 miles north of San Luis

Rey at Camp Pendleton.

LOMITA is a small community just west of Long Beach.

Lomita Landing Strip: This was a small air field one mile west of Lomita that was used as a sub-base to Long Beach AAF. It was operated by the Air Transport Command. After the war the air field blossomed into a first class airport called Torrence Municipal Airport.

LONG BEACH/SAN PEDRO/TERMINAL ISLAND: This is the Los Angeles Harbor area and was the center of military activity in the L.A. area. All along the coast there were various naval facilities, shipbuilding and repair facilities, docks, wharves, Coast Guard facilities, supply depots and, in places, working oil fields. Many people believed that if the Japanese ever bombed or attacked the west coast this would be a primary target area.

The "Lane Victory": This is a WW II "Victory" Ship anchored permanently in San Pedro, and restored as a memorial to the veterans of the Merchant Marines who served in WW II. A "Victory" ship is a later version of the more famous "Liberty" ship but with certain modifications to make it faster and more suitable for postwar commercial use. The "Lane Victory" is virtually unaltered since its WW II days. It is in working condition and cruises are offered. The ship, now a National Historic Landmark, served also during the Korean and Viet Nam Wars and is used frequently in movie and TV productions. Aboard ship is a gift shop, library and museum. Address: US Merchant Marines of WW II, Berth 94, Los Angeles Harbor, PO Box 629, San Pedro, CA 90733. Phone: 310/519-9545. Hours: daily 9:30-4:30. Admission charged. Free parking.

Long Beach Municipal Airport (Daugherty Field) was four miles NE of downtown Long Beach off I-405. In Dec. 1941, a few days after the attack on Pearl Harbor, this airport was one of 7 air fields in California that received combat-ready fighter units of the 4th AF. Their mission was to defend the area from enemy attacks. Those attacks never came and the fighters eventually departed. The Air Transport Command soon established a large air terminal at the airport and used the air field in its

C-47 transport planes under construction at Douglas Aircraft Co., Long Beach.

ferrying operations. Douglas Aircraft Co. had a large plant here building B-17, B-26 and A-26 bombers and C-47s. The Navy also used the field for a variety of purposes. After the war the facility became Long Beach International Airport.

Los Angeles Maritime Museum: This fine museum, in San Pedro, traces the maritime history of west coast from the earliest days of sail to the present. There is a respectable amount of material on the WW II era including models of the Liberty Ship "Lane Victory" and the luxury liner "Queen Mary", both anchored in the area. Address: Berth 84; Foot of 6th St., San Pedro, CA 90731. Phone: 310/548-7618. Hours: Tues.-Sun. 10-5. Closed Jan. 1, Thanksgiving and Dec. 25. Donations requested.

Fort MacArthur: This is a WW I-era fort at the south end of the Palos Verde Peninsula in San Pedro that was activated during WW II to protect the entrance to Los Angeles Harbor and San Pedro Bay. The fort was named after Lt. General Arthur MacArthur, father of General Douglas MacArthur. Seven large gun batteries were built along with several smaller gun emplacements. During WW II several of the fort's major batteries and other defenses were improved to be secure against air attacks. The fort controlled other coastal defense positions along the coast from Point Vincente on the tip of Palos Verde Peninsula to Coast Mesa, 25 miles to the south. Two of these positions were armed with 14" railroad guns and the others had smaller guns, or anti-aircraft guns, or observers or searchlight teams. The fort was also used early in the war as a reception center, and at the end of the war it served as a re-deployment and separation center.

In mid-Dec. 1941 the fort also became a training center for war dogs.

After the war Fort MacArthur was used for training by the Army Reserve, but in the 1970s it was closed. Some of the land was turned into parks built around the old batter-ies and gun emplacements. A WW II-era 16" covered battery remains at White's Point Park at the corner of Paseo Del Mar and Western Ave.

A WW II 155mm "Long Tom" gun position, once part of the WW II defenses of Fort MacArthur, is now in Angel's Gate Park. In the distance is the Korean Bell of Friendship presented to the U.S. by the government of South Korea in 1976. The iron sculpture between the bench and the Bell is the work of a local artist who has his workshop in one of the fort's old gun batteries which is out of the picture, about 100 yards to the left, behind the bench.

Fort MacArthur Military Museum: This is a small museum in the old WW I-era Osgood-Farley battery at Angel's Gate Park which was once part of the fort. There is also a small museum in the park devoted to veterans of the Korean War.

Queen Mary Seaport: This is a city-owned, history-oriented, entertainment center located at the end of I-710 on the Long Beach waterfront with the "Queen Mary" ocean liner as the center's main attraction. The ship was built just before the war and was one of the last great ocean liners of her day. When the war came she was converted into a troop transport and carried thousands of GI's to Europe. After the war she carried thousands home again plus a cargo or two of war brides. She was one of the fastest ships afloat and could outrun any Axis submarine, therefore she usually sailed alone and unescorted. The tactic worked because she was never attacked. After the war she became a floating hotel, convention center and museum with numerous displays on board relating to her WW II service. Guided tours of the ship are available. On shore is a large shopping area, restaurants and rides for kids. Address: Pier J, PO Box 8, Long Beach, CA 90801. Phone: 310/435-3511. Hours: daily 10-6. Admission to the center is free but there is a charge for parking.

Terminal Island: This strategically located island in Los Angeles Harbor was one of the few places in the continental U.S. were martial law was declared during WW II. It was declared on Dec. 8, 1941, the day after the attack on Pearl Harbor because U.S. military authorities thought they had a very explosive situation on their hands. The island was shared by a major U.S. Naval base, major oil installations and a sizeable community of ethnic Japanese fishermen. It was believed that the potential for sabotage by the ethnic Japanese was so great that the military had to intervene. Under martial law the activities of the ethnic Japanese were closely watched and their persons, homes and boats were liable to search at any time. No concrete evidence was ever obtained that the Japanese residents of Terminal Island were disloyal but, still, their presents was intolerable to the U.S. military.

On Feb. 1, 1942 government authori-ties conducted a sur-prise raid on the island and rounded up all ethnic Japanese males. They were taken into custody and shipped off to the enemy alien internment camp at Ft. Lincoln, ND because the relocation camps, planned for the ethnic Japanese, were not yet ready. When the relo-cation camps were completed the women and children were evacuated from Termi-nal Island and sent to relocation camps and their menfolk soon fol-lowed. Following the

removal of the ethnic Japanese, two cannery buildings previously used by the ethnic Japa-nese were taken over and used by the Navy.

U.S. Naval Air Station, San Pedro, Terminal Island, CA: In the 1930s the Navy began using Reeves Field on Terminal Island as one of its 10 Naval Reserve Air Bases providing primary flight training to Navy pilots. The Navy subsequently acquired the field and some land adjoining the Naval Operating Base (NOB) and established the U.S. NAS, San Pedro, Terminal Island. In the late 1930s the station was expanded. The station serviced seaplanes attached to battleships and cruisers as well as land based planes. In March 1939 the station began overhauling all Navy planes associate with Navy ships in the Los Angeles-Long Beach area. In Sept. 1940 the station became a receiving station for the Naval Operating Base and in Sept. 1941 was placed under the command of the NOB and remained there for most of the war. In Oct. 1941 the station acquired an Aircraft Delivery Depot which received new Navy planes produced by the local aircraft manufacturers. The planes were thoroughly inspected by Navy personnel, test flown, equipped with communications gear and armed for combat. They were then ferried to various locations for use. The station also loaded aircraft aboard small aircraft carriers and other ships. In Jan. 1942, with Japanese air attacks a possibility, Army AAF P-38 and P-40 fighter planes, along with some Marine Corps fighter planes, arrived on the station to beef up its defenses. That same month barrage balloon were placed over the station and Navy patrol planes operating from the station began conducting anti-submarine patrols along the coast. In June 1942 the Naval Air Transport Service (NATS) arrived and established schedules military transport service to cities such as Seattle, Corpus Christi, Chicago, New York City and Washington, DC. All the while, flight training continued at the station. In 1944, with fewer aircraft being purchased by the Navy, the Aircraft Delivery Depot began doing more aircraft modification. The station continued receiving, servicing and repairing fleet aircraft until the end of hostilities. By 1947 activity at the station had declined but it remained in Navy hands as a U.S. Naval Reservation throughout most of the Cold War.

U.S. Naval Operating Base, San Pedro: In 1846, during the war with Mexico, the U.S. Navy briefly established a naval base at San Pedro but it was abandoned after that war. The Navy returned in 1917 to build a training station and a submarine base. By the late 1920s the facility was specializing in servicing Navy auxiliary ships and was no longer a submarine base. In 1939, with the onset of WW II, a massive and long-term construction program began to convert the facility into a naval operating base, a sizeable ship yard and a major fuel depot. As a result, here was constant construction at the base for a period of about 10 years. In Aug. 1941 construction began on the Terminal Island Dry Dock facility, the base's main entity, and was not completed until 1945. During the war the base acquired piers, warehouses, a Marine Barracks, large cranes, a boiler shop, a plate shop, massive above-ground and underground fuel storage facilities, a net depot, an ammunition depot, a large Navy hospital, a prison, a degaussing range, a radio station, an air field, numerous smaller facilities and a variety of schools. The lack of available space limited the base from expanding in size so it was never intended that it become a home port for many of the Navy's ships. Nor was it to become a major operating base compared to those at San Diego, Puget Sound and Pearl Harbor. Ship repair was the largest undertaking at the base during the war. From Feb. 1943 to Aug. 1945 the base docked 406 ships, performed 303 major repairs and overhauls including work on 9 battleships, 14 heavy and light cruisers, 46 destroyers, 31 DEs and 30 oilers. The base also made a major conversion to the famous hospital ship "Hope" and built five floating dry docks that were used at various locations in the western Pacific. The base also became an important convoy assembly point and loaded cargo ships. At the beginning of the war the base was a receiving center and near the end of the war, a demobilization center.

With the end of hostilities the base was kept busy for several years deactivating, converting, moth-balling or selling ships. In 1947 a Naval Reserve Armory was established on the base. Also in that year the name of the base was changed to U. S. Naval Operating Base, Long Beach and, for decades to come, remained one of the Navy's most important facilities on the west coast. During the last years of their service lives, during the 1980s and early 1990s, the WW II battleships "Missouri" and "New Jersey" were based here. In the 1990s NOB, Long Beach was closed.

LOS ALAMITOS is 6 miles east of Long Beach.

U.S. Naval Air Station, Los Alamitos: This base was one mile SE of Los Alamitos and began in 1928 as a tent camp with an airstrip for the training of naval reserve aviation personnel. In 1939 fleet aircraft began using the base and a period of expansion began that lasted several year. It also became an auxiliary field to NAS, San Diego. By 1943 more fleet personnel were being trained here than reservists so the base was upgraded to a Naval Air Station. Aircraft maintenance facilities were added and the base began servicing aircraft from the carriers "Lexington", "Saratoga" and the old "Langley". By 1945 NAS, Los Alamitos had become one of the Navy's most important air stations.

After the war the training of reserve air personnel again became the base's primary mission although some fleet air units remained. In 1972 the base was converted to the Armed Forces Reserve Center and Army and National Guard units moved in. During WW II NAS, Los Alamitos had several outlying fields:
• Haster Farm Airport, 1.5 miles NE of Westminster
• Horse Ranch Field, 2 miles E. of Los Alamitos
• Palisades Airport, 2 miles east of Costa Mesa
• Mile Square Farm, 4 miles SE of Westminster

ONTARIO is just east of Pomona.

Ontario Army Air Field, 1.5 miles east of downtown Ontario, was used by the 4th AF as a training field for fighter pilots. In the postwar years the airport became Ontario International Airport.

PASADENA, five miles NE of Los Angeles, is the home of the famous Rose Bowl which was used in early 1942 as a temporary assembly point for the ethnic Japanese before they were moved on to the regular assembly centers and then on to the relocation camps. For a time, some 500 people were housed here. Pasadena also had a large military hospital during the war, McCornack General Hospital.

POMONA is 25 miles east of Los Angeles.

Pomona Assembly Center For Ethnic Japanese: This was the Los Angeles County Fairgrounds on the north edge of Pomona. It processed ethnic Japanese from May 7 to Aug. 24, 1942. During that time its population reached a maximum of 5434. Nearly everyone processed here was sent to Heart Mountain, WY. On Sept. 4, 1942 the center was turned over to the Army's Ordnance Motor Transport Agency and became known as the Pomona Ordnance Depot. The depot stocked a wide variety of ordnance materials and for much of the war serviced the California/Arizona Maneuver Area (CAMA) (Desert Training Center), just east of Pomona. The depot had a prisoner of war camp holding about 1150 POWs who worked at the depot.

RIVERSIDE is five miles south of San Bernardino.

Camp Haan: This Army camp, south of Riverside, was opened in Jan. 1941 as a training camp for artillery, coast artillery and anti-aircraft units. It was located west of March Field across SR 215. At first it was mostly a tent camp, but permanent wooden barracks and other buildings were added. By Nov. 1941 most of the men who trained here had been assigned to coastal defenses in the Los Angeles and San Francisco Bay area. When the attack came on Pearl Harbor a month later, and fears of an invasion of the U.S. west coast were at their height, it would have been these men who would have been our first line of defense had it happened.

In March 1942 Camp Haan was reorganized as an Army Service Depot and in late 1942 a prisoner of war camp was built here for 1200 Italian POWs. The POWs worked at Camp Haan and in the surrounding citrus orchards. In April 1945, German POWs arrived at Haan to replace the Italians. Later in the war Camp Haan had an 800-bed debarkation hospital which received wounded coming in from the Pacific theaters of operation. At its peak, Camp Haan had a population of 80,000 people.

After the war the camp became a separation center and in 1946 was closed. Many of the wooden buildings were sold and moved to other locations and the land was divided. Parcels went to March Field and to create the Riverside National Cemetery on Van Buren Blvd. Land was also used for a housing development, Arnold Heights, named after WW II Air Force General, "Hap" Arnold. Some of the land remains unused and a number of building foundations, streets and sidewalks can be seen from SR 215.

March Field: This air field, 9 miles SE of

The foundation of the guard house at the main gate of Camp Haan as viewed from S.R. 215.

Riverside, was the oldest AAF base in the west at the beginning of WW II and was headquarters for the 4th AF. The air field began operating in March 1918 as an Army training field for air cadets and became known as March Field in honor of a young Air Corps officer, Lt. Payton C. March, Jr., who had been killed in a crash in Texas.

Lt. Col. "Hap" Arnold commanded the base from 1931 to 1936, and many other Air Force officers, who were to gain fame in WW II, served here.

As WW II approached, the b ase was expanded and became a training base for heavy bomber crews. On Dec. 7, 1941 one of the units stationed a March Field was the 17th Medium Bomb Group. This unit, which was equipped with B-25 bombers, was moved a few days later to Pendleton Field, OR. There is early 1942 General Jimmie Doolittle approached the men of the 17th and asked them to volunteer for a secret and dangerous mission. Most of the men volunteered and the mission turned out to be the famous Doolittle bombing raid on Japan in Apr. 1942.

Later in the war, fighter pilot training was added at March as was a recruit reception center and a camouflage training center. March Field had more expansions during the war and Camp Haan was built adjacent to the base across SR 215. March Field remained a very active base into the post-war years, and in 1948 was taken over by the US Air Force and renamed March Air Force Base. It's mission changed several times and was one of the US Air Force's major installations in the west throughout the Cold War.

March Field Museum: This is a fine museum on the grounds of March AFB with about 40 aircraft ranging from WW I bi-planes to jets. Many WW II models are in the collection including a P-59 jet, America's first jet fighter. Other displays trace the history of March AFB and the US Air Force. There is a library, theater and gift shop. The museum is easily accessible from SR 215. Address: 16222 Interstate 215, March Field, CA 92518-2400. Phone: 909/655-3725. Hours: Daily 10-4, closed Jan. 1, Easter, Thanksgiving and Dec. 25. Free.

SAN BERNARDINO is 50 miles east of Los Angeles. Dursing the war the city had two defense plants, the Morrow Aircraft Corp. which built training aircraft and the Western Stove Co. which made incendiary bombs. The Army's Mira Loma Supply Depot was also in San Bernardino.

San Bernardino Army Air Field: This facility

began before the war as Municipal Airport, San Bernardino under Army Air Corps jurisdiction. During the summer of 1941 it became a training base to meet the needs of the 30,000 Pilot Training Program. In Dec. 1941, within days after the attack on Pearl Harbor, combat-ready fighter planes arrived to protect the Los Angeles area from enemy attack. In July 1942 the airport was renamed San Bernardino Army Air Field. During the war the Air Transport Command used the field and in 1943 maintenance operations for gas turbine engines were added. This lead, after the war, to the base becoming one of three major maintenance facilities for jet engines. The base was taken over by the US Air Force in 1950 and was renamed Norton Air Force Base after Capt. Leland Norton, a WW II bomber pilot who, on his 16th mission over Germany, ordered the crew of his crippled plane to bail out just before perishing with the craft. Norton AFB operated as a supply and maintenance base for the US Air Force for several decades and was closed in the 1990s.

SAN GABRIEL, an affluent residential community just east of Los Angeles, was the home town of General George S. Patton, Jr. The church which he and his family attended has a unique memorial honoring the General.

"The Patton Window": This is a stained glass window in The Church of Our Savior (Episcopal) in San Gabriel dedicated to the memory of General Patton. It depicts St. George, the General's namesake, slaying a dragon whose belly is covered with green swastikas. In the dust clouds rising from the

"The Patton Window" of The Church of Our Savior, San Gabriel, CA.

struggle are the names of Patton's victorious battles. Also in the church are windows to the General's mother and father as well as several plaques to him and other members of his family. On the church grounds is a life-sized statue of the general in a garden setting. Address: The Church of Our Savior, 535 W. Roses Rd., San Gabriel, CA 91775. Phone: 818/282-5147. Hours: No regular hours, but church personnel are generally willing to receive visitors if the church is not in use. A phone call to the church office is suggested.

SAN PEDRO: (See Long Beach/San Pedro/Terminal Island above)

SANTA ANA is 14 miles east of Long Beach. (For Santa Ana Army Air Base, see Costa Mesa above. For U.S. Naval Air Station (LTA), Santa Ana see Tustin below).

Orange County Army Air Field: This was Orange County's local airport, five miles south of downtown Santa Ana, when it was taken over by the AAF as a training base. It also served as base for Navy blimps. In the postwar years it became John Wayne Airport.

SANTA MONICA, directly west of Los Angeles, was the home of one of the world's leading aircraft manufacturers, Douglas Aircraft Co.

Douglas Aircraft Co. and Clover Field: When the war started Douglas Aircraft Co. was the world's leading manufacturer of commercial aircraft. Its famous DC-3 air liner, used the world over, was made here at Douglas's main plant at Clover Field (now Santa Monica Airport).

The DC-3 was ideal as a military cargo plane and several versions evolved, the most famous of which was the C-47. This aircraft, sometimes called "The Gooney Bird", became the workhorse of the U.S. and Allied military air transport systems. The Douglas plants, here and elsewhere, cranked out thousands of them, and under a Lend-Lease arrangement, blueprints of the plane were sent to the Soviet Union and hundreds were made there by the Soviets.Douglas also built a larger cargo plane, an expanded version of the C-47, called the C-54. Bombers and fighter planes also rolled out of Douglas plants in Santa Monica, El Segundo and Long Beach. In the summer of 1943 Clover Field was chosen by the AAF to be one of six locations in the country as a Redistribution Center for veterans returning from overseas who were being assigned to new state-side duties. The veterans were housed in local resort hotels. After the war Douglas moved away from Santa Monica, but its memory is forever etched in the history of the town.

Museum of Flying: This is an air museum established in 1989 at Santa Monica Airport to perpetuate the aviation history of the city. It is built on the site of the original Douglas Aircraft Co. facility at the field. Some 20 aircraft are on display including several important Douglas-made planes. Dwight Eisenhower's DC-3 is one of them. Address: 2772 Donald Douglas Loop North, Santa Monica, CA 90405. Phone:

The Museum of Flying in Santa Monica, CA on the former site of the Douglas Aircraft Co.

310/392-8822. Hours: W.-Sun. 10-5. Closed Jan. 1 and Dec. 25.Admission charged.

SOUTH GATE, five miles SE of Los Angeles, had a General Motors plant that built M-5 Light Tanks at the rate of 500 per month.

TUSTIN is just east of Santa Ana.

U.S. Naval Air Station (LTA), Santa Ana was 3.5 miles SE of Santa Ana. It was commissioned in Oct. 1942 as one of two new blimp bases on the west coast. The other was at Tillamook, OR. Blimps were used to patrol America's coastline primarily to watch for enemy submarine. At first 6, then 12 blimps operated out of the station. Large, all-wood hangers were built to house the blimps and at the time of their construction were the world's largest clear span wooden buildings. These hangers became a necessity when the strong Santa Ana winds blew in from the desert disrupting blimp operations. The station had 6 mooring circles and its own helium generating plant.

After the war the station was reduced in status as blimp operations were phased out. In 1951 it was given over to the Marines and became U.S. Marine Corps Air Station, Tustin (helicopters). In the 1990s the base closed. Two of the huge blimp hangers remain at the base and can be easily seen from surrounding roads.

VAN NUYS is a section of Los Angeles in the San Fernando Valley.

Birmingham General Hospital: This was an Army hospital built in Van Nuys in late 1943 and early 1944 to serve as both a general hospital and a debarkation hospital. It had 1777 beds, of which 800 were devoted to debarkation activities. The hospital specialized in general medicine, NCS syphilis, rheumatic fever and psychiatry. The hospital had a small prisoners of war compound. In March 1946 the hospital was transferred to the Veterans Administration.

Van Nuys Airport: This airport, three miles NW

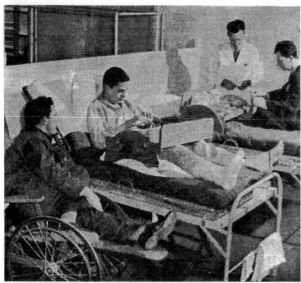

Wounded Veterans at Birmingham General Hospital were employed to sort parts for Northrop Aircraft Corp. (See page 21.)

operated by the Wartime Civil Control Administration (WCCA), an agency of the Army's Western Defense Command. When the voluntary relocation program proved to be a failure the camp was transferred to the War Relocation Authority (WRA) and converted into a relocation camp. It was designed to hold 10,000 people and operated at, or near, that capacity during its existence. The residents worked in agriculture inside and outside the camp. The camp had its own farm area just to the south and a hog farm .5 miles further south. Guayule, a rubber-producing plant, was grown in several locations as part of a government-sponsored experimental program to grow natural rubber in the U.S. America's main supply of natural rubber had been lost when the Japanese invaded SE Asia. The camp also had a camouflage net factory which was the only factory of any kind in any of the camps.

Conditions at Manzanar were similar to those at the other camps although Manzanar had a golf course where some of the other camps did not.

In 1943 famed photographer Ansel Adams visited the camp and took 240 photographs. These photographs have since become well-known and are one of the best photographic records of the camp.

Replica of the original camp sign made for a Japanese-made TV movie entitled "The Two Motherlands. The original sign has been lost.

Manzanar closed in Nov. 1945. All of its buildings, except for the camp auditorium, were torn down or sold and moved. Many of those moved remained in use for years. The auditorium later became an Inyo County equipment shop. Visitors can drive through the camp on well-defined but crumbling roads. There are many foundations, two stone guard houses at the main entrance and the cemetery with an impressive monument.

EASTERN CALIFORNIA MUSEUM OF INYO COUNTY, in Independence, 6 miles north of Manzanar, has displays, artifacts, photographs, etc. on Manzanar. While in Independence visitors will see many of the old camp buildings still in use. Some of them include the west wing of the VFW Hall, the Willow Motel, the Ranch Apartments, the Sierra Baptist Church and the pink maintenance building behind St. Vivian's Catholic Church. Museum address: 155 Grant St., Independence, CA 93526. Phone: 619/878-

of Van Nuys, was a local airport before the war and was utilized by Timm Aircraft Corp. which built military trainer planes and cargo gliders. The field was taken over by the 4th AF and used extensively by the Army and Navy during the war. The AAF trained fighter pilots here in night fighting. The airport had two sub-bases; Grand Central Air Terminal, Glendale and Oxnard Landing Strip, Oxnard. After the war the AAF departed and the airport again became Van Nuys Airport.

MANZANAR RELOCATION CAMP FOR ETHNIC JAPANESE was located 50 miles south of Bishop and 9 miles north of the small community of Lone Pine on the west side of Hwy. U.S. 395. It first opened on Mar. 21, 1942 as one of two reception centers (the other was at Poston, AZ) to receive and assist ethnic Japanese evacuating the west coast during the short-live and ill-fated voluntary relocation program. It was first

Three views of Manzanar— Top left: Sign on U.S. Hwy 395 approaching the camp from the south. Top right: Manzanar Cemetery. The short posts around the monument are simulated tree trunks made of concrete. Debris on the monument is dead flowers. Bottom: The stone building to the left is one of two guardhouse at Manzanar's main gate. To the right of center is a stone monument with a plaque, and to the far right is the camp's former auditorium, which became the Inyo County Highway Dept. equipment shop. It is the only original wooden building remaining at the camp.

The Ranch Apartments at Locust and Hay Sts. In Independence is made of camp building purchased at the time of the camp's closure and moved to this location.

2010 Hours: W.-Sun. 10-4. Closed Tuesdays and holidays. Donations requested.

MARYSVILLE is 40 miles north of Sacramento.

CAMP BEALE was 12 miles east of Marysville. It was activated in late 1942 as the home of the newly formed 13th Armored Div. The base was huge, with many maneuvering areas for tanks towards its eastern end. In the maneuvering areas were simulated enemy bunkers, dragon's teeth and simulated European roads and bridges. Many of these training obstacles remain and can be seen from the local roads. Waldo Rd. is especially good.

After the 13th Div. left Camp Beale, the camp was used to train the 81st and 96th Infantry Divisions and various Army replace-

Concrete dragon's teeth, a tank obstacle used in training tank crews, Camp Beale, CA.

A simulated European bridge at Camp Beale used to train tank crews.

ment units. Beale had a large prisoner of war camp holding 1200 POWs many of them German naval personnel. The POWs worked on the base and on surrounding farms.

After the war the camp was used as a redeployment and separation center and eventually given over to the US Air Force and renamed Beale Air Force Base. Much of the acreage was sold off. Beale AFB operated continually throughout the Cold War.

EDWARD F. BEALE MUSEUM, on the grounds of Beale Air Force Base, preserves the history of Beale from its WW II beginning to the present. There are a number of aircraft at the museum, some of them WW II vintage. Inside the museum are additional displays including a scale mock-up of Camp Beale during WW II, and an exhibit on the all-black "Tuskegee Airmen". Address: 9 SRW/CCX, Beale AFB, CA 95903. Phone: 916/634-2038. Hours: M-F 9-5, Sat. 10-4, closed holidays. Free.

MARYSVILLE ARMY AIR FIELD, three miles south of town, was taken over the AAF and used for only a very short time. It was then transferred to the Air Technical Service Command and eventually vacated. After the war it became Yuba County Airport.

MARYSVILLE ASSEMBLY CENTER FOR ETHNIC JAPANESE: This center

The concrete solitary confinement blockhouse in the disciplinary compound of Camp Beale's prisoner of war compound.

was located 6 miles south of Marysville and about 1.5 miles south of Yuba County Airport. It operated from May 8 to June 29, 1942 toreceive and process the ethnic Japanese in the area that were being evacuated to relocation camps to the east. Its peak population reached 2451 people. Everyone processed here went to the relocation camp at Tule Lake, CA. On June 16, while the last ethnic Japanese were being processed, the center was turned over to the Army's VII Corps which used it for the duration of the war.

MENDOCINO is on California's northern coast about half way between San Francisco and Eureka.

U.S. NAVAL AUXILIARY AIR STATION, MENDOCINO, five miles SE of Little River, CA was the area's local airport known as Mendocino County Airport. It was taken over by the Navy early in the war and used as an auxiliary field for NAS, Alameda.

MERCED is in the San Joachin Valley midway between Stockton and Fresno. It is also the entrance to Yosemite National Park.

MERCED ASSEMBLY CENTER FOR ETHNIC JAPANESE: This was the local fairgrounds, one mile SE of Merced. The camp operated from May 8 to Sept. 15, 1942 receiving and processing local ethnic Japanese being evacuated to the relocation camps. At its peak, the center housed 4508 people. Nearly everyone processed here went to the relocation camp at Granada, CO. On Sept. 30, 1942 the center was transferred to the 4th Air Service Area Command.

MERCED ARMY AIR FIELD, 7 miles NW of town, was first known as Air Corps Basic Flying School, Merced. In Sept. 1941 it became one of the fields utilized to meet the needs of the 30,000 Pilot Training Program. As the original name indicated, it provided basic air training for beginning pilots and crewmen. In April 1942 it was renamed Merced Army Air Field. Many pilots and crews were trained here during the war including a number of Women's Air Service Pilots (WASP). During the summer of 1945, when most other air fields were winding down, Merced was expanded to accommodate the large air tankers then coming into service. When the war ended Merced was home to several air tanker squadrons and remained a training center for pilots and air crews.

In Jan. 1948 the facility was taken over by the US Air Force and renamed Castle Air Force Base in honor of a WW II pilot and Medal of Honor winner, Brig. Gen. Frederick W. Castle who was killed on Christmas Eve, 1944 while lead-

The Castle Air Museum at Castle Air Force Base, Merced, CA.

ing a 2000-bomber raid over Germany. Castle AFB remained a training and tanker base for several decades and was eventually closed in the 1990s. Auxiliary air fields used by Merced AAF during the war were:

- Aux. #1, Merced Airport, 2.5 miles NW of Merced
- Aux. #6, Merced Auxiliary Air Field, 1.5 miles SW of Merced
- Aux. #?, Mariposa Airport, 4.5 miles NW of Mariposa

CASTLE AIR MUSEUM is on the corner of Buhach and Santa Fe in Atwater, CA, and displays a large collection of aircraft from WW I to the present. Many WW II models are in the collection including B-17G, B-18, B-23, B-24M, B-25, B-29 bombers; A-26 Invader attack bomber; C-46F Commando, C-47 Skytrain, C-54 Skymaster transports; AT-6 Texan, C-45 Expediter and BT-13 Valiant trainers. Address: PO Box 488, Atwater, CA 95301. Phone: 209/723-2178. Hours: Summer daily 10-6, winter daily 10-4. Closed Jan. 1, Easter, Thanksgiving and Dec. 25. Donations accepted. Location: Leave U.S. 99 at the Buhach Rd. Exit, take Buhach south to Santa Fe Dr., turn east on Santa Fe Dr., proceed 200 yards and the museum is on the south side of Santa Fe Dr.

MODESTO is located 25 miles SE of Stockton on SR 99.

HAMMOND GENERAL HOSPITAL was built by the Army in Modesto during 1942 to treat war wounded. The hospital was of temporary wooden construction and had 2540 beds. It specialized in neurology, general and orthopedic surgery, neurosurgery and psychiatry. In Dec. 1945 it was closed and the assets tuned over to the state.

MOJAVE is 60 miles NE of Los Angeles in the Mojave Desert.

MUROC ARMY AIR FIELD was SE of Mojave. It began in 1933 as the Army Air Corps' Muroc Lake Bombing and Gunnery Range for crews training at March Field. In 1937 the Army Air Corps maneuvered here. The range was primarily for the use of the 2nd AF, but the 4th AF used it during the early years of the war. In 1942 AAF units moved in to do testing of new aircraft and the base underwent a confusing series of name changes: Muroc Bombing Field, Muroc Lake Army Air Base,

Muroc Army Air Base and finally Muroc Army Air Field. The latter name is the one it retained from Nov. 1943 to the end of the war. In 1942 a part of the base was designated Muroc Flight Test Base, a top secret operation. It was located on an 18,000 foot by 21,000 foot hard dry lake bed. On Oct. 18, 1942, America's first jet fighter, the XP-59 flew for the first time from one of Muroc's runways. On Jan. 8, 1944 another jet, the XP-80, was tested here. It had a British-made Halford jet engine, considered to be the best jet engine at the time. The XP-80 attained the speed of 500 mph in level flight, the first U.S. plane to do so. The production model P-80 evolved from this plane and these tests. In May 1945 B-29 bomber crews began training here because of Muroc's long runways.

After the war, the base came under US Air Force control and in Feb. 1948 was renamed Muroc Air Force Base. The base continued as a aircraft test center. On July 5, 1948 one of the base's test pilots, Capt. Glen W. Edwards, a WW II veteran of 50 missions in North Africa, was killed in the crash of a prototype YB-49 "Flying Wing". In Dec. 1949 the base was renamed in his honor as Edwards Air Force Base.

The base operated throughout the Cold War as one of the US Air Force's main test centers for aircraft, rockets and missiles. It also cooperates with NASA on space programs. NASA has its own facilities at the base, the NASA Dryden Flight Research Facility.

Flight Test Historical Museum: This museum is an Air Force Field Museum on the grounds of Edwards AFB and is, at the time of

publication, an interim museum until a larger facility can be acquired. Its mission is to interpret the history of the Flight Test Center, Edwards AFB and its antecedents, and the history of USAF flight testing. The museum has over 60 aircraft but virtually all of them are postwar. The most prominent WW II aircraft here is a P-59B, America's first jet fighter plane, which was developed at the end of WW II. Address: Bldg. 7211, 1100 Kinchelow, Edwards AFB, CA 93524-1032. Phone: 805/277-8050. Hours: Tues.-Sat. 9-5, closed Jan. 1, Thanksgiving and Dec. 25. Free.

U.S. MARINE CORPS AIR STATION MOJAVE was one mile east of town on SR 58 and before the war was the Kern County Municipal Airport. In 1942 the Marines leased the airport and converted it into a training base for carrier pilots. During that year 32 different Marine Corps air units trained here. By early 1944 operational fighter squadrons flying F4F Wildcats arrived at the station and the facility underwent another expansion. Later in the year Army and Navy pilots trained at Mojave MCAS as part of a joint training program on amphibious operations.

After the war the station was phased out and in 1947 was returned to the County and renamed Mojave Airport. Many WW II buildings remained for years at the airport including some Quonset Huts and a hanger.

MONTEREY is at the southern end of Monterey Bay. In Dec. 1941, when fears of a Japanese invasion gripped California, the Army had concluded that if the enemy planned to invade in the San Francisco area, the likely place for the first landings would be somewhere along the 40-mile stretch of beach of Monterey Bay between Santa Cruz and Carmel.

FORT ORD, just east of Monterey, began in 1917

Top: The Bell XP-59, America's first jet aircraft. Flown here at Muroc Army Air Field for the first time on Oct. 1, 1942. Right: The General Electric Type 1A Turbo Jet Engine used in the XP-59.

Fort Ord had hundreds of WW II buildings like this one in good repair and in use until the fort closed.

as Gigling Field Artillery Range, an artillery range an maneuver area for troops stationed at The Presidio of Monterey. In 1933 it was renamed Camp Ord and in 1938 the first permanent buildings were built. Camp Ord expanded steadily for the next two years and almost doubled in land area. By Aug. 1942 it was designated Fort Ord, a permanent base, and became the home of the Army's reactivated 7th Infantry Division. The 7th trained at Ord until 1943 and then went to the Aleutian Islands of Alaska. The fort then became a replacement depot and a staging area for Army units going overseas. Fort Ord had a prisoner of war camp holding over 1000 POWs.

As the war wound down Fort Ord received returning divisions from overseas to be deactivated or to be sent on to other places. Various post-war missions followed and in 1974 Fort Ord became home once again to the 7th Infantry.

In 1994 Fort Ord was closed and its assets and land used for many purposes. There were hundreds of WW II buildings here and in use to the very last.

THE PRESIDIO OF MONTEREY was first constructed by the Spanish in 1770 and therefore is one of the oldest military sites in the U.S. It's long history parallels that of California. With only 406 acres, it was limited in its usefulness during WW II. It was, however, the headquarters of the 3rd Army Corps and was used as a reception center for inductees, and in 1945 it became a school for soldiers scheduled to do occupation duty. In 1946 the Presidio became the Army's Language School and retained this mission for several decades.

U.S. Army Museum, Presidio of Monterey: This is a small museum on the Presidio grounds. There are displays on the post's long history and its role as a language school. There are special displays on General "Vinegar Joe" Stilwell, who lived nearby in Carmel, and on Lt. General Arthur MacArthur, father of General Douglas MacArthur. The elder MacArthur was post commander here in 1907. Address: AFZW-DC-P-Museum, Presidio of Monterey, Monterey, CA 93944-5006. Phone: 408/647-5414. Hours: M-F 9-12 and 1-4. Closed Federal holidays. Free.

U.S. NAVAL AUXILIARY AIR STATION, MONTEREY, 3.5 miles SE of Monterey was Monterey Peninsula Airport. During the war it was an auxiliary air field to NAS, Alameda.

U.S. NAVAL POSTGRADUATE SCHOOL was located on the grounds of the old Hotel Del Monte within the city of Monterey. The elegant old hotel opened in 1880 and in 1942 was leased to the Navy with an option to buy. The Navy used it as a pre-flight training school for Naval air cadets throughout the war. A curriculum of marine engineering was also added during the war. After the war the Navy bought the hotel and its 600 acres of land and enlarged the school. In 1951 the Naval Academy's postgraduate school moved here from Annapolis, MD. In the postwar years the school ranked academically with the best graduate universities in the country. Some 80% of the Navy's postgraduate students attended the school.

MORGAN HILL is 10 miles south of San Jose.

FLYING LADY RESTAURANT, WAGONS TO WINGS MUSEUM is a privately owned resort complex that consists of a restaurant decorated in an aviation motif, a golf course and a transportation museum. In the museum's collection are several WW II-era planes. In the Flying Lady Restaurant are photos and paintings of aircraft, posters and aircraft paraphenalia. Hanging from the restaurant's ceiling, are 104 large-scale model planes. Address: 15060 Foothill Rd., Morgan Hill, CA 95037. Phone: 408/779-4136 or 408/227-4607. Hours: Museum, W-Sun. 10-8, closed Jan. 1 and Dec. 25. Museum admission is free.

MUROC (See Mojave, above)

OAKLAND: (See San Francisco and the San Francisco Bay Metropolitan Area).

PALM SPRINGS is 80 miles west of Los Angeles.

PALM SPRINGS ARMY AIR FIELD was 2.5 miles east of Palm Springs and was used by both the Army and Navy. The AAF's Air Transport Command and the Naval Air Ferry Command trained pilots here in C-47 transports. The field had a large air freight terminal and was used for ferrying. Many of the field's personnel stayed at the comfortable Lapaz Guest Ranch nearby. In the spring of 1944 the ATC's training operations moved to Brownsville, TX.

TORNEY GENERAL HOSPITAL came into being during the summer of 1942 when the Army purchased the El Mirador Hotel in Palm Springs and converted it into a 1600-bed general hospital. During the war Torney specialized in general medicine, rheumatic fever and general and orthopedic surgery. During the summer of 1943 the Army transferred the hospital to the AAF. About 250 prisoners of war worked at the hospital. In Nov. 1945 the facility was turned over to the Federal Works Administration.

PALMDALE is 35 miles north of Los Angeles in the Mojave Desert.

PALMDALE ARMY AIR FIELD, three miles NE of the town, was used by the 4th AF as a sub-base to Muroc AAF. It was retained after the war and became known as US Air Force Plant #42.

PASO ROBLES is 30 miles north of San Luis Obispo.

ESTRELLA ARMY AIR FIELD, five miles NE of Paso Robles, was the town's local airport before the war and was used by the 4th AF as a sub-base to Santa Maria AAF. After the war it once again the town's local airport.

CAMP ROBERTS, 12 miles north of Paso Robles on Hwy 101, was built by the Army in 1940/41 as a training camp for infantry and artillery replacements, and as a school for cooks and bakers. The peak capacity reached during the war was 36,000 troops, plus a prisoner of war camp with about 900 POWs. This was a segregated camp so negro troops also trained here. Camp Roberts was deactivated in 1946, but opened again for the Korean War at which time the 7th Armored Division was reactivated and trained here. After that war the camp continued its mission as a training camp but on a reduced scale. In 1971 it was turned over to the California National Guard.

This monument now stands on the site of Camp Stoneman. It is on Harbor St. between E. Leland Rd. and Atlantic Ave. in Pittsburgh, CA. (See page 26.)

The Civil Engineer Corps/ Seabee Museum at Port Hueneme, CA.

PINEDALE (SEE p. 14)

PINE VALLEY, 25 miles east of San Diego, had a small Marine training camp operating in an old CCC camp. Marine signal companies and transportation companies trained here. Because Pine Valley was in a heavily forested area, the Marines were given some training in fighting forest fires. During Oct. 1943 a major fire broke out in nearby Hauser Canyon and the Marines were called out to help. One group of Marines was caught by a sudden change in the wind and 8 of their number perished and a dozen others were injured. Today, a monument and plaque stand in Hauser Canyon honoring the 8 who died.

PITTSBURGH is 20 miles east of Oakland on the San Joachin River.

CAMP STONEMAN was built by the Army's Transportation Corps in March 1942 adjacent to the town of Pittsburgh as one of 8 staging centers in the U.S. Thousands of GIs resided here awaiting orders to proceed to one of the embarkation centers in the San Francisco Bay area for overseas duty. At times Camp Stoneman housed 21,000 troops. After Italy changed sides in the war, Italian Service Units were employed at the camp, and in Jan. 1946, 2250 German prisoners of war were billeted here awaiting repatriation to Germany. The Camp operated throughout the Korean War, again as a staging center. By the time it was closed in 1954, 2.5 million troops had passed through. (See photo, page 25.)

POMONA: (See Los Angeles and the Los Angeles Metropolitan Area)

PORT CHICAGO: (See San Francisco and the San Francisco Bay Metropolitan Area)

PORT HUENEME is a deep-water seaport just south of Oxnard.

U.S. NAVAL CONSTRUCTION BATTALION CENTER, PORT HUENEME. Soon after the local citizens of Port Hueneme improved their port facilities with private funds, the U.S. Navy purchased them, acquired additional land, and began building an Advanced Base Depot (ABD) to supply the needs of the Navy's construction battalions (SeaBees) operating in the Pacific. The depot received supplies, stored them in huge warehouses and then shipped them overseas as needed. SeaBee units came and went through the port also. A private company, the Pacific Naval Air Bases Co., operated the depot throughout the war under contract with the Navy. The depot expanded regularly and by 1945 it could accommodate up to 21,000 base personnel and SeaBees in transit. The docks could handle 9 cargo ships and two tank landing craft simultaneously, and the rail yard could hold up to 2000 boxcars.

After the war, Port Hueneme was designated a permanent installation. The Navy took over operations and as other Naval depots closed down around the country some of their operations and personnel came here. Throughout the Cold War Port Hueneme was the Navy's main ABD on the west coast.

CEC/SEABEE MUSEUM is on the grounds of Port Hueneme Naval Construction Battalion Center. It is housed in two WW II Quonset Huts and was established in 1947 as a lasting monument to the Seabees and the Navy's Civil Engineer Corps (CEC). On display are numerous weapons, uniforms, tools, instruments, underwater equipment, Arctic equipment, vehicles, etc. used by the Engineers and Seabees. Heritage Park, across the street from the museum has on display several WW II amphibious vehicles. Museum Address: Building 99, Port Hueneme, CA 93043. Phone: 805/982-5163. Hours: M-F 8-4:30, Sat. 9-4:30, Sun. 12:30-4:30, closed holidays. Free.

PORTERVILLE is 25 miles SE of Visalia in the San Joachin Valley.

PORTERVILLE ARMY AIR FIELD was located three miles SW of the town and was a sub-base to Lemoore AAF. The field had an AAF Western Signal Aviation Unit Training Center.

REDDING is a county seat in north-central California.

REDDING FIELD, 7.5 miles SE of town, was Benton Airpark before the war. The Air Technical Service Command leased the field for the duration of the war and it operated as a subpost of Hamilton Field. Redding Field was used as a refueling base and was home to various Air Force operational units during the war. It was returned to the city of Redding after the war and became Redding Municipal Airport.

RIVERSIDE: (See Los Angeles and the Los Angeles Metropolitan Area)

SACRAMENTO is the capital of California and was a city of 106,000 people at the beginning of the war.

CALIFORNIA CITIZEN SOLDIER MUSEUM is in Sacramento's old riverfront district. It is dedicated to preserving and honor the rich legacy of California's militia and military history with special emphasis on the California National Guard. The museum has on display, and in its library, over 30,000 military-related documents, papers and memorabilia. A significant number of displays are devoted to the WW II era. Address: 1119 2nd St., Sacramento, CA 95814. Phone: 916/442-2883. Hours: T-Sun. 10-5. Closed some holidays. A modest admission is charged.

CAMP KOHLER was an Army Signal Corps replacement training center and depot established near Sacramento in Dec. 1942. In 1944 the depot was chosen by the 4th AF, even thought there was no air field here, to be an intransit depot for AAF men and equipment being transferred from Europe to the Pacific. The sudden end to the war in the Pacific made this operation short-lived. The camp was closed by the Signal Corps in March 1946, but was soon taken over by the Army Corps of Engineers. They stayed only until Sept. 1947. After that the camp was closed again and its assets sold.

MATHER FIELD was 12 miles east of Sacramento. It was built during WW I as a pilot training base and was used by the Army Air Corps for various purposes in the years between the wars. In 1941 the field was expanded and became a training base for single-engine pilots and navigators. Mather had one auxiliary air field, Lincoln Airport, three miles NW of Sacramento. In 1943 the training of B-25 bomber crews began and in 1944-45 it became a port of aerial embarkation to the Pacific in preparation for the expected transfer of large numbers of men and aircraft from Europe to the Pacific. After the war the base was made a permanent base by the US Air Force and in 1948 renamed Mather Air Force Base. The training of navigators became its special. In the 1990s, Mather was closed.

McCLELLAN FIELD (SACRAMENTO AIR DEPOT) was 10 miles NE of Sacramento. In 1935, at the time is was established, it was known as Pacific Air Depot and was one of only four such air depots in the country. In 1938 the base was renamed Sacramento Air Depot and underwent a major expansion as a repair and overhaul facility for P-38 and P-39 fighter planes. The planes were serviced on an assembly line basis. In 1940 an assembly line was added to overhaul P-40 fighters. In Dec. 1941, soon after the attack on Pearl Harbor, P-40s, B-26s and B-17s began arriving at the field to be armed and prepared for immediate shipment overseas. Some B-17s came direct to McClellan from the factories. During this time most of the AAF planes that went to the Pacific Theater were prepared at McClellan. In March 1942 General Jimmy Doolittle's B-25s arrived at McClellan for arming in preparation for their famous Tokyo raid. From here the planes went to USNAS, Alameda to be loaded aboard the aircraft carrier "Hornet". During the war numerous planes arrived here from all over the U.S. to be armed and otherwise prepared for shipment overseas to combat areas. After the war McClellan became a storage center of several types of aircraft including B-29 bombers. The base was renamed McClellan Air Force Base in 1948 and it's repair and overhaul mission continued throughout the Cold War. McClellan was closed in the 1990s after the end of the Cold War.

PBY Catalina seaplanes under construction at Consolidated-Vultee Co.

SACRAMENTO ASSEMBLY CENTER FOR ETHNIC JAPANESE: This center was located 6 miles NE of Downtown Sacramento just east of McClellan AFB in a former migrant workers' camp. It operated from May 6 to June 26, 1942 processing the local ethnic Japanese being evacuated to relocation camps further east. At its peak, the center housed 4739 people. Most of the people processed here went to the relocation camp at Tule Lake, CA. On July 30, 1942 the center was turned over to the Army's Signal Corps and used by them for the remained of the war.

SACRAMENTO SIGNAL DEPOT, located at Fruitridge and Perkins-Florin Rds., was built in 1942 as an Army receiving, storing, repairing and shipping facility for Signal Corps equipment. In 1962 the depot was renamed Sacramento Army Depot and operated for many years under that name and eventually was closed in the 1990s.

SACRAMENTO MUNICIPAL AIRPORT, four miles south of Sacramento, was used as a sub-base to Chico AAF. It was used jointly by the 4th AF and the Western Training Flying Command.

SAINT NICOLAS ISLAND is 115 miles SW of Los Angeles and the most westerly of southern California's offshore islands. In 1944 the island was investigated by officials of the "Manhattan (Atomic Bomb) Project" as a possible site for testing the first atomic devices. The site was rejected in favor of the White Sands area of New Mexico.

SALINAS is a farming center just east of Monterey, and during the war had a relatively high number of ethnic Japanese in the area.

SALINAS ARMY AIR BASE, three miles SE of town, was a subpost to Fort Ord during the war. It was a processing center and a training field for Army pilots in reconnaissance and observation duties in small planes. The Air Transport Command also used the field and had an air freight terminal here.

SALINAS ASSEMBLY CENTER FOR ETHNIC JAPANESE: This was the California Rodeo Grounds, one mile north of downtown Salinas. It operated as an assembly and processing center for the local ethnic Japanese from Apr. 27 to July 4, 1942. At its peak it housed 3586 people. Most of the people processed here went to the Colorado River Relocation Camp at Poston, AZ. On July 24, 1942 it was turned over to the VII Army Corps which used it for the duration of the war. After the war, it again became the California Rodeo Grounds.

SAN BERNARDINO: (See Los Angeles and the Los Angeles Metropolitan Area)

SAN CLEMENTE ISLAND/U.S. NAVAL AUXILIARY AIR STATION, SAN CLEMENTE ISLAND.

This is an uninhabited island 60 miles off the coast of southern California and about halfway between Los Angeles and San Diego. The entire island was an auxiliary air station to NAS, San Diego and had been used for years before the war as a bombing and gunnery range, and for amphibious training. At the north end of the island is Castle Field, an outlying air field to NAS, San Diego. In the postwar years several old WW II ships fulfilled their last missions here as target ships and were sunk in the waters around the island. Some of those ships became accessible to scuba divers.

SAN DIEGO and the SAN DIEGO METROPOLITAN AREA: San Diego had, long before the war, become a "Navy town" because of the many naval and Cost Guard facilities here. Early in the war San Diego was chosen as the new headquarters of the Pacific Fleet after the headquarters left Honolulu. During the first weeks of the war fears of an invasion and/or air attacks were strong here as they were elsewhere in California. At that time the city's only air defenses were the guns on the ships in the harbor. This was soon corrected as the Army moved in as soon as it could to provide adequate air defenses. Arrangement were made between the U.S. Government and the Government of Mexico to allow joint teams of U.S. Army officers and Mexicans Army officers and soldiers to patrol the Mexican peninsula of Baja California. The teams were platoon-size units and patrolled all the way to the southern tip of the peninsula. There were persistent rumors early in the war that the Japanese might have secret air bases in Baja California, but no evidence of this was ever found. The American officers were required to wear civilian clothing and all U.S. markings had to be removed from U.S. Army vehicles and other equipment to accommodate Mexico's neutrality laws.

The Consolidated-Vultee Corp., San Diego's largest aircraft maker, made two of the war's most famous planes, the B-24 Liberator bomber and the PBY Catalina sea plane. At the beginning of the war the B-24 was America's longest-range bomber and it became an absolute necessity to America's war plans. Demand was so high for the bomber that Consolidated-Vultee set up the world's first moving production line to product the planes on an assembly-line basis. But even this modern production method wasn't enough to meet demands, so other production facilities were set up around the country to produce B-24s. The B-24 remained America's premier long-range bomber until Boeing's B-29 and Consolidated's own B-32 were introduced near the end of the war. Development of the B-32 was delayed by production and quality problems, and only 214 B-32s were produced. Of these, only 14 saw action during the last months of the war before production was canceled.

The PBY, like the B-24, was a long-range plane that could land on water or land. It was designed for patrol and rescue work, but it too could drop bombs when called upon to do so. It was very much in demand and used in large numbers by the U.S. Navy and Coast Guard and by several Allied nations.

Another aircraft maker in San Diego was Ryan Aeronautical Co. who produced the PT-22 primary trainer used to train thousands of

A Panama Mount on the ocean side of Point Loma. It held a WW I-vintage 155mm artillery piece that could be operated to track a moving ship. It could also shoot into Mexico in the event of a Japanese invasion from the south. In the foreground are the remains of a trench and a corrugated metal shelter in which the crew could take refuge. Out of the picture and below is the remains of a concrete ammunition storage bunker.

A WW II base line station used to determine the range and position of an enemy vessel and to direct artillery fire. The rough concrete pattern on its top side is camouflage. Visitors taking the ranger-guided park tours at Point Loma can go into this station.

A 60" search light installation at Point Loma. In operation, the square cover slides to the side on rails and the searchlight rises out of a concrete pit below.

Army and Navy pilots. They also produced the SOR-1 Scout plane and had a highly respected flying school, the Ryan School of Aeronautics. The school was one of the first in the country to be selected by the Air Corps, in 1939, to train Army pilots.

The aerospace industry and the Navy remained major factors in San Diego's economy throughout the Cold War and San Diego served as the home to many of the Navy's Pacific Fleet operations and warships.

CABRILLO NATIONAL MONUMENT, at the tip-end of Point Loma Peninsula has several interesting WW II coastal defenses. During the war two 16" covered batteries were built on the ocean side of Point Loma along with four Panama Mounts. One of the 16" batteries remained in use by the military after the war, but not as a coastal defense battery. Two of the Panama Mounts remain and can be explored. They are on the ocean-side of Point Loma about 1/2 mile north of the lighthouse. Access is from Gatchell Rd. Address of Cabrillo Natl. Monument: 1800 Cabrillo Natl. Monument Dr.,

San Diego, CA 92106. Phone: 619/557-5450. Hours: daily 9-5:15 with expanded hours in summer. Admission charged.

CAMP CALLAN was an Army camp, built in 1940, to train coast artillerymen and anti-aircraft gunners. It was three miles north of La Jolla on Torrey Pines Mesa. At its peak the camp housed 7500 people. In Nov. 1945 it was closed and declared surplus. The present-day Torrey Pines Golf Course is built on a part of the camp's land.

FORT EMORY was a battery of two 16" coastal guns at the south end of Dan Diego Bay adjacent to Imperial Beach. It was a subpost of Fort Rosecrans. Construction began in 1942 and continued throughout the war years. The battery was completed but the guns were never installed. It still exists and is on the grounds of the Navy's Imperial Beach Radio Station.

CAMP GILLESPIE was a county airport on the northern edge of El Cajon, an eastern suburb of San Diego. During the early part of WW II land were purchased by the government to build Camp Gillespie as a training camp for paratroopers. Three 256 foot-high towers were built from which the paratroopers jumped. The camp was also an auxiliary air field to U.S. Marine Corps Air Station, El Toro. After the war the camp was turned over to the county to use as a local airport known as Gillespie Field. In 1954-55 the towers were removed.

The San Diego Aerospace Museum, in Balboa Park, occupies one of the hangers at the airport and has a restoration facility for vintage aircraft there. At times, vintage aircraft can be seen at the hanger and operating on the field.

CAMP KEARNEY and CAMP ELLIOTT: Both of these camps became part of the U.S. Naval Air Station, Miramar which was created after the war primarily from the Army's Camp Kearney, and the Marine Corps' Camp Elliott.

Camp Kearney began during WW I as a training base for Army infantry units. Between the World Wars it was used as a blimp base and a bombing range.

Camp Elliott was a large base of 26,034 acres, leased by the Marine Corps before the war from the city of San Diego, as a training base for large Marine units. It became a subpost of the U.S. Marine Corps Base, San Diego (see below) after that facility could no longer expand. Camp Elliott, directly east of Camp Kearney, was also limited in its ability to expand, so in 1942 the Marines acquired a much larger base further north near the community of Oceanside, Camp Joseph H. Pendleton.

At the beginning of WW II the Army's Camp Kearney was transferred to the Navy. On the northern half of the site the Marines built an air station named Marine Corps Air Depot, Miramar, and on the southern half the Navy built an auxiliary air station, calling it U.S. Naval Auxiliary Air Station, Camp Kearney, under the control of the U.S. NAS, San Diego. The Navy's Air Ferry Command also used the station. This arrangement existed throughout the war. In 1946-47 most of the land that had been Camps Kerney and Elliott was combined into one naval facility and in 1952 the entire complex was renamed U.S. Naval Air Station, Miramar. The station then served throughout the Cold War.

CAMP JOSEPH H. PENDLETON is a very large Marine base 15 miles north of San Diego. The base was acquired in 1942 by the Marine Corps as a tactical training area for large Marine units. Camp Pendleton had a long stretch of ocean frontage suitable for amphibious training and open and varied terrain inland suitable for battalion-sized infantry maneuvers, tank maneuvers and artillery ranges. It was the largest Marine base on the west coast and in many respects was comparable to the huge Marine training base on the east coast, Camp Lejeune, NC.

Construction began at Camp Pendleton in May 1942 and the camp's facilities expanded rapidly. The first major Marine unit to train here was the 3rd Marine Division under General Lemuel Shepherd. The 5th Marine Division followed the 3rd Division as did other Marine units and some Allied forces. During the war virtually all types of training operations were conducted here; amphibious, ground, air and support services. In 1944 the camp's population peaked at 86,749 Marines, sailors, civilians and others.

When the war ended most Marine units returning from the Pacific passed through Pendleton to either separate or go on to other assignments. Activities at the Camp rapidly declined after this, but some training continued and the nuclei of many units remained. Activity at the camp surged with the Korean War and again during the Viet Nam era. Throughout the Cold War Camp Pendleton remained an active home of the Marines on the west coast.

Amphibian Vehicle Museum: This outdoor museum is on the grounds of Camp Joseph H. Pendleton and displays amphibious vehicles used by the Marines over the years. There are also some captured Japanese amphibious vehicles. With over 30 vehicles, this is one of

Left: The grave site of Marine General Holland M. "Howlin' Mad" Smith. Right: A group grave of three airmen killed in a plane crash on Oct. 29, 1943. This grave is not far from that of General Smith's.

The Amphibian Vehicle Museum at Camp Pendleton, CA. It is one of the largest collections of amphibious vehicles in the world.

the largest such collections in the world. Most are from WW II. Hours: daily during daylight hours. Free. Location: From I-5 take the Camp Pendleton exit to the Camp's main gate. Proceed along Vandergrift Blvd. approximately 9 miles to Rattlesnake Canyon Rd. Turn right to the museum which is 1.3 miles ahead on the north side of the road.

REAM FIELD was just south of Imperial Beach and 35 miles from the Mexican border. It began operating before WW I as a bare-bones Army air field used for gunnery and landing practice. After WW I the Navy acquired the field and used it for training and for emergency landings. Soon after the attack on Pearl Harbor the Navy converted the field into an auxiliary air station under NAS, San Diego. Once completed in 1943 the station was used for the rest of the war by 22 different Navy air groups. In 1945 Ream Field was closed, but in 1950 the Navy reopened it as a helicopter base, although other units were stationed here too. The base, known then as U.S. Naval Air Station, Imperial Beach, operated throughout the Viet Nam war and in 1974 was disestablished.

FORT ROSECRANS was a 19th century Army post at Ballast Point on the east side of the Point Loma Peninsula. It was built on the site of several earlier forts, the earliest of which dated back to the 1700s during the Spanish period. During WW II Fort Rosecrans was the Army's headquarters for the coastal defenses in and around San Diego. In Dec. 1949 the fort was declared surplus by the Army and turned over to the Navy and eventually became a part of the Navy's Submarine Support Facility which functioned throughout the Cold War. The site can be viewed at a distance from the heights of Point Loma.

FORT ROSECRANS NATIONAL CEMETERY is a very beautiful National cemetery straddling both side of Cabrillo Memorial Dr. on Point Loma. It is the final resting place of Marine General Holland M. "Howlin' Mad" Smith, considered the father of amphibious warfare. As commander of the Marine's 5th Amphibious Corps, he trained and later lead his men in the assaults on Attu, Kiska, Tarawa, Makin, Kwajalein, Eniwetok, Saipan and Tinian.

SAN DIEGO AEROSPACE MUSEUM and **THE INTERNATIONAL AEROSPACE HALL OF FAME** in Balboa Park is a large and excellent museum that memorializes the important people and major advances in the field of aviation and aerospace. There are about 60 aircraft at the museum, most of which are inside the museum's spacious building. Many are from WW II and some were built here in San Diego. The museum's exhibits are laid out in chronological order with an extensive WW II section. The International Aerospace Hall of Fame, which is a part of the museum, honors most of the great names in aviation including many individuals from WW II. Some of the WW II notables are; Jimmy Doolittle, "Hap" Arnold, Howard Hughes, Chuck Yeager, Werner von Braun, Carl Spaatz, Willi Messerschmitt, John Northrop and Donald Douglas. The museum has a library, a theater and a gift shop. Address: 2001 Pan American Plaza, Balboa Park, San Diego, CA 92101. Phone: Museum, 619/234-8291; Hall of Fame, 619/232-8322. Hours: daily 10-4:30. Admission charged.

SAN DIEGO MUNICIPAL AIRPORT (LINDBERGH FIELD) was used during the war by the Army, Navy and Coast Guard. It was s sub-base to San Bernardino AAF and there was a Coast Guard air station here.

U.S. MARINE CORPS BASE, SAN DIEGO was first activated in Dec. 1914 as the home for the Marines in the San Diego area. It was called Marine Barracks, San Diego. Up to that time, the Marines did not have a permanent home at San Diego. Throughout WW I, and in the

Two-story WW II barracks, once a part of Fort Rosecrans, remained in daily use for decades after the war. The downtown San Diego skyline is in the distance.

A San Diego-made PBY-5A Cataline mounted on pylons in the courtyard of the san Diego Aerospace Museum.

The long archway of the old Spanish-style building in which the museum is located at the U.S. Marine Corps Recruit Depot. To the right is the rear door of the museum. To the left is a large and attractive court yard.

years between the wars, the base was the home of the Marines in the San Diego area.

Several years before WW II the base had reached its limit of expansion since it was surrounded on all sides by either the city of San Diego or water. But, expansions continued at its subposts, Camp Elliott and eventually at Camp Pendleton. As various units and commands moved from the main base to the subposts, the main base began to be used more for training and educational activities. During WW II these were the primary functions performed here.

In Jan. 1948, the base was named U.S. Marine Corps Recruit Depot and made the Marine Corps' primary training base for recruits on the west coast. Several advanced schools for Marines also located here, and the facility operated throughout the Cold War.

U.S. Marines Command Museum: This museum is on the ground of the U.S. Marine Corps Recruit Depot in one of the beautiful old Spanish-style buildings. It is dedicated to the preservation of the history and traditions of the Marine Corps. The museum emphasizes the Marine slogan "First to Fight", and the entire history of the Marine Corps is presented in displays and exhibits with the WW II era getting its full share. There are exhibits on Marine training, Marine aviation, the Women Marines, the Navajo Code Talkers, uniforms, documents, posters, flags and small arms. Address: Marine Corps Recruit Depot, San Diego, CA 92140. Phone: 619/524-6038. Hours: Tues.-Sun. 10-5. Free. Location: Enter at Gate 4 on Pacific Hwy. at Witherby St., 1/4 mile south of the interchange of I-5 and I-8.

U.S NAVAL AUXILIARY AIR STATION, BROWN, 5.5 miles SE of Otay, CA was a local airport before the war. It was used by the Navy as an auxiliary air station to NAS, San Diego. The Navy departed after the war and the station became a civilian field called Brown Field.

U.S. NAVAL AUXILIARY AIR FACILITY, DEL MAR (LTA), one mile NE of Del Mar, CA., was a small blimp base and an auxiliary field to U.S. NAS, Santa Ana (LTA). The station also had a landing field for small aircraft.

U.S. NAVAL AIR STATION, SAN DIEGO was on the extreme northern end of the Silver Strand Peninsula on North Island. This very strategic piece of real estate has a long history associated with aviation beginning in 1910 when aviation pioneer Glenn Curtiss established an flying camp here. In 1917 the U.S. Government acquired the land to be used as a joint Army and Navy air field for the training of pilots for WW I. During WW I the Navy's role became dominant on the island because of its proximity to other naval installations in the area and the fact that the Navy declared its facilities here a permanent naval station. NAS, San Diego's main mission was to train pilots and aircraft mechanics. From 1919 to 1939 the air station was often in the news as the base from which famous aviators of the time flew to, or from, in their headline-making adventures.

As the Navy acquired aircraft carriers and dirigibles NAS, San Diego became even more important and underwent several expansions. It acquired deep water docking facilities capable of berthing aircraft carriers.

Within days after the Japanese attack on Pearl Harbor Army combat-ready fighter units were rushed to NAS, San Diego as part of the San Diego area defenses.

During WW II NAS, San Diego was the Navy's primary air station in the San Diego area. It was used both for training and as a support base for naval operations.

In 1955 the name of the facility was changed to U.S. Naval Air Station, North Island. In 1963 the early aviation sites on North Island were officially designated as the "Birthplace of Naval Aviation" by resolution of the House Armed Services Committee.

NAS, North Island functioned throughout the Cold War. NAS, San Diego had the following outlying fields during WW II:
* Booming Field, 2.5 miles SE of Coyote Wells
* Border Airport, 12.5 miles SE of San Diego
* Borego Hotel Field, 34 miles NW of Brawley
* Clark's Dry Lake, 65 miles NE of San Diego at the west end of the lake
* Coyote Wells North Field, 13 miles NE of Coyote Wells
* Coyote Wells South Field, 3 miles east of Coyote Wells
* Jacumba Hot Springs Airport, 1 mile E. of Jacumba Hot Springs
* Rosedale Airport, 6 miles north of San Diego

* San Nicholas Island Air Field, on the north end of San Nicholas Island, 90 miles SW of Los Angeles

U.S. NAVAL AMPHIBIOUS TRAINING BASE was located on the Silver Strand between the Pacific Ocean and San Diego Bay just south of Coronado. It was acquired by the Navy in June 1943 as a training base for amphibious warfare and was used for that purpose throughout the war. It became known as the home of the "Alligator Navy". Several types of amphibious landing vehicles were called "alligators".

The base was retained by the Navy after the war, and in 1946 was renamed U.S. Naval Amphibious Base. The facility was active throughout the Cold War.

U.S. NAVAL OPERATING BASE, SAN DIEGO, began in 1920 along the southern end of San Diego's waterfront. This is the Navy's most important base in San Diego and the heart of Naval operations in the southwestern United States. In 1921 the base became the headquarters of the 11th Naval District with offices in the Naval Supply Depot complex at the foot of Broadway on Harbor Drive, a site it occupied for decades after the war. In the 1920s and 1930s the naval base expanded as did the other naval facilities in the area, and during the early part of the war its facilities mushroomed after San Diego was made the home of the Pacific Fleet. During the war NOB, San Diego provided the Pacific Fleet with virtually everything it needed; ship building, repairs, refitting, supplies, fuel, replacements and numerous other services. The base commander was responsible for coordinating all naval operations in the area to ensure maximum support for the Fleet.

Those responsibilities and functions are basically the same throughout the Cold War. The 11th Naval District Command covered a 6-state area, and San Diego was home port for dozens of U.S. warships.

The base itself extends from the San Diego-Coronado Bay Bridge southward along the eastern shore of the Bay into the northern part of National City.

U.S. NAVAL REGIONAL MEDICAL CENTER, SAN DIEGO was located in Balboa Park and was a huge Navy-run medical facility. In 1914 the Marines set up a field hospital in Balboa Park as part of the Panama-California Exposition and never left. In 1919, in an effort to draw more Navy installations to San Diego, the city fathers donated 17.35 acres of park land, which included the site of the Marine's field hospital, to the Navy for a 250-bed hospital.

During WW II, buildings were put up one after the other until the medical center consisted of 241 buildings with 10,499 beds on a total spread covering 247 acres. Over 172,000 patients were treated here during WW II with the peak load coming in Dec. 1944 with 12,000 patients. The Korean War and the Cold War kept the hospital in active use for decades and it continued to expand in the postwar years.

U.S. NAVAL TRAINING CENTER, SAN DIEGO, at the north end of San Diego Bay, began in 1919 when the city donated land to the Navy to build the training center. From its earliest days the Center trained raw recruits giving them 16 weeks of "Boot Camp". There were also four schools here, one each for radiomen, yeomen, buglers and band.

In 1939 the Navy expanded the Center by filling in 130 acres of the tideland and built additional facilities. By the time the U.S. became involved in the war the Center could train 25,000 recruits at a time, plus give schooling to other personnel in a variety of subjects. Because so many new recruits went through the Center, it gained the nickname "Cradle of the Navy".

After the war, recruit training declined, but specialized training schools increased. The Korean War brought the Center back up to capacity as a "Boot Camp". During the Cold War years the Center operated almost continually as a "Boot Camp".

SAN FRANCISCO and the SAN FRANCISCO BAY METROPOLITAN AREA:

When WW II started, the San Francisco Bay area was one of the most important seaport, commercial and manufacturing centers in the country. With a dozen or so major shipyards, scattered around the Bay, it was #1 in America in shipbuilding. What Los Angeles was to airplanes, San Francisco was to ships.

For over a decade before the war the Bay Area had been growing at a manageable rate of about 10% a year, but when the area's industry began to boom in 1942 many of the Bay communities had severe problems coping with the sudden changes.

In the months just before the war the area's shipyards were busy building ships. The government's twin programs of building a two-ocean Navy, while at the same time building hundreds of cargo ships, called "Liberty" ships, had just gotten under way and the area's shipyards had numerous orders for new ships. This stimulated other local industries and thousands of workers flocked to the Bay Area seeking the available jobs. Thus, when the U.S. went to war in Dec. 1941 the Bay Area's industries were already at, or near, their capacities and her cities were crowded with people.

When the U.S. went to war ship orders surged and more workers and military personnel flocked to the area. The Bay Area was in no position to absorb such a surge, but absorb it must, and absorb it did, although the ordeal was painful.

Shortages of many goods and services soon developed. There was inflation, lack of housing, crowded highways, an increase in vice and crime, and the faltering and sometimes failing of basic city services. Everyone's quality of life diminished and before long the Bay Area was one of the worst areas in the nation in which to live and work. As housing became impossible to find people began living in tents, sheds, garages and their cars. Boarding houses and hotels rented beds by the hour. . "hot beds" they were called. Soldiers waiting to be shipped out to the Pacific had to put up tent camps in the city's parks while they awaited transportation. Schools in some communities went to two shifts, day-care for pre-schoolers became a major problem. Absenteeism, alcoholism, divorces and suicides rose. Many workers simply gave up and went home. And, to make matters worse, the powerful labor unions in the area ordered strikes and work stoppages with

alarming regularity. One particularly bad strike in May 1942 idled 11 shipyards. Labor unrest was to plague the Bay Area throughout the war. The Bay Area acquired a nation-wide reputation as being an area in trouble. Consequently, defense work, and workers, that might have come to Bay Area went elsewhere.

As the war progressed, living and economic conditions slowly improved, but many hard lessons had been learned. The end result was that San Francisco and the other Bay Area communities emerged from the war with some of the most experienced and

The northern gun position of Battery Davis at Fort Funston. It is open and may be explored by visitors.

One of Ft. Funston's base end stations used in sighting the fort's big guns. This base end station is typical of base end stations along the west coast in that they were mounted on high bluffs. On the east coast, base end stations were usually placed in tall towers.

powerful urban planning commissions in the country. After the war, these commissions were given power and money. Slums, worn-out factories, ugly waterfronts, dilapidated housing projects and the like were swept away or rebuilt. With time, the Bay Area became clean, attractive, coordinated and a fine place to live in the postwar years.

Fort Funston, on the Pacific side of San Francisco, was established in 1898 as Laguna Merced Military Reservation to be a part of the coastal defenses of the Bay area. At that time Battery Davis, a dual open-platform gun position, was built. In the late 1930s Battery Davis was modernized by covering it over and mounting new 16" rifled coastal guns. Davis was one of the first such projects completed and it became a model for other defense batteries being modernized. In 1948 Fort Funston's guns were removed and in 1950 the fort was made into a park. In the postwar years Ft. Funston and Battery Davis were opened to the public.

The Holocaust Center of Northern California: This Holocaust center records the history of the Holocaust and has a museum, library and archives which are open to the public. The library and archives have over 8000 volumes plus posters, films, videos and oral histories. Address: 639 14th Ave., San Francisco, CA

94118. Phone: 415/751-6735. Hours: Sun., M & W 10-4, Tues. noon-6, Thurs. noon-8.

Colin P. Kelly, Jr. Street: Before the war this street, just south of the entrance to the Bay Bridge, was called Japan Street. Soon after the attack on Pearl Harbor it was renamed in honor of America's first hero of WW II, Capt. Colin P. Kelly, Jr. who, on Dec. 9, 1941, as the pilot of a B-17 bomber, scored a direct hit on a Japanese transport ship north of the Philippines. Kelly and another member of his crew perished in the attack. It was widely reported at the time that Kelly had sunk the Japanese battleship "Haruna", and was posthumously awarded the Distinguished Service Cross. It was only later in the war that his exploit was clarified.

Lincoln Park: This beautiful park is in the northwest corner of the city, and has two interesting WW II monuments. One is the Holocaust Monument, which is located on Legion of Honor Dr. across from the Palace of the Legion of Honor. It commemorates the victims of the Nazi Holocaust. Its creator was the famous artist, George Segal.

The other monument is the U.S.S. "San Francisco" Monument which is located near the end of El Camino Del Mar street, west of the Veterans Admin. Hospital. It honors the crew and captain of the U.S. cruiser "San Francisco"

The Holocaust Monument in Lincoln Park created by artist George Segal.

The Monument to the U.S. Cruiser "San Francisco". Parts of the monument consist of the ship's bridge which still bears holes made by Japanese shells.

In 1977 the fort became a large community center in which a wide variety of projects and events take place. Many of the old buildings remain in use and the fort is a National Historic Landmark.

The "Jeremiah O'Brien" Liberty Ship, a relic of WW II, is permanently anchored at Fort Mason's Pier 3 and is open to the public. It is the only one of 2751 Liberty Ships made during the war that has survived unaltered. A five-hour Bay Cruise is held each May with a buffet luncheon and a Seaman's Memorial Ceremony commemorating the seamen of WW II. Address: Fort Mason Center, Buchanan St. & Marina Blvd., San Francisco, CA 94123. Phone: 415/441-3101. Hours: M-F 9-3, Sat-Sun 9-4. Admission charged.

The Presidio of San Francisco: This was one of the most beautiful military posts in the country situated on 1500 acres of San Francisco's prime real estate on the south shore of the Golden Gate waterway. It began as a Spanish fort in 1776 which makes it one of the oldest military sites in the country. At the time of WW II it was the headquarters of the 4th Army, which comprised the 7th and 9th Corps and the Army's Western Defense Command which covered 9 states and the Territory of Alaska. It was from here that the military operations were planned for the recapture of the Japanese-held islands of Attu and Kiska in the Aleutian Islands of Alaska. Also during the war the Presidio was home to several of the Army's most important commands. The small national cemetery on the post holds more Congressional Medal of Honor Winners than any other cemetery on the west coast.

The Presidio functioned as an Army post throughout the Cold War and in 1994 was transferred to the National Park System. The headquarters of the U.S. 6th Army remained at the Presidio but most of the post's facilities were converted to civilian uses.

Letterman General Hospital, which later became known as Letterman Army Medical Center, is on the grounds of the Presidio and is one of the Army's largest and most prestigious hospitals. The first buildings were built in 1898 and the hospital has served the Army and the people of San Francisco ever since. It has a nursing school for Army nurses which began in 1918. During WW II Letterman received and treated many wounded servicemen returning from the Pacific. In 1945 alone, 72,000 patients were treated. There was a branch prisoner of war camp at Letterman holding 175 POWs who worked at the hospital. Letterman was fully operative throughout the Cold War but closed when the Presidio closed.

The Presidio National Park Museum, on the grounds of the Presidio at the intersection of Lincoln Blvd. and Funston Ave., traces the history of the Presidio from its Spanish days to the present. Only a few of the displays at the museum are devoted to WW II. The most interesting of which is a full-scale mockup of a WW II coastal defense bunker. Address: Building 2, Presidio of San Francisco, CA 94129-5000. Phone: 415/556-1865. Hours: W-Sun. 10-5. Free.

Fort Winfield Scott, now known as Fort Point National Historic Site, is directly under the southern end of the Golden Gate Bridge. The brick fort was built by the Army in 1861 as Fort Point and, at the time, was the main defense for San Francisco Harbor. In 1882 the fort was renamed Fort Winfield Scott. During WW II Fort Winfield Scott was, of course, not suitable as a coastal fortification because of its brick

which was badly damaged during the Battle of Guadalcanal on the night of Nov. 12/13, 1942. Many of the crew and the ship's captain, Rear Adm. Daniel J. Callaghan, were lost. Parts of the ship's bridge are incorporated into the monument and still bear the shell holes received during the battle.

Fort Mason: This old fort is at Buchanan St. and Marina Blvd., and is on the site of a Spanish gun battery built in 1797. The site was used as a military post until Fort Mason was closed in 1972. During both World Wars and the Korean War Fort Mason was a major embarkation center for Army troops going overseas. In WW II over 1.5 million troops and 23 million ton of cargo passed through Fort Mason. McDowell Hall was the headquarters of the Army's Western Department, and it was from here that General John DeWitt directed the defenses of the west coast and the evacuation of the ethnic Japanese during the early days of WW II. At one time in early 1942 Gen. DeWitt considered moving his headquarters out of San Francisco because of its vulnerability to attack. Salt Lake City, Utah was considered for the new site, but this plan never materialized.

The Liberty Ship "Jeremiah O'Brien", anchored for years at Fort Mason, is now located at the San Francisco Maritime State Historical Park. The ship is open to the public and is in operating condition.

One of two observation posts at Fort Point overlooking the entrance to San Francisco Bay. The massive steel work above is the south end of the Golden Gate Bridge. The steel beams protruding from the roof of the observation post supported camouflage.

construction. Nevertheless, search lights and 3" guns were mounted on its old bulwark to guard the anti-submarine nets that spanned the entrance to the harbor. The fort is open to the public, but historical emphasis is on its early days and not on WW II.

By walking under the bridge to the Ocean side of Fort Point, one will discover two small concrete observation posts dug into the hill side overlooking the entrance to the harbor.

The West Coast Memorial is a large monument on the west side of the Presidio at the junction of Washington, Harrison and Lincoln Blvd. on a promontory overlooking the Pacific Ocean. It commemorates the 413 men of the U.S. armed forces who lost their lives in the U.S. waters off the west coast during WW II and whose bodies were never recovered. The name, rank and branch of service of all 413 are engraved in the monument. Directly behind the monument is an abandoned concrete gun emplacement.

San Francisco Airport: This is San Francisco International Airport. In 1927 the airport was built as San Francisco's municipal airport and named Mills Field Municipal Airport of San Francisco. It was built almost entirely on land reclaimed from the bay. In 1931 it was renamed San Francisco Airport. This was the name it had when, in Dec. 1941, the U.S. military took it over for the duration of the war. It operated as a military airport throughout the war with limited use being given to the needs of commercial airlines. The Air Transport Command operated here and had an air freight terminal. In 1944 the field was chosen to be an intransit field for AAF planes and crews transferring from Europe to the Pacific. The sudden end to the war in the Pacific, though, cut this activity short. Soon after the war, the airport was returned to civilian authority.

San Francisco Maritime State Historic Park, The National Maritime Museum and the **WW II Submarine "Pampanito":** This is a very unique state park with a maritime museum and several historic ships. The National Maritime Museum is on the park grounds at the foot of Polk St., directly across from Ghirardelli Square, and has many displays on the water transportation of the area since the early 1800s. There are several displays in the museum on WW II, but its emphasis is more on commercial maritime history rather than on military maritime history.

Five blocks to the east, on the east side of Fisherman's Wharf, is the WW II submarine "Pampanito". It is owned and operated by the museum and is open to the public. Address: The National Museum Association, Presidio of San Francisco, Building 275, Crissy Field, San Francisco, CA 94129. Phone: to the museum, 415/556-3002; to the "Pampanito" 415/929-0202. Hours: Mid-May thru mid Oct. daily 9-9, rest of year F-Sat 9-9. Admission to the museum if free, admission is charged to the "Pampanito".

San Francisco Shipyard: This ship yard was on the Bay side of San Francisco just north of Candlestick Park. It began as a privately owner dry dock in 1868. It prospered and expanded through the years and in 1939 the government purchased the facility and contracted Bethlehem Steel Co. to operate it. Eleven days after the attack on Pearl Harbor the Navy took complete control of the ship yard to use as a repair facility exclusively for its own ships. During the war the San Francisco Shipyard repaired and/or overhauled some 600 ships with a workforce that peaked at 18,000.

The ship yard continued in operation after the war under Navy control. In 1970 the facility was renamed U.S. Naval Shipyard, Hunters Point and continued to function during most of the Cold War.

San Francisco War Memorial: This is a complex of several buildings at Van Ness and McAllister Sts. in San Francisco's Civic Center. In these buildings the United Nations came into being after WW II. Delegates from the victorious Allied nations met here from Apr. 25 to June 26, 1946 to draw up the U.N.'s new constitution. On June 26, 1945 a ceremony was held in the Herbst Theater and representative of 50 nations signed documents creating the United Nations Organization. A large mural in the theater depicts the event, and United Nations Plaza, across from the theater, commemorates the Organization.

ALAMEDA is a city on the eastern shore of San Francisco Bay consisting mostly of Alameda Island. During the war two of Alameda's ship yards built ships for the Navy. The General Engineering Co. (ship yard) built mine sweepers and net tenders, and the Bethlehem Steel Co., Shipbuilding Division, built merchant ships. Alameda is also the home town of General Jimmy Doolittle. On Jun. 30, 1942 a plane in which Admiral Chester Nimitz was riding crashed in the Alameda Estuary near Alameda and the Admiral narrowly escaped death.

U.S. Naval Air Station, Alameda: In 1934 the city of Alameda built an air strip called Benton Field on reclaimed land at the north end of the island. It was built for two reasons; for the immediate use of Pan American Airways, and as an incentive to attract the Navy to the community of Alameda. The Navy studied the site, accepted Alameda's offer, and in 1938 began building a large air station here that could support four aircraft carrier groups, five patrol squadrons, two utility squadrons, have facilities for complete plane and engine overhaul, piers to dock two aircraft carriers and several outlying air fields. The new naval station, named U.S. Naval Air Station, Alameda, became the Navy's "Aviation Gateway to the Pacific". Construction wasn't yet complete when the U.S. went to war in Dec. 1941, but the air station's personnel began performing wartime duties with what they had available. Offshore and inshore air patrols were begun, air cover for convoys was provided and the station became a ferry point for fleet air units going elsewhere.

In late March 1942 the aircraft carrier "Hornet" arrived at NAS, Alameda and 16 Army B-25 bombers were hoisted aboard. The Hornet then departed under great secrecy on April 2. These were the planes of General Jimmy Doolittle's Raiders that bombed Tokyo and

The West Coast Monument overlooks the Pacific Ocean from the grounds of the Presidio and commemorates the 413 American servicemen who perished in west coast waters during WW II and whose bodies were never recovered.

other cities in Japan on April 18, 1942.

During WW II, this was one of the Navy's busiest air stations with air units, carrier groups, supplies, numerous naval personnel and sometimes VIP's passing through on their way to the Pacific or to points east. Actually, construction never stopped at NAS, Alameda during the war and by 1945 it was a huge facility with 3600 officers and 29,000 enlisted personnel.

In late 1943-early 1944 the AAF established a large intransit air depot in Alameda to handle the logistics of moving large numbers of AAF personnel, planes and equipment from Europe to the Pacific in preparation for the final assault on Japan. It was the largest new construction project undertaken by the AAF at this time. The air depot included many warehouses, wharves, rail sidings and deep-water docks. With the sudden end to the war in the Pacific, though, this facility saw little use.

The naval air station continued in full operation after the war and became home to many Navy commands and service units. In 1967 the station's air field was named Nimitz Field in honor of Adm. Chester Nimitz. NAS, Alameda continued in full operation throughout the Cold War and was one of the Navy's most important facilities on the west coast. In the 1990s NAS, Alameda was closed. Outlying fields for NAS, Alameda during WW II were:

- Crescent City Airport, 3 miles NW of Crescent City
- Concord Outlying field, 2 miles NE of Concord (on the grounds of Concord Naval Weapons Station)
  San Luis Obispo Airport, 2 miles SE of San Luis Obispo

ANGEL ISLAND and FORT McDOWELL: Angel Island, just north of San Francisco off the coast of Marin County, has been many things through the years; farm land, a quarry site, a Civil War camp, a quarantine station, a detention camp, an immigration station, a fort, a prison, a World War I Army camp, a prisoner of war camp, an enemy alien detention center, a port of embarkation and a missile base.

One interesting facet of its long history occurred in the early 1920s when some 19,000 Japanese "picture brides" were processed through Angle Island on their way to marry young Japanese men who had immigrated to the U.S. some years earlier. Many of these women would spend time in the Japanese Relocation Camps of WW II.

At the start of WW II there was a Civil War-era fort, Fort McDowell, on the island occupied by the U.S. Army and a number of unused immigration buildings. Immigration activities had ceased in 1940 when the administration building burned and immigration activities moved to San Francisco. In March 1941 the U.S. Government seized all German, Italian and Danish merchants ships in American waters and some of the merchant seamen were sent to Fort McDowell for internment under the terms of the Geneva Convention. They were housed in the old immigration buildings for a few months and then transferred to other Internment Camps. Later, though, the buildings were used again as a prisoner of war compound for German, Italian and Japanese POWs.

Fort McDowell served as one of several embarkation centers in the Bay area for troops going to the Pacific, and at the end of the war Fort McDowell became a processing center for troops returning from the Pacific. Post engineers built a huge sign on Mount Ida saying "WELCOME HOME" in 60' letters.

In the post-war years Angel Island was used as a Nike Missile Base. In 1962 the Nike base closed and in 1965 the Army ceded the island to the state of California to be used as a state park. The visitor's center on the island has several displays and some historical artifacts on the island's history including some items from its WW II days.

BENICIA is on the north shore of Carquines Strait at the north end of San Francisco Bay.

Benicia Arsenal: This facility began as an Army post named Benicia Barracks in 1849 and gradually evolved into an Army arsenal. In 1864 it became the site where the Army's camels, from the unsuccessful Camel Corps experiment, were sold at auction. Most of the camels went to zoos. The two "Camel Barns", in which the camels were kept, were preserved. One is a local history museum. In 1928 Benicia Arsenal was one of the first arsenals in the country to get remote steel and concrete storage igloos for ammunition. These igloos proved to be very successful and were widely used during WW II.

When WW II started

Benicia Arsenal was expanded and its ammunition supply moved inland to Utah The Arsenal then functioned as a supply and distribution depot and repair center. German prisoners of war worked at the arsenal and 8 of them who died here are buried in the arsenal's cemetery. The arsenal functioned until 1964 when it was closed by the Army.

BERKELEY, north of, and adjacent to, Oakland, is the home of the University of California. Before and during the war much of the early scientific work on atomic energy was done here at the University of California, Berkeley.

Lawrence Hall of Science: This is a hands-on general science museum on the campus of the University of California covering many subjects including the early discoveries in the field of atomic energy. The Hall is named in honor of Professor Ernest O. Lawrence who, while at the University, conducted some of the early experiments in atomic energy that lead to the development of the atomic bombs of WW II. Specifically, Lawrence developed the principal of electromagnetic separation of uranium-235 used in the Hiroshima bomb and discovered the element, Plutonium, which made the Nagasaki bomb possible. Displays in the Hall of Science discuss Lawrence's work and show some of his methods and equipment. Address: Univ. of California at Berkeley, Centennial Dr., Berkeley, CA 94720. Phone 510/642-5132. Hours: M-F 10-4:30, Sat.-Sun. 10-5, closed Labor Day, Thanksgiving, Dec. 24-25. Admission charged.

CONCORD is 14 miles NE of Oakland. The town's local airport, 1.5 miles to the NW, was taken over and used for a while by the AAF's Air Technical Service Command. It was named Concord Army Air Field. After the war it became Buchanan Field, a civil airport.

GOLDEN GATE NATIONAL RECREATION AREA and **FORTS BAKER, BARRY AND CRONKITE:** The Golden Gate National Recreation Park extends for some 35 miles along the Pacific coast both north and south of the Golden Gate. Over the years much of the land was used by the military for forts and coastal defenses, many of which have been preserved and became part of the Park. One of the largest concentration of coastal defenses in the country can be seen and explored along the southern shore of Marin County within the Park. To reach this area, take the first exit north of the northern end of the Golden Gate Bridge and proceeding west along the Park's coastal road. The road crosses lands once belonging to Forts Baker, Barry and Cronkite which were side-by-side along the southern tip of the Marin Peninsula. There are covered and open gun positions, mortar pits, command posts, base line stations and WW II buildings. Virtually all of these coastal defenses were used to some degree during WW II. All guns have been removed, but the massive earthworks and concrete structures are there to see.

Fort Baker, the easternmost fort, was built during the Civil War and covered most of the southern shore of the Marine Peninsula. In 1904 Fort Baker was divided in two and its western portion became Fort Barry. In 1937 Fort Cronkite was built west of, and adjacent

Entrance to the Lawrence Hall of Science on the Univ. of California, Berkeley.

to, Fort Barry. All three forts were active during WW II and consisted primarily of the coastal defenses.

After WW II, Forts Barry and Cronkite and the portion of Fort Baker west of Hwy. 101 were given to the Golden Gate National Recreation Area. The portion of Fort Baker east of Hwy. 101 remained an active Army post.

Most of the newer WW II gun emplacements will be found at Fort Cronkite. Some of them took most of the war years to build only to be abandoned at the end of the war.

HAYWARD is SE of Oakland on the eastern shore of San Francisco Bay.

Hayward Army Air Field: This air field, two miles SW of Hayward, was the community's local airport known as Russell City Airport. It was taken over by the 4th AF and served as a subbase to Hammer Field, Fresno. After the war it became Hayward Air Terminal.

LIVERMORE, 15 miles east of Hayward, is the home of the prestigious Lawrence Livermore National Laboratory.

U.S. Naval Air Station, Livermore: This NAS was built in 1942 four miles east of Livermore to relieve overcrowding of the naval air facilities at Oakland Municipal Airport. The primary mission of the base was to train pilots. Up to Oct. 1944 some 4000 cadets trained here in N2S trainers known as "Yellow Perils". By late 1944 the Navy needed fewer pilots, so training operations ended and the station was given several new tasks; servicing fleet air units preparing for overseas operation, storing aircraft, repairing aircraft and the training of Navy and Marine air reservists.

After the war the station closed down in stages and was decommissioned altogether in 1946. NAS, Livermore had the following outlying fields during the war:

* Abel Field, 1 mile NE of Milpitas
* Brown Airport, 7 miles NW of Tracy
* Brown-Fabian Airport, 3.5 miles west of Tracy
* Cope Field, 2 miles NE of Pleasanton
* Gelderman Airport, 4 miles north of Dublin
* Heath Airport, 3 miles south of Irvington
* Linderman Airport, 9 miles NW of Tracy
* Livermore Airport, 2 miles NW of Livermore
* May's School Field, 4.5 miles NE of Livermore
* Rita Butterworth Airport, 3 miles NE of Pleasanton
* Spring Valley Airport, 2.5 miles NW of Pleasanton
* Wagoner Airport, 1.5 miles SW of Livermore

MARIN CITY, just north of Sausalito, was a town built by the government during the war to house 6000 workers at nearby ship yards. Construction of the town began in 1942. Schools, shopping centers, churches, parks, sewer systems, etc. were all built according to a master plan. Marin City was considered to be one of the best of the federal housing projects built in the Bay area during the war.

MENLO PARK is midway between San Francisco and San Jose.

Dibble General Hospital: This 1868-bed hospital was built for the Army in Menlo Park in late 1943-early 1944 to treat war wounded. It specialized in plastic surgery, ophthalmologic

surgery, psychiatry and care for the blind. In June 1946 the hospital was transferred to the Federal Public Housing Authority.

OAKLAND, the "other" big city in the San Francisco Bay area on the eastern shore of the Bay, was a major seaport, manufacturing center and home to several shipyards and existing military facilities when WW II began. Because of its well-developed port facilities, Oakland became a major embarkation center for both troops and war materials going overseas. Like other cities in the Bay area, the residents of Oakland suffered from the sudden and overwhelming influx of people and war-related activities.

Mountain View Cemetery: Henry J. Kaiser, the famous shipbuilder of WW II, is buried in this cemetery in the Main Mausoleum. His resting place is an elegant marble sarcophagus beside a beautiful inside court yard inside the mausoleum.

Dr. Ernest O. Lawrence, whose early work on atomic energy made possible the atomic bombs of WW II (see Berkeley, Lawrence Hall of Science, above), is buried in the Chapel of Memory adjacent to the entrance of the cemetery. Location: 5000 Piedmont Av., Oakland, CA.

Oakland Army Terminal: This huge Army terminal was on the Oakland waterfront just south of the eastern

Top: A pre-war open gun position used to guard the naval mine field in the waters off the Golden Gate. The Golden Gate Bridge is to the left. Second: Two base end Stations used to direct the fire of the guns. Third: A pre-war Mortar pit now used as a picnic area. The high earthworks make a fine windbreak against chilly ocean breezes. Bottom: A covered 16" gun position built during WW II.

entrance to the San Francisco-Oakland Bay Bridge. Construction was begun in Jan. 1941 and the base was commissioned on Dec. 8, 1941 (one day after the Pearl Harbor attack). Its mission was to ship the Army's men and material into the Pacific areas of operation. During the war tens of thousands of soldiers and 25 million tons of supplies flowed through this terminal. In Jan. 1944 it was renamed the Oakland Army Base. Also in 1944 Italian Service Units, comprised of former Italian prisoners of war, began to work here. At the end of the war, the base served as a reception center for service personnel returning from the Pacific. After that, it was a major distribution point for war surplus material. The Oakland Army Base functioned throughout the Cold War and was closed in the 1990s.

Oakland Municipal Airport: This is now the Oakland International Airport. It began in 1926-27 as a city airport designed to serve Oakland and the eastern Bay area. In 1928 the Navy established a reserve base at the airport and by the time the U.S. went to war, Oakland Municipal Airport was a large and busy airport. Nevertheless, the military took it over and the AAF based P-40 fighter planes here soon after the attack on Pearl Harbor as part of the Bay area's defenses. The AAF's Air Transport Command operated here as did the Army's Air Technical Service Command. The Navy built an air station at the NW end of the airport known as U.S. Naval Auxiliary Air Station, Oakland, for the use of the Naval Air Transport Service. Various additions and expansions were made to the airport during the war, and in late 1945 it was returned to civilian authorities.

There are three private operations at the airport which are WW II related.

The Aerial Advertising Company, at the Oakland Intl. Airport, owns several Stearman PT-17 primary trainers. These are open cockpit biplanes built in the early 1940s to train Army pilots. The planes are painted in the Army colors and insignias of that time. The company does aerial advertising, fly-overs and motion picture and TV work with the planes. They also offer rides to interested parties. Address: 8433 Earhart Rd., PO Box 2272, Oakland, CA 94614. Phone: 800/235-3571 (CA only) or 510/568-1299.

Otis Spunkmeyer Air is a company at the airport that operates two WW II-era DC-3 airliners with a luxuriously modified interior to hold 18 passengers. The company specializes in nostalgic sky tours over the Bay area, aerial parties for special occasions, client entertainment, employee rewards or sightseeing. They fly low and slow over the Bay area. Address: 8433 Earhart Rd., North Field, Oakland, CA 94614. Phone: 800/938-1900 or 510/667-3800.

The Western Aerospace Museum is also on the grounds of the Oakland Intl. Airport and displays several aircraft including a WW II Grumman TBM Avenger, a Stearman PT-13, a rare Short Solent flying boat and a Buecker Junge Meister German trainer. There are exhibits on Jimmy Doolittle, a model plane collection, a Norden Bombsight, a library, the

Oakland Aviation Hall of Fame, a display on the 8th AF, a display on the Eagle Squadron and a gift shop. Address: 8260 Boeing St., Building 621, North Field, Oakland Intl. Airport, Oakland, CA 94614. Phone: 510/638-7100. Hours W-Sun. 10-4, closed weekdays and holidays. Admission charged.

U.S. Naval Regional Medical Center, Oakland: This Navy Hospital began in 1942 as a temporary hospital to handle battle casualties returning from the Pacific. At first it consisted of 25 wooden barracks built on the site of the Oak Knoll Golf Course. Expansions were made during and after the war and the hospital evolved into a modern regional hospital handling naval personnel needing specialized care from a 10,000 square mile area of California and Nevada. In the 1990s NRMC, Oakland was closed.

U.S. Naval Supply Depot, Oakland: This depot began in 1940 when the city of Oakland sold 500 acres of marshlands to the Navy for $1.00. The Navy reclaimed the land and built several large warehouses to store war materials destined for overseas shipment. By Dec. 15, 1941, 8 days after the attack on Pearl Harbor, the Depot was opened for business. It expanded during and after the war and acquired several subposts. In the late 1940s it was renamed U.S. Naval Supply Center, Oakland and operated throughout the Cold War as one of the Navy's most important and most modern supply facilities.

PORT CHICAGO: This little town on the south shore of Suisun Bay no longer exists, but its name will forever remain a part of WW II history because of a terrible disaster that occurred there in July 1944.

U.S. Naval Magazine, Port Chicago: This facility was established in 1942 on the south shore of Suisun Bay near the small town of Port Chicago. It was a subpost of the Naval Ammunition Depot, Mare Island and was used as a transshipment point for supplies and naval ammunition. In 1944 the Navy acquired more land and began storing large amounts of ammunition at the Magazine. On July 17, 1944 a terrible accident occurred at Pier #1 where two cargo ships were being loaded with ammunition from a train parked on the pier. In rapid succession, three tremendous blasts vaporized the ships and train. Three hundred and twenty men were killed, 390 more injured and buildings in the area, including most of the town of Port Chicago, were flattened. The cause of the blasts was never determined. It was the worst such accident in the U.S. during the war.

The Naval Magazine continued in operation after the blast and into the post war years. In 1957 the depot was renamed U.S. Naval Weapons Station, Concord. Pier #1 was never

Newly launched Victory Ships being outfitted at the California Shipbuilding Corp. early 1944.

rebuilt and its broken pilings were left in place and can be seen protruding above the water. There is a redwood monument nearby listing all the names of those killed in the blasts. With prior permission visitors will be escorted to the site. Many of the station's WW II storage igloos can be seen along SR 4 which bisects the station.

RICHMOND, on the NE shore of San Francisco Bay, was a port city and industrial town of 23,000 people before the war. Unfortunately it was to become so overwhelmed by war work and people that it became one of the most troubled communities in America. Its fine harbor attracted four major shipyards including Henry Kaiser's first and most famous yard[3]. In addition, 55 old and new factories operated in this relatively small town. During 1941 and 1942 people flocked to Richmond in unprecedented numbers. By 1943, Richmond's population rose to 150,000 and the city simply couldn't cope with the problems. People were reduced to living in tents, cardboard shacks, greenhouses, theaters and even in the open under bushes and behind fences. Government agencies, the shipyards and many public and private organizations pitched in to build houses, dormitories, streets, schools, sewers and everything else necessary for survival, but they never caught up. It was only at the end of the war when some of the industries began to shut down, that Richmond became a normal community again. The city slowly recovered in the post war years.

SAN BRUNO is one of the small communities south of San Francisco.

Golden Gate National Cemetery: In this beautiful

[3] This shipyard set a world record in building a ship; 4 days and 15 hours. Ten days later that Liberty ship, fully loaded, passed under the Golden Gate Bridge on its way to the Pacific war zones.

Three of America's best known naval heros of WW II are buried side-by-side in the Golden Gate National Cemetery, San Bruno, CA.

national cemetery, on the northern edge of San Bruno, are buried three of America's best known naval heros of WW II, Admirals Chester W. Nimitz, Raymond A. Spruance and Richmond Kelly Turner. They are buried side-by-side with their wives in a prominent location, yet their headstones are no more elaborate than those of the thousands of other servicemen buried here. Wandering the cemetery, a visitor will see graves of many other high ranking officers, Medal of Honor winners and Italian and German prisoners of war. Address: 1300 Sneath Ln., San Bruno, CA 94066. Phone: 415/589-7737. Hours: daily 8-5, Memorial Day 8-7.

Tanforan Assembly Center For Ethnic Japanese: This was the famous Tanforan Racetrack on the east side of San Bruno. The center operated from Apr. 28 to Oct. 13, 1942 processing the Bay Area's ethnic Japanese being evacuated to the relocation camps. At its peak, 7816 people resided here. Most of those processed here went to the Central Utah Relocation Camp at Abraham, UT. The race track eventually became Tanforan Park Shopping Center.

SAN JOSE is at the southern end of San Francisco Bay.

San Jose Airport: This was the town's local airport 2.5 miles east of town. It was used by the 4th AF and the Civil Air Patrol.

SAN RAFAEL is in Marin County on the NW shore of San Francisco Bay.

Hamilton Field: This air field was north of San Rafael on San Pablo Bay. Hamilton Field was built in 1929 on donated land for the specific purpose of defending the Bay Area and was headquarters for the 4th AF. It was also one of only a few fully operating AAF bases on the west coast when the U.S. went to war. Planes from Hamilton Field were active from the very first days of the war patrolling and protecting the U.S. west coast. Most of Hamilton's planes were fighters and patrol planes.

It was from this field, on the evening of Dec. 6, 1941 that 12 B-17 bombers left for service in the Philippines. Their first stop was to be Hawaii. When they arrived over Hawaii on the morning of Dec. 7 they found themselves caught up in the midst of the Japanese attack.

They were low on fuel, had no ammunition for their guns and were being shot at by both the Japanese planes and U.S. anti-aircraft guns. They scattered and set down wherever they could, but not before one plane was shot down and two others damaged.

The Field had a AAF regional hospital and an AAF debarkation hospital. In June 1942 many of Hamilton's combat planes suddenly moved westward to Hickam Field in Hawaii to defend the Hawaiian Islands against the Japanese invasion fleet steaming for Midway. Other combat planes from eastern fields moved on to Hamilton Field to defend California. When the Japanese were defeated at Midway, Hamilton's planes returned and the planes from the eastern bases returned to their respective bases. In 1943, Hamilton became a training center for replacement pilots and crews. In Dec. 1944 the 4th AF was charged with defending a large part of the west coast against the Japanese bombing balloons. In the next few months over 500 sorties were flown from Hamilton Field following up balloon sightings. Most of them were false alarms. Also in 1944 Hamilton Field became an intransit field for aircraft being transferred from Europe to the Pacific. The sudden end to the war in the Pacific cut short this activity.

Hamilton Field became Hamilton Air Force Base after the war and was closed in the 1990s.

SANTA RITA, 13 miles east of Hayward, didn't exist during the war.

Camp Parks and Camp Shoemaker: In Nov. 1942 the Navy built Camp Parks side-by-side with Camp Shoemaker just north of what today is the community of Santa Rita. Camp Parks was used for tactical training of SeaBee units moving in from the east and destined for service in the Pacific area. Camp Shoemaker was used as a naval training base and a distribution center.

After the war the camps were put into caretaker status and much of Camp Shoemaker was leased to the state of California which then built a prison called Santa Rita Rehabilitation Center. During the Korean War the remaining facilities were turned over to the US Air Force and Parks Air Force Base was created. When

peace returned, the US Air Force gave the property to the Army, who again named it Camp Parks. Camp Parks eventually became an Army Reserve facility. Location: In the NW quadrant of the intersection of I-580 and Camino Tassajara, just north of Santa Rita and five miles west of Livermore.

SUISUN BAY: The western end of Suisun Bay is used as a mothball anchorage of surplus war ships. The ship, tightly cluster together, can be easily see from the Benicia Bridge to the east. At I-680 and Lake Herman Rd, there is a vista point, with adequate parking, from which the ships may be viewed. Watch for the signs on I-680.

SUNNYVALE is 8 miles NW of San Jose.

Moffett Field: In 1931 the Navy accepted free land from Santa Clara County and began building a huge dirigile base which became known as U.S. Naval Air Station, Sunnyvale. The most impressive structure to go up was "Hanger One". It covered 8 acres, was 1133' long, 308' wide, 198' high with two 600 ton "orange peel" doors that moved on rails. It could house the Navy's biggest dirigibles and be seen from miles away. The military missions of dirigibles was to do patrol work, escort convoys and bomb enemy ships and territory. Later that year the landing field at the station was named Moffett Field in honor of Rear Adm. William A. Moffett who was lost in the crash of the dirigible "Akron". It was by this name that the station became best known. When the dirigible era ended Moffett Field was turned over to the Army Air Corps and became a basic training center. In 1939 Moffett Field received another tenant, the Ames Aeronautical Laboratory, a research facility that specialized in high speed wind tunnel testing.

When the U.S. went to war and Japanese submarines appeared off America's west coast, the need for anti-submarine defense became paramount and Moffett Field was given back to the Navy to be used as a blimp base. In Jan. 1942 the first blimps began patrolling California's coastal waters. These were the first blimps in action anywhere in the U.S. Blimp activities increased at Moffett and two blimp hangers were built in late 1942 and the base had 8 mooring circles. Blimp crews also trained here.

In early 1945 a major overhaul facility was built here to service transport planes. In Mar. 1945 a Japanese bombing balloon, recovered intact near Echo, OR, was tested here. That balloon is now one or two such balloons in the Smithsonian Museum.

After the war the blimps were phased out, more air transport units moved in as did prop driven and jet fighter squadrons. During the Cold War Moffett remained an active air station and in its last years of operation was known as Onizuka Air Force Base.

The Ames Aeronautical Laboratory expanded and eventually became part of NASA and was renamed NASA Ames Research Center. "Hanger One" has been designated as a naval historic site, but Moffett Field, after all its days of glory, was closed in the 1990s.

The NASA Ames Research Center has a visitor's center with a number of displays on the history of Moffett Field and Ames, and offers tours of the facilities which include Hangar One. Address of the NASA visitor's Center: Mail Stop TO-27, Moffett Field, CA 94035. Phone: 415/604-6497. Hours: M-F 8-4:30, closed holidays. Free.

TIBURON is on the bay side of Marin County's Tiburon Peninsula.

U.S. Naval Net Depot, Tiburon: This naval depot began in 1904 as a coaling station but was phased out as the Navy converted to diesel powered ships. During the 1930s the old station was still Navy property but was being used by the California Nautical School (now the California Maritime Academy at Vallejo). When war started in Europe the Navy canceled the School's lease and reactivated the old station as a facility to make, service and store naval nets and booms, and train men to handle them. In Aug. 1940 the station was commissioned as U.S. Naval Net Depot, Tiburon. One of its first jobs was to make a 6000 ton, 7 mile-long net to protect the San Francisco Harbor entrance. On Dec. 7, 1941 the net was 85% complete. It was rushed to completion and laid in the Bay's waters from Sausalito to the San Francisco Marina. In Jan. 1943 another training facility opened at the Net Depot at Paradise Cove, the Floating Drydock Training Center, Tiburon. Here, naval personnel were trained in overseas ship repair which was usually done in floating drydocks.

After the war the depot was used until the early 1970s when was closed down all except for a 3-acre site used to test instruments. The former drydock training area became Paradise Beach County Park.

TREASURE ISLAND: This island was "made" in 1937 for several reasons. First, by building the island some dangerous shoals were eliminated, and a dumping place was provided for materials then being dredged from various other places in the Bay; second, it served as the site of the 1939-40 Golden Gate International Exposition; and third, after the Exposition, it was to become San Francisco's new airport, serving both land planes and seaplanes. Treasure Island is connected to the natural island of Yerba Buena by a causeway and thus to the mainland via the San Francisco-Oakland Bay Bridge.

The beginning of WW II in Europe, however, prevented the third part of the plan from being implemented. In early 1941 the Navy acquired Treasure Island, named it U.S. Naval Station, Treasure Island and converted it into a reception and embarkation center and headquarters for the 12th Naval District. During peak periods of WW II the center processed up to 12,000 men a day, and after the war, many a sailor received his discharge papers here.

Also during the war four Army seaplanes, designated as C-98s, operated out of the seaplane base, which was the man-made cove between Treasure Island and Yerba Buena Island. These planes were pre-war Pan American "Clippers". The "Clippers" kept their peacetime colors and names as camouflage to make

it appear that they were still is commercial service.

Treasure Island remained a naval reception and embarkation center throughout the Cold War and had as many as 10 other naval agencies on board. In the 1990s NS, Treasure Island was closed.

Treasure Island Museum: This museum, situated at the causeway entrance to Treasure Island, is in one of the original buildings built from the 1939-40 Golden Gate International Exposition. It has displays relating to the Navy, Marines and Coast Guard, and the world's largest collection of memorabilia from the 1939-40 Golden Gate International Exposition. Address: Building One, Treasure Island, San Francisco, CA 94130. Phone: 415/395-5067. Hours: daily 10-3:30, closed Jan. 1, Easter, Thanksgiving Dec.25. Free.

VALLEJO, at the NE corner of the Bay and the entrance to Carquines Strait, was another Bay area town where urban growth went out of control during the war. The Navy's Mare Island naval base, with its huge ship yard and other naval operations, was the main culprit. Tens of thousands of workers flocked to Vallejo. They found jobs, but no place to live. By 1944 Vallejo's population, which had been 20,000 in 1940, had grown to 100,000. Conditions were eased only by the ending of the war and the departure of the war workers.

California Maritime Academy: This is a state college, founded in 1929, to train men and women for careers in supervisory positions on commercial ships in the maritime industry. It was first located near Tiburon, but in 1940 it moved to Morrow Cove south of Vallejo. During the war the Academy trained men at an accelerated pace and most of the Midshipmen entered the U.S. Navy as commissioned officer upon graduation. The Academy's training ship, the "Golden Bear", was built in 1940 as the cargo/passenger ship, but in 1941 it was converted into a Navy attack transport and served throughout the war in the South Pacific. She was turned over to the Academy after the war and named the "Golden Bear".

U.S. Naval Shipyard, Mare Island: Mare Island has been a U.S. Navy base ever since the island was purchased by the U.S. Government in 1853. By the 1940s it had one of the Navy's largest ship yards, building and repairing a wide variety of warships. There was also a large ammunition depot on the Island, a large hospital, a naval prison, a radio station, a Marine barracks, a large naval security group activity which included the substation of Skaggs Island five miles NW of Mare Island and many smaller activities. During the war 391 new ships were built here and 1227 ships of all type were repaired including ships from Allied nations. The ammunition depot not only stored ammunition but also renovated all types of naval ammunition. After the war many inactive ships came to Mare Island for repair and maintenance and some of the Navy's submarines and submarine tenders were mothballed for a while in the Mare Island Strait. NS, Mare Island remained very active

The periscope from the WW II U.S. submarine "Baya" in the Vallejo Naval & Historical Museum. One may view much of Vallejo and nearby Mare Island through the periscope.

throughout the Cold War with more than two dozen commands and activities operating within its boundaries. In the 1990s the ship yard was closed.

The Vallejo Naval & Historical Museum: This museum, near downtown Vallejo, records the history of Vallejo and its close association with the naval base at Mare Island. There are displays on Mare Island's history including its role in WW II. The museum has a working periscope from the WW II submarine "Baya" through which one can view the town of Vallejo and Mare Island. Address: 734 Marin St., Vallejo, CA 94590. Phone: 707/643-0077. Hours: Tues.-Sat. 10-4:30. Modest admission charged.

YERBA BUENA ISLAND: This is a large rugged island in the San Francisco Bay about midway between San Francisco and Oakland and is connected to both cities by the San Francisco-Oakland Bay Bridge. The island has been military property since the 180s. During WW I it was a naval training center. During WW II the naval facilities on the island were placed under the command of the adjacent NS, Treasure Island. In 1941 the Coast Guard built a depot on the island which remained in operation throughout the Cold War. In the postwar years Yerba Buena Island was used primarily as a residential area for Navy and Coast Guard families.

SAN JOSE: (See San Francisco and the San Francisco Bay Metropolitan Area)

SAN LUIS OBISPO is an old Spanish mission town near the coast and about half way between Los Angeles and San Francisco.

CAMP SAN LUIS OBISPO, five miles west of town was established in 1928 as Camp Merriam

The oil facility at Ellwood, CA after the Japanese submarine shelling attack of Feb. 23, 1942. Note the damage to the oil rig and pump house, lower center.

for the California National Guard. Just before the U.S. entered WW II, it was taken over by the Army who expanded the post into a training base for infantry units up to division size. The Army renamed the facility Camp San Luis Obispo. The California National Guard, and units from Nevada and Utah, were housed here and later became the Army's 40th Infantry Division. In 1942 a battalion of Filipino troops was trained here. The camp also had a 200-man prisoner of war compound. In 1946 the camp was returned to the state and again became a National Guard camp. The name, Camp San Luis Obispo, was retained. In 1951 the camp was taken over again by the Army for the Korean War, and was returned to the state in 1965.

SANTA ANA: (See Los Angeles and the Los Angeles Metropolitan Area)

SANTA BARBARA is 100 miles NW of Los Angeles.
Some U.S. military leaders saw Santa Barbara County as a likely spot for an enemy invasion designed to isolate Los Angeles from the rest of the U.S., or as a staging area for occupying the city. In Sept. 1944 Santa Barbara was one of five resort areas4 in the U.S. where the Army Service Forces leased large hotels and converted them into rest, relaxation and redistribution centers for service personnel returning from overseas and awaiting new assignments.

HOFF GENERAL HOSPITAL was built by the Army in Santa Barbara in 1941. It was a 1141-bed facility that specialized in general and orthopedic surgery and services for the deaf. It treated the Army's war wounded throughout the war and in Nov. 1945 was turned over to the Federal Public Housing Authority.

⁴The others were Lake Placid, NY, Asheville, NC, Miami Beach, FL, and Hot Springs, AR.

JAPANESE SUBMARINE SHELLING: At about 7 pm, on the evening of Feb. 23, 1942, the Japanese submarine I-17 surfaced close to shore off the small community of Ellwood, about 12 miles west of Santa Barbara, and began shelling an oil storage and pumping facility with its deck gun. Patrons and the owner of a nearby roadside cafe heard the shelling and rushed to the beach. There they stood and watched as the sub fired its last few shots. The submarine crew fired about 25 shells in a 15 minute period from about one mile out and then withdrew, but not before leaving a phoney periscope bobbing in the water to confuse the Americans. At the time of the shelling President Roosevelt was addressing the nation in one of his "Fireside Chats". U.S. military reaction to the attack was swift and dramatic. Planes from Bakersfield soon appeared over the area and dropped flares, but could not find the sub. The west coast military leaders, fearing additional attacks or perhaps an invasion, ordered all coastal cities from San Diego to Monterey blacked out. They also ordered all radio stations off the air and traffic stopped along highway 101. News of the attack spread like wildfire, especially in Los Angeles and hundreds of thousands of people were jittery and expecting the worst. That night the "Battle of Los Angeles" occurred ... a false air raid that was to be the worst and most intensive in the country during the war.

Tokyo, wanting to make the most of the attack, began propaganda broadcasts saying "The U. S. War Department officially announced that Santa Barbara, California was devastated by enemy bombardment . . .". Actually, the damage was very slight, estimated to be only $500 at the time. Only an oil derrick and the main pier were hit.

For the next few days souvenir hunters swarmed over the site looking for shell fragments. One Army officer, Capt. "Barney" Hagen was wounded in the hand when he picked up an unexploded fuse and it went off in his hand. He later received the Purple Heart medal. For the next few months land values in the Ellwood area plummeted and hundreds of pounds of genuine and not-so-genuine shell fragments were sold throughout southern California.

The attack also serve as a stimulus in another matter, the evacuation of the ethnic Japanese. The evacuation was just getting under way and the attack convinced many American that evacuating the ethnic Japanese was the right thing to do.

The damaged pier was removed and some of the lumber salvaged from it was used to build a restaurant on the north side of Hwy. 101.

The oil facility still exists and looks much as it did in 1942. A sign has been placed at its entrance commemorating the event. Location: There is an unmarked road coming south (towards the Ocean) off of Hollister Ave. just before Hollister crosses Hwy. 101 and ends at Calle Real. The unmarked road gives access to the Sandpiper Golf Course. Continue down that road about 1/2 miles until it ends at the oil facility's entrance.

U.S. MARINE CORPS AIR STATION, SANTA

BARBARA was 8 miles west of Santa Barbara. It began as a civilian airport in the mid 1930s, and when the U.S. went to war the Marine Corps took it over to train Marine pilots and gave it its wartime name. Ever mindful of the Japanese submarine attack at nearby Ellwood, the beach area was regularly patrolled by the Marines and a plane was kept at the ready loaded with depth charges. In Jan. 1947 the Marines departed and the station again became the Santa Barbara Municipal Airport.

SANTA MARIA is 30 miles SE of San Luis Obispo.

SANTA MARIA ARMY AIR BASE
, 3.5 miles south of town, was Santa Maria's local airport before the war and had a well-known flying school called the Santa Maria School of Flying. In May 1939 the School was one of 9 schools contracted by the Air Corps to train Air Corps pilots. When the U.S. went to war the AAF took control of the airport giving it its wartime name. The base continued as a primary training field and was also used by combat-ready P-38 fighter units to protect the west coast. The Navy also used the base. After the war the field became Santa Maria Airport again.

SANTA MARIA MUSEUM OF FLIGHT is adjacent to the Santa Maria Airport and displays several WW II vintage aircraft and other memorabilia of that time. Since the P-38 fighter plane played such an important role in Santa Maria's life during WW II, there is quite a bit of information on that plane. Address: 3015 Airpark Rd., Santa Maria, CA 93456. Phone: 805/922-8758. Hours: Apr. thru Nov. F-Sun. 9-4, rest of year F-Sun. 10-4, closed Jan. 1 and Dec. 25. Donations. Location: On the NE edge of Santa Maria Airport off Skyway Dr. and just north of the airport terminal. Watch for sign on Skyway Dr. at Hanger St.

SANTA ROSA is 40 miles north of San Francisco.

SANTA ROSA ARMY AIR FIELD, 6 miles NW of Santa Rosa, was built in 1942 and pilots were trained here in P-38 fighters. In 1946 the field was turned over to the county and became the Sonoma County Airport. In the terminal restaurant is a scale model of the air field as it appeared during the war.

U.S. NAVAL AUXILIARY AIR STATION, SANTA ROSA was 2.5 miles SW of town. It served as an auxiliary base to NAS, Alameda and had an outlying field 1.5 miles north of Cotati, CA.

SEBASTOPOL, 8 miles west of Santa Rosa,
was one of many places where Japanese bombing balloons landed. Sebastopol's balloon was discovered in a snow bank on Jan. 4, 1945 and one of the first ones found. It was examined in place and then, fearing it carried bacterial agents, was packed in ice and sent to the Naval Research Laboratory in Washington, DC. The balloon did not have bacterial agents aboard but it did further advance the knowledge of the people at the Laboratory as to what was really happening.

STOCKTON, 50 miles east of Oakland, is an
inland seaport in the heart of the San Joachin Valley. At the start of the war its port facilities, highway system and rail connections were well developed so it was only natural that it would

become a major shipping point for military supplies going overseas. There were also several ship yards at Stockton. The George Polcock Co. made sub chasers and Colberg Bros., Inc. made mine sweepers and salvage vessels. There were also many ethnic Japanese in the area.

STOCKTON AREA ARMY DEPOTS: The Army had several depots in the area, the main ones being Lathrop Holding and Reconsignment Point, Lathrop Engineering Depot, and a subpost of the California Quartermaster Depot at Oakland. These depots worked closely together during the war and they were around-the-clock operations receiving, storing, packing and shipping a wide variety of military items. A main prisoner of war camp was located here holding over 1500 POWs who worked at the depots. After the war the depots were consolidated into one and named Sharpe Army Depot.

STOCKTON ASSEMBLY CENTER FOR ETHNIC JAPANESE: This was the San Joaquin County Fairgrounds 1.5 miles SE of downtown Stockton. It operated as an assembly center from May 10 to Oct. 17, 1942 and, at its peak, held 4271 residents. Most of the people processed here were went to the relocation camp at Rohwer, AR. After the center closed it was turned over to the 4th AF and became an air depot.

STOCKTON FIELD, 6 miles SE of town, was Stockton Municipal Airport before the war and one of the best developed airports in the country. In May 1940 the Army contracted a privately-owned flying school here to provide elementary and advanced flight training for AAF pilots. The Air Transport Command also operated from the field and had an air freight terminal here. After the war it again became Stockton Municipal Airport. Auxiliary fields during the war were:

- Aux. #1, Kingsbury Field (Lodi Air Park), 6 miles SW of Lodi
- Aux. #2, Modesto Airport, 2 miles SE of Modesto
- Aux. #3, New Jerusalem Airport, 8 miles SE of Tracy
- Aux. #5, Tracy Airport, 3.5 miles south of Tracy
- Aux. #6, Franklin Airport, 5.5 miles SE of Franklin

U.S. NAVAL SUPPLY DEPOT OAKLAND ANNEX, STOCKTON: By the end of 1943 the Naval Supply Depot Oakland had expanded to its limit so a 1500 acre annex was built on Rough and Ready Island near Stockton. The depot operated until 1965.

TAFT (See Bakersfield)

TULARE is half way between Fresno and Bakersfield. Many ethnic Japanese lived in the area, mostly on small farms. During the brief period of voluntary relocation, Feb. and Mar. 1942, many more ethnic Japanese moved into the county which was just east of the restricted Western Defense Area. When the order came for the forced evacuation of the ethnic Japanese, Tulare acquired one of the assembly center.

RANKIN AERONAUTICAL ACADEMY, 6 miles SE of Tulare, was a contract pilot training school for the AAF. It had an auxiliary field, Tulare Airport, three miles SW of town.

TULARE ASSEMBLY CENTER FOR ETHNIC JAPANESE: This center was the local fairgrounds located 1.5 miles south of Tulare on Hwy. U.S. 99. It operated from Apr. 20 to Sept. 4, 1942 and, at its peak, housed 4978 residents. Most of the people processed here went to the relocation camp at Gila River, AZ. On Sept. 15, 1942 the center was turned over to the VII Army Corps. Later, a prisoner of war camp was established here with 245 POWs working in agriculture.

TULE LAKE, in northern California, just south of the Oregon border, was a very small community in 1942 when it was chosen to be one of the sites to receive a relocation camp for the ethnic Japanese.

This monument on the east side of SR 139 just north of the community of Newell marks the location of Tule Lake Relocation Camp. None of the buildings in the background are original camp buildings. Note the lone chimney to the right of the monument. It is original.

"Flying Goose" housing development comprised of about 100 of the camp's barracks. Each home is privately owned and occupied. The "Flying Goose" was used as a movie site for the filming of the movie "Back to Manzanar".

The camp later became the systems's only segregation camp for trouble-makers and anti-American die-hards.

Just prior to the war an irrigation project had made much of the land in the area suitable for farming and the land was being homesteaded. When the war came, however, homesteading was stopped. In 1947 it was resumed again with veterans being given preference. Each new homesteading family was given two barracks buildings from the relocation camp to help them start out and many of those buildings remained in use. For decades after the war, ironically and for whatever reasons, no ethnic Japanese lived in the area.

TULE LAKE RELOCATION CAMP was located 8.5 miles south of the town of Tule Lake and just north of the small community of Newell on the east side of SR 139. County Rd. 113, which runs off to the east from SR 139, marks the northern boundary of the camp. The camp was built to hold 16,000 people and had 7400 acres of newly irrigated fertile farmland. The first evacuees reached the camp on May 27. The camp was similar to the other relocation camps until the summer of 1943 when the situation at Tule Lake changed dramatically.

In June 1943 the WRA decided to transfer the trouble-makers from all of thme camps to one camp, and Tule Lake was chosen as that camp. Between Aug. and Oct., 1943 twenty-three train-loads of people and their belongings came and went from Tule Lake. The original residents of Tule Lake were moved out to other camps and the trouble-makers were moved in. Tule Lake's security was increased and it became the most prison-like of all the camps. It also became the largest with some 18,000 residents.

It was soon discovered that the most troublesome individuals had to be segregated from the less troublesome, so a new compound was created within the camp with higher fences and more guard houses and the worst trouble-makers were put here. Those individuals openly displayed their loyalty to Japan and the Emperor and their hatred of the U.S. Many of them renounced their U.S. citizenship. They organized themselves into para-military organizations inside their compound and marched about in military formations, wearing makeshift "uniforms", singing patriotic Japanese songs, celebrating Japanese holidays, cheering Japanese victories, and longing for the day when they could return to Japan and join the Japanese armed forces. Dec. 8, the date of the attack on Pearl Harbor in Japan, was celebrated each year in a sunrise ceremony.

Tension at the camp was always high. On Nov. 3, 1943, during a celebration of Emperor Meiji's birthday (Hirohito's grandfather), a group of WRA truck drivers was attacked by club-wielding Kibei and beaten. The Army

One of two Panama Mounts of Battery #2 being washed away by the sea. The Battery was installed here to protect an oil field and railroad and highway bridges across the Ventura River.

moved in and took control the camp, imposed strict controls and punished the attackers. It wasn't until mid-Jan. 1944 that conditions became stable enough for the Army to depart and return the camp to WRA control.

Those who had taken the drastic step of renouncing their U.S. citizenship could not, according to U.S. law, regain it nor could they remain the U.S. after the war. Also, those who renounced their U.S. citizenship automatically became enemy aliens, and therefore wards of the Immigration and Naturalization Service (INS) who ran the enemy alien internment camps. Correspondingly, the renunciants were transferred to the INS camps, and were marked for deportation to Japan after the war.

During the summer of 1945, with an American victory over Japan becoming ever more certain, and finally, with Japan's sudden surrender, many residents at Tule Lake had second thoughts about their future and became more cooperative. Still though, there were thousands who were troublesome to the last.

Tule Lake was the last relocation camp to close on Mar. 20, 1946. Most of those individuals who wanted to remain in the U.S., even though they had been troublesome, were allowed to stay, while those who wanted to return to Japan, and those who were ordered deported, were taken to various west coast ports and sent off to Japan.

Nothing much remains at the site of the original camp except for a few foundations and chimneys. There is a monument on the east side of SR 139, just north of Newell, marking the camp's location.

About 100 of the camp's barracks buildings were moved to a location north of the old camp site and organized into a housing development called "Flying Goose". The relocated and refurbished buildings were sold to individuals and were owned and occupied by local families. In the postwar years the housing development was used as a movie location for the filming of the movie "Back to Manzanar".

The camp officers' club still exists. It's in the town of Tule Lake on S.R. 139 and became a grocery store called the Homestead Market.

TURLOCK is 12 miles SE of Modesto.

TURLOCK ASSEMBLY CENTER FOR ETHNIC JAPANESE: This was the local fairgrounds on the NW side of town on U.S 99. It operated as an assembly center from Apr. 30 to Aug. 12, 1942 and, at its peak, housed 3661 residents. Almost everyone processed here was sent to the relocation camp at Gila River, AZ. The center was turned over to the Army's 9th Service Command on Aug. 24, 1942.

TWENTYNINE PALMS is 75 miles east of San Bernardino.

U.S. NAVAL AUXILIARY AIR STATION, TWENTYNINE PALMS, was five miles north of town at the south end of a large dry lake. It was established in 1944 by the Navy as an auxiliary station to NAS, San Diego to train air crews in bombing and strafing. The aircraft landed on the lake bed except in wet weather, when they used a runway of steel mats. After the war, the Navy left, but in 1952 came back to reclaim its air station and began building a large Marine base, U.S. Marine Corps Air Ground Combat Center, Twentynine Palms which became one of the Marine Corps' largest air stations.

VENTURA is a coastal town 50 miles NW of Los Angeles.

BATTERY 2 and CAMP SEASIDE: Within days of the submarine attack at Santa Barbara, the 2nd Battalion of the 144th Field Artillery (Calif. Natl. Guard) was rushed from Ft. MacArthur at San Pedro to the mouth of the Ventura River. There they began building Panama Mounts for their WW I-vintage 155mm artillery guns, installed a searchlight and put up tents. The location was designated Battery 2, and by early March, 1942 it was ready to defend the vital highway and railroad bridges across the Ventura River and a nearby oil field. A temporary camp was built on the east side of the river at the Ventura County Fairgrounds called Camp Seaside.

By Jan. 1944 the threat of enemy action had greatly diminished and Battery 2 and Camp Seaside were deactivated.

Two of the Panama Mounts still exist on the west side of the river but are slowly being eroded by the sea. When they were built, they were about 100 yards inland. This area became part of Emma Wood State Beach. The Mounts are at the water's edge about 100 yards west of the mouth of the river.

VERNALIS is 20 miles south of Stockton. During the war it had U.S. Naval Auxiliary Air Station, Vernalis, 2.5 miles south of town. The station was an auxiliary field to NAS, Alameda.

VICTORVILLE is 30 miles north of San Bernardino.

VICTORVILLE ARMY AIR FIELD was 7 miles NW of Victorville. The facility began in June 1941 as a training base to meet the needs of the 30,000 Pilot Training Program and was named Air Corps Advanced Flying School. In Feb. 1942 it became a bombardiers' school and in Apr. 1943 was renamed Victorville Army Air Field. A radar observers school was also located here. In 1945 Victorville AAF was converted to a storage facility for B-29s, AT-7s and AT-11s. The US Air Force acquired the base in 1948 and used it as a jet training center. In 1950 it was renamed George Air Force Base, remained operative throughout the Cold War and closed in the 1990s.

During the war Victorville had the following auxiliary fields:
- Aux. #1, Hawes Airport, 1.5 miles SW of Hawes
- Aux. #2, Helendale Airport, 6 miles NE of Helendale
- Aux. #3, Mirage Airport, 15 miles NW of Victorville
- Aux. #4, Grey Butte Airport, 19 miles west of Victorville

WATSONVILLE is 25 miles NE of Monterey.

CAMP MACQUAIDE: This was a small temporary base built in 1940 on the coast to train artillerymen. It operated throughout the war, and in 1946 was used for a while as an Army disciplinary barracks. Eventually it was sold and some of its buildings were acquired by the Monterey Bay Academy and the Seventh Day Adventists.

U.S. NAVAL AUXILIARY AIR STATION, WATSONVILLE (HTA) was 2.5 miles NW of town and an auxiliary to NAS, Alameda. After the war it became a local airport.

U.S. NAVAL AUXILIARY AIR STATION, WATSONVILLE, (LTA), a blimp base four miles SE of town, was also an auxiliary to NAS, Alameda.

WINDSOR is 7 miles NW of Santa Rosa.

CAMP WINDSOR, just west of town, had been built in the 1930s as a migrant workers camp. In 1943 it was converted into a prisoner of war camp for low-risk POWs who worked in local agriculture. The POWs were allowed considerable freedom and fraternized easily with the local people. Camp building foundations can be seen on the north side of Windsor River Road at River Oaks Ln.

YOSEMITE NATIONAL PARK, in west-central California, had a Navy convalescent hospital during the war and for several years thereafter.

COLORADO

President Roosevelt visited Camp Carson in 1943. Here he watches an amphibious landing exercise.

Colorado, like most western states, experienced substantial economic and population growth during World War II. One segment of her economy, however, that of mining, suffered from a severe manpower shortage. Mining production actually declined in 1944 because of this problem.

Colorado's manufacturing and agricultural sectors grew at a considerable rate and the Government built several major new installations in Colorado and generously expanded those that already existed. Many Mexican laborers were brought in to work in agriculture. There were three main prisoner of war base camps in the state and at least 28 branch camps. The POWs, also, were used extensively as agricultural workers. Colorado had one relocation camp for ethnic Japanese. In early 1945 several Japanese bombing balloons came down in the state.

Most of the military bases built or enlarged during the war remained in operation after the war and contributed significantly to Colorado's economy. Colorado also became the home state of the new US Air Force Academy.

COLORADO SPRINGS is at the foot of Pike's Peak.

CAMP CARSON, just south of town, was built in 1942 and named after the famous Army scout, Kit Carson. It was a training camp for mechanized infantry units up to division size. The 71st, 89th and 104th infantry Divisions trained here as well as engineers, tank units, decontamination units, mountain troops, and mule packers.

In Jan. 1943 a 3000-man prisoner of war compound was added, and then enlarged to hold 8000 POWs. In May 1943, Womens Army Corps (WAC) units began to train at Carson. In 1944 Italian Service Units began working at the Camp. After the war Camp Carson became a base for the Army's mountain troops and in the postwar years it became the home of the 4th Infantry Div. Many of the WW II build- ings remained in use well into the postwar era.

PETERSON FIELD was 6.5 miles east of Colorado Springs and before the war was Colorado Springs' municipal airport. In May 1942 the AAF took over the field, named it Air Support Command Base, and in May 1943, established the headquarters of the 2nd AF here. The field was renamed Peterson Army Air Field in honor of 1st Lt. Edward J. Peterson who perished in the crash of his P-51 fighter here at the air field in Aug. 1942. Eight months later the field was renamed again as Peterson Field. This was a training base that first trained photo reconnaissance personnel, then heavy bomber crews, then fighter pilots and finally flight instructors. It had a air-to-air gunnery range at Trinidad, CO that it shared with Lowry AAB, Pratt AAF in KS and Dalhart AAF in TX, and a bombing and gunnery range at Buckley Field it shared with that field.

After the war Peterson Field was returned to civilian control, but after a brief period, the AAF reactivated the military facilities as a part of the Continental Air Forces which, in 1946, became the Strategic Air Command (SAC). The runways were shared between the AAF and the municipal airport. All the facility was taken over by the US Air Force in 1948 and in 1976 the Air Force named the facility Peterson Air Force Base. The base remained fully active throughout the Cold War.

Edward J. Peterson Air and Space Museum: This is a base museum tracing the history of aviation in the Colorado Springs area, the history of Peterson AFB and the history of the North American Aerospace De- fense Command (NORAD). Address: 3rd Space Support WING/PACM, Peterson AFB, CO 80914-50000. Phone: 719/554-4915. Hours: Oct. through April Tues.-F 8:30-4:30, Sat. 9:30-4:30; May through Sept. Tues.-F 8:30-4:30, Sat. 9:30-4:40. Free.

PIKES PEAK GHOST TOWN: This museum covers the early history of Colorado and the local area. One of the items on display is an interesting WW II relic, President Franklin D. Roosevelt's 1942 bulletproof V-12 Lincoln limousine. After President Roosevelt's death, President Truman used the car for a while. Address: 400 S. 21st St., Colorado Springs, CO 80907. Phone: 719/634-0691. Hours: Memorial Day to Labor Day M-Sat. 9-6, Sun. 1-6. Rest of the year reduced hours. Admission charged. Location: at the corner of U.S. Hwy. 24 west and S. 21st St.

US AIR FORCE ACADEMY: The US Air Force Academy didn't exist during WW II. It was built in 1954 after the Air Force became an independent branch of the armed services. The Academy is 12 miles north of Colorado Springs. Visitors are welcome to tour the grounds and visit the Barry Goldwater Visitors Center. Many of the buildings and other facilities are named after famous individuals of WW II. Visitors may roam the Academy grounds from dawn to dusk.

In the Academy's cemetery, off Parade Loop Drive, are many veterans of WW II including Air Force Generals, Carl Spaatz, Curtis LeMay, Donavon Smith and George Stratemeyer. There are several memorial walls at the cemetery bearing plaques honoring various air units, most of which are from WW II. Address: HQ USAFA/XPAG, US Air Force Academy, Colorado Springs, CO 80840-5241. Phone: 719/472-2025 and 2555. Visitor's hours: June

A Curtiss P-40 fighter plane serves as a monument to the Flying Tigers, American volunteers who used these planes in combat against the Japanese in China before the U.S. entered the war. Petersen AFB, Colorado Springs, CO.

President Franklin D. Roosevelt's 1942 bullet-proof V-12 Lincoln Limousine. The car was also used by President Harry S Truman.

Memorial walls at the US Air Force Academy cemetery bearing plaques honoring various air units. Most of the units are from WW II.

through Aug. daily 9-6, rest of year daily 9-5. Closed Jan. 1, Thanksgiving and Dec. 25. Free.

DENVER is the capital of Colorado and was one of the west's boom-towns during the war.

BUCKLEY FIELD, 13 miles east of Denver, was built in 1942 as a basic flight training facility. The field had the Arctic Training School detached from the main base and located at Echo Lake on the slopes of Mt. Evans at 10,600 ft. At this location AAF personnel, scheduled to go to Alaska, were trained in the care and maintenance of aircraft in frigid weather. Schools operating on the field consisted of an armament maintenance school, a chemical warfare school and a post-engineering school. The field had an AAF regional hospital, a 62,000 acre bombing and gunnery range SE of Denver known as "Old Lowry Bombing & Gunnery Range" and a precision bombing range near the base. In 1945 a camouflage center moved here from March Field in CA. In 1946 the AAF began pulling out of Buckley and the field was declared surplus. It was subsequently acquired by the Navy as a naval air station to service a

variety of the Navy's needs in the Rocky Mountain area. The Navy renamed the facility U.S. Naval Air Station, Buckley Field. In 1959 the Navy departed and the base went to the Colorado Air National Guard. The base is over-run with prairie dogs.

FITZSIMONS GENERAL HOSPITAL, in Aurora, CO, an eastern suburb of Denver, was built in 1918. Just before the war a new 8-story main hospital building was added and opened Dec. 3, 1941, four days before the Japanese attack on Pearl Harbor. Some of its first patients were casualties flown in from Hawaii. Its mission during WW II was to serve the military personnel and their dependents in the Denver area. During WW II the hospital had a 3417-bed capacity and specialized in general medicine, tuberculosis, general and orthopedic surgery, thoracic surgery, deep x-ray therapy and psychiatry. Over 300 prisoners of war worked at the hospital.

The hospital continued in operation in the postwar years and expanded to become Fitzsimons Army Medical Center. In 1955 President Eisenhower was a patient here fol-

lowing a heart attack.

The hospital operated throughout the Cold War.

FORT LOGAN, three miles SE of downtown Denver, was an old Army post built in 1888. During WW II is was a reception center, a post for Army engineers and a sub-post of Lowry Field. Logan housed some AAF technical and clerical training facilities that moved in from Chanute Field, IL. It also had an AAF convalescent hospital. At the end of the war Fort Logan served as a re-deployment and separation center. In the 1960s the fort was given to the state.

LOWRY FIELD, 6 miles SE of downtown Denver, began in 1937 as the Army's Air Corps Technical School, Denver Branch, an off-shoot of the Air Corps' technical training facilities at Chanute Field, IL. In 1938 it was renamed Lowry Field and acquired a 64,000-acres bombing and gunnery range SW of the field. From 1937 to 1940 Lowry Field and Chanute Field were the primary Army air fields in the country training Air Corps technical personnel. Training here included photography, armament, clerical work, bombardiers and technical instructors. The field became the administrative headquarters for the AAF's Technical Training Command and there was an air freight terminal here operated by the Air Transport Command. In mid-1943 a major expansion began and Lowry became a flying base specializing in transition training for pilots and crews from other planes into B-29 bombers. B-29 flight engineers[1] were also trained here. These missions, and those of technical training,

[1] The B-29 was the first Air Force plane to require flight engineers.

WW II buildings at Buckley Field in good repair and in use. Note the prairie dogs in the foreground. They are everywhere on the base.

continued into the postwar years. In 1948 the US Air Force acquired the facility and renamed it Lowry Air Force Base.

Lowry became the temporary location of the US Air Force Academy in the years just before the completion of the new Academy facilities at Colorado Springs. Base facilities also served intermittently as President Eisenhower's Summer White House in the years 1952-55. Throughout the Cold War years Lowry specializes in technical training much as it had during WW II. In the 1990s, at the of the Cold War, the base was closed.

ROCKY MOUNTAIN ARSENAL, 12 miles NE of downtown Denver, was built in 1941 on 20,000 acres of land by the Federal Government and operated by the Remington Arms Corp. This 200-building facility manufactured, stored, renovated and shipped intermediate and toxic products, including poison gases, and incendiary weapons. Research and development on these products was also done here. At its peak the arsenal employed 20,000 people and was Colorado's 4th largest community. It had a branch prisoner of war compound with about 300 POWs.

After the war the arsenal was put on standby basis and then reactivated in 1950 for the Korean War. About this time the arsenal began to make nerve gas, which has become a very controversial issue in local politics ever since it was announced to the public in 1954. The arsenal operated throughout the Cold War.

STAPLETON AIRPORT, five miles NE of town, was Denver's municipal airport before the war. Located at the field was the Continental-Denver Modification Center which operated under the direction of the Army's Air Technical Service Command. The Air Transport Command also used the field and had an air freight terminal here. After the war the airport became Stapleton International Airport.

the camp residents could walk to town and buy things in the stores. One Granada merchant operated a thriving fish market catering to the Japanese's love of fresh fish.

After the war the camp's buildings were sold and/or removed or torn down. Many concrete foundations and camp roads remain at the

Top: The "Amache" sign on U.S. 50 west of Granada directing visitors to the old camp site. Above, left:: Building foundations and roads remain at the camp. All original buildings are gone. visitors may drive or walk freely through the camp, but beware of rattlesnakes. Above, right: The Japanese cemetery at Camp Amache. The small brick mausoleum contains the remains of a high-born Japanese lady who died suddenly at the camp, and whose ghost, it is said, still roams the camp. The monument commemorates the 31 members of the camp who joined the U.S. armed forces and who were killed during the war. It was erected in the Denver Central Optimists Club.

GRANADA is in the SE corner of the state.

CAMP AMACHE: This camp, 1.5 miles west of Granada, was the only Japanese relocation camp in Colorado. Construction of the camp began in early 1942 to house 8000 people and its first residents arrived in Sept. of that year. The camp's population rose to 7318 making it the smallest camp in the system. Many of the residents were farmers from the Sonoma Valley and Merced areas of California. Deep wells were drilled and nearby fields irrigated so that the farmers could continue to ply their trade. As a result, the residents grew much of their own food. The little town of Granada prospered very well during the war because

camp site as does the Japanese cemetery. There is a low-income housing development at the east end of the camp and the city dump at the west end. The Big Timber Museum in Lamar, CO, 17 miles west of Granada, has displays on Camp Amache.

Visitors may drive or walk through the camp, but are advised to be vigilant for rattlesnakes. To reach the camp, drive .8 miles west of Granada on U.S. 50 and turn south on a dirt road at the "Amache" sign. Proceed .5 miles south until the road ends at a "T". This is the main entrance to the camp.

GREELEY, 50 miles north of Denver, was the site of one of Colorado's three main prisoner of war camps. The camp was located just west of Greeley and held about 2300 German POWs, most of whom worked in agriculture, forestry or on military bases. Nothing remains of the camp except two stone pillars at the former main gate.

LA JUNTA (The Junction) is 60 miles SE of Pueblo.

LA JUNTA ARMY AIR FIELD
, 4.5 miles NE of town, was established by the 2nd AF as one of the training bases for the 70,000 Pilot Training Program. The base closed down soon after the war and turned over to

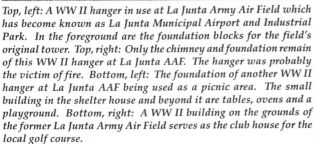

Top, left: A WW II hanger in use at La Junta Army Air Field which has become known as La Junta Municipal Airport and Industrial Park. In the foreground are the foundation blocks for the field's original tower. Top, right: Only the chimney and foundation remain of this WW II hanger at La Junta AAF. The hanger was probably the victim of fire. Bottom, left: The foundation of another WW II hanger at La Junta AAF being used as a picnic area. The small building in the shelter house and beyond it are tables, ovens and a playground. Bottom, right: A WW II building on the grounds of the former La Junta Army Air Field serves as the club house for the local golf course.

the community to become La Junta Municipal Airport. Some of the original buildings remain.

Auxiliary air fields serving La Junta AAF were:

- Aux. #1, Rocky Ford Airport, 2.5 miles NE of Rocky Ford
- Aux. #2, Las Animas Airport, 6 miles SE of Las Animas
- Aux. #4, Arlington Airport, 3.5 miles NW of Arlington

LEADVILLE is 75 miles SW of Denver in the Rocky Mountains.

CAMP HALE: This camp was built to be the home of the Army's 10th Mountain Division. The camp's altitude of 9500 feet and mountainous landscape provided the troops with suitable terrain upon which to practice their skills in mountain warfare. Camp Hale opened in Nov. 1942 and eventually housed 15,000 military personnel and 5000 mules. Along with its mission to train troops in

mountain climbing, skiing, mule skinning, etc. the base was used to test new weapons and other materials to see how they performed at high altitudes and in arctic-type weather.

Camp Hale had a prisoner of war branch camp with more than 2000 German POWs. The 10th Division left Camp Hale in 1943 and served in the mountains of Italy.

After the war Camp Hale was used sporadically by the Army. In 1957 its Mountain and Cold Weather Training Command was moved to Fort Greely Alaska, and in 1964 Camp Hale was closed.

PUEBLO was Colorado's second largest city at the time of WW II. Most of Pueblo's factories converted to war work including the Colorado Fuel and Iron Corp. which produced 155mm shells.

PUEBLO ARMY AIR BASE was 7 miles NE of town on U.S. Hwy. 50. It was operated by the 2nd AF as a training base for bomber crews flying B-17s, B-24s and B-29s, with B-24 training predominating. After the war the facility became Pueble Memorial Airport.

Fred E. Weisbrod Aircraft Museum and The International B-24 Memorial Museum: Both of these museums are in front of the terminal at

the Pueblo Memorial Airport. The Weisbrod Museum has more than two dozen aircraft on display. Planes from WW II include a B-29A, C-47, B-26C and A4D-2. The International B-24 Memorial Museum is a one-of-a-kind museum dedicated solely to the B-24 Liberator bomber. The history of the B-24 is told in a 300-foot-long display called the "Honor Gallery Hall of Liberator Legends". Address: 31001 Aviation Ave., Pueblo, CO 81001. Phone: 719/543-3605. Hours: The Weisbrod Museum, daily 9-dusk; the B-24 Museum M-F 10-4, Sat. 10-2. Donations requested.

PUEBLO ORDNANCE DEPOT, 15 miles east of Pueblo on U.S. Hwy. 50, was built in 1941-42 to receive, store and ship munitions for the Army. It was soon realized that the Depot's mild dry climate was ideal for storing machinery outside. Thus, the depot became a major storage facility for Army vehicles and artillery pieces.

After the war the Depot stored a wide variety of items including missiles and remained one of the largest Army depots in the west.

TRINIDAD is in south-central Colorado near the New Mexico border.

CAMP TRINIDAD was one of Colorado's three main prisoner of war camps. It held approximately 2500 German POWs, most of whom worked in local agriculture.

CONNECTICUT

At the beginning of the war Connecticut's economy was well diversified into manufacturing, commercial, agricultural and military sectors. The state had 2936 manufacturing establishments, and in 1940 was 3rd in the nation in aircraft production. The state was a leader in the manufacture of submarines, small arms ammunition, machine tools, brass products and the mineral, mica, which was used in the aircraft industry. Her manufacturing sector converted almost totally to war production and there was a constant shortage of manpower. Her agricultural sector produced tobacco, dairy products, poultry, hay, potatoes and grain crops. In 1942 Connecticut was first in the nation in war production per capita.

Despite the upsurge in war production and military operations in the state, the state's population did not surge as it did in other states. By the end of the war Connecticut's population was only 2% higher than at the start. When the war came suddenly to an end in Aug. 1945, many war contracts were canceled and Connecticut's manufacturing sector was hard hit.

BRIDGEPORT and **STRATFORD**: This area, on the SW coast of Connecticut, was the state's most industrialized area during WW II. Bridgeport had 147,000 people and Stratford about 3,000.

Major manufacturers in the town were the Vought-Sikorsky Division of United Aircraft Co., which made a variety of military aircraft for the Army and Navy, Remington Arms. Co. which made rifles, small arms ammunition and propellers, Bridgeport Brass Co. which made shell casings, and the Auto Ordnance Corp. which made Thompson sub-machine guns … "Tommy Guns".

BRIDGEPORT AIRPORT, 3.5 miles SE of town, was used by the Navy during the war.

IGOR I. SIKORSKY GRAVE SITE: St. John's Greek Catholic Cemetery in Stratford is the final resting place of aircraft pioneer Igor I. Sikorsky.

Born in Russia, Sikorsky became a successful engineer there pioneering multi-engine aircraft. He fled Russia during the Bolshevik Revolution and came to the U.S. where he developed trans-oceanic flying boats (Clippers). In 1939-40, he developed the western hemisphere's first successful helicopter. Address: 2610 Nichols Ave., Stratford, CT.

GROTON and **NEW LONDON**: These two towns are on either side of the mouth of the Thames River. New London had about 30,000 people and Groton about 5,000. In Groton was one of America's most important industrial facilities, the Electric Boat Co. (later General Dynamics), was the largest supplier of submarines to the U.S. Navy during the war producing a total of 74 subs. The company also built 398 Patrol-Torpedo (PT) Boats during the war.

On Aug. 3, 1941 President Roosevelt left the U.S. Naval Base at New London on his private yacht, the "Potomac", for what was publicized as a vacation along the New England coast. The "Potomac" sailed to a point off Martha's Vineyard and the President transferred to the cruiser "Tuscaloosa". He then sailed to the naval base at Argentia, Newfoundland for a secret meeting with British Prime Minister, Winston Churchill on Aug. 9-12. This meeting produced the famous Atlantic Charter which was a statement of principles calling for the rights of all nations to have free elections and be free from foreign pressures.

Later in the war, New London was one of several U.S. ports considered by Hitler and the German naval staff as a target for a major submarine assault. The attack was never carried out, however.

The WW II submarine "Gunnel" being launched at the Electric Boat Co., Groton, CT.

NATIONAL SUBMARINE MEMORIAL is an outdoor memorial on the Groton waterfront on Thames St. just south of the I-95 Gold Star Memorial Bridge. It's main attraction is the well-preserved conning tower of the U.S. submarine "Flasher". There are plaques at the Memorial relating to the submarine service and a memorial to the 52 submarines that went down during WW II.

FORT TRUMBULL is near the southern end of the New London waterfront. It is an old masonry fort built in 1839, on the site of two previous forts. In 1910 the Army turned the fort over to the Coast Guard, and during WW II the Coast Guard used it as a maritime service training station. After the war the Coast Guard gave it to the Navy who used it for many years as the U.S. Navy Underwater Sound Laboratory.

U.S. COAST GUARD ACADEMY: The U.S. Coast Guard Academy, just north of New London on the west back of the Thames River, is comparable to the academies of the other armed forces in that it trains men and women for careers as officers in the Coast Guard and offers Bachelor of Science degrees. The present Academy was established in 1910. During WW II the Academy trained men at an accelerated rate. The regular four year course was reduced to three and the Academy expanded to train more cadets. On Dec. 19, 1941, two weeks after the attack on Pearl Harbor, the 30 senior members of the class of 1942 were "graduated" early and sent off immediately to sea duty. The class of 1943 was graduated in June 1942. Those cadets going through the Academy on the wartime three-year programs received about 85% of the pre-war training program. During their last month at the Academy the cadets were given a concentrated program in anti-submarine tactics and patrol operations. Some graduates went on to various universities for selected post-graduate work.

After the war a German bark-rigged sail-

F4U Corsairs being made for the Navy on a production-line basis at Vought Sikorsky Div.

The U.S. Coast Guard Academy as it appeared during WW II.

ing ship, the "Horst Wessel", built in Germany in 1936 and used by the German Navy to train sailors, was acquired as war reparations by the Academy. The Coast Guard renamed her "Eagle" and she remained in service for decades. When in port she was usually open to the public. The Academy has a seasonal Visitors' Center with special displays and a multimedia show, and there are periodic cadet parades. For information, phone 860/444-8270.

U.S. Coast Guard Museum: This fine museum, in Waesche Hall on the Academy grounds, preserves the history of the Coast Guard and its three predecessors, the Revenue-Cutter Service, the Lighthouse Service and the Lifesaving Service. On display are uniforms, field equipment, ship and airplane models, photographs, paintings, flags, figureheads and various other artifacts. There is a library with 150,000 volumes, and a gift shop. Address: U.S. Coast Guard Academy, New London, CT 06320-4195. Phone: 860/444-8511 and 860/444-8270. Hours: May through Oct. M-F 9-4:30, Sat. 10-5, Sun. noon-5. Closed major holidays. Free.

U.S. NAVAL AUXILIARY AIR STATION, GROTON was three miles SE of Groton and served as an auxiliary to NAS Quonset Point, RI.

U.S. NAVAL BASE AND SUBMARINE BASE, GROTON, north of Groton on the east bank of the Thames River, was first acquired by the Navy in 1868. In 1898 it became a coaling station and during World War I was converted to a submarine base and greatly expanded. In the years between the wars much of the Submarine Service's research and development work on salvage and rescue work was done here. During WW II the base expanded to 286 buildings and became a full operating base for U.S. submarines. Personnel at the base worked closely with the Electric Boat Co. in the construction of new submarines.

In the postwar years the base expanded again with the advent of nuclear powered submarines, and by 1959 was the world's largest submarine base.

The base remained fully operative throughout the Cold War and became the home port of the U.S. Navy's Submarine Group 2, one of the most powerful naval flotillas in the world.

Nautilus Memorial and Submarine Force Library and Museum: This is a large memorial library and museum located just outside the main gate of the submarine base at one end of the USS Nautilus Pier. The library serves as the repository of the records and history of the U.S. Submarine Force and has a collection of over 10,000 books, papers, diaries and other publications. In the museum are working periscopes, an authentic submarine control room, two theaters, models, submarine parts, personal memorabilia, photographs, submersible vehicles, maps, documents and an extensive model wall tracing the development of U.S. submarines.

Outside is one of the largest displays of WW II submarines in the country. Included are the "Kairyu"(Japanese), the "Maile" (Italian) and the "Seehund" (German) midget submarines. Address: Box 571, Naval Submarine Base New London, Groton, CT 06349-5000. Phone: 860/449-3174 and 3558, and 800-343-0079 (tape recording). Memorial hours: mid-Apr. to mid-Oct. W-M 9-5, Tues. 1-5. Rest of year, W-M 9-4. Closed Jan. 1, Thanksgiving and Dec. 6-17 & 25. Library & Museum hours: mid-Apr. through mid-Oct. W-M 9-5, Tues. 1-5. Rest of year W-M 9-4. Closed Jan. 1, May 2-6, Thanksgiving & Dec. 5-11 & 25. Free.

FORTS H. G. WRIGHT, MICHIE AND TERRY: These forts are on Fishers Island which is part of New York state but accessible only by ferry from the Groton/New London area. These are old Army coastal defense forts built around 1900. Fort Wright is the main fort and Forts Michie and Terry are subposts positions. The forts were active as coastal defenses before America's entry into the war and remained so during the war. After the war the forts were inactivated. In the summer, during the postwar years, National Guard Units trained here.

HARTFORD, Connecticut's capital, was also her largest city and a major manufacturing center. Some of the important manufacturers were the United Aircraft Corp. whose divisions were Pratt & Whitney Mfg. Co. wich made aircraft engines; Hamilton Standard Co. which made aircraft propellers and Vought-Sikorsky Aircraft Co. which made aircraft. Colt's Patent Fire Arms Mfg.Co. made pistols, 50 caliber machine guns and 37mm anti-aircraft guns; the Royal Typewriter Co. made aircraft engine deflectors; Underwood-Elliott-Fisher Co. made M-1 car-

This 1940 advertisement by United Aircraft Corp. shows that they manufactured aircraft, aircraft engines and aircraft propellers.

Fifty foot cutaway model of the WW II submarine "Gato" in the USS Nautilus Memorial Submarine Force Library and Museum.

bines and Cheney Bros., Co., in the suburb of Manchester, made parachutes.

BRAINARD FIELD, three miles SE of downtown, was built in 1920 and was Hartford's state-owned local airport at the time of the war. It was taken over by the AAF and used for military purposes during the war. After the war it was returned to the state and again became Hartford's main city airport.

NEW HAVEN, on the south-central coast was, during the war, a thriving industrial town and seaport. The Winchester Repeating Arms Co. was one of the largest manufacturer in the country of the M1 "Garand" rifle, the standard weapon of the U.S. infantry, and the Marlin Firearms Co. made sub-machine guns.

NEW HAVEN ARMY AIR FIELD. This was New Haven's local airport at the start of the war. It was taken over by the AAF and used by both the Army and the Navy. After the war the military departed and the airport again became New Haven's local airport.

NEW LONDON: (See Groton and New London)

NEW MILFORD, 9 miles north of Danbury, was a small unincorporated community during WW II. In early 1942 a camp was built near New Milford to house children from New York City. Military authorities feared that New York City might be bombed and it would be prudent to evacuate as many children as possible. Their program was based on a British plan under which thousands of children were evacuated from London during the Blitz of 1940. The camp was never used.

NORWICH is 12 miles north of Groton/New London.

MOHEGAN PARK AND MEMORIAL ROSE GARDEN, east of town on SR 32 is a 350 acre park overlooking the city. Its Memorial Rose Garden was created to honor those who died in WW II and is in full bloom from late June to early July. The Park is open all year.

STRATFORD (See Bridgeport and Stratford)

WESTBROOK is 18 miles west of New London on I-95.

THE COMPANY OF MILITARY HISTORIANS is a museum that has one of the largest collection of men's and women's military uniforms in the U.S. They range for WW II to the present. Also on display are medals, awards and military musical instruments. Address: N. Main St., Westbrook, CT 06498. Phone: 860/399-9460. Hours: Tues.-F 8-3:30, closed major holidays. Free.

WINDSOR LOCKS is 12 miles north of Hartford.

BRADLEY FIELD, two miles west of town, was built for the 1st AF in 1941 as a training base for fighter pilots and first called Windsor Locks Air Force Base. Within a year, however, it was renamed Bradley Field in honor of a young pilot who was killed at the field, Lt. Eugene Bradley. During the war pilots trained here in P-39 and P-47 fighter planes. It had a small branch prisoner of war camp with about 250 POWs. In 1946 the base was taken over by the state and converted into a commercial airport. Its location, about half way between New York City and Boston, made it an ideal diversion airport in bad weather. In the postwar years the field became Bradley International Airport and home of the Connecticut Air National Guard.

The B-29A bomber at the New England Air Museum.

NEW ENGLAND AIR MUSEUM, just north of Bradley International Airport, is a fine air museum with a large collection of vintage aircraft and one of the major aircraft museums in the country. The collection included aircraft from the days of WW I to rockets. Some of the WW II planes in the collection include a B-25H, B-29A, A-24B, A-26C, F6F-5K Hellcat, FM-2 Wildcat, P-47D, P-51D, XF4U-4 Corsair, Kawanishi N1K2-J and a Macchi MC.200. There are early helicopters, jets and gliders. Inside the museum is a collection of vintage aircraft engines, an exhibit honoring aviation pioneer Igor Sikorsky and the firms he was associated with, ballooning exhibits, flight simulators and many other items of interest. Address: Bradley Intl. Airport, Windsor Locks, CT 06096. Phone: 860/ 623-3305. Hours: daily 10-5, closed Dec. 25 and Thanksgiving. Location: Exit I-91 at SR 20 (exit 40), and proceed west on SR 20 to SR 75, go north on SR 75 to Suffield at the north end of Bradley Intl. Airport, then west on Suffield to the museum.

DELAWARE

Although Delaware is one of the smallest states in the Union its 266,000 citizens contributed significantly to America's victory in WW II. Delaware's diversified economy produced many items of war and the state was outstanding in the production of chemicals and related products thanks to the heavy concentration of such industry in the northern part of the state. Delaware's shipbuilding industry contributed significantly to the war effort and her farms, canneries and packing houses supplied Americans at home and overseas with meat, fruits and vegetables. Delaware's modest rubber industry specialized, among other things, in tire retreading, and the retreaders worked long hours keeping American cars on the road when new tires became almost impossible to purchase.

Some 30,000 Delaware citizens, or 11.3% of her population, served in the armed forces, all 11 of her civilian airports were taken over by the military and there was enemy submarine action along her coast.

All during the war the citizens of Delaware practiced blackouts and dimouts, and near the end of the war, when it was believed that German rockets might be launched against the U.S. east coast from submarines, her citizens prepared for rocket attacks.

When the war ended, there was a brief economic upheaval as war contracts ended and service personnel came home, but the State readjusted well and the events of WW II are now a part of Delaware's colorful history.

BETHANY BEACH, on Delaware's coast 6 miles north of the Maryland state line, had a Coast Guard radio direction-finding station and a branch prisoner of war camp with 127 POWs who worked in the area. On the beach was an Army training area for anti-aircraft gunners known as Bethany Beach AAA Station.

DELAWARE CITY is on the Delaware River, 12 miles south of Wilmington.

FORTS DELAWARE AND DUPONT: Fort Delaware is a massive, pentagon-shaped, granite stone fort on Pea Patch Island in the Delaware River. Today it is a state park and open to the public, but it was used for a time during WW II. The present fort, the successor of earlier forts, was completed in 1859. During WW II several coastal defense weapons were mounted at the fort, but in 1944 the guns were removed and the fort abandoned as a coastal defense position.

Fort DuPont, two miles NW of Delaware City, was built in 1864 as an auxiliary coastal defense battery and a subpost of Fort Delaware. During WW II it became the dominant Army post in the area and Fort Delaware became its subpost. Fort DuPont was headquarters for the Army's 1st Engineers when WW II started and was soon expanded into an aviation engineering base and performed that mission throughout the war. Fort DuPont had Delaware's only main prisoner of war camp which held about 1300 POWs. The fort was decommissioned in Dec. 1945 and given to the state. In the postwar years it became known as the Governor

Bacon Health Center.

DOVER, Delaware's state capital, was a town of only 5500 people during the war.

DOVER ARMY AIR BASE was on U.S. 113 SE of, and adjacent to, Dover and was called Municipal Airport, Dover Airdrome. In Dec. 1941 the 1st AF took it over and during the war gave it three different names; Dover Army Air Base, Dover Subbase and Dover Army Airfield. The base also changed missions several times. In Dec. 1941 and early 1942 it was a base for combat-ready fighter planes defending the east coast. During 1942-43 its mission was that of anti-submarine patrol. It was then closed for expansion from Feb. to Aug. 1943, and from Sept. 1943 to Sept. 1944 P-47 fighter pilots trained here. After that, until May 1945, the base was used by the Air Technical Services Command in the AAF's air-launched rocket program. In 1946 it became inactive, but was reopened in 1950 by the US Air Force and named Dover Air Force Base. From then on throughout the Cold War, it remained an active Air Force base.

DOVER AFB HISTORICAL CENTER: This is a small, but growing, museum on the grounds of Dover AFB. Of interest is a B-17G bomber, painted in WW II colors, which was used as a drone director in the Air Force's flying bomb program of the 1950s. There is a C-47A used in the D-Day invasion and in the Berlin Airlift of 1948. Another aircraft, a Douglas C-54M was used in the Pacific during WW II and in the Berlin Airlift after it was modified to haul coal. Address: 436 MAW/CCEC, Dover AFB, DE 19902-5144. Phone: 302/678-6614. Hours: M-F 9-3. Free.

LEWES is just west of Cape Henlopen at the entrance to Delaware Bay. Within the city limits was a Coast Guard Station that had, during the war, a radio direction-finding station and a lifesaving station. Lewes' small airport was used by the military.

FORT MILES, on the coast two miles east of Lewes, was a WW II coastal defense position built on the site of several earlier coastal forts. The present coastal defenses were constructed during the early part of WW II and manned by Army Coast Artillery units. Two 8" railroad guns were also brought into position at Fort Miles.

Personnel at Ft. Miles worked closely with the people at Aberdeen Proving Ground, MD in secretly testing the newly developed proximity fuses in anti-aircraft ammunition. This new type of ammunition became very useful to the Allies late in the war against the German V-1 "Buzzbomb" rockets and the Japanese Kamikazes in the Pacific.

Fort Delaware on Pea Patch Island at Delaware City.

Inside the fort was a secret 3761 square-foot casement that housed the mine field controls for the entrance to Delaware Bay, and a sophisticated communications system. There was also a branch prisoner of war camp here with 280 POWs.

After the war the post was used by the Army Reserve to train anti-aircraft gunners. Some of Fort Miles' facilities were eventually incorporated into Cape Henlopen State Park including a WW II watch tower. In 1958 the Army turned Fort Miles over to the local Civil Defense command and only then was the existence of the fort's secret casement revealed to the public.

SLAUGHTER BEACH is a coastal town about 6 miles east of Milford.

FORT SAULSBURY, on the western shore of Delaware Bay near Slaughter Beach, was built during WW I as a 2-battery coastal defense position. It was armed with 12" naval guns and manned by Coast Artillery units during WW II. These guns could reach every acre of water in Delaware Bay. The fort had a branch prisoner of war camp with 263 POWs. After the war the batteries were sold to a private owner who modified them into a refrigerated cold storage facility for pickles.

WILMINGTON had been, for many years, Delaware's largest city and industrial center. At the start of the war the city's population was 112,500, or 42% of Delaware's total population. The city had become known as the "Chemical Capital of the World", due primarily to the E. I. du Pont de Nemours & Co., one of the world's largest chemical companies, which was headquartered here.

By the beginning of WW II Du Pont was involved in the manufacture of many types of explosives. During the war the company became involved in the production of another explosive, of sorts, when it contracted with the U.S. Government to design, build and operate the Hanford Engineer Works near Richland, WA. The Hanford plant produced plutonium, the explosive component of atomic bombs.

Despite its size, Du Pont was not the largest employer in Wilmington. That honor went to the Dravo Shipyard of Christiana, a suburb of Wilmington. During the war Dravo built hundreds of ships and cranes for the U.S. Government and the Allies. There were other shipyards in the Wilmington area, notable the American Car & Foundry Co. which built minesweepers, cargo ships, barges and tank lighters, and Pusey & Jones Corp. which built cargo ships.

DELAWARE GENERAL ORDNANCE DEPOT was an old pre-war depot near Wilmington. It was used to store ammunition during the war for the AAF. Many igloos were built at the depot for this purpose.

NEW CASTLE ARMY AIR BASE, 6 miles SW of Wilmington was, before the war, New Castle County Airport. It was leased by the Army Air Corps in mid-1940 to become the home of the

newly-created Air Ferry Command whose mission was to ferry new aircraft overseas to Europe and Africa. The field had facilities for servicing and maintaining transport aircraft and a large air freight terminal. The Air Ferry Command grew dramatically during the war and other fields around the country were acquired. After the war this air field was returned to its owners and became the Greater Wilmington Airport.

U.S. COAST GUARD CUTTER "MOHAWK" AND THE BATTLE OF THE ATLANTIC MEMORIAL: This is a floating WW II memorial in the form of a WW II Coast Guard cutter. The cutter "Mohawk" was built for the Coast Guard in Wilmington in 1934 by the Pusey & Jones Corp. It was originally an ice-breaker and rescue

vessel, but during WW II was modified to do convoy escort and anti-submarine duties in the North Atlantic. It performed its mission admirably during the war and in the early 1980s was brought to Wilmington, restored to its wartime appearance and opened as a memorial to the men and women who gave their lives in the Battle of the North Atlantic. The "Mohawk" is still an operating ship and takes part in many water-born ceremonies and events all along the east coast. Address: Mohawk, Inc., 901 Washington St., Wilmington, DE 19801. Phone: 302/658-8760. Hours: Sat. only 9-3 in the summer. Donations requested. Location: The "Mohawk" is at the foot of King St. on the Christiana River next to Wilmington's restored Victorian era railroad station.

DISTRICT OF COLUMBIA

Newspapers, magazines and other publications of the World War II years repeated six words over and over again. They were: Berlin, Tokyo, Rome, London, Moscow and Washington. These were the capital cites of the six most powerful nations on earth, and it was in these cities that the most powerful men on earth directed the course of the war, the lives and fortunes of millions of people and, in there day, the future of mankind. Five of the cities paid the high price of war by being heavily bombed and three were captured by the enemy. Only Washington survived intact, yet the cost of war bore heavily on the city and its citizens in other ways.

In the years before the war, Washington experienced a rapid growth and had become plagued with many of the problems that are associated with such growth. Nearly 50,000 people a year, many of them southern negroes, flocked to the city hoping to find jobs. This surge of people created a shortage of housing, a great strain on city services and on the city's welfare roles because the people came faster than new jobs were being created by the city's two major industries, government and tourism. As a result, there was much poverty, despair and crime in the nation's capital.

When war erupted in Europe and the U.S. began building its military strength throughout the nation, there was a rapid increase of government jobs in Washington. Unemployment quickly disappeared and soon there was a labor shortage, but the problems of overcrowding remained. The lure of jobs brought tens of thousands more to the city and made the overcrowded conditions even worse. The 1940 census counted 663,091 residents in Washington, of which 65,437 were Federal employees. By the end of 1941 it was estimated that the city's population had mushroomed to over one million and the number of Federal employees had grown to 200,000, and neither had peaked. Housing was still terribly short despite the fact that the city administration and Federal Government had, together, built 23,500 new housing units and 1000 dormitories.

When the U.S. entered the war the influx of people surged again, a large percent of them women. Apartments and hotel rooms became impossible to find and landlords rented rooms by the shift. Servicemen on weekend passes slept on park benches, in bus and railway stations because they couldn't find hotel rooms. On the Potomac and other waterways flotillas of boats sprang up with people lived on them full time. City services strained to keep up. Cabs were impossible to find, busses crowded, hospitals full, police and firemen overworked and the city often smelled badly because the sewer system couldn't handle the volume. The phone system was so overloaded that the phone

company ran ads asking people not to use the phones any more than necessary. A popular saying at the time was that Washington had the charm of the North and the efficiency of the South.

As in most east coast cities there were great fears of enemy attacks. This was not unreasonable because both the Germans and Japanese had plans to attack Washington if the opportunity presented itself. Many buildings were sandbagged and anti-aircraft guns and search lights were put on tops of roofs and at strategic locations.

The crime rate soared to 2.5 times that of New York City and some newspapers labeled Washington as the "Murder Capital of the U.S." All the while, new housing units were being built at a rapid pace, and hundreds of temporary wooden buildings of all shapes and sizes were constructed to house the sprawling government agencies. These temporary government buildings were called "Tempos" and were everywhere. The most conspicuous group of "Tempos" was on the Mall on both sides of the reflecting pools, around the Washington Monument and running from the Capitol Building to the Lincoln Memorial. Two temporary foot bridges were built across the reflecting pools for pedestrian traffic. These structures were truly an eye-soar in an otherwise beautiful city, but they were a necessity of war. President Roosevelt hated them and longed for the day when they could be removed. Unfortunately, he didn't live to see it. Some of them remained until the 1960s.

Nearly every branch of government expanded during the war, and new agencies were created one after the other and almost always known by their acronyms. There was the WPB, OPA, WMC, BEW, NWLB, ODT, WSA, OCD, OPC, OWI, CAS, OEW and the never-to-be-forgotten PWPGSJSISIACWPB (Pipe, Wire Products & Galvanized Sheet Jobbers Subcommittee of the Iron & Steel Industry Advisory Committee of the War Production Board). Some agencies not directly related to the war effort were moved out of town for the duration and their vacated space quickly filled. The Patent Office went to Richmond, VA, the Securities and Exchange Commission went to Phila-

The Washington Monument blacked out except for an airplane beacon on top. To the right is an anti-aircraft gun on top of a nearby Federal building.

delphia and the Farm Credit Bureau went to Kansas City.

During the summer of 1942 the 8 German saboteurs who landed by submarine in Florida and on Long Island, NY were tried and convicted in Washington. Six of them were sentenced to death by electrocution and the sentence was carried out on Aug. 17, 1942 in Washington's old Red Brick Jail.

New construction was everywhere in Washington. Whole new communities were built to house the new arrivals. Washington spread outward into Maryland and Virginia and became a metropolis.

Since Washington was basically a southern city it was also a segregated city and conditions for negroes were worse than for whites. As was happening in other parts of the country, the negroes in Washington were beginning to organize and press for equal rights, better jobs and better living conditions. During the summer of 1943 an organization called the "Committee on Jobs for Negroes in Public Utilities" organized a number of demonstrations, marches and sit-ins to press their demands. These actions created an extremely tense situation in the city for months, especially during, and immediately after, the tragic race riots in Detroit. Fortunately, no race riots occurred in Washington and neither did things change substantially for the negroes, but the government and the nation was alerted to the plight of the American negro and the negroes had gained unity and experience that they would use in the decade immediately following the war.

As the war neared an end and some of the wartime agencies began to cut back or close down, conditions in Washington improved slowly, but never returned to what old-timers called normal. With the end of the war, Washington's population began to decline, but as the realities of the Cold War began to emerge, it began to climb again. The growth was slower this time, and more manageable. By 1950 Washington was a city of 802,000 people, up from 663,000 in 1940.

Washington, DC is full of World War II sites in the form of monuments and museums. Many Washingtonians live in homes built during the war and many wartime government buildings and military facilities built during the war are still in use. And yes, some of the "Tempos" are still around.

NOTE: FOR WASHINGTON-AREA SITES OUTSIDE OF THE DISTRICT OF COLUMBIA SEE THE LISTINGS "WASHINGTON, DC AREA" IN MARYLAND AND VIRGINIA.

DEAN ACHESON GRAVE SITE: Oak Hill Cemetery, at 28th & R Sts. NW, is the final resting place of Dean Acheson, a close associate of Presidents Roosevelt and Truman. During the early stages of the war he was on the committee to Defend America by Aiding the Allies and was an active supporter of the "Destroyer-For-Bases Deal" with Great Britain and Lend Lease. From 1941 to Aug. 1945 he served in Roosevelt's and Truman's Cabinets as Assistant Secretary of State, and from 1949 to 1952 he was President Truman's Secretary of State.

BLAIR HOUSE, just across the street from the White House, was bought by the U.S. Government during WW II to house the steady stream of foreign dignitaries and VIPs who came to visit the White House. The Blair House, built before the Civil War, has a long history as the home and/or temporary residence of many famous people. In 1948-53 President Harry S Truman and Mrs. Truman lived in the house while the White House was being renovated. The Blair House has been used as the official U.S. guest house for visiting heads-of-state. Address: 1651 Pennsylvania Ave. Closed to the public.

BOLLING FIELD was in southeastern DC at the confluence of the Potomac and Anacostia Rivers. In 1937 the Army built Bolling Field after moving its Air Corps operations from a site immediately to the north where it had been sharing air facilities with the Navy since 1917. Four new runways were built along with ground facilities and the field was in operation when WW II started in Europe. During late 1939 and early 1940 new American-made warplanes that had been sold to Britain and France were flown to Bolling and here turned over to British and French air crews who would then fly them to Europe.

During all of WW II Bolling Field served as the headquarters of the Continental Air Forces, headquarters for the AAF Staff Squadron, as a defensive base for the nation's capital and as a provider of air transportation for important military and governmental personnel in the area. Existing combat air units were also

The Dumbarton Oaks Conference, Aug. 1944. U.S. Secretary of State, Cordell Hull, center, rear table, addresses the opening session.

trained at the field and it had a debarkation hospital. In 1948 the field was taken over by the US Air Force and renamed Bolling Air Force Base, and during the 1950s and 1960s its mission changed from flying to one of administration. In 1968 all flying stopped except for helicopters. The Air Force Band and Air Force Presidential Honor Guard were quartered at Bolling.

DUMBARTON OAKS: This is the former estate of Robert Woods Bliss which was donated the District of Columbia in 1940 and became a meeting place for various groups and organizations. During Aug.-Sept. 1944 it was the site of a high-level meeting between representatives of the U.S., Britain, The Soviet Union, Nationalist China and other nations to discuss the creation of a permanent international organization to maintain peace in the postwar years. The initial agreements worked out here lead to the creation of the United Nations. Dumbarton Oaks eventually became the Center for Byzantine Studies. Address: 1703 32nd St. N.W., Washington, DC. 20007

JAPANESE EMBASSY: The Japanese Embassy of 1941 is still the Japanese Embassy today.

On Sunday, Dec. 7, 1941, an angry crowd of Americans gathered outside the Japanese Em-

Dec. 7, 1941. The staff of the Japanese Embassy burns its secret documents.

bassy at 2514 Massachusetts Ave. shouting insults and shaking their fists at the Japanese diplomats inside. District of Columbia police kept order and there were no injuries or property damage. Puffs of smoke rose from the Embassy's backyard all day long as the diplomats burned their secret papers and made ready to vacate the property for the duration of the war. A few days later the Japanese diplomats and their families departed Washington under heavy guard and were taken to remote luxury hotels to await their return to Japan in exchange for American diplomats from Tokyo. The Embassy was reopened in 1952 by the Japanese.

JEWISH WAR VETERANS NATIONAL MEMORIAL MUSEUM AND ARCHIVES: This museum honors Jewish soldiers who fought in all U.S. wars, and its archives and library serve as a national repository for the collection of objects, documents and memorabilia of those veterans. On display are posters, uniforms, U.S., German and Japanese weapons, medals, letters, personal GI field equipment, a tribute to Jewish chaplains including a portable ark and altar, and a tribute to decorated Jewish veterans including two WW II Medal of Honor winners. Address: 1811 R St. NW, Washington, DC 20009-1659. Phone: 202/265-6280. Hours: M-F 10-4:30. Closed Jewish and federal holidays. Donations accepted.

FORT LESLEY J. McNAIR (See U.S. Army War College and Fort Lesley J. McNair below)

NATIONAL ARCHIVES: The National Archives is the depository of the official and historical records of the United States. Included in it hundreds of millions of documents are many records from WW II including the personnel records of every individual separated from the U.S. armed forces. There are many WW II documents that were once classified including captured German and Japanese documents. The Archive's film library included film of the Battle of Midway, the German concentration camps, Nurenberg Trials and the personal home movies of Eva Braun, Hitler's mistress and eventual wife of 37 hours. There is a small display at the Archives which is constantly changing and not necessarily devoted to the history of WW II. The Archives has branches at Suitland, MD and St. Louis, MO. Address in Washington: National Archives and Records Administration, Washington, DC 20408. Phone: 202/523-3000. Hours: M-F 8:45-10 pm. Sat. 9-5. The Central Research and Microfilm Rooms have slightly different hours. Free.

NATIONAL BUILDING MUSEUM: This is a large museum that traces the history of America's past and present architecture and building arts. On display in the museum is a WW II Quonset Hut, typical of thousands built in the U.S. and overseas during the war. Address: 4th & F Sts., NW, Washington, DC. Phone: 202/272-2448. Hours: M-Sat. 10-4, Sun. noon-4, closed Jan. 1, Thanksgiving, Dec. 25. Free.

NATIONAL FIREARMS MUSEUM: This is a large firearms museum created and operated by the National Rifle Association. Its purpose is to present the history, technology and lore of firearms as a part of America's history. The Museum has one of the largest firearms collections in the U.S. In the WW II collection

are many representative models of American, British, Soviet, German, Italian and Japanese arms used during the war. Address: 1600 Rhode Island Ave. NW, Washington, DC 20036. Phone: 202/828-6253. Hours: daily 10-4. Closed Jan. 1, Easter, 4th of July, Thanksgiving, Dec. 24-25. Free.

WALTER REED ARMY MEDICAL CENTER was during WW II, and is now, one of the world's outstanding medical facilities. It began in 1909 and during WW I expanded considerably to treat the Army's wounded returning form Europe. In the years between the wars it continued to grow and during WW II the Center incorporated some of the surrounding buildings in the area. Thousands of GIs were treated here as well as many well-known military and governmental leaders such as Dwight Eisenhower, George C. Marshall and Harry S Truman. Dwight Eisenhower died here in March 1969. Location: Georgia Ave. and Aspen St. NW.

National Museum of Health and Medicine: This museum is on the ground of the Walter Reed Army Medical Center and displays medical equipment, actual and simulated body parts, medical techniques, drawings, life masks, curiosity items and other things related to the medical profession. Military medicine is emphasized and many of the tools and procedures used by military medical practitioners are exhibited. Address: Armed Forces Institute of Pathology, Walter Reed Army Medical Center, Building 54, 6825 16th St. NW, Washington, DC 20306-6000. Phone: 202/576-2348. Hours: May 1 to Oct. 31, M-F 9:30-5, weekends and holidays 11:30-5:30; Nov. 1 to Apr. 30, M-F 9:30-4:30, weekends and holidays 11:30-4:30. Free.

FRANKLIN D. ROOSEVELT MEMORIAL: This is a modest memorial of white Vermont marble commemorating the nation's wartime president. It is located between 7th and 9th Sts. N.W. on the Pennsylvania Ave. side of the National Archives.

SMITHSONIAN MUSEUM; NATIONAL AIR AND SPACE MUSEUM: This is , perhaps, the finest air museum in the nation. Collected here, under one roof, is a dazzling array of flying machines and spacecraft including some of the most famous aircraft in aviation history. There are displays on early flight, flight testing, air transportation, jet aviation, vertical flight and lunar exploration. The four-story museum has some 20 halls, each with its own aviation theme. The museum has over 300 aircraft and displays about 75 at any given time on a rotating basis. Those not on display are stored at the Paul E. Garber restoration and storage facility in nearby Suitland, MD. Many of the WW II aircraft and displays are on the second floor. There is a display that simulates the hanger deck of an aircraft-carrier complete with WW II naval aircraft. In the balloon collection are Japanese bombing balloons recovered from sites in the western United States. Address: 6th & Independence Ave. SW, Washington, DC 20560. Phone: 202/357-2700. Hours: daily 10-5:30 with hours extended at times during the spring and summer, closed Dec. 25. Free. Location: On the Mall between 4th and 7th Sts. on Independence Ave.

SMITHSONIAN MUSEUM; NATIONAL MUSEUM OF AMERICAN HISTORY: This large museum on the Mall depicts the scientific, cultural and political development of the United States. Two sections of the museum contain significant displays on WW II. They are the Hall of American Maritime Enterprise and the Hall of Armed Forces History. Exhibits in these halls cover the entire history of the U.S., with the WW II displays worked into chronological order. Some of the finest and rarest artifacts of WW II are displayed here. Tours are available. Address: National Museum of American History, Washington, DC 20560. Phone: 202/357-2025. Hours: daily 10-5:30, closed Dec. 25. Free.

THE STATLER HOTEL: When the hotel was constructed in the early 1940s a large Presidential Ballroom was built on the mezzanine and it became the place where President Roosevelt came when he wanted to meet with the press. To facilitate the President's arrival a large elevator was installed into which the presidential limousine could be driven and raised to the mezzanine with the President still inside. The President, who couldn't walk, could then get out of the limousine and into a wheel chair in a private room thus shielding these awkward moments from the gathered reporters. The President would then be wheeled into the Ballroom for the press conference.

The hotel became known in later years as the Captial Hilton and the elevator was removed, but the Presidential Ballroom still exists at the Hotel. Location: NE corner of 16th and K Sts. NW.

U.S. ARMY INDUSTRIAL COLLEGE was located at Fort McNair and was an educational institution whose mission it was to train armed forces personnel in the procurement of military supplies, economic warfare, military strategy, mobilization of the Nation's economy in time of war and overall economic and governmental planning as it pertains to the military.

The need for such an organization grew out of the experiences of WW I and in 1924 the Army Industrial College was established here in buildings that had been vacated by the Army's Engineering School which had moved to Fort Belvoir, VA. Both Army and Navy officers were trained here. The College grew in size and scope until Dec. 24, 1941 when it was abruptly closed and its faculty and student body assigned to mobilization and combat duties. In Dec. 1943 the College reopened for the purpose of training military personnel in the need to terminate war contracts, dispose of surplus military property and prepare for postwar readjustment problems. By the end of 1945 the College had a student body of about 4000 and played a major role in the scaling down of the U.S. armed forces. In early 1946 the College reverted to its pre-war curriculum, was put under joint control of the Army and Navy. The College trained selected senior officers and civilians throughout the Cold War, had branches in several major cities and correspondence courses. In the postwar years it was renamed The Industrial College of the Armed Forces.

U.S. ARMY WAR COLLEGE and **FORT LESLEY J.**

"Generals Row" at Ft. McNair.

McNAIR: The U.S. Army War College is on Greenleaf Point at the confluence of the Potomac and Anacostia Rivers and for decades had provided advanced and specialized training for Army officers in military, political, economic and other areas. During WW II the Army's General Headquarters was also here along with other Army organizations as well. To differentiate between the school and the other activities, the post was given the dual names of Army War College (School) and Army War College (Post). All the while the school continued in its mission of training high level Army officers. During the early part of the war parts of "Operation Torch", the Allied invasion of North Africa, were planned here.

In 1946, with experiences gained during WW II, it was agreed that closer coordination between military and political leaders could be attained if both high level military people and government people, especially State Department personnel, were trained together. Thus in that year the State Department agreed to participate in the operation of the school and the school's name was changed to the National War College, the name it retained in the post-war years. In 1948 the post was renamed Fort Lesley J. McNair in honor of the WW II general and commander of Army ground troops who was killed in action in Normandy.

Throughout the Cold War the National War College trained mature and experienced governmental and military individuals in small classes on such topics as U.S. foreign policy, foreign policies of other nations, international laws, pacts and agreements, international relations, world political, economic and military strategies, atomic weapons, scientific developments and general world order.

There are currently two other colleges on the post, the Industrial College of the Armed Forces (see above) and the Inter-American Defense College. Many of America's highest ranking military officers live at Fort McNair in "Generals Row", a row a 15 stately all-brick, multi-storied, single-family, white pillared homes facing the parade ground.

U.S. CAPITOL BUILDING: This is one of America's most familiar buildings and the working place of the legislative branch of the American Government. It has a long and glorious history paralleling that of the United States and is a "must see" stop for every Washington tourist.

During WW II it functioned as the meeting place of Congress without interruption and was host to many famous visitors and events. It was here that heads-of-state addressed Congress, that Lend-Lease, conscription, emergency legislation and new taxes were enacted; that America's neutrality laws were made and altered as the nation moved closer to war; and, it was here, on Dec. 8, 1941, that President Roosevelt gave his "Day of Infamy" speech and called for the Congress to declare war on Japan, an action the Congress promptly agreed to a few hours later.

During the war the building was heavily guarded, sandbagged in some areas and blacked out at times. In Sept. 1939 an undetonated bomb was discovered and disarmed in one of the lobbies. Still, the building was kept open to the public, but on a reduced schedule.

U.S. HOLOCAUST MEMORIAL MUSEUM: This new museum, authorized by Congress in 1980 and funded by private means, serves as a living memorial to the six million Jews and millions of other victims of Nazi fanaticism before and during WW II. The museum's 36,000 square foot permanent exhibition tells the story of the Jews, Gypsies, Poles, homosexuals, handicapped, Jehovah's Witnesses, political and religious dissident and Soviet prisoners of war who were systematically annihilated in a massive state-sponsored genocide. At the west entrance to the museum is the General Dwight D. Eisenhower Memorial Plaza honoring the American commander of the Allied forces in western Europe and the millions of men who served under him and who put an end to the Nazi tyranny. Address: 100 Raoul Wallenberg Place SW (formerly 15th St. SW) Washington, DC 20560. Phone: 202/488-0400, advanced tickets 800-551-7328 and 202/432-7328. Hours: Daily 10-5:30 with last admission at 3:30. Closed Yom Kippur and Dec. 25. Free.

U.S. NAVAL AIR STATION, ANACOSTIA: This Naval Air Station began in 1917 when the War Department authorized the Navy to use the Anacostia Flats, a drained swamp area, at the confluence of the Potomac an Anacostia Rivers as a seaplane base. The Army was also to have access to the land facilities.

After WW I the air station was retained and other naval activities moved onto the station including a unit using pigeons for air to ground communications. In 1935 the Army was forced to give up its interests in the facility and move several miles south to build Bolling Field.

During WW II NAS, Anacostia expanded considerably and became a primary training base for naval aviation. The Navy's photography department, which had been on station since 1919, expanded into a large operation called the Photographic Science Laboratory (later the Naval Photographic Center). A printers' school was established to augment the needs of the Photographic Science Lab. The testing and development of naval aircraft continued during the war and an organization called the Tactical Air Intelligence Center was created in which personnel from the Navy's air arm, the AAF and the British Royal Air Force catalogued, overhauled, rebuilt and evaluated captured Japanese equipment. In 1943 the testing and intelligence operations moved elsewhere and Anacostia became a part of the Navy's Proficiency Flying Program, a program to provide desk-bound Navy pilots flight time to maintain their skills. About this time Naval Air Reserve Training Units (NARTU) began operating from the station. During the winter of 1944-45, when the Japanese bombing balloons started descending on the western states, Hawaii and Alaska their remnants were sent here for identification and evaluation.

The Army's first successful helicopter, the Sikorsky YR-4A, flies past the Capitol dome, May 30, 1943.

The bas-reliefs on the walls of the U.S. Navy Memorial depict the history of the U.S. Navy as well as its duties and activities.

After the war NAS, Anacostia became an important NARTU base, acquired an intelligence school, an aircraft maintenance facility and a parachute packing and survival equipment operation. The base continued to serve Washington's VIPs when naval air travel was called for. By the late 1950s, however, it was determined that air congestion in the Washington area was reaching its saturation point and NAS, Anacostia was closed in 1961.

U.S. NAVY MEMORIAL is located on Pennsylvania Ave. between 7th and 9th Sts. There is a large circular courtyard, the floor of which is a map of the world, made of granite, that powerfully illustrates the size of the earth's ocean areas in relation to the land areas. The statue of the Lone Sailor, stands in the court yard depicting the ordinary U.S. Navyman. A series of bas-reliefs on low walls surrounding the court yard depict various historic naval events. There is a visitors center, a theater and a gift shop. The U.S. Navy Band plays concerts at the Memorial on a regular schedule during the spring and summer. Address: U.S. Navy

Memorial Foundation, 701 Pennsylvania Ave. NW, Suite 123, Washington, DC 20004-2608. Phone: 800/821-8892 or 202/737-2300. Hours: Memorial open 24 hours a day. Visitors Center open 10-6 and to 7:45 during band concerts. Free.

WASHINGTON NATIONAL CATHEDRAL: This is a new cathedral, the 6th largest in the world, and its tower is the highest point in Washington. Buried on the grounds of the Cathedral are several famous people including Cordell Hull, the U.S. Secretary of State during all of WW II. Hull served in the Spanish-American War, became a senator from Tennessee, and was selected by President Roosevelt in 1933 to be Secretary of State. It was Hull who was personally involved in negotiations with Japanese diplomats when Japan attacked the U.S. on Dec. 7, 1941 and to whom the Japanese handed their declaration of war. On Nov. 7, 1941, Hull had warned the President and the Cabinet that the U.S. could be attacked "anywhere by Japan at any time". Hull retired in Nov. 1945 due to failing health and soon afterwards was awarded the Nobel Peace Prize for 1945.

WASHINGTON NAVAL YARD, located in southeastern DC on the north bank of the Anacostia River, was one of the first naval facilities erected after the establishment of the U.S. Navy. The Naval Yard served the nation in one way or another since 1800. Before WW II the Yard began to make large guns and through the years this activity came to dominate at the Yard. Ship building eventually ended and the Yard concentrated on the research, development and manufacture of large naval guns.

When war in Europe broke out in Sept. 1939 gun manufacturing at the Yard was curtailed in accordance with industrial mobilization plans drawn up in 1937, and the Yard concentrated primarily on research, development and testing of large guns. The actual guns were manufactured elsewhere. After the U.S. entered the war, the Yard took on the additional activity of repairing battle damaged weapons. Other activities at the Yard during the war included the manufacturing, loading and assembly of naval ammu-

nition, the operation of the U.S. Navy Deep Sea Diving School and the Experimental Diving Unit. The Yard was also the headquarters for the newly created Potomac River Naval Command. In the 1960s rockets began to replace guns as the Navy's main offensive weapons and the Yard slowly phased out of gun operations altogether and into various administrative roles. Of special interest to WW II buffs is the Archives Branch of the Naval Historic Division which is located here and has an immense holding of WW II naval records. The Washington Naval Yard is a National Historic Landmark and under the protection of the National Park Service. Over 200,000 tourist visit the Yard and its museums each year.

U.S. Marine Corps Museum: This is one of two museum on the grounds of the Washington Naval Yard. It is in building 58, which was the former Marine barracks. Displays are arranged in chronological order with considerable attention given to WW II. The centerpiece of the WW II display is an extensive exhibit on the famous flag raising at Iwo Jima. Other displays in the museum include small arms, field artillery, communication equipment, scale models of aircraft, boats, tracked vehicles, flags, uniforms, documents, photographs, painting, dioramas and much more. Address: Marine Corps Historical Center, Washington Naval Yard building 58, 9th & M Sts. SE, Washington, DC 20374-5000. Phone: 202/433-3840/3267/3534. Hours: M-Sat. 10-4, Sun. and holidays noon-5. Closed Jan. 1, Inauguration Day, Dec. 25. Free.

U.S. Navy Museum: This museum, on the grounds of the Washington Naval Yard, is the second largest museum in the District of Columbia. Only the Smithsonian Museum is larger. It is one of 17 Navy museums throughout the country and the only general U.S. Navy museum which presents an overview of U.S. Naval history. Exhibitions commemorate the Navy's wartime heros and battles as well as its peacetime contribution and humanitarian service. The museum is housed in two buildings and has an outside display which includes the postwar destroyer "Barry" and the conning tower of the WW II U.S. submarine "Balao". WW II highlights of the museum include gunmounts from WW II fighting ships, an F4U Corsair fighter plane, a Japanese suicide "Baka" Bomb, a bullet-riddled wing of a Kamikaze plane that crashed on the deck of the U.S. carrier "Enterprise" in 1945, naval mines, coast-defense artillery, navigational equipment, a submarine room with a working periscope, a complete collection of U.S. Navy decorations and awards, displays on the attack on Pearl Harbor, submarine warfare, a salute to the British Royal Navy, many ship models including several builder's models and a large gift shop.

The museum has an extensive submarine display which include three Axis mini subs from WW II; a German "Seehund", an Italian "Maiale SSB" and a Japanese "Kaiten II". Address: Washington Naval Yard, Building 76, Washington, DC 20374-0571. Phone 202/433-4882. Hours: M-F 9-4, weekends and holidays 10-5. Free.

SUMNER WELLES GRAVE SITE: Rock Creek

A 16" gun being manufactured at the Washington Naval Yard in 1944.

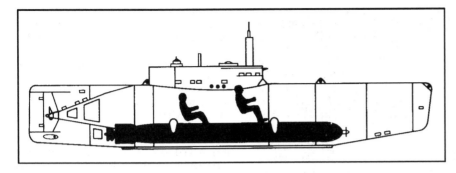

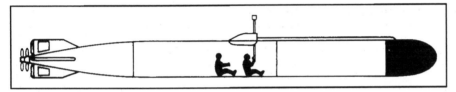

Top: The German "Seehund" (seal) mini submarine. These subs were built in 1944, carried two men and two torpedoes and operated against Allied shipping in the English Channel, especially in the Antwerp area. Center: The Italian "Maiale SSB" mini sub is actually a manned torpedo carrying two divers. They were launched from a conventional submarine and could enter protected harbors by going under the nets. They would approach their target remove the front portion of the torpedo which was the explosive charge, attach it to their intended victim, set a timer and withdraw. Bottom: The Japanese "Kaiten II" was launched from a conventional submarine, from warships or from land. They were used for a variety of purposes, but were slow, large enough to be easily detected and vulnerable to attack.

for all the activities required of the Executive branch of the Government. Every room was occupied and many people on the White House staff had to find space elsewhere in Washington. Some of the congestion in the White House was relieved with an expansion program that enlarged the east wing, west wing and the basement.

The Roosevelts, nevertheless, remained in the White House throughout the President's terms in office.

It was here in the White House, on the afternoon of April 12, 1945, that Vice President Harry S Truman learned from the lips of Eleanor Roosevelt that her husband had died in Georgia and that he was now President of the United States.

When Franklin Roosevelt's body was returned to Washington it was placed in the East Room where services were held and thousands of mourners paid their respects.

Several months later, at 7 pm Aug. 7, 1945, President Truman, flanked by Cordell Hull, James Byrnes and about a dozen other top governmental officials, announced to reporters gathered in the Oval Office that Japan had surrendered and that WW II had ended.

The White House is open to the public, and about one million people go through it each year. Address: 1600 Pennsylvania Ave., Washington, DC: Phone: 202/456-7041. Hours: Tues.-Sat. 10-noon. Free. Between Memorial Day and Labor Day advance tickets are required and may be obtained from the booth on the Ellipse at Constitution Ave. and 16th St.

First Division Monument: This monument is on the corner of Pennsylvania Ave. and 17th St. near the White House grounds. It commemorates the U.S. Army's 1st Division.

Second Division Monument: This monument is in the SW corner of the of The Ellipse near Constitution Ave. and 17th St. It commemorates the U.S. Army's Second Division.

Cemetery, near the junction of New Hampshire Ave. and No. Capital Ave., NW, is the burial place of Sumner Welles, a close associate of President Roosevelt. Welles served in the Cabinet as Under Secretary of State from 1937 to 1943. In 1940 he made a much publicized trip to the warring capitals of Europe in an unsuccessful attempt to mediate peace. In 1942 he represented the U.S. at the Rio Conference in Rio de Janeiro. In 1943 Welles worked on the preparatory planning for the United Nations Organization, but during the summer of that year he had a disagreement with his superior, Secretary of State Cordell Hull, and resigned.

WHITE HOUSE: It's hard to think of a more famous building in America than the White House. It is the home of the President and his workplace during his term in office. During WW II it was occupied by two presidents and their families, Franklin D. Roosevelt and Harry S Truman. The Roosevelts live here from 1933 until 1945 and the Trumans lived here briefly in 1945, then moved out while it was renovated, returned in 1953, and stayed until 1957.

During the war years many important war decisions were made here and when the President addressed the nation on radio in is "Fireside Chats", he broadcasted from the White House. Many of the most important and powerful people in the world came as visitors. This too was the meeting place of the Presidents' Cabinets.

During the first days of the war, the White House, like many other places in the U.S., was thought to be vulnerable to attack. On the day

that war came to the United States, Sunday Dec. 7, 1941, the Roosevelts were at home in the White House. Franklin was upstairs in the Presidential Suite with his close friend and aide Harry Hopkins, and Mrs. Roosevelt was hosting a luncheon for a ladies' organization. Within hours of the attack the Secret Service and high ranking Army officers descended on the White House to begin preparing it for war.

One of the first measures taken to protect those in the White House was to issue gas masks to everyone. The President hung his on the arm of his wheel chair. The Army insisted that anti-aircraft guns be put immediately on the roofs of buildings surrounding the White House. This was done, but some of the guns were wooden dummies because there weren't enough guns in the Army's arsenal to meet the needs. It was also discovered, a year or so later, that the ammunition hastily placed beside some of the real guns was the wrong calibre.

Soon after the Pearl Harbor attack construction began on a bomb shelter at the White House. It had 9' thick ceilings, an emergency diesel powered generating system, a ventilating system in case of gas attacks and an escape tunnel that ran to the U.S. Treasury building across the street.

The White House was prepared for, and participated in, trail blackouts along with the rest of Washington. Parties, receptions and other social activities not related to the war effort were cut back at the White House and the President and Mrs. Roosevelt reduced their participation in outside social activities.

The White House itself was much too small

FLORIDA

When World War II started the state of Florida was a rural southern agricultural state with a few modest-sized cities, lots of empty land, very few modern military establishments and a string of old Spanish forts dotting its 1146-mile coastline. In early 1940 the state had only 8 military installations but by late 1943 it would have approximately 170. Despite this lack of military protection in the pre-war years, polls showed that the people of Florida were the most pro-interventionist in the nation.

Florida's economy was based on fruits, vegetables, grain crops, tobacco, meat packing, dairy products, sugar cane, lumber, pulp and paper manufacturing, naval stores (turpentine and rosin), cigars, phosphate, lime, limestone, winter tourism and some manufacturing is the larger cities like Jacksonville and Tampa. Settlers were still moving into Florida to homestead the land. The state had a young Senator named Claude Pepper serving his second term. Senator Pepper would serve in the U.S. Senate, without interruption, well into the 1980s making him one of the longest-serving members of Congress in U.S. history.

Florida had been hard hit by the Depression so there were many WPA, PWA an CCC units operating in the state.

The war brought many changes to the state and many bloody sea battles to her coasts. German saboteurs landed successfully on her eastern shore. Air fields, training camps, naval bases, shipbuilding facilities and other manufacturing operations came to Florida during the war bringing a new and important dimension to the state's economy. Early in the war both the Army and Navy took great interest in Florida's strategic location for operational purposes and in her good weather for training purposes. At first the services squabbled over available sites in Florida, but eventually the Army and Navy came to an understanding and divided the state between themselves. The Navy took jurisdiction over the east coast with some exceptions in the Miami and Jacksonville areas, and the Army took over the interior and west coast with the exceptions of the Keys and some areas around Pensacola. The dividing line between their respective spheres of operation, agreed to on Sept. 19, 1942, was known as the Stratemeyer-Towers Line.

Florida became a good friend to the British Empire by welcoming some 8000 British airmen who were trained on here soil. More British airmen were trained in Florida than in any other state.

When wartime sugar rationing hit the U.S., Florida's sugar cane industry shifted into full gear and produced as much sugar as it could to help alleviate the shortage.

When the Army, Navy and Coast Guard needed housing and training facilities, many of Florida's resort hotels were utilized for that purpose. During the first months of the war, before the training camps were ready, 40% of Florida's tourist space was leased by the military to house the incoming recruits and military personnel. This bought about a sudden disruption in the tourist business and a mass of cancellations from would-be tourists for the 1941-42 winter season. By the summer of 1942, though, the military began to vacate the hotels and the 1942-43 winter season looked much brighter. Therefore, Florida's aggressive tourist industry, seeing its patriotic duty quite clearly and hoping to make the best of a bad situation, proclaimed the state to be a rest and recreational area for weary war-workers. Ads in northern newspapers announced that "Civilians need furloughs too" and a trip to Florida was "A Blitzkrieg of joy". Florida ads along the heavily populated U.S. east coast hinted that Florida, with its lack of heavy industry and wide-open spaces, was a safe place to be in case of air raids. By the beginning of the 1943-44 season tourism began to boom. Transportation problems had eased and many northern war-workers really were weary and in need of rest. During this tourist season Florida's beaches were crowded as never before despite the barbed wire, night-time curfews and military regulations[1]. Betting records were set at the dog and horse tracks and the night clubs were jammed. People were having so much fun in Florida that northern newspapers and magazines were often critical of this unpatriotic behavior in the midst of a war.

Florida's long-suffering negro population experienced prosperous times during the war as their labor was actively sought by farmers, contractors, factories, the tourist industry and the military services. This newfound economic and social importance would serve them well in the coming struggle for civil rights.

Florida emerged from the war much different than before. Industry and the military had come to stay and the state's image as a year-around vacationland began to blossom as workers from the north, with healthy bank accounts, treated themselves to those long overdue vacations that the Florida advertisements promised. Homesteaders resumed their trek into the state in quest of free land with war veterans now being given special preferences. Increasing numbers of retirees eyed the state's easy climate, recreational opportunities and other comforts. For several years after the war, Florida was the second fastest growing state in the Union after California.

Florida is full of WW II sites and relics both on land and in her coastal waters.

APALACHACOLA is a coastal town 55 miles SE of Panama City.

APALACHACOLA ARMY AIR FIELD, two miles west of town, was the local airport. It was taken over by the Eastern Training Flying Command in late 1942 and operated as a sub-base of Tyndall Field in Panama City. There was a flexible gunnery school here. After the war the airport was returned to civilian use.

ARCADIA is 40 miles east of Sarasota.

CARLSTROM FIELD, 7 miles SE of Arcadia, had been a WW I Army Air Corps training field and had been idle since the 1920s. When the Embry Riddle Co., a private flying school, contracted

[1]Some people avoided going into the water for fear of hitting a naval mine or being captured by an enemy submarine.

with the British Government to train RAF pilots in 1941, the company leased the field and later purchased it. The Riddle Aeronautical Institute, a subsidiary of Embry Riddle Co., did the actual training. The training program was modeled after that used by the AAF at Randolph Field, TX. Carlstrom, therefore, became one of the dozen or so airfields around the country known as "Little Randolphs" using the Randolph program.

DORR FIELD, 12 miles east of Arcadia, was also used by, and later purchased by, the Embry Riddle Co. to train RAF pilots.

AVON PARK: (See Sebring)

BANANA RIVER: (See Cape Canaveral Area)

BARTOW: (See Lakeland/Winter Haven/Lake Wales/Bartow area)

BOCA RATON: (See Miami/Fort Lauderdale/Boca Raton area)

BONITA SPRINGS is in south Florida 12 miles north of Naples.

BONITA SPRINGS ARMY AIR FIELD was activated late in 1942 and used by the Army for the duration of the war.

BROOKSVILLE is a farming community 35 miles north of Tampa.

BROOKSVILLE ARMY AIR FIELD, 7.5 miles SW of town, was activated in 1942 to accommodate B-29 bombers as an auxiliary field for Drew Field in Tampa. It also had a tactical bombing school which operated under Orlando Air Base. In 1944 the field was closed and returned to the local community.

BUSHNELL is 45 miles west of Orlando.

BUSHNELL ARMY AIR FIELD, three miles SE of Bushnell, was a small training field used by the military for field trial projects. It was a sub-base to Orlando AAB. The field was returned to the community after the war.

CAPE CANAVERAL AREA: During WW II Cape Canaveral was mostly a wilderness area except for a lighthouse, built in 1868, on the tip of the cape. The largest communities in the area were Titusville, Pop. 2200, and Cocoa, Pop. 3100, along highway U.S. 1 on the west bank of the Indian River. The huge space center, so well associated with the Cap Canaveral name, evolved after the war. German submarines were very active off the Cape during the war.

JOHN F. KENNEDY SPACE CENTER: After the war, the U.S. government needed a site to begin testing long range missiles such as the Germans had developed during the last months of the war. The U.S. had about 100 captured V-2 German rockets with which to begin their program. After some initial test at White Sands, NM it was decided to build a permanent test site at Cape Canaveral because of its remoteness from large populations and good climate. In 1949 Pres. Truman signed an executive order establishing the "Joint Long Range Proving Grounds" at Cape Canaveral. Facilities were soon built and the testing of the German rockets began. From this beginning evolved the present-day John F. Kennedy Space Center. Exhibits at the Visitor's Center and Air Force Space Museum explain the early

A German V-1 "Buzzbomb" on display at the Air Force Space Museum, Cape Canaveral, FL. An engine for a German V-2 rocket is on display inside the museum.

beginning of the complex.

U.S. NAVAL AIR STATION, BANANA RIVER was 15 miles south of Cape Canaveral off SR A1A on the Banana River. The air station was built during 1939-40 by the Navy to be a sub-post of NAS Jacksonville. The Banana River location, 9' above sea level, had suitable water area to handle large seaplanes taking off and landing in an east-west direction[2] and in poor visibility. The station was used for operational purposes and patrols from its first days of operation. At first only PBM Martin Mariner seaplanes flew from NAS, Banana River, but in 1943 landing strips were built and land planes began operating here. A few blimps also operated out of the station. Most of the pilots and aircraft stationed here participated in the "Hunter-Killer" units developed during the war to hunt down German submarines along the U.S. coasts. In the fall of 1943 the station became a training base for PBM pilots and crews and a group of Fighting French naval officers was trained here in PBMs at this time. At times, the cadets and instructors were pressed into service to help hunt down German subs. In 1944 an Aviation Navigation Training School opened here and even as the war began to wind down the station continued to grow because this was an especially good facility for the training of night fighters. A major aircraft repair and maintenance facility was also built on the station.

The station slowly phased down during 1946-47, but in 1949 the Air Force and Navy began a joint operation at the station under Air Force direction testing and tracking long range missiles fired from Cape Canaveral. In 1951 the US Air Force took over the station and renamed it Patrick Air Force Base. It continued to operate in support of Cape Canaveral.

CARRABELLE is 50 miles SW of Tallahassee.
CAMP GORDON JOHNSON, on James Island four miles east of Carrabelle, was an Army amphibious assault training base the operated during the latter part of the war. It began as Carrabelle Flight Strip, an auxiliary field for Dale Mabry Field in Tallahassee, but was converted early in the war to Camp Carrabelle and used for the training of Army service forces. In Jan. 1943 the camp was renamed Camp Gordon Johnson and became an assault training base. The camp had a prisoner of war camp

[2]Most of the "calm" water sites along Florida's east coast were not wide enough to permit east-west take-offs and landings.

holding about 600 POWs who worked on the base. The flight strip continued in use for training and operational purposes. In 1946 the camp was declared surplus.

CLEWISTON is a small community on the SW shore of Lake Okeechobee.

CLEWISTON AIRPORT (RIDDLE FIELD), 8 miles west of town, was used by the AAF during the war to train both U.S. and British pilots. The training pro-gram was directed by Riddle-McKay Aeronautical College and offered primary and advance flight training. The Airport had a prisoner of war branch camp with the POWs working in agriculture.

CORAL GABLES: (See Miami/Fort Lauderdale/Boca Raton area)

CROSS CITY is 45 miles west of Gainesville.
CROSS CITY ARMY AIR FIELD, one mile east, was activated by the AAF in mid-1942 as an auxiliary base for Dale Mabry Field, Tallahassee and a sub-base to Alachua AAF, Gainesville. The base also had several schools under the direction of Orlando AAB.

DAYTONA BEACH is on the Atlantic coast of Florida 80 miles south of Jacksonville. Its 23 mile-long hard sand beach was famous as a raceway and many world records were set here in the early days of automobile racing. The city had a large WAC training center, one of three such centers in the country[3]. It opened Dec. 1, 1942 and provided basic training for enlisted women. Eighty five local apartments and hotels were rented by the Government to house the women.

Daytona Beach also had an Army Signal Corps school and a unit of the Civil Air Patrol (CAP) that flew coastal patrols and other missions. Later in the war many of the rented hotels and wartime barracks buildings were converted into Army convalescent facilities to relieve overcrowding from several of the Army's hospitals and to provide convalescence in a non-hospital atmosphere.

U.S. NAVAL AIR STATION, DAYTONA BEACH, three miles SW of town, was Daytona Beach's municipal airport before the war. In 1941 the Navy took it over and made it into an operational training base for advanced Navy pilots. These men and their planes were used as a reserve force that could be called out as needed to do battle with, enemy submarines along the coasts. The pilots trained in SNC-1 Falcons, SBD-4 Dauntlesses, F4F and FM-1 Wildcats and F6F Hellcats.

In 1946 the Navy withdrew and returned the airport to the city. During the war the station had the following outlying fields:
- Bunnell (Bulow) Air Field, 20 miles NW of Daytona Beach
- New Smyrna Airport, 3 miles NW of New Smyrna
- Tonoka Airport, 3.5 miles SW of Ormond

DELAND is 20 miles SW of Daytona Beach.
U.S. NAVAL AIR STATION, DELAND, 2.5 miles NE of town, was taken over by the Navy and used as an operational training field and a rest center. A fleet air detachment was also stationed here. The station had an outlying field, Spruce Creek Airport, 3.5 miles north of Sansula. After the war the airport was returned to the community.

DUNNELLON is 20 miles SW of Ocala.
DUNNELLON ARMY AIR FIELD, five miles east of town, was used by the Air Technical Service Command as a sub-base to Alachua AAF and as an air support school of applied tactics under Orlando AAB. The Field was returned to the community after the war.

FORT LAUDERDALE (See Miami/Fort Lauderdale Area)

[3] The other two were at Ft. Des Moines, IA and Ft. Oglethorpe, GA.

WACs in training at one of Daytona Beach's hotels. Here the WACs jump into the hotel's pool with their clothes on and use barracks bags as life preservers.

FORT MYERS is on the SW coast of the Florida peninsula.

BUCKINGHAM ARMY AIR FIELD, 10 miles east of town near the community of Buckingham, was activated in mid-1942 by the Eastern Flying Training Command to train aviation gunners.

FORT MYERS AIR BASE was four miles south of town. It was taken over by the 3rd AF for the 50,000 Pilot Training Program to train fighter pilots and was operated as an auxiliary base for Sarasota AAF. Also, during the summer of 1942, B-24 bomber crews trained here with the help of personnel from Morrison Field in long-distance flying across the South Atlantic Ocean and the African wilderness. The 3rd AF departed from the field after the war and the facility became known as Page Field Airport.

FORT PIERCE is on the east coast 40 miles north of West Palm Beach.

U.S. NAVAL AMPHIBIOUS TRAINING BASE, FORT PIERCE was located on the coastal beaches opposite Ft. Pierce. The U.S. Navy learned from the invasion of Tarawa in the Pacific that they needed teams of men operating underwater to scout intended invasion sites and destroy underwater defenses. This lead to the creation of Naval Combat Demolition Teams (NCDT), later redesignated Underwater Demolition Teams (UDT) or "Frogmen". The first NCDT units assembled and trained here in mid-1943 and were eventually used for the first time in combat at Normandy. During that invasion 46% of their number became casualties. By war's end there were 35 UDT units. After the war UDT teams served in Korea. By the Viet Nam War, the UDT teams had evolved into the Sea, Air, Land Teams (SEALS).

UDT-Seal Museum: This museum is on North Hutchinson Island off Hwy. A1A at Pepper Park on one of the beaches used to train the Navy's "Frogmen". It is the only museum in the world that traces the history and development of the "Frogmen" of WW II and their evolution into the Navy's SEALS. On display are boats, submersible vehicles, scuba gear, weapons, demolition apparatus and other related items used then and now. Address: 3300 North A1A North Hutchinson Island, Fort Pierce, FL 34949: Phone: 407/489-3597. Hours: Tues.-Sat. 10-4, Sun. noon-4. Admission charged.

FORT WALTON BEACH (See Valparaiso/Ft. Walton Beach Area)

GAINESVILLE is in northern Florida 60 miles SW of Jacksonville.

ALACHUA ARMY AIR FIELD, five miles NE of town, was Gainesville Municipal Airport before the war. It was taken over by the Air Technical Service Command and used for an air support school of applied tactics under Orlando AAF. After the war the airport again became Gainesville Municipal Airport.

HOMESTEAD is 25 miles SW of Miami.

HOMESTEAD ARMY AIR FIELD, five miles east of Homestead, was South Dade County Airport before the war. In Oct. 1942 the Air Transport Command took control of the field which had been used by Pan American Air Ferries Corp., a subsidiary of Pan American Airlines, contracted with the U.S. Government to ferry military aircraft overseas. In the early part of

The four saboteurs who landed at Ponte Vedra; Werner Thiel, Hermann Otto Neubauer, Herbert Hans Haupt and Edward Kerling. All four were captured, tried, convicted and executed in Washington, DC in Aug. 1942.

the war Homestead AAF was the starting point for transport aircraft being ferried to the China-Burma-India(CBI) theater for operations over the "Hump". Ferrying operations to many places in the world continued at Homestead AAF throughout the war and, in 1943, the field was expanded to train transport pilots and crews. At first, training was conducted in all types of U.S. transports, but later the field specialized in 4-engine aircraft. In Sept. 1945, the field was badly damaged by a hurricane which resulted in its being inactivated in Dec. 1945. In 1954 it was reopened by the US Air Force, renamed Homestead Air Force Base, and used as an active Air Force base throughout the Cold War and the home of several combat-ready air squadrons. The base was extensively damaged again by another hurricane in Aug. 1992 and later closed.

IMMOKALEE is in southern Florida 30 miles SE of Fort Myers.

IMMOKALEE ARMY AIR FIELD, two miles NE of town, was the local airport before the war. It was activated by the Air Transport Command in Dec. 1942 and shared with the Eastern Flying Training Command. It served as an auxiliary field to Sarasota AAF, Homestead AAF and Hendricks Field, at Sebring, FL. After the war it became Immokalee's local airport again.

JACKSONVILLE AND THE JACKSONVILLE AREA: Jacksonville, on the NE Atlantic coast of Florida, was Florida's second largest city during WW II, a major seaport and an important industrial, commercial, financial, transportation and shipbuilding center.

FORT CLINCH #3, 10 miles north of Jacksonville at the north end of Amelia Island, was a pre-Civil War fort built at the mouth of Cumberland Sound. During WW II it was used as a communications and security post. It became a state park after the war.

JACKSONVILLE ARMY AIR FIELD, 7 miles north of town, was Jacksonville Municipal Airport before the war. The AAF took over much of the airport in early 1941 as a sub-base for MacDill Field and used it as an air support base. In 1946 most of the airport was turned over to the Navy with the Army retaining a small operation for servicing Army aircraft. The Navy called their facility the U.S. Naval Auxiliary Air Station, Jacksonville, #1, and it served as an auxiliary to NAS, Jacksonville. Eventually the airport was returned to civilian control and became Jacksonville International Airport.

PONTE VEDRA BEACH: THE LANDING OF THE

GERMAN SABOTEURS: During the night of June 16/17, 1942 a team of four German saboteurs were landed by the German submarine U-584 at Ponte Vedra beach within sight of a Coast Guard watchtower, but unnoticed by the American. They quickly buried their supplies which consisted of several hundred pounds of TNT, delayed-timing detonators, incendiary pistols, explosive pens, electric matches, acids and bombs disguised as pieces of coal. From the beach they took a bus into Jacksonville and checked into a hotel. They wore American-made clothes, had forged documents and $170,000 in cash.

Four days earlier a similar team had landed on Long Island, NY. All 8 of the saboteurs had lived in America for several years before the war and knew the language and customs well. The two teams were to coordinate their activities and sabotage a long list of targets in the US. The Florida team was to sabotage plants and dams at Muscle Shoal, AL, rail lines between New York and Chicago, and between New York City and St. Louis, MO and to poison the New York City's water supply with hydrogen cyanide[4].

A few days after their arrival, both teams were captured, jailed, tried and convicted. Six were executed and the remaining two were given long prison terms.

U. S. NAVAL AUXILIARY AIR STATION, CECIL FIELD was 16 miles SW of Jacksonville. It was built in 1941 as an auxiliary air station for NAS, Jacksonville and served as an advanced training base for pilots and crew of fighters, bombers and carrier groups. The base had a gunnery school and a school for Landing Signal Officers.

After the war, operations at the station phased down although training of Navy flyers and Reservists continued on a peacetime basis. During the Korean War Cecil Field was home to two jet-equipped attack squadrons and, soon afterward, was designated as one of the Navy's four Master Jet Stations. The Station remained operational throughout the Cold War and was closed in the 1990s.

U.S. NAVAL AUXILIARY AIR STATION, GREEN COVE SPRINGS, two miles SE of Green Cove Springs, FL, a southern suburb of Jacksonville, was the community's local airport before the war known as Benjamin Lee II Field. The Navy acquired the airport in 1940 as an auxiliary air station for NAS, Jacksonville. Training began in seaplanes, but training in land-based was soon added and quickly became the bigger of

[4] This was one of the very rare instances during WW II when chemical warfare was used.

the two operations. At one time in 1942 the station had over 400 planes in inventory and was one of the largest naval training station in the country in numbers of cadets. As the war neared an end, training at the station phased down rapidly and in Sept. 1945 the Navy returned the airport to the local community.

U.S NAVAL AUXILIARY AIR STATION, MAYPORT, at the mouth of the St. Johns River, was built in 1941 to serve as an aircraft carrier basin servicing carriers and their planes. Patrol craft, blimps, rescue vessels, submarines and minesweepers operated out the station at various time during the war along with the carriers. After the war the station underwent several changes and for a few years was operated by the Coast Guard, but eventually reverted again to the Navy and remained active throughout the Cold War.

U.S. NAVAL AIR STATION, JACKSONVILLE is just south of downtown Jacksonville on the west shore of the St. Johns River at its widest point. During WW I the site was occupied by Camp Clifford Foster, an Army camp. Between the wars the camp was used by the Florida National Guard. In 1939 the citizens of Jacksonville bought Camp Foster and offer it, along with additional land, to the Navy as a naval air station. The Navy accepted the offer and in Oct. 1940 the air station was commissioned as a naval aviation training center. After Pearl Harbor, the station underwent a huge expansion which eventually included 700 buildings, three runways over 6000', aircraft overhaul and repair facilities, seaplane ramps, an 1800-bed hospital, auxiliary bases, a bombing range and a variety of operations at 37 outlying fields. During the war over 11,000 pilots and 10,000 crewmen trained here. Primary flight training was given in N3N Stearmans and intermediate training in SNJ Texans, SNC Falcons and various observation aircraft. The final phase of training required the pilots and crews to fly actual patrol and attack mission along the coast against enemy submarines. On these missions PBYs, TBF Avengers and various fighter planes were used.

Several Navy Commands operated here and the base had numerous schools. Sailors and Marines were trained as machinist mates, radiomen, ordnancemen, metalsmiths, electricians, photographers, storekeepers, parachute riggers, cooks, and other classifications. Several hundred German prisoners of war worked at the station.

When the war ended, pilot and crew training moved to NAS, Pensacola and NAS, Jacksonville became a fleet support base and the Navy's largest separation center in the U.S. southeast. The station remained very active in the post-war years and serve a wide variety of the Navy's needs. Outlying fields in the area during the war were:

- Bostwick Airport, 1 mile NW of Bostwick
- Branan Airport, 7.5 miles SW of Orange Park
- Fernandina Airport, 4 miles south of Jacksonville
- Fleming Island Airport, 2.5 miles NE of Russell
- Herlong Airport, 3.5 miles SW of Marietta
- Jacksonville Air Field #2, 9 miles east of Jacksonville
- Kay Larkin Airport, 3 miles NW of Palatka

- Middleburg Airport, 3 miles NE of Middleburg
- St. Augustine Airport, 4 miles NW of St. Augustine
- St. Marys Airport, 2 miles NW of St. Marys, GA.
- Switzerland Airport, 1.5 miles SE of Switzerland
- Whitehouse Airport, 13 miles west of Jacksonville.

KENNEDY SPACE CENTER, John F.: (See Cape Canaveral Area)

KEY WEST AND THE FLORIDA KEYS:
This beautiful string of islands at the southern end of Florida was one of the most strategic military locations in the continental U.S. during the war because around the Florida Keys flowed the great bulk of America's Gulf coast sea trade and from the Keys American planes and ships could reach deep into the Caribbean. Hundreds of ships a year passed through the Straits of Florida between the Keys and Cuba making it a prime hunting ground for enemy submarines in wartime, and an area that had to be defended, at all cost, by the Americans. During late 1940, after France had been defeated and it was feared that she might join the Axis, American intelligence reported that Key West, America's southernmost city, could be bombed by Axis planes from the French island of Martinique in the Caribbean. France did not join the Axis, but the threat was real, nevertheless.

The Navy had, for many years, maintained a major naval base at the city of Key West near the western end of the Keys. From Key West Navy ships and planes penetrated deep into the Gulf of Mexico and the Caribbean guarding U.S. and Allied interests.

During the spring of 1942, when the U.S. Naval leaders concluded that coastal and inter-hemisphere convoys would become a necessity, Key West was chosen as a convoy assembly point. The city's natural harbor was too small to hold the number of ships that some convoys would contain so an expanse of water off the city's north shore was made into a safe anchorage ringed off by a huge mine field. Some 3500 mines were laid between April 24 and May 2, 1942 to create the anchorage, and soon afterwards the first convoy was formed inside the anchorage and sailed from it on May 15. During the war many convoys would come and go out of the Key West anchorage.

Note: The following WW II sites are given in geographic order from east to west along the Keys.

MARATHON FLIGHT STRIP: Running parallel to the main highway through Marathon Shores is an 8000 foot airstrip built by the Navy during the war as an outlying field for NAAS, Boca Raton. In those days, Marathon was a wide open city with 13 bars and no schools or churches. After the war Marathon became a very respectable community and the flight strip serves as the local airport.

U.S. NAVAL AUXILIARY AIR STATION, BOCA CHICA: This had been Boca Chica's local airport before the war. It was taken over by the Navy to become an auxiliary field to NAS, Key West and was used to train pilots and crews of land- and sea-based aircraft in anti-

submarine warfare, torpedo bombing and as night fighters. In March 1945 the Station was merged with, and became a part of, NAS, Key West.

Note: The following sites are all in Key West.

KEY WEST BARRACKS, on the west shore of Key West, was built in 1831 to house the garrison of Fort Zachary Taylor. The Post was repeatedly abandoned and reoccupied through the years. In 1893 the Barracks were occupied and manned continuously by the Army until 1947 when it was turned over to the Navy. During WW II soldiers were housed here. The Barracks and Fort are open to the public, but there are very few displays concerning WW II. Address: Fort Zachary Taylor State Park, Key West, FL 33040. Phone: 305/294-2354. Hours: daily 8-sunset. Admission charged.

KEY WEST LIGHTHOUSE MUSEUM is located at the entrance to Key West Harbor in the former lighthouse keeper's quarters. The lighthouse, built in 1847, can be visited by those willing to climb to the top. In the garden is a Japanese 2-man submarine captured at Pearl Harbor on Dec. 7, 1941. One of the two men aboard became America's first prisoner of war during WW II. Address: 938 Whitehead St., Key West, FL 33040. Phone: 305/294-0012. Hours: daily 9:30-5, closed Dec. 25. Admission charged.

LITTLE WHITE HOUSE: In 1946 President Harry S Truman made a visit to the U.S. Naval Base, Key West (see below) and was very impressed with the Key West area as a possible presidential retreat. As a result, the former commandant's quarters were remodelled as a winter vacation home and Truman returned several times between 1946 and 1952 and spent a total of 174 days here. His wife, Bess, seldom accompanied him. She referred to Truman's time here as "a man's thing". During the time Truman used the house it became known as "The Little White House". Truman called the White House in Washington, DC "the great white jail". The house fell into disrepair after the naval base closed, it but has been restored and is open to the public. It is furnished as it was when the Truman's resided here. Address: 111 Front St., Key West, FL 33041. Phone: 800/352-5397 and 305/294-9911. Hours: daily 9-5. Admission charged.

U.S. NAVAL AIR STATION AND NAVAL BASE, KEY WEST: This naval station was established in 1823 to combat pirates and has a long and colorful history that reflects the history of the area. In early 1939, with war threatening in Europe, President Franklin Roosevelt and his Chief-of-Staff, Adm. Wm. D. Leahy, made a personal visit to the station, which was abandoned except for a radio station, and concluded that it should be reopened as a submarine base. In Nov. 1939 the submarine base began to function. In Dec. 1940 a naval air station came into being here to serve as both an operational and training base. Also, in that month one of the Navy's three sound schools was transferred here from New London, CT. The sound school had four destroyers and three "tame" submarines used in the training of sound men. Beginning in the spring of 1942 the destroyers were, from time-to-time, pressed into service to track suspected enemy submarines in the area and the trainees went along to learn from the first-hand experience. Many naval sound men from foreign nations were also trained here.

In Jan. 1942 the station became the headquarters for the 7th Naval District and in Feb. the Navy's Gulf Sea Frontier was established here. In June, 1942, however, the Headquarters of the 7th Naval District and Gulf Sea Frontier were moved to Miami because Key West was considered to be too vulnerable to enemy attacks.

In Dec. 1943 the station expanded onto Boca Chica Key to the east creating an auxiliary air station. Activities at the station peaked during the summer of 1944 as did the station's population which by then, had reached 4000. Blimps operated from the station, it had a major naval hospital and extensive repair facilities.

After the war activites at the station declined when a series of cutbacks began in 1948, but the station continued to function throughout the Cold War.

KISSIMMEE (See Orlando area)

LAKE CITY is in northern Florida 50 miles west of Jacksonville.

U.S NAVAL AIR STATION, LAKE CITY, three miles SE of town, was the private air field of the Lake City Flying Club and was taken over by the Navy in early 1942 to be 1 of 7 satellite fields supporting training and operational activities at NAS, Jacksonville. The station was used to train both Navy and Marine pilots in PV-1 Venturas and later in PV-3s. NAS, Lake City had one outlying field, Lake Butler Airport, two miles SE of Lake Butler. In May 1945 NAS, Lake City was placed in caretaker status and returned to its former owners in 1946.

LAKELAND/WINTER HAVEN/LAKE WALES/BARTOW AREA: This is a cluster of small communities in a lake-studded area 30 to 50 miles east of Tampa. Lakeland was the largest town during the war with some 22,000 people.

BARTOW ARMY AIR FIELD, five miles NE of Bartow, was Bartow's local airport before the war. It was taken over by the 3rd AF in early 1942 as a sub-base and fighter pilot training field for Sarasota AAF.

CORONET AIRPORT was used by the AAF as an auxiliary field.

HALDEMAN-ELDER AIRPORT, four miles SE of Lakeland, was activated in 1942 as an auxiliary training field of Lakeland AAF.

LAKELAND ARMY AIR FIELD, five miles SW of Lakeland was a pre-war civilian airport known as Drane Field. It was taken over by the 3rd AF as a sub-base for MacDill Field. Lakeland AAF had a flying school, Lincoln Flying School, which had contracted early in the war with the Army Air Corps to provide elementary and advanced flight training for Air Corps pilots. Later, operational training was conducted by the 3rd AF in B-24 bombers. In 1946 the field was returned to the community.

Experimental Aircraft Association Education Center: This unique organization, located on the north side of Lakeland Field near I-4, has a museum displaying primarily experimental, Homebuilt and classic aircraft. A few WW II planes are also on display. The center is closely associated with the Experimental Aircraft Association of Oshkosh, WI. Address: 3838 Drane Field, Rd., Lakeland, FL 33807. Phone: 813/644-2431. Hours: daily 9-5. Free.

LAKELAND MUNICIPAL AIRPORT, two miles north of Lakeland, was used by Lincoln Flying School in the training of AAF pilots. It had an auxiliary field, Coronet Airport, 1.5 miles east of Plant City, also used by Lincoln.

LAKE WALES: This community had three local air fields, Oliver Parker Field, Southwest Field and Wells Field. All three were taken over by the 3rd AF as auxiliary fields for Sarasota AAF and used for training. They were collectively known as Lake Wales Army Air Field. After the war they were returned to their owners.

WINTER HAVEN ARMY AIR FIELD, 2.5 miles SW of town, was Winter Haven Airport before the war. It was taken over by the 3rd AF in Dec. 1942 as an auxiliary training field for Sarasota AAF. Also located here was a branch prisoner of war camp with over 200 POWs who worked in the local citrus industry.

LEESBURG is 35 miles NW of Orlando.

LEESBURG ARMY AIR FIELD, 4.5 miles east of town, had been the local airport before the war. It was taken over by the Air Technical Service Command in mid-1942 and served as a sub-base to Alachua AAF, Gainesville and had a fighter command school of applied tactics under Orlando AAB. A branch prisoner of war camp was located here with about 200 POWs working in local agriculture. In late 1944 the AAF left the field and returned it to the local community. Seven miles NW of Leesburg, was a companion facility known and Leesburg Service Center.

MARIANNA is in the Florida panhandle 60 miles west of Tallahassee.

MARIANNA ARMY AIR FIELD was 4.5 miles NE of town. It was established by the 3rd AF in mid-1942 for the 50,000 Pilot Training Program for the training of air crews in light bombers. It had an advanced flight training school and a gunnery school. Auxiliary fields were:

- Aux. #1, Ellis Airport, 2 miles SW of Ellis
- Aux. #2, Malone Airport, 15.5 miles north of Mariana
- Aux. #3, Bascom Airport, 15.5 miles NE of Mariana
- Aux. #4, Alliance Airport, 14 miles SE of Mariana

MELBOURNE is 20 miles south of Cape Canaveral.

U.S. NAVAL AIR STATION, MELBOURNE, two miles NW, was built by the Navy and commissioned in Oct. 1942. It provided advanced flight training for Navy pilots in SNJ Texans, F4F Wildcats and F6F Hellcats. Flying from catapults was also taught here. The field had two satellite fields at Valkaria and Malabar. The U.S. bureau of Aeronautics had a facility at the station testing both engines and aircraft. In Nov. 1944, with pilot requirements being met, the station began to phase down. With space available, 250 prisoners of war were brought in and worked in the laundry. The station was put in caretaker status in Feb. 1946 and in Nov. was turned over to Melbourne and Eau Gallie for use as their municipal airport. Outlying fields in the area were:

Malabar Airport, 9 miles NW of Malabar and Valkaria Airport, 2.5 miles south of Malabar.

MIAMI/FORT LAUDERDALE/BOCA RATON AREA: When war came to the U.S. Miami was Florida's second largest city with 172,000 people with that many again in surrounding communities. The war escalated the military's interests in the area 10-fold. Here was one of the most militarily strategic locations in the country, with a good climate and large hotels which were seasonally empty in the summer. Both the Army and the Navy found the hotels ideal places to gather large numbers of men and women for training and organizing into military units while they awaited transfer to military facilities which were being built elsewhere in Florida and the southern U.S. Beginning in early 1942 large numbers of service personnel were sent to the Miami area and housed in the area's hotels and apartments leased by the government. At its peak the military services occupied all, or part of, 326 hotels and apartment buildings housed 82,000 service personnel. During Jan., Feb. and Mar., 1942 the tourist business remained relatively good in the area as many people came down from the north thinking this might be their last chance for a winter vacation for some time to come. In some of the hotels, both tourist and military personnel were accommodated. In the spring of 1942 when the tourist season began to wind down, the vacant rooms were quickly filled by in-coming military personnel. The military services stayed on in the area's hotels and apartments for most of the war establishing many schools and training programs in the Miami area. Programs were held in the hotels where the service personnel lived, in local colleges and universities, at local air ports and existing military facilities. In 1943, when veterans began returning to the states, the 3rd AF set up one of its three Redistribution Centers here to receive airmen from overseas, give them a period of rest and relaxation, and send them on to new assignments. In Sept. 1944 the Army did likewise setting up one of its five Redistribution Centers in Miami Beach.

The Miami area, like other major cities suffered manpower shortages, so German prisoners of war were brought in to work in the city's services. One of their principal duties was to collect trash.

Some manufacturing companies built new factories in the area giving it a welcome industrial base which it had not had before the war. The area emerged from the war in a very strong economic position. The tourist business boomed in the early post-war years, more industry moved in, many of the military installations stayed due to the Cold War and by 1950 the population of the area had doubled.

BOCA RATON ARMY AIR FIELD, two miles NW of Boca Raton, was known as Griffith Field before the war. It was taken over in mid-1942 by the Eastern Technical Training Command as a school for radio and radar operators and a training field for B-17 co-pilots. The radar school taught radarmen to direct bombings through overcast. During the postwar years the field became Boca Raton Municipal Airport.

THE HOLOCAUST MEMORIAL, at Dade Blvd. and Meridian Ave. in Miami Beach, is dedicated to the 6 million Jews who died at the hands of the Nazis in WW II. The memorial consists of a 42-foot high bronze arm reaching for the sky with people attempting to climb the arm. There is a black granite wall bearing the names of those who perished, vignettes displaying victims helping victims, an eternal flame and a meditation garden. Phone: 305/ 538-1663. Hours: daily 9-9. Free.

MIAMI 36TH STREET AIRPORT was a municipal airport prior to the war. In early 1941 two Army Air Corps reconnaissance squadrons moved onto the field and lived in tents awaiting transfer to MacDill Field in Tampa, then under construction. With the escalation of the war during 1941 MacDill's responsibilities grew to the point where it could not accept the units stationed here. Therefore, they stayed on and the airport was taken over by the AAF in mid-1942 to be used as an operational field for coastal patrols and anti-submarine activities. The first sizeable contingent of military aircraft at the field consisted of 4 B-18s, 12 B-25s, 10 B-34s and 2 A-29s. The airport continued in operation as the area's main commercial airport with runways and facilities being shared with the military. It also served as a ferrying point for Lend Lease planes going overseas, had a large AAF storage and maintenance depot and served as a training field. Some military operations remained at the field until the early 1950s, but they eventually departed. The airport became Miami International Airport.

MIAMI ARMY AIR FIELD (See U.S. Naval Air Station, Miami and Miami Army Air Field, below)

PAN AMERICAN AIRWAYS FACILITY, CORAL GABLES: For several years before the war Pan American Airlines had operated a large seaplane facility on the Coral Gables water front. In mid-1940 the Army contracted with Pan Am to train 850 Air Crops navigators at the facility while Air Crops training facilities were being built elsewhere. After the American navigators departed, the British, in May 1941, contracted with the Pan Am facility to train 150 of their airmen as navigators. During the summer of 1941 Pan Am went into the ferrying business for the U.S. Government. Three Pan Am subsidiaries were setup for the purpose of ferrying Lend Lease aircraft to our Allies: Pan Am Air Ferries Co. flew planes from Miami to Khartoum, Sudan; Pan Am Airways Co. flew them to points in west Africa; and Pan Am Airways-Africa, Ltd. delivered planes elsewhere in Africa. When the U.S. entered the war, Pan Am extended it ferry services to Cairo, Egypt and Tehran, Iran.

U.S. NAVAL AIR STATION, FORT LAUDERDALE was the area's local municipal airport before the Navy took it over in the summer of 1942 to use as a training base for torpedo bombers. The base was commissioned on Oct. 1, 1942 and the first cadets trained in TBF Avengers. Navy air-sea rescue boat crews were also trained here and throughout the three years that training was conducted here 720 pilots were intentionally or accidentally dunked to give both the pilots and air-sea rescue boat crews experience. There was also a radar school here.

Late in the war when escort aircraft carriers became plentiful, the "USS Solomons" was attached to the station to give the pilots, then in training, actual experience taking off from, and landing on, an aircraft carrier. Heretofore, take offs and landings had been practiced on simulated carrier decks on land. The station had two auxiliary fields, U.S. Naval Auxiliary Air Field, North Pompano, which later became Pompano Beach Airport, and U.S. Naval Auxiliary Air Field, West Prospect, which later became Ft. Lauderdale Executive Airport. NAS, Ft. Lauderdale was disestablished in Sept. 1945, returned to its owners and became Fort Lauderdale-Hollywood International Airport. Outlying fields during the war were: North Pompano Airport, 1.5 miles NE of Pompano West Prospect Airport, 2.5 miles NW of Oakland Park.

U.S. NAVAL AIR STATION, MIAMI AND MIAMI ARMY AIR FIELD, 6 miles NW of Miami, was a dual airport before the war with a history of service to the armed forces. One airport was known as Pan American Airport, owned jointly by the U.S. Army and Pan American Airlines Co., and the other was known as Intercontinental Airport. They were also called East and West fields. The main dual east-west runways of the two airports adjoined each other providing a pair of extra long runways. Since 1931 a Naval Reserve air facility functioned here and in the late 1930s the Navy added blimp facilities at the field. In Aug. 1940 all of the facilities at the airport were expanded rapidly and the Navy began flight training for regular Navy personnel in F2-A Buffalos, SCB Helldivers, and BD and TBD torpedo bombers. Other expansions followed and eventually the airport had large medical, supply, assembly and repair departments, a Marine Corps air station, a Coast Guard air station, a Navy air gunners school, a floating drydock, a radio station, a recruiting station, an operational flight school, a small craft training center, a supply pier, a target towing unit and a training aids library. The naval station became headquarters for the 7th Naval District, the Navy's Gulf Sea Frontier (after June 1942), Inshore Patrol, Registered Publications Issuing Office, Office of Naval Procurement and Port Director. Naval flight training continued throughout the war with cadets eventually training in SBD Dauntlesses, TBF Avengers and PB-4Y Liberator heavy bombers. In the latter months of the war escort carriers were assigned to the station to give the Navy pilots actual experience of taking off and landing on a carrier deck. After the war the regular Navy units pulled out one-by-one and their facilities were turned over to the Navy reservists. A Marine air wing remained until 1958. The AAF used the field during the war as a port of aerial embarkation and an air depot. After the war the airport became one entity known as Opa Locka Airport. During the war NAS, Miami had the following outlying fields:
• Forman Airport, 6.5 miles SW of Ft. Lauderdale
• Master Airport, 1 miles NW of Miami

One of the flyable P-51D Mustangs owned by the Weeks Museum.

• North Perry Airport, 6.5 miles west of Hollywood

WEEKS AIR MUSEUM: This is a fine air museum dedicated to the preservation and restoration of aircraft from the beginning of flight through the end of the WW II era. There are nearly 40 airplanes on display, most of which are in flying condition. WW II planes in the collection include two P-51D Mustangs, a DeHavilland Mosquito bomber, Grumman TBM Duck 2-seater amphibian, Grumman TBM Avenger torpedo bomber, B-17G, B-29, P-40E and more. Address: 14710 SW 128th St., Miami, FL 33186. Phone: 305/233-5197. Hours: W-M 10-5. Closed Tuesdays, Thanksgiving and Dec. 25. Admission charged. Location: at Kendall-Tamiami Executive Airport in SW Miami near the Zoo.

NAPLES is on the SW coast of the Florida peninsula.

NAPLES ARMY AIR FIELD, 1.25 miles NE of Naples, was the town's local airport, and was utilized by the Eastern Flying Training Command as a gunnery school and as a sub-base to both Tyndall Field and Buckingham AAF. At war's end, the field was returned to the community and became Naples Municipal Airport.

OCALA is 30 miles SE of Gainesville on I-75. Silver Springs, an eastern suburb of Ocala, is in a lush tropical-like area of the state with many clear lakes and streams. It was here that the Navy made wartime jungle survival films to show to Navy and Marine personnel going to the South Pacific.

TAYLOR FIELD, one mile SW of Ocala, was the town's local airport. During the summer of 1942 the 3rd AF began using it as a primary flight training school. After the war, the AAF departed and it once again became the local airport.

ORLANDO AREA: This area is in central Florida, about half way down the Florida peninsula.

GOTHA FIELD, at Windermere, FL 9 miles SW of Orlando, was one of the several auxiliary fields serving Orlando AAF and the School of Applied Tactics. It was used as an ordnance depot.

HOLOCAUST MEMORIAL RESEARCH & EDUCATION CENTER OF CENTRAL FLORIDA: This Holocaust center has a museum, library and archives relating the history of the Holocaust. The library has some 2500 volumes plus periodicals and videotapes. Address: 851 N. Maitland Ave., Maitland, FL 32751. Phone: 407/628-0555. Hours: M-Thurs. 9-4, Fri. 9-1,

A B-24 bomber awaits restoration at the Flying Tigers Warbird Air Museum's restoration shop.

1st & 3rd Sun. ea. month 1-4.

KISSIMMEE ARMY AIR FIELD, two miles west of Kissimmee, FL, served as an auxiliary field for Orlando AAB and the School of Applied Tactics. Bombardment training was conducted here. After the war the field was declared surplus and later became Kissimmee Airport.

Flying Tigers Warbird Air Museum: This fine air museum on the west side of Kissimmee Airport is of special interest to WW II buffs in that it has its own restoration facility and specialized in the restoration of WW II aircraft. At any time there are WW II aircraft in the shop undergoing restoration and visitors may watch the work in progress. Restored planes and some unrestored planes are on the premises to view. The aircraft in the shop and display areas are ever-changing so each return trip to this museum offers new warplanes to be seen. Also on display are engines, armament, air frames, photos, models; and there is a gift shop. Address: 231 Hoagland Blvd. (Airport Rd.), Kissimmee, FL 32741. Phone: 407/933-1942. Hours: M-Sat. 9-6, Sun. 9-5. Admission charged. Location: Hoagland Rd. intersects with Hwy 192 just west of Dyer Rd. which leads to the Kissimmee Airport terminal. Take Hoagland Rd. south from Hwy 192 to the museum.

ORLANDO ARMY AIR BASE, 2.5 miles east of town, was Orlando's municipal airport. In late 1940 an Army Air Corps[5] Composite Group, known as the Air Corps Tactical School, moved to the airport from Maxwell Field, AL to do experimentation and training in the latest

---

[5] The Army Air Corps was reorganized in June 1941 and became the Army Air Forces. Each Army Air Force was numbered from then on i.e. 1st Air Force, 2nd Air force, etc.

tactics of aircraft interception. From this beginning evolved, in Nov. 1942, the School of Applied Tactics had the mission to monitor, accumulate and study the latest developments in Allied[6] and enemy technological and tactical developments from around the world and integrate them into the AAF's operations and training. This mission made Orlando one of the most prestigious air facilities in the AAF during the war. A huge expansion was undertaken at the field an in the surrounding area. A simulated combat theater of operations of about 8000 square miles was created in central and western Florida and used to carry out complicated aerial maneuvers. Facilities were constructed at Orlando AAB to provide for training in air defense, offensive and defensive bombardment, air support, and several air services. Twelve new auxiliary fields were built in the surrounding area and existing fields were acquired as sub-bases. Many combat veterans were employed here as instructors. Selected Army and Navy personnel were sent here to be trained in the latest air tactics and doctrines. Air intelligence officers and air inspectors were also trained here. Some of the school's graduates were sent on to other air facilities as instructors, but most went on to combat units. A large library of maps, documents, books and reports was developed during the war years.

By mid-1943, with the need for combat pilots declining, the School concentrated more on training personnel in communications, intelligence, logistics, administration and medical specialties. Also in 1943, training of B-29 bomber crews began at the field and a prisoner of war branch camp was set up with 700 POWs working on the air fields and in local agriculture.

In the postwar years the military operations at Orlando AAB were phased out and the air field eventually returned to the community to become Orlando Executive Airport. Land north of the field was given to the Navy and eventually became Orlando Naval Training Center.

PINECASTLE ARMY AIR FIELD, 2.5 miles SE of the community of Pinecastle was activated in late 1942 by civilian interests as Orlando's second municipal airport. It later became an auxiliary air field for Orlando AAB and was used for demonstrations and test development. The headquarters school of the School of Applied Tactics was here. After the war Pinecastle AAF became McCoy Air

---

[6] U.S. Air Force personnel worked very closely with the British who had developed an effective unified air defense system.

Force Base, and still later it was returned to the community and became the area's largest airport, Orlando International Airport.

U.S. NAVAL AIR STATION, SANFORD was 2.5 miles SE of Sanford, FL which is about 15 miles north of Orlando. Construction of the new station proved difficult and expensive due to the high water table, lack of local labor and shortage of materials, especially lumber. Nevertheless, the station began operations in mid-Dec. 1942 and crews soon began training in PV-1s and SNB 2-engine bombers. In 1944 the Navy decided to use Sanford as a training station for fighter pilots and bomber training operations were moved to Beaufort, SC. Fighter pilots at Sanford then began training in FM-1s. Other facilities at Sanford included a large cold storage plant that provided fresh and frozen vegetables to the other Navy facilities in the area. On Oct. 15, 1944 a hurricane passed over the station but did minimal damage. In July 1945, German prisoners of war arrived to work as mechanics, in the mess halls and on the grounds. In Feb. 1946 the station was put into caretaker status and in May it was disestablished. The site then became Sanford's local airport and a vocation school and a health center were constructed. In 1951 the Navy came back to Sanford and used it as an operational base for fighter squadrons and blimps as well as crash boats operating on the St. Johns River. In 1968 the station was again disestablished and returned to the community.

During WW II NAS, Sanford had outlying fields of Osceola Airport, 1 mile west of Osceola and Titusville-Cocoa Airport, 6 miles south of Titusville.

WINTER GARDEN FIELD, near the community of Winter Garden, a western suburb of Orlando, was activated by the 3rd AF in Dec. 1941 as a searchlight training center under Orlando AAB. The field had been a local airport and was returned to the community after the war.

PALATKA, 40 miles south of Jacksonville, is the birthplace of Gen. Joseph "Vinegar Joe" Stilwell. He was born here in 1883. During WW II Stilwell was the U.S. commander in the China-Burma-India theater, and later was commander of the U.S. 10th and 6th Armies. In 1962 an Army Reserve training camp near Palatka was named in his honor, Camp Stilwell.

PANAMA CITY is on the Gulf coast of Florida's panhandle. During the war the J. A. Jones Shipbuilding Co. here built cargo vessels.

TYNDALL FIELD was 8 miles SE of Panama City on a long peninsula bounded on the SW by the Gulf of Mexico and on the NE by an arm of St. Andrews Bay. The field was activated by the Eastern Flying Training Command in early 1941 as a gunners school to relieve overcrowded conditions at the Air Corps' other gunnery school near Las Vegas, NV. The first staff arrived just days before the Japanese attacked at Pearl Harbor. The first classes began in Feb. 1942 and during that year the school graduated 8091 gunners. The number of graduates increased considerably in the next two years. French and Chinese gunners were also trained here. The base grew in size and became the AAF's second largest gunnery school after Las Vegas. In 1948 the facility was

An instructor at Orlando AAB explains the air defense grid system.

taken over by the US Air Force, renamed Tyndall Air Force Base and continued in operation in during the Cold War.

THE PENSACOLA AREA: This area is at the western end of Florida's panhandle on the Gulf coast. By the time WW II started the area had a number of long-established military installations in the area. Early in the war a new Army camp was built nearby in Okaloosa County to train and utilize conscientious objectors.

FORT McCREE, on the west shore of the entrance to Pensacola Bay, was completed in 1842 and was still operational when WW II started. Several of the old batteries were armed and manned during the war and a new battery, No. 233, was built at Perdido Key, but its 6" guns were never delivered. Much of the fort has been eroded by the sea but some of the old foundations can be seen at low tide. A main ship channel now flows across the fort's former parade ground.

FORT PICKENS, on the western end of Santa Rosa Island was built in the early 1800s to protect the entrance to Pensacola Bay. Before and during WW II it was used extensively by the Army Coast Artillery Corps . . which was very unusual for such an old fort. In the late 1930s the fort was the largest training post for coast artillery in the U.S. and the largest Army post in Florida. It continued to be a training post during the war, as well as an active coastal defense for Pensacola Bay. Battery Worth had four tour-of-the-century mortars in operation until 1942, Battery Trueman had two 1905 vintage 3" rapid-fire guns that were manned until 1946, Battery Cooper had four 155 mm gun emplacements built around the old battery that were operative until the spring of 1945. Battery Langdon, which had two 12" guns, was covered over during the war. A new battery, No. 234, was constructed during the war, but its 6 inch guns were never put in place. In May 1947 Fort Pickens and the other Pensacola forts were deactivated and declared surplus. The fort was transferred to the National Park Service and opened to the public. Address: Gulf Islands Natl. Seashore, 1801 Gulf Breeze Pkwy., Gulf Breeze, FL 32561. Phone: 904/934-2635. Hours: Apr. through Oct. daily 9-5, rest of year daily 8-4. Closed Dec. 25. Admission charged.

U.S. NAVAL AUXILIARY AIR STATION, BRONSON FIELD was 12 miles SW of Pensacola and an auxiliary field to NAS, Pensacola. It had two outlying fields; Faircloth Airport, 3 miles NW of Lillian, AL and Kaisers Tract, 3.5 miles NE of Elberta, AL.

U.S. NAVAL AUXILIARY AIR STATION, CORRY, five miles SW of Pensacola, was an auxiliary field to NAS, Pensacola built by the Navy five miles north of town in 1922 and later moved to its present location in 1927. Corry had an outlying field, Pensacola Field #8, four miles NW of Muscogee.

U.S. NAVAL AUXILIARY AIR STATION, ELLYSON, 7.5 miles north of Pensacola, was an auxiliary field to NAS, Pensacola. It had an outlying field, Spencer Airport, 2 miles NE of Pace.

U.S. NAVAL AUXILIARY AIR STATION, SAUFLEY, 8.5 miles NW of Pensacola, was an auxiliary

field to NAS, Pensacola. It had the following outlying air fields:

- Helm Airport, 12 miles NW of Pensacola
- Pensacola Field #1, 14 miles NW of Pensacola
- Pensacola Field #5, 3 miles SE of Gonzales
- Pensacola Field #6, 2.5 miles north of Gonzales
- Pensacola Field #7, 7 miles NW of Pensacola
- Pensacola Field #9, 1.5 miles south of Gonzales

U.S. NAVAL AUXILIARY AIR STATION, WHITING (NORTH & SOUTH FIELDS) was 6.5 miles NE of Milton. Whiting was commissioned in 1943 as an auxiliary field to both NAS, Pensacola and Eglin AAF. There were two identical fields, north and south, with the station's building between. In the postwar years the field was expanded and became a separate naval air station known as U.S. Naval Air Station, Whiting Field and was used to train Navy pilots. During WW II the station had the following outlying fields:

- Choctaw Airport, 7.5 miles SE of Bagdad
- Holley Airport, 1.5 miles south of Holley
- Milton "T" Airport, 3.5 miles NE of Milton
- Pensacola Airport, 4 miles NE of Pensacola
- New Brewton Airport, 3.5 miles south of Brewton, AL
- Old Brewton Airport, 2.5 miles north of Brewton, AL
- Site #1, 6 miles WSW of Evergreen, AL
- Site #16, near Atmore, AL
- Site #20, 6 miles SW of Evergreen, AL

U.S. NAVAL AIR STATION, PENSACOLA (CAVALIER FIELD): The site occupied by NAS Pensacola, 6 miles west of the town of Pensacola, was first occupied by the Navy in 1825 as a naval shipyard. In 1913 and the Navy the Navy decided that the Pensacola station should be converted into a station for the Navy's newly-acquired aircraft. On Feb. 2. 1914 the first airplane flew from Pensacola . . and they've been flying from the station ever since. By the mid-1930s Pensacola was one of the Navy's best developed air stations with many services and training facilities. In 1936 training activities accelerated considerable as a result of the rising threats of war in Europe. From 1939 to 1945 Pensacola was one of the Navy's most productive training facilities. Over 28,000 Navcads were trained here along with 2755 British and 58 French air cadets. In emergencies, station personnel were called upon to fly operational missions in the area and along the coasts. The station also had Class A Service Schools training aviation machinist's mates, photographers and aviation metalsmiths. The Navy's only School of Aviation Medicine was located here, and the station had a major aircraft repair center overhauling Navy planes. The Naval Air Transport Service and Naval Air Ferry Command also operated here during the war.

NAS Pensacola continued as one of the Navy's most important installations in the postwar years, and was home to important naval commands and ships and the Navy's famous air demonstration team, the Blue Angels.During WW II the station had the following outlying fields:

- Bagdad Airport, 2.5 miles SW of Bagdad
- Brewton Municipal Airport (new), 3.5 miles

Simulated flight deck of a WW II aircraft carrier. National Museum of Naval Aviation, Pensacola, FL.

north of Brewton, AL
- Brewton Airport (old), 2.5 miles north of Brewton, AL
- Site #16, 6 miles NW of Atmore, AL
- Site #21, 2.5 miles north of Crestview

Fort Barrancas: This fort, on the grounds of NAS Pensacola, is one of three forts built in the early 1800s to protect the Pensacola Navy Yard and the town of Pensacola. During WW II it was continuously garrisoned by the U.S. Army as a coastal defense post. After the war it is open to the public. Address: NAS Pensacola, 32508. Phone: 904/452-2311. Hours: Apr. thru Oct., daily 9:30-5; rest of year daily 10:30-4; closed Dec. 25. Free. Location: near the National Museum of Naval Aviation.

National Museum of Naval Aviation: This is a large museum on the ground of NAS Pensacola. It traces the history of naval aviation from 1911 to the space age and has over 100 Navy, Marine and Coast Guard airplanes on display inside and outside of the museum. WW II planes include a PBY-5 Catalina, PB2Y-5R Coronado, PB4Y-2 Privateer, SB2C-5 Helldiver, SBD-3 Dauntless, A1-H Skyraider, A4D-1 Skyhawk and others. There is a Hall of Fame honoring Navy men who have received the Congressional Medal of Honor and a 500-seat multi-media theater. A display in the West Wing highlights Carrier Aviation during WW II. Address: Box 33104 Bldg. 3465, NAS Pensacola, FL 32508. Phone: 904/452-3604 and 800/327-5002. Hours: daily 9-5. Free. Location: Exit I-10 at Exit #2 south on Pine Forest Rd., follow NAS Pensacola/Museum signs to the museum.

PERRY is 45 miles SE of Tallahassee.

PERRY ARMY AIR FIELD, 3.5 miles south of town was the town's local airport. It was taken over by the 3rd AF early in the war to be a sub-base for Tallahassee's Dale Mabry Field. Later in the war it became an operation base for fighters. After the war the air field was returned to the town of Perry.

PUNTA GORDA is 20 miles north of Ft. Myers on the Peace River.

PUNTA GORDA AIRPORT, four miles east of

Left:The observation deck on the "Ferdinand Magellan". President Roosevelt spoke from this platform many times. Right: The dining area in President Roosevelt's bullet-proof Pullman car.

town, was Charlotte County Airport before the war and was activated in early 1942 by the 3rd AF as an auxiliary field for Sarasota AAF. The airport served as a gunnery training base and an advanced training field for fighter pilots. It was returned to Punta Gorda after the war.

RICHMOND HEIGHTS, 19 miles SW of Miami, wasn't on the map when WW II started but their was a small sawmill community in the area called Richmond.

U.S. NAVAL AIR STATION (LTA), RICHMOND, was 1 of 8 new lighter-than-air stations planned by the Navy for coastal defense around the U.S. It was commissioned Apr. 20, 1942 and had 6 mooring circles, 6 air ships, two utility nonridgids, three large blimp hangars, barracks, mess halls, an administration building, a helium plant, repair and maintenance facilities, sewage plant, a small hospital, a pigeon loft and an all-negro 17-piece station band. The station eventually became the largest blimp base on the east coast. In the early morning hours of July 15, 1942 one of Richmond's blimps, newly equipped with radar, had an encounter with a German sub just south of the Keys. This was one of the rare times during the war that blimps and subs tangled with each other. The blimp picked up the sub in the darkness on radar and moved in to investigate. Upon determining that the sub was German, the blimp's pilot made a run at the sub dropping depth charges. The sub, U-134, was one of the few in the German Navy at the time with an anti-aircraft gun. The sub therefore fired back at the blimp puncturing its envelope with many holes. The blimp, slowly losing gas, dropped gently into the water and the sub sped off with little or no damage. The blimp's crewmen were rescued the next day, but not before one man was lost. This was the only blimp lost to enemy action in U.S. waters during the war.

In March 1943 an LTA school for enlisted men began operating at the station, and in Nov. 1943 the Naval Helium Plant Operators School opened here. The station became something of a show-case for the Navy's 7th Naval District and had a steady stream of foreign visitor from Allied nations. On Oct. 17, 1944 a hurricane swept through the area doing some damage to the station. Soon afterwards, a microseismic facility was constructed at the station to detect and track hurricanes. In June 1945, with the war over in Europe, the station began to

phase down, but on Sept. 13, 1945 a fierce tropical storm hit the station during which high winds and subsequent fires destroyed all three hangars and 9 airships. With this, the phase down of the station was accelerated and in Nov. 1945 the station went into caretaker status. In March 1947 the station was inactivated and the property transferred to the University of Miami, the Coast Guard and the Federal Aviation Administration (FAA). In the postwar years the Miami Zoo occupied part of the grounds of the old station.

The Gold Coast Railroad Museum: This museum is built on the concrete floor of one of the NAS, Richmond's blimp hangars, and the museum's parking lot is the landing pad. The museum has a very interesting relic of WW II, Franklin Roosevelt's bulletproof Pullman car. The Pullman car, named the "Ferdinand Magellan" and now a National Historic Landmark, was rebuilt in 1942 from an ordinary Pullman car manufactured in 1928. The car was equipped with 5/8" armor plate all around, 3" bulletproof glass, two escape hatches, an elevator on the observation deck to lift the President up and down in his wheel chair[7], and the interior was modified for the President's convenience. The outward appearance of the car was made to look like an ordinary Pullman car for security purposes. Also at the Museum is Signal Corps Communication Car #1401, a converted

---
[7] The elevator was removed after President Roosevelt's death.

baggage car, that usually accompanied the "Ferdinand Magellan" providing the President with rapid worldwide communications, including the ability to address the nation by radio if necessary. The Pullman was presented to President Roosevelt Dec. 18, 1942 and designated "U.S. Car #1". Roosevelt used the car many times, travelling over 50,000 miles in it. Several famous WW II personalities, such as Winston Churchill, rode in the car with the President. When President Roosevelt died in Warm Springs, GA, the car was part of the funeral train that brought his body to Washington. Mrs. Roosevelt rode in it then. The President's body was in another car. After Roosevelt's death, President Truman used the car, and later, Presidents Eisenhower and Reagan used it. Museum Address: 12450 SW 152nd St., (Coral Reef Dr.) Miami, FL 33177. Phone: 305/253-0063. Hours: M-F 10-6, Sat.-Sun. & holidays 10-5. Closed Holloween week, Thanksgiving and Dec. 25. Admission charged. Location: The museum can be reached through the main entrance to the Metrozoo.

SAINT PETERSBURG (See Tampa/St. Petersburg Area)

SARASOTA, 65 miles south of Tampa, had 11,000 people in 1940.

SARASOTA ARMY AIR FIELD, 3.5 miles north of town, had been the Sarasota-Bradenton Airport before the war. It was taken over by the 3rd AF in Feb. 1942 for use as an operational base, and a training base for replacement pilots in fighter-bombers. During the early months of the war a Civil Air Patrol (CAP) units operated out of the field carrying out submarine patrols. Sarasota AAF grew into a large base and eventually had sub-bases at Bartow, St. Petersburg, Ft. Myers, Tampa and auxiliary fields at Immokalee, Lake Wales, Punta Gorda and Winter Haven. After the war the airport was returned to its civilian status.

SEBRING is 65 miles SE of Tampa in a citrus-

Camp Blanding in Nov. 1940.

growing area.

AVON PARK ARMY AIR FIELD, 10 miles NE of the town of Avon Park had been Avon Park Municipal Airport before the war. The airport was taken over in Sept. 1942 by the 3rd AF as a sub-base of MacDill Field and converted into a training base for heavy bomber crews. British and Americans both trained here. This was one of several AF bases in Florida where the cadets and instructors were used in emergencies for anti-submarine patrols. After the war Avon Park AAF was returned to the community.

HENDRICKS FIELD, located 6 miles east of Sebring, was activated in early 1942 by the AAF as a training base for B-17 bomber crews to meet the requirements of the 30,000 Pilot Training Program. By 1946 Hendricks Field had been declared surplus by the AAF. The field had, as auxiliary fields, Conners Field at Okeechobee and Imokalee Municipal Airport at Imokalee.

STARKE is 35 miles SW of Jacksonville.

CAMP BLANDING: The Army began constructing Camp Blanding 10 miles east of Starke, in 1939 as a division-sized training camp and reception center. The camp was, during 1940, the largest construction project in the state of Florida. Blanding was used during the war for the basic training and field training of the following units: 1st, 29th, 30th, 31st, 36th, 43rd, 63rd, 66th, 79th Infantry Divs. and the 508th Parachute Inf. Regiment. Some artillery units trained here, and during the latter part of the war infantry replacement units trained here. The camp had a main prisoner of war camp holding 1200 German POWs who worked at Camp Blanding. In 1943 a POW camp for German naval personnel was also established here. It was one of four such camps in the country[8]. There was also an air field on the base known as Crystal Lake Air Base. Housing was a constant problem in the area during the war and for that reason the Army abandoned the camp soon after the end of hostilities and turned it over to the Florida National Guard.

CAMP BLANDING MUSEUM AND MEMORIAL PARK: This 13-acre museum and park is on the grounds of Camp Blanding near the camp's main entrance. The museum is a WW II restored barracks with displays and exhibits telling the history of Camp Blanding, the units that passed through the camp and how the soldiers lived while at the camp. In the park is a 15 foot monument of an infantryman honoring Florida Guardsmen who served in WW II. Also in the park are tanks, half-tracks, trucks, jeeps, artillery pieces and a picnic area.

KEYSTONE HEIGHTS ARMY AIR FIELD, four miles NW of Keystone Heights, was activated in mid-1942 by the Air Technical Service Command as an auxiliary air field to Jacksonville AAF and to Alachua AAF, Gainesville. It became inactive after a short period of use.

STUART, on Florida's east coast 30 miles north of West Palm Beach, was home to U.S. Naval Auxiliary Air Station, Witham. NAAS Witham was 1.5 miles SE of Stuart and was an auxiliary field to NAS, Vero Beach.

[8]The others were Camp Beale, CA, Camp McCain, MS and Papago Park, AZ.

An aircraft hangar under construction at MacDill Field in 1939.

TALLAHASSEE, in the north-central part of the state, is Florida's state capital and during the war had a population of 16,000.

DALE MABRY FIELD, three miles west of town, was Tallahassee's pre-war municipal airport. It was taken over by the 3rd AF in 1941 as a combat command base primarily for fighter planes. The field had auxiliary fields at Thomasville and Harris Neck, GA. There was a branch prisoner of war compound here holding about 150 POWS who worked on the base. After the war the field was returned to the community and is once again Tallahassee Municipal Airport.

TAMPA/ST. PETERSBURG AREA: These cities, and several smaller ones, are clustered around Tampa Bay on the western coast of the Florida peninsula. Tampa was the state's third largest city during the war and had a well-developed and diversified industrial base that included three shipyards, the Tampa Shipbuilding Co., which built ammunition and cargo ships, the Tampa Shipbuilding & Engineering Co. which built minesweepers and Tampa Marine Repair Co. which built and repaired smaller ships.

St. Petersburg, the other big city on Tampa Bay, was about half the size of Tampa and was primarily a retirement and tourist community. As Florida geared up for war St. Petersburg provided many hotels and apartments as temporary living quarters for service personnel awaiting assingments to camps still under construction.

FORT DADE, on the south end of Egmont Key at the entrance to Tampa Bay, was built during the Spanish-American War and occupied by the Army until 1936. In that year it was abandoned. It was reactivated again early in WW II, manned by the Army's Coast Artillery Corps and equipped with modern coastal defense and anti-aircraft weapons. In 1946 it was again abandoned.

FORT DE SOTO, on Mullet Key at the mouth of Tampa Bay, was built during the Spanish-American War. The fort was inactivated in 1922 and in 1938 was about to become a part of a county park when the War Department reactivated it. It became a subpost of MacDill Field and was used as an AAF bombing and gunnery training center. The eastern part of Mullet Key became a bombing and gunnery range. After the war the AAF abandoned the fort and it became the centerpiece of Fort

DeSoto Park which encompasses all of Mullet Key and several nearby islands. Address: Fort DeSoto Park, Tierra Verde, Box 3, St. Petersburg, FL 33715. Phone: 813/866-2484.

DREW ARMY AIR FIELD, five miles west of Tampa, had been a secondary airport for Tampa before the war known as Drew Field. In 1940 it was leased to the Federal Government as a subpost of MacDill Field for the duration of the war, or for 25 years. In May 1940 heavy bombers began operating temporarily out of Drew until MacDill Field, then under construction, would be ready to receive them. In Feb. 1941 the bombers withdrew to MacDill and in mid-1941 Drew became a separate base and a replacement training center with an auxiliary field of its own at Waycross, GA. Drew also became the headquarters for the III Fighter command. The base had an engineering aviation unit training center for heavy bombers, a school for air raid warning units, a regional AAF hospital and a branch prisoner of war camp with about 400 POWs who worked on the base. It also served as an AAF personnel depot. In March 1946 the base was returned to the city of Tampa and eventually became the city's main airport, Tampa International Airport.

HILLSBOROUGH FIELD, 7 miles NE of Tampa, served as a bombing and gunnery range for Sarasota Army Air Field and an auxiliary field to Drew Field. The area later became a part of Hillsborough River State Park.

MacDILL FIELD, at Gadsden Point SW of Tampa, was built for the Army Air Corps in 1939/40 and was first named Southeast Air Base, Tampa. In Dec. 1939 the name was changed to MacDill Field. This site was selected because bombers stationed here could reach deep into the Caribbean while the base itself would be relatively safe from carrier-born enemy aircraft operating along Florida's east coast. The 44th Bomb Group was activated here in Jan. 1941 flying B-24 bombers. Operations in B-17 and B-18 bombers began in Feb. 1941. In late 1941 MacDill became the headquarters for the 3rd AF, and in Dec. Training activities were later conducted at the field with cadets and instructors being on call in emergencies for anti-submarine activities. There was an engineer training school here, an air freight terminal and in late 1944 B-29 bomber crews began training here because MacDill had the long runways needed for these huge bombers.

The field also had a branch prisoner of war camp here with 500 POWs working on the base. In 1948 the US Air Force took over the field and renamed it MacDill Air Force Base. It remained active throughout the Cold War.

PASSAGE KEY, a small island at the mouth of Tampa Bay, was used during the war as a bombing and gunnery range by airmen at Sarasota Army Air Field.

PINELLAS ARMY AIR FIELD, 10 miles north of St. Petersburg, was activated early in the war as a sub-base of Sarasota AAF. It had a technical training school and trained replacement fighter pilots and air crews. After the war the air field was converted to a civilian field and became St. Petersburg-Clearwater Intl. Airport.

Yesterday's Air Force Air Museum: This air museum, located at the St. Petersburg-Clearwater Intl. Airport, has on display more than a dozen aircraft of the Army, Navy and Coast Guard. There are also military vehicles, fire trucks and weapons systems. Address: 16055 Fairchild Dr., Clearwater, FL 34622. Phone: 813/535-9007. Hours: Tues., Thurs., and Sat. 10-4; Sun. 1-5; closed M, W, & F. Admission charged.

TAMPA BAY HOLOCAUST MEMORIAL MUSEUM & EDUCATION CENTER: This is a museum and resource center commemorating the Holocaust of WW II. Art and artifacts of the Holocaust are on display and the resource center offers lectures, speakers, teacher training, tours, etc. Address: 5001 Duhme Rd., St. Petersburg, FL 33708. Phone: 813/392-4678. Hours: M-F 10:30-4, Sun. noon-4.

USS "REQUIN" SUBMARINE MEMORIAL: This WW II submarine serves as a floating memorial in Tampa. The "Requin" was completed too late to see action during WW II, but was used by the Navy and Navy Reserve until 1971. Address: PO Box 261704, Tampa, FL 33622. Phone: 813/223-7981. Hours: Inquire locally. Location: Moored on the Hillsboro River behind Curtis Hixon Hall at the Kennedy Blvd. Bridge.

ALBERT WHITTED AIRPORT, on St. Petersburg's water front, was used by the Coast Guard during the war. It had an outlying field, Piper-Fuller Airport, 5 miles NW of St. Petersburg.

VALPARAISO/FORT WALTON BEACH

AREA: Valparaiso, in the Florida panhandle 45 miles east of Pensacola, was a community of less than 300 people and none of the other communities in the area were much larger. In addition to being sparsely settled, the area had good flying weather and the degree of isolation the Army Air Corps was seeking for the construction of a facility that was to hold many military secrets.

EGLIN FIELD began in 1935 when the Army Air Corps acquired land and a small airport donated by a local citizen. The Air Corps named the facility The Valparaiso Bombing and Gunnery Base and it was used by pilots from Maxwell Field, AL. In 1937 the base was renamed Eglin Field. In 1940 the Army Air Corps saw the need for a large research and development facility to relieve the crowded conditions at Wright Field in Ohio, and Eglin was selected as the new site. The Air Corps acquired the Choctawhatchee National Forest

as an expansion to their bombing and gunnery ranges and began building a major R & D facility in the Valparaiso area consisting of laboratories, technical buildings, test centers, hangars, long runways, living quarters and many support facilities. Construction at the base continued throughout most of the war and by the end of 1944 Eglin was the second largest air facility in the U.S. It covered over 500,000 acres, had 882 buildings, 30 miles of runways, 10 auxiliary air fields, 53 land and water bombing and gunnery ranges and numerous off-base and detached installations. Because of the nature of the work being done at the base, most of which was secret, Eglin became an autonomous facility within the AAF. It was here in March 1942 that General Jimmy Doolittle's "Raiders" trained in secrecy for their raid on Tokyo. Each of Doolittle's B-25 crews was required to complete two successful take-offs from a simulated aircraft carrier deck with their planes fully loaded. The simulated carrier deck was simply two white lines painted on the ground 700 feet apart. On March 26, 1942 Doolittle's planes began leaving Eglin for the Sacramento Air Depot at McClellan Field, CA to be armed for their attack on Japan.

During the war the personnel at Eglin did exhaustive testing of new airplanes, engines, guns, electrical and mechanical systems, etc. to see if they would stand up under combat conditions. Eglin worked closely with the Air Force Tactical School at Orlando on problems of air defense. British officers and technicians frequented the facility. There was also a branch prisoner of war camp with over 300 POWs who worked on the base.

Over time, Eglin evolved into a center for the development of new weapons and equipment as well as testing items made by others. During the war captured enemy equipment was tested here and immediately following the collapse of Germany in May 1945, German long range V-2 rockets were evaluated here. Modifications were made to several of the rockets and attempts were made to use them as guided missiles controlled by radar to bring down B-17 drones. Eglin was taken over by the US Air Force in 1949 and renamed Eglin Air Force Base. It remained one of the nation's top military R & D facilities throughout the Cold War.

HURLBURT FIELD, 6 miles west of Ft. Walton Beach, was built in 1941 as an auxiliary field for Eglin Field. It was first named Eglin-Hurlburt Airdrome. During 1944 the name of the field was changed twice; first to Hurlburt Field and then to Eglin Auxiliary Field #9. In 1948 the US Air Force named it Eglin Air Force Auxiliary Field #9 (Hurlburt Field). Hurlburt, as it was generally called, was larger than most auxiliary fields and served as the headquarters for the Electronics Section of Air Proving Ground Command and as a radar countermeasure training facility. After a brief postwar decline the field was fully activated in the 1950s and became a BOMARC missile site and a training center for special air warfare, unconventional warfare and counter-insurgency warfare training. It later became the home of the Air Commandos and several other commands.

Hurlburt Field Memorial Air Park: This is an

outdoor air park on the grounds of Hurlburt Field with about a dozen vintage aircraft on display. Some of the planes are from WW II.

US AIR FORCE ARMAMENT MUSEUM, SW of Valparaiso on SR 85, has on display a wide variety of planes, bombs, missiles, tanks, other vehicles of war and over 5000 Air Force armament items ranging from WW I bombs and machine guns to Viet Nam era missiles. Many items from both enemy and Allied nations are on display. WW II planes on display include a B-17G, B-25J, P-51D and a P-47N. Address: 100 Museum Dr., Eglin AFB, FL 32542-5000. Phone: 904/882-4062. Hours: daily 9:30-4:30. Closed Jan. 1, Thanksgiving, Dec. 25. Free.

VENICE is 18 miles south of Sarasota on the Gulf of Mexico.

VENICE ARMY AIR FIELD, 1.5 miles south of town, was the town's pre-war airport and was used jointly by the 3rd AF and the Air Technical Services Command. It had a training school for air depot personnel, provided service work for Army aircraft and hosted a combat fighter command. The field had a branch prisoner of war camp with 200 POWs who worked at the field. After the war the field was returned to the local community.

VERO BEACH is on the east coast 60 miles north of West Palm Beach.

U.S. NAVAL AIR STATION, VERO BEACH, one mile NW of town, was built by the Navy in 1942 as a training field for scout bomber pilots and crews. British pilots and crews also trained here. A Marine Air Warning Squadron operated from the field patrolling Florida's east coast. In Dec. 1944 the training program was changed to night fighter aircraft. In 1947 the station was deactivated and became a local airport. During the war the station had an auxiliary field, NAAS, Witham at Stuart and two outlying fields, Ft. Pierce Field, 3.5 miles NW in Lucie County and Roseland Airport, 1 mile south of Roseland.

WEST PALM BEACH AREA: This area is on the SE coast of the Florida peninsula. During the early part of the war the area's hotels and apartments were used to house military personnel as they awaited transfer to the many military installations being built in Florida.

MORRISON FIELD was activated by the AAF in Jan. 1942 as an air embarkation base for South America and the South Atlantic, and as headquarters for the South Atlantic Sector of the Army Air Transport Command. In Feb. 25 DC-3 airliners commandeered from U.S. commercial airlines arrived at Morrison together with experienced DC-3 pilots for an accelerated training program in preparation for flying the "hump" (the Himalaya Mtns.) from India to China. In April the men and planes departed for India. Meanwhile, in late Feb. a school for ferry pilots was set up here, the first in the nation. Ferry operations and ferry pilot training continued at Morrison throughout the war. In March 1942 the first flight of Lend Lease B-25 bombers going to the Soviet Union flew from Morrison Field with Pan American Airline crews at the controls. Ferry and military transport operations continued at Morrison throughout the war and Morrison handled one of the largest volumes of this type of traffic in the country. When hostilities ended the field was returned to the local community and eventually became Palm Beach International Airport.

CAMP MURPHY, now Johnathon Dickson State Park on U.S. 1 north of Jupiter, was a training camp run by the Army's Signal Corps to provide Army, Navy and Marine Corps personnel with specialized radar training.

Several WW II buildings remained in use in the park well into the postwar era.

WILLISTON is 15 miles south of Gainesville.

MONTBROOK ARMY AIR FIELD, three miles south of town, was activated in early 1942 by the Air Technical Service Command as a sub-base to both Orlando AAB and Alachua AAF, Gainesville. A bombing school was located here. In late 1944 the AAF vacated the field and returned it to its owners.

WINTER HAVEN (See Lakeland/Winter Haven/Lake Wales/Bartow Area)

ZEPHYRHILLS is 20 miles NE of Tampa.

ZEPHYRHILLS ARMY AIR FIELD, located one mile SE of town, was activated by the 3rd AF in mid-1942 as a sub-base for both Orlando AAB and Alachua AAF, Gainesville, and had an air defense school. The field was vacated by the AAF after the war and returned to its owners.

GEORGIA

Georgia is the largest state east of the Mississippi. During WW II it was very "southern" and rural, and the state's economy, based mainly on agriculture[1] except for the large industrialized area around Atlanta, had suffered badly during the Great Depression. The state's political system was firmly in the hands of the conservative wing of the Democrat Party with racial segregation the law of the land. In Washington the state's outspoken senator, Walter F. George, was a bitter and nationally-known opponent of Franklin Roosevelt and his New Deal policies of the liberal wing of the Democrat Party. One of George's main complaints was that the Government wasn't doing enough in the field of national defense. George's views were widely publicized by the nation's media because he held the powerful position of chairman of the Senate's Foreign Affairs Committee. George's critics discounted much of his rhetoric because two of the nation's largest military camps, Ft. Benning and Ft. Stewart, were in Georgia and a national military buildup would greatly benefit his state. In the end, George's views prevailed thanks to the actions of Hitler, Mussolini and Tojo.

Georgia's contribution to the national economy consisted mostly of agricultural crops such as cotton, tobacco, potatoes, grain, fruit, sugar cane, nuts, meat; forests produced like lumber and paper products and minerals such as clay, stone, cement, silica, slate, talc, umber, iron ore, manganese, mica, bauxite, coal, peat, asbestos and gold. Georgia lead the nation in the production of four minerals, barite (Barium ore), ochre (pigment in yellow coloring compounds), kaolin (used in making porcelain, medicines and paper) and fuller's earth (used in wool processing and refining of fats and oils). In manufacturing the state produced textiles, processed food, cotton seed oil, lumber and wood products. The war greatly benefitted Georgia's economy due to the influx of many manufacturing plants and military installations and the state emerged from the war more prosperous than before.

In 1942 the shooting war came to Georgia's coast when German submarines became active there. In 1943 the state became the first in the nation to allow 18-year-olds to vote.

ALBANY is a county seat in the SW part of the state.

ALBANY AIRPORT, four miles SW of town, was

[1] Forty percent of Georgia's farms were operated by tenants or share croppers.

one of the airports where Army Air Crops pilots were trained in 1940-41 under contract with a private flying school. In this case Darr Aero Tech did the training. French pilots also trained here. After the war the air field became Albany's Municipal Airport.

TURNER FIELD, four miles NE of town, was activated in July 1941 by the AAF as a school for navigators. Later, elementary and advanced pilot training in twin engine craft were offered at the field. French pilots also trained here. The field had a branch prisoner of war camp with about 500 POWs working on the field and in local agriculture. The field remained operational for some years after the war and became Turner Air Force Base. In 1967 the base was taken over by the Navy to become U.S. Naval Air Station, Albany. In 1974, however, during a Pentagon cut-back, NAS, Albany was closed. Turner had the following auxiliary fields during WW II:

• Aux. #1, Leesburg Airport, 8.5 miles NE of Leesburg
• Aux. #2, West Smithville Airport, 4.5 miles SW of Smithville
• Aux. #3, West Leesburg, Airport, 2.5 miles SW of Leesburg
• Aux. #6, North Smithville Airport, 3.5 miles NE of Smithville
• Aux. #7, Cordele Municipal Airport, 1.5 miles NE of Cordele
• Aux. #8, Vidalia-Lyons Airport, 3 miles SE of Vidalia
• Aux. #9, Tifton Municipal Airport, 2 miles SE of Tifton

AMERICUS/ANDERSONVILLE AREA: These are two small communities about 10 miles apart and 50 miles SE of Columbus.

ANDERSONVILLE NATIONAL HISTORIC SITE, just south of Andersonville on SR 49, is the site of the infamous Andersonville Prison of the American Civil War. Here, 32,000 Union soldiers were crammed into a prison compound built to hold 10,000. Conditions were deplorable and thousands died due to the overcrowding and lack of food and medical attention that the impoverished Confederate Government could not provide. On the grounds of the restored prison is a small museum dedicated to American POWs of all wars including WW II. The WW II display is the largest after that of the Civil War. A major part of the WW II display tells the story of the American nurses and other American women interned under horrible conditions by the Japanese at the Los Banos and Santo Tomas

camps in the Philippines. On the wall of the museum near the front door is a plaque commemorating the 9 American POWs who were killed at Hiroshima by the first atomic bomb blast. At the Visitors' Center, there are additional displays, a slide presentation and a gift shop. Address: Rt. 1, Box 85, Andersonville, GA 31711. Phone: 912/924-0343. Hours: Daily. Site open 8-5, museum open 8:30-5. Closed Dec. 25. Free.

SOUTHER FIELD, near Americus, was an elementary pilot training field for the 3rd AF. It had a branch prisoner of war compound with about 400 POWS who worked in agriculture and the forests.

ATHENS is a county seat 60 miles east of Atlanta.

NAVAL SUPPLY CORPS MUSEUM is located in an old Carnegie Library on the grounds of the University of Gieorgia. The museum traces the history of the Navy's Supply Corps, which began at the University, and explains its mission. On display are shipboard and field equipment, uniforms, mess hall cooking equipment, ship models, navigational equipment, ordnance, small arms, photos, paintings, flags and more. Address: Prince Av. and Oglethorpe St., Athens, GA 30606-5000. Phone: 706/354-7349 or 588-7349. Hours: M-F 9-5, closed major holidays. Free. Location: Two miles east of the Athens bypass, off the Athens/Jefferson Rd. exit.

ATLANTA AREA: Atlanta, the state capital, was the largest city in Georgia during the war, the largest manufacturing center and pacesetter for Georgia's economy and political climate. During the war it was the largest manufacturing center in the South. In nearby Marietta there was a new major aircraft manufacturing facility operated by Bell Aircraft Co. which began the war building B-17 bombers and ended the war building B-29s. In Atlanta and the surrounding area hundreds of manufacturing plants turned out a wide variety of items for America's war effort.

ATLANTA MUNICIPAL AIRPORT (Candler Field): Atlanta's local airport, 8 miles south of town, was taken over by the AAF's Air Transport Command but assigned to the Air Technical Service Command. In 1941 AAF personnel were trained here in reconnaissance and observation operations. The Navy used the field from time-to-time and a large air freight terminal was located here. Delta Airline Co. had an aircraft modification center here and modified over 1000 aircraft during the war

Patients at Lawson General Hospital are given calisthenics by one of the hospital's therapists.

including B-29s. The AAF departed after the war and the airport become Hartsfield Atlanta International Airport.

ATLANTA GENERAL DEPOT: This depot was built in 1941 just south of the Atlanta suburb of Conley. The depot warehoused a wide variety of materials for the Army and specialized in repairing and rebuilding war-damaged and worn equipment for the Army Engineer and Ordnance Corps. In early 1942 the Ordnance Automotive School was transferred here from nearby Ft. McPherson and both American and Allied personnel were trained in large numbers. There was a prisoner of war branch camp here with about 560 POWs working at the depot and in the forests. In 1944 the depot had a training program for former Italian POWs who had volunteered to work in the Italian Service Units. The Italians were taught basic military courtesy and regulations, how to take commands in English and how to use U.S. equipment. The Depot remained in full operation in the postwar years and expanded into the maintenance of aircraft. In 1962 the name was changed to Atlanta Army Depot. In 1973/4 the Depot was decommissioned and reorganized into an Army post and became the home of the U.S. 2nd Army and other units. It became known at Ft. Gillem and served as a subpost of Ft. McPherson.

LAWSON GENERAL HOSPITAL: This was an Army hospital located at Chamblee, an Atlanta suburb 10 miles NE of town. It was built in 1941 of temporary wooden construction and had 2514 beds. Lawson was associated with Ft. McPherson and specialized in neurology, amputations, neurosurgery and deep X-ray therapy. The hospital was declared surplus by the Army in June 1946 and transferred to the Veterans Administration and Federal Public Housing Authority.

FORT McPHERSON was first established Atlanta in 1867 on the site later occupied by Spelman College. It was moved to its present location, about four miles SW of downtown Atlanta, in 1885. During WW II the fort, relatively small in size for an Army post, served as an induction and reception center for IV Corps. It was one of the largest induction an reception centers in the country and processed hundreds of men daily on a production line basis. The post hospital was used extensively during and after the war to treat wounded veterans. Fort McPherson continued in operation for many years after the war. It had two subposts during WW II, Ft. Gillem, in SE Atlanta, and Ft. Buchanan in Puerto Rico.

MARIETTA FIELD, 2.5 miles SE of Marietta, had no official beginning, but grew out of the AAF's needs to cooperate with the Bell Aircraft Co. which was building bombers at its huge government-owned facility here. The AAF's Air Service Command established the first AAF units at the factory in Oct. 1942, and in June 1943 Marietta Airfield (aka Rickenbacker Field) was established as an AAF facility at the company's air field. The AAF facility adjoined the Bell Aircraft Corporation's property and was almost totally surrounded by it. In Sept. 1943 the field was put directly under the command of the Commanding General, AAF. The mission of the personnel at Marietta Field was to work with Bell Aircraft Corp. in the development and construction of the military aircraft being built at the plant and eventually take delivery of the planes produced. Transition pilot training was conducted here by the Eastern Flying Training Command. One of the planes built here was the B-29 Superfortress, the largest plane in the AAF's arsenal. Since a B-29 weighed twice as much as a B-17, longer and stronger runways were needed. Therefore, the testing of various runway designed was done here at Marietta including runways that could be built in China with coolie labor.

In 1948 the field was taken over by the US Air Force and renamed Marietta Air Force Base. In Feb. 1950 the name was changed again to Dobbins Air Force Base in honor of Capt. Charles M. Dobbins, a native of Marietta, who was killed in Sicily on July 11, 1943. Dobbins AFB remained active after the war and in the 1950s the Navy moved its U.S. Naval Air Station, Atlanta here from its former location in Chamblee, GA. The Navy built its own facilities, but both facilities shared the runways. The dual base then served throughout the Cold War.

U.S. NAVAL AIR STATION, ATLANTA: The site this station occupied during WW II, 8.5 miles NE of Atlanta near at Chamblee, GA, was first occupied by the Army during WW I and used as an Army training camp. The Army abandoned the site after that war and it lay dormant until March 1941 when the Navy took it over and converted it into a naval reserve aviation training station to meet the Navy's 15,000 plane program of that year. The Navy built runways, hangars and other facilities. In late 1942 a school to train pilots in all-weather flying and control tower operators was establishing here. Thousands of Navy and Marine pilots acquired this specialized training at NAS, Atlanta during the war. Thousands more all-weather flight instructors were trained for the Navy, Marines, AAF, British and Free French. The Navy's Air Ferry Command also operated from the field. In 1946 the station became a naval reserve air station again and all-weather training operations were continued. In 1955 the Navy moved its operations to Dobbins Air Force Base near Marietta, GA where they shared the longer runways with the Air Force. This facility then became the DeKalb-Peachtree Airport. During the war the station had the following outlying fields:

- Gainesville Airport, 1.5 miles south of Gainesville
- Greensboro-High Point (Lindley Fd.), 8 miles NW of Greensboro, NC
- Greenville Municipal Airport, 1.5 miles NW of Greenville, NC
- Memorial Airport, 2.5 miles SW of Spartanburg, SC
- Rome Airport, 3 miles NW of Rome
- Spartanburg Airport, Spartanburg, SC

AUGUSTA is in east central Georgia on the SC state line.

AUGUSTA ARSENAL was a pre-war Army arsenal located three miles from town at the Harrisonville RR Yards. When the war started this arsenal still had an inventory of Civil War caissons. The arsenal was utilized throughout the war to store ammunition and general supplies. Its personnel also did maintenance work on ammunition.

AUGUSTA-RICHMOND COUNTY MUSEUM: This museum, in downtown Augusta, has a full-room display on the WW II cruiser "Augusta". This warship saw action in the Mediterranean and at Normandy and was host to several high level conferences among Allied leaders. A dinner menu bearing the signatures of Franklin Roosevelt, Winston Churchill, Gen. George Marshall, Adm. Ernest King and others is on display from one of the conferences. Address: 540 Telfair St., Augusta, GA 30901. Phone: 706/722-8454. Hours: Tues.-Sat. 10-5, Sun. 2-5. Closed holidays. Admission charged.

DANIEL FIELD, four miles west of downtown, was Augusta's local pre-war airport. It was taken over by the AAF in 1941 and used for training and as a replacement depot. There was a rehabilitation center here and the field had a branch prisoner of war camp with about 1200

POWs working on the field and in the nearby forests. After the war the air field was returned to the community.

CAMP GORDON, 15 miles SW of town, was activated 12 days after the Japanese attack on Pearl Harbor. The camp had been built to train Army divisions. During the war the 4th and 26th Infantry Divs., and 10th Armored Div. trained here one after the other. All three of these divisions served in Gen. George Patton's 3rd Army in Europe. In 1942 Camp Gordon acquired a school for training military police. Many civilians were also trained here in police work. The camp had an Army disciplinary barracks and a main prisoner of war camp. The camp's cemetery contains the graves of 23 German POWs and one Italian POW who died while at the camp. After the war Camp Gordon became a separation center and in 1948 the Army's Southeastern Signal School was established here. In 1956 it became a permanent Army installation and was renamed Fort Gordon. In 1974 the Army concentrated the bulk of its communication training here and in the postwar years Fort Gordon became one of the largest military communications and electronics training centers in the world.

U.S. Army Signal Corps and Fort Gordon Museum: This museum is on the grounds of Fort Gordon and focuses on the history of communications within the U.S. Army and tells the story of the Signal Corps since its beginning in 1860. Permanent displays feature early telephones made by Alexander Graham Bell and prototype wireless equipment made by Marconi. Other displays include a large exhibit on the 10th Armored Div. highlighting its activities during WW II[2]. Outside the museum are heavy weapons and tracked vehicles. Address: ATZH-DPM, Bldg. 36305, Ft. Gordon, GA 30905-5020. Phone: 706/791-2818 or 780-2818. Hours: M-F 8-4; Sat., Sun. & holidays noon-5. Closed Easter, Independence Day, Thanksgiving, Dec. 25, and Jan. 1. Free. Location: From I-20, take I-520 south to Deans Bridge Rd. (US-1). Go south on Deans Bridge Rd. five miles to gate #5. Museum is on the left hand side of the road two miles inside gate #5 at 37th St.

OLIVER GENERAL HOSPITAL came into being when the Government purchased the multistory Forest Hills Hotel in Augusta in late 1942. It was converted into an Army hospital and many wooden buildings were built to the rear of the former hotel making it a 2240-bed hospital. Oliver specialized in general medicine and orthopedic surgery. After the war Oliver was transferred to the Veterans Administration.

BAINBRIDGE is an agricultural community in SW corner of Georgia.

BAINBRIDGE ARMY AIR FIELD, 6 miles NW of town, was the town's pre-war airport. It was occupied by the 3rd AF in 1941 as a training field for the 50,000 Pilot Training Program. The field had a branch prisoner of war camp holding about 250 POWs who worked in the forests. After the war the air field became the

[2]Spiro T. Agnew, future Vice President of the U.S., served as a company commander in this division. He served in combat in Europe and won the Bronze Star.

Oliver General Hospital was a large Army General Hospital converted from the Forest Hills Hotel.

local airport again. Auxiliary fields during the war were:

- Aux. #1, Donalsonville Airport, 1 mile south of Donalsonville
- Aux. #2, Reynoldsville Airport, 2 miles SW of Reynoldsville
- Aux. #3, Faceville Airport, 3.5 miles south of Faceville
- Aux. #4, Vada Airport, 3 miles NE of Vada
- Aux. #5, Babcock Airport, 3.5 miles NE of Boykin
- Aux. #6, Commodore Decatur Airport, 2 miles west of Bainbridge

BRUNSWICK AND JEKYLL ISLAND: Brunswick is on Georgia's south-central coast. During the war it had two shipbuilders, the Brunswick Marine Construction Corp. which built cargo ships and steel tugs and J.A. Jones Shipyard which built Liberty ships.

JEKYLL ISLAND: In 1886 a group of America's wealthiest men, including John D. Rockefeller, J.P. Morgan, Jay Gould and Joseph Pulitzer bought Jekyll Island and turned it into an exclusive hunting preserve and get-away for themselves and their friends. They built a large clubhouse, elaborate "cottages" and pier facilities on the island's west side where they could dock their yachts. Those who had residences on the island became known as the Jekyll Island Club, or just "The Club". By the 1940s the facilities had come into the hands of their children and heirs who took much less interest in the Island's amenities than had their elders. Nevertheless, there was a very active social life on the island and it was still very exclusive. After the U.S. entered the war and German submarines began operating along the Georgia coast, maintaining the island and the life-style it represented became untenable. The island, which at that time had no causeway to the mainland, was undefendable. It was feared that a German raiding party could easily come ashore and kidnap, or otherwise harm, some of America's most prominent citizens. Also, the continuation of such an opulent life-style in the midst of a war was considered unpatriotic. The wealthy owners and residents of the island could see these dangers and prepared for the closing down of "The Club". Besides, their help had left for higher paying factory jobs, there were shortages of fuel, and among other things, many of their yachts were being requisitioned by the Navy or put in storage for the duration. The end came in April 1942, and some say it came in a most dramatic way. The story is still told in the area that it was Gen. George S. Patton who shut down the island. Patton was in Georgia at the time and the story goes that President Roosevelt personally ordered Patton to close the island because Patton, a multi-millionaire, was one of their own. It is reported that the General arrived on the island around dinner time on that fateful night in April, went straightaway to the club house where some of the residents were dining, signed the guest register, dramatically slammed it shut, and announced in a commanding voice that "The Club" was closed for the duration.

J. P. Morgan's yacht, "Corsair". It was turned over to the Coast Guard during the war.

Whether or not this story is true, the fact remains that the island was vacated soon afterwards and remained virtually abandoned during the rest of the war. It is also claimed that club's guest register, with the General's signature in it, has been preserved. Remaining on the island were a few Coastguardsmen who patrolled the beached and lived in the sumptuous cottages. The buildings deteriorated due to neglect and vandalism, and by the end of the war the former owners showed no interest in returning. Eventually the state bought the island and turned it into a state park. It has become a popular resort for vacationers, tourists and golfers. There's a small museum on the island that tells the full history of the island with a brief display on its end during WW II.

U.S. NAVAL AIR STATION, GLYNCO (LTA): This air station, 6 miles north of Brunswick, was built by the Navy as a blimp station in 1942 to combat the enemy submarine menace off the U.S. east coast. It became fully operational in Jan. 1943 with two large all-wood blimp hangars, two mooring circles, 12 blimps, a helium plant and other necessary buildings. By this time, however, the worst of the submarine warfare along the east coast had passed. Yet, the station's existence, and other anti-submarine measures taken by the U.S. armed forces, insured that if and when enemy submarines returned they would do so at great risk. Blimps from NAS, Glynco continued to carry out coastal patrols and air-sea rescues for the remained of the war. In July 1945 the station was reduced to an air facility and became a storage and salvage yard for some 800 Navy aircraft. German prisoners of war, awaiting transportation to Europe, were brought in to work in the yard. The station was reduced to standby status after the war, but in 1951 was made operational again as a blimp station for the duration of the Korean War. From 1952 on, the Navy moved other operations to the field including jets, and for several years in the 1950s is was the only naval station in the country operation all types of aircraft; blimps, propeller planes, jets and helicopters. In 1973, during a Defense Dept. economy program, NAS, Glynco was disestablished and eventually became a local airport, Glynco Jetport.

U.S. NAVAL AIR STATION, ST. SIMONS ISLAND: Before the war this was Malcolm McKinnon Airport on the southern end of St. Simons Island about 8 miles east of Brunswick. In 1942 the Navy took over a part of the field and built a small air station for the training of Navy and Marine officers and enlisted men in the operation of Combat Information Centers (CIC). These are the units aboard warships that participate in the control the fleet's aircraft, sometime under the most trying conditions of combat. NAS, St. Simons Island was never very big in comparison with other naval stations. The station had several radar stations in the area, its own aircraft, classrooms, mockups of destroyer and cruiser CICs and, since most of the flying was over water, a Coast Guard Air-Sea Rescue Unit. Much of the training was copied after, and coordinated with, the British Navy's equivalent aircraft control center at Yeovilton, England. Commercial airlines and local pilots continued to use the field alomg

with the Navy during the war. At war's end the station was rapidly scaled down . . so rapidly in fact that a personnel shortage developed in March 1946 and some German prisoners of war, awaiting transportation back to Europe, were brought in temporarily to perform some of the necessary jobs to keep the station operational. In 1947 the Navy withdrew altogether and Malcolm McKinnon Airport continued operating as a civilian airport. During the war the station had an outlying field, St. Marys Airport, 2 miles NW of St. Marys, GA shared with NAS, Jacksonville.

Sterling silver on display in the Hall of Flags at the National Infantry Museum, Ft. Benning, GA. The silver pieces were awarded to individual servicemen for outstanding service.

COLUMBUS is in the west-central part of the state on the Alabama state line.

FORT BENNING, just south of Columbus on U.S. 27, is known as the "Home of the Infantry". In 1826 the Army chose the site for its Infantry School of Instruction, but this venture was short-lived and the school closed in 1828. In 1918 the Army returned and built a temporary infantry training facility which had branched off from Fort Sill, OK. In 1919 several Army schools were combined and moved here to become the Army's new Infantry School. The Army liked the area's terrain and climate for infantry training so in 1922 the post was enlarged and renamed Fort Benning. Benning was continually expanded during the 1930s, which was very unusual for those money-tight depression years. During those years the Army's Tank School was located here, but eventually moved to Fort Knox, KY. Yet, armored tanks continued to train here. As war loomed in Europe, construction spurted again. The Fort became a huge reception center for IV Corps and the home of the 1st and 4th Infantry Divs. It had the largest Officer Candidate School in the country, an airborne training school and its own air field, Lawson Field, three miles SW of Ft. Benning operated by the AAF's I Troop Carrier Command. One of the Army's first airborne units, the 509th Parachute Infantry Battalion, trained here and was the first American parachute unit to go into

action in WW II, jumping into North Africa in Nov. 1942. The Fort continued to expand during WW II and thousands of infantrymen and paratroopers trained here. In 1945 the post population peaked at 90,000. There was a 2200-man prisoner of war camp here with the POWs working on the post and in agriculture. During 1944-45 Italian Service Units (ISU) worked at the camp. In the latter months of the war one of several secret re-education schools for German POWs was set up here to train Germans who were willing to work for the American occupation government in Germany when they returned home. Fort Benning functioned throughout the Cold War and was home of the famed U.S. Army Infantry School which became the nation's undisputed representative of infantry doctrine, tactics and weapons. The Infantry School's motto is "Follow Me".

National Infantry Museum: This excellent museum, on the grounds of Ft. Benning, follows the American foot soldier across more than two centuries of history. His victories, defeats and day-to-day life are interpreted in the paintings, sculptures and artifacts on display. In the Hall of Flags on the museum's main floor is a display containing the signature of every U.S. president, a weapons collection depicting the evolution of the infantryman's rifle, a collection of band instruments, an exhibit honoring the famous infantry general Omar Bradley and more. Address: Bldg. 396, Attn: ATZB-DPT-MUS Ft. Benning, GA 31905-5273. Hours: M-F 8-4:30, Sat.-Sun. 12:30-4:30.

Some of the WW II equipment on display at Georgia Veterans Memorial State Park.

Phone: 706/545-2958/4762. Free. Location: At the end of I-185 turn onto Dixie Rd. and proceed approximately one mile to First Division Rd. Turn right and proceed approximately one mile to Baltzell Av. Turn right, museum is on Baltzell Av.

CORDELE is 60 miles south of Macon on I-75.

GEORGIA VETERANS MEMORIAL STATE PARK is 9 miles west of town on US 280 and was established as a permanent memorial to all U.S. veterans. It is a typical state park with facilities for camping, hiking, boating, fishing, golfing and picnicking. The park has a small military museum and a significant outdoor display of military equipment and aircraft. Items of several wars are on display, but the WW II display is the largest. The museum is named after Gen. Courtney Hodges, a Georgia native, who commanded the U.S. 1st Army at the Battle of the Bulge. Address: Rt. 3 Box 382, Cordele, GA 31015. Hours: Museum daily 8-4:30, park daily 7 am-10 pm. Phone: 912/273-2371. Free.

DOUGLAS, in the south-central part of the state, is home to South Georgia College. The college had an air field and a flying school which was contracted by the Army Air Corps during 1940-41 to provide elementary flight training for Air Corps cadets.

DUBLIN is 60 miles SE of Macon on I-16.

DUBLIN AIRPORT, 4.5 miles NW of town, became a training field for the AAF early in the war and was an auxiliary field to Columbia AAF, Columbia, SC. The Navy also used the field on occasions. The base had a branch prisoner of war camp with about 300 POWs who worked in the surrounding forests and at other tasks. The airport was returned to the local community after the war.

FORT OGLETHORPE is in the NW corner of the state about 10 miles SW of Chattanooga, TN.

FORT OGLETHORPE, 9 miles east of the town of Fort Oglethorpe, was built in 1903 on the Chickamauga battlefield of the Civil War. During WW II the fort was a reception and induction center for IV Corps, a training camp

WAC recruits undergoing basic training at Ft. Oglethorpe.

The 24th Infantry Division & Fort Stewart Museum at Fort Stewart near Hinesville, GA.

for cavalry regiments and had a Provost Marshal Officer Candidate School. In 1942 Oglethorpe became one of three training centers in the country of enlisted WAACs (later WACs)[3]. In late 1942 the fort was one of the first Army camps to have a prisoner of war camp because it had available space when POWs began arriving in this country in large numbers from North Africa. The camp held about 300 POWs who worked on the base. The fort remained a U.S. military reservation throughout the Cold War.

HINESVILLE is a county seat 35 miles SW of Savannah.

CAMP STEWART sprawled for 280,000 acres north of the town of Hinesville. It was named after Revolutionary War General Daniel Stewart, the great-great-grandfather of Eleanor Roosevelt, and is the largest military installation in side east of the Mississippi River. It was established in 1940 as a training camp for anti-aircraft units, a mission it fulfilled throughout the war. The camp had its own air field, Camp Stewart Army Air Field, 3.5 miles NE of Hinesville, which also served as a sub-base for Chatham AAF. There was a main prisoner of war compound here with about 400 POWS who worked on the base. Camp Stewart reached its peak population in 1943 with 55,000 residents. Near the end of the war it became a demobilization center. The Army retained the camp after the war and in 1953 it became a training camp for armored, anti-aircraft and mechanized infantry units. In 1956 it was designated Fort Stewart and continued in operation throughout the Cold War.

24th Infantry Division and Fort Stewart Museum: This museum is on the grounds of Fort Stewart and pays tribute to the 24th Infantry Div., a postwar resident, and records the history of Fort Stewart. The 24th Infantry Div., known as the "Hawaiian Div." was in residence at Schofield Barracks, Hawaii on Dec. 7, 1941 when the Japanese attacked the islands. Some of the displays in the museum

[3] The other two centers were Ft. Des Moines, IA and Daytona Beach, FL.

tell of those days. Outside is The Museum Park with tanks, anti-aircraft guns, searchlights and other large weapons, many of them from WW II. The museum maintains a branch museum at Hunter Army Airfield which includes a replica of a WW II-era ready room of the 8th AF. Museum Address: Wilson & Utility Sts., Fort Stewart, GA 31314. Phone: 912/767-4480. Hours: daily 10-6. Closed Jan. 1, Thanksgiving, Dec. 25. Free.

JEKYLL ISLAND (See Brunswick/Jekyll Island)

MACON is in the geographic center of the state.

COCHRAN FIELD, 10 miles south of Macon, later became Lewis Burgess Wilson Airport. It was operated by the AAF's Personnel Distribution Command during the war as a training field. It also had an AAF convalescent hospital. Auxiliary fields during the war were:

- Aux. #2, Perry Airport, 5 miles east of Perry
- Aux. #3, Harris Airport, 3 miles NE of Ft. Valley
- Aux. #4, Byron Airport, 3 miles west of Byron
- Aux. #5, Myrtle Airport, 4 miles east of Myrtle

HERBERT SMART FIELD, five miles east of town, was a local airport before the war. It was occupied by the AAF at the time Wellston Depot (Warner Robins AAF), was being built. Some of the units scheduled to operate out of the depot used Smart Field until their air field was ready. Later, Smart Field became an auxiliary field to Warner Robins AAF for the duration of the war.

WARNER ROBINS ARMY AIR FIELD was 14.5 miles SE of Macon and 1.5 miles NE of Warner Robins, GA. It was activated in 1942 by the AAF to be used by both the Air Technical Services Command and the Air Transport Command. A large air depot opened here in March 1942, and was first known as Wellston Depot, after the nearby hamlet of Wellston. In Sept. 1942 the depot was renamed Warner Robins Air Depot after Brig. Gen. Augustine Warner Robins who had devised a system of cataloging AAF supplies that the AAF had recently adopted[4]. Gen. Warner Robins died in June 1940 while serving as the commandant of the Air Corps Training Center at Randolph Field, TX. The air depot soon acquired a basic flight training center and the enlarged facility

[4] The Robins System is still used today by the Air Force.

was named Warner Robins Army Air Field. Eventually the town of Wellston changed its name to Warner Robins, GA. During the war, both the depot and training facilities grew rapidly. The depot became one of the first three air depots in the country to acquire an engine overhaul facility. The training center acquired a medical service school, a chemical warfare training center, an air freight depot, an AAF regional hospital and a signal training school. After the war the base continued in operation and was renamed Robins Air Force Base in 1948. It later became the Air Logistics Center and was the largest single industrial complex in Georgia.

Museum of Aviation: This museum, on the grounds of Robins Air Force Base, is one of the largest air museums in the country. The museum has a large display of aircraft, mostly of U.S. make, and many of them from WW II. Some of the aircraft are inside the spacious museum along with exhibits of small arms, ordnance, uniforms, field equipment, navigational equipment, communications equipment, a Norden bomb sight, flags, photos, paintings, captured enemy equipment and more. The Georgia Aviation Hall of Fame is here honoring distinguished Georgia airmen. Address: PO Box 2469, Warner Robins, GA 31099. Phone: 912/926-6870/4242. Hours: Tues.-Sun. 10-5, closed Jan. 1, Thanksgiving and Dec. 25. Free. Location: Entrance to museum is off SR 247 south of Russell Pkwy.

CAMP WHEELER was an infantry replacement training camp 7 miles SE of Macon. It was established during WW I and reactivated for WW II. Wheeler had a main prisoner of war camp with 1500 POWs working at the camp and in the area. The camp was closed in Jan. 1946.

MOULTRIE is a county seat 30 miles SE of Albany.

SPENCE FIELD, five miles SE of town, was a local air field taken over by the AAF in 1941 to meet the needs of the 30,000 Pilot Training Program. The field offered basic flight training. There was a branch prisoner of war camp here holding 500 POWs who worked at the field and in the local food industry. After the war, the field was returned to its owners. Wartime auxiliary fields were:

- Aux. #1, Berlin Airport, 3 miles SE of Berlin
- Aux. #2, Norman Airport, 3.5 miles NW of Norman Park
- Aux. #3, Moultrie Municipal Airport, 7 miles south of Moultrie
- Aux. #4, New River Airport, 6 miles SW of Nashville

ROME is in the NW corner of the state. In front of City Hall is a bronze replica of the famous Roman statue of the she-wolf nursing Romulus and Remus, the founders of Rome, Italy. This statue was give to the city of Rome, GA in 1929 by Benito Mussolini.

BATTEY GENERAL HOSPITAL was built in Rome in 1943. It had 1826 beds and specialized in general medicine, orthopedic surgery and psychiatry. In 1945 the hospital was transferred to the state.

SAVANNAH, on the northern coast of Georgia at the mouth of the Savannah River, was Georgia's second largest city during the war. The city had two shipyards during the war building minesweepers and merchant ships.

CHATHAM ARMY AIR FIELD, 7 miles NW of Savannah, was Savannah Municipal Airport #2 before the war. During the war it was operated by the 3rd AF as a sub-base to Hunter Field and provided crew training in heavy bombers. In late 1944 Chatham was expanded to be an operating field for B-29 bombers. There was a branch prisoner of war camp here with over 200 POWs who worked on the field. After the war the air field became Savannah Intl. Airport.

HUNTER FIELD was SW of, and adjacent to Savannah. Before the war it was a local air field that had been leased by the Army Air Corps in Oct. 1940 to become an operational field for a light bombardment group from Barksdale Field, Shreveport, LA. At that time, living facilities at the field were almost non-existent and the officers and men lived in tents. Hunter was closely associated with Camp Steward and came under the control of the 3rd AF. It was the home of the 3rd AF Staging Wing and was also used by the Air Transport Command which had a large air freight terminal here. Hunter was an aerial port of embarkation, had an AAF regional hospital and a branch prisoner of war camp here with 550 POWs working on the base. Hunter Field remained operative after the war.

SAVANNAH QUARTERMASTER DEPOT was built in Savannah early in the war for the Quartermaster Corps, but was loaned to the Army Ordnance Corps for the storage of ammunition, a function it performed throughout the war.

FORT SCREVEN is 20 miles SE of Savannah on Tybee Island. The fort was built in 1897 to defend the entrance to the Savannah River and was occupied by the Army until 1945. Its Battery Garland has became a museum and is part of the Tybee Museum which contains the fort, an old lighthouse and the keeper's cottage. Address: Tybee Museum, 30 Meddin Dr., Tybee Island, GA. Phone: 912/786-5801. Hours: Apr. through

Sept. daily 10-6, rest of year M-F noon-4, Sat.-Sun. 10-4. Closed Jan. 1, Thanksgiving and Dec. 25. Admission charged.

SHIPS OF THE SEA MARITIME MUSEUM, in downtown Savannah, is a museum devoted primarily to sailing ships. It does, however, have displays and models on some ships of WW II. Of interest is a 13 foot model of the cruiser "Savannah" of WW II and a model of the WW II U.S. freighter "Juliette Low", named in honor of the founder of the Girl Scouts and a Savannah resident. Address: 503 E. River St. and 504 Bay ST., Savannah, GA 31401. Phone: 912/232-1511. Hours: daily 10-5, closed Jan. 1, St. Patrick's Day, Thanksgiving and Dec. 25. Admission charged.

THOMASVILLE is a county seat 40 miles west of Valdosta.

FINNEY GENERAL HOSPITAL was built in Thomasville in 1943 to treat war wounded. The hospital was of temporary tile and gypsum board construction and had 1994 beds. Finney specialized in general medicine, syphilis, general and orthopedic surgery and psychiatry. In Dec. 1945 it was transferred to the Veterans Administration.

THOMASVILLE ARMY AIR FIELD, 8.5 miles NE of town, was controlled by the 3rd AF as an operating base and a training field for fighter pilots. It was a sub-base to Dale Mabry. The field had a branch prisoner of war camp holding over 200 POWs who worked on the field.

TOCCOA is a mountain community in the NE corner of the state.

FORT TOCCOA, near the city of Toccoa, was a temporary training camp used by the Army during the war. It was activated in Jan. 1943 and provided basic training for new recruits. Paratroopers were also trained here. The fort was closed in Feb. 1944.

VALDOSTA is 70 miles west of Savannah on I-75.

MOODY FIELD, 10 miles NE of town, was established in June 1941 by the 1st AF as a training base for air crews of light bombers. In Feb. 1942 the field acquired an advanced pilot training school and had a branch prisoner of war camp with about 500 POWs who worked on the field and in agriculture. Moody was retained after the war and in 1948 was renamed Moody Air Force Base by the US Air Force. During the Cold War Moody AFB served the Air Transport Command and the Tactical Air Command. Auxiliary fields during the war were:

- Aux. #1, Rocky Ford Airport, 9 miles SE of Quitman
- Aux. #2, Lake Park Airport, 1 mile SW of Lake Park
- Aux. #3, Bemis Airport, 5 miles NE of Bemis
- Aux. #5, Valdosta Municipal Airport, 2.5 miles south of Valdosta

WARM SPRINGS is in west-central Georgia 25 miles NE of Columbus.

LITTLE WHITE HOUSE STATE HISTORIC SITE: This is the small cottage built by Franklin Roosevelt for his personal use whenever he came to Warm Springs. Roosevelt liked coming here because he felt that the local waters were beneficial to his health and strengthened his

Some of the displays at Warner Robins Air Force Museum, Warner Robins, GA.

The Little White House at Warm Springs, GA. President Franklin Roosevelt's private residence and the place where he died, April 12, 1945.

legs which were crippled by polio in 1921. This house was the only house he ever built for himself. FDR personally selected the site, used it first as a private picnic grounds and later built the cottage. During his years in office many notable people visited the cottage as FDR's guests. On April 12, 1945[5], FDR was sitting in the living room of the house with two other people writing a speech and having his portrait painted by one of the visitors. He suddenly put his hand to his head saying "I have a terrific headache", and then lapsed into unconsciousness. He had had a cerebral hemorrhage and died soon afterwards. He was taken to Washington, DC for a state funeral and then buried at his family estate in Hyde Park, NY.

The cottage, the nearby servants quarters and other structures have been preserved as they were when FDR lived here. Two of his automobiles, especially equipped with hand controls, are on dis-

[5] Hitler and Mussolini also died during April 1945

play along with many other personal items. The cottage is open to the public and guides are available to answer questions. There is a 12-minute movie "FDR in Georgia", a snack bar and a gift shop. Address: Warm Springs, GA 31830. Phone: 706/655-3511. Hours: daily 9-5 except Thanksgiving and Dec. 25. Last tour begins at 4:15. Admission charged. Location: On SR 85W 1/4 mile south of the Warm Springs traffic light.

FRANKLIN D. ROOSEVELT STATE PARK, five miles SE of Pine Mountain, is a 10,000-acre park named after Warm Springs' famous resident. Camping, picnicking, hiking, boating, fishing and swimming are available at the park.

WARNER ROBINS (See Macon)

WAYCROSS is in the SE corner of the state.

WAYCROSS FIELD, four miles NW of town, was the local airport which was taken over by the 3rd AF for the duration of the war as a training field for fighter pilots. It was a sub-base of Drew Field, FL and had a branch prisoner of war camp with about 250 POWs who worked in agriculture. After the war the field was returned to the community.

IDAHO

Senator William E. Borah of Idaho at the Republican National Convention in 1936 during his unsuccessful bid for the Republican nomination for president.

For a state with only 534,000 people, Idaho made a meaningful contribution to America's war effort. There were several major military installations in the state, several important manufacturing operations, a relocation camp for ethnic Japanese and about 20 prisoner of war camps. POWs proved to be a significant source of labor in the state which had vast agricultural potential and so few people. Many Mexicans were employed in Idaho also, especially in the sugar beet industry. The State had a sizeable number of ethnic Japanese, most of whom lived in the Snake River Valley. Since Idaho was not included in the west coast military defense zone, Idaho's ethnic Japanese were not required to relocate. There continued presents in the state caused no major problems and they lived, for the most part, in harmony with their non-Japanese neighbors.

All eight of the states major airports were used by the military as well as many smaller air fields. The state produced grain, beet sugar,

hay, potatoes, gold, silver, copper, lead and zinc. In early 1942 known deposits of tungsten were developed in Idaho when America's usual supply of this important alloy was cut off from Spain. Before the war there were strong isolationist sympathies in Idaho personified by Idaho's popular Senator, William E. Borah, who was one of the best-known leaders of the isolationist movement in America. During his long career in Washington he ran for President, opposed America's participation in the League of Nations and the World Court but, ironically, supported many of President Roosevelt's liberal New Deal policies. Borah did not live to see America go to war. He died in 1940 while still in office. In the later months of the war, Idaho, like the other western states, was subjected to the Japanese bombing balloon campaign, but they caused virtually no damage in the state.

AMERICAN FALLS is in the Snake River

Valley 20 miles SW of Pocatello. Remnants of two Japanese bombing balloons were found near this community; the first on Feb. 13, 1945 when fragments of an envelope and shrouds were found, and the second on Mar. 13, 1945 when an envelope, 19 shrouds and ballast gear were found.

ATHOL is in Idaho's panhandle 20 miles north of Coeur D'Alene.

U.S. NAVAL TRAINING STATION, FARRAGUT: This inland naval training station is now Farragut State Park and only a handful of the original structures of this once large naval station remain. Soon after the U.S. entered the war the Navy saw the need for three new training stations and this site on a peninsula at the southern end of Idaho's Lake Pend Oreille, was selected[1]. It comprised 4050 acres of virgin forest land and was far enough inland to be

[1] The other two sites were Bainbridge, MD and Sampson, NY.

This is the former brig, the largest remaining WW II structure at NTS, Farragut. The dark vertical wooden panels cover the original barred windows. The structure became the park's maintenance building.

About 100 WW II barracks buildings stand mothballed and furnished at Gowen Field ready to receive National Guardsmen and Reservists from 11 western states in the event of a national emergency. The barracks buildings stand out because they are painted in different pastel colors.

safe from a possible enemy attack. Construction began in April 1942 and the station was commissioned on Aug. 2, 1942. On Aug. 17 President Roosevelt paid a visit to the station during his secret tour of the U.S. The station had 6 separate boot camps, each training new recruits in 6 to 8 week programs. At its peak Farragut had 650 frame buildings, plus 538 family housing units and several dormitories for station personnel. Farragut's population reached 65,000 people and was larger than any city in Idaho. It also was the second largest naval training center in the world. The station had schools for hospital corpsmen, cooks and bakers, electricians, gunner's mates, class C instructors and small boat handlers. There was also a main prisoner of war camp here holding 825 German POWs. During the war over 293,000 men and women trained here. In Sept. 1945, with all training ended, Farragut became a distribution and separation center. Because of its remote location, however, very few servicemen were processed. In 1946 the Navy abandoned the site and parts of it became a state park and Farragut College and Technical Institute, which survived only until 1949. A small area was retained by the Navy near Bayview and became the U.S. Naval Acoustic Research Detachment Facility.

The Park Office has an interesting and informative display on NTS, Farragut and a drive around the park will reveal many foundations and the few remaining structures. Address: Farragut State Park, East 13400 Ranger Rd., Athol, ID 83801. Phone: 208/683-2425. Open year around. Motor vehicle entrance fee required.

BOISE, in the SE corner of the state, is the capital of Idaho and the state's largest city. On Feb. 25, 1945 a Japanese bombing balloon, still very much intact with a live demolition charge still aboard, was discovered near the city.

BOISE BARRACKS, 1.5 miles NE of downtown Boise, became a Veterans Administration Hospital and the Idaho State Veteran's Home after the war. The Barracks, the successor of two earlier military installations known as Camp Boise and Fort Boise, was founded in 1863 as a temporary encampment for U.S. soldiers protecting emigrant trains against Shoshone Indians. The post became permanent and was named Boise Barracks in 1879. From 1939 the post was used as an Idaho National Guard encampment and a training center. The post also had its own air field. In Mar. 1944 the post was closed and much of the land sold off. The post's hospital remained in operation and became a V. A. Hospital and Veteran's Home. Many of the beautiful old stone buildings remain in use.

GOWEN FIELD was four miles south of downtown Boise off of present-day I-84. Before the war it was known as Boise Air Field and was the area's local airport. In Dec. 1940 the airport was taken over by the Army Air Corps as a training field for pilots and crews of medium bombers. In 1941 the field was renamed Gowen Field. In Dec. 1941, just days after the Japanese attacked Pearl Harbor, a squadron of B-26 bombers stationed at Gowen was rushed to Alaska because Japanese invasion fears there. Meanwhile Gowen became a sub-base of Walla Walla AAF, WA and served as a training base for B-17 crews. In 1946 the Idaho Air National Guard acquired most of the WW II facilities on the southern section of Gowen Field and retained its wartime name. New commercial air facilities were built on the north side of the field and became Boise Municipal Airport. During the height of the Cold War Gowen Field was designated as an assembly center of National Guard and Reserve units from 11 western states in the event of a national emergency. For this purpose about 100 WW II barracks buildings were preserved and mothballed standing ready, fully furnished, to receive and house a sudden influx of service personnel. The barracks were all painted in different pastel colors. Also at Gowen Field five WW II hangars remained in use for several decades.

CALDWELL is 22 miles west of Boise on I-84. **WARHAWK AIR MUSEUM** is a privately-owned air museum located at Caldwell Industrial Airport along the east side of I-84. On display are two P-40 fighters, a P-40E Kittyhawk and a P-40N Warhawk. Also on display is a P51-D, other aircraft, engines, captured enemy equipment, uniforms, posters, photographs, a Norden bombsight, WW II sweetheart and mothers pins, V-Mail and war stamps, snow skis for a P-51 and much more. Address: Caldwell Industrial Airport, 4917 Aviation Way, Caldwell, ID 83605. Phone: 208/454-2854. Hours: Vary, please phone. Admission charged.

IDAHO FALLS is in the Snake River Valley 50 miles NE of Pocatello. It was one of almost two dozen Idaho communities that had branch prisoner of war camps with POWs working in local agriculture. On Aug. 9, 1945 remnants of a Japanese bombing balloon were found near the town consisting of an envelope, a gas relief valve and a number of shrouds.

KETCHUM, 70 miles north of Twin Falls, is the site of the famous Sun Valley Resort. The resort was founded in 1937 by Averell Harriman, the former Chairman of the Board of the Union Pacific Railroad, as a ski resort for the wealthy. Because of the war the resort closed in 1943, but in June of that year, it was taken over by the Navy and used as a hospital. It operated under the name U.S. Naval Convalescent Hospital, Sun Valley with 1800 beds for enlisted men and 300 for officers. Meanwhile, its founder Harriman, became an important member of President Roosevelt's Administration. In 1946 the resort was returned to its owners.

KOOSKIA is in Idaho's panhandle 60 miles SE of Moscow.

KOOSKIA INTERNMENT CAMP, was located 29 miles east of Kooskia on U.S. 12 at the mouth of Canyon Creek as it empties into the Lochsa River. The camp was built in 1935 as a prison camp for Federal prisoners working on the Lewis and Clark Highway (U.S. 12). It was know as Lochsa Federal Prison Camp and was one of only two such camps in the nation.

One of two P-40 fighters on display at the Warhawk Museum, Caldwell, ID.

During the early part of WW II the camp was converted into an internment camp for male Japanese aliens and held about 150 internees. The first aliens arrived in May 1943 and, like the Federal prisoners before them, were employed, if they chose to work, on road building. Others worked in the camp. Those working on the roads were paid $50.00 a month, and those working in camp were paid $25.00 a month. It was an open camp where the guards did not carry weapons and the internees were free to roam the immediate area with minimal supervision. The guards and their families lived 1/2 mile away in what became the U.S. Forest Service's Apgar Campground. Most people at the camp agreed that, under the circumstances, life was good here. This was confirmed by the fact that there were no escape attempts. In 1945 the aliens departed and the camp was closed. Over the years the buildings have been demolished or relocated elsewhere.

MINIDOKA RELOCATION CAMP, (See Twin Falls)

MOUNTAIN HOME is in the Snake River Valley 50 miles SE of Boise.

MOUNTAIN HOME ARMY AIR FIELD was built by the 2nd AF between Nov. 1942 and mid-1943 as a training base for pilots an crews of heavy bombers. The field had extra long runways and specialized in training for blind landings. Crews used the huge Boardman Bombing Range near Boardman, OR and the Craters of the Moon Air Force Range near Carey, ID. In Feb. 1945 the field was placed under the command of the 4th AF and in April 1945 it passed to the Continental Air Command and became a sub-base of Gowen Field and then a sub-base of Walla Walla Field, WA. In 1948 the Air Force took over and renamed the facility Mountain Home Air Force Base. From 1950 on, the base closed and reopened several times.

POCATELLO is in the Snake River Valley near the SE corner of the state and was the state's second largest city during the war.

POCATELLO ARMY AIR BASE, west of Pocatello off of present-day I-84, was built by the 2nd AF and began, in Oct. 1942, training pilots and crews in B-17 and B-24 bombers. All phases of crew training was done here; pilots, navigators, bombardiers and gunners. In Feb. 1944 fighter pilot training in P-39s and P-48s was added.

Three of the huge factory buildings of the former U.S. Naval Ordnance Plant, Pocatello. These, and several more like them, remained in use as part of an industrial park. In the foreground is Naval Ordnance Plant Park, a city park that was once a part of the naval plant.

Some foreign pilots trained here including a squadron of Mexican fighter pilots, flying P-47s, who later served in the Southwest Pacific. The base also had a branch prisoner of war camp holding German and Italian POWs. In Dec. 1944 training ended and the base eventually became inactive. In 1949 the City of Pocatello acquired the base for use as it's main airport calling it Pocatello Regional Airport. In the terminal is a sizeable display on Pocatello Army Air Base with WW II uniforms, artifacts and photos.

U.S. NAVAL ORDNANCE PLANT, POCATELLO: This was a huge, sprawling plant north of downtown Pocatello on Quinn Rd. (US 91). It was built by the Navy early in the war to reline and otherwise service large naval guns. The plant also made new guns. Pocatello's access to good rail transportation was a factor in locating the plant here. In 1950 the plant was sold to various buyers. Most of it became an industrial park known as Gateway West Industrial Park and a city park known as Naval Ordnance Plant Park. The entire complex is still known to the local people as "The Gun Factory".

SUN VALLEY, (See Ketchum)

TWIN FALLS is on the Snake River in south-central Idaho. On Feb. 8, 1945 fragments from an envelope of a Japanese bombing balloon were found near the city.

MINIDOKA RELOCATION CAMP (HUNT RELOCATION CENTER): This was one of several relocation camps built by the U.S. Dept. of Justice in 1942 to house the ethnic Japanese forced to evacuate the military security zone established along the U.S. west coast early in the war. The camp was located about 15 miles NE of Twin Falls just north of the community of Eden. It was administered by the War Relocation Au-

thority, a civilian agency, and guarded by Army Military Police. It was designed to hold 10,000 people and, at its peak, actually held 9397 people. It operated from Aug. 10, 1942 to Oct. 28, 1945. Most of the residents came here from the states of Washington and Oregon via the Portland, OR and Puyallup, WA Assembly Centers. The camp was known locally as the Hunt Relocation Center or "Hunt Camp", a name that remained in use for many years. Most of the camp's buildings are gone, but a few can be seen on the grounds of the camp and in the surrounding area. Most of the camp's land is in private hands and is being farmed. To find the camp exit I-84 at SR 50 and proceed north to its junction with SR 25. Take SR 25 4.4 miles west to a paved road leading north and a sign reading "Hunt 2.5 miles". Proceed north on the paved road 2.5 miles to the camp. In Jerome, ID, 15 miles west of the camp, the Jerome County Historical Museum has displays and information on the relocation camp. The Museum is located at 220 N. Lincoln and is open all year M-Sat. 1-5. Phone: 208/324-5641.

The stone guard house and a lone chimney of the visitors reception center mark the entrance to Minidoka Relocation Camp. This sign tells some of the history of the camp.

This WW II hangar remained in use at the former Pocatello Army Air Base well into the postwar era. It is accessible from Thunderbolt via Grumman.

One of many building foundations that can be seen in the camp area. To the rear is a large potato storage cellar.

ILLINOIS

When people spoke of America as being the "Arsenal of Democracy" during WW II, they were referring to states like Illinois. The state produced almost every type of weapon used in the war; ships, planes, tanks, trucks, munitions, small arms, steel, diesel and aircraft engines, telephone equipment and thousands of other items of war. Most of these things came from the Chicago metropolitan area which was one of America's great industrial centers. In 1940 Chicago was the nation's second largest city and had over 9000 manufacturing plants scattered throughout the four adjoining counties. In those counties, as well as throughout the state, many new manufacturing firms came into being and existing ones expanded to meet the ever-increasing demands of the war. Some plants ran around-the-clock; there was plenty of overtime for the workers, but there was almost always a shortage of workers despite the fact that the state's population grew by about 318,000 during the war years. Illinois became 6th in the nation in war expenditures among the 48 states. By the fall of 1944 production at Illinois' four great munitions plants began to slow, but in Dec. 1944 when the Battle of the Bulge erupted in Europe, they quickly cranked up again to full capacity.

At the start of the war Illinois had over 320,000 registered enemy aliens, most of whom lived in the Chicago area. The great majority of them proved to be peaceful and cooperative. Some, however, were interned and others watched by the police and FBI.

Illinois was a major food producer. Its farms produced corn, soybeans, oats, hay, fruits, vegetables and meat. Coal was mined in the southern part of the state and in the Salem-Centralia area, where oil had been discovered in the early 1930s, there were some 3000 producing oil wells making Illinois third in the nation in oil production. Illinois had 8 major prisoner of war camps and dozens of branch camps. Illinois was represented in President Roosevelt's Cabinet by two native sons, Harold L. Ickes, Secretary of the Interior and Frank Knox, Secretary of the Navy. The state had a young Congressman, named Everett McKinley Dirksen, who would go on to serve many years in the House of Representatives and Senate. Dirksen became somewhat of a legend in Washington because of his homey wit, boyish mannerisms and rumpled appearance.

AURORA, on I-88, is 35 miles west of Chicago.

GRAND ARMY OF THE REPUBLIC & VETERANS MILITARY MUSEUM: This museum, in downtown Aurora, is devoted primarily to Civil War history, but has significant collections of WW I and WW II items. Address: 23 Downer Place, Aurora, IL 60507. Phone: 312/897-7221. Hours: M, W & Sat. noon to 4. Free.

CARBONDALE is in the SW corner of the state.

ILLINOIS ORDNANCE PLANT was built in 1941 by the Federal Government to product munitions for war. It was operated by the Sherwin-Williams Corp. and made large calibre artillery shells and 100 lb bombs. In 1946 the plant was phased down and declared surplus, but during the Korean War it was reactivated and continued in operation throughout the Cold War.

CHICAGO METROPOLITAN AREA:

Chicago was America's second largest city during the war and it and its suburbs contained more than half the citizens of the state. The city was a major industrial, commercial and trade center, and the largest railroad hub in the world. The area had been hard hit during the Great Depression but with the onset of war in Europe business began to boom. By 1941 the production of steel, war materials, munitions and consumer goods dominated all phases of Chicago life. In Melrose Park, 12 miles west of Chicago's downtown Loop, a huge new factory was built by the Government and operated by the Dodge Div. of Chrysler Corp. to produce aircraft engines. It was the world's largest aircraft engine plant at the time of its construction with floor space equaling all of the combined floor space of the other aircraft plants in the country. Production at the Dodge plant was just getting under way when the Japanese attacked Pearl Harbor in Dec. 1941. The plant eventually reached a productivity of 1500 engines a month.

Other well-known firms operating in Chicago were Douglas Aircraft Co. which make transport planes; Press Steel Car Co. made Sherman tanks; Ford Motor Co. made T-22 armored cars; The Pullman-Standard Co. made submarine chasers for the Navy, troop cars for the Army, aircraft wing assemblies, M-3 tanks for the British, 81 mm mortars and 105 mm shells; International Harvester Co. made trucks, heavy tractors, torpedoes, bomb fuzes and shells; Ingersoll Steel Disc Div. made amphibian tractors, amphibian tanks and amphibian cargo carriers; Diamond T Motor Car Co. made 57 mm mobile anti-tank vehicles, military trucks and other military vehicles; Oliver Farm Equipment Co. made naval gun barrels and 155 mm shells; Henry C. Grebe & Co. made Navy tugs and mine sweepers, Rock-ola Co. and Quality Hardware & Machine Co. made M-1 carbines and the Wm. Wrigley, Jr. Co. packed "K" Rations at the rate of two million a month. In early 1942 the AAF took over Chicago's largest hotel, the Stevens, on Lake Shore Dr. This 3000-room, 27-floor hotel was used to house and train up to 9700 air recruits.

In 1942 one of Chicago's own, Donald M.

Nelson, a high level executive of the Sears Roebuck Co. was called to Washington to become head of the War Production Board (WPB). That agency coordinated and directed America's wartime production and was one of the most powerful agencies in the Government, and Nelson was its "Czar". Also during 1942 several federal agencies, with 2951 people, moved to Chicago from Washington, DC to relieve overcrowding there. A year later more federal agencies moved to Chicago and an additional 14,000 people came with them.

In June 1942 German spies landed on America's east coast at two locations with plans that involved Chicago. One of the spies, Hans Schmidt, had instructions to buy a small farm outside Chicago where the group could meet and store explosives and other supplies. Another spy, Ernst Burger, was to start a commercial art studio in Chicago to be used as the headquarters for the northern group's operations. The spies were caught, however, before they could carry out their plans when one of them made contact with family members still living in Chicago.

Another Chicago native, Douglas Chandler, a pro-Nazi American who migrated to Germany before the war, broadcasted German propaganda to Allied troops during the war under the name of "Paul Revere". He was also known as the "American Lord Haw Haw"[1]. After the war, another famous Axis propaganda broadcaster made Chicago her home after serving a prison term. She was Iva Toguri D'Aquino, better known as "Tokyo Rose". She operated a flower shop in downtown Chicago.

Of all the big cities in the U.S., Chicago was the most receptive to relocated ethnic Japanese from the west coast. Many of those people found work and general acceptance here.

Despite the wartime boom conditions Chicago did not suffer a severe housing shortage like many other large cities. This was quite remarkable considering the fact that the city's population increased about 43% by 1945. There were, however, shortages of fuel, rubber and other items and the city's public transportation system was stretched to the limit. Near the end of the war, with building materials in short supply, Chicago then begin to experience a housing shortage. There was a

[1] A reference to William Joyce, a British citizen, who was known as "Lord Haw Haw". Joyce (born in New York City) became the most famous of several British and American propaganda broadcasters for the Nazis.

The world's largest aircraft engine plant in Melrose Park consisted of 19 major buildings on 500 acres of land.

constant manpower shortage in Chicago and ways were sought to relieve it including the use of prisoners of war and the importation of foreign laborers. The powerful unions, though, fought these efforts whenever possible, but were forced by the pressing needs of war, to accept non-union workers in many places. After V-J Day, however, the unions began to exert their muscle and a long period of labor unrest followed in the early postwar years.

THE CHICAGO DAILY TRIBUNE NEWSPAPER: This is one of America's great newspapers. It was, however, staunchly pro-Republican and pro-isolationist in its views. As a result it was very critical of President Franklin Roosevelt, his "New Deal" liberalism and his conduct of the war. The paper's owner, Col. Robert McCormick, was outspoken in his anti-Administration views and was a member of America's largest isolationist organization, the "America First Committee". The newspaper not only criticized the Roosevelt Administration, but tried to sabotage it whenever possible. Throughout the war, the Tribune was distributed, along with other U.S. newspapers, to prisoner of war camps in the U.S., and its strong anti-Administration stance became a revelation in the workings of democracy to the Nazi and Fascist POWs who had been exposed only to the totalitarian political systems of the homelands. On the other hand, some camp commanders felt that the newspaper was an embarrassment and had it quietly banned from their camps.

CHICAGO MUNICIPAL AIRPORT (Midway Airport) is 9 mile SW of the Loop. It was built in 1926 and was the area's main commercial airport before and during the war. By 1939 the airport had become the second busiest in the nation after Newark (NJ) Mun. Airport. Although it remained a commercial airport during the war it was used extensively by both the AAF & Navy. The airport had military air terminals and the AAF's Air Technical Service

Command and Air Transport Command operated here, as did the Naval Air Transport Command. After the war, when the City of Chicago bought Orchard Place Airport to use as a newer and larger regional airport, the name of this field was changed to Midway in honor of the Battle of Midway. Midway Airport then became Chicago's second airport.

CHICAGO QUARTERMASTER DEPOT was a large pre-war Army depot located at 1819 W. Pershing Rd. During the war it made, repaired, stored and distributed military clothing and related items.

ENRICO FERMI GRAVE SITE: Oakwood Cemetery at 71st and S. Cottage Grove Ave. is the final resting place of Enrico Fermi, the famous scientist who first achieved a controlled nuclear chain reaction. Fermi's great achievement, which was achieved here in Chicago, was instrumental in the development of the atomic bomb which brought an early end to WW II.

FIRST DIVISION MUSEUM is located in Wheaton, IL, 25 miles west of downtown Chicago. It is one of two museums on the grounds of Cantigny, the 500-acre estate of the late Col. Robert R. McCormick, editor and publisher of the Chicago Daily Tribune. Col. McCormick commanded an artillery battalion of the First Infantry Div. during WW I and was instrumental in founding the museum. The museum traces the history of the Division and its predecessors from 1776 to the present and has a significant number of WW II items on display. Address: 1 South 151 Winfield Rd., Wheaton, IL 60187. Phone: 708/668-5185. Hours: Tues. through Sun. from Memorial Day to Labor Day, 10-5 and 10-4 rest of year. Closed Jan. 1, Thanksgiving and Dec. 25. Free. Location: From the East-West Tollway take Naperville Rd. north for 1/2 mile to Warrenville Rd. Turn west on Warrenville for three miles to Winfield Rd. Proceed north on Winfield two miles to Cantigny.

GARDINER GENERAL HOSPITAL, 1660 E. Hyde Park Blvd., was, before the war, the elegant 12-story Chicago Beach Hotel on Chicago's lake front. Early in the war it was taken over by the AAF and used to house trainees. In 1943 it was transferred to the Army and converted into Gardiner General Hospital to treat war wounded. The hospital specialized in general and orthopedic surgery. In 1946 it was retained by the Army and used as the

This is a postwar view of Fifth Army Headquarters in Chicago which was formerly the Chicago Beach Hotel.

headquarters for the U.S. 5th Army. The former hotel and two adjacent twin 22-story apartment buildings also used by the Army were called the Army's only "vertical post".

HOLOCUAST MEMORIAL FOUNDATION OF ILLINOIS MUSEUM, LIBRARY AND RESOURCE CENTER: This Foundation is dedicated to recording and remembering the Holocaust. There is a museum which displays a large collection of memorabilia donated by Holocaust survivors and those who helped liberate the Nazi concentration camps at the end of the war. The museum displays painting, photographs, sculptures, woodcuts, a Wall of Remembrance, special exhibits and displays on Jewish communal life in pre-war Europe. Address: 4255 Main St., Skokie, IL 60076-2063. Phone: 708/677-4640. Hours: M-Thurs 9-4:30, F 9-3. Donations accepted.

MIDWAY AIRPORT (See Chicago Municipal Airport)

MUSEUM OF SCIENCE AND INDUSTRY, in Jackson Park at 57th St. and Lake Shore Dr., is one of the largest and foremost science museums in the country. Among its numerous exhibits are several WW II displays, the most important being the German submarine U-505 which was captured by the U.S. Navy in June 1944 off the coast of West Africa. Visitors may board the submarine and walk through it. There is a 20-minute narrative on the dramatic capture of the sub, plus artifacts from the sub, such as its log book and personal belongings of the crewmen. The museum also has scale models of several WW II ships. In the Museum's airplane collection is a British Spitfire and a German Stuka Dive Bomber. All aircraft are indoors. Address: 57th & Lake Shore Dr., Chicago, IL 60637-2093. Phone: 312/684-1414. Hours: M-F 9:30-4 and Sat., Sun. & holidays 9:30-5:30. Closed Dec. 25. Admission charged.

O'HARE INTERNATIONAL AIRPORT: (See Orchard Place Airport)

ORCHARD PLACE AIRPORT (O'Hare International Airport) is 14 miles NW of downtown Chicago off I-90 and I-294. The airport, first known as Orchard Place Airport,

The main entrance to the Chicago Quartermaster Depot.

The first batch of CCC applicants arrive at Ft. Sheridan, IL during the early days of the Depression.

was built by the Government in 1942 for the testing and delivery of new aircraft built by the Douglas Aircraft Co. whose assembly plant was adjacent to the field. The airport was used by both the AAF and Navy. In 1946 the airport was declared surplus and was bought by the City of Chicago and expanded into a second metropolitan airport to help relieve crowding at Chicago Municipal Airport (Midway Airport). In 1949 Orchard Place Airport was renamed O'Hare Field in honor of Chicago native Navy Lt. Edward "Butch" O'Hare who, in Feb. 1942, shot down five Japanese planes in four minutes over Bougainville Island. O'Hare was later killed in action in the Pacific. In Dec. 1958 the airport was renamed Chicago O'Hare International Airport and eventually became Chicago's primary airport.

FORT SHERIDAN is on the shore of Lake Michigan north of, and adjacent to, Highland Park, IL. It was activated in 1887. At the time of the Spanish-American War, the fort was commanded by the father of Gen. Jonathan Wainwright and young Jonathan spent part of his boyhood here. Between the wars the fort was commanded for a time by Col. Robert McCormick, who later became editor and publisher of the Chicago Daily Tribune. Gen. Mark Clark also lived at the fort as a boy and attended school in nearby Highland Park. The fort was small in comparison to other Army posts so it was used as a reception center for the Army's 6th Corps. The fort processed over 500,000 men for the Army. The Fort had a subpost, Camp Haven, which consisted of 164 acres on the shore of Lake Michigan and was used to train anti-aircraft gunners. There was a main prisoner of war camp at Fort Sheridan holding about 1600 POWs who worked on the post. As the war ended, the fort became a separation center, and the first servicemen discharged under the military's new point system were discharged here on May 10, 1945. The fort separated over 500,000 service personnel between July 1944 and March 1947. In the postwar years the Fort served as the headquarters for both the 4th Army and the Army's Recruiting Command. It also provided logistic support for Army Reserves units in the

area. In the 1990s the fort was closed.

CAMP SKOKIE was a small Army camp located between Skokie and Glenview, IL just north of Chicago. It was a training post for military police and had a prisoner of war compound holding about 400 POWs who worked on the post. Camp Skokie was declared surplus in Nov. 1945.

U.S. NAVAL AIR STATION, GLENVIEW, NW of, and adjacent to, the city of Glenview, IL, was built as a civilian airport in 1937 and called Curtiss-Reynolds Airport. In 1940 the Navy moved onto the airport and created a small reserve training facility called U.S. Naval Reserve Aviation Base, Glenview, Chicago. In 1942 the base was expanded to become a primary flight training center for Navy and Marine pilots. On Jan. 1, 1943 the base was renamed U.S. Naval Air Station, Chicago. Expansion and construction at the station continued throughout the war and the station became a major training base for carrier pilots. At one time the station had 15 outlying fields, two small aircraft carriers in Lake Michigan and a large bombing and gunnery range in Lake Michigan. The most popular trainer at the station was the N3N-3 "Yellow Peril". In May 1944 the name of the station was changed again to U.S. Naval Air Station, Glenview, and later that year the headquarters of the Naval Air Primary Training Command moved onto the station from Kansas City. After the war the station reverted to training Navy and Marine reservists and became home to the Naval Air Reserve Training Command (NARTC) headquarters. In the 1990s, the station was closed.

U.S. NAVAL TRAINING STATION, GREAT LAKES was 34 miles north of Chicago on the shore of Lake Michigan. This facility was built by the Navy in 1911 as part of the Navy's inland recruiting and training program. During the 1930s the station became very inactive, but with the outbreak of war in Europe in Sept. 1939 the station reopened as a training facility and had a sizeable influx of new recruits, but only a modest expansion in facilities. As a result overcrowding resulted and training programs had to be reduced from 8 weeks to 6, and at time even 4 weeks. In Dec. 1941 the station began to expand and construction proceeded until 1944 at which time the station could handle up to 100,000 recruits in training. By the end of the war the station had over 1000 buildings and 1350 acres of land. In the postwar years the station continued in operation and became the Navy's largest training center. It also became the headquarters for the Ninth Naval District and acquired service schools in electronics, fire control, gunnery, instructor training and propulsion engineering.

UNIVERSITY OF CHICAGO: During the war

almost all major universities in the U.S. made scientific and scholastic contributions to the war effort. One scientific breakthrough, however, made here at the U. of Chicago, stands out above all the rest. On Dec. 2, 1942, a group of scientists, working in a make-shift laboratory under the stands of the University's football field, obtained the world's first controlled nuclear chain reaction. This discovery proved that it was feasible to make the fissionable element plutonium out of uranium and thereby produce an extremely powerful bomb using the explosive power generated by the splitting of plutonium atoms. The experiments were directed by Enrico Fermi, an Italian-born, Nobel Prize winning physicist who had fled Fascist Italy in 1939 because his wife was Jewish. Fermi became a member of the "Manhattan Project", America's program to create an atomic bomb, and served as the Project's chief consultant for all nuclear physics experiments.

The football stadium is gone, but a bronze marker marks the spot where the famous experiment took place. The marker is on the east side of S. Ellis St. in the middle of the block between 56th and 57th Sts.

Room 405, Jones Laboratory: This room is a National Historic Landmark because in 1942 it was in this room, then a science laboratory, that the man-made element of plutonium was first isolated and weighed. This was another of the important discoveries that lead to the development of the atomic bomb. Jones Laboratory is on the east side of S. Ellis St. several building south of 57th St.

VAUGHN GENERAL HOSPITAL was built in Hines, IL, a suburb of Chicago, in 1944 to treat the Army's war wounded. This was a 1900-bed hospital which specialized in general medicine, general and orthopedic surgery and psychiatry. In Apr. 1946 it was transferred to the Veterans Administration.

DANVILLE is in east-central Illinois on I-74 near the Indiana state line. In the 400 block on Hazel St. is a World War II Memorial financed, in part, by the collection and sale of aluminum cans. In the 500 block of Hazel St. is a joint Korean and Viet Nam Wars memorial. Hazel St. is a north-south street five blocks east of Gilbert, which is US 136 and SR 1.

EAST SAINT LOUIS AREA: This area, on the eastern bank of the Mississippi River opposite St. Louis, MO, consists of a cluster of small towns of which East St. Louis is the largest. In Granite City there was a large Army depot called the Granite City Ordnance Depot, and in East St. Louis the Army's Chemical Corps had a large plant making chemicals for military use. The Alcoa Aluminum plant in the area was targeted by the two groups of German saboteurs that landed by submarine on the U.S. east coast in June 1941. The saboteurs were caught before they could carry out their plan.

CURTISS-STEINBURG FIELD (PARKS AIRPORT) was three miles south of downtown East St. Louis. It was the area's local airport and was home to Parks Air College, the first certified aviation school in the U.S. In May 1939 Parks was one of the air schools contracted by the Army Air Corps to give elementary flight training to Air Corps cadets. The airport and

One of two remaining concrete water towers at Camp Ellis. This one is used as a grain elevator. This house in Ipava, IL was a former camp building. It was moved to town and became a private home.

college survived well into the postwar years. The airport became St. Louis Downtown Parks Airport and the college became Parks College of St. Louis University.

SCOTT FIELD was 23 miles SE of East St. Louis off I-64 and 8 miles NE of Belleview, IL. Scott Field was one of five Army Air Corps bases remaining from WW I, and from 1919 to 1938 was used for lighter-than-air training. After 1938 the base was converted to handle heavier-than-air craft. By 1940 the need for technically trained Air Corps personnel began to outstrip the training capacity of Chanute Field (the Air Corps' main technical training facility at Rantoul, IL), so part of the training load was shifted to Scott Field. A school, known as the Air Corps Institute, was established here and operated by the Eastern Technical Training Command. The Institute trained aircraft and auto mechanics, radiomen, engineers, meteorologists and other specialists. Also, courses in basic education were offered to enlisted men in such fields as mathematics, drafting, chemistry, English, grammar. etc. The Institute offered correspondence courses for enlisted men, the only such school of its kind in the Army. During the war as many as 15,000 service personnel were in training here at various times. Early in the war Scott served as a reception center for the VI Corps Area. The field also served as a transport base under the Air Transport Command and had an AAF regional hospital. The Army's Jefferson Barracks in St. Louis, MO was annexed by Scott Field and became a recruit training center and a communications school. After the war the Institute and the other operations were scaled back but remained in operation. In 1948 the air field was taken over by the US Air Force and renamed Scott Air Force Base. In 1950 the Institute became very active again due to the Korean War. By the 1960s air transport operations at Scott AFB had become the dominant operation and the base eventually

became headquarters for the Military Airlift Command, the successor of MATS. In the following years the base became home to as many as 40 other service commands.

ELWOOD (See Joliet)

FULTON COUNTY is 40 miles SW of Peoria and west of the Illinois Rivere.

CAMP ELLIS was located in western Fulton County between the communities of Table Grove and Ipava on the north side of highway US 136. The camp was built in 1942 as a training camp for Army supply units. In 1943 a large prisoner of war camp was built at the camp to hold 2000 POWs who worked at the camp and in agriculture. At the end of the war Camp Ellis was cut back drastically and in 1950 was abandoned altogether. Its buildings were moved and/or dismantled, the salvageable lumber was sold and the land returned to farming. Only a few foundations, chimneys, a couple of postwar buildings and two water towers remain at the camp site.

GALESBURG is a county seat 45 miles NW of Peoria on I-74.

MAYO GENERAL HOSPITAL was an 1855-bed Army hospital built in Galesburg in 1944 to treat war wounded. It specialized in general medicine, neurology, neurosurgery and vascular surgery. In Sept. 1946 it was transferred to the state of Illinois.

JOLIET is 35 miles SW of Chicago with a sizeable Czech population. During the war a new housing development in the

city was named "Lidice" in honor of the small village in Czechoslovakia and its citizens. In 1942 a high-ranking SS leader, Gen. Reinhardt Heydrick, was assassinated in the Czech village by members of the Czech Resistance. Out of revenge, the Nazis executed every man and boy in the village, some 200 individuals, irregardless of age, and 56 women. The other women were sent to concentration camps and the young girls placed in correctional homes. The entire village of Lidice was levelled.

CAMP DES PLAINES, located SW of Joliet on the west side of then highway 66 in Grundy County, was established in the fall of 1942 to house laborers brought in from Jamaica and Barbados because of the general labor shortage. The camp also housed a special Army unit guarding the locks on the Illinois Waterway. In 1945 the camp was abandoned and then dismantled in 1948.

ELWOOD ORDNANCE PLANT, 10 miles south of Joliet and just west of the small community of Elwood, IL, was built by the Federal Government in 1941 and operated by a private contractor to produce the explosive Tolvol and other ordnance items. The plant began producing on Dec. 2, 1941 only five days before the Japanese attacked Pearl Harbor. On June 5, 1942 an explosion occurred at the plant killing 49 workers. The plant also loaded shells and bombs. In 1944 the plant was renamed Joliet Arsenal and later Joliet Army Ammunition Plant. It operated for many years thereafter.

KANKAKEE is 50 miles south of Chicago.

KANKAKEE ORDNANCE WORKS was built by the Federal Government in 1940-41 to make explosives and was run by the E. I. DuPont de Nemours Co. This site was selected because it was close to various acid manufacturers in

A smaller and newer hanger sits on the concrete floor of a larger and long-gone WW II hangar at George Field.

The Heritage in Flight Museum at Lincoln, IL. Its building was formerly at Camp Ellis in Fulton County and housed German prisoners of war.

Chicago and St. Louis. Acid was a vital ingredient in the manufacture of the plant's products. The plant began production in Sept. 1941 manufacturing TNT, DNT, Tetryl, Lead Azide, Sodium Azide and Oleum.

LAWRENCEVILLE is in SE Illinois 10 miles west of Vincennes, IN.

GEORGE FIELD, four miles east of Lawrenceville, was built by the AAF in 1942 as part of the 50,000 Pilot Training Program. It began operating in Oct. 1942 and was named in honor of Brig. Gen. Harold "Pursuit" George who commanded the US Air Force in the Philippines in 1941 and early 1942. Gen. George was killed in April 1942 in Australia. George Field was a training base for light and medium bomber pilots. In May and June of 1943 a devastating flood on the nearby Wabash River made the field unusable for several weeks. At the time it was called the "Battle of George Field". In Aug. 1944 the Field's mission changed to that of training Troop Carrier Command pilots and it retained this mission throughout the remainder of it military use. In early 1945 the field was closed, and in 1948 it was deeded over to the city of Lawrenceville to become Lawrenceville Municipal Airport. It later became a regional airport known as Mid-America Air Center, or by a secondary name, Lawrenceville-Vincennes International Airport. The Indiana Military Museum in Vincennes, IN has an exhibit on the wartime activities of George Field. During the war George Field had the following auxiliary fields:

• Aux. #1, Auxiliary Field #1, 11 miles north of Vincennes, IN

• Aux. #2, Emison Airport, 3.5 miles SW of Oakton, IN

• Aux. #3, Presbyterian Church Airport, 4 miles NW of Lawrenceville

• Aux. #?, Walesboro Airport, 1 mile west of Walesboro, IN

LIBERTYVILLE is 8 miles SW of Waukegan.

U.S. SERBIAN CHURCH MONASTERY CEMETERY: This is the resting place of King Peter II of Yugoslavia. Yugoslavia was one of the Allied nations during WW II. Peter had come to power suddenly in March 1941 at age 18 in a palace coup that ousted his pro-Axis uncle and Regent, Prince Paul. The next month, on April 7, the Axis nations invaded Yugoslavia from all sides and the boy-king and his cabinet fled to London and established the Yugoslav Government-in-Exile. After the war Tito, Yugoslavia's outstanding wartime guerilla leader, and the Communists took control in Yugoslavia and abolished the monarchy. Peter lived in this monastery after the war and died here at the aged of 47.

LINCOLN is a county seat 30 miles NE of Springfield on I-55.

HERITAGE IN FLIGHT MUSEUM is a small museum on the grounds of the Logan County Airport which is NE of town about one mile from the city center. The museum has an interesting collection of WW II memorabilia and some items from WW I. It is housed in a wartime building relocated here from Camp Ellis where it housed German prisoners of war. Address: Logan county Airport, Lincoln, IL 62656. Hours: 10-5 Sat. Donations accepted.

LINCOLN ORDNANCE DEPOT, in Lincoln, went into production in June 1942 making percussion primers and soon expanded to make detonators, assemble fuses and load boosters for 155 mm shells. Later in the war Lincoln became a master depot.

MOLINE/ROCK ISLAND: These are two of the four cities that make up the well-known Quad-Cities of Illinois and Iowa. The other cities are Davenport and Bettendorf on the Iowa side of the Mississippi River. The area's two largest private manufacturer's, the John Deere Co. and the International Harvester Co. both make tanks, tank parts, military tractors and other vehicles. IHC also made artillery guns and cannons.

ROCK ISLAND ARSENAL is an old Government-owned arsenal on Arsenal Island in the Mississippi River. Its first military use was in 1816 when Ft. Armstrong was built here during the Black Hawk War. The Arsenal was build in 1862 during the Civil War. Since its inception the Arsenal has manufactured a wide variety of military weapons, ranging from small arms to large artillery pieces and tanks. During WW II it produced to its maximum capacity and many of the workers were women. M-2 medium tanks were produced here in modest numbers. The arsenal is well-maintained and has a park-like atmosphere. There are many large and well-preserved stone and brick factory buildings, service buildings and homes for the administrators and military officers. Most of the buildings remained in use well into the postwar years. Various pieces of military hardware are located around the grounds and at Rodman Av. & East Av. is Memorial Park which displays a collection of artillery guns, tanks, rocket launchers and other military items. The Arsenal is open to the public and tours are available.

Rock Island Arsenal Museum: This is a large museum in one of the old stone factory buildings on the grounds of the Arsenal. The museum tells the history of Rock Island and the Arsenal and preserves and displays many of the items manufactured here. The museum

The Rock Island Arsenal Museum is located in one of the well-preserved old stone factory buildings and is the second oldest Army museum in the nation. An American casualty of war. This M-4 Sherman tank was put out of action during the Battle of the Bulge. Note the shell cavities on the sloping front upper plate.

German prisoners of war picking asparagus in Illinois.

was established in 1905 making it the second oldest Army museum in the country after that at West Point. The museum was closed during WW I and WW II to provide additional manufacturing space. The current museum has been in its present building since 1948. Over 1100 U.S. and foreign weapons are on display. Address: Rock Island Arsenal, Rock Island, IL 61299. Phone: 309/782-5021/5182. Hours: daily 10-4, closed Jan. 1, Thanksgiving and Dec. 24 & 25. Free.

NAUVOO is on the west-central edge of the state on the Mississippi River.

JONATHAN BROWNING HOME AND GUNSHOP is in downtown Nauvoo. Browning was the inventor of the Browning Automatic Rifle (BAR), a powerful but light-weight machine-gun-like weapon used by nearly every squad of infantrymen in the U.S. Army during WW II. Browning was also the inventor of many other automatic weapons. These structures are recreations of Browning's original home and gunshop and there is an extensive gun collection. Address: Main St., Nauvoo, IL 62354. Hours: Memorial Day-Labor Day daily 9-6, rest of year 9-5. Free.

QUINCY is on the west-central edge of the state on the Mississippi River.

ALL WARS MUSEUM is on the grounds of the Illinois Veterans Home, one of the largest and oldest such homes in the nation. Exhibits in the museum span American military history from the Revolution to the present with a sizeable display on WW II. Address: 1707 N. 12th St., Quincy, IL 62301. Phone: 217/222-8641. Hours: W-Thurs. 1-4, Sat.-Sun. 9-noon and 1-4. Free.

RANTOUL is 12 miles north of Champaign-Urbana on I-57.

CHANUTE FIELD, one miles SE of Rantoul, was built in 1917 and was one of the few WW I air fields to be retained by the Army Air Corps after that war. It was a training field for pilots during WW I and became an aircraft storage field afterwards and home to the Air Corps' Air Service Mechanics School for enlisted men. By the late 1930s the field had become the Air Corps' most important, and only, technical training field for enlisted men and officers up to the rank of first lieutenant. The Air Corps Technical School, as it was then called, was operated by the Eastern Technical Training Command and offered a wide variety of aircraft-related technical training courses. The School also offered training courses for Air Corps officers in such subjects as staff duties, basic Army and Navy tactics related to air operations, the proper deployment of air units in operations against the enemy and a number of refresher courses. As the U.S. Air Corps grew, so did Chanute Field and by 1937 the base was overcrowded. As a result, some of its schooling operations were transferred to Scott Field in East St. Louis, IL and Lowrey Field, CO. During the war Chanute spun off a number of technical training teams that were sent to other air fields to become nuclei for training schools at those fields. All during the war the Chanute trained enlisted men and young officers in large numbers. Unfortunately, Chanute got the reputation as being a dumping ground for airmen who, for whatever reason, couldn't make the grade as pilots or members of air crews. A saying arose expressing this view, "Don't shoot 'em, Chanute 'em". Despite this handicap, Chanute turned out over 200,000 technicians during the war. In 1945 Chanute became a separation center, but once that task was completed, the field again became a technical training base. Chanute was eventually taken over by the US Air Force and renamed Chanute Air Force Base. More schools came to the base and Chanute AFB continued to be a technical training facility throughout the Cold War. It was closed in the 1990s.

ROCK ISLAND (See Moline/Rock Island)

ROCKFORD is in the north-central part of the state.

CAMP GRANT was a WW I Army training camp established in 1917 four miles south of Rockford. It was a large camp with 1515 buildings and a troop capacity of 42,800. Between the wars it was used by the Illinois National Guard which was the Army's 33rd Div. With the onset of WW II the Federal Government reclaimed the camp and used it first as a reception center for the VI Corps Area and then as a training camp for replacement medical personnel. The camp had a main prisoner of war camp holding about 1700 German POWs who worked at the camp, in agriculture and at local food processors. After the war the camp was disposed of. Parts of it became Rockford's main airport, and industrial park and a forest preserve.

ROCKFORD ORDNANCE PLANT, built in Rockford during the war, was located at 2800 N. Main St. It produced shell casing for 105 and 155 mm shells under the management of W.F. and John Barnes Co. Production was cut back after the war but revived again for the Korean War. In 1960 the facility was declared surplus and sold.

SALEM is in the south-central part of the state 70 miles east of East St. Louis. Salem claims to be the birthplace of the GI Bill of Rights. A tentative outline of the plan that eventually became the GI Bill of Rights was drawn up in the local American Legion Hall in Nov. 1943. The plan was promoted by the American Legion National Headquarters and several powerful political leaders, including President Roosevelt, and became law in June 1944. A bronze plaque in the American Legion Hall commemorates the event.

SAVANNA is in the NW corner of the state on the Mississippi River.

SAVANNA ORDNANCE DEPOT was built in 1918 on the east bank of the Mississippi River 8 miles north of town and was very active during WW I. It was, however, scaled back drastically in the 1920s and 1930s and by early 1939 had only 143 employees. With the onset of WW II the Federal Government revitalized the depot and expanded it into one of the largest ammunition storage depots in the U.S. The depot received, stored, loaded and issued a wide variety of ammunition to the U.S. armed forces. The depot also had an ammunition maintenance school. By late 1942 employment at the depot peaked at 7195. After the war the depot was again scaled back but had a resurgence of activity during the Korean and Viet Nam Wars. It then continued in operation throughout the Cold War.

SPRINGFIELD, near the geographic center of the state on I-72 and I-55, is the capital of Illinois. During the war the Illinois State Fairgrounds, three miles north of downtown at Sagamon Av. and I-55 Bus., was taken over by the AAF and used as a specialized storage depot. This was not uncommon. In many states state fair gounds were canceled for the duration of the war and the unused buildings and spacious grounds made ideal storage facilities for war supplies. In Springfield's case, the fairgrounds depot was run by the Fairfield (Calif.) Air Technical Service Command who promptly departed after the war and returned the fairgrounds to its original use.

Surplus WW II bombs were buried at Savanna Ordnance Depot after the war as a means of storing them.

INDIANA

During WW II Indiana was a major producer of both war materials and food. Virtually all of the state's larger cities had manufacturing plants and they turned out things like iron and steel, airplanes, tanks, gasoline and diesel engines, automobiles and trucks, railroad cars, farm machinery, electrical machinery, refrigerators, tires, glass products, chain, saws, pharmaceutical, landing craft, munitions and bombsights. The state's mines and wells produced coal, oil, limestone, cement and clay products. The state's flat and fertile farms produced grain, livestock and vegetables. Indiana prospered very well during the war. Indiana became 7th in the nation in the production of war supplies. In the SW part of the state newly-found gas and oil deposits were exploited and in 1941 alone 260 new oil wells and 57 new gas wells were brought in.

Indiana was home to several well-known WW II personalities including Ernie Pyle, war correspondent; Claude Wickard, President Roosevelt's Secretary of Agriculture; Senator Homer Capehart; Elmer Davis, Head of Office of War Information; Paul V. McNutt, head of the War Manpower Commission, Gen. Lewis B. Hershey, Director of the Selective Service; General Walter Bedell Smith, Secretary of the U.S. Joint Chiefs of Staff, American Secretary of the Anglo-American Combined Chiefs of Staff and Eisenhower's Chief of Staff; and Wendell Willkie, Republican presidential candidate in 1940. The German saboteurs who landed on the U.S. east coast in June 1942 had plans to sabotage some of the locks on the Ohio River which forms Indiana's southern boundary. The saboteurs were caught before they could carry out their plans.

CHARLESTOWN is in the SE corner of the state on the Ohio River.

INDIANA ARSENAL AND HOOSIER ORDNANCE WORKS: The Indiana Arsenal was built by the E. I. Dupont de Nemours Co. for the Federal Government in 1941. It is located just east of Charlestown between SR 62 and the Ohio River. The Arsenal make smokeless gun powder, diphenylamine & barium nitrate. The Jefferson Proving Ground at nearby Madison, IN tested much of the powder produced here. Also on the grounds of the arsenal was another manufacturing operation, the Hoosier Ordnance Works, run by the Goodyear Engineering Co., which used powder made at the arsenal to make howitzer charges for 75 mm, 105 mm and 155 mm shells. The Hoosier Ordnance Works was the largest plant of its kind at the time. About 1000 prisoners of war worked at the arsenal and in the surrounding area. In 1944 a third facility was built on the Arsenal grounds to make rocket propellent. In Oct. 1945 the arsenal was inactivated, but then reactivated again for the Korean War. It remained in operation for several decades thereafter under various contract operators. In 1961 it was renamed the Indiana Ordnance Plant and later became known as the Indiana Army Ammunition Plant.

COLUMBUS is a county seat 35 miles south of Indianapolis.

ATTERBURY ARMY AIR BASE was on the north edge of town. It was built in late 1942 soon after Camp Atterbury, 10 miles to the NW, was completed. The air field was to provide air support for the ground troops training at Camp Atterbury and was to be known as the Columbus Air Support Command Base. By Dec. 1942, when the field was ready for use, intended use of the field was canceled. The field then sat idle until Feb. 1943 when it was turned over to the 3rd AF who made it a sub-base of Godman Field, Ft. Knox, KY. It was then renamed Columbus Army Air

This is the original chapel at Atterbury AAB. It is to be the only WW II structure preserved. All the others are to be torn down eventually.

Base and provided training for B-26 bomber crews. In Apr. 1943 the name of the base was changed again to Atterbury Army Air Field and sometime later to Atterbury Army Air Base. In May 1944 the base was transferred to the I Troop Carrier Command who made it a sub-base of Bowman Field, Louisville, KY and used it as a training facility for glider pilots. During this time the base was also used by reconnaissance planes operating with the 106th Inf. Division which was then in training at Camp Atterbury, and as a stop-over base for military planes flying across country. In Aug. 1944 the base became an arrival point for transport planes bring wounded back from France who were being taken to Wakeman Hospital at Camp Atterbury. In Mar. 1944 training in medium bombers was transferred to Freeman Field, but glider training continued. In Feb. 1946 Atterbury AAB was placed on stand-by. In 1949 it was used by the Air Force Reserves, and in 1954 it became Bakalar Air Force Base, named in honor of Lt. John Bakalar, a native of Hammond, IN, who was killed in France in 1944. Eventually the base was turned over to the city of Columbus to become Columbus Municipal Airport

Atterbury-Bakalar Air Museum: This is a new museum on the grounds of the Columbus Municipal Airport, just west of the terminal, which preserves the history of the field from its beginning to the present. Most of the displays in the museum relate to the field's WW II history and its days as an Air Force base. Address: 4742 Ray Boll Blvd., Columbus, IN

The Indiana Arsenal, later known as the Indiana Army Ammunition Plant, can be seen easily from SR 62. It stretches for miles along the east side of the road and consists of many large buildings spaced well back from the road and far apart from each other.

This was Ernie Pyle's home in Dana, IN. It is now a state historic site.

47203. Phone: 812/372-4356. Hours: Sat. 10-4, Sun. 1-4. Donations requested.

CRANE, 30 miles SW of Bloomington, did not exist before the war.

U.S. NAVAL AMMUNITION DEPOT, CRANE was built by the Navy in 1940-41 on rolling and forested land, much of which was wilderness and already government-owned. This site was selected because it was safe from enemy carrier-born air attacks[1], had a good water supply and had good rail and road connections to the east coast. The depot was to be a permanent installation with the mission to manufacture, store, prepare and issue all types of ammunition to the Atlantic Fleet. It was planned from the beginning to be a very large depot (the largest in the world at the time) able to produce and store as much naval ammunition as all the existing naval depots on the east coast combined. A large part of Crane's operation was to operate and maintain various types of ammunition loading and processing plants, so in reality it was also a naval arsenal. Building the depot was a massive undertaking. Roads, rail spurs and utilities had to be cut through wilderness and rough terrain, and supplies and laborers acquired from great distances. Private homes were built for the Navy personnel and workers and these eventually became the community of Crane, IN. The depot's processing plants

[1] At the time most of the Navy's ammunition depots were along the U.S. coasts close to major naval bases, and therefore vulnerable to air attacks.

assembled and loaded bombs, torpedoes, depth charges, star shells, mines and medium and major calibre projectiles. NAD Crane loaded the very first rockets used by the navy during the war. In Mar. 1944 NAD Crane became an assembly point for Navy crews awaiting assignment to some of the Navy's smaller vessels. While they awaited their new assignments many of the sailors were put to work in the depot and the processing plants to ease the constant labor shortage. In 1944 NAD, Crane reached its peak employment of 10,000 people.

When the war ended the depot became extremely busy receiving carloads of ammunition being returned from the war zones, mothballed ships and munitions contractors. NAD, Crane continued in operation without interruption throughout the Cold War. In 1975 it was renamed the U.S. Naval Weapons Support Center, Crane.

DANA is in the west-central part of Indiana near the state line.

ERNIE PYLE STATE HISTORIC SITE: This is the birthplace of Ernie Pyle, America's best-known WW II correspondent. Pyle, a Pulitzer Prize winning newspaper columnist, wrote from the eyes of the common soldier and gave the folks back home a truthful and realistic account of what was happening in the heads and hearts of their loved ones at the front. Pyle was killed by a Japanese sniper in 1945 and his death was such a great loss that it was announced personally by President Harry S Truman. Pyle is buried in Hawaii. His home is restored and open to the public and displays many of Pyle's personal belongings. Address: G.D. 1995, Dana, IN 47847-0345. Phone: 317/665-3633. Hours: Tues. & Sat. 9-5, Sun. 1-5. Closed holidays except Memorial Day, July 4 and Labor Day. Free. Location: On SR. 71 one mile north of US 36 in Dana.

EAST CHICAGO/GARY/HAMMOND are adjacent communities in the NW corner of the state on Lake Michigan. It was a heavily industrialized area, known for steel production and heavy industry. Among the major companies in the area that produced for the war were U.S. Steel Corp., which made artillery shells, armor plates, steel coils, bars, etc.; the General American Transportation Co. which built tank lighters, steel barges and 90 mm high explosive shells; the Pullman Standard Car Co. which made M-4 Sherman tanks, tank parts and 105 mm & 155 mm howitzer carriages; the East Chicago Armor Plate Plant which made cast armor plate and the American Steel Foundry Co., which built the world's largest foundry during the war to make steel castings. Many of the castings made here were the upper bodies of Sherman tanks. Because this was a "smoke stack" industrial area the local civil defense people hit upon a novel idea to protect the area in case of an air attack; it was to intentionally blanket the area in smoke. One test was made in Jan. 1941 and declared successful.

EDINBURGH is 25 miles south of Indianapolis.

CAMP ATTERBURY, one miles west of town, was built in 1942 as a training camp for division-sized infantry units. It was the largest training camp in Indiana. Troops began training here

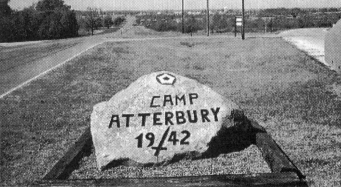

Left: This small chapel was built by Italian prisoners of war in their compound at Camp Atterbury. It has been maintained through the years and is used on special occasions. Above: This rock, carved by Italian prisoners of war at Camp Atterbury, rests at the camp entrance where it was originally placed in 1943. Sometime after its installation, the camp authorities realized that the dagger was an Italian military dagger pointing at the "heart" of Atterbury.

in July 1942. The divisions trained were the 83rd, 92nd, 30th and 106th Inf. Divs. in that order. The camp had a number of schools training military police, medical units, supply depot troops, ordnance units, engineers, quartermaster units and signalmen. There was a very large hospital at the camp named Wakeman Hospital. In July 1944 the WAC Medical Department Enlisted Technicians' School move in Wakeman from Hot Springs, AR. Wakeman was expanded into a 10,000-bed convalescent hospital and later became a general hospital to receive wounded flown in directly from Europe. Planes carrying the wounded would land at Atterbury Army Air Base north of Columbus, IN and the wounded would be brought to Wakeman in ambulances. In early 1943 a 3000-man prisoner of war camp was built here for Italian POWs. The POWs worked at the camp and in agriculture. At the

entrance to the camp is a stone, with the camp's name on it, carved by the POWs. After Italy changed sides in the war, the Italian POWs were moved out and in May 1944 German POWs moved in and remained at the camp until June 1946. In Mar. 1943 a school for Rangers, elite commando-type combat units, was set up here by the 83rd Inf. Div. In 1944 Atterbury became a separation center. The camp and Wakeman Hospital closed down after the war and were turned over to the Indiana National Guard. A little chapel built by the Italian POWs is preserved and still used on special occasions. Johnson County Museum of History at 135 N. Main St., Franklin, IN has a room devoted to the history of Camp Atterbury.

Camp Atterbury Veterans Memorial: This is an outdoor memorial and display honoring the thousands of servicemen and women who passed through Camp Atterbury from its beginning in WW II to the present. The main feature of the memorial is a limestone wall bearing the crests of the 10 major units that utilized the camp. Surrounding the memorial wall are 18 pieces of WW II equipment, a reflecting pool, walkways and a 6' bronze statue of a GI pointing the way.

ELWOOD, 30 miles NE of Indianapolis, was the birthplace of Wendell Willkie, the Republican presidential candidate in 1940. In Willkie Park at 400 N. Anderson St. is a granite memorial to Willkie.

EVANSVILLE is in SW Indiana on the Ohio River.

EVANSVILLE MUNICIPAL AIRPORT, now Dress Regional Airport, is on US 41 north of town. Before the war it was the town's local airport, built in 1930. In 1942 the Federal Government built a large aircraft factory at the Airport, run by Republic Aviation Co., to produce P-47 fighter planes. The first plane was produced in Sept. 1942 and by war's end the plant had produced about 6000 P-47s. The airport remained in private hands during the war, but was shared with Republic and the military services. After the war the aircraft plant was sold to International Harvester Corp. to make refrigerators.

EVANSVILLE ORDNANCE PLANT: This plant was a pre-war automobile assembly plant making Plymouth cars and Dodge trucks and located

at Stringtown Rd. and Maxwell Ave. When auto production was halted Chrysler retooled the facility to make .45 caliber ammunition by a new process using casings made of steel rather than brass, which was in short supply. The plant was renamed the Evansville Ordnance Plant. Unfortunately, the steel cartridges were not received well by the GIs in the field who blamed them for frequent gun jamming. This problem was never verified, but the War Dept. gave in to the GI's prejudices and discontinued the steel cartridges when brass became more plentiful. The Evansville Ordnance Plant then retooled again and rebuilt Sherman tanks, trucks, scout cars, half-tracks, gun motor carriages and made incendiary bombs. After the war it sold to a new owner and was used again as a manufacturing plant.

EVANSVILLE SHIPYARD: This was a 40-acre shipyard on the north bank of the Ohio River at Wabash St. near downtown Evansville. It was constructed by the Missouri Bridge & Iron Co. and built landing ship, tanks (LSTs). The yard produced 171 LSTs and 31 smaller vessel during the war and, at its peak, employed 19,600 people. The yard closed down after the war and on Jan. 26, 1946 suffered an ignominious end when it was completely destroyed by fire. In the postwar years most of the 40 acre site became a parking lot.

FORT WAYNE is a large city in the NE corner of the state.

ALLEN COUNTY WAR MEMORIAL COLISEUM, on US 30 Bypass, is a memorial to the servicemen and women who died in WW I, WW II and the Korean War. It seats 10,000.

BAER FIELD, 6.5 miles SW of town, was built in 1941 to serve as a home for combat-ready pursuit (fighter) units. In June 1941 units of the 31st Pursuit Group arrived at the field. The 31st was the first group in the AAF to be equipped with P-39 Airacobras. Beginning on the afternoon of Dec. 7, 1941 the entire 31st Pursuit Group was rushed to the east coast to defend America's eastern frontier. The vacated field was then assigned to the 3rd AF and became a staging field with the mission to receive and prepare medium bomber units for shipment overseas. In March 1943 the field was reassigned again to the I Troop Carrier Command and performed a variety of tasks

Wendell Willkie began his campaign in his home town of Elwood, IN. Here he rides in triumph down Elwood's main street after receiving the Republican nomination for President.

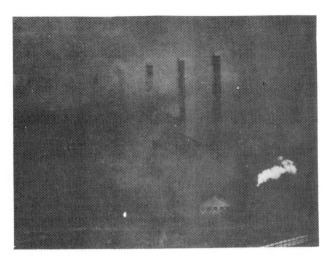

From Left: The great "smokeout" of Jan. 1942. An effort to hide vital war plants from enemy bombers, conducted in the East Chicago/Gary/Hammond area of Indiana (See page 83). Yard locomotives and factory smoke stacks begin to blanket emit smoke in the picture to the left. In a short time a heavy blanket of smoke covers the factories. How the smoke was generated was a military secret.

from giving new recruits basic training to shipping Troop Carrier units and glider troops overseas. In June 1945, after the end of hostilities in Europe, the field was made a Central Assembly Station with the mission of receiving troops from Europe and preparing them for transfer to the Pacific. This mission was cut short by the sudden surrender of Japan. In Sept. 1945 Baer Field became a separation center and in 1948 it passed to the US Air Force and served as an Air Force base until after the Korean War. The air field then became the area's main airport known as Ft. Wayne International Airport.

Greater Fort Wayne Aviation Museum: This museum is on the second floor of the Airport Terminal at Ft. Wayne International Airport. It has displays on the aviation history of NE Indiana and the history of Baer Field. Hours: daily 7 am-10 pm.

CASAD ORDNANCE DEPOT was located three miles east of the town of New Haven on the north side of SR 14/US 24 & 30. It was built in 1942 by the Federal Government to receive, store and ship a wide variety of war material ranging from small arms to 240 mm mobile guns. The depot handled projectiles, anti-aircraft guns, machine tools, automobiles, tanks, tank destroyers, parts and Lend Lease items scheduled for shipment to the Soviet Union. The depot was two miles long with easy access to main highways and two rail lines. The depot had four different names prior to its being named Casad Ordnance Depot in April 1943, the name it carried throughout the remainder of the war. Labor was always in short supply so prisoners of war were used and soldiers from nearby Camp Scott were sometimes pressed into service as depot workers. The depot remained active in the immediate postwar years but eventually parts of it were sold off to form an industrial park. The part of the depot retained in Government hands became known as the Strategic Materials Depot and stockpiled strategic minerals and ores for use in future national emergencies.

CAMP THOMAS A. SCOTT was located at the SE edge of Ft. Wayne opposite the International Harvester Co. between Wayne's Trace Rd. and the Pennsylvania RR. It was established in May 1942 to train the 750th Railway Operating Engineer Battalion whose mission was to provide rail service behind American lines in combat zones. As a major part of their training the men worked with actual civilian railway crews. The 750th Battalion departed in Nov. 1944 and the camp was converted into a branch prisoner of war camp. After the war the POWs were repatriated and in the summer of 1946 the camp was used for emergency veteran housing. The camp was finally closed in Oct. 1949 and the buildings removed or sold off. Virtually no trace of the camp remains.

HAMMOND (See East Chicago/Gary/Hammond)

INDIANAPOLIS, in the geographical center of the state, is the capital of Indiana. Some of the major manufacturers in the city were the Allison Div. of General Motors which made aircraft engines[2], including some of the early jet engines; the Curtiss-Wright Corp. which was the nation's largest manufacturer of propellers; the Marmon Herrington Co. which made trucks, armored cars, light tanks, tractors and axles and Bridgeport Brass Co. which made brass cartridges. Like many cities, Indianapolis gave up its state fairgrounds to the military for the duration of the war. The Indiana State Fairgrounds, on E. 38th St., became an AAF sub-depot of the Fairfield, OH Air Service Depot specializing in the storage of aircraft engine parts and technical books.

FORT BENJAMIN HARRISON was NE of, and adjacent to, Indianapolis. It was built in 1905-06 to be the home of the Army's 10th Infantry Regiments. During WW I it was an Army training camp and after that

[2] Allison engines were used in the P-38, P-39 and P-40 fighter planes.

war it became the permanent home of the 11th Infantry Regiment. With the onset of WW II Fort Harrison, too small for infantry training, become an induction and reception center. The fort then acquired the Army Finance School, a Finance Replacement Training Center, a chaplin's school, a school for cooks and bakers, a 1000-bed general hospital, a medical technicians school, a military police school, a disciplinary barracks and a special training center to provide periodic field training for office-bound GI's. In Jan. 1944 the fort established a prisoner of war camp for 250 Italian POWs. By 1944 finance operations became the dominant activity at the fort when the Finance School and the Finance Replacement Training Center were merged to form the Army Service Forces Training Center (ASFTC). The general hospital, Billings Hospital, also became a major entity receiving wounded from overseas for long-term treatment. In May 1944 the Italian POWs were transferred elsewhere and about 300 German POWs took their place. The Germans worked at the fort as did the Italians before them. In Feb. 1945 the POW camp was closed and the POWs sent to Ft. Knox, KY. At the end of the war the post became very busy because the ASFTC was deluged with a mountain of accounting work necessary to close the financial records of the hundreds of thousands of service personnel leaving the Army. And, Billings Hospital received a heavy influx of GIs who had been Axis prisoners of war and were in need of medical attention. By early 1946 most of Billings' patients had been released or sent to other facilities and in Mar. 1946 the hospital was transferred to the Veterans Administration. By July 1946 the activities of ASFTC had declined and it was moved to St. Louis, MO. In the 1950s the ASFTC returned from St. Louis and Fort Harrison evolved into the Army Finance Center (AFC) and became known as the "Home of the Army Dollar". In the 1990s Fort Harrison was closed.

INDIANA WAR MEMORIAL PLAZA occupies a five-block area in downtown Indianapolis between Meridian, Pennsylvania, New York and St. Clair Sts., and is the largest of its kind in the world.

These brick buildings at Ft. Harrison, later used for family support services, comprised the core of the fort's prisoner of war camp. They were built in 1925 as part of Camp Edwin F. Glenn, a Citizens Military Training Program facility. This was one of the Army's programs to train Reserve citizen-officers in the days of strong isolationist and anti-militaristic sentiments.

The Indiana War Memorial Building in downtown Indianapolis.

Contained within the Plaza is a Memorial Building, a park, a cenotaph honoring Indiana's war dead, fountains, a 100 ft. obelisk and the National headquarters of the American Legion.

War Memorial Building: This is a multi-story limestone edifice that serves as the main focus of the Plaza. It is at the south end of the Plaza between Vermont and Michigan Sts. In the lower concourse of the building is the Military Museum which focuses on Indiana's military history and has many artifacts from WW I and WW II. Address: 431 N. Meridian St., Indianapolis, IN 46204. Phone: 317/635-1964. Hours: daily 8-4:30, closed Jan. 1, July 4, Thanksgiving and Dec. 25. Free.

INDIANAPOLIS CHEMICAL WARFARE DEPOT: This depots stored poison gas and because of it, kept a very low profile lest this knowledge unduly alarm the people living in the area. The depot was located in a group of three pre-war leased buildings at 2060 Northwestern Ave.,

but there were no signs identifying it, no listed phone number and all visible military activities were kept as concealed as possible. The depot operated from May 1942 to June 1946. It also stored gas masks, gas-proof clothing, desensitizing chemicals, flame throwers and other items of a chemical nature. Labor was in such short supply at the depot that in Jan. 1945 the depot managers reluctantly accepted 63 German prisoners of war as laborers. At the end of the war the depot was closed and its inventory shipped to Huntsville, AL. For many years thereafter, people in the area did not know what had been stored at 2060 Northwestern Ave.

STOUT FIELD, three miles SW of downtown Indianapolis at S. Holt Rd. and Minnesota, was built by the city in the 1920s as a municipal airport and a home for the Indiana National Guard. In 1928 the city realized it needed a larger airport and with expansion possibilities at Stout limited, the city bought 1000 acres two miles to the west to build a new and larger municipal airport. Stout Field was then turned over to the state to be used primarily by the National Guard and as a secondary commercial airport. The Indiana National Guard was nationalized in 1940 and in early 1942 the AAF leased the nearly empty airport from the state and converted it into the headquarters of, and a training field for, the newly created I Troop

Carrier Com-mand. The mission of the new Comand was to transport by air paratrooper, airborne infantry units, equipment and evacuate wounded. C-47s, C-53s, and later C-46s, became the Command's standard equipment and pilot and crews trained in those aircraft. The field became a stop-over field for other military aircraft flying coast-to-coast and an arrival field for wounded being flown in from combat areas to be treated at Ft. Benjamin Harrison's Billings Hospital. As the activities of the I Troop Carrier Command increased, and the capacity of Stout Field reached its limits, other fields around the country were acquired to train additional TCC pilots and crews. As more gliders became available Stout Field became a testing field for newly produced gliders and in June 1944 acquired a glider pick-up school. After the war the I Troop Carrier Command headquarters was transferred to Greenville, SC and Stout Field stood vacant. For a while its barracks were used as emergency housing units to ease a local housing shortage. In 1947 the field was returned to state control and again became the home of the Indiana National Guard. By 1977 all flying at the field ended and much of the land not used by the Guard was sold off to become an industrial park. The National Guard has a display of some WW II equipment near the main gate.

U.S. NAVAL ORDNANCE PLANT, INDIANAPOLIS was located at E. 21st St. and Arlington Ave. This large factory building was built in 1942 to manufacture the secret Norden Bombsight, considered at the time to be the best in the world. The entire factory was air conditioned at a time when air conditioning was very rare. The plant was operated by the Lukas-Harold Corp. and during the war produced 14,000 bombsights as well as flight gyros, torpedo directors and gunsights. At its peak the plant employed 6900 people. In Sept. 1945 the factory was taken over by the Bureau of Ordnance and began making shipboard and airborne fire control devices. In 1978 the Navy returned and converted the factory into a large research, development and test center on sophisticated electronic and mechanical devices, many of which were for guided missiles. The factory then operated under several names. In the 1900s the facility was closed.

USS "INDIANAPOLIS" MEMORIAL, 714 N. Senate Ave, commemorates the cruiser, USS Indianapolis, which was torpedoed and sunk in the Pacific on July, 30 1945 by a Japanese submarine. The ship had just delivered America's first atomic bomb to Tinian Island. The ship sunk quickly and her brief distress signal was not heard. As a result most of her crew died in the water due to exhaustion, injury, thirst and sharks. Only 317 survived out of a crew of 1197. The names of all 1197 crewmen are inscribed on the monument. The monument is on the east bank of the Downtown Canal at the end of W. Walnut St. which runs west from the 700 block of N. Senate.

JEFFERSONVILLE, in south-central Indiana, is on the Ohio River opposite Louisville, KY. During the war it had a large boat-builder, the Jeffersonville Boat & Machine Co. that built sub chasers, LSTs and YO Boats for the U.S. Navy.

Stout Field's WW II runways remain in use in a number of unique ways. The foreground shows the original concrete runway, right, and topped with asphalt, left, for use as a road in the industrial park. In the background the runway is used as a parking pad for equipment of the Indiana National Guard. In other areas of the industrial park runways are used as warehouse floors and foundations.

The main entrance to the post-Civil War-era quadrangle at the Jeffersonville Quartermaster Depot. This building was used by the Quartermaster Corps during WW II and well into the postwar years. It is now in private hands.

JEFFERSONVILLE QUARTERMASTER DEPOT: This is a huge depot with a unique post-Civil War-era quadrangle building located in the two-block area between 10th and 12th Sts. and Watt and Mechanic Sts. near downtown Jeffersonville. From this location the depot spreads out to the north and west covering more than a hundred acres with dozens of warehouses built during WW I and WW II. The depot began in 1864 an as Army hospital. By the 1930s the facility had become a quartermaster depot an auto repair facility, a manufacturer of tents and other canvas items and a sheet metal shop. The depot stored many of the items it made plus thousands of other items purchased from contractors. During WW II the deopt expanded adding a machine shop, foundry, woodworking shop, printing shop and manufacturing facilities to make field kitchens, mess furniture, agricultural equipment, more items of leather and canvas and more articles of clothing. Many of the personal items used by GIs were made here; canteens and canteen covers, shelter half tents, meat cans, canteen cups, pistol belts, haversacks, cartridge and magazine belts, entrenching shovels and every GI belt the Army issued. In 1943 the depot was charged with the task of buying and storing sporting goods. The depot also had a training center for quartermaster personnel and a research and development facility that constantly strived to improved quartermaster items. The depot handled some 27,000 different items during the war and peak employment reached 5000 people, about half of them women. Also working at the depot were negro service units and German prisoners of war. In the early postwar years the depot was very busy receiving, sorting, repairing and disposing of items returned from all over the world. The Army abandoned the depot in the late 1950s and most of the buildings, including the Civil War-era quadrangle, were sold.

LAPORTE is in NW Indiana.

KINGSBURY ORDNANCE PLANT, 7 miles SE of town, was built in 1940-41 as an ammunition loading plant and operated by the Todd and Brown Corp. Production began in Aug. 1941 and for the duration of the war the plant produced tens of millions of round of ammunition ranging from 20 mm to 75 mm. The plant was one of the earliest to be inactivated in Jan. 1945 as the supply of munitions began to meet projected needs. In 1946, however, the plant was re-activated to make bombs, land mines, primers, fuses, mortar rounds and medium-caliber ammunition. It produced these products until 1959 at which time it was permanently closed and many of the buildings sold off. Portions of the facility became an industrial park, a wildlife area and an Army Reserve facility.

MADISON is a county seat in SE Indiana on the Ohio River.

JEFFERSON PROVING GROUND, 7 miles north of town, was a huge fan-shaped tract of land 17.5 miles long, three miles wide at the south end and 6 miles wide at the north. The site was chosen in 1940 to be an extension of the Aberdeen Proving Grounds in Maryland which, since before WW I, had been the Army's only facility for field testing munitions. The Madison site was chosen because it was a flat remote area, yet near enough to major industrial centers, with good transportation facilities available and suitable weather. It was also close to the newly-built Indiana Arsenal at Charlestown, IN whose power it would test. Construction began in Dec. 1940 and in May 1941 the first firings began when the facility was only 40% complete. The main components of the proving grounds were the administrative, technical and living areas, the firing lines, the impact and recovery fields and a large air field from which large bombers could operate to test airborne ordnance. Administrative personnel came from Aberdeen and at its peak of operations JPG employed 1200 people, 22% of them women. JPG worked closely with the Indiana Arsenal testing nearly ever batch of powder produced. JPG continued in operation throughout the Cold War but was closing in 1995. An extensive cleanup, that will continue until 2021, is underway to make the land safe and usable again.

NEWPORT is in west-central Indiana near the Illinois state line.

NEWPORT ARMY AMMUNITION PLANT was built in 1942 to produce various explosives including RDX, an explosive more powerful than TNT. The facility was operated during the war by the E.I. DuPont de Nemours, Corp. After the war the plant continued in operation for years making and storing deadly VX nerve gas. With the end of the Cold War the question as to how to dispose of the nerve gas became a highly controversial local issue.

PERU is 60 miles north of Indianapolis.

U.S. NAVAL AIR STATION, BUNKER HILL, 7 miles west of Peru on U.S. 31, was built in 1942 by the Navy as a permanent air station to provide primary pilot training to Naval Reserve air cadets. Twenty six outlying fields were acquired by the station, many of them no more than a grass field. The first landing strips built at the air station were of steel mats, but these were eventually replaced by concrete runways. The station was commissioned in July 1942 as U.S. Naval Reserve Aviation Base, Peru, but the name was soon changed to U.S. Naval Air Station, Peru. In 1943 it was changed again to U.S. Naval Air Station, Bunker Hill after the small community of Bunker Hill, IN one miles east of the station. More than 6000 Navy and Marine pilots trained here during the war including 800 British pilots from the Royal Navy. On one of the runways was a painted flight deck of an aircraft carrier. The cadets dubbed it "USS Cornfield". At war's end, all training ended and the station was placed in caretaker status. In 1951 the US Air Force took over the station, named it Bunker Hill Air Force Base and used it throughout the Cold War. In 1968 it was renamed Grissom Air Force Base and in the 1990s it was closed.

Grissom Air Museum and Airpark: This is a fine private museum on the grounds of the old air base with an interesting display of aircraft from WW II and later. WW II aircraft include a B-17G, C-47 and a B-25J. Address: 6500 Hoosier Blvd., Grissom AFB, IN 46971. Phone: 317/688-2654. Hours: Museum, M, W, F & Sat. 10-4. Airpark open daily dawn to dusk.

RUSHVILLE is 30 miles east of Indianapolis

The grave of Wendell L. Willkie, 1940 Republican presidential candidate and, later, special emissary of President Roosevelt to several important Allied leaders. (See page 88.)

Aerial view of Freeman Field during the war.

and during 1940 it had a brief period of glory when it was chosen as the site of the National Campaign Headquarters of the Republican Party for the Republican presidential candidate, Wendell Willkie. Willkie's wife was from Rushville and when he returned to Indiana he spent much time here.

WENDELL WILLKIE GRAVE SITE: Easthill Cemetery, on SR 44 east of town, is the final resting place of Wendell Willkie and several members of his family. At the main entrance to the cemetery is a plaque honoring Willkie.

SEYMOUR is midway between Indianapolis and Louisville, KY on I-65.

FREEMAN FIELD, two miles south of town, was built by the CAA as an emergency landing field before the war. It was taken over by the AAF in 1942 as part of the 70,000 Pilot Training Program to provide advanced flight training for crews of multi-engine aircraft. The field was expanded and first called Seymour Army Air Field. Pilots began training in Oct. 1942 in AT-10 and Beechcraft Model 26 twin-engine trainers before the field was fully operational. The field was renamed Freeman Army Air Field in May 1943 in honor of Capt. Richard Freeman, a well-known pre-war aviator from Winamac, IN. Freeman Field was a segregated base so negro units served here performing service duties. In Jan. 1944 Freeman Field became the first AAF field in the nation to train helicopter pilots and mechanics. The first class of helicopter pilots graduated in Aug. 1944. Also in early 1944 a "Little Bryan"[3] instrument flying school was set up at Freeman, and later a school to train WACs in control tower duties was established. Between Jan. and Dec. 1944 Womens Airforce Service Pilots (WASPs) served at the field flight testing aircraft undergoing maintenance. Also by 1944 the field had schools for aircraft mechanics and radio technicians. In Mar. 1944 flight training operations from Atterbury AAF were transferred here. In late 1944, however, the need for twin-engine pilots diminished and operations at the field declined rapidly, and by Feb. 1945 the field had became inactive. During its years as a training field some 4000 pilots received their wings here and the field had the lowest accident rate for its type in the Eastern

[3] So named because it was one of several off-shoots of the instrument flying school originated at Bryan, TX.

Flying Training Command. In Mar, 1945 the field was reactivated by the Air Technical Service Command (ATSC) to provide consolidation of, and advanced training for, the 477th Bombardment Group, an all-negro unit, which was undergoing training at two different locations. This unit stayed only a few months and in May 1945 the field was inactivated again. In June 1945 the field was reactivated a third time and made a collecting point for captured enemy aircraft and aeronautical equipment which was tested and evaluated. Two of the German planes tested here were the JU 290 4-engine bomber, Germany's equivalent to the U.S. B-29, and Germany's first operational jet, the Me 262. In Nov. 1945 the ATSCs glider laboratory came to Freeman to test new gliders and try new towing methods. During 1946-47 military operations phased down and in Apr. 1947 the field became inactive once again, this time for good. The city of Seymour acquired the field and converted it into its municipal airport and a large industrial park. Freeman had five auxiliary fields during the war:

- Aux. #1, Walesboro Airport, 1 mile SW of Walesboro
- Aux. #2, St. Anne Airport, 2.5 miles NE of North Vernon
- Aux. #?, Grammar Field in Bartholomew County
- Aux. #4, Millport Airport, .5 miles NW of Millport
- Aux. #?, Zenas Field in Jackson County

SOUTH BEND is in north-central Indiana. Among the major companies producing war material were the Studebaker Corp. which produced the Cyclone aircraft engine used in B-17 bombers, trucks and the Weasel cargo carriers. The Oliver Farm Equipment Corp. made gun barrels, 20mm to 155 mm shells, projectiles and shot and the Bendix Corp. made aircraft parts.

TERRE HAUTE is in west-central Indiana on the Wabash River. One of the major manufacturers in the city was Commercial Solvents, Corp. which produced penicillin for the needs of the armed forces.

TERRE HAUTE ORDNANCE DEPOT was located two mile NE of Terre Haute on Fruitridge Ave. and adjacent to the Chicago, Milwaukee, St. Paul and Pacific Railroad. It was built in 1942 as a storage, rebuilding and modification facility for military vehicles and equipment. It also stored spare parts for the vehicles and prepared both vehicles and parts for overseas shipments. Many of the depot workers were women. After the war the depot was made a permanent Army installation and was used for many years thereafter.

VIGO ORDNANCE PLANT was built in late 1942 by the Federal Government to load shells and bags and produce detonators with powder made by the nearby Wabash River Ordnance Plant. The Vigo Ordnance Plant was operated by ConCan Ordnance Corp., a subsidiary of Continental Can Co., and began production in Feb. 1943. It operated only 9 months and was then shut down. This made it one of the last ordnance plants in the nation to open and one of the first to close. In Jan. 1944 the plant was leased to Delco Radio Div. of GM to produce radios and another part was used for ammunition storage. In May 1944 the Army started up a small production line to make smoke bombs but in Nov. 1945 it was inactivated again.

WABASH RIVER ORDNANCE PLANT was built

The Commercial Solvents Corp. plant is Terre Haute was one of several in the country that mass-produced penicillin for the military.

in 1942 near Terre Haute by the Federal Government to produce the powerful explosive, RDX, for the U.S Navy and the British. RDX is 30% more powerful than TNT, but also more sensitive. This was the first plant in the country to produce RDX and was built on the model of British plants which used the batch method of producing the explosive. Before the plant was completed, however, a second RDX plant was begun at Kingsport, TN which used a newly developed process to producing RDX quicker and cheaper. As a result, production of RDX at this plant was ended in late summer 1943. Later that year the plant was converted into a back-up manufacturer of heavy water for the Manhattan (atomic bomb) Project. In Oct. 1945 the plant was inactivated.

VINCENNES is in SW Indiana on the Wabash River.

INDIANA MILITARY MUSEUM, NE of Vincennes, has a large collection of vehicles and artifacts from the Civil War to the present, but the majority of the collection is from WW II. There are articles of clothing and personal items belonging to Gens. Ira Eaker, James Gavin, Omar Bradley, George Patton, Dwight Eisenhower, Mark Clark, Maxwell Taylor, James Van Fleet and Admirals William Halsey, Eugene Fluckey and Robert Carney. The museum has displays on the cruiser USS "Vincennes" and George Field which was just across the state line in Illinois. Address: 4305 Bruceville Rd., Vincennes, IN 47591. Phone: 812/882-8668. Hours: Outdoor displays daily 8-5. Indoor displays (summer) daily noon-5, winter inquire. Donations requested. Location: From the clover-leaf interchange of US 150/41 and US 50 proceed south of US 50 past the

Holiday Inn 1/4 mile to the first intersection. Turn east and the road quickly becomes a "Y". Take the north (left) arm of the "Y"which is Bruceville Rd. and proceed about two miles to the museum.

USS "VINCENNES" MUSEUM is in Vincennes City Hall. The museum commemorates the four ships of the U.S. Navy that have carried the Vincennes name. Two of these ships, both cruisers, fought in WW II. The USS "Vincennes" (CA-44, 1936) saw action in the Pacific early in the war which included escort duty for the carrier Hornet on the Doolittle Tokyo Raid. This ship was later lost off Guadalcanal. The second "Vincennes" (CL-64, 1943) saw action in the western Pacific in 1944-45. Address: Vincennes City Hall, Vigo St. and Lincoln Memorial Bridge, Vincennes, IN 47591. Hours: M-F 9-4. Free.

IOWA

During the war Iowa was one of the America's great food-producing states. Iowa is in the heart of the grain belt and produces corn, soybeans, wheat, oats, barley, potatoes, hogs, cattle, sheep, horses and mules. In 1940 Iowa had 210,000 farms, 9,651,000 hogs, 4,688,000 cattle and 2,538,000 people. During the war the state had several prisoner of war camps and many of the POWs helped to produce Iowa's food. The state was a great producer of meat products and much of the canned meat produced in Iowa found its way overseas to feed our GI's at the front. Iowa was one of several states that began to produce hemp for the war effort when America's supply of this important imported fiber was reduced due to shortages of shipping. The state also had several manufacturing centers, the largest of which were Burlington, Cedar Rapids and Ankeny. Minerals produced in the state were coal, cement, gypsum, sand & gravel and stone. In 1940 Iowa's favorite son, Henry A. Wallace became Vice President of the United States after having been hand-picked by President Roosevelt to be his running mate. Iowa was also the home state of America's only living ex-president, Herbert Hoover, who held several important governmental and UN posts during and after the war which involved the distribution of food to the war's victims and refugees. Another Iowan of prominence, from Sioux City, was Harry Hopkins, President Roosevelt's most trusted advisor during most of the war. Hopkins had distinguished himself early in the Roosevelt Administration by creating a huge welfare program to put people back to work at the beginning of the Great Depression. Hopkins also administered the Lend Lease Program, met with Churchill and Stalin on FDR's behalf, served as FDR's liaison with the Chiefs of Staff and, for a while, lived in the White House with the Roosevelt family. Truman also used Hopkins as an advisor. Dubuque, Iowa was the home town of Frederick W. Kaltenbach, an Iowan who distinguished himself in a very different way. He was one of several Ameri-

can turncoats who made propaganda broadcasts for Germany.

Near the end of the war Iowa was subjected to Japanese bombing balloon attacks. These attacks did no serious damage and due the great secrecy surrounding the attacks most Iowa citizens didn't even know they were being attacked.

ALGONA is in north-central Iowa 40 miles north of Ft. Dodge.

ALGONA PRISONER OF WAR CAMP, now Algona Airport, was 1.5 miles NW of town at the junction of US 18 and US 169. It held up to 5000 German POWs who worked mainly in agriculture and forestry. In their spare time several German artisans built an elaborate Nativity Scene, that upon completion, was displayed for the 1945 Christmas season at the edge of the camp near the road where passers-by could see it. In 1946 the POWs departed and the camp was closed and dismantled, but the nativity scene was saved.

ALGONA NATIVITY SCENE, built by German prisoners of war at the nearby Algona Prisoner of war Camp, is on permanent display in its own building at the Kossuth County Fairgrounds. The figures are half-lifesize and were made of surplus wire, plaster and concrete. The scene took more than a year to complete. Several of the former POWs who worked on the project returned to Algona after the war and were treated by the townspeople as celebrities. The Nativity Scene is open to the public daily from 2 pm to 9 pm from the

The Nativity Scene made by German prisoners of war at Algona POW Camp during the war is preserved and on display at the Kossuth County Fairgrounds.

first Sunday in Dec. to New Year's Eve and by appointment the rest of the year; phone 515/295-7163. Donations requested. The Fairgrounds is locate south of town. Take US 169 (Phillips St.) south to E. Fair St. Turn on Fair St. 1 block to Fairgrounds entrance. The Nativity Scene building is at the west end of the fairgrounds.

BOONE is 35 miles NW of Des Moines.

MAMIE DOUD EISENHOWER BIRTHPLACE: This is the birthplace of Mamie Doud Eisenhower, wife of General Dwight D. Eisenhower, Supreme Allied Commander in Europe and later President of the United States. This modest Victorian residence has been restored and opened to the public. It is one of only two homes of first ladies so preserved1 in the U.S. The first floor of the home is decorated in furnishings of the times when Mamie lived here. Much of the furniture came from members of the Doud family including the bed in the master bedroom in which Mamie was

The birthplace of Mamie Doud Eisenhower. This is one of only two preserved homes of American first ladies in the U.S.

Schick General Hospital was built in 1942-43 to care for wounded servicemen of WW II. After the war the facility was sold to private interests and its buildings utilized for a variety of purposes. This part of the hospital is an apartment complex.

born in 1896. The basement has been converted into a museum and library displaying many of Mamie's personal belongings and items relating to Mamie's childhood and adult life. There are also exhibits on the General. Address: 709 Carroll St. Boone, IA 50036. Phone: 515/432-1896. Hours: Apr. & May Tues.-Sun. 1-5. June-Oct. daily 10-5. Rest of year by appointment. Admission charged. Location: The home is a few blocks NE of downtown Boone. Carroll is a north-south street five blocks east of Division St., the town's main north-south street. Proceed north on Carroll to the 700 block.

BURLINGTON is in the SE corner of Iowa on the Mississippi River.

IOWA ORDNANCE PLANT, on SR 79 just west of town, was built in 1941 by the Federal Government to load bombs, shells, projectiles, primers, detonators and fuses. It was one of the larger manufacturing plants in Iowa and was run by the Day & Zimmerman Corp. The plant got off to a bad start when, in Dec. 1941, only months after opening a serious explosion occurred and took the lives of 13 workers. The plant was retained by the Government after the war and operated throughout the Cold War. In the postwar years it became known as the Iowa Army Ammunition Plant.

CLINTON is in the east-central Iowa on the Mississippi River

SCHICK GENERAL HOSPITAL This was a 2014-bed hospital built by the U.S. Army in 1942-43 to care for wounded personnel. All of the buildings are brick and the hospital was intended to be semi-permanent. The hospital specialized in general medicine, CNS syphilis, general and orthopedic surgery and psychiatry. About 200 prisoners of war worked at the hospital. In 1946 it became a veteran's hospital but eventually closed and the buildings were sold off. Most of them remain and are used for a variety of purposes; apartments, nursing home, handicapped employment center, senior citizen center, art museum and a county museum. Schick is located north of downtown at North 4th St. and 25th Ave. North.

Clinton County Historical Museum: This museum is in the former morgue building of

the hospital. It traces the history of Clinton County and has considerable information on Schick General Hospital. Address: Root Park off 25th Ave. South, Clinton, IA 52732. Phone: 319/242-1201,6797,4544. Hours: Sat. & Sun. 1:30-4:30. Other times by appointment. Donations accepted.

DES MOINES is in the south-central part of the state and is Iowa's capital. The Iowa State fairgrounds, three miles east of downtown, was taken over by the AAF and converted into s specialized air depot for the duration of the war. On display in the State of Iowa Historical Building, 600 E. Locust St., are fragments of one of the Japanese bombing balloons that came down in the state.

DES MOINES MUNICIPAL AIRPORT, now Des Moines International Airport, is SE of downtown on 64th Ave. & Fleur St. It was home to the AAF's 132nd Tactical Fighter Wing during the war, but remained an operating civilian airport. The Air Transport Command and Air Technical Service Command operated at the field, and there was a military air freight terminal. In the postwar years the Iowa Air National Guard operated from the airport.

DES MOINES ORDNANCE PLANT was built in Des Moines in 1940-41 by the Federal Government to make 30 and 50 calibre ammunition. This plant was highly automated and produced millions of round per day. It was run by the United States Rubber Co.

FORT DES MOINES, five miles south of downtown at Chaffee and Army Post Rd. (SR 5), was built in 1900-03 as an Army cavalry post. From 1920 through WW II the 14th Calvary shared the post with a field artillery unit. Early in WW II the fort served as a reception center

for the 7th Corps Area and in 1942 became the first training center in the country for the newly formed Women's Army Auxiliary Corps (WAAC)2. This event gave the fort considerable notoriety and some 65,000 women eventually trained here. In 1946 the fort was closed and used as a temporary housing project. In 1958 the Army returned and made it the home of the Iowa Sector of the XIV Army Corps, an Army Reserve Training Center and various other military and civilian agencies. Some of the fort's land has been converted into a county park and golf course.

CAMP DODGE, 12 miles NW of downtown Des Moines, has been the home of the Iowa National Guard since WW I. The Guard was mobilized during WW II and became a part of the 34th Infantry Div. After the war the Iowa National Guard returned to Camp Dodge.

The Iowa Gold Star Museum: This museum is on the grounds of Camp Dodge and collects, preserves and interprets material reflecting Iowa citizens' contributions to the nation's defense. The museum displays artifacts, weapons, uniforms, photos, paintings, and large maps showing the areas in which the 34th Inf. Div.

2 The WAAC later became the Women's Army Corps (WAC) and two other WAC training centers were added, one each at Daytona Beach, FL and Ft. Oglethorpe, GA.

1 The other is the home of Abigail Adams in Massachusetts.

The Iowa Gold Star Museum at Camp Dodge honors Iowa's citizen soldiers and has considerable information on the WW II activities of the 34th Inf. Div. which was comprised, in part, by the Iowa National Guard.

The grave of Henry A. Wallace, Vice President of the U.S., 1941-44.

This WW II hangar remained in use at Sioux City Municipal Airport for decades after the war.

fought in WW II. Address: Camp Dodge, Johnston, IA 50131. Phone: 515/242-5313. Hours: M, W & F 1-4:30: Donations accepted.

HENRY A. WALLACE GRAVE SITE: Glendale Cemetery, four miles west of downtown Des Moines on University Ave., is the final resting place of Henry A. Wallace, Vice President of the U.S. from 1941 to 1944. Wallace also served as Secretary of Agriculture, Chairman of the War Production Board, Secretary of Commerce and an independent presidential candidate in 1948. Wallace was a prominent agricultural economist and editor before going into politics.

OTTUMWA is in the SE corner of the state 80 miles from Des Moines.

AIRPOWER MUSEUM is on County Rd. H41 10 miles SW of Ottumwa. It is located on the Antique Airfield which was built in 1965 to look like a typical grass-field airport of the 1930s. The museum displays a collection of planes, all privately owned, from WW I to postwar WW II. The emphasis is on light aircraft and the majority of WW II aircraft on display are trainers. Address: Rt. 2, Box 172, Ottumwa, IA 52501. Phone: 515/938-2773. Hours: M-F 9-5, Sat. 10-5, Sun. 1-5. Donations requested.

U.S. NAVAL AIR STATION, OTTUMWA was five miles north of town at the junction of US 63 and SR 389. It was built during the summer of

1942 to provide primary flight training to Naval Reserve Air Cadets (NAVCADS). At first, the base was called Naval Reserve Air Base, Ottumwa and the first planes, N3N "Yellow Peril" trainers, arrived in Sept. 1942. In Jan. 1943 the station was given its wartime name. Up to 1000 cadets trained here at a time and the station had 10 outlying fields. For a time a young Naval officer named Richard M. Nixon was the station's legal officer. At the end of the war the station served as a separation center. In 1947 it was decommissioned and became Ottumwa Industrial Airport, an industrial center and an apartment complex.

SIOUX CITY is in the west-central part of the state.

SIOUX CITY ARMY AIR BASE: This was Sioux City's new municipal airport, built in 1939-41, when it was taken over by the 2nd AF for use as a training facility for B-17 and B-24 bomber crews. The Air Transport Command had operations here including a military air freight terminal. The air field also continued to serve as the local airport during the war. In Nov. 1948 the air base was returned to the City with areas reserved for the Iowa Air National Guard and the US Air Force Reserves. The airport is located 8 miles south of downtown Sioux City on I-29.

WATERLOO is 90 miles NE of Des Moines. One of the community's families, that of Thomas and Alleta Sullivan, was to suffer a terrible loss that was to become one of the great tragic stories of WW II. On the night of Nov. 13, 1942 a Japanese submarine torpedoed the U.S. cruiser "Juneau" in the waters off Guadalcanal. The torpedo hit the ship's magazine which exploded causing the ship to sink in 16 seconds. All but 10 members

of the crew perished. Among those who died were the five sons of Thomas and Alleta Sullivan. The brothers had enlisted in the Navy together and had requested that they be allowed to serve on the same ship. The deaths of the Sullivans, which so devastated this one family, caused the Navy to revise its regulations and henceforth forbid family members from serving together on the same ship or airplane. Thomas and Alleta Sullivan and their lone surviving sibling, Genevieve Sullivan, buried their grief as best they could and eventually went on several tours to promote the sale of War Bonds. In 1943 the Navy named a newly-built destroyer in their honor and their mother christened it. That destroyer, the USS "Sullivan Brothers", saw action in WW II and is on permanent display at Naval Park, Buffalo, NY. In Feb. 1944 Hollywood made a movie of the Sullivan Brothers, called "The Fighting Sullivans", which was shown throughout the country and resulted in a surge of enlistments for the Navy. After the war the Sullivan Brothers were honored further on a U.S. postage stamp and the city of Waterloo named its new convention center and a park in their honor. The Sullivan Brothers Park is located at the corner of East 4th and Adams St. in their old neighborhood. A monument was also erected at St. Mary's grade school which the brothers attended. In Waterloo the **Grout Museum**, 503 South St., maintains permanent displays on the brothers.

The tower and operations building built by the Navy in 1942 remained in use at Ottumwa Industrial Airport for many years.

When the Sullivan Brothers were in New York City they spent a night on the town and visited Jack Dempsey's famous establishment on Times Square. There, they posed with the former heavy weight champion of the world.

KANSAS

Food and airplanes ... that's what Kansas produced most of during the war. This large state is in the geographic center of America and the heart of the Grain Belt. During the 1930s the state fell on hard times as a result of the Great Depression and the western part of the state became part of the famous "Dust Bowl". Many farmers abandoned the land and by 1940 the state's population had declined 4.3% from 1930. In the late 1930s, however, the state's economy began to grow again and with the coming of war, Kansas became a significant producer of basic food stocks such as wheat, oats, barley, hay, livestock, butter, fruit, soybeans, flax, grain sorghum and potatoes. She also produced petroleum products, natural gas, coal, cement and a variety of manufactured goods, foremost of which were airplanes. In the Wichita area a cluster of light aircraft manufacturers had evolved before the war and within a short time this industry was booming. By 1943 the state became the nation's third largest producer of military aircraft after California and New York. And, later in the war it was here in Kansas that B-29 Superfortresses were built. The state's mineral production rose significantly also and by war's end the state was third in the nation in zinc production, fifth in salt, sixth in lead and tenth in cement. In the western part of the state her oil, coal and natural gas resources were actively exploited and there was much wildcat drilling. By 1945 these efforts had paid off and Kansas counted 53 new oil and gas pools.

Kansas was represented in President Roosevelt's Cabinet in the late 1930s by a Kansas native, Harry H. Woodring, Secretary of War.

Although Kansas was about as secure from enemy attacks as any state in the union the state did come under attack on one occasion when a Japanese bombing balloon came down harm-

lessly in the NE corner of the state near Bigelow.

The end of the war saw the state in a strong economic position with a continuing demand for her food products. The aircraft industry declined for a while, but then revived as the need for civilian and military aircraft grew during the postwar years.

ABILENE is 85 miles west of Topeka on I-70.

THE EISENHOWER CENTER is a large complex of five major buildings honoring Abilene's, and Kansas', favorite son, Dwight D. Eisenhower. Ike, as he was known throughout most of his life, grew up in Abilene. He left Abilene as a young man seeking a career in the Army and rose to be the Supreme Allied Commander in Europe during WW II and later President of the United States. He returned from time-to-time to Abilene to visit, and finally returned in death. Ike, his wife Mamie and their first-born son, Doud Dwight Eisenhower, are buried on the grounds of the Center in a chapel known as the Place of Meditation. The other major buildings of the Center are the Eisenhower Family Home, the Museum, Presidential Library and Visitor's Center. The Eisenhower home stands on its original site on 4th St. and is furnished with much of the original furnishings and fixtures. The museum consists of five major galleries and contains items associated with Eisenhower, his family and his career. The Library houses the private and official papers accumulated by Eisenhower during his two terms as President. The Visitor's Center orients the visitors, explains the facilities and services offered and shows a motion picture on Eisenhower's life. Address: The Eisenhower Center, Abilene, KS 67410. Phone: 913/263-4751. Hours: daily 9-4:45, closed Jan. 1, Thanksgiving and Dec. 25. Admission charged to the Museum. Other buildings free. The Center is located two miles south of the Abilene exit off I-70 on SR 15 (Buckeye Ave.)

WORLD WAR II HALL OF GENERALS WAX MUSEUM is one block south of the Eisenhower Center and features life-sized wax models of famous U.S. generals and admirals of WW II. In the display are Gens. Eisenhower, MacArthur, Adm. Nimitz and others. A brief biography of each man is provided. There is a large gift shop associated with the museum. Address: 100 SE 5th St., Abilene, KS 67410. Phone: 913/263-

Life-sized wax figure of Adm. Chester W. Nimitz at the World War II Hall of Generals Wax Museum.

4194. Hours: daily Mar.-Sept. 8-8, Oct.-Feb. 9-5. Admission charged to the museum.

COFFEYVILLE is in the SE corner of the state on the Oklahoma state line. Wendell Willkie, the 1940 Republican candidate for president, taught school here before he came to prominence as a businessman and politician. And, when he began his presidentail campaign in 1940 he launched it from here. His association with Coffeyville is remembered with exhibits in the Dalton Defenders Museum, 113 E. 8th St. Hours: Memorial Day-Labor daily 9-7, rest of year 9-5. Admission charged.

COFFEYVILLE ARMY AIR FIELD, 4.5 miles NE of town was established by the 3rd AF in 1942 as part of the 50,000 Pilot Training Program to train pilots, combat air crews and aerial photographers. Coffeyville AAF had an auxiliary field, Edna Airport five miles north of Edna, KS which it shared with Independence AAF.

CONCORDIA is 50 miles north of Salina.

CONCORDIA PRISONER OF WAR CAMP was built near Concordia and held about 2300 German POWs who worked mostly in agriculture. Little remains of the camp except for its water tower and some building foundations. The Cloud County Historical Museum, 635 Broadway, has a permanent display on the POW camp. Hours: Tues.-Sat. 1-5, closed major holidays. Donations requested.

DODGE CITY is in the SW corner of the state.

DODGE CITY ARMY AIR FIELD, 6 miles NW of town, was built in 1942 for the 70,000 Pilot Training Program to train pilots and crews in medium bombers, primarily B-25s. In 1945 the

In this two-story white house, President Eisenhower and his brothers grew to manhood Their mother lived there until her death in 1946.

Left: The concrete runway at Dodge City AAF is abandoned and overgrown with weeds and the WW II hangar in the distance is abandoned and decaying. Above: Many chimneys can be seen on the site of the Dodge City AAF but the buildings they served are long gone.

AAF departed and the air field and its buildings were used for a variety of commercial and civilian purposes. Location: Proceed west of Dodge City on US 50 2.3 miles from its junction with US 50 Business to an unnamed paved road with signs giving directions to Rex Stanley Feed Yard, Inc. and Santa Fe Trail Suburbans. Proceed north on this road 2.1 miles to the air field site which is on either side of the road.

GALENA is in the SE corner of Kansas five miles west of Joplin, MO.

JAYHAWK ORDNANCE WORKS was built by the Federal Government in 1941 two miles NE of Galena to make ammonia and nitric acids which were used in explosives.

GARDEN CITY is in SW Kansas 50 miles NW of Dodge City.

GARDEN CITY ARMY AIR FIELD was 9 miles SE of town on US 50. It was established as an AAF training field in 1942 as part of the 70,000 Pilot Training Program. After the war the field was turned over to the community to become its local airport, Garden City Municipal Airport. In the terminal is a small display on the air field's WW II days. Garden City AAF had three auxiliary fields in the area, all constructed of steel landing mats.

GREAT BEND is in central Kansas 90 miles NW of Wichita.

GREAT BEND ARMY AIR FIELD, 4.5 miles SW of town, was built in 1942 for the 2nd AF as an operational training base for very heavy bombers, primarily B-17s and B-24s. In late 1943 the air field became one of four in Kansas[1] to train B-29 crews in newly-built B-29s being produced in Wichita. After the war the air field became Great Bend's municipal airport.

HAYS/WALKER AREA: Hays is 93 miles west of Salina on I-70. Early in the war it had a local airport with a civilian flight training school that was contracted by the Air Corps early in the war to train Army pilots. Walker is 13 miles east of Hays.

WALKER ARMY AIR FIELD, 1.2 miles NW of Walker, was built in 1942 for the 2nd AF and was known for a time as Hays-Walker Air Field. It was an operational training base for the crews of very heavy bombers, primarily B-17s and B-24s. The field had a small prisoner of war camp holding about 75 POWs who worked in agriculture. In late 1943 Walker AAF became one of four fields[2] in Kansas to train crews of B-29 bombers being produced in Wichita. Through the years the field has been abandoned.

HERINGTON is 70 miles SW of Topeka.

HERINGTON ARMY AIR FIELD, 10 miles NE of town, was built in 1942 for the 2nd AF for use as an operational field for P-38 fighter units in support of Ft. Riley. In Dec. 1942, soon after the base became operational, it was converted to a staging field for heavy bomber units preparing to leave for overseas

[1,2] The other 3 were at Pratt, Salina and Walker, KS.

Many WW II building foundations remain at Garden City Municipal Airport and there are a few WW II buildings in various stages of use and decay. The fire hydrant in the foreground is part of the air field's original water system remained in use well into the postwar era.

duty. Accord-ingly, the field's runways were lengthened and three large hangars were built. By Apr. 1943 Herington AAF was processing B-24 bomber units for overseas departures. The field also had a branch prisoner of war camp with about 200 POWs. During the summer of 1944, the field began processing B-29 units for overseas operations. In the postwar years the air field was used by private planes.

HUTCHINSON is 40 miles NW of Wichita. Cessna Aircraft Co. had a plant in the city making cargo gliders for the military.

U.S. NAVAL AIR STATION, HUTCHINSON was 9 miles south of town. It was built by the Navy in 1942 and first called U.S. Naval Reserve Air Base, Hutchinson with a mission to provide ground school and primary flight training for Naval Reserve Aviation Cadets (NAVCADS). The first training planes used were N2S-3 and N2S-4 trainers. In Jan. 1943 the name of the facility was changed to U.S. Naval Air Station, Hutchinson and shortly thereafter the training aircraft were upgraded to N2S-5s. In June 1944 the station acquired another school training air crews in PB-4Y Liberator bombers. Students from Allied nations were also trained here. The station had a small prisoner of war camp holding about 100 POWs who worked in

The tower and operations building at NAS, Hutchinson remain but are no longer used.

The U.S. Cavalry Museum is in Ft. Riley's old hospital building (1854) and traces the history of the U.S. Cavalry from the Revolutionary War to 1950.

agriculture. By the end of the war some 5000 Navy and Allied personnel had been trained here. The station was disestablished soon after the war but was reopened in 1952, again as a training base. In 1958 it was disestablished again and turned over to the community of Hutchinson. It then became a secondary local airport, an industrial park and had a branch of Hutchinson Community College. The station is difficult to find. Proceed to the small town of Yoder SE of Hutchinson on SR 96. From Yoder go south on S. Yoder Road .9 miles to the first paved, but unmarked cross road. Proceed west 1.0 mile on that road to the former main gate which can be identified by the boarded-up brick guard house. The station is to the west and south of the guard house. NAS Hutchinson had the following outlying air fields (OLF):

- OLF #1 Hutchinson OLF #1, 4 miles NE
- OLF #? Newton Airport, 3 miles north of Newton
- OLF #? Searcy Field, near Stillwater, OK.

INDEPENDENCE is in SE Kansas 15 miles north of Coffeyville.

INDEPENDENCE ARMY AIR FIELD, 5.5 miles SW of town, was built in 1942 as a training field for the 70,000 Pilot Training Program. The field was retained after the war and used for the storage of surplus aircraft. At that time the field was operated by the Air Technical Service Command. Independence AAF had five auxiliary fields in the area during the war.

JUNCTION CITY is in east-central Kansas 60 miles west of Topeka.

FORT RILEY, two miles east of Junction City, was established in 1853 on the north bank of the Kansas River to protect wagon trains and settlers heading west along the Santa Fe Trail. In 1887 Ft. Riley was made a permanent school for cavalry and light artillery. Cavalry activities grew steadily at the fort and it soon became known as the "Cradle of the Cavalry". In 1936 the 13th Cavalry Regiment, one of several at the fort, was mechanized marking the beginning of the modernization of the cavalry from horses to tanks. For several years both horse-mounted and mechanized cavalry units trained here. In 1941 another camp, called Camp Forsyth, was established on the west side of the Ft. Riley reservation to become the home of the Cavalry Re-

placement Training Center. In 1943 horse-mounted cavalry training ended altogether but mechanized cavalry training continued. By the end of the war some 150,000 horse-mounted and mechanized cavalrymen had trained here. In addition to cavalry training the fort had an air field, Marshall Field, operated by the 3rd AF, where air observation units trained as support units for the cavalry. Ft. Riley also had a main prisoner of war camp holding 1800 German POWs. The POWs sent to this camp were selected for their willingness to cooperate with the Americans and were, therefore, guarded very lightly. Most of the POWs worked at the fort or in agriculture. In the postwar years Ft. Riley became the home of the 1st Infantry Div. (Mech.), had a correctional activity and an NCO Academy. At Exit 301 and I-70, the entrance to the fort, there are various pieces of WW II and more modern equipment displayed on a hillside overlooking the exit. They can be seen from I-70 and paths lead up the hill to the various pieces from a parking lot.

U.S. Cavalry Museum: This fine museum is on the grounds of Ft. Riley and chronicles the colorful history of the American mounted horse soldier from the Revolutionary War to 1950. WW II artifacts make up only a small part of the museum's displays, but several pieces of WW II-era mechanized equipment are on the grounds outside the museum. Address: Building 205, Ft. Riley, KS 66442-5000. Phone: 913/239-2737. Hours: M-Sat. 9-4:30, Sun. noon-4:30. Closed Jan. 1, Easter, Thanksgiving and Dec. 25. Free.

KANSAS CITY, Kansas, the smaller of the two Kansas Cities, is on the eastern border of the state on the west bank of the Missouri River. Located here were two aircraft manufacturers, North American Aviation Corp. which made B-25 bombers and Commonwealth Aircraft Co. Inc. which made troop carrying gliders. Being a river town with good transportation, Kansas City had two military depots during the war, the Kansas City Medical Depot and the Kansas City Quartermaster

Sub-Depot, a sub-depot of the Kansas City Quartermaster Depot in Kansas City, MO. The sub-depot was located at 4th & Santa Fe Sts. in K.C.,KS.

FAIRFAX FIELD, 2.5 miles north of downtown Kansas City on the western bank of the Missouri River, was Kansas City's pre-war municipal airport. During the war it was the site of the U.S. Government's Assembly Plant #2, operated by North American Aviation Corp. which built B-25 bombers. The air Technical Service Command and the Air Transport Command operated from the field in cooperation with North American. After the war the US Air Force took over the field for use by the U.S. Air Defense Command. After that the field reverted again to being a commercial airport, Fairfax Municipal Airport. In the late 1980s the airport was closed and the site developed into an industrial complex.

U.S. NAVAL AIR STATION, OLATHE was five miles SW of Olathe, KS, a SW suburb of Kansas City. It was built in 1942 to serve as an auxiliary airport but was soon upgraded to a naval air station. NAS, Olathe was commissioned in Oct. 1942 as a primary flight training facility for naval aviation cadets. The cadets trained in N2S Kaydets, N3N "Yellow Perils", NP Spartans and N2S-5s. In May 1943 a tornado destroyed over 100 aircraft and damaged many of the buildings. While the station was recovering its mission was expanded and it became the Continental Headquarters for the Naval Air Transport Command (NATS) and Transport Squadron 3 (VR-3) whose planes were supplied by Trans World Airlines, and VR-9, whose planes supplied by Pan American Airways. These planes, which flew servicemen to and from the various fighting fronts, were serviced and maintained at Olathe. By the fall of 1944 both primary flight training and transport operations declined and the station was reduced to servicing station aircraft and transients. All flight training ended in late 1944 and in late 1945 the NATS squadrons moved out and the station became a training base for Navy and Marine reservists from several state. In 1970 reserve flight training ended and the station became a commercial airport and an industrial park. During WW II NAS, Olathe had 14 outlying fields.

Old Olathe Naval Air Museum: This museum is on the grounds of the naval air station in the former homes of the station's commander and executive officer. On display are artifacts and memorabilia related to the history of the air station including pews from one of the station's

This large WW II hangar and adjacent building at the former NAS, Olathe are unused and slowly decaying.

chapels and the station's 1940 fire truck. Address: 1 Navy Park Dr., Industrial Airport, KS 66031. Phone: 913/829-1956. Hours: Open weekends only.

WINTER GENERAL HOSPITAL was built in Shawnee, a western suburb of Kansas City, in 1943 to treat the Army's war wounded. This was a 1771-bed facility that specialized in general medicine, general and orthopedic surgery and psychiatry. The hospital had a branch prisoner of war camp with about 160 Italian POWs who worked at the hospital. In Nov. 1945 the hospital was transferred to the Veterans Administration.

LAWRENCE is midway between Kansas City and Topeka on I-70.

THE MEMORIAL CAMPANILE OF THE UNIVERSITY OF KANSAS: This is a 120' bell tower on the campus of the University of Kansas dedicated to those who fought in WW II. It houses a 53-bell carillon and is one of only two carillons in Kansas. The bells of the carillon are played on various occasions. On the ground floor is a Memorial Room where the names of the 276 Kansans who gave their lives during the war are engraved on the walls. The Campanile is located in the heart of the campus opposite Spencer Library on Memorial Drive.

SUNFLOWER ORDNANCE WORKS was 13 miles east of Lawrence on SR 10 near the town of Eudora. It was built in 1942 to produce smokeless powder, but as the plant neared completion it was modified to produce rocket powder. The plant was run by the Hercules Powder Co. and grew to be the world's largest producer of rocket powder. It produced most of the rocket powder used by the U.S. Army and large quantities of the powder were sent to the Soviet Union[3] under Lend Lease. The plant also made sulfuric and nitric acids, nitroglycerin, nitrocellulose, TNT and oleum.

[3]The Red Army relied heavily on rocket propelled artillery and perfected a very effective multiple rocket launcher, the Katyusha Rocket Mortar, that could fire from 32 to 48 rockets in rapid succession to saturate an enemy-held area. The Germans called the Katyusha "Stalin's Pipe Organ".

Its peak employment reached 12,000 during the war. In 1946 production was scaled back drastically but the plant remained operative. The ordnance plant operated throughout the Cold War as the Sunflower Army Ammunition Plant. In the 1990s, after the Cold War, it was closed.

LEAVENWORTH is 15 miles NW of Kansas City on the Missouri River. On the Missouri River was a shipbuilder, the Missouri Valley Bridge & Iron Co. which built tank landing craft (LSTs) for the Navy.

FORT LEAVENWORTH is north of, and adjacent to, the city of Leavenworth. It was built in 1828 to protect settlers and the area's transportation routes. After the Civil War a disciplinary barracks was established and eventually became a large and permanent entity at the fort. In 1881 Gen. Wm. T. Sherman established the School of Application for Infantry and Cavalry at the fort and through the years this facility evolved into the U.S. Army Command and General Staff College, one of the most prestigious schools in the U.S. Army and usually reserved for high level officers. In 1926 Dwight Eisenhower attended the College and graduated 1st in his class. In the late 1930s Gen. George Marshall commanded the fort for a short time. At the beginning of WW II the fort became an induction center and a reception center for the 7th Corps. The Disciplinary Barracks and the Command & Staff College, of course, were very active during the war. The Disciplinary Barracks incarcerated U.S. servicemen who committed violent crimes and major felonies. Some servicemen were executed. Prisoners of war convicted of similar crimes were also imprisoned here and some of them were executed. The Command & Staff College increased its curriculum and accelerated its programs to turn our more graduates faster. During the war some 18,000 officers from all branches of the U.S. armed forces and several Allied nations went through the College. There was a main prisoner of war camp here and an air field, Sherman Field, operated by the 3rd AF. At the end of the war

the fort became a separation center. After that the fort continued to function much as it did in the past. It remained the home of the Command & Staff College and the Disciplinary Barracks and became a National Historic Landmark.

Frontier Army Museum: This museum is on the grounds of Ft. Leavenworth opposite Bell Hall. It chronicles the founding and long history of the fort and, of course, has exhibits on the fort during WW II. Address: Andrews Hall, Gibbons & Reynolds Aves., Ft. Leavenworth, KS 66027. Phone: 913/684-3191. Hours: M-F 9-4, Sat. 10-4, Sun. & holidays noon-4, closed Jan. 1, Easter, Thanksgiving, Dec. 25. Free.

LIBERAL is in the SE corner of Kansas on the Oklahoma state line.

LIBERAL ARMY AIR FIELD, 1.5 miles NW of town, was built in 1942 for the 70,000 Pilot Training Program to train pilots and crews in four-engine bombers, primarily B-24s. In 1946 the field was declared surplus and became a civil air field, Liberal Airport.

Mid-America Air Museum: This fine museum is on the grounds of Liberal Airport in the former Beech Aircraft Co. factory building. It has a collection of over 60 aircraft. WW II equipment in the collection include a B-24, B-25, P-47, A-20, F4U-4, Link Trainer, several training planes and one of the few Japanese Zeros in the country. Address: 2000 W. 2nd St., Liberal, KS 67905. Phone: 316/624-5263. Hours: M-F 8-5, Sat. 10-4, Sun. 1-5. Closed Jan. 1, Thanksgiving and Dec. 25. Admission charged.

PRATT is in south-central Kansas 70 miles west of Wichita.

PRATT ARMY AIR FIELD, 4.5 miles north of town, was builtfor the 2nd AF as a training field for the crews of heavy bombers, primarily B-17s and B-26s. In late 1943 it was one of four fields in Kansas[4] converted into training centers for the crews of newly-built B-29 bombers manufactured in Wichita. Pratt's runways were lengthened and five large hangars (an

[4]The other 3 were at Great Bend, Salina and Walker, KS.

Below: This rare B-29 hangar at Pratt AAF, which was made mostly of wood, burned to the ground one windy night in April 1991 leaving the field with only two of the original five hangars. One of the remaining hangars is in the background.

Above: This long and wide WW II concrete runway at Pratt AAF is used for a very unusual purpose ... a cattle feed lot. Feed lots are notoriously muddy and by building them on a concrete surface the mud is eliminated. This lot holds hundreds of head of cattle destined for market.

An interior view of the Combat Air Museum.

unusually large number of B-29 hangars) were built to accommodate the huge planes. After the war Pratt AAF was turned over to the community and became Pratt Municipal Airport.

SALINA is a county seat 100 miles west of Topeka on I-70 and I-135.

CAMP PHILLIPS was built near Salina in 1942 by the Army as a training camp for division-sized units. The camp was used for only two years and closed in late 1944. It had a small branch prisoner of war camp holding about 300 POWs who worked in agriculture.

SMOKY HILL ARMY AIR FIELD was four miles SW of town. It was built in 1942 for the 2nd AF to train the crews of heavy bombers and as a staging field for air units going overseas. It had a regional AAF hospital and an air freight terminal. The Air Transport Command also operated from the field. One of the pilot skills taught here was blind landings and for that reason Smoky Hill had extra long runways. The runways proved their worth in another way because in 1944 Smoky Hill AAF was one of four air fields in Kansas[5] converted to train air crews for newly-built B-29 bombers coming from the factory in Wichita. In the postwar years the US Air Force used the field as a base for the Strategic Air Command (SAC). In the 1960s the field was closed, turned over to the city of Salina and subdivided into a community airport known as Salina Municipal Airport, an industrial park and a school.

TOPEKA, in the east-central part of the state, is 50 miles west of Kansas City and the capital of Kansas.

TOPEKA ARMY AIR FIELD, 7.5 miles south of town, was built in early 1942 for the 2nd AF

[5]The other 3 were at Great Bend, Pratt and Walker.

and operated by the Continental Air Force as an operational and staging field for combat-ready bomber units. The first bombers to operate from the field were B-24s and the last were B-29s. New B-29s, produced in Wichita, were also flight-tested here beginning in 1944. The Air Transport Command also operated from the field and had an air freight terminal at the field. The US Air Force took over the field after the war and for a while it was operated by the Strategic Air Command (SAC). In 1973 the field was turned over to the community to become a commercial airport known as Forbes Field.

Combat Air Museum: This is a large museum with a large aircraft collection at Forbes Field housed in two hangars, one of WW II vintage and the other postwar. Part of the collection is in the WW II hangar and part of it is outdoors. The postwar hangar is the museum's restoration shop. WW II aircraft represented in the collection include two A-26s, two B-25s, two C-47s, a Catalina PBY, F9F, AT-6 Harvard, AT-6 Texan, one of only two existing No. American O-47B observation planes, a Spanish-built Heinkel He 111 and a Messerschmitt Bf-109 replica. Also on display are missiles, engines, bombs, rockets and scale models. Address: Hangars 602 & 604, Forbes Field, Topeka, KS 66619. Phone: 913/862-3303. Hours: M-Sat. 9:30-4, Sun. 10-4:30. Closed Jan. 1, Easter, Thanksgiving and Dec. 25. Admission charged.

WALKER (See Hays/ Walker Area)

WICHITA is in the south-central part of the state. Of foremost importance to the U.S. military was the cluster of aircraft manufacturers who had established themselves in the Wichita area in the pre-war years. The

leading companies were Beech, Cessna, Lear, Mooney and Culver Aircraft Companies. These companies specialized in light aircraft and all built military aircraft during the war. The largest aircraft manufacturing operation, however, was a huge new factory built by the Federal Government at Wichita Airport to build B-29 bombers.

WICHITA AIRPORT, 5.5 miles SE of town, was Wichita's pre-war airport. In 1942 the Federal Government built a huge aircraft factory here to produce B-29 bombers, America's largest, highest flying and super-long-range bomber. The plant was run by Boeing Aircraft Co. and produced up to 30 bombers a month on an assembly line basis[6]. Tis plant also built PT-17 Kaydet bi-wing primary trainer used by both the Army & Navy. This was the largest factory in Wichita and one of the largest in the country. The airport also had a large air freight terminal and was used by the Air Transport Command and the Naval Air Transport Service. In 1946 B-29 production ended. In 1951 the US Air Force established Wichita Air Force Base here and used it to train bomber crews. In 1954 the base was renamed McConnell Air Force Base in honor of two Wichita brothers, 2nd Lt. Thomas L. McConnell and Capt. Fred McConnell, Jr., both combat air veterans of WW II. McConnell AFB was active throughout the Cold War.

Kansas Aviation Museum: This museum is in the pre-war terminal building of Wichita Airport which is on the National Register of Historic Places. The museum highlights the importance of Kansas in the history of aviation and displays aircraft and artifacts from the earliest days of aviation. Some of the displays relate to WW II. Address: 3350 George Washington Blvd., Wichita, KS 67210. Phone: 316/683-9242. Hours: Tues.-F 9-4, Sat., Sun., & holidays 1-5, closed Easter, Thanksgiving and Dec. 25. Donation requested. Location: The museum is on the NW corner of the air field at the southern end of George Washington Blvd.

WINFIELD is 35 miles SE of Wichita.

STROTHER ARMY AIR FIELD, five miles SW of town, was established in 1942 for the 2nd AF as a part of the 70,000 Pilot Training Program to provide basic flight training. The air field had an auxiliary field, South Air Field, five miles west of Arkansas City. After the war the field was utilized by the General Electric Co. as a service center for GE aircraft engines.

[6]There were two B-29 assembly lines in the country, this one and one at Boeing's plant in Renton, WA. The Wichita plant built 1595 B-29s during the war.

KENTUCKY

During the Great Depression of the 1930s virtually every segment of Kentucky's economy was depressed. One of the state's counties filed for bankruptcy and others had defaulted badly on their debts. The economic situation was eased somewhat by the presence in the state of many WPA and CCC operations. The state's economy rebounded nicely, though, during the war as demand grew for Kentucky's products of grain, tobacco, potatoes, whiskey, livestock, horses, coal, oil, natural gas, asphalt, and cheap electricity. Kentucky's coal industry, one of the state's largest employers, was unsettled and often turbulent during the war because of labor problems. Labor troubles were frequent in the 1930s and when the war started in Europe in Sept. 1939, Kentucky's coal producing region in the eastern part of the state, was in a state high tension. Earlier in the year John L. Lewis, the controversial President of the United Mine Workers (UMW), had lead the union's coal miners in a strike that was long and bitter. Violence erupted and in May 1939, Kentucky's Governor, A. B. "Happy" Chandler, had to send in troops to restore order. The onset of the war did little to improve labor relations in the coal industry. The industry was still plagued with wildcat strikes, work slowdowns and threats of strikes. On one occasion, when strikes threatened to shut down a large segment of the industry, President Roosevelt responded by threatening to send in Federal troops to keep the mines open and producing for the war effort. The Union backed down and the miners kept working. Working conditions in the mines were often deplorable and dangerous and a primary source of much of the trouble. In 1945 alone, there were 153 mining fatalities. After the war the mine owners vigorously promoted automation in the mines which put many miners out of work and weakened the strength of the unions. Governor "Happy" Chandler went on to become a senator and later a very popular commissioner of

United Mine Workers' President, John L. Lewis, lecturing a Senate sub-committee.

This fenced compound at Ft. Knox was used during the war to hold prisoners of war. It was used as a detention center for years afterwards. The buildings are of WW II vintage.

baseball. Another popular Kentucky politician, Alben Barkley, was a Kentucky senator during the war and Senate Majority Leader. After the war he became Harry S Truman's Vice President during Truman's second term, 1949-53. Truman also had a Kentuckian in his Cabinet, Frederick M. Vinson, Treasury Secretary. Yet another Kentucky politician, Andrew Jackson May, made himself very unpopular during the war. May, a member of the House Military Affairs Committee, announced to the press in June 1943 that the Japanese were setting their depth charges too shallow to affect U.S. submarines. The Japanese, of course, picked up this bit of information and used it to their advantage. Adm. Charles Lockwood, Commander of U.S. submarines in the Pacific, claimed that May's careless statement cost the lives of over 800 U.S. submariners and the loss of 10 subs.

Kentucky was one of the targets of the German saboteurs who landed by submarine on the U.S. east coast in June 1942. They had plans to destroy some of the locks on the Ohio River and damage power plants in the TVA system. The saboteurs were caught before they could carry out their plans.

After the war Kentucky's economy slipped back into the doldrums, but not as bad as before the war. The war, though, helped add one more facet to the state's economic diversification . . tourism.

BURGIN is a very small town 8 miles north of Danville.

DARNELL HOSPITAL was a pre-war hospital for mental patients that was taken over and enlarged by the Federal Government in March 1942 to care for military mental cases who needed closed ward treatment. About 140 prisoners of war worked at the hospital. Darnell was returned to the state of Kentucky in Dec. 1945 and remained a mental hospital until the early 1980s when it was converted into a prison known as Northpoint Training Center. The facility is on the east side of SR 33, 6 miles north of Danville.

COVINGTON/NEWPORT AREA: This is a cluster of several Kentucky towns on the

Ohio River opposite Cincinnati, OH.

KENTON COUNTY AIRPORT was a local airport taken over the AAF early in the war and used as an auxiliary air field to Lockbourne AAB in OH. After the war this airport blossomed into Greater Cincinnati International Airport. There are no signs or references at the airport relating to its WW II history.

FORT THOMAS was located on South Ft. Thomas Ave. in the community of Ft. Thomas, KY which is east of, and adjacent to, Newport, KY. Ft. Thomas, an infantry post, was built in 1889-90 to replace an older military installation which was subject to frequent flooding. During WW II it became an induction center, replacement depot and military hospital. In 1946 it was converted into a veteran's hospital. No signs of its WW II days remain.

FORT KNOX is 25 miles SW of Louisville on US 31W and it is here that a large part of America's gold reserves are stored. During WW II the fort was not only America's gold warehouse but was also one of America's foremost training centers for armored units. The area that became Ft. Knox was first used by the Army in 1903 for large-scale maneuvers. In 1922 the fort was utilized as a training center for Army Reserve officers, a Citizens Military Training Camp and a Kentucky National Guard facility. In 1931 the fort's varied terrain was recognized as a suitable site for the training of the Army's newly created "Mechanized Cavalry Brigade" and in Nov. of that year the Brigade came to Ft. Knox. One of the Brigade's staff officers was an up-an-coming young colonel named George S. Patton, Jr. As the importance of armored units grew, so did Ft. Knox. In 1932 the fort became a permanent garrison and more armored units were soon in residence. In 1936 the U.S. Bullion Depository was completed on the grounds of the fort and the name of Ft. Knox began it long-standing connection with gold. When WW II started in Europe in 1939 the importance of the new German "Blitzkrieg" tactic, based on the massive used of armored units, was quickly recognized and the importance of Ft. Knox sky-rocketed. In 1940 the U.S. Army's Armored Force was

Graves of the Buckner family: Simon Bolivar Buckner, Jr., left front; his wife Adele Blanc Buckner, right front; Simon Bolivar Buckner, Sr., General in the Confederate Army and Governor of Kentucky, left rear; his wife Delia Clairborne Buckner, right rear.

created and Ft. Knox became the headquarters for the 1st Armored Corps, the 1st Armored Division, the Armored Force Board and the Armored Force School. The fort expanded rapidly and by 1943 was America's foremost armored training center. The 1st, 2nd & 5th Armored Divisions trained here as did dozens of other armored units. Fort Knox was a segregated post so negro soldiers also trained here. Some of the last horse-mounted cavalry units trained here during and the war and until July 1950 when all horse units were discontinued. The fort had its own air field, Godman Field, which was used to support activities of the armored units and as an operational training field for the crews of medium bombers. There was a main prisoner of war camp holding 2500 POWs who worked at the fort. The fort also had an Armored Replacement Training School and a disciplinary barracks. After the war, the fort remained very active and continued to train armored units throughout the Cold War. Many WW II buildings remained at the fort in what is known as the "WW II District" in the area of Eisenhower Ave. and 4th Division Rd.

Patton Museum of Cavalry and Armor: This is an outstanding museum on the grounds of Fort Knox and is one of the largest in the U.S. Army Museum System. It is dedicated to the preservation of historical materials relating to the U.S. Army's cavalry and armored units, and has several galleries laid out in chronological order tracing the history of the cavalry branch from its beginning to the present. The Patton Gallery is dedicated to Gen. George S. Patton, Jr. and displays many of his personal items including his famous ivory-handled pistols, a jeep specially modified by Patton for his personal use and the 1938 Cadillac sedan in which he was riding when he was fatally injured in Dec. 1945. Keyes Park, adjacent to the museum, has many pieces of armored equipment on display from the U.S.

and foreign nations. Address: Fayette Ave., Ft. Knox, KY 40121-0208. Phone: 502/624-3812. Hours: May thru Sept. M-F 9-4:30, Sat.-Sun. and holidays 10-6; rest of year M-F 9-4:30, Sat.-Sun. 10-4:30. Closed Jan. 1, Dec. 24/25 and Dec. 31. Free: Location: Enter Fort Knox at the Chaffee Ave. Gate. The Museum is near this gate.

U.S. Bullion Depository: This is America's "Gold Vault" on Bullion Blvd. on the grounds of Ft. Knox. This bomb-proof structure was build in 1936 of granite, steel and concrete by the U.S. Treasury Dept. It is managed by the Department of the Mint and houses much of America's gold reserves. During WW II many of the gold reserves of overrun and threatened nations in Europe were sent to the U.S. for safekeeping and some of them were stored here. No visitors are allowed in the Depository which can be seen from U.S. Hwy. 31W. **FRANKFORT**, 20 miles NW of Lexington, is the capital of Kentucky.

GENERAL SIMON BOLIVAR BUCKNER, JR. GRAVE SITE: Frankfort State Cemetery, on E. Main St. (US 60), is the final resting place of WW II General Simon Bolivar Buckner, Jr., a native of Kentucky. He is buried on a high bluff overlooking the Kentucky River and within 100 yards of Daniel Boone. Buckner was a West Point graduate and career Army officer. He was Army commander in Alaska early in the war and played an important role in the recapture of the Aleutian Islands. He later served as commander of the 10th Army which invaded Okinawa in Apr. 1945. Bucker was fatally wounded on Okinawa on June 18, 1945 by an enemy artillery shell.

KENTUCKY MILITARY HISTORY MUSEUM, near downtown Frankfort, is in the Old State Arsenal built in 1850 to house the weapons and equipment of the Kentucky State Militia. The museum emphasizes the military service of Kentucky units from the Revolution to the present. One of the WW II display honors Kentuckians that fought in the Philippines and on Bataan, and were forced to take part in the infamous Death March. Also on display is a plaque taken from the Landsberg Prison jail cell which Adolph Hitler occupied during his imprisonment in 1923. The cell had been made into a Nazi shrine. Address: Capitol Ave. and E. Main St. (US 60), Frankfort, KY 40602. Phone: 502/564-3265. Hours: M-F 9-4, state holidays noon-4. Closed Easter, Thanksgiving. Dec. 24/25 and Jan. 1. Free.

This is the 1938 Cadillac sedan in which Gen. was riding when he was fatally injured in an accident on Dec. 9, 1945. It is on display at the Patton Museum.

The Patton Museum at Ft. Knox, KY.

The Kentucky Military History Museum, Frankfort, KY.
(See page 99.)

HENDERSON is on the Ohio River 8 miles south of Evansville, IN.

CAMP BRECKINRIDGE, 16 miles south of Henderson on US 60, was built in 1942 as a training camp for infantry units up to division size. It was a large camp and at its peak housed 40,000 people. The camp had a main prisoner of war camp holding German 3000 POWs who worked on the base, in agriculture and in a cannery. Breckinridge was deactivated in 1949, but reopened for the Korean War and was used again to train infantrymen. From 1954-1963 it was a training camp for the Kentucky National Guard. It was then parcelled out to various organizations. In 1965 a Job Corps Camp opened here using many of the old barracks buildings. The officers club became a dance hall, the base chapel became the church of a local congregation and the camp's water system was used by all. There are plaques on US 60 at the former main entrance of the camp telling of the camp's history. One plaque honors baseball star Jackie Robinson who began his professional baseball career while stationed here.

KIMMEL HOMESTEAD: In the 500 block on Green St. in Henderson is a roadside plaque identifying the homestead of Adm. Husband E. Kimmel who was commander of the U.S. Pacific Fleet in Hawaii when the Japanese attacked Pearl Harbor. Much of the blame for the disaster was placed on Kimmel and he was relieved of command 10 days after the attack. A subsequent investigation censured him and forced him into retirement. Kimmel became a bitter man and directed much of his bitterness, both privately and publicly, towards President Franklin Roosevelt claiming that Roosevelt, in his desire to see the U.S. become involved in the war, purposely withheld vital information from him which increased the severity of the Pearl Harbor disaster. Later in the war one of Kimmel's three sons, Manning Kimmel, was captured by the Japanese and suffered a horrible death, along with several others, by being doused with gasoline and burned alive. Admiral Kimmel, upon hearing of his son's death, said publicly "Now that son of a bitch (Pres. Roosevelt) has killed my son". The Kimmel home was torn down after the war and the site is occupied by an automobile dealership.

OHIO RIVER ORDNANCE PLANT was in West Henderson between highway US 60 and the river. It consisted of a complex of several buildings constructed in 1941-42 to produced anhydrous ammonia for explosives. The plant was operated by the Atmospheric Nitrogen Corp. and employed about 1500 people. Some of the buildings remain and are in private hands as part of an industrial center.

HOPKINSVILLE is in the SW Kentucky 55 miles west of Bowling Green.

CAMP CAMPBELL, 12 miles south of Hopkinsville, was a huge Army base straddling the Kentucky-Tennessee state line. Although 2/3 of the post is in Tennessee the fort is identified as being in Kentucky. Camp Campbell was built early 1942 and used for the training of division-sized armored units. The 8th, 12th, 14th and 20th Armored Divisions trained here as did 26th Infantry Div. and the IV and XXII Armored Corps. By war's end over 250,000 men had passed through the camp. Campbell had its own air field, Campbell Field, which accommodated aircraft operating in support of the ground forces training at the camp. Training in 4-engine bombers was also conducted at the field. After the war the air field was taken over by the U.S. Air Force and renamed Campbell Air Force Base. During the war Camp Campbell had three prisoner of war camps holding up to 4000 POWs. Those POWs who were allowed to work did so at the camp, in agriculture, in a stone quarry and in coal yards. At first there was only one POW camp at Campbell, but when troubles erupted with hard-core Nazi POWs throughout the nation the Army ordered the construction of several new camps and the segregation of the troublemakers. Campbell was designated as a site for one of the new segregation camps. Later a 3rd camp was built at Campbell to hold another category of POW, anti-Nazi Germans whose well-being had been threatened by other German POWs. Individual German POWs, who felt threatened, could request transfer to this camp.

When the war ended, Camp Campbell became a redeployment center. The first large unit to return to the camp was the XVIII Airborne Corps commanded by Gen. Matthew Ridgeway. It remained here until it was inacti-

Above: In the foreground is a foundation of a WW II building that is being used to store firewood. To the right are two restored camp buildings used as private residences. In the background is a WW II building falling down in decay, and the chimney to the left rear stands alone with the foundation of a WW II building that no longer exists.

This former Camp Breckinridge WW II building foundation today makes a convenient parking pad for a mobile home.

This WW II era building is the Welcome Center at Ft. Campbell. It is one of many WW II buildings that remained in use at the Fort.

vated in 1946. In 1949 the 11th Airborne Div. returned from occupation duty in Japan and took up residence at Camp Campbell. In 1950 the camp became a permanent military installation and was renamed Fort Campbell. In 1956 the 11th Airborne left and the famous 101st Airborne Div. moved to Fort Campbell and became the Fort's resident throughout the Cold War.

Don F. Pratt Museum: This is a fine museum on the grounds of Ft. Campbell and centers on the history of the 101st Airborne Div. It is named in honor of Gen. Don F. Pratt, assistant division commander of the 101st Airborne Div. who was killed in a glider crash during the Normandy invasion. The museum related the history of Ft. Campbell and has many WW II items on display including one of only three gliders remaining in the U.S. actually used during WW II. An adjacent air park contains monuments and several WW II aircraft used by the 101st. Address: 26th & Tennessee Ave., Ft. Campbell, KY 42223-5000. Phone: 502/798-3215/4986. Hours: daily 9:30-4:40. Closed Jan. 1 and Dec. 25. Free. Location: Enter Ft. Campbell at Gate 4 on US 41 Alternate.

LEXINGTON is a large city in the east-central part of the state.

LEXINGTON SIGNAL DEPOT was 10 miles east of downtown Lexington on Briar Hill Pike (SR 57). It was built early in the war to receive, store, repair and issue the Signal Corps' com-

munications and electronic equipment. The depot had its own air field, Creech Army Air Field, and a branch prisoner of war camp holding about 240 POWs who worked at the depot. The depot was used continually from WW II to the end of the Cold War. In 1962 its name was changed to Lexington Army Depot and after that to Blue Grass Army Depot. In the 1990s the depot was closed.

LOUISVILLE, in north-central Kentucky on the Ohio River, was Kentucky's largest city. West of town a new war-related industry sprang up comprising a number of large plants that made a variety of newly discovered prod-

The former Lexington Signal Depot as it appeared in later years under the name Blue Grass Army Depot.

ucts of synthetic rubber such as "Neoprene", "Koroseal" and "Buna S". This area became known as "Rubbertown".

BOWMAN FIELD, four miles east of downtown Louisville on Taylorsville Rd. (SR 155), was built in 1919 to be Louisville's local airport. Bowman Field was taken over by the I Troop Carrier Command and used as a training field for air evacuation units and glider pilots. It also had a school of aviation medicine which trained Army nurses assigned to the AAF. A headquarters for

the Personnel Distribution Command was here as well as an AAF convalescent hospital and a military air freight terminal operated by the Air Transport Command. After the war the airport was returned to its pre-war owners and became Louisville's secondary airport. Bowman had one auxiliary air field during the war, Blue Grass Airport, 6 miles west of Lexington.

100th Division Museum: This is a small museum in the 100th Division's headquarters building on the east side of Bowman Field. The museum has displays and memorabilia tracing the history of the division from its beginning in WW I to the present. Address: Bldg. #3, 3600 Century Division Way, Louisville, KY 40205. Phone: 502/454-2901. Hours: M-F 8-4:30, closed holidays. Free.

LOUISVILLE AIRPORT, four miles south of downtown Louisville at the junction of I-65 and I-264, was built to be Louisville's new commercial airport in 1941. But, upon completion was taken over by the Air Technical Service Command for the duration of the war. The Federal Government built a large aircraft factory at the field to make newly designed C-76 transport planes which were made of wood in an effort to save aluminum. Before the plant became operational, however, the shortage of aluminum eased and the C-76 program was canceled. The plant was then used to make various modifications to military aircraft and was operated by Consolidated-Vultee Corp. After the war the field was returned to its civilian owners and the Government-built factory was sold to the International Harvester Co. for the manufacture of engines. In the postwar years the airport became known as Standiford Field, Louisville's primary airport.

LOUISVILLE ARMY MEDICAL DEPOT, 6.5 miles south of downtown Louisville, was on the east side of National Turnpike (SR 1020). This was a complex of 10 large warehouses on 400 acres of land and was built originally as a storage facility for ammunition. In July 1943 it was converted to a medical depot to receive, store and issue supplies for the Army's Medical Corps. Thereafter, it was known as "the largest drugstore in the world" and distributed medical supplies to all branches of the U.S. armed forces. There was a small branch prisoner of war camp here holding about 200

This trophy case in the Pratt Museum holds momentos from both Hitler and Hermann Goering including a pair of Goering's trousers.

Many of the buildings of Nichols General Hospital remain in use. These buildings comprise part of the Nichols Apartment complex 3620 Manslick, Rd.

POWs working at the depot. The depot was sold in 1961 and became the Louisville Industrial Center, 7601 National Turnpike.

NICHOLS GENERAL HOSPITAL was built in late 1942 on Manslick Rd. five miles SW of downtown Louisville. It was a 1717-bed hospital intended to be a temporary and used to treat wounded service personnel. Nichols specialized in neurology, general and orthopedic surgery and neurosurgery. It was turned over to the Veterans Administration in March 1946 and was later sold. Many of the WW II buildings continued in daily use.

U.S. NAVAL ORDNANCE PLANT, LOUISVILLE is located on Southside Dr. (SR 1020), 5.5 miles south of downtown Louisville. The plant was built in 1941 as a permanent facility to assembly and test 5" guns for the Navy. The plant was also designed to manufacture 20 mm and 40 mm projectiles and other components such as torpedo tubes, 6" triple turret slides, 8" and 12" slides, the plating of gun barrels, loading machines, rocking platforms for training use and anti-torpedo nets. It had 7 large factory buildings and supporting facilities amounting to about one million sq. ft. of floor space. The facility was operated by the Westinghouse Electric & Manufacturing Co. A 250-acre test site was acquired on the grounds of Ft. Knox and used to test the guns assembled in the Louisville plant. In July 1945 employment peaked at 4000 people. The plant continued in operation as a Navy gun plant during the postwar years making many of the same components it

made during the war and adding new dimensions such as the manufacture of Missile motors.

NEWPORT (See Covington/Newport)

PADUCAH is in the western part of Kentucky on the Ohio River.

ALBEN W. BARKLEY MUSEUM is near downtown Paducah in an historic Greek Revival House that is a Kentucky Landmark and listed on the National Register. The museum honors Paducah resident Alben W. Barkley who, during WW II, was Kentucky's Senator and the Senate Majority Leader. After the war Barkley became Harry S Truman's popular Vice President and gained the nickname "Veep". The museum houses papers and memorabilia from Barkley's public and private life. In the living room of the house, called the Barkley Room, is Barkley's desk and chair, his Vice-Presidential flag, a picture of Harry S Truman donated by Mrs. Truman, a "Barkley for President" banner and other items of interest. Address: 6th & Madison Sts., Paducah, KY 42001. Phone: 502/554-9690, 443-5707. Hours: Sat. & Sun. 1-4, other times by appointment. Donations requested.

A second and smaller display of memorabilia on Alben Barkley can be seen at Whitehaven, a remodeled mansion serving as a state welcome center, at

the junction of I-24 and US 45. The center is open 24 hours, and the information desk operates daily 8-6.

KENTUCKY ORDNANCE WORKS, west of town on Bethel Church Rd. (SR 1321) was a complex of manufacturing buildings constructed at the beginning of the war to produce TNT. Some of the buildings remained in the area including two of the old drop towers.

RICHMOND is 20 miles south of Lexington.

BLUE GRASS ORDNANCE DEPOT is south of Richmond about five miles on the east side of U.S. 25/421. It was a huge place and its fence ran for several miles along the U.S. highway and SR 499. It was built in 1942 to store ammunition and general supplies for the Army. For two years during the war it was operated by Firestone Tire & Rubber Co. The rest of the time it was operated by the Federal Government. The depot was retained after the war and in 1962 was renamed Blue Grass Army Depot. Later it was known as the Lexington-Blue Grass Army Depot. During the Cold War the depot stored large quantities of war chemicals including deadly nerve gases.

STURGIS is in NW Kentucky 35 miles SW of Evansville, IN.

STURGIS FIELD, 1.5 miles east of town, was the area's local airport before the war. It was taken over by the I Troop Carrier Command and used as a sub-base of George Field, IL for training purposes. In the postwar years the field became known as Sturgis Airport.

Entrance to the former Blue Grass Ordnance Depot at Richmond, KY. The depot stores many deadly chemicals from the Cold War era and admission to the site is restricted.

LOUISIANA

Louisiana was a troubled state before the war. The Great Depression of the 1930s had racked her fragile agrarian economy and the state's political house was in disarray. In June 1939 the state's Governor, Richard W. Leche, was forced to resign in the face of a corruption scandal. He was succeeded by the Lt. Governor, Earl K. Long, brother of the late Huey Long who was assassinated in 1935. Huey Long had been a charismatic and controversial ex-Governor, ex-Senator and Presidential aspirant. Huey Long's popularity did not necessarily carry over to his brother, Earl, who had long been Huey's political opponent, and now was somewhat tainted by his association with Leche. In the 1940 state elections Earl Long was defeated in his bid for re-election by Sam Houston Jones, an acknowledged leader of the reformers. Governor Jones and the reformers pushed through a sweeping reform law doing away with the state's archaic system of political patronage, loop-holes that permitted the misuse of state funds and unfair taxation.

Meanwhile, with the war having begun in Europe and America beginning to built its defenses, Louisiana's economy began to prosper. The state had a widely diversified agricultural base and all segments began to grow. The state produced cotton, sugar cane, rice, corn, oats, soybeans, peanuts, potatoes, vegetables, citrus fruit, dairy products, livestock, hay, malt liquor, sea food, lumber and pulp.

In late 1942 prisoners of war began to arrive in the state is large numbers and were put to work in the sugar cane industry to help ease the nation-wide sugar shortage. By war's end Louisiana had one of the highest concentration of POWs of any state in the U.S[1]. Louisiana's manufacturing sector also prospered and produced lumber products[2], paper, corrugated boxes, bags, cotton seed derivatives, rice products, refined sugar, canned vegetables, tropical clothing, ice, petroleum products and chemicals. As the war progressed new metal-working industries evolved in the state especially in the New Orleans area, and for the first time in its history, Louisiana became a major shipbuilding state. The construction of new military bases, and the expansion of existing ones brought more new jobs and stimulated the state's commercial base even further. The influx of thousands of service personnel and war workers swelled the state's population and caused housing shortages in several areas. New roads, air fields and factories were built, and an all-important road and railroad bridge was rushed to completion across the Mississippi River at Baton Rouge. During Aug.-Sept.-Oct. 1941, 500,000 soldiers came to Loui-

[1]Other than the towns mentioned here, the following communities had prisoner of war camps: Arabi (a suburb of New Orleans), Eunice, Franklin, Gueydan, Hahnville, Kaplan, Lockport, Mathews, Port Sulphur, Reserve, St. Martinville, Terrebone County, Thibodaux, West Monroe, Whitehall and Youngsville.
[2]Louisiana was 3rd in the nation at the time in lumber production.

Oil, water and mud blow from a newly discovered Louisiana oil well.

siana to participate in large-scale Army maneuvers that covered most of northern Louisiana and parts of neighboring Texas and Mississippi. In 1942 a second large-scale Army maneuver was held in the state. The brightest spot in the state's economy, however, was her mineral wealth. Oil companies had actively been exploring in the state for oil and natural gas for several years, and new fields were being discovered with considerable regularity. By 1941 it was clear that Louisiana would soon be a major oil-producing state, so an interstate oil pipeline was begun at Baton Rouge to supply Louisiana's oil to the U.S. east coast. The state's other minerals also became important to the war effort especially sulphur.

By 1945 the state had gained two new industries, the manufacture of synthetic rubber and fish farming. After V-J Day unemployment and labor unrest began to plague the state. Yet, the state's seaports were still very busy receiving returning GIs from overseas along with tons of war material. Demands for the state's products remained high in the postwar years and tourism was on the rise. Louisiana's new oil wealth continued to spark her economy and was supported by strong demands for chemicals and agricultural products. Throughout the 1940s and 1950s the state remained economically strong, prosperous and politically peaceful.

ALEXANDRIA in the geographic center of the state on I-49. By WW II Alexandria had become a substantial military center because of all the military bases in the area. Most of the military bases were training facilities and during the war some 7 million service personnel trained in the Alexandria area. Alexandria suffered a severe housing shortage because of the influx

of so many military people and their families. Famous generals such as Dwight Eisenhower, Mark Clark and George Patton resided in the city at various times. They stayed at the Hotel Bentley in downtown Alexandria and much overseas planning took place in that hotel.

ALEXANDRIA ARMY AIR FIELD was five miles NW of Alexandria. The base began in 1939 as an emergency landing strip for the Alexandria-Pineville Municipal Airport. In 1942 it was taken over by the 3rd AF and expanded into a training base for B-17 bomber crews. In 1943 it was transferred to the 2nd AF which continued to use it for B-17 crew training, and to the Air Transport Command which operated an air freight terminal. In 1946 the AAF turned the field over to the local community and it became Alexandria's Municipal Airport. In 1950, however, at the beginning of the Korean War, the US Air Force took over the airport and used it again to train bomber crews naming it Alexandria Air Force Base. In late 1954 the name was changed to England Air Force Base in honor of Lt. Col. John B. England, a highly decorated WW II P-51 ace who flew 108 missions and was credited with 19 kills including four in one mission. England AFB remained active until after the end of the Cold War and was closed in the 1990s.

CAMP BEAUREGARD, five miles from Alexandria, was established in 1917 on the site of the first University of Louisiana. It was used as an infantry training camp and in 1920 was transferred to the Louisiana National Guard. The National Guard used the camp until WW II when it again became a reception center for the 4th Army Corps Area and a training camp for regular Army units. During the war the camp was the home of the V Corps of the 3rd Army. The 32nd Infantry Div., consisting of the Wisconsin and Michigan National Guards, trained here. After the war the camp reverted to the Louisiana National Guard.

CAMP CLAIRBORNE, 18 miles SW of Alexandria, was built in 1940 as a division-size infantry training camp and was used extensively during the Army's large-scale maneuvers in Louisiana. The 34th Infantry Div., comprised of the National Guards of Iowa, Minnesota, North Dakota and South Dakota, trained here. The 32nd Infantry Division also trained here, and in Aug. 1942 the famous 101st Airborne Div. was activated here. The camp had a main prisoner of war camp holding about 900 POWs who worked at the camp. Clairborne was deactivated in Dec. 1945 and in 1947 most of its assets were sold at auction.

ESLER FIELD, 10.5 miles NE of Alexandria, was an old CCC camp. In 1941-42 it was converted to an air field and was associated with Camp Beauregard in the training of reconnaissance and observation personnel. Later, the field became a training center for B-25 bomber crews and a maneuver station for Camp Beauregard. Esler was also home to the 3rd AF's 1st Tactical Air Division. In 1945 the field was occupied by the Tactical Air Command of the 3rd AF.

This oil pipeline was built during the war to supply Louisiana's oil to the U.S. east coast. The pipeline began at Baton Rouge.

Esler had one auxiliary field, Lafayette Municipal Airport, one mile SE of Lafayette, LA. After the war Esler became a commercial airport.

CAMP LIVINGSTON, 15 miles north of Alexandria, was a large camp within Kisatchie National Forest. It was built in 1940-41 as a reception center for the 4th Corps Area and a tent camp for the training of Army ground forces. Later, wooden buildings and paved streets were constructed as well as a large hospital which had 81 buildings, two miles of corridors and covered 9 acres. Livingston was a segregated camp and many negro troops trained here. The camp also had one of the few all-negro hospitals in the Army. The 32nd Inf. Div., comprised of the Michigan and Wisconsin National Guards, was one of the first major units to train here. Later the 38th Inf. Division received battle readiness training here. At its peak, some 14,000 men were in training a the camp. Livingston had a main prisoner of war camp with about 3300 POWs who worked mostly in the sugar cane fields. There was also an internment camp for enemy aliens holding about 900 Japanese aliens from the U.S., Hawaii, Panama, Costa Rica and Peru. In Nov. 1945 Camp Livingston was deactivated. Two years later some 4500 buildings were sold and in 1957 the Government transferred 12,500 acres of the camp to the Louisiana National Guard.

BASTROP was a farming community of 6600 people, 18 miles NE of Monroe. It was one of the several towns in Louisiana that had a prisoner of war camps not associated with a military facility. Bastrop's camp held about 550 POWs who worked primarily in local agriculture.

BATON ROUGE, the capital of the state, is located in the SE part of the state on the Mississippi River 70 miles NW of New Orleans. It is an inland seaport able to service ocean-going vessels. During the war the city had several large oil refineries which supplied large quantities of petroleum products to the U.S. armed forces and those of the Allies. Baton Rouge's oil refineries played a significant role in the Battle of Britain in the fall of 1940 by supplying much of the 100 octane aviation gasoline used by the Royal Air Force.

BATON ROUGE ARMY AIR BASE, 5.5 miles north of downtown Baton Rouge, was the city's local airport, Harding Field, when it was taken over by the AAF. It was operated by the Air Technical Service Command during the war and was turned back to the local authorities in Sept. 1945 and became known as the Baton Rogue Metro Airport.

LOUISIANA NAVAL WAR MEMORIAL (Museum) is located on the east bank of the Mississippi River opposite the Centroplex at Government and Front Sts. The museum features the naval history of Louisiana and the lower Mississippi River area from colonial days to the present. The centerpiece of the museum is the WW II destroyer USS "Kidd" which saw considerable action in the Pacific. The ship is anchored permanently in the Mississippi River and is not only open to the public but also offers tours, parties and overnights, primarily to school children. The children can sleep on the ship much as the sailors did when the "Kidd" was a fighting ship during WW II. The "Kidd" was named in honor of Rear Adm. Issac C. Kidd, who died aboard the battleship Arizona during the Japanese attack on Pearl Harbor. Another WW II trophy at the museum is a P-40 fighter plane painted in the colors of the famous Flying Tigers of wartime China. This is one of the actual fighters used by the Flying Tigers under the command of Gen. Claire Chennault, who grew up in Louisiana. A number of other displays are dedicated to Chennault and the Flying Tigers. Address: 305 S. River Rd., Baton Rouge, LA 70802. Phone:504/342-1942. Hours: daily 9-5, Thanksgiving 1-5, closed Dec. 25. Admission charged.

CAMP PORT ALLEN: This was the fairgrounds of the town of Port Allen across the river from Baton Rouge. It was turned into a prisoner of war camp and housed about 600 POWs who worked mostly in agriculture. The fairgrounds was located to the rear of the town's court house.

DE RIDDER is a county seat 55 miles SW of Alexandria.

DE RIDDER ARMY AIR FIELD, three miles west of town, was taken over by the AAF and used as a training field for observation and reconnaissance personnel. It was returned to the community of De Ridder in late 1945. De Ridder AAF had an auxiliary field, Gillis Field, 10.5 miles north of Lake Charles, LA.

DONALDSVILLE, 25 miles south of Baton Rouge on the Mississippi River, was one of several towns in Louisiana to have a sizeable branch prisoner of war camp not associated with a military installation. Donaldsville Camp held about 700 POWs who worked mostly in the sugar cane fields.

HAMMOND is 40 miles east of Baton Rouge on I-12 and I-55.

HAMMOND FIELD was taken over by the 3rd AF and used as an auxiliary field for Key Field, MS. Hammond Field had a small prisoner of war camp holding about 225 POWs who worked in agriculture and the forests. In 1946 the field was vacated by the AAF.

HOUMA is a unique delta town 45 miles SW of New Orleans in the heart of Cajun country. It was also strategically located for anti-submarine activities in the Gulf.

U.S. COAST GUARD AIR STATION, HOUMA AND U.S. NAVAL AIR STATION, HOUMA (LTA): These

The WW II destroyer, USS "Kidd", on permanent display at the Louisiana Naval War Memorial.

The Louisiana Naval War Memorial, Baton Rouge, LA.

Blimp of the type that operated out of NAS, Houma (LTA).

two military facilities existed side-by-side at a private airport outside Houma. The Coast Guard facility was established first as a base for amphibious planes patrolling the Gulf coast. On Aug. 1, 1942 a plane from CGAS, Houma sank the German submarine U-166 off the Louisiana coast. In 1943-44 the Navy built NAS, Houma (LTA) as a blimp base with a mission to patrol the Gulf coast and protect U.S. shipping in the area. In Apr. 1944 a sudden gust of wind forced open a huge blimp hangar door and blew three blimps out of the hangar to their destruction. Then, in Aug. 1944 one of the station's blimps was lost over the Gulf in a severe thunderstorm. Only one of the 13 men aboard survived. In Oct. 1944, a light carrier air group arrived to operate in conjunction with the blimps. The station had a branch prisoner of war camp with the POWs working on the post. In 1947 the blimps departed and the NAS was inactivated and renamed NAS, Houma which remained active until 1948. During that time conventional aircraft operated from the field.

JEANERETTE, 30 miles SE of Lafayette, was a small farming community of 3400 people during the war with its own prisoner of war camp. The camp held about 500 POWs who worked in agriculture.

LAKE CHARLES is in the SW corner of the state on I-10 in the heart of Cajun country.

LAKE CHARLES ARMY AIR FIELD, 3.5 miles ESE of town, was established by the 1st AF in late 1941 as a training field for the 30,000 Pilot Training Program. Its mission was to train air crews for light bombers. In 1946 the field was declared surplus.

LEESVILLE is 50 miles SSW of Shreveport.

CAMP POLK, 6 miles SE of Leesville, was built in early 1941 to meet the needs of the Army's large scale maneuvers from 1940 through 1944. It comprised 95,406 acres of varied terrain consisting of rolling hills to a dense jungle-like environment. The 3rd Armored Division was the first to train here, followed by the 9th and 11th Armored Divs. The 7th & 8th Armored Divs., 11th Airborne Div., the 95th Infantry Div., and part of the newly formed 5th Women's Army Auxiliary Corps (WAACs), also trained here. In 1945 Polk was enlarged and divided into North Camp Polk and South Camp Polk about five miles apart. The camp had a main prisoner of war camp that grew steadily and

by the end of the war held 4000 POWs. Polk was closed in Dec. 1946, but was partially reopened in 1948 to accommodate summer training of the National Guard and Army Reserves. In 1950 Polk became fully activated for the Korean War. After that, it was closed and opened several times as a training center as national emergencies and defense budgets dictated. In Nov. 1955 the camp was designated Fort Polk and eventually became Louisiana's largest military installation.

Fort Polk Military Museum: This museum is on the grounds of Fort Polk in a WW II mess hall and relates the history of the fort and the divisions that served here. Displays include tanks, armored vehicles, artillery pieces, helicopters, small arms, uniforms, field equipment, maps, medals, mines, rockets and other military items. Address: PO Box Drawer R, Ft. Polk, LA 71459-5000. Phone: 318/531-7905. Hours: Wed.-Fri. 10-2, Sat. & Sun. 9-4. Closed Jan. 1, Thanksgiving and Dec. 25. Free. Location: The museum is reached through the main gate of Fort Polk, five miles south of Leesville off US 171.

MONROE is in the north-central part of the state on I-20.

SELMAN FIELD, five miles east of town, was the community's local airport before the war. It was taken over by the Central Flying Training Command in 1941 as part of the 50,000 Pilot Training Program and used to train navigators and bombardiers. In 1946 the AAF departed and returned the field to the community of Monroe.

NEW ORLEANS is, and always has been, the state's largest city, seaport, manufacturing center, cultural center and tourist center. Like many major cities, it experienced a large influx of war workers and service personnel that greatly strained the city's housing, schools and other services. The city was the headquarters of the 8th Naval District and the Gulf Sea Frontier Command. One of the city's race tracks was used to train Coast Guard horse patrols. The local jockeys were employed as trainers the Coastguardsmen were housed in the Southern Yacht Club (higher ranks) and a local penitentiary (lower ranks) until facilities could be built for them. Consolidated-Vultee had an aircraft plant in the city making seaplanes, Delta Shipbuilding Co. and Louisiana Shipbuilding, Inc. built cargo ships, Jones & Laughlin Steel Co. built Landing Ship Tanks (LSTs), and a local manufacturing giant,

Andrew Jackson Higgins.

The prisoner of war camp at Camp Polk.

Higgins Industries, built aircraft, PT boats, tank lighters, engines and landing craft known as "Higgins Boats". Higgins' founder, Andrew Jackson Higgins, became a local hero whose fame rivalled another famous shipbuilder, Henry Kaiser.

New Orleans was also the gathering place for small ships, landing craft and submarines made in the U.S. between the Appalachian and Rocky Mountains. Those vessels were usually made on one of the tributaries to the Mississippi River on in the Great Lakes, and upon completion, were sailed down river to New Orleans and thence to the battle zones of the world.

New Orleans was host to several branch prisoner of war camps. Only the most trustworthy POWs were sent here because escape was facilitated by the presents of the large seaport and the frequent arrival and departure of ships from neutral nations. In time, the most trustworthy of the trustworthy were granted passed and spent much of their time and money whooping-it-up in the French Quarter.

Lake Pontchartrain, just to the north of the city, was used as an air-to-air gunnery range and a test and training facility of naval vessels.

JACKSON BARRACKS, located on the left bank of the River about five miles south of downtown New Orleans, was built in 1834 and known then an New Orleans Barracks. Its first use was as a port of embarkation for U.S. troops fighting in the Second Seminole War in Florida. After that, the Barracks had a long and colorful history and was the site of a Civil War battle. In 1866 it was re-named Jackson Barracks and in 1922 was turned over to the state. During WW II the U.S. Army used it as an embarkation facility and a sub-post of the New Orleans Port of Embarkation. After the war the facility was used by the Louisiana Air and Army National Guards.

Louisiana Military History and State Weapons Museum: This museum is the official National Guard Museum of the state of Louisiana and is housed in the old powder magazine at Jackson Barracks. During WW II the magazine was used to house German prisoners of war from the Afrika Korps. On display in the museum are some 300 U.S. and foreign weapons from 9 major U.S. wars, including WW II. Of particular interest is a copy of the official transcript from the post-WW II Nuremberg Trials. Address: 6400 St. Claude Ave., New Orleans, LA 70146-0330. Phone: 504/278-6242. Hours: M-F 8-4, closed holidays. Free.

LA GARDE GENERAL HOSPITAL was a 1176-bed Army general hospital located at 421 Robert E. Lee Blvd. It was built in 1941 as a temporary facility to treat war wounded. The hospital specialized in general and orthopedic surgery and psychiatry. Near the end of the war La Garde increasingly became a debarkation hospital receiving wounded directly from the battle fronts. In Dec. 1945 the hospital was turned over to the Veterans Administration.

THE NATIONAL D-DAY MUSEUM: This is a $30 million museum-to-be that will be built in New Orleans and opened in early 1997. As the name implies it will specialize in telling the story of the Allied invasion on France, June 6, 1944 . . D-Day. Upon entering the museum visitors will be offer a 40-minute wide-screen film which will bring to life what the individual sailor and soldier experienced during the momentous hours of June 6, 1944.

The museum will have four exhibit-laden galleries. Gallery I will relate the details of the outbreak of WW II and chronicle America's remarkable mobilization and war production efforts. Gallery II will cover preparations and planning for the D-Day invasion. Galleries III and IV will detail the story of the actual invasion and relate the events of the remained of the war in Europe. Mail address: The National D-Day Museum Administrative Office, 925 Common St., Suite 800, New Orleans, LA 70112. Phone: 504/527-6012.

NEW ORLEANS ARMY AIR BASE, 6 miles NNE of downtown New Orleans, consisted of two components, a cantonment bounded by Franklin Ave., Leon C. Simon Dr. and the Inner Harbor Canal, and the newly-built airport on the south shore of Lake Pontchartrain. The facility was built in 1941 and was nearing completion when the U.S. went to war. In early 1942 AAF bombers arrived at the field to operate as patrol planes along the Gulf coast. The runways were short for the bombers, but they flew from the field anyway. In July 1942 the base was reassigned to the Air Service Forces and was used to train boat companies, signalmen and quartermasters. The Air Transport Command operated out of the field and had a freight terminal here. The Naval Air Transport Service also used the field. In Jan. 1944 the Army's Transportation School moved here from Camp Palauche and in Feb. 1944 the base was converted to a staging area for the New Orleans Port of Embarkation as well as a replacement training center. The air field's runways were too short for modern military aircraft and too expensive to expand, so the field was turned over to the city and became New Orleans Lakefront Airport. The cantonment was retained and in 1947 renamed Camp Leroy Johnson in honor of Sgt. Leroy Johnson of Canne Creek, LA, a Congressional Medal of Honor winner during WW II. The camp remained small during the postwar years and was used mainly for transportation and personnel services. It was finally closed in 1964 and the land utilized for a park, a university and residential areas.

NEW ORLEANS PORT OF EMBARKATION was an Army shipping facility located on the left bank of the Mississippi River at its junction with the Intracoastal Waterway about three miles from downtown New Orleans. It consisted of three huge concrete terminal buildings, each 6 stories high. The facility had five berths with additional storage space for loading and unloading ocean-going vessels simultaneously. The AAF had it own port of embarkation facilities at Poland and Dauphine Sts. From these locations both men a material were dispatched to overseas locations, and after the war, were received back again. The facility had a main prisoner of war compound holding over 1200 POWs who worked at the port. In the postwar years two of the buildings were sold to private owners and the third turned over to the Navy to become a part of the New Orleans Naval Support Activity.

CAMP PALAUCHE was built in 1941-42 on leased land between the town of Harahan and the Huey P. Long Bridge north of Jefferson Hwy. The facility was originally called Camp Harahan and had about 300 buildings. It was designed to be a staging area for Army troops departing through the New Orleans Port of Embarkation, but in late 1942 it was converted into a training center for port troops, railroad operating troops and hospital service personnel. In 1943 the Army's Transportation School moved here from Mississippi State College, Starkesville, MS where it had originated. In Jan. 1944 the school moved on to New Orleans AAB, and near the end of the war Camp Palauche was used as a prisoner of war camp for POWs being returned to Europe. The camp was abandoned by the Army in 1946 and the area became part of a commercial and industrial area.

U.S. NAVAL RESERVE AVIATION BASE, NEW ORLEANS/U.S. NAVAL AIR STATION, NEW ORLEANS: This naval air facility, built in 1940-41, was 8 miles SSE of downtown New Orleans near the small community of Belle Chase served as a reserve air training facility known as U.S. Naval Reserve Aviation Base, New Orleans. In July 1942 primary flight training began at the base to relieve some of the congestion at NAS, Pensacola, FL. In Jan. 1943 the name of the base was changed to U.S. Naval Air Station, New Orleans and the next month a Primary Flight Instructor School was established here. The new school proved to be very successful and was enlarged. Aircraft used were the N3N "Yellow Peril", N2S Stearman and SNV Valiants. At the end of the war the flight instructor school continued in operation and several carrier and Marine air groups were assigned to the station. From Sept. 1945 to Sept. 1946 the station served as a separation center. By June 1946 the naval reservists had returned and the training of reserve pilots became the station's primary function. Summer training of Naval Reservists from the surrounding states became a regular activity. During the Korean War the station was used again to train Navy and Marine pilots, but reverted to the training of reservists after that war. It continued as a reserve air training facility throughout the Cold War and acquired another new name, U.S. Naval Air Station, Belle Chase. During WW II the station had 8 outlying fields.

U.S. NAVAL STATION, ALGIERS/U.S. NAVAL STATION, NEW ORLEANS: The Navy first used this site, two miles east of downtown New Orleans on the right bank of the Mississippi River, in 1803 as a naval base. That facility lasted 15 years. In 1901 the Navy returned to build a more permanent naval station naming it U.S. Naval Station, Algiers after the nearby community of Algiers, LA. The main asset of the station was a large state-of-the-art dry dock which was used to repair and service large warships and some commercial ships. USNS, Algiers was very active during WW I, but fell on hard times and was closed in 1933. With the advent of war in Europe USNS, Algiers was reopened in Dec. 1939 and functioned as before utilizing the old, but still very serviceable, dry dock. In March 1940, however, the dry dock was disassembled and taken to Pearl Harbor, Hawaii. A multitude of other uses was then found for USNS, Algiers. In Sept. 1940 the Coast Guard moved onto the station and set up a training facility. In July 1941 a large naval supply department was established here to outfit the many new naval vessels being built in the Mississippi River Valley and along the Texas coast. In Feb. 1942 an armed guard training facility was established to train naval personnel as gun crews on merchant ships. A month later a naval section base was established at the station to outfit, inspect and make seaworthy small naval craft such as yard mine sweepers, patrol boats, submarine chasers and small mine layers. In Dec. 1942 the station began modifying Landing Ship Tanks (LSTs). In 1943 the station continued to receive new tenants. A new brig was built and a prisoner rehabilitation program begun, the supply department was enlarged into a depot, a small dry dock was received and the repair of training ships begun, the armed guard training school was enlarged, a facility was acquired on Lake Pontchartrain as part of a PT-boat program, a firefighting school was set up and facilities for training sailors from Allied nations was established[3]. By 1944 the acquisition of new facilities ended, but those that had been established here flourished and some were expanded. During 1944 4154 vessels were supplied by the station and another 245 outfitted. The station's population peaked in Jan. 1945 with 80,000 enlisted personnel and 900 officers. In May 1945, with the war having ended in Europe, many of the armed guard crews returned for refresher courses and reassignment to the Pacific. With the end of the war in the Pacific, however, activities at USNS, Algiers declined and the station was realigned to serve as a destroyer base and naval reserve training facility. In 1947 the station was renamed U.S. Naval Station, New Orleans and continued to serve a variety of naval functions. In 1966 the name changed again to the F. Edward Hebert Defense Complex, and still later it became known as the New Orleans Naval Support Activity.

PATTERSON is 50 miles SSW of Baton Rouge.

WEDELL-WILLIAMS MEMORIAL AVIATION MUSEUM is located on SR 182 two miles NW of town at Williams Memorial Airport. The museum preserves and displays relics of Louisiana's aviation history. WW II planes on

[3] Many French sailors were trained here which was intentional because of the area's French heritage and history. Britons, Russians, Norwegians, Brazilians and Greeks were also trained.

display include President Dwight Eisenhower's Aero-Commander, a Boeing-Stearman A75N1 Kaydet (PT-17), a half-scale replica of a Focke-Wulf Fw 190 and a half-scale replica of P-47 Thunderbolt. Address: PO Box 394, Airport Circle, Patterson, LA 70392. Phone: 504/395-7067. Hours: Tues.-Sat. 10-4. Admission charged.

RUSTON is in north-central Louisiana 30 miles east of Monroe.

CAMP RUSTON was built in late 1942 as a prisoner of war camp to house German POWs expected to arrive from the North African campaign. The camp was completed in early 1943 and the POWs had not yet arrived, so it was used temporarily as a training center for women newly recruited into the WAACs. The WAACs left in late June 1943 and the POWs began arriving soon afterwards. Camp Ruston operated as a POW camp for the remained of the war housing up to 4000 POWs. Most of the POWs worked in the nearby forests or on military installations. When, in late 1943-early 1944 it was realized that pro-Nazi POWs had to separated from non-Nazi and anti-Nazi POWs, Camp Ruston was selected to be a camp for non-Nazi officers. After the war the camp was closed.

SHREVEPORT is in the NW corner of the state on I-20 and I-49.

BARKSDALE FIELD, 6 miles east of downtown Shreveport, was one of the Army Air Corps' few pre-war air fields. It had been built in the early 1930s on donated land as a tactical air base and a home for several of the Air Corps's operational pursuit plane units. Its original mission was to protect the U.S. Gulf coast. In 1939-40 light bomber units replaced the pursuit units. From 1940 to mid-1941 an Air Corps flying school operated at the field which included a navigators training program operated by Pan American Airways under government contract. During the summer of 1941 the navigator program's personnel were divided into three components and each sent to other air fields to become the nucleus of new navigator schools. From 1942 through 1945 the field was operated by the 3rd AF and dedicated to the training of bomber crews and replacement crews of heavy and very heavy bombers. Advanced pilot training was also offered. In July 1942 B-17 bombers began operating out of the field on anti-submarine patrols along the Gulf coast. Barksdale was also home to the III Tactical Air Command and had an AAF Chemical training center and a

Military Police training center. The field also had an AAF Guards School, a chemical training center, a school for cooks & bakers and an AAF regional hospital. The Air Transport Command operated an air freight terminal here and the Navy used the field for ferry operation. There was a prisoner of war camp at Barksdale holding about 550 POWs who worked on the post. In late 1944, Barksdale's runways were lengthened and the field became a training base for B-29 and B-32 bomber crews. Barksdale was retained after the war, turned over to the US Air Force and became Barksdale Air Force Base. It operated throughout the Cold War providing a wide variety of services for the Air Force.

Eighth Air Force Museum: This fine museum on the grounds of Barksdale Air Force Base is named after the 8th AF which was one of the largest and most famous air units of WW II. The 8th AF came to Barksdale in the post-war years and brought its fame with it. The museum, of course, highlights the history of the 8th AF, but also has many exhibits from the pre-war and postwar eras. WW II aircraft in the museum's collection include a B-17G, a B-24J, B-29, P-51D, C-47 and an AT-11. Address: PO Box 10, Barksdale AFB, LA 71110. Phone: 318/456-3065/3067. Hours: M-F 9-4, Sat. 10-4, Sun. noon-4. Closed Jan. 1 Thanksgiving and Dec. 25. Free.

LOUISIANA ORDNANCE PLANT was 22 miles east of Shreveport on I-20 near Minden. LA. It was one of several shell loading plants built by the Government in 1941 and run by a private contractor. The plant remained active throughout the Cold War and was known as the Louisiana Army Ammunition Plant.

SLIDELL is in the eastern Louisiana near the Alabama state line.

CAMP VILLIERE, four miles NW of town, was built in 1942 as a small arms range for trainees at Camp Palauche in New Orleans. The camp had barracks, messing facilities, gun ranges and a small air field. After the war the camp was used by both the Army and the Louisiana National Guard. In the 1960s it became a tactical training center for Camp Leroy Johnson. Later, the camp was turned over to the Louisiana National Guard.

TALLULAH is in the NE corner of the state on I-20 about 20 miles west of Vicksburg, MS.

CAMP TALLULAH was another of the prisoner of war camps in Louisiana located near small towns. The camp held about 500 POWs who worked in local agriculture and the nearby forests. After the war the camp was closed.

MAINE

Of all the states in the nation, Maine is geographically closest to Europe. That made the state an important link in America's connections with her European Allies. Early in the war, before the U.S. became involved, important air routes were established from Maine to Scotland across the North Atlantic to carry Lend Lease aircraft and essential materials, supplies and personnel. There were two main air routes from Maine to Scotland; a northern route via Labrador-Greenland-Iceland-Scotland for planes of limited range, and a shorter and more southerly route via Newfoundland-Scotland for planes with longer range. Supplies and personnel were also flowed from Maine to new bases and weather stations in the far northeastern part of the continent. In this respect, commercial airline companies were employed to establish regular air service to many remote locations. American Airlines and Northeast Airlines lead the way by establishing routes from Maine to points in Northern Canada, Labrador, Baffin Island, Greenland and Iceland.

Maine's strategic location was also important to America's defenses. Military forces stationed in Maine were in a position to intercept German submarines approaching the U.S. from Europe, and aircraft and ships from Maine provided vital convoy escort services along sections of the North Atlantic convoy routes.

Maine's shipbuilding industry contributed significantly to the Allies' war effort. Many small shipbuilders dotted the Maine coast with larger ship yards in the Portland area and the Portsmouth Navy Yard at Kittery. Most of the yards were busy from the beginning of the European war building ships for the U.S. armed forces and the Allies.

Besides air routes and ships, Maine provided a host of other commodities for the war effort; potatoes, grain, apples, seafood, lumber, pulp, paper, boots & shoes, cotton & woolen cloth, stone, sand & gravel and clay. When high quality European peat became unavailable, peat deposits in Maine were exploited. Maine's primary source of income, tourism, suffered during the war because of gas and rubber rationing, but the wartime economy more than made up for the losses in revenue.

When the U.S. went to war activities in Maine spurted to new heights. Fears of invasion and air attacks were strong in the state and blackouts and dimouts became a regular occurrence. German submarines, for the most part, by-passed Maine's waters until 1943. Since many of Maine's citizens were experienced seamen the Federal Government contracted with the state government to convert the state's normal college at Castine into a school for sailors. The school was subsequently renamed the Maine Maritime Academy and was run by retired naval officers and financed by the Federal Government. As the war progressed the state experienced shortages of housing in the bigger cities and strains on city services. There was a severe shortage of teachers, especially in shipbuilding areas, and during 1944 83 schools closed and others experienced overcrowding. Skilled labor and farm labor was also scarce. To help out on the farms, prisoners of war were employed at many locations in the state.

In 1940 a young woman, Margaret Chase Smith (R), was elected to the House of Representatives to fill the seat held by her late husband. Smith became a very popular politician and was one of the first members of Congress to pressure the Navy to recruit women. The Navy complied and Mrs. Smith gained the title "Mother of the WAVES". She went on to serve in the U.S. Senate in the 1950s and 60s becoming the first woman in history to be elected to both houses of Congress.

BANGOR is in the south-central Maine on the Penobscot River.

DOW FIELD, two miles west of downtown Bangor, was the city's municipal airport before the war. The AAF bought the airport and named it Dow Field. In mid-Jan. 1942, a month after the U.S. entered the war, the 1st AF sent B-17 and B-18 bombers to Dow to begin deep ocean patrols into the Atlantic. The Navy, who had responsibility for such patrols, did not have aircraft available and the Army patrols were to be temporary. The Army planes flew 600 miles out looking for enemy submarines and then returned. In the spring of 1942 Dow became a staging field for AAF units being transferred to England. Generally 4-engine planes staged at Dow and then went on to bases in Newfoundland and then to England. Two-engine and single-engine planes generally went to Presque Isle and across the northern route where distances between bases were less. This arrangement, however, was not rigidly adhered to. The Air Transport Command also operated out of Dow Field and had an air freight terminal here. Some training was done at Dow. The air field remained active for many years after the war under the name Dow Air Force Base. Eventually the base was closed and it became Bangor International Airport.

BAR HARBOR AND THE FRENCHMAN

BAY AREA: Bar Harbor is a picturesque fishing village on the east side of Mt. Desert Island at the entrance to Acacia National Park. The community had an air field that was strategically located, and during the early months of 1942 a Civil Air Patrol (CAP) units operated out of the field doing anti-submarine patrols. Later, the Navy moved in and took over the field replacing the CAP.

HANCOCK POINT is a small fishing village at the north end of Frenchman Bay on the point of a small peninsula. Here, on the night of Nov. 29, 1944, the German submarine U-1230 landed two German spies. The spies then walked north four miles to highway U.S. 1, flagged a motorist and paid him $6.00 to drive them to Bangor where they took a train to New York City. They had $60,000 cash in their possession, a radio, code books and forged documents. Their mission, planned to last two years, was to gather important information in NYC, especially concerning ship movements, and radio it back to Germany. Unfortunately for the spies they were seen walking along U.S. 1 by a local woman, Mrs. Mary Forni, who thought them suspicious because the wore "city clothes" and were carrying bundles. She alerted the FBI who subsequently discovered their landing site and soon picked up their trail. Both spies were caught a month later on Dec. 30, 1944 in NYC. They were tried, convicted and sentenced to be hanged. Their sentences, however, were commuted to prison terms and eventually both were released and returned to Germany. One of the spies, Wm. C. Colepaugh, a U.S. citizen, returned to the U.S. and lived in Connecticut.

U.S. NAVAL AUXILIARY AIR STATION, BAR HARBOR: This was the area's local airport built in 1934-36. It was located on SR 3 on the mainland 9 miles NW of Bar Harbor near the small community of Trenton. In early 1942 volunteer civilian pilots and planes of the Civil Air Patrol began operating out of the field doing anti-submarine patrols. In May 1942 the CAA improved the runways and in 1943 the Navy leased the field as a base for inshore patrols. It was named U.S. Naval Auxiliary Air Facility, Bar Harbor and was an auxiliary to NAS, Brunswick. The Navy improved the field further and for the next year OS2U-3 observation planes flew patrols from the field. Near the end of 1944 use of the field was given over to the Royal Navy which had air units based at NAS, Brunswick. The British pilots used NAAF, Bar Harbor for intensive deck landing practice. The facility was closed during the winter of 1944-45, but was opened again for use by the Royal Navy in the spring of 1945. From time-to-time, during its brief career, NAAF, Bar Harbor also hosted blimps from NAS, South Weymouth, MA. In 1946 the facility was returned to the local community to serve once again as the area's local airport.

U.S. NAVAL RADIO STATION, WINTER HARBOR: The Mt. Desert Island and Frenchman Bay area of the coast has the unique feature of being an exceptionally good area for receiving long distance radio signals. This feature was recognized before WW I and a Navy radio receiving station was built at Otter Point on Mt. Desert Island. In 1935 the radio station was moved to Winter Harbor on the east shore of Frenchman Bay across from Bar Harbor. During WW II the station was enlarged and became an important link in the Navy's world-wide radio communication system. In 1944 it became a Supplementary Radio Station to the Communication Station, Boston. The station remained active throughout the Cold War and became known as Naval Security Group Activity, Winter Harbor.

BATH/BOOTHBAY HARBOR/BRUNSWICK AREA:

Bath is 30 miles NE of Portland on the west bank of the Kennebec River 12 miles inland from the sea. It has been a shipbuilding center and home to the famous Bath Iron Works which had a long history of building ships for the U.S. Navy. During the war the Bath Works, along with its subsidiary in East Brunswick, built destroyers, large merchant ships and other ships for the Navy. Bath, like other major shipbuilding towns in Maine, suffered from overcrowding during the war. Boothbay Harbor, a picturesque coastal village and popular tourist center, 10 miles ESE of Bath, also had a shipbuilding enterprise, the Frank Sample, Jr. Corp. which built wooden mine sweepers for the Navy. Brunswick, 8 miles west of Bath, was the site of a large naval air station.

FORT BALDWIN: This is an old fort 12 miles south of Bath at the mouth of the Kennebec River. It is on the west bank of the river near the community of Popham Beach. The fort was built in 1905-08 as a coastal defense position to protect the entrance to the river. Fort Baldwin was armed and manned during WW I, but by WW II the guns had been removed. The fort was nevertheless used in another way. One of the several concrete fire control towers built along the Maine coast was constructed on the grounds of the fort and served as a base end station for area coastal defenses. After the war the fort became known as Fort Popham[1] and Fort Baldwin Memorial and opened to the public.

U.S. NAVAL AIR STATION, BRUNSWICK, 1.5 miles SE of Brunswick, ME, was a local airport before the war. The Navy took it over in late 1942 to use as a base for anti-submarine air patrols working in conjunction with destroyers from the Destroyer Base, Casco Bay in the Portland area, and the blimp base at South Weymouth, MA. The airport needed extensive work which was done during the winter of 1942-43 and was ready for operations by April 1943. By then, however, the submarine menace along the east coast had subsided and the station was turned over to Royal Navy to use as a training base for British and Canadian pilots learning to fly American-made airplanes. When the British and Canadians departed after the war the air facilities were returned to the community to be used again as a local airport and much of the station's housing facilities were leased to the University of Maine and Bowdoin College for temporary student housing. With the onset of the Korean War and the new threat of Soviet submarines operating in the North Atlantic, NAS, Brunswick was recommissioned in 1951. It became a fully active naval air station again and remained active until after the end of the Cold War. During WW II NAS Brunswick had as an outlying field, Portsmouth Airport, three miles west of Portsmouth, NH.

CAMPOBELLO ISLAND, NEW BRUNSWICK, CANADA: This Canadian island, just across the border from Lubec, ME, has an important WW II site worthy of note.

ROOSEVELT CAMPOBELLO INTERNATIONAL PARK, on the western end of the island, was the site of the 34-room summer home of the Franklin D. Roosevelt family. It was here, in Aug. 1921 that Franklin Roosevelt was stricken with polio at the age of 39. The Roosevelt family used the summer home less and less after Franklin became president and the demands of the job consumed most of his time. The home has been preserved and opened to the public. The Roosevelt International Bridge,

[1]Ft. Popham is a Civil War-era fort.

Franklin Roosevelt at age 25 near his summer home on Campobello Island.

built in 1962, connects Lubec, ME with Campobello Island. Park open daily 9-5. Estate open May 28 thru Oct.-9 daily 9-5. Phone: 506/752-2922. Free

HOULTON is on the NE edge of the state near the Canadian border about 40 miles south of Presque Isle.

HOULTON ARMY AIR FIELD, 2.5 miles east of town, was the town's local airport before the war. It was purchased by the U.S. Government in 1941 as an aerial port of embarkation for Lend Lease aircraft going to Britain. When the U.S. entered the war, Houlton became one of the AAF's staging fields on the air routes across the North Atlantic to England. The field was not used as extensively as its neighbor to the north, Presque Isle AAF, or Dow Field at Bangor, and was inactivated in 1945. The field had a large prisoner of war camp holding about 1200 prisoners of war who worked on the field, in the forests and in agriculture. After the war the air field became Houlton's local airport again.

KITTERY is in the SW corner of the state across the Piscataqua River from Portsmouth, NH. It is the home of the Portsmouth Naval Shipyard which is named after, and generally associated with, Portsmouth, NH. The shipyard, however, is in Maine just south of Kittery on Seavey Island.

FORT FOSTER, on Gerrish Island at the mouth of the Piscataqua River, was built in 1900 as a coastal defense position. During WW II the fort's Battery Bohlen was armed with three 10" rifles on disappearing mounts and Battery Chapin mounted two 3" guns. There were also two fixed and two mobile anti-aircraft guns at the fort. Fort Foster was closed after the war and became a park and recreation area.

KITTERY HISTORICAL AND NAVAL MUSEUM, near downtown Kittery, preserves and interprets the history of the Kittery area and the Portsmouth Naval Shipyard. Some of the items on display pertaining to the ship yard are documents, ships' plans, photographs, paintings, dioramas, ships' logs and many models of ships built at the yard. The museum has a library with many original manuscripts. Address: Rogers Rd., Kittery, ME 03904. Phone: 207/439-3080. Hours: Memorial Day thru Oct. 31, M-F 10-4, rest of year by appointment. Admission charged. Location: From I-95 take exit 2 to SR 2365. At the traffic circle follow

signs to US 1N, then make the first right after the traffic circle onto Rogers Rd.

PORTSMOUTH NAVAL YARD: Shipbuilding and the export of mast timber began in the Portsmouth area in the 17th Century. In 1800 the U.S. Government acquired land on Dennett's Island for the purpose of building a naval ship yard. Construction of the yard went slowly and it was not until 1814 that the keel of the first ship laid. By 1900 the yard had grown considerably and was a major naval ship yard. In 1903 the yard acquired one of the Navy's first radio stations and during Aug. and Sept. 1905 the yard's newly-completed Supply Building was with site of a high-level diplomatic conference, hosted by the U.S. Government, that lead to the end of the Russo-Japanese War[2]. In 1915 the yard built its first submarine at a cost much less than that being charged by private shipyards. This established the yard as a competitive submarine builder. During WW I, and soon afterwards, the yard launched 6 submarines. The yard was then slow during the 1920s, but in 1933 began building submarines again. On May 23, 1939, one of the yard's new submarines undergoing tests, the "Squalus" foundered off the coast. A dramatic rescue of part of the sub's crew followed and was highly publicized. A movie was later made based on the "Squalus" rescue. Despite the tragedy, the yard continued to build submarines and during WW II built 67 of them. The yard built ships other than submarines and did repair work on many U.S. and foreign ships. In Dec. 1943 the yard reached it peak employment of 20,466. In May 1945, when the war ended in Europe, four German submarines, operating in the western Atlantic at the time, put in at Portsmouth to surrender. The last of these to surrender was U-234, a cargo submarine on its way to Japan with a German-made items included a supply of heavy water and uranium for Japan's nuclear bomb project. Two Japanese officers were aboard, and since Japan was still at war with the U.S., they asked to be allowed to commit suicide rather than surrender. The Germans gave their permission and the two men subsequently went out onto the sub's deck, doused themselves with luminal and burned them-

[2]The Japanese opened that war with a surprise attack on the Russian fleet as it lay at anchor in a Russian harbor. With the Russian fleet out of action, the Japanese fleet ruled the seas of East Asia and Japan subsequently won the war.

selves to death.

In Sept. 1945 the name of the yard was changed to the Portsmouth Naval Shipyard and, along with the other naval facilities in the area, was combined into a new entity, the U.S. Naval Base, Portsmouth. The yard continued to turn out submarines in the postwar years including nuclear-powered subs and other vessels. The yard operated constantly throughout the Cold War, but was closed in the 1990s.

"Squalus/Sailfish" Memorial: This memorial, on the grounds of the Portsmouth Naval Yard, consists of the conning tower of submarine SS-192 which began life as the "Squalus". As related above, the "Squalus" sank off the coast of Maine in 1939 taking the lives of half its crew. The "Squalus" was eventually raised, repaired, renamed "Sailfish" and saw action during WW II. As "Sailfish", she won 9 battle stars and a Presidential Unit Citation.

LEWISTON is 30 miles north of Portland.

U.S. NAVAL AUXILIARY AIR FIELD, LEWISTON, 4.5 miles SW of town, was the area's pre-war airport. It was taken over by the Navy and used as an auxiliary air field for NAS, Brunswick. After the war NAAF, Lewiston was returned to the community and again became a local airport.

LUBEC (See Campobello Island, New Brunswick, Canada)

PORTLAND, on the SW coast of Maine on the Atlantic Ocean, was Maine's largest city during the war and the state's leading industrial, commercial, trade and cultural center.

The city had close ties to Canada because it handled much of Canada's trade during the winter when Canadian ports were frozen in. This relationship continued throughout WW II.

An oil pipeline was completed from Portland, ME to Montreal, Quebec in 1941 to provide oil to that city in the winter and to reduce the need for sea travel which could (and did) become vulnerable to enemy submarines.

In Nov. 1941 a pipeline was laid from Portland to Montreal, Quebec to transport oil to Canada. Portland was a major shipbuilding center. Its three largest shipbuilders, all in So. Portland, were Todd-Bath Iron Shipbuilding Co., South Portland Dry Dock & Repair Co. and New England Shipbuilding Corp. All built merchant and cargo ships during the war. One of the Liberty Ships build by the New England Shipbuilding Corp., the "Jeremiah O'Brian", has been preserved and is on permanent display at Ft. Mason in San Francisco, CA. In South Portland there was a large Coast Guard Station with a depot, training center and radio direction-finding station. In Dec. 1941, soon after the U.S. entered the war, the Navy sent mine layers to Portland to mine the harbor against enemy vessels. German submarines, however, by-passed Portland for more lucrative targets further south. In early 1942 the Army put together an emergency air patrol organization called the I Air Support Command. It operated out of the Portland area using a collection of military and civilian planes to patrol Maine's southern coast. This Command operated for several months until it was replaced by regular military personnel and aircraft. Like most shipbuilding towns, Portland suffered a severe housing shortage and an overload of city services during the war.

FORT ALLEN PARK, on Eastern Promenade in east Portland, overlooks Casco Bay. In the park is a memorial to the cruiser "Portland" which saw much action in the Pacific during the war. The memorial consists of the "Portland's" mast, bell and open bridge. A monument and plaque list the ship's battle record.

FORT LEVETT, on the south side of Cushing Island, is about 3.5 miles from downtown Portland. The 125-acre coastal defense position was built in the 1890s. During WW II Battery Bowdoin had three 12" rifles, Battery Kendrick had two 10" rifles, Battery Ferguson had two 6" pedestal rifles and Battery Foote, which was encased during WW II, had two 12" rifles. Ft. Levett was a sub-post of Ft. Williams during the war. Levett's guns were removed beginning in 1943 and in 1957 the reservation was sold to a private investor.

FORT LYON, located on Cow Island, is about four miles from Portland. It was built in the 1900s and had two batteries, both of which were armed during WW II. Battery Bayard mounted three 6" rifles and Battery Abbot had three 3" rifles. During the war Fort Lyon was a sub-post of Ft. Williams. After WW II the fort was declared surplus and turned over to the city of Portland.

FORT McKINLEY is a coastal defense position located on the east side of Great Diamond (Hog) Island in Casco Bay. It was built in the 1890s to defend the entrance to Hussey sound. The fort had 9 batteries and 21 guns ranging form 3" to 12" rifles and mortars. The fort was fully

garrisoned during WW II, and was a sub-post of Ft. Williams. After the war Ft. McKinley was declared surplus and turned over to the city of Portland which sold it to a private investor.

FORT PREBLE is an old coastal defense position on the mainland 1.5 miles SE of Portland. It was built in 1808 and by WW II had become obsolete and was unarmed. During WW II it was used, however, to house military personnel. It was a sub-post of Ft. Williams. In 1950 Ft. Preble was declared surplus and became part of a vocational training school.

FORT WILLIAMS, 6 miles south of Portland at Cape Cottage, was built in 1873 as a coastal defense battery. It was upgraded to a fort with several batteries of its own in 1898-99. By WW II the fort was still partially armed with some 50-year-old rifles, up to 12", mounted on disappearing carriages. The guns were left in place until 1943 and then sold for scrap. Ft. Williams served as the headquarters for Portland's coastal defenses during the war. The fort was gradually phased out and in 1962 was declared surplus. It was turned over to the town of Cape Elizabeth and became a park.

U.S. NAVAL DESTROYER BASE, CASCO BAY: In 1940 the U.S. Government instigated the Neutrality Patrol, which was the use of U.S. warships to escort U.S. and foreign (mainly British) vessels travelling in the North Atlantic west of Iceland. Because of this, U.S. destroyers used as convoy escorts, began using the broad expanse of island-dotted water outside Portland harbor as an anchorage. There were no Navy shore installations so the destroyers were serviced by Navy tenders and oilers. In early 1942 the Navy built oil storage facilities on Long Island and enlarged them in 1943. Also in 1942 a seaplane ramp and hangar were built on Long Island to handle PBY Catalinas which cooperated with the destroyers on convoy duties. This facility was named U.S. Naval Auxiliary Air Field, Long Island and was attached to NAS, Brunswick.

It was from Casco Bay, in Oct. 1942, that the covering force for the U.S. task force departed heading for the invasion of French Morocco in North Africa. The covering force consisted of the battleship "Massachusetts", cruisers "Tuscaloosa" and "Wichita" and four destroyers.

In 1944 the name NAAF, Long Island was changed to U.S. Naval Air Field, Casco Bay. The facility also served as a base for air-sea rescue boats and target drones. Additional facilities were built on the south side of Peaks Island to service the destroyers and the Navy took over the Maine State Pier in downtown Portland to use as a supply pier. Together, all these scattered facilities comprises the destroyer base. After the war, the Navy gave up or dismantled its facilities and in 1946 the base was closed.

PRESQUE ISLE is in the NE corner of Maine near the Canadian border. This was one of the most militarily strategic locations in all of the U.S. because it was the easternmost community in the U.S. of reasonable size and the closest point in the U.S. to air destinations in eastern Canada, Greenland, Iceland and Scotland.

PRESQUE ISLE ARMY AIR FIELD, 1.5 miles WNW of town, was the area's local pre-war airport.

It was purchased by the Federal Government in 1941 to use primarily as a staging field for Lend Lease aircraft going to Britain. Later, after the U.S. entered the war, it's operations were expanded to handle U.S. and Allied aircraft flying over the North Atlantic air routes to Europe. Together with Dow AAF at Bangor, Me, Presque Isle AAF handled the majority of military aircraft, lend lease craft, air freight and passenger service flying these routes. These two field became America's main ports of air embarkation over the North Atlantic. Generally 4-engine planes departed from Dow and single-engine and twin-engine planes left from here. This, however, was not always adhered to. Beginng in June 1942, the bulk of the 8th AF departed for Europe through Presque Isle. The field also receive aircraft returning form Europe. There were two main air routes to Europe from Presque Isle: the northerly route to Goose Bay, Labrador-Bluie 1 or Bluie 6, Greenland-Reykjavik, Iceland-Prestwick or Stormways, Scotland; and a more southerly route to Harmon Field or Gander, Newfoundland and then on to Prestwick or Stormways, Scotland. The commercial air carrier, Northeast Airlines, was contracted by the Government to open regular air service out of Presque Isle to places like Gander, Moncton, Goose Bay, Stephenville, Argenta, Reykjavik, the Azores, Frobisher Bay, Baffin Island & Churchill, Manitoba. Most of Northeast's flights serviced U.S. and Allied weather stations. As part of its operations, Presque Isle AAF had a debarkation hospital and a large air freight terminal. The air field was used for many years after the war, but was eventually abandoned by the military and returned to the community.

ROCKLAND is on the west shore of Penobscot Bay near the ocean.

U.S. NAVAL AUXILIARY AIR FIELD, ROCKLAND, three miles SSE of town, was the town's local airport before the war. It was taken over by the Navy and used as an auxiliary field to NAS, Brunswick. At the end of the war the Navy gave up the field and it became the area's local airport again.

SANFORD is in SW Maine 28 miles SW of Portland.

U.S. NAVAL AUXILIARY AIR FIELD, SANFORD, four miles SE of town, was established as an auxiliary field to NAS, Brunswick. After the war the field was abandoned. During WW II NAAF, Sanford had an outlying field, Portsmouth Airport, 3 miles west of Portsmouth, NH.

MARYLAND

The state of Maryland had, like many states in the Union, suffered economic hardships through the Great Depression. It the late 1930s, however, Maryland's economy was reviving nicely. In the late 1930s a major program was under way in Maryland to build new bridges and improve highways. In 1941 the Ritchie Memorial Bridge at Annapolis was completed connecting Baltimore, the state's largest city, with Annapolis, the state's capital. Baltimore was one of the nation's major seaports and a major industrial center. War plants moved into Maryland in record numbers during the war causing the need for even more roadwork to accommodate the upsurge in traffic and increased population. Maryland had a 20% increase in manufacturing in 1942 alone, and this sector of her economy grew steadily throughout the war. The state's diversified economy produced ships, airplanes, manufactured goods, coal, coke, limestone, lime, slate, asbestos, granite, basalt, seafood (oysters & crabs), grain, tobacco, canned fruits & vegetables, meat, steel, munitions, airplanes, tinware, men & boy's clothing, breads & baked goods. The state was dotted with many truck farms producing vegetables for the big cities along the east coast. The state had a popular Senator in Washington, Millard Tydings (D), who had served continuously since 1927.

After the war Maryland continued to prosper and its population continued to increase especially in the Baltimore-Washington, DC corridor.

ABERDEEN/EDGEWOOD: These two towns are 20 and 30 miles respectively NE of downtown Baltimore near the north end of Chesapeake Bay. Their names are synonymous with the nation's most famous and oldest proving grounds and arsenal. The towns were very small during the war. Aberdeen had only 1500 people and Edgewood even less.

ABERDEEN PROVING GROUND (APG) AND EDGEWOOD ARSENAL, about 10 miles apart, both originated in 1917 and developed separately during WW I, WW II and into the postwar years until 1971 when they were merged.

APG was established in 1917 as the Army's primary test and evaluation center for research, development and testing of arms, ammunition, tracked & wheeled vehicles and other military equipment. APG comprised some 80,000 acres of land and water areas and was the Army's only proving ground for the development and acceptance of munitions and components. In 1921 the Army's Ordnance School was established at APG and became the primary educational facility for personnel operating and working at Army ordnance plants and depots throughout the country. APG operated continuously between the wars and was the storage ground for many of the Army's large weapons. In the late 1930s, operations picked up rapidly and the facility was expanded. The expansion, however, didn't keep pace with operations and by 1940 APG had become over-crowded, so some of its operations were spun off to

new proving ground in Indiana, Arkansas and Ohio. APG had a replacement training center for the Ordnance Corps training both white and negro troops.

In the late summer of 1941, after the British defeat at Dunkirk, hundreds of artillery pieces and tanks, many of them obsolete models from WW I, along with tons of ammunition, were

Tear gas being sprayed from an airplane for instructional purposes as Edgewood Arsenal.

Flame thrower being tested at Edgewood Arsenal.

Negro war workers at Edgewood Arsenal during the war filling shells with white phosphorus. The chemical had to be handled under water because it burned when exposed to air.

shipped, post haste, to England to replenish the British Army. In 1942 APG became very involved in the preparations for America's first major offensive, the invasion of North Africa. The Army's new anti-tank recoilless rocket launcher, known as the "Bazooka", was tested here along with floating tanks and mobile artillery pieces. These items, and more, were used in the invasion. Other weapons developed or tested here include recoilless rifles, 4.5" "Calliope" rocket launchers, proximity fuses, 240 mm mobil howitzers, M-26 Pershing tank, the "Tom Thumb" mortar for use in jungles, the 914 mm "Little David" mortar for use against the Siegfried Line, armor plate, armor piercing shells and welding & riveting processes. Captured enemy equipment was also evaluated here. Near the end of the war APG personnel proved that 155 mm shells and larger were ideal from closing the entrances to the caves from with the Japanese so often fought in the Pacific area. As a result, utilization of 155 mm guns dramatically increased in the field and production of guns and shells surged around the country. During the war APG operated 24 hours a day, test fired over 14 million rounds of ammunition from approximately 120,000 different guns and dropped over 100,000 test bombs. The ammunition and bombs came from manufacturers all over the country. Also tested here were vehicles ranging from Jeeps to heavy tanks, and guns from small arms to heavy artillery pieces. Near the end of the war the world's first electronic computer, "ENIAC", was put into operation here under a veil of secrecy.

APG's work force peaked in 1943 with over 30,000 military personnel and 5000 civilians, many of them women.

Edgewood Arsenal was built in 1917 as a "Mother Arsenal" specializing in chemical warfare weapons and was officially known as The Army Chemical Center. It was built on a peninsula, 8 miles long by two miles wide, jutting into Chesapeake Bay. By the end of WW I the arsenal was huge by the standards of the time with 558 buildings, 14.8 miles of paved roads, 36 miles of rail lines and had its own air field. During that war the arsenal made poison gasses and other chemicals. Between the wars Edgewood produced munitions off-and-on and stored most of the nation's supply of poison gasses. In the late 1930s Edgewood became very active again when war erupted in Europe. In 1940 proposals were made to move the arsenal inland where it would be safer from air attacks, but this didn't happen. Instead, the arsenal expanded and began producing a wide variety of chemicals. In Dec, 1941, just after the attack on Pearl Harbor, the arsenal received an order to supply gas masks for everyone in Hawaii. Its personnel shipped out every gas mask in inventory, called in gas masks from several Army units and shipped them out, and began round-the-clock production of new masks. In 1942 the name of the facility was changed to The Chemical Warfare Center. During the war the center produced 63 different types of chemicals including toxic gasses, incendiary bombs, smoke devices and signalling devices. The center also loaded shells, bombs and grenades. In early 1942 the bombs dropped on Japan by Doolittle's Raiders came from here. In addition to making chemicals the center developed launching devices, mechanical flame throwers and the war's largest incendiary bomb that could cover an area 100 yards by 40 yards with flames. It was called "The Ball of Fire" or "Hitler's Hotfoot". The center had an extensive medical facility developing and testing medicines, ointments, clothing, detection kits and other protective devices. A large chemical school, which began in 1920, operated here training U.S. and Allied personnel from all branches of service in the use and handling of the chemical weapons. Edgewood was a segregated post so negro troops also trained and worked here. In May 1945 a tragic accident occurred at the center when some white phosphorous exploded killing 13 people and wounding 51. The center's work force peaked in Mar. 1943 at 3,420 military and 10,710 civilian personnel. Many women were employed at the center, and after 1944 there was a prisoner of war camp here with about 700 POWs employed at the center.

In 1946 the center was renamed the Army Chemical Center, but in 1962 regained its old name, Edgewood Arsenal. In 1971 it merged with Aberdeen Proving Ground.

U.S. Army Ordnance Museum: This museum is in the Aberdeen Area of the Aberdeen Proving Grounds. It is an outstanding museum in that it has the most complete collection of weapons in the world. Exhibits, both inside and outside, provide a tour through the evolution of many types of weapons. Some of the fascinating weapons on display include a 20 ton bomb designed to penetrate German submarine pens which had a 50' covering of concrete and earth; "Anzio Annie", a huge German railway gun used against the Allies at Anzio; a Soviet T-34 tank, the Soviet Union's most effective tank; a 1941 British Churchill tank; a German Tiger tank from 1942 and a King Tiger tank from 1944 and a post-war atomic cannon. There are also displays of side arms, shoulder arms, machine guns, flame throwers, bazookas, mines, chemical and biological weapons, field artillery, anti-aircraft guns, landing craft, tracked vehicles and much more. Address: U.S. Army Ordnance Center and School, Aberdeen Proving Ground, MD 21005-5201. Phone: 410/278-3602/2396. Hours: Museum; Tues.-Fri. noon-4:45, weekends 10-4:45. Grounds are open daily 9-sundown. Closed holidays. Free. Location: Leave I-95 at exit 85 onto SR 22. Follow signs to Aberdeen Proving Grounds Military Police Gate.

ANNAPOLIS in on the eastern shore of Chesapeake Bay 20 miles south of Baltimore and 25 miles ENE of Washington, DC. It is Maryland's capital and home of the U.S. Naval Academy.

The town had very little industry except for the Annapolis Yacht Yard which, during the war, built small boats, especially patrol-torpedo (PT) boats. Many of the yard's PT boats went to Britain and the Soviet Union under Lend Lease.

U.S. NAVAL ACADEMY AND THE SEVERN RIVER COMMAND: The U.S. Naval Academy, which occupies 300 acres of land on the south shore of the Severn River, was established in 1845 as a government-operated four-year military college to train officers for the Navy and Marine Corps. Its students are called "midshipmen" and upon graduation receive a bachelor of science degree and commissions in the Navy as ensigns, or in the Marine Corps as 2nd lieutenants. Before WW II the Academy was only one of several naval commands in the Annapolis area. The others were; the Naval Engineering Experimental Station, a naval radio station (one of the most powerful in the world); a naval post-graduate school; a small seaplane base known as Naval Air Facility, Annapolis and the office of the Supervisor of Shipbuilding. On Dec. 8, 1941 the Secretary of the Navy, Frank Knox, consolidated these operations into a single command called the Severn River Naval Command under the Superintendent of the Naval Academy. Security at the various facilities was increased and at the Academy itself one company of sailors and one company of Marines were armed and posted as guards while midshipmen were assigned to operate the 5" guns mounted along the Academy's seawall. Furthermore, arrangements were made with nearby Ft. Meade to send soldiers to the defense of the Academy if it was attacked. The Academy's flotilla of small boats, manned by midshipmen, was pressed into service patrolling the waters around Annapolis.

Just before the U.S. entered the war the Academy's curriculum had been shortened from four years to three years and summer cruises and leave time cut back. This schedule was maintained throughout the war. During the first months of the war many of the regular duty naval officers, who were serving as instructors, were called to duty elsewhere, so the Academy called in reserve officers, retired officers and civilians to replace them. The Academy's new teaching staff proved to be very effective and prided itself in keeping up with the rapid changes in naval warfare, especially naval aviation. Each year of the war the Academy turned out more graduates than the year before. The Feb. 1941 graduating class was 399 and by June 1945 the graduating class reached 1046. About 100 Quonset huts were built on the Academy grounds to house the additional students and Academy personnel. The Academy suffered a labor shortage during the war so many women were hired and prisoners of war were brought in to operate the Academy's dairy and serve as groundskeepers.

The Engineering Experimental Station, on the north shore of the Severn River, operated independently of the Academy and did much testing during the war on non-ordnance items such as metallurgy, welding, chemistry, captured enemy equipment, jet assisted takeoffs for aircraft and rockets. From 1942 until his death in 1945, the famous rocket scientist, Dr. Robt. H. Goddard, worked with the station on rocketry.

The Naval Air Facility, Annapolis, adjacent to the Engineering Experimental Station operating about 15 seaplanes for the benefit of the Severn River Command.

The Severn River Command's hospital, in early 1942, received some of the first naval battle casualties suffered in the Pacific. They were sent here to relieve crowding in west coast hospitals and to bring some of the wounded men closer to their homes.

The mission of the Command's radio station was to broadcast a steady stream of messages and information to U.S. ships at sea throughout the war. This information was picked up by distant naval radio stations and relayed to every part of the globe. Ships at sea

Adm. Ernest J. King, Commander-in-Chief of the U.S. Fleet and Chief of Naval Operations is buried on the grounds of the Academy.

could receive this information without revealing their locations. The radio station was considered by the Navy (as well as the citizens of Annapolis) to be a prime target for sabotage, so it was heavily guarded and well lite at night as a precaution against sabotage. As backup, the Navy leased commercial transmitters in New Jersey and New York to use in case the Severn River station ever went down. The radio station also had a school to train fleet radio operators.

After the war the Severn River Command terminated and the Academy became an independent naval facility once again. It continued on its wartime schedule for a while, but in 1947-48 returned to its peacetime schedule. Since then the Academy has resumed its role as the Navy's primary educational facility for training new officers.

Buried in the Academy's cemetery are two famous WW II personalities, Adm. Ernest J. King, C-in-C of the U.S. Navy and Chief of Naval Operations during the war, and Adm. Husband E. Kimmel, Commander of the Pacific Fleet at the time of Pearl Harbor. The grounds of the Academy are open to the public until 9 pm and guided tours are offered from the visitor's center. For tour information, phone: 410/267-3363 or 263-6933.

Naval Academy Museum: This fine museum is located in Preble Hall on the Academy grounds. It contains two galleries of exhibits tracing the history of the Academy and demonstrates the role of the Navy in war and peace. On display are ship models, paintings, photographs, ships' instruments, weapons, medals, manuscripts, uniforms, naval artillery pieces, vehicles, aircraft and much more. The WW II era is well represented in the museum's collection. The museum has a large library and offers guided tours and educational programs. Address: U.S. Naval Academy, Annapolis, MD 21402-5034. Phone: 301/216-2108/2109. Hours: daily M-Sat. 9-5, Sun. 11-5. Closed Jan. 1, Thanksgiving & Dec. 25. Free. Access to the museum is through gate 1 of the Academy.

BAINBRIDGE (See Port Deposit)

BALTIMORE is in the north-central part of the state on Chesapeake Bay. At the beginning of the war it was Maryland's largest city and industrial center, a major shipbuilding center, the nation's third largest seaport in total waterborne commerce and the nation's 7th largest city. The onset of war in Europe bought a welcome surge of prosperity to the city which had suffered considerably during the Great Depression. Baltimore benefitted nicely from the Lend Lease Act of 1941 because much of the Lend Lease material sent to Britain went through this port. Baltimore's shipbuilding industry boomed and by 1941 all of her ship yards were busy and some of them were expanding. From 1942 through 1945 they worked around-the-clock. A total of 608 new vessels was launched in Baltimore during those three years of which 383 were Liberty Ships and 94 Victory Ships. Hundreds more ships were repaired. Three of the major shipbuilders were the Bethlehem-Fairfield Shipyard[1], General Ship Repair Co. and the Maryland Drydock Co. Smaller yards
[1]This ship yard launched the first Liberty Ship, the "Patrick Henry" on Sept. 27, 1941.

turned out patrol-torpedo boats, landing craft, submarine chasers, and other small craft. Some of Baltimore's port facilities were taken over by the military services and used exclusively to ship military supplies and some personnel. At the Clinton St. Pier the U.S. Maritime Commission and the Navy jointly operated a net depot that installed heavy cable nets on merchant ships as a protection against torpedoes. There was a constant labor shortage along the Baltimore waterfront so later in the war prisoners of war were brought in to work in the warehouses and on the docks. In 1942 part of Gen. Patton's forces embarked from Baltimore for the Allied landings in North Africa. After V-E Day, Baltimore's port was busy receiving returning troops and equipment and the port's facilities served as a giant liquidation center for surplus war materials.

Many other wartime activities went on in Baltimore. It was the headquarters for the Army's 3rd Corps, had a large aircraft manufacturer, the world's largest magnesium extrusion plant and over 100 other manufacturing plants. Like most shipbuilding and manufacturing communities around the U.S., Baltimore suffered serious housing shortages and severe strains on city services. Emergency housing was built, new roads were built and both factories and schools staggered shifts to avoid traffic congestion. Baltimore was a racially mixed city during the war. One third of its population was negro. There were sizeable Italian and German communities, and because of a unique clause in the state's constitution, Baltimore was required to have at least one German-language newspaper. This clause was repealed in 1944.

One Baltimore native, Adm. Raymond A. Spruance, rose to a high position in the Navy during the war. Spruance was one of the heros of the Battle of Midway, became Adm. Nimitz' Chief of Staff and later commanded of the U.S. 5th Fleet which saw action in most of the major battles of the Pacific.

THE OSS IN BALTIMORE: Because of its proximity to Washington, DC, which was the headquarters of the super-secret U.S. spy agency known as the Office of Strategic Services (OSS), Baltimore was used as a training ground for U.S. spies. Several estates, hotels and schools in the Baltimore area were taken over by the OSS for use as spy schools. These schools were usually camouflaged to appear as research and development centers or rehabilitation facilities for wounded servicemen. Some of the facilities used as schools included the Huntsmans' Inn, The Hillside, Filson Manor, Inverness Farm and Oldfields School. At Filson Manor, for example, OSS agents were taught blackmail, forgery, bribery techniques, wire tapping, poison-pen letter writing, lock-picking, safe-cracking, Morse code and code deciphering. Upon completion of their classroom work some of the agents were sent into the city and practice their new skills by trying to infiltrate closely guarded war plants, power plants and factories, and apply for jobs using fake identification. Their successes were then used to point out security problems to management.

FORT ARMSTRONG was a 45-acre coastal defense position, built in 1898, at Hawkins Point near the west end of the Francis Scott Key

Bridge. In late 1917 its guns were removed and in 1923 it was turned over the city of Baltimore and made into a park. During WW II the Navy took over the old fort and used it as an ammunition storage facility. In 1947 it was returned to the city, but in 1952 the Army took it over and set up anti-aircraft guns in the fort. Within a few years the guns were removed and the fort was turned into a park again.

BALTIMORE ARMY AIR FIELD: This was Baltimore's new municipal airport completed in Nov. 1941. A month later, when the U.S. went to war, fighter planes were sent to the airport according to pre-arranged plans for the defense of the Baltimore area. The planes remained at the airport for some time during which the Army designated the facility as an army air field. The airport continued to operate, though, as a commercial airport. In the postwar years the airport became the Baltimore-Washington International Airport.

BALTIMORE MARITIME MUSEUM is located on Baltimore's Inner Harbor on Pier 4 at the end of Pratt St. This museum has three WW II ships, all of which saw action in WW II and are now open to the public. They are the submarine "Torsk", the lightship "Chesapeake" and the Coast Guard cutter "Taney". Nearby, at Pier 1 at the end of Clinton St., is another WW II ship berthed and open to the public. It is the Liberty Ship "John W. Brown". Maritime Museum address: Pier 4, Pratt St., Baltimore, MD 21202. Phone for the Maritime Museum: 410/396-3854/5528; for the "John W. Brown" 410/558-0646. Hours for the Maritime Museum: Daily 9:30-4:30; for the "John W. Brown", by appointment only. Admission charged.

CURTIS BAY ORDNANCE DEPOT, 7 miles south of downtown Baltimore, was built in 1917 on the west bank of Curtis Bay Creek across from the Curtis Bay Coast Guard Station. Between the wars the Curtis Bay Ordnance Depot was used to store ammunition. The depot became very active in 1941 as a facility for loaded gun powder in bags for large guns. At that time much of its production went to the British under Lend Lease. After the U.S. entered the war the depot expanded its operation to load small arms ammunition into clips, magazines and belts for all branches of service. The plant also served as a backup ammunition storage facility for Ft. Armstrong at Hawkins Point. Most of the plant's workers were negroes and women and employment peaked at 1800. After the war the depot became a receiving point for small arms ammunition being returned. Its personnel then removed the ammunition from the clips, magazines and belts and stored it for future use. In the postwar years the facility became known as the Curtis Bay General Services Administration Depot.

ALLEN W. DULLES GRAVE SITE is in Greenmount Cemetery, one mile north of downtown Baltimore on North Ave. Dulles (1893-1969) was a high ranking agent in the Office of Strategic Services (OSS), and later a director of the Central Intelligence Agency (CIA), the OSS's successor. During the war, Dulles was sent to Switzerland and became very successful in relaying information back to Washington on military installations inside Germany. In the latter months of the war he was instrumental in ar-

ranging for the surrender of the German forces in Italy. In 1953 President Truman appointed him director of the CIA.

HOLABIRD SIGNAL DEPOT, three miles ESE of downtown Baltimore, was built in 1918 as a repair facility for military equipment, and known then as Mechanical Repair Shop Unit 306, Quartermaster Corps. It remained active between the wars under several names. In Aug. 1942 it became known as Holabird Ordnance Base and was used for an interesting array of activities. Just before WW II much of the testing on the new vehicle known as the "Jeep" was done here. Depot personnel also worked on developing long-wearing rubber tires and the use of synthetic rubber for various automotive applications. Between 1941-43 the depot stored and test-drove thousands of new Army vehicles. Special European-style block roads were construction at the depot for this purpose. The depot stocked numerous automotive parts and had a large repair facility for Army-owned locomotives, railroad cars, cranes and railroad equipment. It also had schools to teach people to drive military vehicles, a school for illiterates and a counter-intelligence school. Holabird had its own air field, Logan Field, just east of the depot. Automotive activity ended suddenly in Sept. 1943 when all such activities were consolidated at Letterkenny Ord. Depot in Pennsylvania. That same month the Army's Signal Corps took over Holabird Ordnance Base to store its equipment and use as a training facility for radio and radar repairmen. The facility's name was changed to Holabird Signal Depot. When the Government began using V-Mail[2], Holabird became the storage facility for the photographic equipment used in the process. Soon after they took over the facility, the Signal Corps began to store the latest models of radar units here. The units were all top secret and kept under heavy guard. Employees working in the radar section were forbidden to use the work "radar" and called the items in their care "electronic equipment".

There was a constant labor shortage at the depot and prisoners of war were used as were high school students working part time. By the end of the war Holabird was the largest military installation inside the Baltimore city limits with 286 buildings on 354 acres of land. When the troops came home, the depot received tons of Signal Corps items from overseas and processed it for re-storage or disposal. In 1947 Holabird was deactivated and its operations consolidated at Middle River Depot. In the 1950s and 60s Holabird was utilized again as an intelligence school and was known as Fort Holabird. In the postwar years the depot was sold to private interests and became known as Holabird Industrial Park. It can be seen on the east side of highways I-95/I-895 just east of the eastern exit of the Ft. McHenry Tunnel.

GLENN MARTIN AIR FIELD was 10 miles east of Baltimore on Eastern Blvd. in the community of Middle River. During the war this was the

[2]V-Mail was the process by which letters and other documents going overseas were photographically reduced onto film for shipment overseas to save shipping space and weight.

site of the Glenn L. Martin factory which built B-26 Marauder medium bombers, PBM Mariner seaplanes and JRM Mars seaplanes. The company was one of the biggest employers in the Baltimore area and also the world's largest manufacturer of power-operated gun turrets for aircraft. The last B-26 rolled off the assembly line on Mar. 31, 1945. Soon afterwards, the factory, which was owned by the Government, was turned over to the Army and, in 1946, became a sub-depot of Holabird Signal Corps Depot. The plant was eventually sold to private interests but the airport continued to be known as Glenn Martin State Airport well into the postwar years.

FORT McHENRY at the entrance to Baltimore's main harbor is, perhaps, the best known fort in America, for it was here that Francis Scott Key penned the words to a poem that would become the words to our national anthem, "The Star-Spangled Banner". Ft. McHenry was built between 1798 and 1803 and has been utilized in every American war up to, and including, WW II. In 1939 the fort was declared a National Historic Site, but when the Coast Guard needed a training center in the Baltimore area at the beginning of WW II the old fort was pressed into active service once again. Here, at this historic site, Coast Guard recruits were trained in coastal patrol work and other duties. In 1944 an old Liberty ship, the "Gaspar De Portola" which had been damaged beyond repair, was beached near Ft. McHenry and the students used it for firefighting training. Fires would be set aboard the ship and the students would rush in with their firefighting equipment and extinguish them. By war's end 28,053 Coastguardsmen had passed through the Ft. McHenry school. The fort has been restored to its pre-Civil War appearance and is open to the public. There is little evidence of its WW II days. Address: End of East Fort Ave., Baltimore, MD 21230-5393. Phone: 410/962-4299. Hours: Early June-Labor Day daily 8-8, rest of year daily 8-5. Closed Jan. 1, & Dec. 25. Admission charged.

FORT MEADE (See Laurel, MD)

U.S. COAST GUARD YARD, CURTIS BAY, 6 miles south of Baltimore, is on the eastern bank of Curtis Creek. The facility began as a Coast Guard station in 1899 and through the years developed into a one-of-a-kind Coast Guard facility in that it actually built Coast Guard cutters, buoy tenders, navigational buoys and other equipment for the Coast Guard, Navy, Army and U.S. Geodetic Survey. It also repaired ships and equipment. In 1939 the yard underwent an expansion and within a year had facilities to repair vessels as large as Navy destroyers. On Nov. 1, 1941 the Navy took over the yard for the duration of the war and expanded it further. Under Navy direction the yard still trained Coastguardsmen and in the early months of the war began training dogs to operate with Coastguardsmen on beach patrols. The yard reverted to the Coast Guard after the war and continued in operation as a ship building and repair center for many years. It also retained its wartime name.

BETHESDA (See Washington, DC area)

CAMP DAVID (See Hagerstown/Thurmont area, Shangri-La)

A national advertisement produced during the war by Triumph Explosives, Inc. of Elkton, MD.

CAMP SPRINGS (See Washington. DC area)
CHELTENHAM (See Washington, DC area)
CUMBERLAND is in Maryland's panhandle on the Potomac River.
ALLEGANY ORDNANCE PLANT was established here early in the war when the Federal Government took over a privately-owned manufacturing firm and converted it into a facility to make 30 and 50 calibre ammunition. The facility was operated by Kelly-Springfield Engr. Co. a division of Goodyear Tire and Rubber Co. Allegany Ordnance operated only until 1943.
EDGEWOOD (See Aberdeen/Edgewood)
ELKTON, in the NE corner of the state off I-95, was a small town of 3500 people during the war. The community was quite unique in that it was the center for fireworks manufacturers. As might be expected, the fireworks companies all got Government ordnance contracts. The National Fireworks Co. made detonator fuzes and high explosive ammunition, the Elk Mills Loading Corp. made incendiary bombs and hand grenades and the Maryland Display & Fireworks Co. made photo flash bombs and float light pellets.
FREDERICK is 40 miles west of Baltimore.

FORT DETRICK, four miles NNE of Frederick, was a small municipal airport in the 1930s and the home of the 104th Observation Squadron of the Maryland National Guard. The field also had a pilot training facility operated by the CAA. In Nov. 1942 the U.S. Chemical Warfare Service moved onto the field and set up a facility to test biological warfare weapons. These weapons were new to warfare and were top secret. The test facility was located at the airfield as part of its camouflage, and it and the air field were collectively named Fort Detrick. The site was chosen because it was close to Washington, DC and Edgewood Arsenal where the weapons were developed. The test facility, was further camouflaged by labelling it a chemical warfare research center. Personnel at Fort Detrick came from several civilian agencies, several U.S. universities and British and Canadian agencies, all of whom were involved in the development of the weapons. During the war Fort Detrick grew considerably and many special-purpose buildings had to be erected. The fort acquired satellite test facilities and plants in Mississippi, Indiana and Utah. The researchers at Fort Detrick studied all known fungi, bacteria and rickettsia for use as weapons against humans, animals and plants. They also studied defenses and delivery systems. During the course of operations there were several accidents that caused employees to get sick, but there were no fatalities or spreading of the agents outside the fort. The fort had a branch prisoner of war camp with about 350 POWs who worked in agriculture and the food industry, and were kept well away from the test facilities.

Fortunately for mankind, biological weapons were not used in WW II and the discoveries made here never had to be put to use. On the positive side, a number of discoveries were made for peacetime use in the fields of medicine and veterinary medicine. Much was learned about airborne diseases, antibiotics, streptomycin, streptothricin, plant growth, weed killers, safety equipment and procedures. Research continued in the postwar years and Fort Detrick became home to other activities. In the postwar years the fort was operated by the U.S. Army Health Services Command and remained a research facility under their direction.

HAGERSTOWN/THURMONT AREA:

These are two communities in Maryland's panhandle region. Hagerstown, the larger community, had a diversified economy including an aircraft factory, operated by Fairchild Aircraft Co. that manufactured cargo planes. Thurmont, 16 miles east of Hagerstown, was the center of a resort area in the Catoctin Mountains.
CAMP RITCHIE was near the small community of Cascade which is 13 miles NE of Hagerstown. In peacetime this was a resort area. Camp Ritchie was established in 1926 as a camp for the Maryland National Guard. In 1940 the Army established a week-end recreation center on the post, but this was soon abandoned and in 1942 the War Department took over the post for use as a field training center for its Military Intelligence Division. Specially selected individuals from the Army and Marines were sent here for secret training as interrogators, interpreters, translators, photo interpreters and counter-intelligence agents. The students were usually well-educated individuals who were fluent in one or more foreign languages. They underwent an 8-week course during which they attended lectures, learned to identify and use enemy equipment and took part in cross-country exercises surviving in the woods where "enemy" troops, dressed in enemy uniforms and using enemy equipment, put obstacles in their way. Because the camp used so much enemy equipment it had top priority on acquiring newly captured equipment. Upon graduation, most of the students went immediately overseas to combat areas.

The super-secret intelligence agency, the Office of Strategic Services (OSS), also used Camp Ritchie. They took over an old CCC camp about a mile from Shangri-La (now Camp David), the presidential retreat. Part of the training of the OSS agents included the use of guns and explosives. As a result, explosions were frequently heard at Shangri-La. In Sept. 1946 Camp Ritchie was returned to the Maryland National Guard. In 1951, however, the camp was taken over by the Army to become a primary and permanent Army communications center. At this time the camp was renamed Fort Ritchie. In the late 1950s a large, top secret underground atom bomb-proof installation was built at Fort Ritchie under Raven Rock Mountain. In 1971 it became the headquarters of USASTRATCOM-CONUS, a high level Army communications facility, that moved here from Alexandria, VA. It is generally believed that the underground facility was to become the Army's primary command post in the event of an atomic attack. For that reason the installation, known officially as "Site R", also became known as "The Underground Pentagon". Information on the installation during the Cold War was scarce and speculative. Fort Ritchie operated well into the postwar years and became an attractive military installation in a beautiful part of the country and a very desirable post for Army personnel.
Brigadier General Leonard J. Riley Memorial Holding: This is a small museum on the grounds of Fort Ritchie. It has displays of communications equipment, field artillery, uniforms, photographs and other items related to Ft. Ritchie. Address: Fort Ritchie, MD 21719-5010. Phone: 301/878-5128. Hours: Tue.,

This was the first laboratory at Ft. Detrick.

Thurs. and the last Sat. of each month, 10-2. Free.

SHANGRI-LA: This is now Camp David, the famous presidential retreat in the Catoctin Mountains near Thurmont, MD. During the Great Depression it was a CCC camp. In early 1942 it was scheduled to be closed when President Roosevelt intervened and ordered that it be converted into a rustic mountain retreat for himself and future presidents. Roosevelt personally named it Shangri-La after the mythical land of the then-popular novel and movie "Lost Horizons". While the camp was being converted, Jimmy Doolittle and his Raiders bombed Japan and when Roosevelt was asked where the U.S. bombers had come from, he quipped "Shangri-La". The CCC buildings were converted into rustic and spartan living quarters for the President and his aides. Here, they would hold important, but informal meetings and talks on the porch of the President's cabin overlooking a beautiful mountain valley. A phone hot line linked the camp with Washington. The President's wife, Eleanor, apparently didn't like Shangri-La because she never came here. When Dwight Eisenhower became president, he used the camp but renamed it Camp David in honor of his father. When asked why he changed the name, Ike replied "Shangri-La was just a little too fancy for a Kansas farm boy". Camp David is not open to the public.

INDIAN HEAD is 20 miles south of Washington, DC on the east shore of the Potomac River.

U.S. NAVAL POWDER FACTORY, INDIAN HEAD was built in 1890 and, as the name suggests, made gunpowder for the Navy. It was located south of Indian Head on a peninsula formed by the Potomac River and Mattawoman Creek. During WW II the plant made gun powder and did research and testing on its products at a proving ground near Dahlgren, VA. The factory expanded during the war and produced several new types of explosives including rocket propellants. Research on mines was done here and there was a school on mine warfare. Many new homes were built in the area by the Government to house workers. The factory suffered from a constant labor shortage and many WAVES were employed here to help relieve the situation. The employees worked

long hours and there were several accidents which cost a total of 6 lives. The facility operated throughout the Cold War and was later known as the U.S. Naval Ordnance Station, Indian Head.

LAUREL is midway between Baltimore and Washington, DC.

FORT MEADE, five miles east of Laurel, was established in 1917 as Camp Meade, an Army training center. In 1928 the camp was declared a permanent post and in 1929 the name was changed to Fort Meade. The fort acquired its own air field, Ft. Meade Air Field. When WW II began Ft. Meade served as a reception center and training facility for large units. In 1940 the 29th Infantry Div. was brought to Ft. Meade from Louisiana to serve as a protective force for Washington, DC. That division, the 76th Infantry Div. and part of the 26th Infantry Div. trained here during the early part of the war. Meade was a segregated base and many negro troops trained here as did French colonial troops from the Western Hemisphere. Meade had many schools, training chaplains, Medical Corpsmen, Military Police, quartermasters, censors, Signal Corpsmen, field artillerymen, coast artillerymen, anti-aircraft units, gas warfare units, special services personnel, tank destroyer units, packers & craters and entertainers & band members. There was also a school for WACs and a large school for cooks, bakers and meat cutters. Ft. Meade had a facility that did research on field rations and on occasions, VIPs from Washington, DC would be invited to the camp to sample newly created rations. This included President Roosevelt who toured the fort in Feb. 1944. In March 1945 the fort's population peaked at 69,746 making it Maryland's fourth largest city at the time. In Aug. 1943 the Army's "Ground Forces Replacement Depot #1" was established here. This was one of two such depots in the U.S. The other one was on the west coast. The Depot received trained replacement personnel from other camps and held them until it was determined where they were needed. While they waited the replacements were given advanced training. For this purpose a mock town was constructed and the men received training in house-to-house fighting. From here, most of the replacements went overseas. During the

war the depot handled about 1.4 million troops.

Fort Meade had a main prisoner of war compound holding 3600 POWs who worked on the fort and in food processing plants. The Enemy POW Information Bureau was here with the responsibility of keeping records on every POW in U.S. custody. The Bureau took care of the POW's belongings, including personal property and money, and handled outgoing and incoming POW mail. It kept records on POW deaths and answered inquiries from families seeking information about relatives in U.S. custody. The Bureau operated a secret interrogation center to interview POWs who were willing to cooperate, or who were thought to have valuable information. The living quarters of these POWs were equipped with electronic bugs and informants were placed in their midst in an attempt to get them to divulge information.

There were also three separate alien internment camps at the fort, one each of Japanese, German and Italian aliens. After Italy joined the Allies in Sept. 1943 Italian Service Units were trained here and some of the units went to work at the Enemy POW Information Bureau and others were sent to work in the Pentagon. At the end of the war the fort served as a separation center and in the postwar years continued to host a wide variety of commands and operations including the headquarters of the U.S. First Army. In one corner of the post the super-secret National Security Agency set up its heavily guarded headquarters.

Fort Meade Museum: This museum is on the grounds of Ft. Meade and chronicles the military history of the Fort and the surrounding area from the days of the Revolution to the present. Of particular interest is a bullet-ridden bust of Adolph Hitler found in the rubble of Berlin, and pieces of the famous Remagen Bridge over the Rhine. Also on display are tracked and wheeled vehicles, field artillery, ordnance, communications and medical equipment, small arms, machine guns, uniforms, medals and more. Address: Attn: AFZI-PTS-MU. Ft. Meade, MD 20755-5115: Phone: 301/677-6966/7054. Hours: W-Sat. 10-4, Sun. 1-4 (subject to change). Free. Access to the museum is through the post's main gate on SR 198.

LEXINGTON PARK AREA: This area is in the south-central part of the state on Chesapeake Bay and the Patuxent River.

U.S. NAVAL AMPHIBIOUS BASE, SOLOMONS ISLAND was located at the end of a small peninsula on the east bank of the Patuxent River near the fishing village of Solomons, MD and across from NAS, Patuxent River. The "island" was government-owned land bounded on three sides by water and only 117 acres in size. Selecting this small a location turned out to be a big mistakes because there was virtually no chance for expansion. The Navy, nevertheless, proceeded with plans to built an amphibious training facility here because the site had good landing beaches at Drum and Cove Points, and sufficient anchorages for transport ships. Furthermore, the location had been personally approved by an expert on amphibious invasions, Gen. Holland M. Smith. It was anticipated that the base would become known as the "Cradle of Invasions". Large-scale land-

Prisoners of war repairing U.S. Army uniforms at Ft. Meade, MD.

ings were new to the Navy and there was much to be learned. NAB, Solomons Island would prove to be a good teacher. From the beginning, the base was under a tight schedule to train men for the upcoming amphibious invasion in North Africa scheduled for Nov. 1942. To meet the deadline many shortcuts were taken in building the base. With no existing military facilities in the area the Navy took over the Reker Hotel and rented several houses to use as administration buildings while the construction of barracks and other facilities proceeded post-haste to accommodate 500 men. Material and labor shortages plagued the construction effort. Meanwhile one transport arrived with 15 or 16 temporary landing craft[3] and training began. Some of the first men trained here later landed the Marines at Guadalcanal in Aug. 1942. On June 10, 1942 NAB, Solomons Island was ordered to expand its facilities to accommodate 2000 men. That number was later increased to 3400, then to 7000 and eventually to 9500. This turned the difficult task of building and preparing the facilities into turmoil. Barracks, mess halls and other necessary buildings were thrown up as fast as possible, but "luxuries" such as sidewalks, paved streets, recreation facilities, an other amenities were non-existent. All the while, training continued as more transports, and finally the proper types of landing craft, arrived. This, however, caused yet another unforeseen problem. The increased number of transports and the maneuvering of large numbers of landing craft interfered with seaplane operations at NAS, Patuxent River across the river.

As many as a 1000 men a week were shuttled back and forth between NAB, Solomons Island and the Norfolk area for the amphibious training programs. It was not a trip the men looked forward to. Word had spread that NAB, Solomons Island was a hellhole of mud, crowded conditions, shortages (including a water shortage) and boredom. To make matters worse, the morale of the officers and men stationed at the base was in a permanent state of depression because the amphibious forces were looked upon in the Navy as a dumping ground for wash-outs and screw-ups. It was sometimes called the "Siberia of the Navy".

In late 1942, after the rush to train men for the North African invasion had passed, the base had a breathing spell and was able to improved its facilities somewhat. But then, training resumed at breakneck speed again for the many amphibious operations being planned in the Mediterranean and the Pacific. Overcrowding and shabby conditions persisted at NAB, Solomons Island. At times there were 15,000 at the base built for 9400. As many as 18,000 men a weeks came in from Norfolk and went out again. Nevertheless, base conditions slowly improved and NAB, Solomons Island acquired a shakedown school, stewards mate school, a marine railroad and a small drydock to maintain landing craft. The station also became one of two locations on the east coast[4]

[3]LSTs, LCIs,LSMs and LCSs, the landing craft that was to be used in North Africa, was not yet available.
[4]The other was NATB, Littlecreek in Virginia.

where newly-built landing craft, manufactured by various ship yards along the east coast, were gathered prior to being taken overseas. After July 1944 the number of trainees at the base began to decline and by Feb. 1945 only 1858 men were trained. The Navy took this opportunity to close the base soon afterwards and close the books on this unhappy experience. Years later the state bought the site and salvaged many of the buildings for other purposes. The area was all but abandoned in the postwar years and little evidence remains of NAB, Solomons Island.

U.S. NAVAL AIR STATION, PATUXENT RIVER, is east of, and adjacent to, Lexington Park at the mouth of the Patuxent River. It was built in 1942-43 as a test center for naval aircraft. Heretofore, naval aircraft were tested at five different locations. NAS, Patuxent River consolidated these operations at one site. The location was chosen because it was remote enough to avoid air congestion with other military air facilities and large cities, was isolated which improved security for secret tests, and had open spaces for gunnery and armaments testing. Also, the area had good highways, water and rail transportation and was close to Washington, DC. The station also had adequate water frontage and operating lanes in the Patuxent River and Chesapeake Bay for seaplanes. During the war the station expanded, acquiring a 12,000' runway, 9 hangars, shelter for up to 200 planes and living space for 14,000 people. The station used Bloodsworth Island in Chesapeake Bay as a bombing and gunnery range. Many veteran carrier pilots, with combat experience in the Pacific, were used here as test pilots. The Naval Air Test Center was the tenant commander of the station and oversaw and managed the numerous tests run on new and updated aircraft. At any given time there was a wide variety of aircraft on station undergoing tests. When hurricanes threatened nearby areas, NAS, Patuxent became the refuge for Navy planes flown out of the hurricane's path. The station became host to numerous support commands and agencies affiliated with aircraft and testing. The Naval Air Transport Command operated here with air routes to Europe and several points in Latin America. The facility continued operating into the postwar years much as it had during the war.

Naval Air Test & Evaluation Museum: This museum in on the grounds of NAS, Patuxent River and is a one-of-a-kind museum in that it is the only museum in the country offering displays on the testing and evaluation of naval aircraft. On display are aircraft, engines, models, test pilot gear, photos and a multitude of components and systems evaluated by the personnel of NAS, Patuxent River, some successfully, some not. Address: PO Box 407, Naval Air Test Center, Patuxent River, MD 20670-5000. Phone: 301/863-7418. Hours: July through Sept., W-Sat. 11-4, Sun. noon-5. Rest of year F-Sat. 11-4, Sun. noon-5. Closed Easter, Thanksgiving and Dec. 25. Free. Access to the museum is through the NAS's north gate at the intersection of SR 235 and Shangri-La Dr. in Lexington Park.

U.S. NAVAL MINE WARFARE TEST STATION, SOLOMONS was about a mile north of NAB,

Solomons Island on the east bank of Patuxent River. The station was built in 1942 at the same time NAB, Solomons Island was being built. This location was chosen because it was close to Washington, DC yet in a remote area conducive to security, and offered deep and sheltered water necessary for the testing of mines. The test station's mission was to conduct research and experimentation on underwater warfare materials and devices, primarily mines and torpedoes, for both offensive and defensive purposes. The station tested underwater devices purchased by the Navy from independent contractors and some captured enemy underwater weapons. There was a small school here to train naval personnel, including some British and Canadian personnel, in the handling and application of underwater devices. Much of the work done at NMWTS, Solomons was secret and the station attempted to maintain a low public profile. In Aug. 1945 the station's population peaked at 1445 enlisted men, 228 officers and 350 civilian employees. During the war NMWTS, Solomons was instrumental in developing and releasing to the Navy about 20 new types of mines. Activity declined rapidly after the war and in June 1947, the station was deactivated.

U.S. NAVAL TORPEDO TESTING RANGE, PINEY POINT was located at Piney Point, MD 9 miles SSW of Lexington Park on a peninsula on the east bank of the Potomac River. Since WW I the Navy had used this area of the Potomac River to test torpedoes operating from a barge. In July 1939 they transferred the operation to shore and built a small station to accommodate about 1000 naval personnel and civilian employees. Throughout the war the station operated under the direction of the Naval Torpedo Factory, Alexandria, VA. Piney Point had an unlimited range over which torpedoes could be tested and was the only torpedo test station in the country with weather that allowed it to be operative the year around. During the war the station was exceptionally busy and handled about 15 times the work load originally anticipated. Since torpedoes are very expensive and complex devices, attempts are made to salvage each one after being tested. This is usually done by filling the war head with air so the torpedo rises to the surface for easy retrieval after each test run. Accurate records are kept on torpedoes and war records show that some 1400 torpedoes tested at NTTR, Piney Point scored hits on enemy targets during WW II. After the war the station was deactivated and abandoned.

PORT DEPOSIT is in the NE corner of the state.

U.S. NAVAL TRAINING STATION, BAINBRIDGE, near the town of Port Deposit, began in 1942 when the Navy acquired the defunct boys schools, known as the Tome School for Boys, for the purpose of converting it into a recruit training facility. This was one of three inland training stations built by the Navy during the war[5]. The 14 stone buildings of the school served as administration buildings and officers' housing and several hundred wooden buildings were erected during the summer and
[5]The other two were at Farragut, ID and in the Geneva/Seneca Falls area of New York.

fall of 1942. Five 5000-man training camps were built with common facilities such as a hospital, officers' compound, storage, utilities and a unique 10,000-seat outdoor auditorium. During the war the station expanded and its wartime population peaked at 35,000 making it the largest naval facility in Maryland. Upon completion of their training some of the new sailors went to advanced schools, or to ships, or to an "outgoing" camp on the grounds of NTS, Bainbridge where they resided until sent elsewhere. NTS, Bainbridge had a number of schools, some of which included schools for quartermasters, signalmen, electrician's mates, clerks, cooks & bakers, stewards, hospital corpsmen, recruit instructors and naval personnel working with private industry. NTS, Bainbridge also had a preparatory school for selected individuals going on to the Naval Academy. In Apr. 1944 NTS, Bainbridge was upgraded to a training center and renamed U.S. Naval Training Center, Bainbridge in anticipation of its becoming a major separation center for sailor and marines at the end of the war and a training facility for personnel operating this and other separation centers. These plans came to pass and by war's end the center was training the last of the 244,277 separation center personnel scheduled to pass through the station. At that same time NTC, Bainbridge was beginning operations as a separation center in its own right. The center's hospital was used as part of the separation center discharging individuals for medical reason, nurses and women reservists. In mid-1947 separation operations ended with the center having separated 47,013 individuals. From then on activities at the center fluctuated up and down. It became very active again during the Korean War only to taper off again after that war. Various operations and commands came and went at NTC, Bainbridge until the early 1970s when it was determined to eventually close the facility. One-by-one NTC, Bainbridge's operations closed down or move out and in 1974 the center was closed.

SANDY SPRING is a small community 18

Harold L. Ickes (1874-1952)

miles north of Washington, DC.

HAROLD L. ICKES GRAVE SITE: Harold Ickes was the Secretary of the Interior throughout the Roosevelt Administration and for a year of the Truman Administration. He lived for many years in nearby Olney, MD and is buried in Sandy Spring in the Friend's Meeting House Cemetery on Meeting House Rd. During the war Ickes took on the additional tasks as solid-fuels administrator, petroleum administrator and coal mines administrator. He was a colorful and outspoken politician and a strong conservationist. He referred to himself as the "Old Curmudgeon". Directions to the grave site: From SR 108, which runs east and west through Sandy Spring, proceed to the center of town and watch for Meeting House Rd. which joins SR 108 in the center of town between a bank and the fire house. Proceed south several hundred feet south on Meeting House Rd. to the cemetery which will be on your left. Ickes' grave is No. F-11.

SILVER SPRINGS (See Washington, DC area)

SUITLAND (See Washington, DC area)

THURMONT (See Hagerstown/Thurmont Area)

WASHINGTON, DC AREA: Already, in the early 1940s, the city of Washington was outgrowing the small area of the District of Columbia and its suburbs were spreading into Maryland. This process was accelerated in Dec. 1940 when the Potomac toll bridge south of DC opened becoming the only bridge across the Potomac south of DC and the main bypass around DC. The coming of the war greatly accelerated the suburban sprawl into Maryland making Montgomery County the fastest growing county in the state. As a result, the people and communities of this part of the state became more closely associated with DC than with the state of Maryland.

OSS OPERATIONS IN THE WASHINGTON, DC AREA OF MARYLAND: The top-secret U.S. spy agency, the Office of Strategic Services (OSS), was headquartered in Washington, DC, and quite naturally kept its small, tight-knit training operations close at hand. Several sites were used in Maryland including the Lothian Farm at Clinton, MD, Smith Point on the Potomac River in Charles County, MD and the Congressional Country Club at Bethesda, MD. The schools were disguised as research or medical facilities to cover their real identities. Lothian Farm was the first OSS school established in Nov. 1941 and graduated its first class in April 1942. The Congressional Country Club specialized in teaching agents to parachute from planes at night and offered refresher courses to veteran agents. After the war the club was used as a separation center for OSS agents.

AIRMEN MEMORIAL MUSEUM is SE of DC in the town of Suitland, MD. and is known as the "all-electronic" museum because of its many participatory computerized exhibits. The museum uses the latest technology in computer graphics, holography and laser technology to tell its story, which is the history of the U.S. Airman. There are three galleries of exhibits which, in addition to the electronic exhibits, include uniforms, equipment, documents, photographs, paintings, medals and a

recreated 1940s orderly room. There is a large video screen upon which visitors may call up and review the service records of family members and friends who served as enlisted men. Address: 5211 Auth Rd., Suitland, MD 20746. Phone: 301/899-3500. Hours: M-F 8-5. Free. Location: From I-95 take exit 7B north on Branch Ave./Silver Hill towards Suitland. Auth Rd. is the first road to the right. Proceed three blocks down Auth Rd. to the museum.

CAMP SPRINGS ARMY AIR FIELD, which became Andrews Air Force Base after the war, was 1.5 miles east of Camp Springs, MD. The site upon which the air field was built was considered, in 1929, as the site for Washington's metropolitan airport, but another site was chosen. In 1942 the AAF acquired the site and built Camp Springs Army Air Field to be its headquarters and a protective air field for the DC area with a secondary mission of training fighter pilots and bomber crews. Camp Springs AAF expanded rapidly during the war because other air fields in the area, such as Bolling AAF couldn't expand. In May 1943 the newly-trained and combat-ready 1st Fighter Group became the first defensive air unit to operate out of Camp Springs AAF. This group soon moved overseas and another newly-trained group took its place. The air field saw a succession of such groups come and go during the war and in that way provided operational experience for pilots who would soon go into combat. The training of replacement pilots in P-47s and other aircraft was also conducted at Camp Springs. The new practice of skip-bombing (the skipping of a bomb across the surface of water into a target) was taught at one of Camp Springs' auxiliary fields at Millville, NJ. The field's main administration building was a unique five-sided, three-story structure and became known in the AF as the "Baby Pentagon". In Feb. 1945 the name of the field was changed to Andrews Field in honor of Lt. Gen. Frank M. Andrews, Commander of U.S. forces in Europe, who was killed in an air crash in Iceland in May 1943. In Apr. 1945 Andrews Field became the headquarters of the newly formed Continental Air Force which, in Oct. 1946, was renamed the Strategic Air Command (SAC). By war's end Andrews Field was one of the largest air bases in the U.S. and served as a separation center processing 18,872 AF men and women. The field remained very active in the postwar years serving the needs of SAC, the Washington establishment and local reserve units. The US Air Force took over the field in the late 1940s renaming it Andrews Air Force Base, and during the Korean War B-25 bomber crews trained here. In 1961 Navy air units moved onto the field when NAS, Anacostia closed in DC. In the postwar years the field became the home of the President's plane, "Air Force 1" and served as the aerial port of entry for visiting foreign heads of state and other official government visitors.

PAUL A. GARBER FACILITY: One mile SW of Suitland, MD, is a preservation, restoration and storage facility for historic aircraft owned by the National Air and Space Museum of the Smithsonian Institute. This facility exists, in part due to the efforts of Air Force Gen. Harold "Hap" Arnold who was determined to preserve

James V. Forrestal

at least one aircraft of every type from WW II. The facility is open to the public as a "no-frills" museum and displays many of its aircraft in the original and unrestored condition. There are over 100 planes from all eras of aviation on display and represent only a small percentage of the total number of aircraft owned by the National Air and Space Museum. In addition to aircraft there are numerous engines, propellers and flight-related objects on display. Outstanding in the collection is the B-29 bomber that dropped the first atomic bomb on Japan, the "Enola Gay". Other WW II aircraft in the collection include a Hawker Hurricane Mk11C, Northrup P-61 Black Widow, Focke-Wulf FW 190F-8, Bell P-39Q and P-63A, de Haviland Mosquito, Douglas B-26B, Fieseler Fi 156 Storch, Grumman F6F-3 Hellcat, F8F-2 Bearcat and TBF-1 Avenger, Lockheed P-38J Lightning, P-47D Thunderbolt, Vought F4U-1D Corsair, Vought OS2U Kingfisher and a German-made Arado 234-B jet. Visitors are escorted through the facility on guided tours and are taken into the restoration area to see aircraft being restored. A limited number of people are accommodated on the tours so it is recommended that visitors phone ahead, especially in the summer months. The facility is neither heated nor air conditioned. Address: Suitland, MD 20746. Phone: 202/357-1552. Hours: Tours M-F at 10 am. Sat. & Sun. 10 and 1. Reservations are required and may be obtained by writing to Tour Scheduler, National Air & Space Museum, Rm. P700, Smithsonian Institute, Washington, DC 20560, or phone 202/357-1400. Free: Location: From I-95 4B exit onto SR 414 east. Proceed three miles to the facility at the Jct. of Old Silver Hills Rd. and St. Barnabas Rd.

NATIONAL NAVAL MEDICAL CENTER, BETHESDA: From 1935 to 1942 the National Naval Medical Center was located in Washington, DC. In 1942, however, the center moved to new and larger facilities about one mile north of Bethesda, MD on Rockville Pike. The 500-bed facility consisted mostly of temporary wooden buildings. It was

dedicated by President Franklin D. Roosevelt[6] on Aug. 31, 1942 and served at first as a naval hospital, medical school and dental school. During the war the center expanded to include a school for naval corpsman and women hospital attendants, a school for hospital administrators and as the home of the prestigious Naval Medical Research Institute. Near the end of the war a specialized school for medical technicians, who were to be involved in demobilization, was set up here. During the war the center grew to 2500 beds and treated mostly naval, Coast Guard and Marine personnel. At times the hospital was very crowded and had to use double-deck beds and space beds closer together than normal. The Naval Medical Research Center (NMRC) made some significant medical advances during the war including research on tropical diseases, the use of acrylic plastic eyes to replace glass eyes, emergency food kits, new uses for penicillin, improved treatment for burns, water sterilization, body armor, insect repellents, photography inside the body and an expendable refrigerator for shipping blood long distances. Also developed was a kit for desalinating sea water that was later mass produced by the Navy and placed aboard every life raft. In all, the NMRC worked on 536 research projects. The hospital itself treated 51,800 patients during the war. NMRC, Bethesda remained very active after the war and opened its doors to other government and service personnel. In May 1949 James V. Forrestal, the Under Secretary of the Navy and later Secretary of the Navy during the war and still later the nation's first Secretary of Defense, leap to his death from the 16th floor of the hospital while a patient there. The hospital operated well into the postwar years and became one of the largest hospitals in the Washington area.

OXON HILL MANOR: This was the home of Sumner Welles, a career diplomat and confidant of President Roosevelt. Welles served as

[6] Roosevelt was later a patient at the hospital in April 1944, a year before he died. He was treated for bronchitis and his doctors recommended that he give up smoking. He didn't, and until the end of his life he continued to cough softly but persistently.

Ambassador to Cuba in 1933, Assistant Secretary of State 1933-37 and Under Secretary of State 1937-43. In early 1940 Welles was sent by FDR to Europe as his personnel emissary during the "phoney war" in an unsuccessful attempt to seek peace. In 1941 Welles accompanied FDR in his meeting with Churchill and in Jan. 1942 represented the U.S. at the Rio Conference of foreign ministers. Because of this and his subsequent relationships with Latin American countries, Welles became known as an architect of the "Good Neighbor Policy", a phrase he is credited with having originated. Later, Welles headed the U.S. body that carried out preparation planning for the United Nations Organization. During the summer of 1943, however, Welles suddenly resigned his post in a dispute with his superior, Cordell Hull, and was succeeded by Edward R. Stettinius, Jr.

Oxon Hill Manor is an elegant estate built by Welles and his wife in 1927 on the site of a famous 18th century manor house. It is on the National Register of Historic Places and is open to the public. Address: 6901 Oxon Hill Rd., Oxon Hill, MD 20745. Hours: Inquire. Phone: 301/839-7782/7783. Location: From the Capitol Beltway, I-95/495, take exit 3A south onto SR 210, which is Indian Head Highway. Immediately south of the interchange take Oxon Hill Road (SR 414) west and proceed to the Manor which will be on the right.

WALTER REED HOSPITAL, FOREST GLEN SECTION (SILVER SPRINGS, MD): This is an annex to Walter Reed Army Medical Center in Washington, DC. During the war, Walter Reed Army Hospital, had a need to expand and bought a girl's finishing school in the community of Forest Glen near Silver Springs, MD. The school was converted into a rehabilitation and convalescent center freeing space at the main hospital for other purposes. The homey atmosphere of the Forest Glen Section was maintained including many of the original decorations, the four-poster mahogany beds and the school's chef. The facility opened in Jan. 1943 and was very busy throughout the war. Expansions brought it up to a 767-bed facility by 1947 and eventually to 1100 beds. The hospital operated

Oxon Hill, the home of Sumner Welles, Under Secretary of State and close associate of President Roosevelt.

Ft. Washington, MD, on the Potomac River across from Mt. Vernon, VA, guarded the approaches to Washington, DC.

throughout the Cold War as an annex to Walter Reed in Washington, DC and became the home of the Army's Prosthetics Research Laboratory.

U.S. NAVAL RADIO STATION, CHELTENHAM was built in 1938 at Cheltenham, MD, 15 miles SE of downtown Washington. It was one of several very powerful radio receiving stations in the country operated by the Navy. During the war its personnel spent much of their time listening to transmission from enemy submarines. The facility operated around-the-clock and employed both naval personnel and civilians. There was a school on the station offering advanced training to radiomen. The station continued in operation throughout the Cold War.

FORT WASHINGTON was south of Washington, DC on the east bank of the Potomac River across from Mt. Vernon, VA. It was built in 1815-23 on the site of another fort, Fort Warburton, which was destroyed during the War of 1812. Ft. Washington was abandoned and reoccupied several times during the 1800s. It 1896 it was reoccupied after a period of dormancy and between 1900-04 was modernized and heavily armed. It then remained occupied continuously until WW II. In Jan. 1942 the Army's Adjutant General School moved to the fort from Arlington, VA. The school's mission was to train Army personnel in the multifold duties and procedures of Army administration. The school also undertook the task of standardizing procedures, forms, Army terms and abbreviations. During the course of the war the school completely revised and shortened the volume of books known as the "Army Regulations". "The Book" or "The Bible", as it was often called, was reduced from 9 sets of books and 10,000 pages to two sets of books with 3000 pages. The school also produced the first Army dictionary and other useful instruction books and manuals. There was a branch prisoner of war camp here with about 200 POWs who worked at the fort. By war's end 35,241 students, both men and women, had passed through the school along with 79 officers from Allied nations. In Aug. 1944 the Adjutant General's School moved to Ft. Lee, VA and Ft. Washington was closed. The fort was turned over to the Veterans Administration who, in 1946, relinquished it to the Department of the Interior who converted it into a park known as Ft. Washington Park.

WESTOVER is on the Delmarva Peninsula 18 miles SSW of Salisbury.

CAMP SOMERSET was a CCC camp built in 1935 on SR 13 near Westover and was abandoned in early 1941. In Dec. 1941 the Army bought the camp to use as a headquarters for Army units being rushed to defend the coastal areas of Maryland and Virginia. The camp was enlarged to house about 1000 soldiers and had four smaller camps under its jurisdiction. Camp Somerset also housed a tank company, artillery company, engineer company, intelligence unit and medical unit ready to go into action at any point along the coast if the enemy threatened. Housing at Somerset was limited so some personnel lived off base in Westover and Princess Anne. In early 1944, with the threat of invasion waning, the camp was closed and the troops sent to Camp Pendleton, VA. In July, however, Camp Somerset reopened as a prisoner of war camp for 1032 German POWs. The POWs had been brought to Camp Somerset purposely to relieve a severe labor shortage in the area. They subsequently worked on farms, in local canning factories, a meat packing house, sawmills and at the local railroad station. The camp served as a POW camp until June 1946 when the POWs were repatriated and the camp closed once again. Later that year the camp was bought by the University of Maryland and in 1947 it was turned into a migrant workers camp, which functioned well into the postwar years.

MASSACHUSETTS

When World War II began in Europe in 1939 the state of Massachusetts had the good fortune of finding itself in the right place at the right time. Its growing industrialized economy, its eager work force, geographic location and political stability all contributed to the boom conditions that the state was about to experience. Massachusetts was one of the most industrialized states in the nation. Over 89% of her population lived in cities of 10,000 population or more and were associated with manufacturing. Foremost among those industries effected by the war were the state's firearms and shipbuilding industries. Before the first shots of WW II were fired, these industries were bustling with government contracts. Other Massachusetts-made products that were soon in great demand were electrical equipment, foundry & machine shop products, machine tools, rubber goods, textiles, clothing, leather, boots & shoes, wool, paper and coke. From her farms came livestock, dairy products, corn, apples, tobacco, cranberries and hay, and the state's seaports produced great quantities of sea food. Massachusetts' mines produced clay, lime and stone. When the import of mica, used in electrical components, was cut off, long dormant deposits of this vital material in Chester State Forest were re-activated.

Geographically the state became important to the defense of New England and the U.S. east coast. Its seaports, especially Boston, became important for convoys and other naval operations in the North Atlantic. Before the U.S. entered the war Massachusetts ports serviced British and Canadian warships and exported Lend Lease goods to Britain and other nations.

When the U.S. went to war in Dec. 1941 the citizens of Massachusetts felt themselves threatened because of their proximity to the North Atlantic convoy lanes and to Europe itself. This was not unreasonable because the Germans had plans on file to attack Massachusetts if the opportunity ever presented itself. Also, the presents of local spies and sabotage was a real concern because the state had 360,416 enemy aliens, the fourth largest enemy alien population in the U.S. In Jan. 1942 Governor Leverett Saltonstall proclaimed a state of emergency in Massachusetts and assumed extraordinary powers provided for the governor in the state's constitution. The state government acted quickly and became the first in the nation to begin civil defense preparations.

The state's fishermen braved the terrors of war and continued to venture far out to sea to bring in the catch. At first they resisted attempts by Government and military officials to act as picket boats and report on activities they saw concerning enemy submarines. The fishermen believed that such activity would make them vulnerable to enemy attacks. This changed, however, in the spring of 1942 when a German sub sank two fishing boats in an unprovoked attack. After that, the fishermen served willingly as observers and as rescue vessels for the Allied ships traversing their fishing grounds. The fishing boats were still relatively safe at sea because they were small, unarmed and, in the minds of the German sub captains, unworthy of an attack which might reveal their sub's position. All the while the fishermen brought home tons of sea food.

The state had many prisoners of war within it boundaries working for the military and in agricultural. In the fall of 1944 the POWs were credited with saving the state's cabbage crop.

The state had several famous national personalities. Perhaps the most famous was Joseph P. Kennedy, the ambassador to Great Britain at the beginning of the war and a power in the National Democrat Party. Three of Kennedy's four sons were in service. One was killed and the other two served with distinction. All three of Kennedy's surviving sons went into politics after the war and one of them, John F. Kennedy, became President. The state also had as one of its senators, Henry Cabot Lodge, Jr. (R) from Beverly. Lodge resigned his Senate seat in 1944 to join the Army. Upon his return he was re-elected to the Senate again in 1946, but then lost his seat in 1952 to John F. Kennedy. In 1960 Lodge was the Republican Party's Vice Presidential candidate with Richard Nixon in his first, and unsuccessful, bid for the Presidency. Other prominent Massachusetts citizens were Joseph C. Grew, U.S. Ambassador to Japan at the time of the Japanese attack on Pearl Harbor, and John W. McCormick, Majority Leader of the House of Representatives. Yet another influential politician was Joseph W. Martin, Jr. (R) from North Attleboro, Minority Leader in the House. A scientist of world renown came from Worcester, MA. He was Dr. Robert H. Goddard, the father of modern rocketry.

When the war ended, Massachusetts' economy showed no signs of letting up. The introduction of the quick-freeze process opened up world markets for the state's fishing industry, the state's electronics business began to blossom, a 6-year state-wide road building program was launched and other segments of the economy remained strong. The state legislature voted a $100 bonus for every Massachusetts veteran and the state's governor made a determined, but unsuccessful, effort to bring

German prisoners of war work on a local paper drive at Ft. Devens, MA.

the permanent home of the United Nations to Boston.

AYER, 30 miles NW of Boston, was an unincorporated during the war.

FORT DEVENS, a division-size training camp, was built one mile south of Ayer in 1917 and at that time was known as Camp Devens. After WW I it became a training center for Army Reserve officers and the Civilian Military Training Corps. In 1931 it was made a permanent Army post and was re-named Fort Devens. In 1940 the fort was expanded to accommodate the draftees from all of New England who had been called into service as a result of America's first peacetime draft. The fort acquired a 1200-bed hospital and its own air field. Fort Devens was a reception center for the 1st Army Corps and was used, as it had been in WW I, as a training camp for division-sized units. The 1st, 32nd and 45th Infantry Divisions trained here as did the 4th Women's Army Auxiliary Corps (WAAC). In 1941 the post's hospital was expanded to 4000 beds and upgraded to a general hospital called Lovell General Hospital. It then treated war wounded from overseas and specialized in general medicine, syphilis and general and orthopedic surgery. The fort had segregated facilities, so negro troops also trained and served here. Furthermore, the fort was used as a staging area for units awaiting shipment overseas through the ports of Boston and New York. In late 1942, Ft. Devens was one of the first Army camps in the country to receive POWs who were beginning to arrive at

Boston. Ft. Devens was to be the only main POW camp in New England, but as more and more POWs flooded into the U.S. that changed. In Feb. 1944 Devens' prisoner of war camp was enlarged to hold 5000 German POWs who had been identified as anti-Nazi Germans. The POWs worked at the fort and at a variety of jobs in the area. In 1945 when U.S. authorities began searching German POW camps for co-operative individuals to work in the future U.S. occupation government in Germany, Fort Devens was used as a screening center for candidates. Of 17,883 German POWs screened, 816 were accepted for administrative posts and 2895 as policemen. These people were sent to other locations for training and then were among the first to be repatriated to Germany. When it came time to repatriate the bulk of the German POWs in the U.S. the Ft. Devens' POW compound became a staging area and processing center for POWs being shipped out. The POW camp remained in operation until late 1946. At the end of the war Fort Devens became a separation center for U.S. soldiers and soon afterwards was put into caretaker status. Lovell General Hospital was scaled back and became the post's hospital once again. Many of Fort Devens' buildings were used as temporary housing for students at the University of Massachusetts. The Fort was reactivated for the Korean War and used once again as a reception center and a training camp. During the Cold War the fort was used by both the U.S. Army and the Army Reserves for a variety of needs. Fort Devens was closed in the 1990s.

U.S. NAVAL AUXILIARY AIR STATION, AYER was 1.2 miles NW of Ayer. It was established by the Navy as a training base and an auxiliary field for NAS, Squantum. After the war the Navy abandoned the facility.

BEVERLY is 17 miles NE of Boston on the north shore of Beverly Harbor across from Salem. One of the town's largest manufacturers was the United Shoe Machinery Corp. which made 37 mm anti-tank guns. The town also had one of the few U.S. Coast Guard Air stations in the country.

U.S. NAVAL AUXILIARY AIR FIELD, BEVERLY was three miles NW of town and was the area's local airport before the war. The Navy took it over to use as an auxiliary field to NAS, Squantum. After the war the field was returned to the community.

BOSTON AREA: Boston is the capital of Massachusetts, its largest city and main economic, industrial and cultural center. At the time of WW II Boston was the 9th largest city in the country. During the war Massachusetts Institute of Technology, in Cambridge, did considerable research on the development of radar, and Harvard University, also in Cambridge, did war-related research on oceanography. Commercially, Boston was one of the nation's great sea ports, a major manufacturing center, a center for the wool trade and an important fishing port. In 1941 Logan Airport, in East Boston, expanded and became one of the most modern in the country. In the harbor, ship channels were dredged to accommodate larger ships and during 1941 several British warships put it at Boston for repairs. Boston's local industries shifted into high gear with a steady influx of defense orders lead by the privately owned shipbuilding companies and the huge Boston Navy Yard. Among the principle independent shipbuilders were the Bethlehem Steel Co. Shipbuilding Div. in Quincy which built a variety of warships[1] and the Quincy Adams Yacht Yard, Inc. which built sub chasers. In Oct. 1941 Boston became a major port shipping Lend Lease goods to England. Also in 1941 a new Coast Guard base was built in the area. About this time the city began to feel the first effects of overcrowding as thousands of war workers and military personnel moved in. These conditions continued throughout the war despite a continuing effort to build new housing units.

When the U.S. went to war in Dec. 1941 Boston became a bee's nest of military activities and suffered a good case of war jitters. On Dec. 9 rumors spread that the city might be bombed. Schools closed, factories were alerted to prepare for air raids and anti-aircraft guns were pulled from storage and hastily placed around the city. In late Dec. AAF fighter planes arrived at Boston airports to protect the city according to a pre-arranged defense plan. Between Jan. 21-24, 1942 Boston participated in the first full-scale urban air defense test that effected cities from Boston to New York. The system was patterned after the British urban defense system and included simulated air raids, blackouts, the movement of people to shelters, air surveillance, air raid warden drills, first aid practice, etc. Some 10,000 volunteers took part in the exercises. By the end of 1942 the number of volunteers in the air defense system had risen to 23,000.

In July 1942, when the Army's Transportation Corps came into being, Boston was one of the first ports it chose as a port of embarkation. This resulted in the Army taking over several commercial piers and warehouses at the waterfront. These facilities, and a debarkation hospital which was built later, comprised the Boston Port of Embarkation (POE), an Army installation. Within a short time men and equipment began flowing through the POE to overseas locations. In late 1942 the first prisoners of war arrived in Boston. They were mostly Germans and Italians captured in North Africa. Throughout the war POWs continued to arrive in large numbers. Some of them stayed in Boston to work on the docks and in the warehouses, but most were sent inland to POW camps. In 1944 daily air freight service was established from Boston airports to 42 cities making Boston a major air hub.

When the war ended, thousands of troops and tons of war material returned through Boston. Logan International Airport expanded again and regular air service was inaugurated to London. When war heros such as Gens. Eisenhower, Patton, Geo. C. Kenny (a Massachusetts resident) and Adm. Halsey come to town they received tumultuous welcomes. Boston continued to prosper and grow well into the postwar years bringing much of the state's economy along with it.

FORT ANDREWS, an 88-acre coastal defense position located on the eastern tip of Peddock's Island, was built in 1898-1901 as one of the main defenses for Boston Harbor. During WW II it served as a sub-post of Ft. Banks. During much of the war Ft. Andrews had a small branch POW camp holding Italian POWs. In 1947 the fort was declared surplus and in 1957 was sold, along with most of Peddock's Island, to private investors and converted primarily into recreational uses.

FORT BANKS, a 43-acre coastal defense position one mile NE of Winthrop, MA at Grover's Cliff, was built in 1899 as one of the main defenses for Boston Harbor. By WW II it had become the headquarters of the harbor's coastal defense command and all the other harbor forts were sub-posts to Ft. Banks. After the war most of the other forts were closed, but Banks remained active until 1950. In 1951, during the Korean War, it was reactivated and supplied with anti-aircraft guns. Banks guarded the skies over Boston until 1966 when it was declared inactive.

BEDFORD ARMY AIR FIELD, two miles south of Bedford, MA, became known in the postwar

In Mar. 1943 the gold-leaf dome of the Massachusetts State House in Boston was painted over with dull gray paint so as not be become a landmark or a conspicuous target in an enemy attack.

[1]The battleship "Massachusetts" (Big Mamie) was built here in 1941 and is on permanent display and open to the public at Battleship Cove, Fall River, MA.

era as Laurence G. Hanscom Field. It was built in 1941 as a civil airport and was known then as Laurence G. Hanscom Field, Boston Auxiliary Airport at Bedford. In 1942 it was renamed Bedford Municipal Airport and in 1943 was taken over the AAF and named Bedford Army Air Field. As Bedford AAF it was used as a test facility for radar and radio research in co-operation with Massachusetts Institute of Technology (MIT), and with Harvard University in research on electronics, geophysics, chemistry and nuclear applications. The field continued as a test center after the war under the US Air Force.

BOSTON ARMY BASE is about two miles SE of downtown Boston on the South Boston waterfront at 666 Summer St. It was built by the War Department in 1918 as a storage and shipping facility. It remained active after WW I and served as a storage facility for Army footwear. For 14 months in 1937-8 it was the headquarters of the U.S. 1st Army. After that it served as headquarters for the 1st Army Corps until 1942 when the Corps moved to new quarters in downtown Boston. Boston Army Base then became a sub-port of the New York Port of Embarkation and served in that capacity until 1946. After that, the base acquired its own command and served again as an Army storage and shipping facility. It also became a training center for Army Reserve officers, ROTC instructors and a communications center. The base operated throughout the Cold War under its original name.

BOSTON NATIONAL HISTORIC PARK: This is a park consisting of a number of historic sites around the Boston area. They include the Boston Navy Yard (Charleston Navy Yard), the Bunker Hill Monument, Dorchester Heights National Historic Site, the Paul Revere House and Faneuil Hall. There are two visitors centers, one at 15 State St. in downtown Boston and the other at the Boston Navy Yard. Most of the sites are connected by a three-mile-long trail that takes the visitor past these and other historic sites. Of interest to WW II buffs is the USS Constitution Museum at the Boston Navy Yard where the WW II destroyer "Cassin Young" is on display and open to the public along with the famous 18th century warship, the "USS Constitution". The "Cassin Young" is named after Capt. Cassin Young who distinguished himself at Pearl Harbor as commander of the "Vestal" and at the Battle of Guadalcanal where he was killed while commanding the cruiser "San Francisco". Also on display at the museum are WW II ship models, uniforms, documents, paintings, flags, navigational equipment, medical equipment and small arms. Address of the "Cassin Young" display: PO Box 1812, Boston, MA 02129. Phone: 617/242-7400. Hours: summer, daily 9-6, spring & fall daily M-F 9-5, winter M-F 10-5 and weekends 9-5. Admission charged. The museum is accessible from I-93 and is well marked along the highway.

FORT DAWES is located on Deer Island in Boston Harbor. It was built as one of Boston's coastal defenses in 1906. In 1940 it was renamed Fort Dawes, became a sub-post of Fort Banks and was armed and manned throughout the war. In 1963 the fort was abandoned

by the Army and turned over to the city of Boston.

FORT DUVALL was a 15-acre coastal defense position on Spinnaker Island at the entrance to Boston Harbor. It was built in 1920 as a part of the overall defenses of Boston. The fort's Battery Frank S. Long mounted two 16" guns with a range of 44,680 yards. The fort was armed and manned all during WW II. After the war the 16" guns were dismantled and moved elsewhere and the fort was put into caretaker status. Years later the property was sold to developers and townhouses were built atop the bunker that once was Battery Frank S. Long.

JOSEPH C. GREW GRAVE SITE: Joseph C. Grew was U.S. Ambassador to Japan at the time of the Japanese attack on Pearl Harbor. He is buried in Forest Hills Cemetery in Jamaica Plain. As early as Jan. 1941 Ambassador Grew passed on rumors to the U.S. State Department of the pending attach on Pearl Harbor. For this reason he gained the title "Prophet of Pearl Harbor". After his repatriation from Japan he served as Undersecretary of State in Washington, DC. Grew was a native of Boston, a graduate of Harvard and a career diplomat.

FORT HEATH is one mile from Ft. Banks and was built in 1899 on Grover's Cliff. The fort mounted three 12" rifles on disappearing carriages. During WW II Ft. Heath was a sub-post of Ft. Banks.

JOHN F. KENNEDY LIBRARY AND MUSEUM in Dorcester honors the memory of John F. Kennedy, the 35th President of the U.S. and a native of Massachusetts. It highlights his life and also traces the career of his brother, Robert F. Kennedy. Included in the displays is a complete account of John F. Kennedy's WW II service and his brush with death as captain of the ill-fated PT-109. Address: Columbia Point, Boston, MA 02125. Phone: 617/929-4523. Hours: Daily 9-5. Closed Jan. 1, Thanksgiving and Dec. 25. Admission charged. Location: Leave I-93 at exit 15 and follow the signs to the University of Massachusetts and the JFK Library.

JOSEPH P. KENNEDY GRAVE SITE: Joseph P. Kennedy is buried in Holywood Cemetery in Brookline, MA. He was U.S. Ambassador to Great Britain at the beginning of the war. He was also a power in the National Democrat Party and father of the famous Kennedy children including John F. Kennedy, the 35 President of the U.S.

LOGAN AIRPORT, at East Boston, was one of the most modern airports in the country during WW II. It remained a civilian airport throughout the war, but both the Army & Navy had operations here. The AAF's Air Technical Service Command operated on the field under the direction of Rome Army Air Field, Rome, NY, and the Air Transport Command used the field and operated a freight terminal.

FORT REVERE is located at the tip of the Nantasket Peninsula in the town of Hull. It was built in 1900 as part of Boston's coastal defenses. During WW II it was manned and

The complete story of John F. Kennedy's WW II service is recorded in this museum including his brush with death as captain of PT-109.

armed. In July 1947 the fort was closed and in 1948 it was declared surplus. It then became a part of Paul Revere Park.

FORT RUCKMAN was a 44-acre coastal defense position located on the tip of the Nahant Peninsula three miles south of Lynn. It was built in 1921 and had powerful 12" guns that could command this part of Massachusetts Bay almost as far as Newburyport. It was operational during WW II as a sub-post of Ft. Banks. In the postwar years it was converted into a park.

FORT MYLES STANDISH was built in 1900 on Lovell's Island in Boston Harbor as part of Boston's coastal defenses. During WW II it became a staging area for troops departing through the Boston Port of Embarkation. At first the troops lived in tents, but eventually wooden barracks were built. Over 1.4 million troops were processed through the fort during the war. In 1946 the fort was inactivated.

FORT STRONG was a coastal 66-acre defense position on Long Island in Boston Harbor. It mounted five 10" rifles and other guns. During the war it was fully armed and manned and operated as a sub-post of Fort Banks. After the war, Fort Strong was closed and declared surplus in 1947.

U.S. COAST GUARD MARITIME TRAINING STATION was located on Gallups Island in Boston Harbor. It was built in 1939 and operated throughout the war but was closed in the postwar years.

U.S. NAVAL AIR STATION, SOUTH WEYMOUTH is 15 miles SE of downtown Boston. It was built in 1942 as a blimp base and had the world's second largest blimp hangar, a structure covering 8 acres. A second and smaller hangar was also built at the station. NAS, South Weymouth had 6 mooring circles, 6 blimps and a landing strip for small aircraft. The blimps patrolled the coast of New England throughout the war. In 1945 blimp operations were discontinued and the station was reduced to a naval air facility and used to store naval aircraft. In 1953 a Naval Air Development Unit moved onto the base to test the military feasibility of blimps in the postwar era, and the station was upgraded again to a naval air station. It also became a training facility. In the early 1960s the Navy decided to discontinue the use of blimps and the testing of blimps ended at the station. The large blimp hangar was torn down and the station turned over to the Navy Reserve.

U.S. NAVAL AIR STATION, SQUANTUM was located on the Squantum Peninsula that thrusts into Boston Harbor south of Boston separating Quincy and Dorchester Bays. The site was first used by the Massachusetts Naval Militia just prior to WW I making it one of the earliest military air fields in the country. During WW I the Navy took over the field and used it for training and for coastal patrols. In 1923 the field reverted to its pre-WW I status of providing primary flight training to naval reservists and in 1930 it was designated a naval reserve air base. In the autumn of 1940, after the fall of France, the Navy began improving the facility to handle larger planes, seaplanes and small ships to augment its flight training program. In May 1943 the station became the home of a Special Project Unit which flight testing new electronic equipment developed at MIT. By Sept. 1943 the facility had four auxiliary air stations and was designated U.S. Naval Air Station, Squantum. At the end of the war the station continued its flight training program, but on a reduced schedule. In March 1946 the station's field was named in honor of a Massachusetts native, Lt. Col. John J. Shea, who had died in the sinking of the carrier "Wasp" in 1942. In 1954 the station was closed and the land and buildings sold.

U.S. NAVAL AMMUNITION DEPOT, HINGHAM was 2.5 miles west of Hingham, MA on the Weymouth Back River. It was built between 1906-13 and during WW I stored small and medium-calibre ammunition for the Navy. It also served as a training center and a quarantine facility for naval personnel with contagious diseases. Between the wars it was mostly inactive, but with the passage of the North Atlantic Neutrality Patrol Act in 1940 the depot was chosen as one of the main ammunition storehouses for U.S. ships carrying out those patrols. Soon the depot was filled with naval ammunition, bombs and other explosives. In 1941 the Navy acquired 3744 acres of land near Cohasset as an addition to the depot and built numerous earthen magazines to store additional ammunition. In time the Cohasset facility outgrew the main depot and became the Navy's major ammunition storage facility on

the North Atlantic coast. At the depot a new 480' wharf was added to facilitate ship loading and the draw-bridge on SR 3A across the Weymouth Back River, which had become a traffic bottleneck, was replaced with a higher permanent bridge. In 1942 an ammunition loading plant was built on the ground of the depot and in 1944 a rocket propellant plant was added. In June 1945 the work force at the depot peaked with 2091 civilian employees and 1096 naval personnel. After the war activity at the depot dropped dramatically and the Cohasset facility was closed. NAD, Hingham, nevertheless, continued in operation into the postwar years and throughout the Cold War.

U.S. NAVAL AUXILIARY AIR STATION, NORWOOD, one mile east of Norwood, MA, was the area's local airport before the war. It was taken over by the Navy to serve as a training field and an auxiliary air field to NAS, Squantum. After the war it was returned to its civilian owners and became Norwood Municipal Airport.

U.S. NAVAL HOSPITAL, CHELSEA was established in 1802 at the NE corner of the navy yard as a hospital for merchant seamen. In 1823 the hospital was moved to a larger site fronting on both the Mystic and Island End Rivers. During WW I the hospital was enlarged with temporary building to 1000 beds. After that war, the temporary building were removed and the hospital served the entire 1st Naval District. During WW II the Navy took over the Marine Hospital (which stood on the original 1802 site) and converted it into quarters for hospital corpsmen. In 1942 several 6-story half-H type wards were built at NH, Chelsea and in 1944 five temporary wards were added. In the postwar years the hospital continued to serve Boston's naval community, but when the navy yard closed in 1974, so did the hospital.

U.S. NAVAL SHIP YARD, BOSTON (ALSO CALLED BOSTON NAVY YARD AND CHARLESTON NAVY YARD) began with the purchase of land at the confluence of the Mystic and Charles Rivers by the Federal Government in 1800 for the purpose of constructing a navy yard. The yard was not completed until after 1812, but from then on, the Boston Navy Yard, as it was most commonly known, remained at the service of the Navy for over 150 years. By the late 1930s the yard had become specialized in the construction of destroyers. Between 1934-1940 the yard built 14 new destroyers and in Sept. 1939, with the onset of war in Europe, the yard received a rush order to reactivate 19 previously mothballed destroyers. In 1940 the Navy Yard acquired a second shipbuilding facilities commonly known as the South Boston Dry Dock. This was an area two miles south of the main yard on the South Boston waterfront that had been used in years past and had

its own large dry dock. This facility eventually became known as U.S. Naval Dry Dock, South Boston. In 1942 a 4th and 5th dry dock were added here to construct destroyer escorts (DE).

In the first 11 month of 1943 the Boston Navy Yard produced a record number of 46 DEs which was more than any other yard in the country. In 1944 the yard shifted its focus to Landing Ship Tanks (LST) and barracks ships known as Auxiliary Personnel Living (APL) while still building some destroyers and DEs. In the spring of 1944 the yard was assigned two unfinished submarines to give yard personnel experience in that type of vessel. An order for 16 new submarines soon followed, but only four were completed and the others canceled because of the favorable progress of the war. In that year the work force at the yard peaked at 50,130 men and women. Beside the U.S. Naval Dry Dock, South Boston the Boston Navy Yard operated several other detached facilities including a fuel depot annex at Orient Heights in East Boston, a pair of marine railways in Chelsea, a degaussing station in Pleasure Bay and a supply annex at Commonwealth Pier in South Boston. In Sept. 1945, under a new reorganization plan, all of the naval facilities in the Boston area, including the Boston Navy Yard, became a part of the newly designated U.S. Naval Station, Boston. Between 1945-47 the yard participated in the demobilization of the wartime Navy and served for a while as an anchorage for mothballed warships. After this, the yard reverted to its traditional practice of repairing and modifying ships with some new construction. By the 1970s, however, the yard had become old, cramped and expensive to maintain, so in 1974 it went into caretaker status and, eventually, parts of the yard were sold off for other purposes. A small portion of the yard still remains as part of the Boston National Historic Park and the home of the USS "Constitution" and the WW II destroyer "Cassin Young".

U.S. NAVAL SHIP YARD, HINGHAM was located on Hingham Bay at Hingham, MA. This facility was built by the Navy in 1942 and operated by the Bethlehem Steel Corp. for the purpose of building small warships. NSY, Hingham had 16 ways and built 92 destroyer escorts and high speed transports, plus 40 Landing Ship Tanks (LST) during the war. At war's end the yard was dismantled.

FORT WARREN was a 28-acre coastal defense position built in 1833 on Georges Island. The fort was operational throughout WW II as a sub-post of Fort Banks and served as the control center for mine laying operations in Boston Harbor. After the war the fort was closed and in 1957 was sold to private developers for recreational use. Eventually it became a part of Boston Island State Park and is open to the public. It is accessible with regular ferry service to the island. The fort is open daily Memorial Day through Oct. 30 from 10-5, and from May 1 to the day before Memorial Day Sat.-Sun. 10-5. Phone: 617/727-5250; for cruise information 617/723-7800. Admission charged.

WATERTOWN ARSENAL is in the town of Watertown 6 miles east of downtown Boston on the north bank of the Charles River. The

Fort Warren on Georges Island in Boston Harbor was the oldest of the Boston-area forts. It was operational during WW II and served as the control center for mine-laying operations in Boston Harbor.

An inspector checks finished top carriages for 37 mm anti-aircraft guns at Watertown Arsenal, MA.

arsenal was built in 1816 as a depot for ordnance and a manufacturing facility for small arms. Through the years the Arsenal expanded its operations to manufacture field artillery, coastal defense guns, gun carriages, specialized steel and other related items. During WW II the Arsenal produced these types of weapons, including anti-aircraft guns, in large quantities. In the postwar years the Arsenal manufactured accessories for Army missiles and atomic cannons.

CAPE COD/FALMOUTH AREA:
Cape Cod is one of New England's great playgrounds, jutting into the Atlantic with miles of beautiful beaches, quaint villages and picturesque bays. In wartime, however, it's geographic location makes it a strategic area for military installations and a tempting target for an invading army. For these reasons Cape Cod

was aggressively patrolled by the Coast Guard and Navy throughout the war and some temporary coastal defense positions constructed. In the early months of the war the Civil Air Patrol participated in coastal patrols from an air field in Falmouth.

CAMP EDWARDS, at the western end of the Cape, was expanded in 1940 by the Army and again in 1942 to become a camp for the training of large units. Camp Edwards had several detached areas including a 796-acre amphibious training area near Cotuit, MA. The 26th Infantry Div., comprised primarily of the Massachusetts National Guard, trained here along with many anti-aircraft and artillery units. Edwards was a segregated camp so many negro troops also trained here. The camp's hospital was expanded to 3200 beds and designated U.S. Army General Hospital, Camp Edwards throughout most of the war. As the war progressed it became more and more of a debarkation hospital receiving war wounded directly from the battle fields. After the war the general hospital reverted to being the camp's post hospital again.

The camp had a large prisoner of war camp holding about 2000 German POWs who worked mostly at the camp. The POWs kept here were not hard-core Nazis, but were, nevertheless, considered the "most Nazi" POWs in New England. In the spring of 1946, when most German POWs were being repatriated, Camp Edwards' POW compound became a staging and processing center for POWs departing for Europe.

During the war the camp's air field, Otis Field, was used by the Navy and operated as U.S. Naval Auxiliary Air Field, Otis, an auxiliary to NAS, Quonset Point, RI. After the war Camp Edwards was inactivated, but in the years that followed it was reopened and closed several times throughout the remainder of the century. Otis Field remained active after the war and became the home of the Massachusetts Air National Guard.

U.S. NAVAL AUXILIARY AIR STATION, HYANNIS, one mile north of Hyannis, was the local airport for Hyannis, MA

before the war. It was taken over by Navy to serve as an auxiliary air field for NAS, Quonset Point, RI. The Navy left after the war and the field again became Hyannis Airport.

FALL RIVER/NEW BEDFORD AREA:
These are two old and historic coastal towns in southern Massachusetts just a few mile apart. Among the major manufacturers in Fall River were the Firestone Rubber & Latex Product. Div. which made barrage balloons and gas masks, and Excel Foundry & Machine Co. which made torpedoes and torpedo parts. On the night of Oct. 11, 1941 a fire destroyed most of the Firestone plant and a huge supply of rubber which was stored inside. The lost rubber amounted to 12% of the nation's supply at the time. Sabotage was suspected, but never proven.

New Bedford was an old whaling and fishing port and her fishermen continued to bring in millions of pounds of sea food to aid in keeping Americans well-fed. The city also had a major manufacturer, Goodyear Fabric Corp., which make barrage balloons.

BATTLESHIP COVE, MARINE MUSEUM AND FALL RIVER HERITAGE STATE PARK: This is a three-in-one attraction. Battleship Cove is an anchorage for several WW II-related warships, the battleship "Massachusetts" (Big Mamie), the submarine "Lionfish", the destroyer "Joseph P. Kennedy, Jr.", an LCM landing craft, a one-man Japanese suicide submarine and two PT boats, PT-617 and PT-796. All of the ships saw action in WW II except the "Joseph P. Kennedy, Jr." which was launched in 1945. This ship was named in honor of the oldest son of Joseph P. Kennedy, U.S. Ambassador to Britain and brother of President John F. Kennedy. Joseph P. Kennedy, Jr. was killed during WW II, and the destroyer named in his honor saw action in the Korean and Viet Nam Wars.

All of the ships are open to the public. Aboard the "Massachusetts" are the official state WW II, Korean War and Viet Nam War Memorials honoring Massachusetts citizens who gave their lives in those wars. Overnight camping on the "Massachusetts" is permitted. Aboard the "Joseph P. Kennedy, Jr." is the Adm. Arleigh Burke National Destroyermen's Museum which tells the history of the ship and has displays on the day-to-day lives of men who served abroad destroyers. The PT boats on display are sister ships to PT-109, the craft commanded by young John F. Kennedy in the

At the beginning of the war this sign existed on Cape Cod near Orleans Beach Rd. reminding residents of the submarine activity off shore during WW I and that fact that enemy shells landed on Cape Cod.

Cantonment construction, Camp Edwards, MA Oct. 1940.

The WW II battleship "Massachusetts" (Big Mamie), on permanent display at Battleship Cove in Fall River. The ship is open to the public and aboard are the official state memorials to those who fell in WW II, the Korean War and Viet Nam War.

Pacific. PT-796 is the only wooden PT boat on display anywhere. There is also a PT boat library at the site containing one of the largest collections of PT boat archives in the country.

The other two attractions at the park are the Marine Museum which recalls the age of sail and steamship travel from colonial days up to 1937, and the Fall River Heritage State Park, an 8-acre urban park with a visitors center and exhibits on Fall River's textile and nautical history. Address of the complex is: Battleship Cove, Fall River, MA 02721. Ships and Museum phone: 508/678-1100. Ships and Museum hours: July 1-Labor Day, daily 9-8; rest of year 9-5. Closed Jan. 1, Thanksgiving & Dec. 25. Admission is charged to ships and museum: State Park phone: 508/675-5758 or 5759. State Park hours: Memorial Day-Labor Day M-F 10-5, Sat.-Sun. noon-8; rest of year W-Sun. 10-4. Closed Jan. 1, Thanksgiving & Dec. 25. Location: From I-195 take exit 5 and watch for signs. Complex is beneath Braga Bridge.

FORT RODMAN is on the tip of a peninsula in the south part of New Bedford jutting into Buzzard's Bay. Built in 1892-98 the fort had four batteries with a fifth one added in 1920. The fort was in caretaker status before WW II, but in 1940 it was reactivated and remained armed an manned throughout the war. In 1947 Fort Rodman was declared surplus.

U.S. NAVAL AUXILIARY AIR FIELD, NEW BEDFORD, 2.5 miles NNE of town, was the city's local airport before the war. It was taken over by the Navy as a training field and an auxiliary to NAS, Quonset, Point, RI. NAAF, New Bedford had an outlying field, Barnes Air Field, three miles NNE of Westfield, MA. After the war NAAF, New Bedford was returned to its original owners and became a local airport again.

FALMOUTH (See Cape Cod/Falmouth Area)

FRAMINGHAM is 12 miles west of Boston.

CUSHING GENERAL HOSPITAL was built in Framingham in 1944 of brick construction and intended to be a permanent hospital facility. It had 1800 beds and specialized in neurology, plastic surgery, ophthalmologic surgery, neurosurgery and psychiatry. In Sept. 1946 it was transferred to the Veterans Administration.

LOWELL is 20 miles NW of Boston.

LOWELL ORDNANCE PLANT was a privately-owned plant in Lowell that was taken over by the Federal Government to make small calibre ammunition. The plant was run by the Remington Arms Co. and one of the plant's main items of production was 50 calibre bullets. The plant closed in 1943.

MANSFIELD is 23 miles SSE of Boston.

U.S. NAVAL AUXILIARY AIR FIELD, MANSFIELD, two miles SSE of town, was established by the Navy as an auxiliary air field for NAS, Squantum. After the war the Navy abandoned the field and it became a local airport.

MARTHA'S VINEYARD is a large island off the south coast of Massachusetts. Because of its strategic location Martha's Vineyard was one of the places where watch towers were built as a part of Massachusetts' coastal defenses. The Army Engineer Corps used some of the boating facilities on Martha's Vinyard and the surrounding sea to train men to handle small boats needed to transport engineer equipment from ships to shore during amphibious operations.

U.S. NAVAL AUXILIARY AIR FIELD, MARTHA'S VINEYARD was the island's pre-war airport when it was taken over by the Navy. The field is located near the geographic center of the island and during the war it was used as an auxiliary field to NAS, Quonset Point, RI. After the war the air field reverted to its pre-war status.

NANTUCKET ISLAND is another large island off the south coast of Massachusetts east of Martha's Vineyard.

U.S. NAVAL AUXILIARY AIR FIELD, NANTUCKET, 2.5 miles SE of the town of Nantucket, was the island's local airport before the war. It was taken over by the Navy and used as an auxiliary air field to NAS, Quonset Point, RI. After the war it was returned to its original owners.

NEW BEDFORD (See Fall River/New Bedford Area)

SPRINGFIELD, in the SE part of the state near the Connecticut state line, was a major manufacturing center with a heavy reliance on the manufacture of small arms. Needless to say, the Spring-

field armsmakers had all the business they could handle during the war. Some of the major arms manufacturers in the city, besides the Springfield Armory mentioned below, were a plant of the Automatic Ordnance Corp. of Bridgeport, CT which made Thompson submachine guns "Tommy Guns", Savage Arms Co. which made 30 calibre rifles and sub-machine gun parts, Smith & Wesson Inc. which made a wide variety of guns and Cheney Bigalow Wire Works which made "Bazookas". J. Stevens Arms Co. of Chicopee, a western suburb of Springfield, made Lee Enfield rifles for the British.

SPRINGFIELD ARMORY is the nation's oldest manufacturing arsenal. It began in 1777 when the Government leased a building in downtown Springfield as a "laboratory" and arms depot. Over the years the Armory became a world-famous design and development center for small arms. During WW II the Armory made some four million M1 Garand rifles, the standard infantry rifle used by the U.S. Army from 1935 to 1958. The Garand was designed at the Armory by John C. Garand a government engineer. Peak production of the Garand rifle reached 1500 rifles a week with a work force of 5381. The Armory became a National Historic Site and is on the campus of Springfield Technical Community College. The old arsenal building, master armorer's house, CO's quarters and a museum are open to the public.

Springfield Armory Museum: This fine museum is on the grounds of the Armory in the main arsenal building which dates back to 1847. It has one of the largest collections of small arms in the world, many of which were designed here. There is a major display on the M1 Garand Rifle and its designer, John C. Garand. Address: One Armory Square, Springfield, MA 01105. Phone: 413/734-8551. Hours: Memorial Day-Labor Day daily 10-5, rest of year Tues.-Sun. 10-5. Closed Jan. 1, Thanksgiving and Dec. 25. Free.

WESTOVER FIELD, 7 miles north of downtown Springfield was built in 1939 and first called Northeast Air Base. It was given its wartime name, Westover Field, in Dec. 1939. This was a 1st AF base used for the training of B-24 bomber crews. On Dec. 8, 1941, however, the day after the Japanese attacked Pearl Harbor, the base became an operational base when I Bomber Command sent a group of armed B-17, B-18 and B-25 bombers to the field to fly

John C. Garand, developer of the M1 Garand Rifle.

coastal patrol missions along the New England coast and up to 600 miles out to sea. In 1942 Westover Field was greatly expanded and in the summer of that year units of the 8th AF staged at Westover during their transfer to Britain under "Operation Bolero". All the while the training of B-24 bomber crews continued and a new school was added to train engineer aviation battalions. The field had a main prisoner of war camp holding about 500 POWs who worked on the field. The Air Transport Command operated at the field using it as a port of aerial embarkation and operating an air freight terminal. The field also had a regional AAF hospital.

Westover survived the war to become Westover Air Force Base and served as one of the Air Force's main bases in the U.S. northeast throughout the Cold War.

TAUNTON is 30 miles south of Boston.

CAMP MYLES STANDISH, within the town of Taunton, was established early in the war as a staging area for troops shipping out of the Boston Port of Embarkation. The camp provided living quarters for up to 40,000 officers and men. It had a main prisoner of war camp holding about 800 Italian POWs who worked at the camp. Later, after Italy became an Ally, four Italian Service Units, totalling about 1000 men, worked at the camp.

In 1948 the camp was deactivated and much of it became a state mental health facility. In 1973 another part of the camp was converted into an industrial area known as Myles Standish Industrial Park.

MICHIGAN

If Michigan had been an independent country during WW II it could have fielded one of the best equipped armies in the world. Virtually everything a modern army needed was made in Michigan. The huge metropolitan area around Detroit was, and had been for two decades, one of the world's great manufacturing centers, and it had spawned manufacturing operations all over Michigan, into the bordering states and into Canada. Before the war, however, Michigan's economy was not healthy. The manufacturing sector of the state's economy, especially the Detroit-based automotive industry, had been badly hurt by the Depression and this brought down other sectors of the economy. When the war started in Europe, and the U.S. Government began building up America's military might, Michigan had lots of manufacturing capacity available and many unemployed workers eager for jobs.

The labor unions in Michigan were among the strongest in the county and during the Depression had repeatedly flexed their muscles calling many strikes and work slow-downs. With the onset of war in Europe and the advent of new prosperity this policy did not change. In 1940 the powerful United Automobile Workers Union (UAW) called a strike against the Chrylser Corp. which lasted 54 days and proved to be the longest and most costly strike, to date, in Michigan's history. This had a bitter and lingering effect that polarized relations between the big manufacturers and the big unions. Frequent smaller strikes, some of them violent, did not help the situation. When the U.S. entered the war President Roosevelt called upon American labor unions to observe a no-strike policy for the duration of the war. The big unions in Michigan generally complied, but throughout the war the state had to content with many local and "wildcat" strikes.

On Jan. 12, 1942 Donald M. Nelson, head of the War Production Board, ordered an end to the manufacture of civilian automobiles for the duration of the war and on Apr. 27, 1942 President Roosevelt, by executive order, placed the entire U.S. economy on a wartime footing. These actions dictated that Michigan's manufacturing plants would produce virtually nothing but war materials in the coming years. During the war practically every urban center in the state had at least one manufacturing plant which converted to war production.

After the Japanese attack on Pearl Harbor, the people and government leaders of Michigan, like many others in the county, feared enemy attacks on their state or sabotage by enemy agents. Michigan had a large number of registered enemy aliens, almost 291,000, or 6.1% of the country's total. For this reason, the state legislature, in early 1942, passed a new law making industrial sabotage a felony. There was also fear that an enemy naval force might penetrate Canada's Hudson Bay and send aircraft to bomb the vital locks at Sault Sainte Marie through which most of the nation's iron ore was shipped. This did not happen, but in Apr. 1942, after German submarines attack targets in Puerto Rico and Curacao in the Caribbean, President Roosevelt stated that the enemy was capable of attacking American cities and specifically mentioned the possibility of Detroit being bombed. Detroit was never a planned target of the enemy as were other U.S. cities, but the people of Michigan didn't know that. Near the end of the war, however, two of Michigan's cities, Grand Rapids and Farmington, did come under enemy attacks by a most unusual source ... Japanese bombing balloons.

Some of the many items produced in Michigan included motor vehicles, trucks, aircraft, ships, guns, tanks, munitions, steel, foundry products, refrigerators, copper, hardware, machine shop products, drugs & medicines, chemicals, lumber & paper, coke, oil, natural gas, iron ore, copper ore, gypsum, cement, stone, salt, corn, wheat, soybeans, field beans, oats, barley, rye, alfalfa, potatoes, fruit, sugar beets and meat.

When victory finally came with the defeat of Japan, the ugly pattern of union strife arose again throwing thousands of people out of work. Also the other big manufacturers began to close down plants temporarily to re-tool again for civilian products thus throwing still more people out of work. Because of the loss of tax revenues and the fact that Michigan's infrastructure was now badly worn due to the effects of the war, the state legislature increased taxes on liquor, horse racing, bank accounts and intangible property.

In the postwar years Michigan's fortunes were mixed. Heavy industry made a concerted effort to move out of the state to areas with a friendlier labor climate. Yet, the general post war economic boom and the military needs of the Korean War, the Viet Nam War and the Cold War kept the state's manufacturing sector in relatively good shape.

ALPENA is in NE Michigan on the shore of Lake Huron.

ALPENA ARMY AIR FIELD, 7 miles west of town, began as a grass landing strip in the 1920s servicing local flyers. By 1931 it had been upgraded to become a recognized airport. Early in WW II it was taken over by the AAF, given its wartime name, and used for training purposes. After the war it was returned to civilian control and the Michigan Air National Guard utilized some of the facilities. Following the war the field became known as Alpena Regional County Airport and the ANG segment was known as Phelps Collins ANG Base.

BATTLE CREEK is in the SW part of the state near the junction of I-94 and I-65. Battle Creek had a large manufacturer, the Clark Equipment Co., which made trucks and industrial tractors for the military.

FORT CUSTER, five miles west of town near the community of Augusta, was established during WW I as Camp Custer to train division-size infantry units. After WW I most of the camp's 2000 building were dismantled and the camp and its remaining facilities were used as a summer training camp for the ROTC and the Citizens Militia Training Corps. In Aug. 1940 it was designated as a permanent Army post and renamed Fort Custer. The fort was then expanded to accommodate approximately 20,000 troops. Early in the war, Custer became a reception center for the 6th Army Corps and inducted some 300,000 men into the Army. The training of large units, including the 5th Infantry Div., also began at this time. Later in the war the fort became a replacement training center and headquarters for the Provost Marshall General's 350th Military Police escort guard and a processing center for prisoners of war. From Nov. 1942 to Oct. 1944 Custer hosted the Military Police Officers Candidate School. The fort had its own air field, Fox Field, a base hospital and a main prisoner of war camp holding about 3700 POWs. At the end of the war the fort became a separation center for individuals coming out of the Army and also for patients being released from Percy Jones General Hospital near downtown Battle Creek. At this time Percy Jones operated the fort calling it Percy Jones Hospital Center. This lasted until 1949 when the fort passed to the control of the U.S. 5th Army headquartered in Chicago. During the Korean War the fort was activated again as a training camp. In June 1953 the fort was

WW II buildings, still in use, can be seen from Fort Custer's main gate. The sign to the right says "Buildings for Sale" ... WW II buildings.

transport planes. The field worked in conjunction with Fort Custer which adjoined the field on the west. After the war the field was returned to the community with a portion of it being reserved for the Michigan Air National Guard. The facility retained the name, Kellogg Field.

BAY CITY/MIDLAND/SAGINAW: These three cities are just a few miles apart near the south end of Saginaw Bay. One of the larger defense contractors in the area was the Defoe Shipbuilding Co. at Bay City which built destroyer escorts, mine sweepers and submarine chasers for the Navy. A Chevrolet plant here made aircraft propellers and Saginaw Steering Gear Div. of General Motors in Saginaw made 30 Cal. machine guns and M1 carbines.

MICHIGAN'S OWN, INC. MILITARY AND SPACE MUSEUM: This is a fine, privately owned, museum in the picturesque and popular tourist town of Frankenmuth. MI, 15 miles SE of Saginaw. The museum honors Michigan veterans of the nation's five foreign wars. There

inactivated by the Army and 7500 acres and many of the buildings were turned over to the Michigan Department of Military Affairs. In the decades that followed parts of the fort were used by the Job Corps, two areas were designated as parks and a third area became an industrial park. In 1968 Fort Custer became a training center for the Army Reserves, the Michigan National Guard and the home of the Michigan Military Academy.

PERCY JONES GENERAL HOSPITAL, at the corner of Washington Ave. and Champion St. near downtown Battle Creek, was a 14-story pre-war medical facility known as the Battle Creek Sanitarium. It went into receivership in 1933 and in 1942 was purchased by the U.S. Army and converted into a general hospital under the new name, Percy Jones General Hospital. The hospital specialized in neurology, neurosurgery, plastic surgery, deep x-ray therapy, the fitting of artificial limbs and general rehabilitation. Percy Jones GH expanded considerably during the war and acquired additional facili-

Michigan's Own Museum, Inc. honors Michigan service men of America's five foreign wars.

ties at Fort Custer. It was eventually designated a hospital center and operated under its own command. Percy Jones Hospital Center functioned until after the Korean War, and in 1953 was permanently closed. During its 11 years of operation the hospital treated over 100,000 military patients. In 1954 the facility became the Battle Creek Federal Center.

KELLOGG FIELD, three miles west of town, was Battle Creek's local airport before the war. In 1942 it was taken over by the short-lived I Concentration Command and five months later transferred to the 3rd AF. It was then assigned to the I Troop Carrier Command for use as a training field for pilots and crews of

are several rooms in the museum each dedicated to a particular war including WW II. One of the specialties of the museum is the collection of uniforms worn by those who are honored here. Many of the uniforms are on display along with the story of their owner. Address: 1220 S. Weiss, Frankenmuth, MI 48734. Phone: 810/652-8005. Hours: Mar.-Dec. M-Sat. 10-5, Sun. noon-5. Admission charged. Location: Weiss is a north-south street south of the Cass River and is the first street east of S. Main St. (SR 83).

TRI-CITY FIELD is about midway between Bay City and Midland off US 10. It was built in 1943 and soon after its dedication was taken over by the AAF and used as a training field and a port of aerial embarkation. During the latter part of the war the field had a large branch prisoner of war camp with the POWs working primarily in the local sugar beet fields. After the war the field was returned to the community and became a large and modern airport known as Tri-City International Airport. In the lobby of the terminal is a large mural showing the air field during its WW II days and telling some of its history.

BENTON HARBOR is in SW Michigan on Lake Michigan and had a relatively large number of manufacturing plants during the war.

The former Percy Jones General Hospital. It was operated by the U.S. Army from 1942 to 1953 as a general hospital treating the wounded of WW II and the Korean War.

Three of the largest were the Dachell Carter Shipbuilding Corp. which made mine sweepers and submarine chasers for the Navy, the Nineteen Hundred Corp. in St. Joseph which made 50 calibre machine guns, torpedo tubes, propeller controls and gunsights, and the Auto Specialties Mfg. Co., also in St. Joseph, which made artillery shells.

DETROIT AREA: The area in and around Detroit was one of America's great manufacturing centers, and the heart of America's automobile industry. The decade before WW II, however, had brought turbulent times to Detroit. In 1929 Detroit was the first major U.S. city to go into a serious depression following the stock market crash of that year. The city never fully recovered until the onset of WW II. During the 1930s the city had large numbers of unemployed, many bankrupt and financially shaky manufacturing companies, intermittent labor trouble and a fluctuating population. Despite these problems, Detroit still produced most of America's cars and trucks. In 1940 the census of that year ranked Detroit as America's fourth largest city with 25% of its population foreign born. 1940 also marked the first year of recovery for the city due to the influx of numerous, and most welcome, defense orders. During 1940-41 there was a great influx of job seekers and the city felt the beginnings of a housing shortage that would get much worse before it got better. During 1941 the city's economy grew rapidly as more and more defense orders came in. Then, in 1942, with the U.S. at war, the economic dam burst and the Detroit area was flooded with defense work. In early 1942 the Federal Government ordered an end to automobile production and a total conversion to war work. Hundreds of millions of dollars worth of new defense work inundated Detroit's already busy manufacturers and tens of thousands of people flocked to the area to fill the well-paying jobs. There were numerous problems in Detroit, however, during 1942. As the auto plants shut down to retool some 400,000 workers were temporarily laid off. There were many small strikes and a major strike at Ford, and the housing shortage was aggravated by the fact that the Federal Government took over many hotels and apartments to house service personnel. By 1943 the Federal Government was deeply involved in the city building housing for the war workers, but a serious housing shortage still persisted. Detroit's small public transit system had become overwhelmed and the area's street were congested with traffic. Wayne County's population was estimated to have soared to 2.7 million, and despite this there was a constant labor shortage. During the summer of 1943 Detroit experienced the nation's worst wartime race riot which required Federal troops to quell. To make matters worse, local and "wildcat" strikes continued to plague manufacturers. Nevertheless, Detroit produced as never before, and 1944 was the year records were set. Yet, there were continuing problems in housing, labor relations and city services. For the first 9 months of 1945 it was more of the same, but after V-J the inevitable began to occur. The defense orders stopped, overtime all but disappeared, the plants began to re-tool again for

civilian products and workers were laid off again by the thousands. Detroit's future, though, looked bright because of the huge pent up demand for consumer goods created by the wartime shortages. Once automobiles began to roll off the assembly lines they sold as soon as they hit the showroom floors. But, the old labor troubles also returned and the manufacturers experienced a new round of large-scale and costly strikes. Despite the postwar problems, Detroit struggled through and continued to be one of the nation's major industrial areas although many of the big manufacturers began to spin off operations into other parts of the county to get away from the area's troublesome labor atmosphere.

WHO MADE WHAT IN THE DETROIT AREA:

- American Cruiser Co. of Detroit made submarine chasers.
- American Forging & Socket Co. of Pontiac, MI made 100 lb bombs and 40 mm shells.
- Cadillac Division of General Motors made M-4 Sherman tanks, M-2 to M-5 light tanks, M-8 howitzer motorized gun carriages, Hydramatic transmissions for many military vehicles and inner assemblies for Allison aircraft engines.
- Chevrolet Motor Division of General Motors made Pratt & Whitney aircraft engines, military trucks, amphibious DUWKs (in coop-

eration with GMC Truck Div.), 6X6 truck axles, tank track parts, 90 mm guns, aluminum & steel forgings, iron & magnesium castings, high-explosive and armor-piercing shells and other military items.
- Chris-Craft Corp. of Algonac, MI made motor boats and landing craft.
- Chrysler Corp. made M-3 medium tanks (see Detroit Arsenal, below), military trucks, marine tractors, Navy pontoons, harbor tugs, aircraft, industrial & marine engines, wing panels, fuselage & nose assemblies, anti-aircraft gun parts, 40 mm machine guns, fire-fighting equipment, air raid sirens, gun boxes, search light reflectors, and other items.
- Consolidated-Vultee Aircraft Co. of Dearborn, MI and Wayne, MI built AT-19 trainer aircraft and L-5 light aircraft.
- DeSoto Division of Chrysler Corp. made aircraft fuselage, nose and wing sections, anti-aircraft gun parts and tank parts.
- Dodge Division of Chrysler Corp. made a wide variety of military trucks, short-wave radar sets and Sperry Gyro-compasses.
- Federal Motor Truck Co. made trucks and a variety of other military vehicles.
- Fisher Body Div. of General Motors made flight instruments, components for aircraft, and components for tanks and large guns.

This advertisement was run in national publications by Revere Copper & Brass Corp. in 1944 entitled "Victory Garden in Detroit". It honored the company's Detroit area customers.

Completed M-3 Grant tanks being loaded for shipment from the Detroit Tank Arsenal.

- Ford Motor Co. made B-24 bombers (see Willow Run Plant and Airport below), gliders, M-4 Sherman tanks, Jeeps, armored cars, various other military vehicles, aircraft & tanks engines, armor plate and many other military items.
- Gar Wood Industries made truck & trailer equipment, hoists, winches, cranes, derricks, road machinery and heating equipment for small boats.
- General Motors Diesel Engineering Division made a wide variety of diesel engines including marine diesels.
- General Motors Truck & Bus Division built military trucks and busses and commercial busses which were badly needed throughout the nation by over-loaded transit systems.
- GMC Division of General Motors made DUWKs in conjunction with Chevrolet and a wide variety of military trucks.
- Great Lakes Engineering Co. of River Rouge, MI made merchant ships.
- Great Lakes Steel Corp. was the world's largest manufacturer of Quonset Huts.
- Hudson Motor Car Co. made gasoline engines, marine engines, 20 mm Oerlikon anti-aircraft guns, machine guns, aircraft wing, motor and tail assemblies and other military items.
- Kelsey Hayes Wheel Corp. of Plymouth, MI made 50 calibre bullets, Browning machine guns, 3" anti-aircraft projectiles and 4" high explosive projectiles.
- Nash-Kelvinator Corp. made Pratt & Whitney aircraft engines, trailers and binoculars.
- Packard Motor Car Co. made Rolls-Royce aircraft engines for P-40s P-51s and several British airplanes, and marine engines for PT boats. Packard's proving ground, 2.5 miles north of Utica, MI, was used by the Army as an auxiliary air field.
- Pontiac Division of General Motors in Pontiac, MI made Oerlikon 20 mm anti-air-

craft guns, 40 mm automatic field guns, naval torpedoes and parts for diesel engines, tanks and trucks.
- Standard Tube Co. made 3" & 3.5" anti-aircraft projectiles and 155 mm shells.
- Yellow Truck & Coach Mfg. Co. of Pontiac made M-7 & T-18 armored cars and and was the primary manufacturer of 2.5 ton 6X6 amphibious vehicles known as DUKWs. In 1943 this plant was taken over by General Motors.

DETROIT TANK ARSENAL, at 28251 Van Dyke Rd. in Warren, MI was, at the time of its construction, the world's largest tank plant. It was built in 1940-1941 in less than a year and began manufacturing M-3 Grant tanks in Apr. 1941. The arsenal was operated by the Chrysler Corp. and the tanks were made on an assembly-line basis much the way automobiles were made. During the war the arsenal produced 25,567 tanks. Chrylser also operated a tank training school associated with the arsenal. In 1946 the name of the arsenal was shortened to Detroit Arsenal. During the Korean War the Arsenal again made heavy military vehicles. In later years the Arsenal was sold to the Chrysler Corp. and it was then used it to produce Plymouth Automobiles.

FARMINGTON BOMBING: On Mar. 25, 1945 fragments of a Japanese incendiary bomb, identical to those carried by Japanese bombing balloons, were discovered in the Detroit suburb of Farmington. It can only be presumed that they came from a bomb dropped by one of the balloons. Since no balloon fragments were found in the area, it must also be presumed that the bombing balloon continued on to the east after dropping the bomb. The bomb did no damage, but proved to be the most easterly bomb ever discovered from a Japanese balloon.

HENRY FORD MUSEUM & GREENFIELD VILLAGE, at Village Rd. and Oakwood Blvd. is one of the great museums of the world. It contains a multitude of artifacts, inventions and memen-

tos of American social and scientific history. Scattered throughout the museum are many displays are items related to WW II. Of interest is President Roosevelt's bullet-proof Lincoln known as "The Sunshine Special" and an early VS-300 Sikorsky helicopter made in 1939 and flown personally by Igor Sikorsky to the museum in 1943 where he landed on the museum's lawn. Address: 20900 Oakwood Blvd. Dearborn, MI 48121. Phone 313/271-1620. Hours: daily 9-5, closed Jan. 1, Thanksgiving, Dec. 25. Admission charged.

HOLOCAUSE MEMORIAL CENTER is on the grounds of the Jewish Community Campus in West Bloomfield, a suburb NW of Detroit. The Center has exhibits, video presentations and dioramas on the Holocaust. There is also an eternal flame, a library and a memorial garden. Address: 6602 W. Maple St., West Bloomfield, MI 48322. Phone: 313/661-0840. Hours: Sun.-Thurs. 10-4. Donations requested.

WILLIAM S. KNUDSEN GRAVE SITE, is located in Acacia Park Cemetery in Birmingham, MI. In 1940 Knudsen, a Danish-born American, was president of General Motors. President Roosevelt called him to Washington to head the National Defense Advisory Commission to advise the Administration on defense production requirements. In Jan. 1941 Roosevelt created another agency, the Office of Production Management (OPM) to oversee U.S. defense production. He appointed Knudsen its director. In 1942 when a new agency, the War Production Board absorbed the OPM, Knudsen was drafted by the War Department to become its production director and was given the rank of Lt. General. Thereafter, Knudsen travelled throughout the county speeding production and settling labor disputes particularly in the aircraft industry. In May 1944 Sec. of War Henry L. Stimson awarded Knudsen the Distinguished Service Medal and called him "the master troubleshooter on the biggest job in the world". Knudsen retired from Government service in 1945 and died in 1948.

ROMULUS ARMY AIR FIELD, SW of downtown Detroit in the town of Romulus, MI, was a regional airport built in 1929 and known as Wayne County Airport. In July 1942 the AAF leased the field and made it the headquarters for the 3rd Ferrying Group whose primary mission was to ferry Lend Lease aircraft to the Soviet Union. Romulus handled mostly P-39 and P-63 fighters which were made by the Bell Aircraft Co. in Buffalo, NY. The planes would be flown from Buffalo to Romulus, refueled and then flown on to Great Falls, MT. From there they flew northward through Canada to Alaska where they were turned over to Soviet pilots who flew them on to the Soviet Union via Siberia. Romulus AAF was greatly enlarged by the AAF in 1944 and had a large aircraft servicing operation and a training program for ferry pilots. The Air Transport Command also operated at the field and had an air freight terminal. In 1947 the AAF gave up its lease and returned the field to its pre-war owners. The air field then became one of the area's main airports, Detroit Metropolitan-Wayne County Airport.

SELFRIDGE FIELD, two miles east of Mt. Clemens, MI on Anchor Bay, was activated as an Army flying field in 1917 and was one of only five WW I air fields to survive until WW II. In 1922 Selfridge Field became a permanent post, and during the 1920s and 1930s it was an operating base for pursuit planes. In Jan. 1940 the first operational fighter group, to fly new P-39 Airacobras, the 31st Pursuit Group, was organized at Selfridge. The group trained here and then moved on to Baer Fd. IN. In Feb. 1942 the 8th Interceptor Command of the newly created 8th AF was activated at Selfridge and later moved to South Carolina for training. Throughout the war the field was used to organize and train new operational and replacement fighter units under the direction of the 3rd AF. Selfridge was a segregated facility and negro troops trained and served here. In 1947 Selfridge was transferrer to the Air Force and became Selfridge Air Force Base. In 1971 it was transferred to the Michigan Air National Guard and remained under their control throughout the Cold War.

Selfridge Military Air Museum: This interesting museum is on the grounds of Selfridge Field and chronicles the history of the base from its beginning in 1917. There is a sizeable collection of aircraft on display, most of it WW II and postwar. Also on display are aircraft engines, aircraft models, paintings, photographs, uniforms, small arms and other artifacts related to the field. Address: 127 TFW/MU, Box 43, Selfridge ANG Base, MI 48045. Phone: 313/466-5035. Hours: Apr. 1-Nov. 1, Sun. 1-5 except Easter. Donations requested.

U.S. NAVAL ORDNANCE PLANT, CENTERLINE was built in the community of Centerline, MI in 1940 to produce medium caliber naval gun mounts and sub-assemblies. It was one or two plants (the other was in Canton, OH) which fed components to an assembly plant in Louisville, KY.

U.S. NAVAL AIR STATION, GROSSE ILE was located on Grosse Ile in the Detroit River at the south end of the island. The station was first established as a seaplane base in 1927. The small naval facility was known as U.S. Naval Seaplane Base, Grosse Ile. In 1932 the state of Michigan bought and leased additional land and gave it to the Navy to establish a permanent naval reserve station. This new facility was known as U.S. Naval Reserve Air Base, Grosse Ile and it provided primary flight training for Naval Reserve pilot candidates. In 1940 British naval air cadets began receiving primary flight training at the station and in 1942, the station was doubled its size. In Dec. 1943 the base was elevated to a naval air station reflecting its increased importance and had 18 outlying fields and a station population of 1400 U.S. and 600 British cadets. Primary flight training ended at NAS, Grosse Ile in Nov. 1944 and the station then shifted emphasis to offering refresher courses to returning pilots and air crews. By late 1945 the refresher training program ended and the station was turned over, once again, to the Naval Reserve for the training of reservists. During the Korean War three of the station's squadrons were called into service. In 1969 the station was closed and eventually became a commercial airport, Grosse Ile Municipal Airport.

Willow Run, the world's largest aircraft factory. The plant, airfield and hangars covered 1300 acres. It had its own vocational training school and hospital.

FORT WAYNE, on the west bank of the Detroit River at the foot of Livernois St., was built in the 1840s to protect the area from British intrusions and command the southern approaches of the Detroit River. During WW II the old fort was used as a support and training facility by the Army. In 1944-45 Italian Service Units worked at the fort. In 1949 the Federal Government deeded the fort to the city of Detroit and it became a historical monument and a museum.

FORT WAYNE ORDNANCE DEPOT/ PALMER WOODS ORDNANCE DEPOT: Ft. Wayne Ordnance Depot was established in Detroit early in the war as a motor supply depot to receive, store and ship automotive-related items to the Army. Being in the heart of the world's largest automotive industrial area the depot was soon overwhelmed. A part of the depot was then separated from the original and became a second motor supply depot known as Palmer Woods Ordnance Depot. Before the war ended, both became master depots. Together they were the world's largest distribution center for automotive parts.

WILLOW RUN PLANT AND AIRPORT: Here, on the outskirts of Detroit near the town of Ypsilanti, one of the greatest industrial achievements of the war was accomplished. The huge Willow Run Aircraft factory and adjoining air field were constructed to mass-produce B-24 Liberator heavy bombers. The plane had been developed by Consolidated-Vultee Corp. of San Diego, CA and an assembly-line facility was established there, but it could not produce enough B-24s to meet the AAF's needs. Hence the need for the Willow Run plant[1]. The plant was built in 1941-42 and was the largest factory in the world at the time. It had more floor space than Douglas Aircraft Co., Boeing Aircraft Co. and Consolidated-Vultee combined. In the U.S. press it was labelled as the "7th Wonder of the World". Willow run was built and operated by Ford Motor Co. and became Ford's most noted contribution to the war effort. During the spring and summer of 1942 tooling problems delayed the start of production and Ford came under strong criticism from several sources. Senator Harry Truman's committee on government waste investigated the plant and some of the plant's critics began to call the facility "Will It Run?". By Sept. 1942, however, the first bombers came off the line,

[1]There were a total of four B-24 plants in the country, the others were at Tulsa, OK and Ft. Worth, TX.

In Sept. 1942 President Roosevelt visited the Willow Run Plant. Here he is shown talking with two midget workers who were used to get into cramped spaces in the wing assemblies.

and once the plant reached its peak efficiency it produced bombers at the rate of one an hour. In 1944 Willow Run alone produced as many planes as the entire Japanese aircraft industry did that same year. As production increased the price of the bombers decreased by 40%.

The plant required a work force of about 100,000. This caused an acute housing problem in the area that persisted throughout the war. The town of Ypsilanti became of city of overpriced houses and trailer parks.

By the time bomber production ended in Dec. 1945 the plant had produced 8685 bombers. After the war the plant was utilized by Detroit's auto makers. The first to use it was the Kaiser-Fraser Automobile Co. Later is was acquired by General Motors and used to produce Hydramatic transmissions.

Yankee Air Museum: This air museum is located at Willow Run Airport at the corner of Ecorse and Beck Rds. It has a large collection of vintage aircraft, many of which are flyable, and its own restoration facility. There is a major exhibit on the building and operations of the Willow Run plant during the war. Visitors may enter the restoration area and watch craftsmen in the process of restoring vintage aircraft. Among the WW II aircraft on display is a PB4Y-2 Privateer, the Navy's version of the B-24 bomber and a rare F7F-3N Tigercat used by the

A PB4Y Privateer, the Navy's version of the famous B-24 Liberator bomber.

Marines. Also in the collection is a B-17G, C-47D, PT-19, PT-23, B-25D, T-6 and BT-13A. Address: PO Box 590, Belleville, MI 48112. Phone: 313/483-4030. Hours: Tues.-Sat. 10-4, Sun. noon-4. Admission charged.

FLINT, 50 miles NW of Detroit, was a heavily industrialized community. The principal manufacturers where Buick Motor Car Div. of General Motors which made Pratt & Whitney aircraft engines, tank transmissions and tank destroyers, Fisher Body Div. of General Motors which made M-4 Sherman tanks and 3" gun motor carriages, and Chevrolet Div. of General Motors which made T17E1 armored cars, M-39 ammunition and personnel carriers, artillery shells and aircraft parts. Chevrolet built a new plant in Flint during the war to produce aircraft engines.

FRANKENMUTH (See Bay City/Midland/Saginaw area)

GRAND HAVEN is on Lake Michigan 25 miles WNW of Grand Rapids.

U.S. COAST GUARD TRAINING STATION, GRAND HAVEN: This was one of the Coast Guard's larger training centers with facilities

on the Grand River and in Mulligan's Hollow behind the present-day Coast Guard headquarters. At the start of the war the Coast Guard cutter "Escanaba", which had been stationed at Grand Haven since 1932, left for convoy duty. Many of its crewmen were Grand Haven residents. On June 13, 1943 the "Escanaba" was torpedoed and sunk while on convoy duty in the North Atlantic. Of the crew of 103 only two survived. Since then, the memory of the ship and her crewmen have been an integral part of Grand Haven's history.

The Coast Guard station was reduced considerably in size in the postwar years and Mulligan's Hollow became a city park and a YMCA facility.

COAST GUARD MEMORIAL PARK is on the shore of the Grand River in front of the present-day Coast Guard Headquarters. It commemorates the Coastguardsmen who have served at Grand Haven and the memory of the Coast Guard cutter "Escanaba" and another cutter "Acacia" sunk by a German submarine in the Caribbean in Mar. 1942. The Tri-Cities Historical Museum at the corner of N. Harbor Dr. and Washington Ave. has displays on the "Escanaba" and other activities in the Grand Haven area during WW II. Museum address: N. Harbor Dr. & Washington Ave., Grand Haven, MI 49417. Phone: 616/842-0700. Hours: Memorial Day weekend to Labor Day, Tues.-Sat. 10-10, Sun. 2-10. May & Oct. Sat. & Sun. 2-5, Sept. Sat. 2-9:30, Sun. 2-5. Admission charged.

GRAND RAPIDS is in western Michigan 60 miles WNW of Lansing. Major manufacturers were Cessna Aircraft Co.

which made cargo gliders, Irwin-Pederson Arms Co. which made M-1 30 calibre carbines, Nash-Kelvinator Corp. which made a variety of military items and Berkey & Gay Furniture Co. which made wooden parts for aircraft. On Feb. 23, 1945 remnants of a Japanese bombing balloon were found near Grand Rapids. The balloon did no damage and, at the time, was the most easterly recovery of a Japanese bombing balloon.

GERALD R. FORD MUSEUM, near downtown Grand Rapids, honors the 38th President of the United States who was a resident of Grand Rapids. The museum traces the private and public lives of President Ford from his birth to the present. Included in the many displays are details on his military career during WW II as an officer in the U.S. Navy. Ford rose from Ensign to Lt. Commander and served aboard the carrier "Monterey" as gunnery officer, assistant navigator and athletic director. Address: 303 Pearl St. NW, Grand Rapids, MI 49504. Phone: 616/456-2674. Hours: M-Sat. 9-4:45, Sun. noon-4:45. Closed Jan. 1, Thanksgiving and Dec. 25. Admission charged.

GRAYLING is in the north-central part of Michigan on I-75.

CAMP GRAYLING, five miles SW of Grayling, has been the home of Michigan's National Guard since 1911. It is a large camp covering parts of three counties. During WW II the camp was used as a mobilization point for the 32nd Infantry Div. which included the Michigan National Guard and units of the Wisconsin National Guard. After the war the camp again became the home of the Michigan National Guard.

GRAYLING ARMY AIR FIELD, 1.5 miles NW of town, was Grayling's local air field, McNamara Airport, when it was taken over by the AAF early in the war as a sub-base to Alpena AAF and an air support field for Camp Grayling. It was given its wartime name but continued to serve Grayling's civilian needs as well. The Navy also used the field at times. After the war, the Army retained the field and it contin-

Coast Guard Memorial Park near downtown Grand Haven commemorates the men and ships of the U.S. Coast Guard which have long been a part of Grand Haven's history.

Interior of the Kalamazoo Air Museum.

This bronze statue, outside the Kalamazoo Air Museum/Guadalcanal Memorial Museum honors the more than 6000 U.S. servicemen who died on Guadalcanal.

ued to serve as Grayling's local airport. For years after the war the field was still called Grayling Army Air Field.

KALAMAZOO is in SW Michigan at the junction of I-94 and I-131. Contributing to the war effort were the Upjohn Co. which made pharmaceuticals for the armed services, Checker Motor Co. which made truck cabs, tank recovery vehicles, trailers and other military hardware, Ingersoll Steel Disc. Div. which made tanks and amphibian tractors, Shakespeare Co. which made machine gun controls, bomb sight parts and fire control equipment, and Kalamazoo Stove & Furnace Co. which made aircraft struts and parachute flares.

KALAMAZOO AIR MUSEUM AND THE GUADALCANAL MEMORIAL MUSEUM: This is two museums in one located at the Kalamazoo Airport. The former is a large air museum with a sizeable collection of aircraft, most of which are of WW II vintage. The latter is a smaller museum within the air museum dedicated to those who served on Guadalcanal. Prominent aircraft among the air museum's collection include a P-40 and four Grumman Cats . . . the Wildcat, Hellcat, Tigercat and Bearcat. Also on display is a B-25H, C-53, P-39Q, P-47D, F4U Corsair, F8J Crusader, BT-13, PT-17, T-28 and a Spanish-built version of the German Bf-109 Messerschmitt. Most of the collection is indoors. The air museum has its own restoration facility and visitors are invited to watch restoration work in progress.

The Guadalcanal Memorial Museum occupies a large room within the air museum with separate sections describing the various phases of the Battle of Guadalcanal, America's first offensive of WW II. The museum contains many artifacts from the actual battle. Outside the air museum is a bronze statue of a GI scratching the name of a fallen buddy on a makeshift cross. This statue is intended to honor the more than 6000 U.S. servicemen who died on the island. Address for both museums: 3101 E. Milham Rd., Kalamazoo, MI 49002. Phone: 616/382-6555. Hours: M-Sat. 10-5, Sun. 1-5, closed holidays. Admission charged.

LANSING is the capital of Michigan. Some of the larger companies in the city were the Oldsmobile Div. of GM which made 75 mm cannons, howitzers, anti-aircraft guns and projectiles, REO Motors, Inc. which made trucks and T-13 armored cars, and Lansing Paint & Color Co. which made explosives.

MIKADO, 11 miles NE of Oscoda, was a community of 125 people during the war. As a patriotic gesture its citizens changed the name of the town to MacArthur. In the postwar years, however, they changed it back to Mikado.

MACKINAC ISLAND is a popular tourist site in the Strait of Mackinac between the Upper and Lower Peninsulas of Michigan. Beginning in 1943 the Grand Hotel, the island's largest and most elegant resort hotel, was used as a convalescent center for war wounded.

MIDLAND (See Bay City/Midland/Saginaw area)

MUSKEGON is in the western part of the state on Lake Michigan 30 miles NW of Grand Rapids. One of the largest defense plants in the city was built new by Continental Aviation & Engineering Corp. to build Rolls-Royce "Merlin" aircraft engines and Ford V-8 engines for tanks. Another company, Brunswick, Balke, Collender Co. made aircraft for the Navy.

USS SILVERSIDES & MARITIME MUSEUM is located on Muskegon's waterfront at the foot of 9th St. The museum's center piece is the WW II submarine "Silversides". This submarine was commissioned Dec. 15, 1941, just 8 days after the Japanese attack on Pearl Harbor, and she fought throughout the war spending all of her time in the Pacific. "Silversides" sank a total of 23 enemy ships to became the third highest-scoring US submarine in the war. After the war "Silversides" was used as a naval reserve training submarine at Chicago and in 1987 she came to Muskegon to be put on permanent display as a National Monument. The museum offers overnight stays aboard the submarine for youth groups. Address: PO Box 1692, Muskegon, MI 49443. Phone: 616/755-1230. Hours: Apr. and Oct. Sat.-Sun. 10-5:30. May thru Sept. M-F 1-5:30, Sat.-Sun. 10-5:30. June thru Aug. daily 10-5:30. Admission charged.

OSCODA is in eastern Michigan near the entrance to Saginaw Bay.

OSCODA ARMY AIR FIELD, two miles NW of Oscoda, began as an Army camp called Camp Skeel in 1931. From 1924 to 1944 the area was used by the Army for winter maneuvers, and after 1927 it was also used for aerial gunnery practice by air crews station at Selfridge Field. In 1942, when it was a sub-base of Selfridge Field, three runways were built and the camp was renamed Oscoda Army Air Field. The facility was then used extensively by personnel and planes from Selfridge Field throughout the war. After the war the air field was taken over by the US Air Force, modernized and renamed Oscoda Air Force Base. In 1953 the base was renamed Wurtsmith Air Force Base in honor of Maj. Gen. Paul B. Wurtsmith, commander of the 13th AF during WW II in the SW Pacific. Gen. Wurtsmith died in the crash of a B-25 in 1946.

SAGINAW (See Bay City/Midland/Saginaw area)

The "Silversides" is the highest-scoring surviving US submarine of WW II.

ROSCOMMON is in north-central Michigan 13 miles SE of Grayling.

CCC MUSEUM, at North Higgins Lake State Park, is not a true WW II site. Rather, it is a preserved pre-war Depression-era CCC Camp. It is significant to WW II, however, in that the buildings seen here are the predecessors to hundreds of thousands of temporary wooden buildings built by the U.S. Government at military installations all over the world. In 1940 the U.S. Government made the decision not to build many permanent buildings at military bases, but instead to build large numbers of temporary buildings based on pre-war CCC building designs. Also, thousands of existing CCC buildings, like those seen here, were pressed into military service during the early part of the war. As the ranks of the CCC declined, camp after camp was abandoned and many of the buildings were torn down in sections and moved to military locations an reassembled. During the summer of 1942 the Federal Government declared all CCC camps in America surplus and turned them over to the War Dept. Some CCC camps were used as they were for small unit training camps, secret training camps, prisoner of war camps and other purposes. One CCC camp in Maryland became President Roosevelt's mountain retreat and became known as Shangri-La (later Camp David). The museum is open all year and is free. Location: The museum is 7 miles west of Roscommon on County Rd. 203 about midway between I-74 and US 27.

SAULT SAINTE MARIE, MICHIGAN AND SAULT SAINTE MARIE, ONTARIO CANADA are twin cities and the site of the vital "Soo Locks" that allow large ships to pass from the lower Great Lakes into Lake Superior. During the war 90% of America's iron ore passed through the Soo Locks, between the months of March and Nov. It came from mines in northern Minnesota and went to steel mills in 7 U.S. states and southeastern Canada. At the beginning of the war there was no other way to transport the necessary amount of ore needed by U.S. and Canadian industry. Existing U.S. railroads could carry only about half of what was needed. Therefore, the locks were seen by both the Americans and Canadians as the second most vital waterway in North America after the Panama Canal, and a tempting target for sabotage or an enemy attack. The latter was thought possible if an enemy aircraft carrier could penetrate Hudson Bay in northern Canada from which bombers could reach the locks. Also a bombing attack from German-occupied Norway by long-range bombers flying the Great Circle Route could not be ruled out, nor could a suicide parachute attack. For these reasons security measures became intense in the area. In Sept. 1939, when the war started in Europe, the four companies of soldiers stationed at the time at Ft. Brady were assigned to guard the locks, and Coastguardsmen from the local Coast Guard station began to actively patrol the approaches to the locks. Machine

guns and search lights were installed above the locks and military guards went aboard every ship as it passed through the locks. By May 1941 the soldiers had been replaced by a Military Police battalion. When the U.S. entered the war, security at the Soo was beefed up. In Apr. 1942 an anti-aircraft artillery regiment and a barrage balloon battalion arrived as did an infantry regiment specially trained to fight paratroopers and guard against sabotage. The latter force replaced the MPs. Also in that month an air defense zone was set up that included almost all of Michigan's Chippewa County and an area in Canada from the Soo northward to Hudson Bay. Only controlled flights, approved in advance, were permitted in this area. In Canada the Canadians set up 266 ground observer posts, manned by 9047 people, north and east of the Soo. And, with Canadian permission, five U.S.-manned radar stations were set up across northern Ontario. No permanent air protection was established at the Soo. Rather, three emergency landing fields were prepared in the area and the 1st AF was assigned the task of keeping available a suitable air units that could be rushed to the area in case of a pending attack. By the end of 1942 7300 U.S. military personnel were engaged in protecting the Soo locks plus those at the radar stations. During the summer of 1942 the Americans and Canadians established a Permanent Joint Board to manage the military defenses of the Soo and the Canadians brought in an anti-aircraft battalion of their own.

During the summer of 1943, with the general reduction of continental defenses, the U.S. force at the Soo was reduced to 2500. In Jan. 1944 both the U.S. and Canada abandoned their ground observer posts and removed their anti-aircraft guns. After that the U.S. soldiers were removed and replaced by a battalion of Military Police, and by the end of 1944 this force was reduced to one company. The Soo locks survived the war free of enemy attacks or acts of sabotage.

FORT BRADY was within the city limits of Sault Sainte Marie on the south bank of the St. Mary's River. It was built in 1892 and was normally manned by a battalion-size regular Army force. But, during WW II it housed many of the soldiers brought into the area to man the local defenses. Near the end of the war the fort was inactivated and in Oct. 1945 it was declared surplus.

CAMP LUCAS was a small camp established by the Army in 1942 about a mile from downtown Sault Sainte Marie at St. Mary's Falls. Its mission was to guard the Soo Locks. The camp was manned until 1960 and closed in 1962.

This is a typical barracks building used at CCC camps all over the country during the Depression. Many of them were used during WW II and the building's design and construction became the fundamental design for hundreds of thousands of temporary wooden buildings built by the Government at military installations all over the world.

MINNESOTA

Lt. Commander Harold E. Stassen while on the staff of Vice Admiral Newton, successor to Adm. Halsey in the South Pacific.

Minnesota contributed in many ways to the war effort. The state had major manufacturing enterprises in the Minneapolis-St. Paul area and rich farms that produced grain, dairy products and meat. Perhaps the state's most outstanding contribution, though, was iron ore, a very important commodity for any nation at war. Minnesota's iron ore mines are in the northern part of the state and were America's main source of this very necessary commodity. Needless to say, the mines were worked feverishly during the war, often around-the-clock.

At the beginning of the war the state's Governor, Harold E. Stassen, the youngest governor in the country, was one of the up-and-coming stars in the Republican Party and a possible candidate for national office. In 1943, however, Stassen resigned as Governor and joined the Navy. He served as a flag officer to Adm. William "Bull" Halsey and took part in four major battles in the Pacific. Before he left the Navy he made the rank of Captain. In 1945, President Roosevelt appointed him as a delegate to the United Nations Conference in San Francisco. In 1948, and again in 1952 he ran unsuccessfully as a candidate for President at the Republican Conventions of those years.

Minnesota, like many other midwestern states, continued to prosper after the war thanks to the continuing demands for the state's products, and many of her wartime military facilities remained active for decades.

AUSTIN is on the SE edge of the state on I-90 near the Iowa state line. Just before the war the town's major meat packing company, the Geo. Hormel Co. developed a meat product called "Spam" packed in small meal-size cans. During the war "Spam" proved to be an ideal way to provide a tasty and nutritious meat

product to servicemen all over the world and to our food-short Allies. Therefore, tons of "Spam" were produced and shipped to nearly every corner of the globe. Almost every GI, airman and sailor ate "Spam" at one time or another during the war.

DULUTH is strategically situated at the western end of Lake Superior and had, by WW II, become a major lake port shipping primarily one product . . iron ore. Minnesota's rich iron ore deposits are west of Duluth, and the bulk of the nation's steel mills, that processed the ore, were east and south of Duluth on or near one of the Great Lakes. Duluth was also a shipbuilding town. Two of the larger companies that built ships for the war effort were Marine Iron & Shipbuilding Co. which built Coast Guard cutters and Zenith Dredge Co. which built Coast Guard cutters and tankers.

CANAL PARK VISITORS CENTER & MARINE MUSEUM: This is a large recreational facility in Canal Park which is on the north shore of the canal connecting Lake Superior with Superior Bay. Inside the visitors center is a fine marine museum which focuses on the maritime history of the Duluth area. Among the museum's exhibits are many references to the WW II era, and a large model ship collection contains models of the ships built in Duluth for the Navy and Coast Guard during the war. Museum address: Canal Park, Duluth, MN 55802. Phone: Museum, 218/727-2497. "Sundew" tour information, 218/727-2497. Visitors Center & Museum hours: Memorial Day weekend- Labor Day daily 10-9; Apr. 1 thru day before Memorial Day weekend and day after Labor Day to mid-Dec. daily 10-6; rest of year Sun.-Thurs. 10-4:30. Free.

LITTLE FALLS AREA of Minnesota is near the geographic center of the state 90 miles NW of Minneapolis/St. Paul.

CHARLES A. LINDBERGH STATE MEMORIAL PARK features the boyhood home of Charles. A. Lindbergh, the world-famous aviator who made the first non-stop flight between New York City and

Paris in 1927. The Interpretive Center traces the history of the Lindbergh family for three generations and displays family artifacts and memorabilia. After the Japanese attack on Pearl Harbor Lindbergh offered went to work for United Aircraft Co. as a technical consultant on the development and production of Corsair and P-38 fighter planes. He was credited with increasing the range of the P-38 to 500 miles. Later in the war, at the request of the War Department, Lindbergh toured the Pacific as a technical consultant and an instructor to fighter pilots. In the course of this work he made many flights as a civilian pilot in fighter planes including about 50 combat missions. During a bombing mission over Guam, in which he was flying escort in a P-38, he shot down a Japanese plane.

After the war, Lindbergh became a consultant to the Chief of Staff of the Air Force and became a Brigadier General in the Air Force Reserves. He went on to serve in many other important posts including being on the committee to select the site for the new Air Force Academy. Lindbergh gained many post-war honors including the Congressional Medal of Honor and the Pulitzer Prize. Address: S. Charles A. Lindbergh Dr., Little Falls, MN 56345. Phone: 612/632-3154. Hours: May 1-Labor Day daily 10-5, rest of year Sun. noon-4.

The main gate at Camp Ripley.

Admission charged.

CAMP RIPLEY, just north of Little Falls, was built in the late 1800s as an Army post named Fort Ripley. In 1931 it became the home of the Minnesota National Guard. Just before WW II Camp Ripley was used as a proving ground for military vehicles and prototypes of the first Jeeps were tested here. In Feb. 1941 the Minnesota National Guard was mobilized and became part of the 34th Infantry Div. The camp was then used by the Army as a training ground for some 10,000 Regular Army troops. Winter combat training was one of the camp's specialties and there was a school for military police. The camp had its own air field which operated in conjunction with the ground troops being trained. After the war the National Guard returned to the camp.

Minnesota Military Museum: This is the official museum of the Minnesota National Guard and is located on the grounds of Camp Ripley. The museum's mission is to preserve the artifacts and history of Minnesota's militia and National Guard, and interpret military history as experienced by citizens of the state. Displays include military vehicles, aircraft, amphibious landing craft, artillery pieces, small arms, field equipment, uniforms, medals, insignias, ordnance and captured enemy equipment. Address: Camp Ripley, Little Falls, MN 56345. Phone: 612/632-6631 ext.374. Hours: Memorial Day to Labor Day Wed.-Sun. 10-5. Rest of year by request. Free.

MINNEAPOLIS/ST. PAUL AREA: These twin cities comprise the political, economic, industrial and cultural heart of Minnesota. The area became an important air link with Alaska and Canada and a transit center for Lend Lease supplies going to the Soviet Union.

GOPHER ORDNANCE WORKS, known in later years as the Twin Cities Army Ammunition Plant, was 10 miles NNW of downtown St. Paul off I-10. The plant was built by the Federal Government early in the war to produce explosives and was one of the largest facilities of its kind in the nation. The plant specialized in the production of oleum, cannon powder and rifle powder and was run by E. I. Du Pont de Nemours Co. There were also several production lines here making small arms ammunition which were run by Federal Cartridge Co. Near the end of the war Gopher became a reclamation depot, reclaiming and repairing ordnance materials that needed such work before shipping and storing. Like most large ordnance plants, Gopher remained active for many years after the war.

HOLOCAUST RESOURCE CENTER OF MINNEAPOLIS has a small museum with displays and artifacts commemorating the great Holocaust of WW II. The center also has a library and archives, and offers educational programs, exhibits, teacher training and interfaith programs. Address: 8200 W. 33rd St., Minneapolis, MN 55426. Phone: 612/935-0319. Hours: M-Thurs. 9-8, Sun. 9-1.

The Minnesota Military Museum at Camp Ripley is the official state museum of the Minnesota National Guard.

MINNESOTA STATE CAPITOL BUILDING: Many state capitol buildings and county seats around the country have relics of WW II sitting on their lawns, but the relic on the lawn of Minnesota's State Capitol Building is quite unique. It is the gun that fired America's opening shots of WW II. The gun is a 4" naval gun removed from the destroyer "Ward" during its conversion to a fast transport. On the morning of Dec. 7, 1941, before the Japanese air attack began, the "Ward" was patrolling the entrance to Pearl Harbor. Suddenly, crewmen of the "Ward" spotted a small suspicious vessel trying to enter Pearl Harbor and sank it with rounds fired from this gun. The suspicious vessel turned out to be a Japanese midget submarine that was positioning itself in order to take part in the coming attack. The State Capitol Building is located at Aurora and Constitution Aves. in downtown St. Paul.

PLANES OF FAME AIR MUSEUM is a large air museum at Flying Cloud Field in Eden Prarie, MN 14 miles SW of downtown Minneapolis. The museum has a large collection of restored and air-worthy aircraft, mostly from WW II. Of special interest in the collection is a rare TP-40N Curtiss Warhawk dual-control trainer and a rare Douglas C-41A transport, the first military version of the famous DC-3 airliner. Also on display is an FM-2 Wildcat, F8F Bearcat, P-38J, P-47D, P-51D, A-26C, B-25J, PT-17, T-6G, N2S-3 Stearman, Supermarine Spitfire and a 1942 Swiss-built EKW C-3605 fighter. Address: 14771 Pioneer Trail (County Rd. #1), Eden Prairie, MN 55347. Phone: 612/941-2633. Hours: Sat.-Sun. 11-5. Call for weekday hours. Admission charged. Location: On the NW corner of the air field.

SAINT PAUL AIRPORT, now Saint Paul Downtown Airport (Holman Field) near downtown St. Paul, was the city's main airport at the time of the war. In Feb. 1942 a British air mission, working in cooperation with the AAF, contracted Mid-Continental Airlines Co., a civilian airline with maintenance operations here, to modify several new Lend Lease B-25 bombers for the British for operation in the North African desert. The work was done outside under tarpaulins and in make-shift sheds. More contracts were given to Mid-Continental and construction on two large government-finances hangars was begun. Soon after modifying the British planes, the facility modified another batch of B-25 bombers by removing the lower turrets and adding extra gas tanks. These bombers were later used on the famous Doolittle Tokyo raid. Mid-Continental merged with Northwest Airlines Corp. (NWA) and the modification center, completed in Dec. 1942, became known as Northwest Airlines-St. Paul Modification Center #12. Each of the two huge hangars, when completed, held 13 heavy bombers undergoing modifications. During the war the center modified mostly B-24 bombers including some used on the famous Ploesti oil field raids in Rumania. During the war 3286 aircraft were modified here with a work force that peaked at 5090 people. The center also had an Ice Research operation, a secret Navy research program and an airmen's transitional training school. After the war the facility was acquired

The 4" gun from the destroyer "Ward" used to sink a Japanese midget submarine at Pearl Harbor on the morning of Dec. 7, 1941.

by NWA and was used for maintenance operations on civilian aircraft.

CAMP SAVAGE was located at the junction of SR 13 & Xenwood Ave. in the Village of Savage, MN, a southern suburb of Minneapolis. It was a temporary camp of 136 acres built in the summer of 1942 by the Army for a unique Military Intelligence Service School. The school's mission was to teach U.S. soldiers, mostly of oriental heritage, the Japanese language. Upon graduation, the soldiers would be used throughout the Army's Intelligence Service and later in Japan as members of the U.S. occupation forces. Minnesota was chosen for the location of the school because there was a very tolerant attitude in the state for peoples of foreign nationalities which, it was felt, would provide an atmosphere of relative peace and security for the teachers and students. Some 6000 Americans of Japanese, Korean and Chinese descent were graduated from the school during

training facility for small and specialized Army units. In 1946 the fort was decommissioned and turned over to the Veterans Administration and Army Reserves. It then became a National Historic Landmark and a state park. In the main building is a history center, but there is little or no references to the fort's role in WW II.

WOLD-CHAMBERLAIN AIRPORT, which later became Minneapolis-St. Paul International Airport, was 6 miles south of downtown Minneapolis. It was the area's main airport before the war and had among its many tenants both Army and Navy operations. The Navy's operation, known as U.S. Naval Reserve Air Base, Minneapolis, was the largest of the military operations at the field. In 1940 the station's reserve squadron was called to active duty and in 1941 the Navy's vacant facilities were utilized to train some 800 pilots under the Civilian Pilot Training Program. After the U.S. entered the war the Navy's facilities were greatly enlarged and the station was given the mission

The Planes of Fame Air Museum as viewed from beneath the wing of a B-25 bomber. This is a large museum with a fine collection of restored and flyable WW II aircraft.

B-24 bombers being worked on at the Northwest Airlines-St. Paul Modification Center.

the war. In 1946 Camp Savage was closed and the school moved to Ft. Snelling. In later years the camp site became an industrial area and very little evidence remained of Camp Savage.

FORT SNELLING is 7 miles SE of downtown Minneapolis at the confluence of the Minnesota and Mississippi Rivers. It was built in 1819 and by WW had evolved into a collection of fine old stone buildings and breastworks, obsolete for modern warfare, but still occupied by the Army. During the war the fort was used as a reception center, supply depot and a

of educating naval aviation cadets in ground school and primary flight training. N3N "Yellow Perils" and N2S Kaydets were used. On Jan. 1, 1943 the station was upgraded and renamed U.S. Naval Air Station, Minneapolis. Its training mission remained the same and in May 1944 NAS, Minneapolis reached its peak population of 3579 people. In Feb. 1944 the Army and Navy cooperated in a joint research project at Wold-Chamberlain to study the effects of precipitation static on aircraft and aircraft equipment and to seek to develop special devices to control hazards in low temperature flying.

The Minnesota Air National Guard had had its main operation at Wold-Chamberlain Field since 1921, and early in the war the AAF came to the field and began using it as a staging area for AAF aircraft flying westward and to Alaska. By late 1942 the AAF had established regular passenger and freight service between Wold-Chamberlain and Fairbanks and Anchorage, Alaska. The field was also used regularly for Lend Lease aircraft being flown to the Soviet Union via Alaska. Both the Army's Air Transport Command and Air Technical Service Com-

One of the few remaining remnants of Camp savage is Shakers Famous Burger Tavern & Grille which occupies one of the camp's WW II buildings.

mand operated here.

All the while, Wold-Chamberlain Field continued in operation as a commercial airport. Northwest Airlines, which was very active at Wold-Chamberlain, established regular air routes, under government contract, to points in Alaska and along the AlCan Highway and the Northwest Staging Route through Canada.

After the war the military operations at Wold-Chamberlain declined and the naval air station was turned back to the naval reserves. Other military operations continued at the field in the postwar years and at times were substantial.

During the war the NAS has several outlying fields, two of which were Cedar Ave. Airport 8.5 miles south of Minneapolis and Fleming Airport, 7 miles SE of Minneapolis.

Minnesota Air Guard Museum: This is an air museum located at the former Wold-Chamberlain Field featuring the history of the Minnesota Air National Guard from its inception in 1921 to the present. The museum has a collection of more than a dozen planes most of which are post-war models. WW II aircraft, however, include a P-51 fighter, AT-6 trainer, L-4H Piper Cub and C-47 transport. Other displays include aircraft models, photographs, uniforms, artifacts and personal belongings of guardsmen. Address: PO Box 11598, Mpls-StP IAP, MN. 55111. Phone: 612/725-5609. Hours: Mid-Apr.-mid-Oct. Sat. 10-4 and Sun. noon-4. Donations requested. Location: NE corner of the airport near the intersection of highways 55 & 62.

The Minnesota Air Guard Museum at Minneapolis-St. Paul International Airport (Wold-Chamberlain Field).

MISSISSIPPI

Mississippi, in America's "Deep South", was one of the "Sun Belt" states that the War Department turned to when the need arose to train hundreds of thousands of new soldiers and airmen. And later, when the need arose to house tens of thousands of prisoners of war the War Department looked again to Mississippi. Here was cheap land, uncongested skies, hardworking people and cooperative state and local governments. Mississippi was an agricultural state with cotton as its principal product, but the market for cotton had never really been good since the end of the American Civil War. As a result, with 67% of the state's population living on farms, many of the state's citizens lived in poverty. In 1936 the state legislature had passed a law called the Balancing Agriculture With Industry (BAWI) act which was designed to attract manufacturing companies to the state. BAWI offered major tax concession to new industrial operations and authorized local communities to sell bonds to help finance new factories. When WW II started in Europe BAWI was beginning to have a positive effect on the state's economy. There were many new manufacturing plants in the state which soon obtained defense contracts which, in turn, produced jobs for Mississippians. And, with BAWI still an attraction, more new manufacturing concerns moved into the state as factories up north filled to capacity with war work and their owners looked for new areas in which to expand.

Just before the war began, in 1939, Mississippi had the good fortune in that oil was discovered in the SW part of the state near Tinsley. Wells were drilled one after the other and by the end of 1944 the state had 450 producing oil wells.

In the fall of 1941 the state became a part of a three-state Army maneuver area[1] in which some 400,000 soldiers tested their new skills and training.

The wartime economy brought increased demands for the state's traditional products; cotton, lumber, corn, oats, sweet potatoes, sugar cane, sorghum, fruit, peanuts, pecans, seafood, clothing, natural gas, sand & gravel and clay products. To man the state's farms, now short of labor, some 20,000 prisoners of war were employed throughout Mississippi working out of four main camps and 15 branch POW camps.

By war's end, Mississippi was enjoying more prosperity than it had known in generations. The oil industry had spawned another major industry, that of chemicals, and with BAWI still in force and a new state right-to-work law (one of the first in the nation), industry continued to move into Mississippi.

BILOXI/GULFPORT/PASCAGOULA

AREA: These are the three largest towns on Mississippi's coast. Biloxi had a new Coast Guard Air Station, built in 1941. In a waterfront park on the Gulf, about a mile west of downtown Biloxi and opposite a local VFW chapter, is a memorial to the WW II light cruiser

[1]The other two states were Louisiana and Texas.

"Biloxi" consisting of the ship's mast and a 40 mm gun mount.

Pascagoula had a sizeable ship yard, the Ingalla Shipbuilding Co. which produces cargo ships, passenger ships and net layers. The town's harbor also became an assembly point for wartime convoys. West of Gulfport is St. Louis Bay. A part of the bay, and a large area of adjoining marshlands, were used as a bombing & gunnery range by the Army Air Forces. This area was known as the Hancock County Range and covered 30,622 acres.

At Pas Christian the U.S. Merchant Marine Cadet Corps had established, in 1938, a school to train officers for the U.S. Maritime Service. This school shifted to a accelerated schedule when the war started and turned out many much-needed maritime officers.

CAT ISLAND WAR DOG CENTER was on Cat Island, 8 miles south of Gulfport. Here, dogs were received and trained by the Army for a variety of military uses. The facility operated through June 1944.

GULFPORT ARMY AIR FIELD, three miles NE of downtown Gulfport, was the city's local airport before the war. It was taken over the 3rd AF and used as a training center for crews of heavy bombers. After the war the AF departed and the field was returned to the community and became Gulfport Municipal Airport.

KEESLER FIELD, two miles west of downtown Biloxi, was acquired by the War Department in early 1941 and was first known as Biloxi Air Corps Technical School for aircraft mechanics. The field was a brand new civil airport that was given to the AAF by the city of Biloxi along with adjoining land. In Aug. 1941 the name of the facility was changed to Keesler Field. When the U.S. went to war in Dec. 1941 Keesler was one of only three AF mechanic's schools in the country. This operation was enlarged rapidly and the field also acquired other operations including a basic training center for AF recruits, a regional AAF hospital and an air-sea rescue school

training replacement crews primarily in B-24s. Mechanics training, however, remained the primary mission of the field. For a while, men for the Chinese Nationalist Air Force were trained here as mechanics. Keesler was retained by the AAF after the war and continued to train mechanics and recruits. In 1947 a large radar school came to the base which, together with the existing schools, made Keesler one the AAF's two largest schools. In 1948 the US Air Force acquired the field and changed its name to Keesler Air Force Base. It continued to serve the Air Force throughout the Cold War remaining primarily a technical and recruit training center.

FORT MASSACHUSETTS is on historic Ship Island 12 miles south of Gulfport. Construction of this brick fort was completed after the Civil War. By WW II the fort was obsolete for military purposes, but was used to train war dogs in cooperation with the War Dog Training Center on nearby Cat Island. Dogs were trained here for work in the Far East by Japanese-American volunteers who taught the dogs commands in Japanese and other Asian languages. The fort was abandoned by the Army after the war and became a part of the Gulf Islands National Seashore operated by the National Park Service. The fort is well preserved and open to the public. Address for the fort: Gulf Islands National Seashore, 3500 Park Rd., Ocean Springs, MS 39564. Phone: 602/875-0821.

U.S. NAVAL ADVANCED BASE DEPOT, GULFPORT was established in June 1942 just west of Gulfport. Its mission was to provide a training facility for Naval Construction Battalions (SeaBees) and to serve as an outloading facility for the Caribbean area. In Oct. 1942 the depot acquired a school for merchant ship armed guards and a cooks & bakers school. The next month the depot became a receiving facility for the SeaBees. In 1944 the depot became a Naval Training Center providing training in basic engineering, diesel,

Naval Construction Battalion 26 in formation at Gulfport in 1942.

radioman, quartermaster and electricians ratings. In 1945 it served as a U.S. Naval Storehouse, and in 1946 the training center was decommissioned. From 1948 to 1952 the depot became a storage facility for certain national stockpile materials such as bauxite, tin, copper, sisal and abaca. In 1952 the naval storage facility was disestablished and the old depot became the U.S. Naval Construction Center, Gulfport with the mission to serve as an operating and training facility for Seabees. It served that role throughout the Cold War.

SeaBee Museum, Gulfport Branch: This is a small museum on the grounds of the U.S. Naval Construction Center, Gulfport in building 60. The museum has artifacts and displays tracing the history of the facility from its beginning in 1942 to the present. Address: U.S. Naval Construction Center, Gulfport, MS 39501: Phone: 601/871-2032. Hours: M-F 11-4, Sat. 10-2. Free. Plans are under way to enlarge the museum and move it to a restored WW II building.

CENTREVILLE is in SW Mississippi near the Louisiana state line.

CAMP VAN HORN, near the community of Centreville, was built by the Federal Government in 1942 and first known as Centreville Cantonment. It was a large camp used as a training center for division-size Army units. It was also a segregated camp so negro troops served and trained here also. In Oct. 1945 the camp was declared surplus and by 1947 most of the buildings and land had been sold off.

COLUMBUS is 80 miles north of Meridian, MS.

COLUMBUS ARMY AIR FIELD, 10 miles north of town, was built by the War Department in early 1941 for the Army Air Corps as a training field for pilots and crews of twin-engine bombers. It was known then as Air Corps Advanced Flying School, Columbus, MS. Later that year, it was renamed Columbus Airfield, and in Feb. 1942 renamed again as Kaye Field. A month later it was renamed yet again as Columbus Army Flying Field and finally in Mar. 1943 it was named Columbus Army Air Field. Throughout most of the war it was operated by the Eastern Flying Training Command and carried out its mission as a training facility. In July 1945 the name of the base was changed once again to Columbus AAF Pilot School (Specialized Two-Engine). In 1946 the field was closed, but then re-activated in 1951 as a contract flying school during the Korean War operated by California Eastern Airways. In 1955 the field was taken over by the US Air Force and became Columbus Air Force Base. It continued as a training facility throughout the Cold War. During WW II Columbus AAF had the following auxiliary air fields:

- Aux. #1, Columbus Aux. Fd. #1, 10 miles NNW of Columbus
- Aux. #2, River Airport, 13 miles east of Aberdeen
- Aux. #3, Caldonia Airport, 13.5 miles SE of Aberdeen
- Aux. #4, Water Works Airport, 4 miles NE of Columbus
- Aux. #5, Columbus Aux. Fd. #5, 3.5 miles NW of Columbus
- Aux. #6, Vaughn Airport, 8.5 miles SSE of Columbus
- Aux. #7, Starkville Municipal Airport, 2 miles SW of Starkville
- Aux. #8, Stinson Airport, 3 miles NW of Aberdeen

COMO is 40 miles south of Memphis, TN.

COMO PRISONER OF WAR CAMP was located in Panola County near Como and held some 2600 prisoners of war who worked mainly in local agriculture. This was onw of the state's four main POW camps.

FLORA is 20 miles NNW of Jackson.

FLORA ORDNANCE PLANT was a large ordnance plant near Flora designed to produce and load powder into bags for heavy artillery. The plant was built early in the war but never put into operation. During the war it was maintained in readiness in the event it was needed. The facility was used, however, as an ordnance training center and as a staging area for Army troops. Up to 15,000 troops resided at times at the plant. In 1945 the plant was finally put into operation as a bag loader, but soon after the war ended the facility was closed and declared surplus. It was sold piecemeal and some of the large buildings were bought my manufacturing firms.

GREENVILLE is 90 miles NW of Jackson on the Mississippi River.

GREENVILLE FIELD, 7 miles NE of town was established by the War Department in late 1941 for the 30,000 Pilot Training Program.

During the war it had a branch prisoner of war camp holding about 270 POWs who worked in agriculture. The field ended training operations earlier than most near the end of the war and was used to store surplus aircraft. During the war the field had the following auxiliary air fields:

- Aux. #1, Yellow Bayou Airport, 5 miles north of Lake Village, AR.
- Aux. #?, Greenville Airport, 3 miles ESE of Greenville
- Aux. #3, Walker Airport, 3.5 miles NE of Leland
- Aux. #?, Avalon Air Field, 1.3 miles SE of Avalon
- Aux. #5, Kimbrough Airport, 4.5 miles east of Lake Village, AR.

GREENWOOD is 80 miles north of Jackson.

GREENWOOD ARMY AIR FIELD, 6 miles SE of town, was established by the AAF for the 70,000 Pilot Training Program. It was operated by the Air Transport Command and used to train transport pilots and crews. Early in 1945 another school came to the field to train ferry pilots for fighter aircraft. The field had a branch prisoner of war camp holding about 300 POWs who worked in agriculture. In 1946 the field was declared surplus. During the war the field had the following auxiliary fields:

- Aux. #?, Indianola Air Field, Indianola
- Aux. #2, Oxberry Airport, 1.2 miles west of Oxberry
- Aux. #4, Cruger Airport, 4.3 miles NE of Cruger
- Aux. #5, Tchula Airport, 2.2 miles SE of Tchula
- Aux. #6, Greenwood Municipal Airport, 3 miles SW of Greenwood

GRENADA is in the north-central part of the state on I-55.

GRENADA ARMY AIR FIELD was a new air field, 3.5 miles north of town at the beginning of the war. It was taken over by the I Troop Carrier Command in 1944 and used for only 10 months. It was then turned over to the Air Technical Service Command to store surplus aircraft and as an air freight terminal. During the war it had a main poisoner of war camp holding about 4400 POWs who worked on the field and in agriculture.

CAMP McCAIN was located 9 miles SE of Grenada near the community of Elliott. It was built in 1942 by the War Department as a training facility for division-size units. This was a segregated camp so negro troops also served and trained here. McCain had a main prisoner of war compound that held both anti-Nazi German POWs and German naval POWs. Most of the POWs worked in agriculture. In 1946 the camp was declared surplus and most of it's land an buildings were eventually disposed of. A part of the camp was retained to become a National Guard facility and retained the name Camp McCain.

GULFPORT (See Biloxi/Gulfport/Pascagoula Area)

HATTIESBURG is in SE Mississippi 60 miles north of the coast.

CAMP SHELBY, 12 miles from town, was established during WW I as a training camp for the 38th Infantry Div. (National Guard). It was closed in 1919, but with the beginning of

Living accommodations at Camp Shelby in 1941.

WW II it was reactivated as a tent camp and enlarged. It became a reception center for the 4th Army Corps and a training camp for division size units. The 38th Inf. Div., which comprised the national guards of Indiana, Kentucky and West Virginia, trained here during 1941. The 38th participated in the first Louisiana Maneuvers during Aug./Sept. 1941, and then went on for amphibious training at Camp Carrabelle, FL. Later, the 37th Infantry Div., comprised of the Ohio National Guard, trained here. In late 1942 Camp Shelby had extra housing capacity available, so it was assigned one of the first prisoner of war camps in the U.S. The camp held about 1200 German POWs who worked at the camp and in the nearby forests. Shelby was a segregated camp so negro troops served and trained here. After WW II Camp Shelby was turned over to the Mississippi National Guard.

JACKSON, near the center of the state, is the state capital.

CLINTON PRISONER OF WAR CAMP was located SE of Clinton, a western suburb of Jackson, MS. It was a main POW camp holding about 3000 German POWs. This camp was unique in that it had a large compound for high-ranking German officers and at one time held 40 German generals including Gen. Jurgen von Arnim, Gen. Rommel's replacement in North Africa. The officer's compound, which was some distance form the enlisted men's compound, was a very comfortable POW camp and sometimes referred to as "the Country Club". Each officer had his own quarters and generals had their own cottages which included the services of German enlisted men as orderlies and gardeners. The officer's also had a social club, tennis courts, a big library, private radios, English classes, escorted tours to universities, ship yards, war plants and U.S. landmarks such as Mt. Vernon, VA. At times they were allowed to go, unescorted, into Jackson. The excellent treatment of high-ranking German officers had its purposes. First, it was expected that captured U.S. officers would be well treated in Germany; and secondly, it was presumed that some of these men would become postwar leaders in

Germany and it was the hope of the U.S. Government that they would return to Germany impressed with the democratic from of government and be a bulwark against German officers being returned from the Soviet Union imbued with Communism. The enlisted men at Clinton had it good too with ample sports programs, a symphony orchestra, jazz band, painting and art exhibits and a camp newspaper. In 1945 a Swiss Legation inspection team and a YMCA inspection team both reported that Camp Clinton was the best POW camp they had seen.

Near the end of the war the POWs were put to work building a huge scale model of the lower Mississippi River basin with the intention that the facility would be taken over by the Army Corps of Engineers after the war and used to study the water flow and flood-control system of this part of the country. Later, a large concrete-testing facility was built on the Camp Clinton site. Most of the old POW camp was absorbed by the U.S. Waterways Experimental Station.

FOSTER GENERAL HOSPITAL was a 1905-bed hospital established by the Army on W. Capitol St. early in 1943 to treat war wounded. It was staffed by 1500 doctors, nurses, technicians and other employees. The hospital had about 100 buildings and specialized in general medicine, rheumatic fever and general and orthopedic surgery. At the end of the war part of the hospital was converted into a 600-bed Veterans Hospital and the remainder of the facility became Veterans Administration state headquarters. The Veterans Hospital later moved to Woodrow Wilson Dr.

JACKSON ARMY AIR BASE, was two miles NW of town and was Jackson's pre-war airport, Hawkins Field. It was taken over by the AAF and used by the 2nd AF for elementary pilot training during the war. Between May 1942 and Feb. 1944 pilots of the Dutch East Indies Air Force trained here in P-40 fighters and B-25 bombers. The base also had an air servicing detachment under the command of the Air Technical Service Command. The Navy used the field occasionally for ferrying operations. After the war the field was returned to the city of Jackson for commercial use and part of the

AAF facilities were turned over to the Mississippi Air National Guard. Hawkins remained Jackson's primary airport until 1963, when Allen C. Thompson Airport was built on the east side of town. During the war the base had two auxiliary fields, Hinds County Airport, 3 miles NNE of Raymond and Lime Prairie Airport, 4 miles NNW of Morton.

WAR MEMORIAL BUILDING, 100 S. State St. is located next to the Old Capitol Building and serves as a monument to the soldiers of Mississippi that served in all of America's wars. The building is open for tour M-F 8-4. Phone: 601/354-7207. Free.

LAUREL is 32 miles NE of Hattiesburg on I-59.

LAUREL ARMY AIR FIELD was located three miles SW of town and was used for training purposes. Near the end of the war it was used as a storage facility of aircraft and after the war it became Laurel's main airport.

MERIDIAN is 85 miles east of Jackson and near the state line.

KEY FIELD, 3.5 miles SW of town, was Meridian's local pre-war airport. It was taken over by the 3rd AF shortly before the war and used as an operational and training base. It became the headquarters of the III Tactical Air Div. and provided for the training of combat air crews and tactical reconnaissance groups. The Navy also used the field for ferrying operations.

In mid-Dec., 1941, just a few days after the Japanese attacked Pearl Harbor, 25 P-40 fighters of the 11th Pursuit Squadron stationed at the field were ordered to report, post-haste, to Fairbanks, Alaska to beef up U.S. defense there. The planes and pilots departed at once, flew to California to have their planes winterized, and arrived in Alaska in early January, 1942.

There were four sub-bases attached to Key, one each at Ozark, AL, Demopolis, AL, Hattiesburg, MS and Laurel, MS. After the war the field was returned to the community and once again became a commercial airport, retaining the name Key Field.

PASCAGOULA (See Biloxi/Gulfport/Pascagoula Area)

MISSOURI

Missouri was the home of one of America's two WW II Presidents, Harry S Truman (Independence, MO) and one of the war's more famous general, Omar Bradley (Clark, MO). When Truman became President he bought another Missourian, Robt. E. Hannegan, into his cabinet as Postmaster General. Another Missourian of note was Donald M. Nelson, of Hannibal, MO and executive of Sear, Roebuck & Co. Early in the war Nelson was appointed by President Roosevelt to head the War Production Board which made him the most powerful man in American industry during the war. In April 1944 Missouri's senator Bennet Champ Clark introduced a piece of legislation in the U.S. Senate that would affect virtually every service man and women in the post war years; the "GI Bill of Rights".

Missouri had a diversified economy and had two large industrial centers, St. Louis and Kansas City. Many other towns in Missouri also had manufacturing plants that produced war materials. The state's farms, estimated at 217,520 in 1939, produced cotton, corn, soybeans, oats, hay, meat and lespedeza seed. Her mines provided lead[1], barite, zinc, cement, coal, stone, clay and lime. Her factories produced aircraft, landing craft, tanks, trucks, munitions, iron & steel, drugs & medicines, clothes, footwear and malt liquor.

During the war prisoner of war camps were plentiful in Missouri and helped the state's farmers plant and harvest the crops. Missouri was one of the intended targets of the German saboteurs that landed on the U.S. east coast in June 1942. They had plans to blow up some of the locks on the Mississippi River in the St. Louis area. The saboteurs, however, were arrested before they could carry out their plans.

After the war Missouri went through an adjustment period like most other states, but recovered rapidly and went on to prosper in the postwar years.

BRANSON is 35 miles south of Springfield near the Arkansas border.

[1]Missouri was one of the leading producer of lead in the U.S. In 1942 the state produced 36% of the nation's total output.

Churchill and Truman together at Westminster College, Mar. 5, 1946. Churchill's exact words were "From Stettin (now the Polish city of Szczecin) in the Baltic to Trieste in the Adriatic, an iron curtain has descended across the Continent. Behind that line lie all the capitals of the ancient states of Central and Eastern Europe . . in what I must call the Soviet sphere, and all are subject . . not only to Soviet influence, but to a very high and in some cases increasing measure of control from Moscow."

RIDE THE DUCKS, is a company 2.5 miles west of town on SR 76, that offers local tours in WW II DUKWs (ducks). These are genuine WW II-era 7 ton 6x6 amphibious vehicles that were used in every theater of war. For military purposes they could carry 5000 lbs of cargo, or 25 men on land, or 50 men on water, make 50 mph on land and 5.5 knots on water. The Ride the Ducks Co. has 25 DUKWs which have been modified to be comfortable and safe for passengers, and offers narrated tours around Table Lake and the Branson area. They also own a collection of other types of amphibious military vehicles and a drive through the collection is included in the tours. During the height of the season Duck tours begin every 15 minutes from the "Duck Dock" at the company's offices on SR 76. The ducks then proceed down the road and into the lake. The meaning of DUKW is: D (1942); U (amphibian); K (all-wheel drive); K (rear wheel axles). Address: SR 76 West, Branson, MO 65616. Phone: 417/334-5350. Hours: Mid-Apr. through Oct. daily 8-5:30. Nov. Sat.-Sun. 10-5. There is a charge for the tours.

DOOLITTLE, 6 miles west of Rolla on I-44, was an unincorporated community before the war on old highway U.S. 66. During the war its citizens chose to name their town in honor of General James Doolittle.

FULTON, 20 miles SE of Columbia, was a college town of about 8300 people during the war. Soon after the war ended, Britain's wartime Prime Minister, Winston Churchill, was invited to speak at Fulton's

Westminster College. In the speech, Churchill coined the phrase, "Iron Curtain", that aptly defined the newly established political and geographical division in Europe between the Communist World and the Free World. This dividing line existed for another 43 years throughout the Cold War and constantly referred to as the "Iron Curtain".

WINSTON CHURCHILL MEMORIAL & LIBRARY is on the grounds of Westminster College and commemorates Churchill's famous "Iron Curtain" speech of Mar. 5, 1946. The Memorial pays tribute to the wartime leader of Great Britain and is the only center in the U.S. devoted to the study of Churchill's life. The centerpiece of the Memorial is an 800-year-old English church built by Christopher Wren and known as St. Mary Aldermanbury. The church was severely damaged in the London blitz of 1940 and left unrestored after the war. In the mid-1960s it was brought here in segments and restored to house the memorial and library. The sanctuary is used regularly for church services and the undercroft of the church comprises the museum, gallery and library. Highlighted in the museum are displays on Churchill's 6 decades of public service and his blueprint for world peace. In Nov. 1990, former President Ronald Reagan added one final touch to the Memorial when he dedicated a transplanted section of the Berlin Wall that had been an actual part of the "Iron Curtain". Address: Westminster College, Fulton, MO, 65251. Phone: 314/642-3361,-6648. Hours: daily 10-4:30. Closed Jan. 1, Thanksgiving, Dec. 25. Admission charged. Location: Proceed to U.S. 54 seven miles south of its intersection with I-70. Turn east on Fulton Rt. F and proceed to Westminster Ave., then north on Westminster Ave. to 7th St. and the memorial.

INDEPENDENCE (See Kansas City/Independence area)

JOPLIN is in the SW corner of the state. For

The military version of the DUKW is in the foreground and the Ride The Ducks version is beyond.

almost 100 years it had been the center of Missouri's lead and zinc mining area. Joplin became a boom town during the war when the mines began working around the clock and people flocked to Joplin to work in the mines. There were several manufacturing plants in the area. One of the largest was the Atlas Powder Co. which made TNT in two locations, Joplin and the northern suburb of Webb City.

CAMP CROWDER, about two miles south of Neosho on U.S. 71, was a training camp for the Army's Signal Corps. The camp was built in 1941 and also provided signal training and infantry training to units of the Army Air Forces. Crowder was a segregated camp so negro troops were trained and stationed here. The camp had a main prisoner of war camp holding about 2000 German POWs who worked primarily in the camp. Crowder was closed after WW II, but reopened for the Korean War. Between 1953-58 Crowder served as a branch of the U.S. Disciplinary Barracks.

KANSAS CITY/INDEPENDENCE AREA:

Kansas City and Independence are twin cities in the west-central part of the state on the Missouri River. To the west was Kansas City, KS. The Missouri twin cities had a diversified economy and ranked high in the marketing of wheat, agricultural products and cattle. There were also several sizeable manufacturing concerns in the area and it was an important transportation center.

During the Depression Kansas City had been ruled by a corrupt Democrat machine politician named Thomas Pendergast. In 1939 Pendergast and four of his associates were convicted of income tax evasion and election fraud and sent off to Leavenworth Penitentiary. The state was obliged to step in and reformed the discredited Kansas City Police Department. All the while, Harry S Truman, Missouri's senator from neighboring Independence, remained unscathed by the scandal, although his name had often been linked with the Pendergast machine in the past. In 1942 Truman's reputation and notoriety soared when he headed a Senate committee that conducted a highly publicized investigation into waste and corruption in the construction of military camps and bases around the U.S. Truman's investigation, which was squeaky-clean, brought forth disclosures of wrong-doing that caused a national uproar and brought about needed reforms. Truman's prestige rose to the point where, in 1944, President Roosevelt selected him to be his Vice Presidential running mate for the coming national elections. Roosevelt was re-elected for his fourth term and Truman became Vice President. On Apr. 12, 1945 President Roosevelt died suddenly in Georgia and Truman acceded to the Presidency. He was the first Missourian to hold that office.

Some of the major manufacturers in the Kansas City/Independence area were North American Aviation Co., which built B-25 bombers, Rearwin Aircraft & Engineering, Inc. which made gliders and Oldsmobile Div. of General Motors which made 75 and 90 mm shells. In early 1942 the Federal Government transferred the Farm Credit Bureau from Washington, DC to Kansas City to relieve overcrowding in Washington. Later in the war the Army estab-

The Lake City Ordnance Plant.

lished its Effects Bureau in Kansas City to handle the personal effects and belongings of soldiers killed or missing in action.

KANSAS CITY QUARTERMASTER DEPOT was located at 601 Hardesty Ave. It was one of the largest Quartermaster depots in the country with large sub-depots in Leavenworth, KS, Omaha, NE, and St. Charles, MO. The Kansas City depot remained active into the 1950s when it was converted into an Army records and archives center known as the Kansas City Records Center. Eventually the center was abandoned by the Army and the old depot was converted into an industrial facility.

LAKE CITY ORDNANCE PLANT was 8 miles east of Independence. It was built in 1940-41 and was 1 of 13 small arms ammunition plants then being built by the U.S. Government. Lake City was operated by the Remington Arms Co. and produced 30 and 50 calibre ammunition, and made more types of this ammunition than any other plant in the country. The plant was retained by the Government after the war and in the postwar years was called Sunflower Ordnance Plant.

TRUMAN FARM HOME is located on Blue Ridge Blvd. in the southern suburb of Grandview. The farm house was built in 1894 and between 1906 and 1917 young Harry S Truman lived here with his family and helped his father farm the surrounding land. The farm land has long been developed but the house remains and has been restored and opened to the public. It is furnished with items of the 1900s including some things that belonged to the Truman family. Address: 12301 Blue Ridge Blvd., Grandview, MO 64030. Phone: 816/881-4431. Hours: June 15-Sept. 15 vary, inquire. Admission charged.

HARRY S TRUMAN HISTORIC DISTRICT: This is an area of near-downtown Independence that was Harry Truman's neighborhood. He knew ever inch of it because he spent most of his life here and walked through the area frequently on his daily morning walks. To tour the district, it is recommended that the visitor obtain

a local map or take a conducted tour. Maps, tickets and tour information are available at the Ticket & Information Center located at the corner of Truman Rd. and Main St. (223 N. Main St.) Independence, MO 64050. Phone: 816/254-7199. Hours: Memorial Day through Labor Day daily 9-5. Closed on Mondays the rest of the year. Tickets are free and given on a first-come-first-served basis.

Historic Independence Square & Independence Square Courthouse: Here in the old courthouse, lawyer Harry Truman began his political career as a County Judge. His court room and office are restored to the period when he presided, and an audio-visual presentation traces his life before he became President. Address: Independence Square, Independence, MO 64050. Phone: 816/881-4431, -4467. Hours: Apr. 15-Nov. 15 Wed.-Sat. 9-5, Sun. 1-5. Rest of year by appointment. Admission charged.

Memorial Building, 416 W. Maple Ave: This was Truman's polling place for over 30 years. Here, on June 27, 1945, Truman gave his first press conference in Independence, MO after becoming President, and it was here that he voted in Nov. 1948 when he won his first elected term as President. In Dec. 1972, when Truman was on his death bed, the building was used as a central communications point, and it was from here that Truman's death was announced and details of his state funeral were covered.

Truman Boyhood Home, 909 W. Waldo: Truman lived in this house as a boy from 1896 to 1902. It is in private hands and not open to the public.

Truman Home, 219 N. Delaware: Harry & Bess Truman lived in this house from the time of their marriage in 1919 until their deaths. During Truman's Presidency this 14-room Victorian house became known as the "Summer White House" because he returned to it frequently. Upon her death in 1982, Mrs. Truman donated the house and grounds to the United States. It is now a National Historic Site and open to the public. It is decorated in period furnishings and in the garage is the Truman's

The Home of President and Mrs. Truman in Independence, MO.

last personal car, a 1972 Chrysler Newport sedan. Harry Truman purchased it new and Bess Truman used it until her death in 1982 at which time the odometer read 18,000 miles. Across the street at 216 N. Delaware is the former home of Harry Truman's aunt, Margaret Noland. It was here that young Harry Truman and a high school classmate, Bess Wallace, would meet to study Latin. Bess Wallace eventually became Mrs. Truman. Phone of the Truman Home: 816/254-9929. Hours: Memorial Day thru Labor Day daily 9-5, rest of year Tues.-Sun. 9-5. Closed Jan. 1, Thanksgiving and Dec. 25. Admission charged.

Truman Library & Museum: This magnificent museum and library is at the north end of the Truman Historic District on U.S. 24 and N. Delaware St. It contains Truman's official and personal papers, memorabilia, artifacts and family belongings. In the court yard, President and Mrs. Truman are buried side-by-side. Of special interest in the museum is a reproduction of the Oval Office of the white House circa 1948 when Truman was President. On the desk is a sign with the motto that Truman made famous, "The Buck Stops Here". The museum has exhibits of Truman's boyhood, his military career in WW I, his life as a civilian soon after-

wards, then as a local politician, senator, Vice President, President and ex-President. Other exhibits offer extensive information on the critical closing months of WW II which were Truman's first months as President. There are also displays on the historic Potsdam Conference and the Korean War which erupted during Truman's last term in office. Other displays include the table upon which the United Nations Charter was signed, a piano Truman played at the White House, china and paintings form the White House, memorabilia form the battleship "Missouri", a presidential limousine, several of Truman's personal cars and several audio-visual presentations. Address: Independence, MO 64050. Phone: 816/833-1400. Hours: daily 9-5. Closed Jan. 1, Thanksgiving and Dec. 25. Admission charged.

KNOB NOSTER is 50 miles ESE of Kansas City on U.S. 50.

SEDALIA ARMY AIR FIELD was two miles south of Knob Noster and 18 miles west of Sedalia, MO. The air field was built new by the War Department early in the war and was first known as Sedalia Glider Base. The facility changed names no less than 7 times between 1942 and 1951. For most of the war, however,

it was known as Sedalia Army Air Field and was used by the I Troop Carrier Command as a training base for glider pilots and crews. It also provided transitional flight training for transport pilots. The field had a branch prisoner of war camp holding about 140 POWs who worked on the base. Sedalia AAF was declared surplus in 1946, but reopened by the US Air Force in 1951 for the Korean War. It remained an active Air Force base after that war and in 1955 was given yet another name, Whiteman Air Force Base. This name honored 2nd Lt. George A. Whiteman, a native of Sedalia, who was the first airman to die in aerial combat in WW II. Lt. Whiteman was stationed at Wheeler Field, Hawaii when the Japanese attacked on Dec. 7, 1941. He attempted to take off in his P-40 fighter plane to engage the enemy but was shot down on take-off and died in the crash.

Whiteman AFB remained an active Air Force base throughout the Cold War. During WW II the Sedalia AAF had as an auxiliary field Kansas City-Grandview Airport, 3 miles SW of Grandview, MO.

LAMAR is in the SW corner of the state 25 miles NNE of Joplin. In 1884 Harry S Truman was born here.

HARRY S TRUMAN STATE HISTORIC SITE consists primarily of the modest 1 1/2-story frame house in which Harry S Truman was born on May 8, 1884. His father, John A. Truman, was a farmer and dealer in livestock. The family lived in this house only 11 months after Harry was born. They then moved to Belton, MO, then to Grandview, MO and finally settled in Independence, MO in 1890. The house measures 20 x 28 feet and has four rooms downstairs and two room upstairs. There is an outdoor smokehouse and a hand-dug well. Address: 11th St. and Truman Ave. Lamar, MO 64759. Phone: 417/682-2279. Hours: M-Sat. 10-4, Sun. noon-4. Closed Jan. 1, Easter, Thanksgiving, Dec. 25. Free. Location: From the intersection of U.S. 71 and U.S. 160, proceed east on U.S. 160 to Truman Ave. Turn north on Truman Ave. 1 block. The Truman house is on the west side of Truman Ave.

LOUISIANA is 50 miles NW of St. Louis on the Mississippi River.

MISSOURI ORDNANCE WORKS near Louisiana, MO was built early in the war and operated by the Hercules Powder Co. to produce synthetic ammonia. The facility had a branch prisoner of war camp holding about 100 POWs who worked in agriculture. In 1945 the plant was acquired by the Bureau of Mines and was converted into a facility to produce synthetic oil from coal and lignite based on recently captured secret German processes. This was the largest of four such plants established in the country at the time.

MALDEN is in the SE corner of the state on U.S. 62 and SR 25.

MALDEN ARMY AIR FIELD was three miles NW of town.

The Harry S Truman Library & Museum, Independence, MO.

It was established by the AAF for the 70,000 Pilot Training Program and was used by the I Troop Carrier Command as a training field. In 1946 the field was declared surplus and eventually became a local airport. During the war it had the following auxiliary air fields:

- Aux. #1, Dexter Airport, 1.5 miles SE of Dexter
- Aux. #3, Risco Airport, 2 miles west of Risco
- Aux. #4, Gideon Airport, 1 mile SE of Gideon
- Aux. #6, Campbell Airport, 3 miles east of Campbell

NEVADA is near the WSW edge of the state 50 miles north of Joplin.

CAMP CLARK was a WW I encampment located four miles SE of Nevada, MO. and was used as a mobilization center for the Missouri National Guard during that war. It was retained by the National Guard after WW I and during WW II it was used to train and again mobilize the Guard. When large numbers of prisoners of war began arriving in the U.S. in late 1942, Camp Clark had available space and thus acquired a main prisoner of war camp holding about 4200 German POWs. Later in the war the POW camp became a center primarily for German NCOs. After the war the Missouri National Guard returned to Camp Clark.

SAINT JOSEPH is 35 miles north of Kansas City on the Missouri River. The town had a large Army Quartermaster Depot at 409-415 3rd St. which was a sub-depot of the Kansas City Quartermaster Depot.

ROSECRANS FIELD was three mile NW of downtown St. Joseph on the west side of the Missouri River. Before the war it was St. Joseph's local airport. In July 1942 the AAF's Air Transport Command (ATC) moved onto the field to establish an air freight terminal and to train pilots and crews in C-46 transports. Many of the pilots were former airline pilots. The ATC did not take over the field, but shared it with the existing civilian tenants. In Sept. 1942 the AAF's Ferry Command also moved onto the field and began training ferry pilots and crews. Training at Rosecrans emphasized long-range flying and flying on instruments. In June 1943 the C-46 training operations moved to Reno, NV where the pilots and crews could get specialized flight training over mountains in preparation for their ultimate destination, the China-Burma-India theater, where they would fly supplies over the Himalayan Mountains (The Hump), from India To China. Meanwhile, Rosecrans field became a training base for pilots and crews in C-47 transports. After the war the AAF left the field and turned part of its facilities over to the Missouri Air National Guard. The main field eventually became known as Joseph-Rosecrans Memorial Airport.

SAINT LOUIS: In 1939, when WW II began in Europe, St. Louis was already a city on the move. It was experiencing a building boom, up 30% over 1938, and the city was well on its way to eliminating industrial smoke pollution that plagued many large U.S. cities at the time. There was also an exciting and bold plan underway to build a national park in downtown St. Louis. Forty square blocks of slums and blighted area on the city's waterfront were to be demolished and turned into the national park honoring Thomas Jefferson and commemorating the great western migration.

The powder magazine at Jefferson Barracks houses a museum.

The metropolitan St. Louis area had long been a major industrial center and as America's war needs increased so did the fortunes of the area's manufacturers. In 1941 the world's largest small-arms ammunition plant was built in St. Louis. Other large manufacturers in the area were the Missouri Shipbuilding Co. which made landing craft, the Chevrolet Motor Div. of General Motors which made 6x6 trucks, Curtiss-Wright Corp. which made cargo planes and A-25s, American Car & Foundry Co. of St. Charles which made M-3 light tanks, St. Louis Car Co. which made tanks, St. Louis Aircraft Corp. which made training planes, Laister Kauffman Aircraft Corp. which made gliders, Fisher Body Div. which made 105 mm howitzers, American Stove Co. which made 500 lb bombs, 40 mm shells and flares, Midwest Piping & Supply Co. which made 1000 lb bombs, Scullin Steel which made 12,000 lb "earthquake" bombs[2], Monarch Metal Weatherstrip Corp. which made 60 mm shells, Amertorp Corp. which made torpedoes, Monsanto Co. made sulfa drugs and other chemicals, National Slug Rejectors (a slot machine manufacturer) made axles for heavy trucks and Universal Match Co. which made aircraft signals.

In late 1941 the Federal Government transferred the Rural Electrification Administration and the Farm Security Administration to St. Louis to relieve overcrowding in Washington, DC.

In 1943, the city lost its mayor, Wm. Dee Becker in a tragic accident. Critics had come down hard on some of the St. Louis-made gliders and declared them unsafe because of a rash of crashes. To prove the critic wrong Mayor Becker offered to ride in one of the gliders over the city. Unfortunately the glider in which he flew lost a wing in flight and came crashing to the ground killing the Mayor and all aboard. Mayor Becker is buried in Belle Fountaine Cemetery on the north side of St. Louis.

JEFFERSON BARRACKS was 10 miles south of downtown St. Louis on the west bank of the Mississippi River. In 1826 the location was chosen as the site for Camp Adams, a large Army central garrison post from which troops could be distributed throughout the Mississippi Valley. Later that year the name of the camp was changed to Jefferson Barracks in honor of Thomas Jefferson who had died on July 4 of that year. Through the years the

[2]One of Scullin Steel's "earthquake bombs was credited with sinking the German battleship "Tirpitz" in a Norwegian fjord.

Barracks expanded and by the late 1930s was an old and historic Army installation and the home of the Regular Army's 6th Infantry Div. It was also the reception center for the 7th Corps area. In 1940 the 6th Infantry moved out, and in Sept. of that year the 11th Army Air Corps took over the Barracks and moved the AAF recruit basic training facility from Scott Fd., IL to Jefferson Barracks. By early 1941 Jefferson Barracks was the Air Corps' largest basic training center in the nation housing some 12,000 men who lived mostly in tents because the existing facilities were inadequate for that number of men. The post also acquired a technical training school for aircraft technicians and a branch prisoner of war camp holding about 430 POWs who worked on the base.

In June 1946 the Barracks was declared surplus by the war Department and eventually became a part of the Jefferson Barracks Historical Park. There is a museum in the old powder magazine, but there is very little reference to WW II.

LAMBERT FIELD, now Lambert-St. Louis International Airport, is 12 miles NW of downtown St. Louis. It was built in 1920 as a private air field, but in 1928 was purchased by the city of St. Louis to serve as the city's main municipal airport. By the beginning of WW II it was a large modern airport. In 1939 James McDonnell started McDonnell Aircraft Co. at the field. His company served as a subcontractor during WW II while developing plans for the production of postwar jet aircraft. Both the Army and Navy shared the field during the war with the commercial tenants. The AAF's Air Technical Services Command operated here as did the Air Transport Command. There was also an AAF air terminal. The Navy had an air reserve unit of long standing at the field that evolved into a naval air station during the war (see U.S. Naval Air Station, St. Louis below). The Naval Air Transport Service and the Naval Air Ferry Command also used the field. The Army left the field after the war turning over some of its assets to the Missouri Air National Guard, while the Navy stayed on for another 12 years.

SAINT LOUIS MEDICAL DEPOT was located at Spruce St. and Tucker Blvd. in downtown St. Louis. This facility stored and distributed medical supplies for the Army. During the postwar years it become known as the U.S. Army Support Center.

SAINT LOUIS ORDNANCE PLANT (U.S. CARTRIDGE): This was a huge plant located at 4300

Lt. Gen. Brehon B. Somerville of the U.S. Army Quartermaster Corps addresses the workers at the new St. Louis Ordnance Plant, July 1942.

Goodfellow Blvd. It was built in 1941 by the Federal Government to manufacture small caliber ammunition and was operated by the U.S. Cartridge Co. The plant was the largest of its kind in the world and at its peak employed 35,000 people. On Dec. 8, 1941, one day after the Japanese attack on Pearl Harbor, the plant produced its first lot of ammunition. Within a year it had produced enough ammunition to supply every U.S. soldier overseas with 1000 rounds of ammunition. At the north end of the plant another facility manufactured 105 mm shells. In June 1945 the plant was closed and much of the machinery sold. In the postwar years the buildings were used to house demobilization personnel records, an Adjutant General's printing center, an Army finance center, a claims and debt subsection, an Army & Air Force aviation picture service. Some of the buildings were sold to private interests. In the early 1950s the manufacture of small arms ammunition was resumed at the plant on a smaller scale than the war years, and in 1966 the manufacture of 105 mm shells was resumed in the north facility by Chevrolet Motor Div. under a Government contract. With time, all the original government-owned buildings were sold to private firms.

SOLDIERS' MEMORIAL MILITARY MUSEUM is located at 1315 Chestnut St. in downtown St. Louis. It was dedicated by President Franklin Roosevelt in 1936 to commemorate St. Louis citizens who died in WW I. The area around the Memorial was later developed into a park named Memorial Plaza honoring St. Louis men and women who died in both WW I and WW II. Across the street from the Soldiers' Memorial Military Museum are memorials honoring those who died in WW II, Korea and Viet Nam. The museum honors all St. Louis citizens who have died in military service since 1800 and has displays of uniforms, small arms, artillery pieces, ordnance, medical equipment, ship and vehicle models, medals, flags, photographs and paintings. Address: 1315 Chestnut St., St. Louis, MO 63103. Phone: 314/622-4550. Hours: daily 9-4:30. Closed Jan. 1, Thanksgiving and Nov. 24-Dec. 25. Free.

U.S. NAVAL AIR STATION, ST. LOUIS began as a naval aviation reserve facility in 1928 on the west side of Lambert Field. By 1941 the Naval Aviation Cadet Training Program (NAVCAD) was well under way and the Lambert facility, which by then was known as U.S. Naval Reserve Aviation Base, St. Louis, was expanded in Jan. of that year to handle its share of Navcads. After the U.S. entered the war and the need for naval aviators increased, NRAB, St. Louis was expanded yet again beginning in Jan. 1942. On Jan. 1, 1943 the facility was upgraded to a full naval air station and named Naval Air Station, St. Louis. Its mission was to provide primary flight training to Navy fighter pilots. Between Mar. and Aug. 1944 the station also trained 732 British Royal Navy and Royal Air Force cadets. By the fall of 1944 the primary flight training program ended and the station was turned over to several naval agencies for their use. These included the Naval Air Transport Service, a Naval Aviation Mobile Training Detachment, a separation center activity and Marine and Navy air reserve training units. After the war NAS, St. Louis came under strong local pressures to close down be-

cause of the increased civilian activities at Lambert Field. The station remained operative, however, and when the Korean War started the station became very active training reservists. After the Korean war a combination of crowded conditions at Lambert Field and Navy budget-cutting spelled the end for NAS. St. Louis and the station was disestablished in Feb. 1958. During the war NAS, St. Louis had the following outlying fields:

- Black Walnut Field, 3 miles east of Orchard Farms
- Creve Coeur Airport, 4 miles NW of Creve Coeur
- Machens Airport, 1 mile NW of Machens
- Meremec Field, 1.5 mile SE of Valley Park
- Sylvan Beach Airport, 2 miles NW of Fenton

U.S. NAVAL AUXILIARY AIR FIELD, SMARTT FIELD, 12 miles NNE of St. Charles, was a local airport before the war known as Neubeiser Field. It was taken over by the Navy early in the war and first used as an outlying field for NAS, St. Louis. Later, Neubeiser was upgraded to a naval auxiliary air field and renamed NAAF, Smartt Field in honor of Ensign Joseph G. Smartt, a naval aviator who was killed at Pearl Harbor. After the war the Navy returned the field to its owners and it became known as St. Charles Smartt Airport.

WELDON SPRING ORDNANCE PLANT, at Weldon Spring, MO, a western suburb of St. Louis, was built in 1940-41 to produce high explosives, primarily TNT, and was operated by the Atlas Powder Co. To house workers the Federal Government built housing developments at St. Charles and Wentzville. Weldon Spring was the nation's largest plant of its kind. It also made DNT and loaded bombs and bags with both explosives. By Jan. 1944 U.S. inventories of TNT, DNT and related bombs reached capacity and more efficient methods of producing TNT had been developed so the Weldon Spring plant was shut down. Six months later, however, it reopened and began producing again in preparation for the final push against Japan. In June 1945, Edward R. Stetinius, the U.S. delegate to the United Nations conference in San Francisco, suggested that the Weldon Spring complex might be used as the new home of the United Nations. Missouri's political leaders lobbied hard for this proposal, but lost

Barracks buildings under construction at Fort Leonard Wood.

out to a site in New York City. A short time later the site was proposed as the site for the new Air Force Academy, but a site in Colorado was selected.

In 1947 part of the Weldon Spring site was acquired by the University of Missouri, another part became a wild life sanctuary and most of the production buildings were acquired by the Mallinckrodt Chemical Works which had developed a process for converting high-grade uranium ore into concentrates and purified compounds.

SAINT ROBERTS is on I-44 70 miles NE of Springfield.

FORT LEONARD WOOD was built in 1940-41 as a division-sized training camp for the 7th Corps area. During its construction the fort was one of the targets of the U.S. Senate's Truman Commission which was investigating waste and corruption in the construction of military bases around the country. The irregularities found here and elsewhere propelled the Missouri Senator into the national spotlight and brought about the creation of a powerful industrial watch-dog commission, the War Production Board, which was chaired by another Missourian, Donald Nelson.

During the war the 6th, 8th, 70th, 75th and 97th infantry divisions trained here as did numerous Army engineer units. The fort had its own air field, a large hospital and a main prisoner of war camp holding about 2700 German POWs. Ft. Wood, as it was known locally, was a segregated camp with training and living facilities for negroes, most of whom were in the Army Engineer Corps. By the time the fort was closed in 1946 it had trained some 300,000 men and women. The fort was reactivated in 1950 shortly after the outbreak of the Korean War as a basic training camp for recruits from 11 surrounding states and as a training facility, once again, for engineer and other technical service units. In 1956 the fort became a permanent installation and served as an Army training post and engineering center throughout the Cold War.

U.S. Army Engineer Museum: This museum is on the grounds of the fort and offers displays related to the fort's history from its beginning in 1940 to the present. The museum building itself is a renovated WW II barracks building. On the grounds around the museum are displayed many types of Army vehicles and equipment including many WW II items. Address: ATZT-PTM-OM Ft. Leonard Wood, MO 65473-5165. Phone: 314/368-4249. Hours: M-Sat. 10-4. Free. Admission to the museum is through the fort's main gate off I-44.

SPRINGFIELD is in the SW corner of the state.
O'REILLY GENERAL HOSPITAL: This was a large military hospital in Springfield treating wounded veterans. It was built in 1941 of temporary wooden construction and had 3232 beds. O'Reilly specialized in neurology, plastic surgery, ophthalmologic surgery and neurosurgery. It had a branch prisoner of war compound holding about 100 POWs who worked at the hospital. In 1946 the hospital was transferred to the Veterans Administration.
VICHY, 10 miles north of Rolla, was an unincorporated community at the start of the war.
VICHY ARMY AIR FIELD, 1.5 miles north of town, was a sub-base to Sedalia AAF and was used by the I Troop Carrier Command for training purposes. The field was vacated by the AAF after the war, but beginning in 1948 the Navy used it as an outlying field to NAS, St. Louis. The airport was eventually abandoned by the Navy and became a local civilian airport.
WEINGARTEN, 50 miles south of St. Louis, was one of the many small community in the U.S. selected to have a main prisoner of war camp. The camp held about 2700 Italian & German POWs who worked in agriculture. After the war the camp was dismantled, but many of the building foundations can still be seen in the area.

MONTANA

The people of Montana call their beautiful state "Big Sky Country". During WW II the Army Air Forces heartily agreed and put thousands of war planes into Montana's "Big Sky" for training purposes and as Lend Lease planes on their way to our wartime ally, the Soviet Union. In the process, the military services used 26 of the state's 106 air fields. In 1942 Montana became the new gateway to Alaska. In that year the Alaskan Highway (AlCan Highway) was completed from northern Alberta, Canada to Fairbanks, AK and a series of air fields, called the Northwest Staging Route, were built and paralleled the highway. These routes were along the eastern slope of the Canadian Rocky Mountains where the land was flat and the routes relatively safe from enemy attacks. Most trucks and aircraft going to Alaska from the "lower 48" now passed through Montana making the state a huge staging area for Alaska-bound traffic.

Montana was not only "Big Sky Country", but it was also "Big Farm Country". Seventy two percent of the state's 560,000 people lived on farms or ranches, making the state a big producer of cattle, grain, potatoes, hay, flaxseed, sugar beets and lumber. Her mines and wells produced copper, zinc, lead, silver, gold, coal and oil. During the war a new and large deposit of chromium was discovered in Custer National Forest.

Before the war Montana was considered an isolationist state, and this sentiment was personified by the state's popular Senator, Burton K. Wheeler. Wheeler was one of the most outspoken isolationists in the nation and often made national headlines because of his strong opposition to President Roosevelt's interventionist policies. When the U.S. was attacked by Japan, however, Wheeler and his constituents in Montana put aside their political views and actively supported the American war effort. Montana's Congresswoman, Jeanette Rankin, also made headlines when, on Dec. 8, 1941, she became the only member of Congress to vote against the U.S. declaration of war against Japan. Rankin was defeated in the next election by a young man named Mike Mansfield. Mansfield went on to become a Montana senator and one of the more powerful men in the U.S. Senate in the postwar years.

Being a big and sparsely populated farm state, Montana suffered a severe farm labor shortage during the war. To help solve this problem many prisoners of war were sent to the state and many Mexican laborers were brought in. The labor shortage never was resolved and persisted in varying degrees throughout the war.

Montana was on the receiving end of the Japanese Bombing Balloons that came down in North America. Thirty-six separate instances are recorded. No significant damage was done, but they were a concern and a nuisance.

CUT BANK is 80 miles NW of Great Falls.
CUT BANK ARMY AIR FIELD, 2.5 miles SW of town, was built for the 2nd AF during the winter of 1942-43 to be one of group of four training bases[1], all in Montana, which worked together in a joint training program. Each base

[1]The other three were Lewiston AAF, Malmstrom AAF and Glasgow AAF.

A WW II hangar in use at Cut Bank, MT.

The pre-war terminal building at Gore Field remains and is used for administrative purposes. Most of the WW II buildings are gone, having been sold at auction or torn down.

A C-47, painted with Soviet Air Force markings, awaits transfer to the Soviet Union. Beyond the C-47 is a B-25 bomber also awaiting transfer.

was to be the home of a B-17 bomber squadron which was to practice mid-air, long distance link-ups with the squadrons stations at the other three fields. This aerial maneuver was a necessary part of overseas operations in order to carry out massive bombing raids. The flat and featureless landscape of eastern Montana also figured into the training program because at night it was very similar to blacked-out England and tested the crew's ability to find their way home in the dark. Unfortunately, Cut Bank AAF had a serious problem in that the runways began to deteriorate soon after construction. The problem came about because the concrete used in them was poured in the dead of winter with frozen aggregate. When warm weather arrived the aggregate thawed and the concrete began to settle and break up. Throughout most of the program work crews had to continually patch the air field's runways. Primarily for this reason the link-up program was discontinued after only five months and Cut Bank AAF was placed on stand-by status while it was determined what to do about the runway problem. Eventually, in 1943, the runways were patched up as best they could be and the base was used as a transit base for Lend Lease aircraft going to the Soviet Union. Most of these planes were fighters and light bombers so their lighter weights did not damage the runways as had the B-17s. In the postwar years the runways were repaired or replaced and the air field remained in use and became Cut Bank's local airport.

GLASGOW is in the NE corner of the state.

GLASGOW ARMY AIR FIELD, .7 miles north of town was the community's pre-war airport and was taken over by the 2nd AF to become one of a group of four training bases, all in Montana, which worked together in a joint training program concerning link-up training for B-17 bomber crews. New runways were built during the very cold winter of 1942-43, and when warm weather came they began to settle and break up. See Cut Bank AAF, above, for details on the program and the runways. After the war the field was returned to the

community. In the post war years, the US Air Force built a large air base near Glasgow, but on a different site.

GREAT FALLS

is in the east-central part of the state, is 65 miles NE of Helena on the Missouri River.

GORE FIELD, 3.5 miles SW of town, was Great Falls' local airport before the war. When the war started the Government leased a large part of the field and acquired additional land. Many new buildings were constructed and the field was then used as a base for ferrying Lend Lease supplies and planes to the Soviet Union via Canada and Alaska. Civilian operations continued at the field and the runways were shared. The Alaska Wing of the Air Transport Command (ATC) operated the field and used Great Falls' local fairgrounds as a sub-depot providing additional warehouse space. From Gore Field thousands of tons of Lend Lease goods and airplanes were flown up the Northwest Staging Route through Canada to Fairbanks Alaska, and eventually to the Soviet Union. Most of the Lend Lease aircraft that passed through Gore were P-39 fighters and C-47 transports. During 1944 Northwest Orient Airlines began operating several air routes out of Gore Field under Government contract adding to the already heavy traffic at the field.

In late 1944 the other large air field in town, Great Falls Army Air Field, or "East Base", as it was more often called, became available, and most of the ferrying operations were moved from Gore to East Base. The depot operations at the fairgrounds were also moved to East Base. One ATC ferrying group, and the Northwest Orient Airlines opera-

tions remained at Gore Field until Nov. 1945. After that, some of the Government assets were turned over to the Montana Air National Guard and most of those remaining were sold at auction. Gore Field was then returned to civilian use and, during the post war years, became Great Falls International Airport.

GREAT FALLS ARMY AIR FIELD ("East Base") was three miles east of town. During the war it was more often referred to as "East Base" and in the postwar years it became Malmstrom Air Force Base. East Base was built for the 2nd AF during the winter of 1942-43 to be one of four training fields for B-17 bomber squadrons practicing aerial link-up maneuvers. Great Falls was the Group headquarters for the four squadrons. See Cut Bank AAF, above for details on the training program and problems with the runways. By Oct. 1943 the bomber training operations ended and in late 1943 the base was turned over to the Air Transport Command to relieve the crowded conditions at nearby Gore Field on the west side of town. Gore was an important ferry station for Lend Lease aircraft going to the Soviet Union via Canada and Alaska. In Jan. 1944 East Base took over the bulk of the Lend Lease operations. Since the planes involved in Lend Lease were lighter aircraft the problems with the runways were reduced. In early 1944 Gore's sub-depot, which had been operating from the local fairgrounds, also move to East Base. During 1944 Lend Lease deliveries to the Soviet Union increased significantly and East Base was busy most of the time handling P-39 and P-63 fighters, A-20 attack bombers, B-25 bombers

Malmstrom Air Force Base Museum, Malmstrom AFB, Great Falls, MT.

The main gate of Ft. William H. Harrison, now the Montana National Guard facility known as Camp Stan Stevens.

A sign at the main gate reminds visitors that this was training camp of the famous First Special Service Force (Devil's Brigade) of WW II.

and C-47 transports being sent to the Soviet Union. The planes were usually flown to East Base directly from the manufacturers. At East Base they were inspected, serviced if necessary, winterized, painted in the Soviet colors and with Soviet insignias and test flown. They were then flown by American ferry pilots up the Northwest Staging Route to Fairbanks, Alaska. At Fairbanks they were turned over to Soviet pilots who flew them to the Soviet Union. East Base also had air routes across Canada to Hudson Bay and Greenland, a debarkation hospital, a mechanics school, an arctic training school and an aircraft modification center. During 1944 East Base reached its peak population of 2300.

At the end of the war Lend Lease operations stopped and East Base became an AAF separation center. In Dec. 1946 a new base commander arrived, Col. John S. Chennault, son of the Gen. Claire Chennault of Flying Tiger fame. In 1948 the base was taken over by the US Air Force and in 1955 was renamed Malmstrom Air Force Base in honor of Co. Einer Axel Malmstrom who had served at the base during and after the war. On his 58th mission over Germany, Malmstrom was shot down and became a POW. Malmstrom died in an air crash in 1954. Malmstrom AFB remained active throughout the Cold War.

Malmstrom Air Force Base Museum & Air Park:
This museum is located on the grounds of Malmstrom AFB just inside the main gate and records the history of the base from its beginning to the present. Included are displays on the various units stationed here, a reconstructed WW II barracks room, small arms, uniforms, dioramas, ordnance, maps, aircraft models, photographs, paintings and more. In the air park are vintage aircraft and missiles. Address: 840 CSG/CDR, Malmstrom AFB, MT 59402-5000. Phone: 406/731-2705,-4044. Hours: June thru Aug. M-Sat. noon-3, Apr.-May and Sept-Oct. M-F noon-3, rest of year M, W & F noon-3. The Air Park is open during daylight hours. Free.

HELENA is in the west-central part of the state and is the capital city of Montana.

FORT WILLIAM H. HARRISON, five miles NW of Helena, was established by the Army in 1895. During WW II it became a training camp for small Army units including one very special elite force, the First Special Service Force. This unit consisted of one Canadian and two U.S.

regiments and was organized at Ft. Harrison. The Force was trained as a commando-like unit which could be dropping into critical areas of Europe, behind enemy lines, and carry out specific missions before being pulled out by Allied aircraft. The First Special Service Force began training at Ft. Harrison in the summer of 1942. Training was intensive and lasted throughout the winter. Norwegian instructors were brought in to provide specialized cold weather training. By spring 1943 the unit was ready for combat and took part in the Kiska invasion in Aug. 1943. After that it went to the Mediterranean area and saw considerable action in Italy & France where it gained a reputation as being one of the best units in the U.S. Army. In Europe the Force acquired another name, the "Devil's Brigade", which was given to it by the Germans because of it ferocity in battle.

After the war Ft. Harrison became the home of the Montana National Guard and the Montana Military Academy. In recent years the name of the fort was changed to Camp Stan Stevens, but it is remembered locally as Fort Harrison, the training camp of the "Devil's Brigade".

CAMP RIMINI was a small camp of 160 acres in Helena established by the Army to train war dogs. It was operated by 20 Army officers and 200 enlisted men and trained mostly sled dogs for work in northern Canada and Alaska.

USS HELENA MEMORIAL, located at Last
Chance Gulch Mall and Wong St., is an outdoor memorial that commemorate the four cruisers that have borne the "USS Helena" name; 1896-1932, 1939-1943, 1945-1972 and 1987 to the present. Both the second and third "Helena" saw action in WW II. The second "Helena" was damaged at Pearl Harbor, but was repaired and fought at Guadalcanal, Savo Island and Cape Esperance where she was sunk by the Japanese with the loss of 168 crewmen. The third "Helena", which was purchased by the people of Montana, served at the end of the war both in the Atlantic and Pacific, and later in Korea. The memorial consists of the propeller, anchor, anchor chain and bell from the third "Helena". Plaques at the memorial give the battle records

The "USS Helena" Memorial in Helena, MT honors the four ships that have borne that name. Two of ships served in WW II.

This was the main hangar at Lewiston AAF. Late in the war its roof was raised to accommodate B-29 bombers, but the B-29s never came.

This was the air field's bombsight safe. After each flight the bombardier was required to remove his top-secret Norden Bombsight from the plane and store it here. The safe was guarded around-the-clock by sentries. The fire plug was part of the air field's original water and sewer system which remained in use for many years.

of the other "USS Helenas" including the second "Helena".

KALISPELL is a picturesque community in the Flathead Valley in the NW corner of the state. On Dec. 11, 1944 a woodcutter and his son found a deflated, but nearly intact balloon, in the forest near town. The gas bag was made of

paper and there was an assortment of shrouds and metal parts, some of which had oriental characters on them. The woodsman called the local sheriff, who called the FBI, who called the Army, Navy and Army Air Forces, who all sent representatives to examine the curious find. The military was very concerned because this was the four such balloon had been found in recent weeks in North America and Hawaii. It was known by now by the U.S. authorities that the balloons were of Japanese origin and carried bombs that were time-released as the balloon free-floated on the winds. What the authorities didn't know as yet was where the balloons were coming from.

Most theories pointed to the balloons being launched form Japan itself, but the possibility that they were being launched from submarines, or warships, or even from a Japanese relocation camp had not been ruled out. On Dec. 14, 1945 the local newspaper in Libby, MT printed the story of the finding and stated that ". . the balloon was large enough to

have carried 6 or 8 men and had Japanese flags at both ends". These things were untrue, but alarmed citizens didn't know it and thought that Japanese saboteurs were in their midst. The Libby newspaper report, and a second report also published in the country[2], were so grossly exaggerated that they became a factor in the decision by the U.S. Government to try to keep future balloon discoveries as secret as possible.

LAME DEER is a small farming community in the SE corner of the state. On Jan. 13, 1945, at approximately 4:00 pm in the afternoon, a Japanese Bombing Balloon was seen coming to earth by local citizens. This was one of the rare times that balloon landings were witnessed. The balloon's gas bag, shrouds and gas relief valve were recovered. No one was hurt.

LEWISTON is near the center of Montana 80 miles SE of Great Falls.

LEWISTON ARMY AIR FIELD, just SW of town, was built for the 2nd AF during the winter of 1942-43 to be one of four training bases, all in Montana, which worked together in a joint training program. Unfortunately, Lewiston's runways were not sound and began to break up in the spring. See Cut Bank above for details of the training program and the runways. Like the other three bases, Lewiston was used for only a short time. Later in the war it was prepared to receive B-29 bombers, but the B-29s never came.

After the war the air field was turned over to the community of Lewiston and became Lewiston Municipal Airport.

MISSOULA is an old gold mining and lumbering town near the west-central edge of the state.

FORT MISSOULA, three miles SW of downtown Missoula on the Bitterroot River, was established in 1876-77 to protect the local settlers from the Indians. The fort was garrisoned continuously until 1898, and thereafter intermittently until WW I, when it served as an Army mechanic's school. Between the wars the fort was used by the Army Reserves and other government agencies, and was the home of the Regular Army's 4th Division until 1941. In that year, the 4th Div. departed and the fort was turned over to the

The Italian compound at Ft. Missoula, MT in 1942.

[2]The first published report was made by the local newspaper in Thermopolis, WY.

This WW II DUKW (Duck) was used for decades after the war in the local logging industry. DUKWs would work in the rivers and lakes pushing logs around.

Immigration and Naturalization Service to become an internment camp for enemy aliens. Before the U.S. entered the war Italian seamen were kept here along with a few Germans. In mid-Dec. 1941, several days after the U.S. went to war, some 650 Japanese aliens arrived from the west coast. As the war progressed more Japanese aliens came to Ft. Missoula from other parts of the country, from other internment camps and from Latin American countries such as Peru, Bolivia and Nicaragua. The Italians, Germans and Japanese were kept in separate compounds because it was discovered that they did not mix well. Many of the internees worked outside the camp in local agriculture, especially the sugar beet industry. From time-to-time they were given passes to go into Missoula. In late 1944, after Italy changed sides in the war, the Italian aliens were released or sent elsewhere, and in early 1944 many of the Japanese aliens were released. The remaining aliens were then sent to other internment camps, and in Apr. 1944 the fort was taken over again by the Army and converted into a medium-security Disciplinary Barracks with a capacity of 1250 prisoners. By late 1946 all the prisoners had been released or relocated and by May 1947 the fort was idle. In the postwar years the fort was utilized by a variety of agencies including the Army Reserves, the National Guard, the ROTC, the U.S. Forest Service, the University of Montana and several county and city agencies.

Historical Museum at Fort Missoula, MT: This museum is in the Fort's old Quartermaster's Warehouse which was built in 1911. It traces the history of the fort and preserves the history of Missoula County and western Montana. The museum's exhibits rotate, and only a few relate to WW II. Address: Bldg. 322, Fort Missoula, Missoula, MT 59801. Phone: 406/728-3476. Hours: Memorial Day-Labor Day, Tues.-Sat. 10-5, Sun. noon-5. Rest of year Tues.-Sun. noon-5. Donations accepted.

POLSON is 50 miles north of Missoula.

THE MIRACLE OF AMERICA MUSEUM, in Polson, has a large and interesting collection of western, pioneer, patriotic and military artifacts including a considerable collection of WW II items. Among the WW II artifacts are small arms, ordnance, posters, captured enemy equipment, uniforms, sheet music, post cards, ads and military vehicles including an amphibious DUKW (Duck) which was used in the logging industry for many years after the war. Address: 58176 Hwy. 93, Polson, MT 59860. Phone: 406/883-6804. Hours: Memorial Day thru Labor Day M-Sat. 8-dusk, Sun. 2-dusk, rest of year M-Sat. 8-5, Sun. 2-6. Location: 3/4 miles south on Hwy. 93 from its junction with Hwy. 35.

SWEETGRASS is in NW Montana on the Canadian border. Here, in the early staged of WW II the Americans and Canadians worked out a unique way to delivery American-made war planes to Britain. U.S. neutrality laws permitted friendly belligerents such as Britain and Canada to purchase American-made war materials but required that they come to the U.S. to accept delivery and transport the war material out of the U.S. at their own expense. This arrangement was called the "Cash and Carry" program and predated Lend Lease. At Sweetgrass two air strips existed side-by-side, one on the American side of the border and the other in Canada. A wire fence was all that divided them. Therefore, U.S.-made planes were flown to the air strip on the U.S. side, a hole was opened in the fence and the Canadians came across the border with a team of horses and dragged the aircraft onto the Canadian air strip. This simple arrangement satisfied the delivery requirements of the U.S. neutrality laws. From Sweetgrass, the planes found their way to England.

NEBRASKA

During WW II Nebraska was a sparsely populated state and almost purely agricultural. It's many farms produced corn, wheat, oats, hay, potatoes, sugar beets, hogs, cattle, chickens and dairy products. The industry that existed was an outgrowth of agriculture such as meat packing, leather goods, milling and confectionery. The state had a small lumbering industry and a few manufacturing firms. In late 1939 oil was discovered in the SW part of the state, but the oil fields were small and Nebraska was not a significant oil producer during the war.

WW II brought significant changes to Nebraska especially in the field of manufacturing. During 1942 there was a great surge of industrial activity in the state with the building of many new war plants in her larger cities, especially in Omaha. Many new military installations were also built in the state. A labor shortage occurred on the state's farms as men went off to military service, and both men and women went to work in the new war plants. To help alleviate the labor shortage, many prisoners of war were sent to the State. Nebraska had five main POW camps and about a dozen branch camps. The POWs worked in all aspects of agriculture.

In July 1944 a group of pilots being trained in Nebraska acquired a B-25 and permission to fly the plane to Boston and New York City over the weekend to visit relatives. While approaching its landing in New York City in fog and drizzle, the plane crashed into the side of the Empire State Building killing 14 people including all aboard the plane. This was one of the most publicized air accidents of the war.

Nebraska was one of the states on the receiving end of the Japanese Bombing Balloon attacks of 1944-45. Five separate instances are recorded of balloons coming down in the state. The balloons did no damage and most of the residents of the state were unaware of the balloon attacks because of the great secrecy surrounding them.

AINSWORTH is in the north-central part of the state.

AINSWORTH ARMY AIR FIELD was the local airport 6.5 miles NW of town. It was used by the AAF as a sub-base for several of the larger air fields in the area.

ALLIANCE is in the center of the state's western panhandle.

ALLIANCE ARMY AIR BASE was built in 1942 4.5 miles SE of town to be one of three training centers in the U.S. for glider-carried infantry troops and paratroopers. Alliance AAB had one auxiliary field, Alliance Airport, the town's pre-war airport, 3 miles SW of town. After the war the new field became Alliance's primary airport and the town's pre-war airport site was abandoned.

ASHLAND is midway between Omaha and Lincoln on I-80.

CAMP ASHLAND, was a Nebraska National Guard tent camp near Ashland, build on 878 acres of land. It was constructed as a temporary camp.

ATLANTA is in the south-central part of the state.

ATLANTA PRISONER OF WAR CAMP was one of five main prisoner of war camps in Nebraska. It was located SW of Atlanta on US 6/34 and held about 2600 POWs who worked in agriculture and other segments of the civilian economy. After the war the camp was torn down and the land returned to farming. A highway marker and a lone chimney mark the camp's location. The Phelps County Historical Society Museum in nearby Holdrege has a large permanent display on the camp. Museum address: One mile north of US 6/34 on US 183, Holdrege, NE 68949. Phone: 308/995-5015. Hours: M-Sat. 10-5, Sun. 1-5. Closed holidays. Donations accepted.

CRAWFORD is in the NW corner of the Nebraska panhandle.

FORT ROBINSON, now Fort Robinson State Park, was located two mile west of Crawford on the White River. The original fort was first established in 1874 as a frontier fort near the Red Cloud Indian Agency. By WW I the Ft. Robinson Reservation was being used as a remount station for the breeding, training and distributing of thousands of horses and mules to the Army. The fort had also become a reception and training center for war dogs. Dogs were received, trained and distributed to all of the military services. The fort had a main prisoner of war camp holding about 2000 POWs who worked primarily on the base. After the war the fort was declared surplus and was converted into Nebraska's largest state park. The park has a small museum which records the history of Fort Robinson. Park Address: PO Box 392, Crawford, NE 69339. Phone: 308/665-2660.

GENEVA/BRUNING/FAIRMONT: These three communities are 50 to 60 miles SW of Lincoln and are close to each other along US 81.

BRUNING ARMY AIR FIELD, 8 miles east of Bruning, was a small air field used by the AAF. It had a small bombing and gunnery range 3 miles to the SW. In 1946 Bruning AAF was declared surplus.

FAIRMONT ARMY AIR FIELD was located three miles south of Fairmont. It was established by the 2nd AF as a training field for very heavy bombers. In Sept. 1944 the 393rd Bombardment Squadron (B-29s) arrived here for training. This was a very special unit because the 393rd was one of the AAF units chosen to deliver the yet-to-be-developed atomic bomb. The Squadron, commanded by Capt. Frederick C. Bock, completed its training here and then went on for further training at Wendover Field,

UT, and then to Tinian Island in the Pacific. On Aug. 9, 1945 Capt. Bock and his crew dropped the second atomic bomb on Japan at Nagasaki. The plane they flew was named "Bock's Car". A few days later Japan surrendered unconditionally. In 1946 Fairmont AAF was declared surplus.

GRAND ISLAND is 90 miles west of Lincoln.

CORNHUSTER ORDNANCE PLANT was a new munitions loading facility in Grand Island built by the Federal Government early in the war. The plant loaded 100 lb bombs and M-104 boosters.

GRAND ISLAND ARMY AIR FIELD, three miles NE of town, was the area's local airport before the war. It was taken over by the 2nd AF and used as an operational training base for crews of very heavy bombers (B-29s). The field had a branch prisoner of war camp holding about 100 POWs who worked in agriculture. After the war the air field was returned to the local community.

HASTINGS is 20 miles south of Grand Island.

HARVARD ARMY AIR FIELD was located three miles NE of the town of Harvard. The air field was built for the 2nd AF and used as an operational training field for the crews of very heavy bombers (B-29s). The field had a branch prisoner of war camp holding about 90 POWs who worked at a variety of jobs in the area. After the war Harvard AAF was declared surplus and abandoned.

U.S. NAVAL AMMUNITION DEPOT, HASTINGS was a huge Navy depot near Hastings that manufactured and stored ammunition for the Navy. It had an extensive system of igloo bunkers that stretched for some 10 miles around the plant. During the postwar years the depot was abandoned by the Navy.

KEARNEY is on I-80 and 50 miles SW of Grand Island.

KEARNEY ARMY AIR FIELD, four miles NE of town, had been the area's local airport before the war. It was taken over by the AAF and used

At Fort Robinson state Park, many of the old fort's buildings remained in use including some which were used for guest lodgings.

A B-29 Superfortress on display at the Strategic Air Command Museum near Omaha, NE.

jointly by the Continental AF and the Air Transport Command. Kearney became a staging field for air units going over seas after completing their state-side training. The field had an air freight terminal and a branch prisoner of war camp holding about 150 POWs who worked in agriculture. After the war Kearney was retained and transferred to the US Air Force. For several years it was part of the Strategic Air Command. Eventually the field was returned to the community and became the area's local airport.

LINCOLN, in the SE corner of Nebraska, is the state's capital city.

LINCOLN ARMY AIR FIELD, five miles NW of town, was the city's local airport before the war. In 1939-40 it was one of the fields used by the Air Corps in their civilian pilot training program whereby Air Corps cadets were taught to fly by private flying schools. In this case the school contracted by the Air Corps was the Lincoln Airplane & Flying School and it offered basic flight training. The contract with the school was terminated, however, because the local weather interfered with the training. Later in the war the air field was taken over by the AAF and used as a basic flight training center for AAF recruits. Still later, Lincoln AAF became a staging field for combat-ready units going overseas. The field had a regional AAF hospital and a school for aircraft mechanics. In Mar. 1945 a Combat Crew Processing & Distribution Center was also established here. In 1946 the field was declared surplus by the AAF and was returned to its civilian owners to become Lincoln Municipal Airport.

McCOOK is in the SW corner of the state near the Kansas state line.

INDIANOLA PRISONER OF WAR CAMP was one of the five main prisoner of war camps in Nebraska. The camp was near the town of Indianola, which is 10 mile east of McCook, and held about 700 German NCO POWs who worked in agriculture and for the military. In May 1945 the POWs were shown films of the horrors discovered in the Nazi concentration camps, and soon afterwards issued a statement condemning their own Nazi Government for committing such atrocities. This was one of only a very few such statements issued by

German POWs in the U.S. After the war the camp was closed and abandoned.

McCOOK ARMY AIR FIELD was 9 miles NW of McCook and had been the city's local airport before the war. It was taken over by the 2nd AF and used as an operational training field for crews of B-17s, B-24s, and later, B-29s. After the war the field was returned to the community of McCook and once again became the local airport.

OMAHA, in eastern Nebraska on the Missouri River, was Nebraska's largest city. Omaha had, during the war, one of the largest stock yards in the Plains States and 12 meat packing companies. One of the larger manufacturing firms in the city was the Omaha Steel Works which made Landing Ship Tanks (LSTs) and 155 mm shells. In 1941 the Coast Guard built a new depot in Omaha.

FORT GEORGE CROOK AND OFFUTT FIELD: Fort Crook was built 9 miles south of Omaha in 1878. The fort was used for various purposes, including a balloon training center during WW I and later a prison. In 1921 the first landing field and hangar were built to accommodate Regular Army and Reserve flight training and the Post Office Department's growing air mail service. In 1924 the air field, which had been called Flying Field, Ft. George Crook, was renamed Offutt Field. By the mid-1930s flying operations had ended at Ft. Crook and between 1935-1940 the post was occupied only by a small detachment of enlisted men. In 1940 the Glenn L. Martin Co. leased all of the field's flying facilities and 503 acres of land to build a new bomber plant. This facility became known as the Martin-Nebraska Co. and

built B-26 bombers, and later in the war, B-29 bombers. The "Enola Gay", the B-29 that dropped the first atomic bomb on Hiroshima, was built here. The company also modified bombers. The Army continued to occupy Ft. Crook during the war using it as a reception center for the 7th Corps Area and an Ordnance Corps automotive school. The fort had a main prisoner of war camp holding some 700 Italian POWs who worked at the fort and elsewhere. The AAF's Air Transport Command also operated from the field and had a freight terminal here. In 1946 the AAF acquired Ft. Crook and used it as a separation center. In 1948 Ft. Crook was acquired by the US Air Force and renamed Offutt Air Force Base. In Nov. of that year the headquarters of the Strategic Air Command (SAC) moved here from Andrews AFB, MD and the air field was greatly expanded to handle the latest and most modern aircraft in the Air Force's arsenal. During the Cold War Offutt became a very large air and missile base and remained SAC headquarters throughout the Cold War.

Strategic Air Command Museum: This is an excellent and modern museum on the grounds of Offutt Air Force Base with a large collection of aircraft and missiles. The museum's emphasis is on the activities of the Strategic Air Command (SAC), but also tells the history of Ft. Crook and Offutt Field. The life and career of General Curtis LeMay, the "Father" of SAC, is highlighted including his role in WW II as commander of the 3rd Air Division in Europe and the XXI Bomber Command in the Pacific. The museum chronicles the history of military air power from the days of the Wright Brothers to the present. Displays at the museum include a cutaway of a B-25 bomber, a model of an airborne command post, a display on the Tuskeegee Airmen, a Link Trainer, nuclear weapons, a display on military intelligence covert operations, small arms and more. WW II aircraft on display include a B-29, one of only four remaining B-36 bombers, one on only three remaining British Avro Vulcans, a B-17, C-47, C-54, T-33, A-26 and a B-25. Address: 2510 SAC Pl., Bellevue, NE 68005. Phone: 402/292-2001. Hours: Memorial Day through Labor Day daily 8-8, rest of year 8-5. Closed Thanksgiving, Dec.

The minesweeper "Hazard" on permanent display at Freedom Park, Omaha, NE.

25 and Jan. 1. Admission charged. Access to the museum it through Offutt AFB's main gate which is well marked on approaching highways.

FREEDOM PARK is one mile south of Epply Airfield on the west bank of the Missouri River. On display here are two ships, the WW II-era minesweeper "Hazard" and the postwar training submarine "Marlin". "Hazard" is a steel-hulled minesweeper of the Admirable class and one of only two such ships remaining out of 106 built. "Hazard" was built in 1944 and served as a minesweeper, a patrol ship, a convoy escort, a radar picket ship and did anti-submarine duties. She served at Okinawa an in several other naval actions. Retired in 1971, the ship was brought here, put on permanent display and has been designated a National Historic Landmark. The "Marlin" was built in 1953 and served until 1974. Also on display in the park is the anchor and anchor chain of the carrier "Wasp", a huge ship's propeller and minesweeping equipment. Address: 1600 Abbott Dr., Omaha, NE 68110. Phone: 402/345-1959. Hours: Apr. through Oct. daily, 10:30-6, weather permitting. Admission charged.

FORT OMAHA, five miles north of downtown Omaha, was a frontier fort built in 1868 and originally known as Sherman Barracks. During WW II the old fort served as the major station of the 7th Service Command Headquarters units. In 1947 the fort was sold and became the home of the Metropolitan Technical Community College.

OMAHA QUARTERMASTER DEPOT at 22nd & Hickory Sts. was a sub-depot of the Kansas City Depot and specialized in receiving, storing and shipping military vehicles.

SCOTTSBLUFF is in the far western part of the state's panhandle.

SCOTTSBLUFF ARMY AIR FIELD, four miles east of town, was the town's local airport before the war. It was taken over by the I Troop Carrier Command and used as a sub-base and training field for Alliance AAF, Alliance, NE. The field had a main prisoner of war camp holding about 2600 German POWs who worked mostly on the base and in agriculture. After the war the air field was returned to the community and again became the local airport.

SIDNEY is on the southern edge of the Nebraska Panhandle on I-80.

SIOUX ORDNANCE DEPOT was built 12 miles NW of Sidney in 1942 and used throughout the war to store poison gases. In 1943 the Army build a hospital at Ft. Crook for the civilian workers. This was one of the few such hospitals built during the war by the army for civilians. After the war the depot was improved and when the Korean War began it was expanded and eventually became the largest Army installation in Nebraska. In 1962 the depot was renamed Sioux Army Depot but its function remained the same as it had been since the depot's beginning in 1942. During the Cold War several ICBM missiles were emplaced on the depot's grounds.

WAHOO is 30 miles west of Omaha.

NEBRASKA ORDNANCE PLANT was built east of Wahoo and just south of the town of Mead in 1941 as a bomb-loading and ammonium nitrate manufacturing facility. The plant was operated by the Nebraska Defense Corp., a subsidiary of Firestone Tire & Rubber Co. Production began in Sept. 1941 and at its peak the plant employed some 3000 people. By Aug. 1945, when production ended, the plant had produced 2,839,778 bombs ranging form 90 lb fragmentary bombs to 4000 lb "Block Busters". In Nov. 1945 the Army Ordnance Corps took over the plant and placed it on a permanent standby status and used it as a storage facility for ammunition components. The plant then operated off-an-on thoughout the Cold War.

NEVADA

Nevada is one of the larger states in the country but during WW II it was the least populated. On Jan. 1, 1940 the head count in the state was estimated to be 110,000 people, 390,000 cattle and 845,000 sheep. Much of the state was desert waste land and mountains . . of little value in peacetime, but not necessarily in wartime. When the military services needed wide open spaces to use as maneuver areas and bombing and gunnery ranges, Nevada's assets fit the bill. The state was a producer of food and raw materials needed in wartime such as meat, wool, leather, manganese, gold, silver, lead, copper, zinc, molybdenum, vanadium, mercury, brucite, antimony, tungsten[1] and emeralds.

Nevada also had some very liberal laws. It was the only state in the Union that permitted state-wide gambling, which during the war, was not a big industry. Gambling was relegated to the back rooms of smoke shops, pool halls and a few bars and dude ranches. The state also permitted local-option prostitution, but this too was not a big industry. The state's marriage and divorce laws were the most liberal in the country and had attracted nation-wide attention to the state. A couple could get married within minutes of crossing the state line and a spouse could get an uncontested divorce after being a resident of the state for only 6 weeks. When war came to the U.S. servicemen and war workers flocked to Nevada in large numbers to made generous use of all of the above. All during the war a steady stream of GIs and their fiances flocked to Nevada from California for last-minute weddings before the man went overseas. In California a couple had to have a medical examination and wait at least three days after obtaining a California marriage license to marry. In Nevada a couple could get married and have a brief honeymoon on a three-day pass.

The boom times for Nevada began in 1940 and never really ended. And, the Federal Government played a big role in starting the boom. Nevada was one of several states in the U.S. southwest were the Federal Government spent more money per capita than any other section of the country. By 1942 the state's mines were working at maximum capacity and new military installations were either in operation or under construction in many parts of the state. At the end of the state's fiscal year of 1942 the state showed a healthy cash surplus, and such surpluses continued throughout the war.

In Washington, DC Nevada had a capable and well-liked senator, Pat McCarran, who brought a whole new industry to Nevada, the refining of magnesium ore. McCarran's memory is still honored in the state today even though he was known before the war as a staunch isolationist.

By late 1944, however, stockpiles of raw materials had accumulated all over the nation and Nevada's mines began to cut production and layoff miners, but the other segments of the state's economy remained strong.

During the winter of 1944-45 Nevada became a target for the Japanese bombing balloons. Eight separate instances are recorded including one of the very first at Yerington, NV. As the war ended, the state's economy remained healthy because the military chose to stay on. And, as military aircraft got faster and weapons became more destructive, Nevada's wide-open spaces became more attractive than ever to the military as testing grounds. By 1946 it was estimated that the state's population had increased by about 50% to 156,000 people. And, another new industry was beginning to emerge ... casino gambling.

BOULDER CITY is in the southern tip of the state on the Colorado River. The city was built by the Federal Government for the workers and their families involved in the construction, and later the operation, of nearby Boulder Dam (Hoover Dam) which had been completed just before WW II began.

BOULDER CITY AIRPORT, two miles SW of town, was the local airport before the war. It was not taken over by any of the armed services, but the Navy used it from time-to-time and had an ammunition depot there.

CAMP WILLISTON was three blocks south of downtown Boulder City. It was built early in the war to house an Army military police battalion assigned to protect Boulder Dam from enemy attacks and sabotage. The camp was called Camp Williston. In Mar. 1941 the 751st Military Police Battalion, consisting of some 800 men, most of whom were negroes, took up residence at the camp. Their duties consisted primarily of patrolling areas around the dam and along the electric transmission lines. The 751st stayed until Mar. 1944 when it departed for further training and eventually overseas duty. The camp was then declared surplus. After the war the site was used for a public park, an elementary school, a junior high school and a high school.

CALIFORNIA/ARIZONA MANEUVER AREA (DESERT TRAINING CENTER): This was a huge

---

[1]Nevada was the leading producer of tungsten ore in the U.S.

This was the primary product of Basic Magnesium, Inc., ingots of magnesium metal. The metal was used in aircraft construction, incendiary bombs, flares and tracer bullets.

desert training ground which stretched from just east of San Bernardino, CA to a point 50 miles west of Phoenix, AZ and from southern Nevada in the north to Yuma, AZ in the south. The Nevada part of the Maneuver Area was south of Searchlight, NV and SR 164 and stretched to the California and Arizona borders. The area was ysed as a huge training ground for armored units preparing for the invasion of French North Africa which took place in Nov. 1942. There were no camps or other facilities built in the Nevada part of the area. For more details on the California/Arizona Maneuver Area, see both California and Arizona.

FALLON is 55 miles east of Reno.

U.S. NAVAL AUXILIARY AIR STATION, FALLON, 5.5 miles SE of town, began as an emergency landing field constructed by the CAA in 1943. Later that year it was taken over by the Navy for use as an auxiliary field to NAS, Alameda, CA to provide advanced flight training for carrier pilots. The Fallon area was excellent for flight training because it had 360 days of good flying weather. Squadron after squadron of Navy flyers passed through NAAS, Fallon taking 2 to 8 week courses practicing gunnery, bombing and torpedo launching at several bombing and gunnery ranges in central Nevada. In 1946 the station was reduced to caretaker status, but in 1953 it was reopened by the Navy as an auxiliary air station, again to NAS, Alameda, CA, and once more offered advanced flight training to naval flyers and reservists. The station's field was named Van Voorhis Field in honor of Lt. Comdr. Bruce A. Van Voorhis, a Navy flyer who, in 1943, won the Congressional Medal of Honor in the Pacific. In 1972 the station was upgraded to a naval air station and remained active throughout the Cold War. During WW II NAAS, Fallon had three outlying fields; Austin

Airport, 7 miles SW of Austin, Lovelock Airport #2, 9 miles SW of Lovelock, and Winnemucca Air Field #2, 6 miles SW of Winnemucca.

HAWTHORNE is 70 miles SE of Carson City.

U.S. NAVAL AMMUNITION DEPOT, HAWTHORNE was built three miles east of town to store ammunition for the Pacific Fleet. At its peak of operation during the war it employed some 6000 people. The depot was retained after the war and was eventually turned over to the Army. In the postwar years it became known as the Hawthorne U.S. Army Ammunition Plant.

HENDERSON, 10 miles SE of Las Vegas, was built by the Federal Government during the war to house workers at a huge new plant built nearby. The Government planned to abandon Henderson and the plant after the war, but the plant survived and so did Henderson. The town was eventually incorporated in 1953 and became a community of over 40,000 people and Nevada's leading industrial center.

BASIC MAGNESIUM, INC. was a huge plant built in 1940-41 near Henderson to produce manganese ingots from ore which was plentiful in nearby Nye County. At the time of its construction Basic Magnesium was the largest plant of its kind in the world. Nevada's wartime senator, Pat McCarran, was instrumental in getting the plant built here and was able to obtain President Roosevelt's personal support on the matter. The plant utilized the cheap electricity generated by newly-constructed Boulder Dam (Hoover Dam) and at peak production employed some 13,000 people. Magnesium is a light and relatively strong metal and was used in aircraft production. It also burns with a very bright light and was used in incendiary bombs, flares and tracer bullets. By Nov. 1944, however, the nation's inventory of magnesium was sufficient and the plant was closed. The Federal Government planned to abandon the plant, but the State of Nevada bought it and then resold it to a private company.

CLARK COUNTY HERITAGE MUSEUM, in Henderson, traces the

history of Clark County and Henderson. The museum has considerable material on WW II because that era was so important in the development of the County. On the grounds of the museum is one of the original houses built by the Federal Government to house the families of the workers at Basic Magnesium, Inc. The house is painted and furnish as it was when it was new in 1941. It is open to the public and one room is devoted to WW II displays and memorabilia. Address: 1830 S. Boulder Hwy. (US 93/95), Henderson, NV 89015. Phone: 702/455-7955. Hours: daily 9-4:30. Closed major holidays. Admission charged.

INCLINE VILLAGE is at the northern end of Lake Tahoe.

PONDEROSA RANCH is an outdoor museum and theme park based on the famous TV program, "Bonanza" and the sets used in producing the shows. Of interest to WW II buffs is a large collection of military vehicles, many of which are of WW II vintage. The vehicles are stored together on an open lot at the west side of the museum. Address: 100 Ponderosa Ranch Rd., Incline Village, NV 89451. Phone: 702/831-0691. Hours: May through Oct. daily 9:30-5. Admission charged.

LAS VEGAS: It is safe to day that this city, in the southern tip of Nevada, made the most dramatic change of any city in the nation between WW II and the present. It is hard to imagine that today's Las Vegas was little more than a dusty desert town during WW II. The things that made Las Vegas great were, of course, casino gambling and entertainment, but it was during WW II that the city got its initial boost on its road to greatness.

In 1940 Las Vegas had a population of 8422, thanks largely to the construction of Boulder Dam. Then came WW II, and along with it the military, and Basic Magnesium, Inc. in nearby Henderson, and 1000s of war workers . . .and the little desert community became a wartime boom town. On top of this, in 1941-42, two new hotel/casinos, the first in Nevada, were built on SR 6 south of town and people flocked in, mainly from California, to gamble. Gas rationing and other restrictions on transportation

This is one of the original homes built by the Federal Government in 1941 in Henderson, NV to house the workers at Basic Magnesium, Inc. It is restored, painted and furnished as it then.

Part of the military vehicle display at Ponderosa Ranch.

soon diminished the out-of-state gambling trade, but for the brief time it existed it proved to be very profitable and the city fathers of Las Vegas had experienced a glimpse of their future. Throughout the war the two hotels on the highway and the traditional gambling spots in the bars and small hotels clustered around the railroad station in downtown Las Vegas survived quite well filling the entertainment needs of the GIs and local war workers. When the war ended and war-weary Americans finally found time for a much-needed vacation, the trek that had ended in 1942 with gas rationing began anew as thousands of people flocked to Las Vegas to gamble and see the shows. As a result, the town blossomed into an adult entertainment center the likes of which the nation had never seen and by 1950 Las Vegas could claim a population of 28,300.

IMPERIAL PALACE CAR COLLECTION: The Imperial Palace, on the famous Las Vegas Strip, has one of the world's finest antique automobile collections which includes several fascinating relics from WW II. On display are Hitler's super-charged bulletproof 1939 770K Mercedes Benz parade car, a 1939 Alfa Romeo sports car given by Mussolini to his mistress, Hirohito's 1935 Packard 4-door limousine, Franklin Roosevelt's 1936 Ford convertible

equipped with hand controls, Eleanor Roosevelt's 1932 Plymouth touring car, Dwight Eisenhower's customized 1952 Chrysler convertible parade car, Douglas MacArthur's 1942 Packard Clipper Custom, Juan Peron's (Argentina) 1938 Packard Dual-cowl phaeton convertible, and Queen Wilhelmina's (Netherlands) 1933 Buick limousine. There are

The Fuehrer riding in his bulletproof 1939 770K Mercedes Benz which is now on display at the Imperial Place Car Collection in Las Vegas.

also several WW II era military vehicles in the collection. Address: 3535 Las Vegas Blvd. So., Las Vegas, NV 89109. Phone: 702/731-3311. Hours of the Auto Collection: daily 9:30 am-11:30 pm. Admission charged.

LAS VEGAS ARMY AIR FIELD was 8 miles NE of Las Vegas and was the town's local airport before the war. Like most small communities in the U.S. the Las Vegas officials were eager to have the AAF take over and improve their local airport. But, the town of Las Vegas had a serious and unique drawback . . its large and legal red light district. At the insistence of the AAF, the city fathers agreed to shut down the district for the duration of the war. The local airport was then taken over by the Eastern Training Flying Command in 1941 as a training field for aerial gunners, the first of its kind in the U.S. Las Vegas Air Field, as it was first known, began operations on Dec. 9, 1941 just two days after the Japanese attack on Pearl Harbor. Most of the early gunners were trained for B-17 bombers. By 1944 the field was training gunners at the rate of 25,000 a year. The top 10 gunners in each class were treated to a free dinner and show at one of the local hotel/casinos.

After the war Las Vegas AAF closed, but reopened by the US Air Force in 1949, just before the beginning of the Korean War, to train fighter pilots. It was renamed Nellis Air Force Base in honor of 1st Lt. William H. Nellis, a resident of Nevada and a P-47 fighter pilot during WW II who was killed in Belgium while flying his 70th mission. Nellis AFB continued in operation in the postwar years.

CAROL LOMBARD CRASH SITE: On Jan. 16, 1942 the famous movie star, Carol Lombard , wife of actor Clark Gable, was killed in a plane crash at Table Mountain near Goodsprings, NV, 20 miles SW of Las Vegas. Lombard was returning to Hollywood after conducting a war bond drive in the eastern part of the U.S. Also killed in the crash were 6 other civilian passengers including her mother and 15 Army ferry pilots returning to the Los Angeles, CA area.

RENO is in western Nevada about 20 miles north of Carson City. During WW II Reno was the state's largest city with a population of 21,300. Reno was the city of choice for most women who came to Nevada to obtain a quicky divorce. In the 1930s and 1940s, the phrase "she's going to Reno", was synonymous with "she's getting a divorce". Reno experienced

In 1942 people lived wherever they could in Las Vegas. Tents like this one rented for as high as $60.00 a month.

A typical truck-mounted turret used at Las Vegas Army Air Field to train aerial gunners.

rain, the pilots would fly back and forth over the Sierra Nevada Mountains west of Reno, and to simulate the primitive conditions in India and China, the field was unlighted at night. The base survived the war and was turned over to the US Air Force and renamed Stead Air Force Base. It was used for several decades by the Air Force and then turned over to the community to be-

substantial growth during the war with the arrival of the military and some war work, but was not a boom town like her southern sister, Las Vegas.

On Mar. 22, 1945 the shooting war came to Reno when a P-63 fighter plane from Walla Walla AAF, WA shot down a Japanese bombing balloon over the city. When the balloon crashed it caused no injuries or property damage.

RENO ARMY AIR BASE was built in 1942 10.5 miles NW of Reno by the 4th AF as a operational base for combat-ready units defending the west coast. After the threats to the west coast diminished the base was turned over to the Air Transport Command and converted into a training base for transport pilots who were destined to be sent to the China-Burma-India (CBI) Theater to fly supplies over the Himalaya Mountains from India to China. To get experience flying over mountainous ter-

This is the Nevada Military Academy at Reno Stead Airport, housed in renovated WW II barracks.

come Reno Stead Airport.

During the war Reno AAB had two auxiliary fields, Douglas-Tahoe Airport, 2 miles NE of Minden, and Minden Municipal Airport 3 miles north of Minden.

TONOPAH is midway between Carson City and Las Vegas.

TONOPAH ARMY AIR FIELD, 8 miles east of town, was the local airport before the war. It was taken over in 1942 by the 4th AF and converted into a training field for crews of heavy bombers. These crews, along with others from surrounding air fields, used the huge Tonopah Bombing & Gunnery Range south of town. After the war the air field was abandoned by the AAF and was one of the very field air fields in the country not reopened as a local airport.

TONOPAH BOMBING & GUNNERY RANGE, SE of Tonopah was established in 1940 by the Army Air Crops and was one of three[2] large general bombing and

[2]The other two were the Boardman Bombing Range in Oregon and Wendover in Utah.

gunnery ranges in the country. Some 3.5 million acres of land, mostly public domain, was acquired and cordoned off to be a practice range for several training air fields in the SW part of the U.S. The range was used throughout the war and retained after the war. In the postwar years the range was partitioned off for a variety of purposes. The range, or parts of it, became the Las Vegas Bombing & Gunnery Range, Nellis Air Force Range, Tonopah Atomic Energy Commission Test Range, The Nevada Atomic Energy Commission Nuclear Test Range, India Springs Gunnery Range and a desert wildlife refuge.

YERINGTON is 20 miles SE of Carson City. During the war it was a town of 1000 people and the center of a rich farming and ranching area. In late Aug. 1944 a strange event happened on a ranch near town. A cowboy working on the ranch owned by Charles Ragsdale noticed a large, partially inflated balloon settling to earth on the ranch's property. He secured the balloon to a fence post and notified Ragsdale. Ragsdale examined the balloon and had no idea what it was so he called the U.S. Naval Ammunition Depot at Hawthorne, NV. No one at the depot, however, showed any interested in the balloon. He then contacted McClellan Army Air Field near Sacramento, CA, and again found no interest. Since the gas bag was made of fine quality rubberized clothe, Ragsdale cut it up to line a watering trough for his cattle. Three months later, in Nov., a group of military men contacted Ragsdale and wanted to know all he could tell them about the balloon. They believed it was a balloon that had been launched in Japan or perhaps by a Japanese ship off shore. Remnants of the balloon were collected, but it was not until after the war, when the records on the Japanese bombing balloon program were examined, that the American authorities really knew what they had. It was then discovered that the Yerington Balloon was one of a few rubberized silk bombing balloons being tested, at the time, by the Japanese Navy. And, it was the only one of its kind known to have reached North America. Since it was a test balloon it did not carry bombs. Rather, it carried weather recording instruments and a radio to relay back to Japan its progress crossing the Pacific Ocean. The Yerington

Carol Lombard sings the "Star Spangled Banner" at her last appearance in Indianapolis, IN on the morning of Jan. 16, 1942. A few hours later she left by plane to return to Hollywood. See page 155.

Balloon was not the forerunner of the many Japanese bombing balloons that later came to North America. Those balloons had paper gas bags and were developed and launched by the Japanese Army. The Yerington Balloon represented the unsuccessful efforts of the Japanese Navy to develop a bombing balloon in competition with the Japanese Army. In Aug. 1944, when the Yerington Balloon came down in Nevada, its radio batteries were dead after the long trip across the Pacific Ocean and the Japanese, themselves, didn't know that their balloon had reached America.
The Yerington balloon soon after it was recovered by rancher Charles Ragsdale.

NEW HAMPSHIRE

New Hampshire is one of our smaller states, but yet, it contributed significantly to the war effort. The large Portsmouth Naval Ship Yard was one of the major shipbuilding yards in the country. The yard is actually in Maine, but most of the people who worked there were from New Hampshire. Somersworth, Laconia, Manchester, Nashua and Claremont were major manufacturing centers producing industrial machinery, boots & shoes, leather goods, textiles & military uniforms. The state's farms, forests and mines produced lumber, wood, pulp, paper, dairy products, poultry, potatoes, fruit, corn, hay, oats, maple sugar & syrup, clay, feldspar, mica, sand, gravel & stone, and the state's fishermen gave us seafood. The production of lumber, sorely needed for wartime construction, doubled in New Hampshire during the war and several new mica mines were opened to meet the demands of the electrical industry.

The state had only two prisoner of war camps during the war, but in the fall of 1944 the POWs were credited with saving the state's apple crop in the face of a severe farm labor shortage.

New Hampshire had a popular senator in Washington, Styles Bridges from Concord, who served in the Senate from 1937 to 1961. During 1947-53 he became Chairman of the powerful Senate Appropriations Committee. Adm. Thomas C. Kinkaid was also from New Hampshire. He particitaped in most of the major battles in the Pacific and became commander of the 7th Fleet.

In 1945 the question of America's participation in the newly organized United Nations Organization was a widely discussed issue in the state. Since New Hampshire had a long history of conducting public affairs via town meetings, the question of the U.S joining the U.N. was put to a town-by-town referendum.

The results showed that of the 204 towns participating, 202 voted in favor of the U.S. joining the U.N.

BRETTON WOODS, in the northern part of the state on U.S. 302, was a popular resort area. During the war there was very little tourist business and lots of available hotel space.

THE BRETTON WOODS CONFERENCE: In early July 1944 high level financial experts from 44 Allied Nations, including the U.S., Great Britain, France, The Soviet Union and Nationalist China, met at the Mount Washington Hotel in Bretton Woods. The old and elegant hotel had been renovated by the Federal Government especially for the Conference which was officially called the World Monetary Fund Conference. Its purpose was to lay the groundwork for stabilizing world currencies, international trade, borrowing, lending and other financial activities in the coming postwar era. The U.S. dominated the meeting because its economy was, by far, the strongest in the world at the time because its industrial base had remained undamaged by the war, and because the U.S. held huge reserves of international credit and more than half of the world's gold. It was obvious to all that the U.S. would emerge in the postwar years with the world's strongest economy. Preliminary talks between the U.S. and British leaders produced outlines for most of the proposals that would ultimately be accepted by the other participating nations. In order to strengthen and stabilize other world currencies, it was agreed at the conference that the price of gold would be fixed at 35 U.S. dollars per once. This would stabilize the price of gold, and most world currencies because most of them were tied to gold in one way or another. It was also agreed that the International Monetary Fund and the

International Bank of Reconstruction & Development would be the primary institutions responsible for financing the rebuilding of the war-torn nations. These proposals were referred to the U.S. Senate which gave quick ratification on July 19, 1944 by a vote of 61 to 16.

Bretton Woods remained a popular resort community after the war and the room in the Mount Washington Hotel, where the Conference took place, is maintained as a small museum.

MANCHESTER is in south-central New Hampshire.

GRENIER FIELD, four miles south of town, was the local airport before the war. It was taken over by the Army Air Corps in the summer of 1940 to serve as a tactical air field for the defense of New England and as a port of aerial embarkation. When the Army Air Corps became the Army Air Forces in June 1941, the field came under the control of the 1st Air Force. In late May and early June 1942 men and planes (mostly B-17s, P-38s and P-39s) of the newly trained 8th Air Force were staging at Grenier in preparation for their transfer to England when orders suddenly came for several units to fly west to McChord Field in the state of Washington. This was part of a global chain reaction in U.S. military preparations for the coming Battle of Midway Island, half way around the world from Manchester, which eventually fought in early June. The chain reaction began when AAF units from Oahu Island in Hawaii moved forward to reinforce Midway and AAF units from the U.S. west coast moved to Oahu to replace them. The air units from Grenier and other fields, in turn, replaced the west coast units. The Battle of Midway turned out to be a resounding victory for the Americans and the units of the 8th AF were soon released from duty on the west coast and returned to Grenier, and then on to England as originally planned.

During most of the war Grenier was used as an aerial port of embarkation for planes, men and freight by the Air Transport Command which had the headquarters here for its North American Division. Some training was conducted at the field.

After the war the field was returned to its pre-war owners and became Manchester Municipal Airport. The Airport's air field retained the name Grenier Field.

PORTSMOUTH, on New Hampshire's coast, was the state's main seaport during the war. The town's main shipyard, the Portsmouth Naval Ship Yard, was not in New Hampshire, however. It was across the river at Kittery, Maine, but most of the people who worked there lived in Portsmouth. During the war the Ship Yard hired numerous extra workers and often worked around the clock. As a result, Portsmouth suffered the typical problems of shipyard towns around the country. There was a severe housing shortage and the city's services were strained to the breaking point.

FORT CONSTITUTION, three miles east of Portsmouth on Great Island, in the community of New Castle. The fort was built by the British in Colonial days. During WW II it was manned and armed as a part of the Portsmouth defenses and was a sub-post of Ft. Williams, ME. Fort Constitution is preserved and open to the public, but there is little evidence of its role in WW II. Address: SR 1B, New Castle, NH 03854. Phone: 603/436-5294/6607. Hours: daylight hours on weekends. Admission charged.

FORT DEARBORN was a coastal defense position build in 1941 near the town of Rye, NH five miles south of Portsmouth. The fort mounted two 16" guns during the war and was one of the primary defenses for the Portsmouth area. Fort Dearborn operated as a sub-post of Ft. Williams, ME. In 1959 Fort Dearborn was declared surplus and in 1961 was turned over to the state and became a part of Odiorne Point State Park.

CAMP LANGDON was a temporary recruiting and training post established by the Army in 1941 near Portsmouth. It was a sub-post of Fort Constitution and was abandoned after the war.

PORTSMOUTH NAVAL SHIP YARD (See Kittery, ME)

FORT STARK, at the southern end of Great Island, was an old coastal defense position built in 1873. During WW II Ft. Stark was used as one of the defenses for Portsmouth. It was, at first, a sub-post of Fort Constitution and later a sub-post of Fort Williams, ME. In 1949 Ft. Stark was declared surplus. Since then it has been preserved and opened to the public. Address: Seacoast Ranger, c/o Wentworth-Coolidge Mansion, Little Harbor Rd., Portsmouth, NH 03801. Phone: 603/436-5294/6607.

WEST MILAN is in the northern New Hampshire 12 miles NNW of Berlin.

STARK PRISONER OF WAR CAMP, near W. Milan, was the site of the largest prisoner of war escape in the country. The camp held about 300 German POWs who were employed in the surrounding forests cutting pulp wood. The escape occurred when 30 POWs, representing about 10% of the camp's population, simply walked away and into the woods in a coordinated escape attempt. Like most escapes, the majority of escapees either returned to the camp on their own or were soon recaptured. One POW, however, made his way to New York City and managed to support himself for several month by painting pictures and selling them to people in Central Park. His freedom ended when a sales clerk in an art supply store, where the escapee had been buying art supplies, became suspicious of the strange artist with a German accent and reported him to the police.

NEW JERSEY

The state of New Jersey was a very impor tant cog in the American War Machine. The state's strategic location, strong agricultural base and large industrial economy were all-important assets during World War II. The northeastern corner of the state is part of the dynamic New York City metropolitan area and the northern shore of New Jersey forms the western shore of the lower Hudson River and the western edge of New York Bay. For some 25 miles in this area the New Jersey shore was lined with piers, docks, warehouses, manufacturing plants and other industrial facilities. Railroads from all over the nation terminated on New Jersey's waterfront making New Jersey one of America's great centers of both rail and water transportation. Inland from this waterfront area sprawled a huge industrial area that stretched half way across the state and down to New Brunswick. In addition, the state had significant industrial areas at Trenton, Camden, and in several small communities opposite Wilmington, DE.

Like most heavily industrialized states, New Jersey was hard-hit by the Depression, but when war began in Europe and the U.S. began to re-arm, the state's industry sprang to life providing well-paying jobs and a multitude of products. By the end of 1941 defense contracts in the state amounted to $465.67 per person, the largest per capita expenditure in the country. During the war the state produced ships, airplanes, munitions, chemicals, electrical machinery, farm machinery, locomotives & transportation equipment, sewing machines, elevators, fabricated metal products, clothing, military uniforms and many other manufactured products. During the war the state ranked fifth in the nation in defense work.

Central and southern New Jersey was primarily agricultural. New Jersey's farmers, long before the war, had gained for the state the title "Garden State". This came about because New Jersey had tens of thousands of acres of carefully cultivated land and thousands of acres of greenhouses growing vegetables and fruit for the millions of people in nearby urban areas. When war came, this segment of the state's economy, too, began producing at its maximum. It was said of New Jersey during the war that the "Garden State" had became one huge "Victory Garden". In addition to fruits and vegetables, the state's farmers produced poultry, dairy products, processed foods, meat, wheat, hay and corn. The state's fishermen did their share by producing tons of sea food.

In southern New Jersey the ethnic Japanese, displaced from the U.S. west coast and Latin America, found one of the very few havens in the country where they were accepted and could get work.

The state also had mineral wealth and its mines producing zinc, iron ore, stone, clay and sand & gravel.

There was plenty of excitement along New Jersey's coast during the war, especially in early 1942, when German submarines ravaged Allied ships along the state's coast. And, there were nearly constant fears of enemy attacks and/or an invasion. These fears were not unfounded because the Axis nations did have plans to bomb and attack New Jersey's northeastern industrial areas if the opportunity presented itself.

New Jersey hosted 8 prisoner of war camps during the war and many POWs who escaped from camps in other parts of the country attempted to made their way to the New York/New Jersey metropolitan area. Some were successful. Also, a New Jersey facility was an intended target of the German saboteurs that landed on the U.S. east coast in June 1942.

The wartime prosperity was generally good for the state. At the end of the war New Jersey ranked 9th in the nation in the value of its manufactured goods.

ATLANTIC CITY, on New Jersey's southern coast was one of the largest tourist centers on the east coast. It had many fine hotels, amusement centers and the famous "Boardwalk". When the U.S. went to war, Atlantic City was one of several tourist towns in the country where the armed forces requisitioned, leased or purchased large hotels to house and train newly recruited men and women until suitable training camps could be built. Between spring and fall 1942 the Army alone took over 47 hotels in the city and the Navy took over several more. Also, Atlantic City was one of the first towns to receive a unit of the Civil Air Patrol (CAP), and it was here that the first CAP over-water anti-submarine patrols were tested and put into service. All the while, Atlantic City continued to be a tourist center although to a lesser degree than before the war.

In 1944 the Army converted some of the hotels it controlled into one of six redistribution centers[1] in the U.S. for returning service personnel. They were given several weeks of morale-lifting rest and relaxation before being sent on

[1]The others were at Lake Placid, NY, Asheville, NC, Hot Springs, AR, Miami Beach and Santa Barbara, CA.

to new assignments. The Army Air Force also acquired 6 hotels and the city's convention center and converted them into its own redistribution center for its personnel. That same year the Army converted the Haddon Hall Hotel into a 3650-bed general hospital to treat war wounded. The facility was called England General Hospital in honor of Lt. Col. Thomas M. England, MAC, USA. It specialized in neurology, amputations and neurosurgery. In June 1946 the Army's lease on the hotel was canceled and the facility was returned to its owners.

U.S. NAVAL AIR STATION, ATLANTIC CITY, 10 miles NW of town, was Atlantic City's new municipal airport before the war. It was taken over by the Navy in July 1942 for use as an operational base for coastal patrol bombers and fighters. Meanwhile, a second air field, an extension of NAS, Atlantic City, was built during late 1942-early 1943 near Egg Harbor City, three miles NW of the main station. The Egg Harbor facility was used for the training of fighter, bomber and torpedo bomber squadrons. A bombing and gunnery range was established over the ocean for use by those pilots training at Egg Harbor. In late 1943 the main station was expanded and converted into a training facility also to meet the increasing needs for naval air units in the Pacific. The station acquired a Fighter Director School which was established at the Brigantine Hotel in Atlantic City. By Apr. 1945, when training operations began to scale back, NAS, Atlantic City had trained 49 squadrons. When the war ended NAS, Atlantic City was retained and several fleet air units took up residence here. The station was used for a variety of purposes in the postwar years and eventually closed in 1958. The main station then reverted to civilian use and became Atlantic City's main airport. During the war NAS. Atlantic City had two outlying fields; Bader Field 1.3 miles WSW of Atlantic City, and Woodbine Air Field, 2 miles SE of Woodbine, NJ.

BELLE MEAD is 8 miles south of Somerville on U.S. 206.

BELLE MEAD SERVICE FORCES DEPOT, near Belle Mead, NJ, was an Army depot occupied jointly by the Quartermaster Corps, Engineer Corps, Ordnance Corps and Signal Corps. It received, stored and shipped items for all of these services. The depot survived into the postwar years and became known as Belle Mead General Depot. In the early 1950s, though, it was inactivated.

BRIDGETON, at the southern end of the state, was the center of a large truck gardening and food processing area. Since this industry are very labor-intensive, the general manpower shortage was a very serious problem here. To get laborers, business leaders, especially those of the Seabrook Farms, Corp., actively recruited ethnic Japanese from the relocation camps in the west. This was one of the very few places in the nation to do so. The ethnic Japanese worked in the fields and in the processing plants and were found to be good workers and caused no trouble. German prisoners of war were also employed in the area. When the war ended and the ethnic Japanese returned to the west coast and the POWs were repatriated to Europe, Seabrook Farms recruited over 100 Peruvian-Japanese who had been forbidden to return to Peru by the Peruvian Government. In addition, they also hired some 2600 ethnic Japanese who had renounced their U.S. citizenship during the war and were trying to regain it in a long draw-out court case. These people found it hard to obtain employment anywhere, but the ethnic Japanese who had preceded them proved to be such good workers, the doors were open to these people. The renunciants, however, were closely watched and not allowed to travel more than five miles from their place of employment.

CAMDEN, on the east bank of the Delaware River opposite, Philadelphia, was heavily industrialized and most of its industry converted to war work including its several ship yards. The area's largest ship yard, the New York Shipbuilding Corp., built large warships including battleships and aircraft carriers. The RTC Shipbuilding Corp. built tankers for the Navy and the Mathis Yacht Building Corp., in nearby Gloucester City, built sub chasers. The Radio Corporation of America (RCA) had major manufacturing facilities at Camden and was one of the leaders in the development and production of radar, submarine detectors and other electronic equipment for the military.

GLOUCESTER INTERNMENT CAMP in Gloucester City was one of two enemy alien internment camps in the U.S.[2] for women. It was run by the Immigration and Naturalization Service.

CAPE MAY is at the

[2]The other was at Seagoville, TX.

southern end of the state guarding the entrance to Delaware Bay.

U.S. NAVAL AIR STATION, CAPE MAY was at the north edge of Cape May at Sewall's Point and fronted on Cold Spring Inlet. A naval air station existed here during WW I, but in 1922 it was turned over to the Coast Guard which used it as a Coast Guard station and a training facility. In 1942 the station was reclaimed by the Navy as an operational base for anti-submarine activities and inshore patrolling. Coast Guard operations, however, continued at the station. NAS, Cape May operated a degaussing range, floating dry cock, radio station, radio direction-finder station, Marine barracks, pigeon station and Frontier base. In 1946 the station was again relinquished to the Coast Guard and remained in Coast Guard hands well into the postwar years.

CARNEYS POINT/PEDRICKTON/SALEM: These towns are in SW New Jersey on the east side of the Delaware River opposite Wilmington, DE.

DELAWARE ORDNANCE DEPOT at Pedrickton was a large old depot that had stored munitions between the wars. During WW II it receiving, storing, maintaining and shipping ammunition for the Army. It was a sub-post of Raritan Arsenal and remained active into the postwar years.

E.J. Du PONT de NEMOURS & CO. POWDER PLANT, CARNEYS POINT: Before the war this plant and Picatinny Arsenal, at Dover, NJ, were among the very few plants in the country producing gunpowder on a full-time basis for the U.S. Army. With the onset of war in Europe and the subsequent buildup of U.S. military forces, these plants quickly reached their production limitations. In 1941 the U.S. Government, therefore, began an ambitious plan to build more powder plants and proving grounds throughout the nation. This plant was expanded during the war, but produced only a fraction of the gunpowder used by the armed forces.

HERCULES POWDER PLANT at Salem was one of several plants in New Jersey owned and operated by the Hercules Powder Co. When war came, the plant's production was almost totally devoted to military needs. The Hercules plants made smokeless cannon and rifle powder, nitrocellulose, dynamite, DNT and special propellant powders.

FORT MOTT, 6 miles NW of Salem on the Delaware River, was built in 1872 as one of the coastal defenses for Philadelphia. When WW II started, the fort was still manned and armed with big, but out-of-date guns. In 1943, when the threat of enemy attacked diminished along the U.S. east coast, Ft. Mott was one of the first coastal defenses to be declared surplus. In 1947 the state purchased the fort and made it into Fort Mott State Park and incorporated most of the fort's land into Killcohook Wildlife Refuge.

DOVER is in north-central New Jersey near I-80.

HERCULES POWDER PLANT, at Kenvil, was one of several plants in New Jersey owned by the Hercules Powder Co. During the summer of 1940 an explosion at this plant occurred revealing that the newly developed small-grain smokeless powder was sensitive to pressure

Officers' quarters at Picatinny Arsenal. This area is referred to as "The Birches".

and that it could only be stored safely in containers that did not exceed a certain depth. This hard-won lesson was used through the munitions industry from then on.

PICATINNY ARSENAL, two miles north of Dover, was opened in 1879 to produce and develop ammunition for the Army Ordnance Corps. Through the years it became one of the Army's primary ammunition sources. The Arsenal not only developed military ammunition, but manufactured, assembled and loaded it in large quantities. During the war the Arsenal was extremely busy and to fill its manpower needs, brought in workers from Jamaica and Barbados. After the war the Arsenal continued in operation and became the nation's most important ammunition research and engineering facility in both the nuclear and non-nuclear fields. In the 1990s the arsenal was closed.

U. S. NAVAL AMMUNITION DEPOT, LAKE DENMARK, 7 miles from Dover, was established by the Navy in 1892 to store and supply naval ammunition needs in the New York area. It was a relatively small facility, only 460 acres, and comprised several hundred storage buildings built rather close together. By 1926 the depot was crammed with left-over WW I ammunition and in the summer of that year a great disaster occurred here. An electric storm started a fire in one of the magazine buildings which exploded and started a chain reaction that destroyed or damaged every building in the depot and set the adjacent woods on fire. The fires burned for a week. This great calamity forced the Navy to re-evaluate its ammunition storage procedures. As a result new and safer storage buildings were designed and future depots were built on much larger tracts of land with the magazines separated much further apart. When WW II began and the Navy began building new ammunition depots across the country, they were built to the specifications developed after the Lake Denmark disaster.

During WW II NAD, Lake Denmark was an active storage facility, and remained a relatively small facility.

LAKEHURST is 30 miles SE of Trenton in the central part of the state. In 1937 the town and its naval station gained world-wide attention when a great disaster befell the new German Zeppelin "Hindenberg". On May 6 of that year the "Hindenberg", after having just crossed the Atlantic Ocean and making a triumphant flight over New York City, burst into flames as it attempted to land at the mooring mast at Lakehurst Naval Air Station. The disaster, caught on movie film, cost 36 lives, destroyed the air ship and contributed to the demise of zeppelins.

U.S. NAVAL AIR STATION (LTA), LAKEHURST, one mile NW of town, was built by the Navy in 1921 on the site of an ammunition proving ground used by the Russian Imperial Government (1918-21) and later by the U.S. Army. In 1921 the Navy, which was just beginning to develop its own zeppelins, chose the site for a lighter-than-air station because it was near the coast, behind natural wind breaks, convenient to both New York City and Philadelphia, and available. Also, the soil could support the huge hangars

A Japanese Bombing Balloon being tested at Lakehurst. The net around the balloon was of U.S. design to retain the balloon during testing.

needed to house zeppelins. Subsequently Hangar #1 was built to house zeppelins and an agreement was soon reached with the Germans for Lakehurst to become the North American terminus for the two German trans-Atlantic zeppelins, the "Graf Zeppelin" and the "Hindenberg." NAS, Lakehurst, thus became North America's first trans-Atlantic international airport. NAS, Lakehurst also became the home port for three American Zeppelins. In 1923 a school was established here to train crewmen for zeppelins, and a parachute school soon followed and survived until 1947. One-by-one, however, the great zeppelins met with tragic ends including the spectacular burning and crash of the "Hindenberg" here in 1937. Soon, the day of the zeppelins was over, but the future of blimps and dirigibles was still promising. Lakehurst, therefore, became a blimp station. In July 1941 28 blimps were assigned to Lakehurst and the construction on Hangars #2 and #3 begun. Other improvements were made and when the U.S. went to war Lakehurst was a fully operational and effective blimp base. Blimps from here conducted coastal patrols and convoy escort throughout the war. There were also a number of conventional aircraft stationed here that performed the same mission. The station had a school for lighter-than-air pilots and crewmen, and trained Canadians and Brazilians as well as Americans. There was also a parachute material school, a radio station, a pigeon station, a photographers school and a Marine barracks. During the war hangars #4, #5 and #6 wer e built to house the large number of blimps operating out of the station. Hangars #5 and #6 ar e the largest single-arch structures

in the world and are made of wood because of the wartime steel shortage. Near the end of the war several Japanese Bombing Balloons, which had been captured intact, were sent here for testing and evaluation.

After the war, blimps faded from military use and helicopters took their place. As a result, Lakehurst became a center for research on helicopters and vertical take-off aircraft. The huge hangars were also used by the Navy from projects that needed lots of space. Hangar #1, for example, housed the world's largest training aid, a 400' long mini-aircraft flight deck used to train sailors for work on carriers.

NAS, Lakehurst remained operational throughout the Cold War and in 1968 Hangar #1 was declared a National Historic Landmark. After 1977 the station was known as Lakehurst Naval Air Engineering Center.

LONG BRANCH (See Sandy Hook/Long Branch Area)

MILLVILLE is in the south-central part of the state.

MILLVILLE ARMY AIR FIELD was an existing air field three miles SW of town when the U.S. went to war. According to a pre-arranged plan it was taken over by the 1st AF for use as a fighter base for the defense of the east coast. Later in the war, when the threats to the east coast, lessened, Millville AAF was converted into a training field for fighter pilots. Although, in keeping with its original use, the training specialized in the bombing of ships. After the war the AAF departed and the air field was returned to the community.

PAVIN STATE PARK PRISONER OF WAR CAMP: There was a prisoner of war camp established in Pavin State Park, 10 miles NW of Millville. The POWs were employed in military-related work and food processing.

NEW BRUNSWICK is 25 miles SW of Newark.

CAMP KILMER, two miles east of New Brunswick, was built in 1942 as a staging camp and processing center for troops shipping out of, and returning through, the New York area ports of embarkation. Camp Kilmer worked closely with Fort Dix and together they represented the Army's largest staging facility. Kilmer had a main prisoner of war camp housing Italian POWs. When the war ended POWs from other camps across the nation were sent here and staged until they could be repatriated to Europe. During the war over one million GIs passed through Camp Kilmer. The camp remained active after the war as an Army Reserve Training Center until 1963 when it was closed.

THE NEWARK AREA: This was the largest urbanized area of the state and a part of the metropolitan area of New York City. Newark was the largest of several cities on the New Jersey side of the Hudson River and New York Bay. Four of New Jersey's 6 largest cities were in this area: Newark, Jersey City, Paterson and Elizabeth. Some of the major manufacturers in the Newark area were Federal Shipbuilding & Dry Dock Co., Kearney, NJ, which made a variety of ships including destroyers; Elco Naval Div. which made PT boats and Electro Dynamic Works which made electric motors & generators, both in Bayonne, NJ and both

This 15' bronze sculpture in Liberty State Park is called "Liberation". It depicts an American soldier carrying a survivor out of a German concentration camp. In the background is the Statue of Liberty.

divisions of Electric Boat Co. of Groton, CT; New Jersey Shipbuilding Co., Barber, NJ, which built a variety of vessels for the Navy; Eastern Div. of General Motors at Linden, NJ which built F4F, FM-1 and FM-2 fighter planes for the Navy; Curtiss-Wright Corp. which built aircraft engines at Wood Ridge, NJ and Caldwell, NJ; Otis Elevator Co. of Harrison, NJ which built aircraft components and artillery recoil mechanisms; Monroe Calculating Machine Co. of Orange, NJ which built aircraft components; Crucible Steel Corp. of Harrison, NJ which made shells and projectiles from 37 mm to 16"; Thomas A. Edison, Inc. of West Orange, NJ which made time fuzes, tracer ammunition and ammunition components; Lionel Corp. of Irvington, NJ which made compasses, binoculars and primer parts; Congoleum Nairu, Inc. of Kearney, NJ which made

incendiary bombs, grenades and torpedo parts; N.J. Fulgent Co. of Metuchen, NJ which made incendiary bombs and aircraft flares and Kincaid Mfg. Co. of Perth Amboy, NJ which made flame throwers, gun barrels and gun parts;

Newark was one of the first cities in the U.S. to practice pre-war blackouts. On May 26, 1941, 6 1/2 months before the U.S. entered the war, the city had a 15-minute test blackout.

The Newark area was one of the areas in the U.S. targeted for Axis attacks if and when the opportunity presented itself. Also, the German saboteurs that landed on Long Island and in Florida in June 1942 planned to sabotage the Pennsylvania Railroad Station in Newark. None of these plans were carried out and Newark did not come under enemy attack during the war.

CAVEN POINT ARMY BASE was an Army port of embarkation built early in the war on 340 acres of land bordering New York Bay, almost due west of the Statue of Liberty. After the war it became a training facility for the New Jersey Army Reserves and eventually was converted into Liberty State Park.

NEW YORK NAVY YARD ANNEX is on a peninsula that juts outs from the eastern shore of Bayonne, NJ for over two miles into New York Bay. This man-made peninsula was built with land fill in 1941 and the Navy established a dry dock and ship repair facility here to service and repair large naval and commercial ships that could not easily pass under the Brooklyn Bridge and reach the New York Navy Yard. Construction of this facility was part of the Navy's "Two Ocean Navy" buildup program begun just before the U.S. entered the war. This facility worked closely with the nearby Bayonne Naval Supply Depot. The Annex survived the war and in the postwar years became more of a cargo terminal than a repair facility known as the Military Ocean Terminal, Bayonne.

NEWARK ARMY AIR FIELD was south of, and adjacent to, Newark. This was Newark's pre-war municipal airport built in 1928. By the 1940s it was one of the nation's most modern and busiest airports. The Army Air Corps had had operations at the airport since 1934 when the Air Corps began carrying mail. In 1942 the 1st AF took over the airport, expanded it, and

used it throughout the war as an operational base for the defense of the east coast, and as an air depot, known as the Atlantic Overseas Air Technical Service Command Control Depot. After the war the air field was returned to the community and became Newark International Airport.

RARITAN ARSENAL was established in 1918 on the north bank of the Raritan River four miles SE of Metuchen and three miles west of Perth Amboy. It was known then as Raritan Ordnance Training Camp or as Camp Raritan. Its mission was to store and ship Army ammunition. Raritan was one of the few ammunition storage facilities retained after that war, and in the 1920s the camp was upgraded to an ammunition repair facility and renamed Raritan Arsenal. During WW II it stored, maintained, repaired and shipped Army ammunition and served as a backup arsenal for Seneca, NY and Letterkenny, MD. Raritan was a segregated camp and many negro troops served here. There was also a branch prisoner of war camp holding Italian POWs who worked at the arsenal. The Arsenal survived until 1964 at which time it was closed and its assets disposed of for educational, industrial and recreational purposes.

U.S. NAVAL MUSEUM/SUBMARINE USS "LING" is located near downtown Hackensack at Borg Park. The WW II-era submarine, "Ling", is the main attraction and serves as a memorial to those who served aboard submarines during WW II. The submarine was commissioned June 8, 1945 and served only during the last months of the war. She was brought to this location in 1973. Other displays include artillery pieces, vehicles, scale models, photographs, ordnance and a collection of Japanese periscopes. Address: 150 River St., Hackensack, NJ 07601. Phone: 201/342-3268. Hours: tours daily 10:15-4. Closed Mon. and Thurs. in Dec. and Jan. Admission charged.

U.S. NAVAL SUPPLY DEPOT, BAYONNE was located at the Bayonne Port Terminal on the Bayonne waterfront. It was purchased by the Navy in 1940 and at the time consisted of 153 acres of land and an existing steel-framed transit building. The mission of the new facility was to relieve the New York Navy Yard of procurement, supply, storage and transfer responsibilities so that that facility could concentrate more on ship building and repairs. The Bayonne depot site had excellent rail connections and was on a good deep-water channel. Soon after purchase construction began on 20 large storehouses, one of which was 7 stories and another 6 stories. The depot was expanded further during the war and by war's end consisted of 26 major buildings, four million square feet of storage space and 5000' of waterfront moorings. The depot handled mostly supplies for the North Atlantic theater and was a backup facility for the Norfolk Supply Depot in the Caribbean. The Bayonne depot also had a school for supply officers, pay clerks and storekeepers.

PEDRICKTOWN (See Carneys Point/ Pedricktown/Salem Area)

SALEM (See Carneys Point/Pedricktown/ Salem Area)

SANDY HOOK/LONG BRANCH AREA:

The former New York Navy Yard Annex, later known as the Military Ocean Terminal, Bayonne.

The WW II submarine "Ling" is on permanent display and open to the public in Hackensack, NJ.

This area, at the northern end of the New Jersey coast, is opposite the entrance to New York Bay. Sandy Hook is a long peninsula 1/2 mile wide and five miles long jutting north into Raritan Bay. Because of its strategic location it has had many fortifications built on it over the years. During WW II some of those fortifications were put to use. A Coast Guard station existed at the northern end of Sandy Hook which contained the oldest lighthouse in America, the Sandy Hook Light, built in 1764. This light was operational during the war. All of Sandy Hook was owned by the Federal Government during WW II, but by 1962 most of the military installations there had become obsolete, so in that year 460 acres of land on Sandy Hook was sold to the state of New Jersey and converted into Sandy Hook State Park.

CAMP COLES, at Lincroft, a short distance west of the Garden State Parkway and Red Hook, was established in 1942 as an adjunct and extension of Fort Monmouth. In Apr. 1945 it was redesignated Coles Signal Laboratory.

CAMP EDISON, at Sea Girt, was a New Jersey National Guard encampment before the war known as Camp Edge. It was a small camp and during the war it was used as a training camp for Signal Corps personnel. Also during the war it was renamed Camp Edison in honor of the then-serving Governor of New Jersey, Charles Edison. After the war Camp Edison was returned to the National Guard and served their needs until 1954.

CAMP EVANS, near Belmar, was a small Army camp established in 1942 as a technical facility for the Signal Corps. In 1945 it was redesignated Evans Signal Corps Laboratory.

FORT HANCOCK, at the north end of Sandy Hook, was built between 1892-95 to be part of the coastal defenses of the New York area. A 500-bed hospital was also built on the fort's grounds. This facility, unusual for a coastal defense post, remained active until 1950. Between the wars, Ft. Hancock was the storage facility for many of the Army's big railroad guns. Soon after the U.S. entered the war these guns were rushed to various parts of the country to serve as mobile coastal defense batteries. During WW II the fort's obsolete coastal guns were removed and anti-aircraft batteries installed making the fort a part of the New York area's air defense system. In 1946 a branch of the Army's Disciplinary Barracks was established here. In 1950 the fort was deactivated, but then reactivated in 1956 and used as a radar and missile site. In 1960 the

old hospital became the Sandy Hook Marine Laboratory. In 1972 the fort was declared surplus and eventually became a part of Sandy Hook State Park.

FORT MONMOUTH, two miles NW of Long Branch, was built in 1917 for the Army's Signal Corps and remained a Signal Corps post throughout its life of service. It was originally named Signal Corps Camp and changed names three more times before 1925 when it was renamed Fort Monmouth. During WW II, Monmouth was the home of the Signal Corps and many of the advancements in electronics made during the war are associated with the Signal Corps Laboratory located here. The fort had one of the largest Officer Candidate Schools in the Army and the prestigious Signal Corps School which trained not only Army officers, but officers from the other branches of service, in signal communications. The fort also had a school training men in one of its oldest forms of communication, pigeons. Also during the war a complete and separate training camp was built on the grounds of Ft. Monmouth, known as Camp Charles Wood, to train Signal Corps personnel. Fort Monmouth remained operational in the postwar years and became one of the leading technological centers in the nation in research, development and training of military communications.

U.S. Army Communications-Electronic Museum:

This museum is on the grounds of Ft. Monmouth. It traces the history and evolution of technological developments of Army communications equipment and methods of communication through the years. Exhibits include Civil War communications equipment, carrier pigeons, early radio, airborne radio, vacuum tubes, radio miniaturization, laser technology, solar cells, fuel cells, batteries and cameras. Address: Kaplan Hall, Building 275, Ft. Monmouth, NJ 07703-5000. Phone: 908/532-4390. Hours: M-F noon-4. Free.

U.S. NAVAL AMMUNITION DEPOT, EARLE, 8 miles WSW of Long Branch, was built between Oct. 1942 and June 1944 to store naval ammunition for the naval facilities in New York area. The new depot removed a hazardous activity from a densely populated area and provided opportunities for expansion in those areas vacated. The site chosen, however, was swampy and construction was difficult and slow. The depot's size was increased and additional storage facilities were built for the Army's use. A two-mile-long pier was constructed and provided berths for both Navy and Army ships. Most of the ammunition stored here was shipped to Europe to supply the Allied advance through Europe in the last year of the war. The depot continued in operation after the war and served the Navy throughout the Cold War.

TRENTON, in the west-central part of the state on the Delaware River, is the capital of New Jersey. Some of the city's largest defense plants were the Eastern Aircraft Div. of General Motors which made the famous Grumman TBF Avenger fighter planes, TBM-1 and TBM-3 fighter planes; St. Regis Paper Co. which made plastic aircraft propeller parts and engine deflectors and L.A. Young Spring & Wire Corp. which made 75 mm shells.

U.S. NAVAL AIR FACILITY, TRENTON five miles NW of town, was the area's local airport before the war, Mercer County Airport. The Navy took it over and used it as one of the links in its ferry operations under the control of the Naval Air Ferry Command. After the war it was returned to the community and became the

The main entrance to Fort Monmouth as it appeared shortly after the end of the war. Russell Hall, the post headquarters, is in the center.

area's main airport, Mercer County Airport.

WRIGHTSTOWN is 15 miles SE of Trenton.
FORT DIX, just south of Wrightstown, was established in 1917 on a 49 square mile tract of land that spanned two counties. It was known then as Camp Dix and was used as a training camp for large Army units. From 1922 to 1933 it served as a training camp for regular Army units, Army Reserve and National Guard units. From 1933 to 1939 it served as a reception, replacement and discharge center for the CCC. In 1939 the facility was made a permanent Army post and renamed Fort Dix. By then it was the home of the 1st Infantry Div. and later the 44th Infantry Div. Ft. Dix became an Army reception center for the II Corps, and later a separation center. It had the first Separation School in the country to train men working in the separation program.

Early in the war the ground units of the newly formed 8th AF staged here prior to being transferred to Britain through the New York ports of embarkation. Later, 10 Army divisions and many smaller units either trained here or staged for shipment overseas. The fort had a large Army hospital, Tilton General Hospital, and a main prisoner of war camp holding about 2600 German POWs who worked at the fort and, in agriculture and the food processing industry. Later in the war Italian Service Units worked at the Fort. At its peak, Fort Dix had a population of 70,000.

Fort Dix had its own air field, Fort Dix Airport, during the war which was used by the AAF for anti-submarine patrols and later as an aerial port of embarkation. In 1948 Fort Dix Airport was acquired by the US Air Force and developed into McGuire Air Force Base which was named in honor of Maj. Thomas B. McGuire, a native of Ridgewood, NJ and a WW II Congressional Medal of Honor winner.

At the end of the war Ft. Dix experienced a very unpleasant incident. The U.S. and Soviet Union had reached an agreement whereby the Soviets would return Americans freed from German prisoner of war camps in their zone of occupation in exchange for Soviet citizens held in this country. Unfortunately, most of the Soviet citizens in the U.S. were prisoners of war captured while servicing in the German Army, and therefore traitors to the Soviet Union. These individuals were rounded up and staged at Ft. Dix in preparation for their return to the Soviet Union. When they realized they were to be returned to the Soviet Union and face possible imprisonment or execution, they became unruly. Many tried to escape and some committed suicide. The Army had to place them under heavy guard and watch them carefully. Eventually the Soviet citizens were sent by train to San Francisco where they were returned by ship to the Soviet Union. The U.S. Government regretted this action and the U.S. soldiers hated this duty, but it was necessary in order to get the Soviet Union to cooperate in returning the Americans in their custody.

In 1947 Ft. Dix became a basic training center for the Army and the home of the 9th Infantry Div. In 1956 the fort was renamed U.S. Army Training Center, Infantry. The post remained active throughout the Cold War and was expanded several times.

Fort Dix Museum. This museum, located at Ft. Dix, tells the history of the fort from its beginning in 1917 to the present. There are displays on the fort's construction, its use as a CCC camp, its activities before and during WW II, unit histories and the role of women at Ft. Dix. Address: ATZD-GCD, Ft. Dix, NJ 08640-5000. Phone: 609/562-6983. Hours: M-F 8:30-4, closed federal holidays. Free.

NEW MEXICO

In the 1940s New Mexico was called the "Sunshine State"[1]. That name was very appropriate because sunshine is an important asset in wartime and it was one of the reasons the U.S. military was attracted to New Mexico. Sunshine and a moderate climate are important in the training of aviators & ground troops, the housing prisoners of war and enemy aliens, and in the conducting of outdoor technical research. Another big asset New Mexico had to offer was its wide open spaces which are ideal for proving grounds and bombing and gunnery ranges.

New Mexico produced significant amounts of agricultural products such as cattle, sheep, wheat, corn, beans, sorghum, cotton, cottonseed oil, hay and lumber. Plus, the state produced a whole smorgasbord of minerals; copper, potash, oil, natural gas, coal, zinc, gold, silver, lead, iron, beryllium, gypsum, manganese, molybdenum, helium gas, mica, perite, pumice, salt, lime, stone, clays, sand and gravel. In 1950 a large uranium ore deposit was discovered in the state which turned out to contain nearly ⅔ of the nation's known reserves of that mineral.

New Mexico was one of several states in the west that received one of the highest influx of Federal dollars per capita during the war. This helped the state's mining industry, communications systems in the form of roads and airports, and manufacturing. Wartime growth in these sectors of the economy helped set the pace for New Mexico's continued growth in the postwar years. The state also had a modest tourist industry before the war and this, too, would prosper in the postwar years.

During the war years the state had 17 prisoner of war camps and two enemy alien internment camps giving it a relatively high per capita population of prisoners of war and interned aliens. Most of those incarcerated worked for the military or in agriculture.

Good fortune smiled on New Mexico during the winter of 1944-45 when the Japanese bombing balloon campaign was under way. Not one bombing balloon was known to have come down in New Mexico, while balloons came down in all of the surrounding states and in Mexico.

New Mexico had a man in President Truman's Cabinet at the end of the war, Clinton P. Anderson, Secretary of Agriculture.

ALAMAGORDO is in the south-central part of the state 80 miles NNE of El Paso, TX. To the north and west of the town was one of the largest desert wildernesses in the nation consisting of thousands of square miles of desolate mountains and dry valleys. Dominating this desolate landscape was a hundred-mile-long natural outcropping of gypsum which, over the eons, had been ground by natural forces into a fine white sand. This phenomenon of nature gave the general area its popular name, "The White Sands Area of New Mexico". When, late in the war, the Federal Government had need of a place to test its most secret of secret weapons, the atomic bomb, it chose the "White Sands" area for the test site, and Alamagordo became the staging and supply area for the test. On July 16, 1945 that test, the detonation of the world's first atomic device, took place at a place called "Trinity" 55 miles NNW of Alamagordo. The blast could be seen and felt by everyone in the town and in many small towns around. No one at the time knew what it was they had witnessed because of wartime secrecy, but when the war ended abruptly one month later the people of Alamagordo were told about that mysterious blast in the desert and that they had witnessed, with their own eyes and ears, the dawn of the atomic age.

ALAMAGORDO ARMY AIR BASE, 8.5 miles SW of town, was built in 1942 by the 2nd AF as a training field for combat air crews of very heavy bombers. The field had a branch prisoner of war camp holding about 300 POWs who worked in agriculture.

On July 16, 1945 the world's first atomic device was detonated at the extreme northwest corner of this huge bombing and gunnery range.

In 1947 the AAF shifted it guided missile program to Alamagordo AAF from Wendover, UT and the name of the combined air field and bombing range was changed to New Mexico Joint Guided Missile Test Range. In 1948 the Air Force took over the facility and renamed it Holloman Air Force Base. In the years that followed, Holloman became an operating missile base and a major test facility for missile experiments. Holloman remained an active Air Force facility throughout the Cold War.

WHITE SANDS PROVING GROUND was a huge tract of land roughly 40 miles wide by 100 miles long north and west of Alamagordo. It was established July 9, 1945, only 7 days before the world's first atomic device was detonated inside its boundaries[2]. The next month, August 1945, while two atomic bombs were being dropped on Japan, scientists from Japan's former Ally, Germany, arrived at White Sands Proving Grounds along with American scientists to, in effect, continue the missile and

[1]Later the name was changed to "The Land of Enchantment."

[2]White Sands Proving Grounds absorbed parts of the Alamagordo Bombing and Gunnery Range.

A German V-2 rocket being tested at White Sands Proving Ground in late summer 1945.

rocket research and development programs which had been going on in Germany throughout the war. At this time, the Germans were far ahead of everyone in the development of missiles and rockets for military use. Heading the group of German scientists was Dr. Werner von Braun, the renowned rocket scientist. With von Braun and the Germans came several captured, and fully operational, V-2 rockets, plus plans and engineering data for future rockets up to the V-10. Within a few days of their arrival the first V-2 ever to be fired in America was launched from here.

In the years that followed, many new buildings and laboratories were built at White Sands Proving Grounds and in 1952 the facility was merged with the Alamagordo Bombing and Gunnery Range. The new facility was almost as large as the states of Connecticut and Rhode Island combined. It was given a new name, White Sands Missile Range, and became America's primary development center and testing range for ground-to-ground missile and rockets. The testing of atomic weapons also continued at the Range.

Trinity Site: This site, 55 miles NNW of Alamagordo inside the White Sands Missile Range, was ground-zero for the first atomic device that was exploded here on July 16, 1945. The device was hoisted to the top of a steel tower and detonated from controls on the ground while military people, and the scientists who had designed it, looked on from distant bunkers. This one blast used up the nation's entire supply of plutonium, but more was in the pipeline. The light from the blast was seen in Los Alamos, Albuquerque, Santa Fe, El Paso, TX, Silver City and Gallup, and thunder from the blast was heard in the latter two cities.

Quite naturally, people inquired as to what had happened. The official reply came from the Commander of the Alamagordo AAB stating that a "remotely located ammunition magazine" had accidently exploded with no loss of life. Even workers and scientists at Los Alamos were given the "ammunition magazine" story, but many of them knew the truth. Gen. Groves, who headed the "Manhattan (Atomic Bomb) Project", sent a coded message to Secretary of War Stimson, who was with President Truman at the Potsdam summit conference, that the device had been a success. Truman then informed Churchill and Stalin.

At the site, only a few feet of the legs of the steel tower remains protruding from the ground. A stone monument commemorates the event and a nearby house, in which the device was assembled, has been restored and is open to visitors. This barren site, however, is not accessible to tourist. One cannot drive to it. Tours to the site are offered only twice a year from the White Sands Missile Range and Missile Park (see below) on the first Saturday in April and the first Saturday in October. Hundreds of people usually attend. For information contact the Public Affairs Office, Bldg. 122, White Sands Missile Range, NM 88002. Phone: 505/678-1134.

ALBUQUERQUE is near the geographic center of the state at the junction of I-40 and I-25. During WW II this was one of the cities of the Great Southwest that was "discovered" by both the military and industry. Sizeable new military bases and factories came to Albuquerque and, with them, many people. Albuquerque's central location in the Great Southwest and its mild climate were contributing factor to its wartime growth. Rapid growth was not easy. During the war the city suffered a severe housing shortage, strains on city services and inflation. By 1950, however, these problems had been resolved and the city's population had more than doubled.

KIRTLAND ARMY AIR FIELD, three miles SSE of town, was the city's new pre-war municipal airport, built in 1939 and known as Oxnard Field. It was purchased by the AAF for $1.00 in late 1941 and renamed Albuquerque Army Air Field. In 1942 it was renamed Kirtland Army Air Field. The facility was used by the 2nd AF during the war as a training base for four-engine bombers crews. It also had an aircraft maintenance facility and a bombardier's school. Air transport operations were conducted at the field by the Air Transport Command and there was an air freight terminal here. Early in the war Trans-World Airlines established a flying school here and trained British pilots. Chinese pilots also received transition training at Kirtland. There was a branch prisoner of war camp holding about 125 POWs who worked at the field and in agriculture. After the war the AAF contracted with the city to share the airport for commercial use along with existing military operations. The commercial facilities were at the west end of the field and the military facilities at the east end. In early 1946 activities at Kirtland shifter to assist the Federal Government's expanding atomic energy program. In 1948 the US Air Force took over the field and named it Kirtland Air Force Base. Within the scope of a 7-year expansion plan (1950-57), Kirtland began to acquire a whole host of new facilities including a new weapons center, several research laboratories, test centers and, in 1955, a 13,370' runway, the longest operational runway in the nation. In 1963 the Air Force sold the western portion of the field back to the city for $1.00, but kept the eastern portion. The western portion eventually became Albuquerque International Airport. Kirtland AFB continued to expand in the 1960s and 1970s and became the home of the Department of Energy's prestigious Sandia National Laboratory. Throughout the Cold War Kirtland AFB was one of the Air Force's

J. Robert Oppenheimer, left, Director of the Atomic Laboratories at Los Alamos, and Maj. Gen. Leslie Groves, head of the "Manhattan (Atomic Bomb) Project", stand at the remains of the steel tower upon which the first atomic device was detonated July 16, 1945.

Replicas of the WW II atomic bombs. "Little Boy" (above) was an all-uranium bomb dropped on Hiroshima and "Fat Man" (right) was a plutonium bomb dropped on Nagasaki.

primary research and development centers.

During WW II Kirtland AAF had two auxiliary fields; Santa Fe Airport, 10 miles SW of Santa Fe and Socorro Airport, 2.5 miles south of Socorro, NM.

National Atomic Museum: This fine museum is on the ground of Kirtland Air Force Base and relates the history of atomic energy. Prominently featured are the activities of the "Manhattan Project" centered in New Mexico that developed, produced and tested the first atomic bomb. On display are replicas of "Little Boy" the atomic bomb dropped on Hiroshima, and "Fat Man", the atomic bomb dropped on Nagasaki. The museum also has a replica of a hydrogen bomb and a 53-minute documentary film entitled "Ten Seconds That Shook the World" featuring news clips from the 1930s and 1940s recreating the era of WW II that concluded with the dropping of the atomic bombs and Japan's surrender. Address: PO Box 5400, Albuquerque, NM 87115. Phone: 505/845-6670. Hours: Daily 9-5, closed Jan. 1, Easter, Thanksgiving and Dec. 25. Free. Access to the museum is through either the Wyoming Blvd. Gate or the Gibson Blvd. Gate.

ERNIE PYLE MEMORIAL LIBRARY is located at 900 South Girard. This is the former home of the famous WW II correspondent and Pulitzer Prize winner Ernie Pyle. It is now a branch of the Albuquerque City Library. Pyle and his wife built the house in the 1930s from plans drawn up by Ernie himself. They lived here until 1940. Inside the library is a bust of Pyle and a small display commemorating his life. Pyle wrote about this house from time-to-time in his columns. Pyle was killed on the island of Ie Shima on April 18, 1945 by a Japanese sniper.

SANDIA BASE was an Army Air Forces facility 10 miles SE of Albuquerque just south of old US 66 as it entered the city. It was used during the war as an air depot training station and a convalescent hospital. In Jan. 1946 this facility came under the control of the Armed Forces Special Weapons Project with the mission to work closely with the Atomic Energy Commission on military matters. In 1959 Sandia Base became part of the Defense Atomic Support Agency, and in 1971 it was incorporated into Kirtland Air Force Base and evolved into Sandia National Laboratory.

CARLSBAD is in the SE corner of the state near the Texas line.

CARLSBAD ARMY AIR FIELD, 6 miles SW of town, was established for the AAF' as part of the 50,000 Pilot Training Program. This was a bombardier training facility which specialized in training bombardiers and air crews in bombing through clouds. Some Chinese aviators were trained here. The field had a branch prisoner of war camp holding about 200 POWs who worked on the base and in agriculture. After the war the air field became Carlsbad's local airport. During the war Carlsbad AAF had an auxiliary field, Carlsbad Air Field, 11 miles south of Carlsbad.

CLOVIS is on the east-central edge of the state.

CLOVIS ARMY AIR FIELD, five miles west of town, was Clovis Municipal Airport when it was taken over by the Government in 1942 for use as a training base for glider pilots. This plan was short-lived and the field became a training field for the crews of heavy bombers, meteorologists and weather reconnaissance personnel. The field had extra long runways and also specialized in blind landings. The air field had a small branch prisoner of war camp holding about 50 POWs who worked on the base. In the latter months of the war Clovis AAF became a training field for crews of B-29s, and in 1945 it became a separation center for the AAF. In 1948 Clovis AAF was taken over by the US Air Force and named Clovis Air Force Base. In 1951-2 it served as an Air National Guard Base, but in 1953 the Air Force returned and the base became part of the Tactical Air Command. In 1957 it was renamed Cannon Air Force Base in honor of General John K. Cannon who, during WW II, commanded air operations during the invasion of southern Europe and later served as Commander-in-Chief of USAFE in the Mediterranean. Cannon AFB remained operational throughout the Cold War.

CAMP WILLIAM REID, near Clovis, was established in Apr. 1942 as a training center for Army railroad units. Army personnel were trained to operate trains in both the U.S. and Europe. Most of them served in North Africa, Italy, France and Germany.

DEMING is in the SW corner of the state on I-10.

DEMING ARMY AIR FIELD two miles SE of town, was the local airport before the war. It was taken over by the 2nd AF as part of the 50,000 Pilot Training Program and served as a training field for bombardiers and as a base for tar-

get towing aircraft. The field had a branch prisoner of war camp holding about 200 German POWs who worked on the field. After the war, Deming AAF was returned to the community of Deming and became not only a civilian airport again, but the local fairgrounds and an industrial park. Deming AAF had three auxiliary fields during the war:
- Aux. #1, Deming Air Field (south), 19.5 miles SW of Deming
- Aux. #2, Deming Air Field (center), 11.5 miles west of Deming
- Aux. #5, Las Cruces Airport, 8.5 miles west of Las Cruces

LUNA MIMBRES MUSEUM, near downtown Deming, is the city's local museum. Just south of the museum is Veteran's Memorial Park dedicated to the memory of those who served in New Mexico's National Guard which was inducted into the Army in Jan. 1941 and sent to the Philippines. They were there when the Japanese invaded and endured the long and bitter struggles on Bataan and Corregidor. Most of the men of the unit were eventually captured and forced to take part in the infamous "Death March". They then spent 40 months as Japanese prisoners of war under horrible conditions. When they were eventually liberated in 1945 some 900 of their original number of 1800 had died. Displays inside the museum give details on the men and their ordeal. Address: 301 S. Silver St., Deming, NM 88031. Phone: 505/546-2382. Hours: M-Sat. 9-4, Sun. 1:30-4, closed Thanksgiving and Dec. 25. Donations requested.

FORT STANTON is 50 miles NE of Alamagordo.

FORT STANTON INTERNMENT CAMP: Ft. Stanton was originally a frontier fort built in the late 1800s to protect settlers from the Indians. By 1899 the threat had ended and the fort was used by the U.S. Public Health Service as a hospital for men of the U.S. Merchant Marine suffering from tuberculosis. In 1940 the Immigration and Naturalization Service (INS) had need of an internment camp to hold the growing number of aliens from the Axis nations being incarcerated in the U.S. under the edicts of the Geneva Convention. Heretofore, enemy aliens had been held at existing INS immigration stations at major U.S. ports of entry. These stations were becoming overcrowded. After a site search the INS chose Ft. Stanton because it was remote from populated areas, in a relatively warm climate and could be put into operation in a short time. This was the INS's first new internment camp of the war. The tuberculosis patients were moved to other facilities and the fort was made ready to house aliens. The first aliens to arrive here, in Jan. 1941, were the seamen from the German ocean liner "Columbus" which was scuttled by its crew off the coast of New Jersey in late 1939. The seamen had first been taken to Ellis Island in New York Bay, then to Angel Island in San Francisco Bay and finally here. After the U.S. went to war, this camp was designated as a camp for hard-core pro-Nazi aliens. Those interned here were kept under heavy guard and seldom allowed to leave the camp. At the end of the war they were all repatriated to Germany and the fort, once again, became a hospital for tuberculosis patients. In 1953, with new treatments available for tuberculosis and the need for such hospitals declining, the fort was sold to the state of New Mexico for use as a state hospital and training center for the mentally retarded.

FORT SUMNER is 55 miles west of Clovis.

FORT SUMNER ARMY AIR FIELD, two miles east of town, was established by the 2nd AF in 1942 for the 70,000 Pilot Training Program and was used as a training field for fighter pilots. It fulfilled this mission throughout the war. The field had a small branch prisoner of war camp holding about 100 POWs who worked in agriculture. The field had two auxiliary air fields; Aux. #5, Ft. Taiban Airport, 7 miles north of Taiban and Aux. #7, Tucumcari Airport, 7 miles east of Tucumcari. After the war Fort Sumner AAF became the area's local airport.

GALLUP is in the NW part of the state on I-10.

WINGATE ORDNANCE DEPOT, 12 miles east of town, was located at Ft. Wingate Military Reservation. Old Fort Wingate was first established in the 1850s but fell into disuse prior to WW I. In 1918 the fort was selected by the Army to be a munitions storage depot after a series of disastrous munitions explosions in the New York area near the end of WW I. Large quantities of surplus WW I munitions were moved here and the post was named Wingate General Ordnance Depot. In the years between the wars Wingate was active shipping munitions to Army units all over the country and to the Panama Canal Zone and the Philippines. In 1936 there was a major expansion of the post with the construction of more magazines and igloos. In 1940, just after the beginning of WW II, the first shipments of US-made munitions to Britain and France came from Wingate. At that time the depot's entire stock of TNT was sold to the British and French. In 1941 Wingate underwent another large expansion and newly manufactured munitions from ordnance plants all over the country poured into Wingate for storage and distribution. Many Indians were employed here. Those Indians who could not read had their time cards and other documents stamped with their cattle brands. On May 7, 1945 the scientists and engineers at White Sands Proving Ground detonated 100 tons of TNT in order to test and calibrate their instruments in preparation for the detonation of the first atomic device. The entire 100 tons of TNT came from Wingate. At the end of the war activity and employment dropped off sharply at Wingate, but resumed again during the Korean War. In the early 1960s the depot was used as a test site for missiles and became a preserve for buffalos. Following that, the depot continued in operation throughout the Cold War and was closed in the 1990s.

HOBBS is in the SE corner of the state near the Texas state line.

HOBBS ARMY AIR FIELD, 6 miles NW of town, was established by the 2nd AF in 1942 for the 50,000 Pilot Training Program. It was operated by the Western Flying Training Command and trained bombardiers and the crews of four-engine bombers. After the war the facility was abandoned as an air field. During the war Hobbs AAF had three auxiliary fields:

- Aux. #1, Knowles Airport, 8 miles north
- Aux. #4, Hobbs Air Field #4, 6 miles SW
- Aux. #6, Hobbs Municipal Airport, 5 miles west
- Aux. #?, Wink Airport, 3.5 miles WNW of Wink, TX

FLYING MUSEUM: This air museum is at the Lae County Airport 8 miles west of Hobbs on U.S. 62/180. It was established by the New Mexico Wing of the Confederate Air Force as a facility to house and display aircraft owned by its members. The museum is in a WW II B-17 hangar moved here from its original site at Hobbs AAF NW of town. The aircraft on display change from time-to-time due to the nature of the organization, but many of the aircraft are of WW II vintage. Address: PO Box 1260, Hobbs, NM 88240. Phone: 505/395-2377. Hours: daily 8-sunset.

LAS CRUCES AREA: This area is in south-central New Mexico just north of El Paso, Texas. During the war the town had a branch prisoner of war camp holding about 260 POWs who worked in agriculture. *where?*

FORT SELDEN STATE MONUMENT, 13 miles north of Las Cruces on I-25, was a Civil War-era fort that played an important role in the development of this area in the latter part of the 1800s. By WW II the fort had long been abandoned. In 1973, however, it become a state monument and was opened to the public. Ft. Selden is significant in WW II history in that Gen. Douglas MacArthur spent several years of his childhood here in the 1880s when his father, Captain Arthur MacArthur, was the post commander.

WAR EAGLE MUSEUM is located at the Santa Teresa Airport in Santa Teresa, NM a western suburb of El Paso, TX. *VISITED 4/25/80am* This is a very fine, privately owned, air museum that is dedicated to collecting, restoring and displaying historic aircraft of the WW II and Korean War eras. Most of the planes are in flying condition. Outstanding in the collection is a TF-P-51D dual control trainer, one of only two in existence and the only one flying. Another outstanding aircraft is the museum's Fieseler Storch F1-156 believed to be the one flown by Otto Skorzeny when he rescued Mussolini. Another interesting aircraft in the collection is a C-47 that was converted into the private plane for the spiritual leader known as the "Rajneesh". Other WW II-era planes

include a P-38, AT-6, P-40, BT-13, F-4U-4, TBM-3E and an A-26. Address: Santa Teresa Airport, Santa Teresa NM 88008. Phone: 505/589-2000. Hours: Thurs. through Sun. 10-4. Admission charged. *$ 5.00 Seniors*

WHITE SANDS MISSILE RANGE MISSILE PARK & VISITORS CENTER is 20 miles east of Las Cruces three miles south of U.S. 70/82. This park has one of the largest collection of missiles in the country. In the Center are displays tracing the history of the White Sands facility from its beginning in 1945. There is a small display of early nuclear weapons along with photographs, rockets, rocket launchers and other related memorabilia. In the Missile Park is a German V-2 rocket similar to those tested at White Sands at the end of the war. Most of the other missiles are of postwar vintage. Address: Building 122, White Sands Missile Range, NM 88002-5000. Phone: 505/678-1134/ 1135/1700. Hours: M-F 8-4. Free.

LAS VEGAS is 40 miles east of Santa Fe on I-40.

CAMP LUNA, near the town of Las Vegas, was built in 1904 as a National Guard encampment. In 1942 it was taken over by the Army Air Forces and used by the Air Transport Command (ATC) as a replacement training center for ATC personnel. This was a non-flying facility. In 1946 Camp Luna was returned to the state.

LORDSBURG is in the SW corner of the state on I-10.

LORDSBURG PRISONER OF WAR CAMP was 6 miles SE of town. It was built early in the war as a main prisoner of war camp and at various times held male Japanese aliens from the U.S. west coast and Hawaii, German prisoners of war and Italian prisoners of war. In their spare time the POWs built a mosaic of the American Eagle at the main gate of the camp. That work of art remained in place for decades. After the war the land and buildings were sold, but remnants of the camp remain in the forms of camp buildings being used as houses and barns. Several large low concrete water tanks remained in use holding water from wells that were drilled during the war to supply the camp. To reach

The War Eagle Museum at Santa Teresa, NM, a western suburb of El Paso, TX.

The road leading to the former Lordsburg Prisoner of War Camp is still called POW Rd.

the camp take I-10 east of Lordsburg and exit at Exit 24 (E. Motel Dr. runs north from the intersection and POW Rd. runs south). Take POW Rd. which runs south from I-10 for .3 miles, then east for 1.4 miles, then south for 1.7 miles where there is a turnoff to the east which leads .1 miles to the camp's main entrance.

LOS ALAMOS, 25 miles NW of Santa Fe, was not a town before the war. It was the Los Alamos Ranch School for Boys, an exclusive boy's school in a forest on top of a huge mesa. By war's end, though, Los Alamos was a small city and world famous. In 1942, this beautiful and isolated spot was chosen personally by Maj. Gen. Leslie Groves and Dr. J. Robert Oppenheimer, the top men of America's super-secret "Manhattan (Atomic Bomb) Project", to be the site of a new science city where the Project's best scientists would gather and work in secret isolation and attempt to produce an ultra-powerful explosive device that the latest

theories and research in atomic science indicated was possible. The school had 790 acres of land with lots of adjacent land for expansion, and existing buildings that could house 500 people immediately. The owner was anxious to sell so the deal was made. The buildings of the school were utilized by the arriving scientists while dozens of new structures were being built to house their sophisticated equipment and their associates who would follow. Los Alamos thus became the "wizard's workshop" of the "Manhattan Project". And in the end, the wizards were successful. Atomic research was going on at dozens of labs around the country, but the Los Alamos lab was the only one focusing on bombs. During the spring of 1944 this lab made the first pieces of purified plutonium metal and in Sept. 1944 it received the first significant quantities of that metal from the Hanford (WA) Engineer Works. Larger quantities of

plutonium then followed. By mid-July 1945 a device had been produced here and was tested in southern New Mexico proving that plutonium was a suitable material for bombs. The plutonium atomic device exploded with a force unlike anything else ever made by man and ushered in a new era called "The Atomic Age". Once proven, the new technology was quickly built into bombs which were rushed to the western Pacific, and on August 6, 1945 the first of these bombs was dropped on the Japanese city of Hiroshima. On August 9, a second bomb was dropped on Nagasaki. Their destructive power was so awesome that the Japanese leaders realized they had no defense against such weapons and within days sued for peace bringing about the sudden and unexpected end to WW II.

After the war, Los Alamos National Laboratory, as it became known, continued as an important research center in the field of atomic science and the development of nuclear energy for both military and peacetime uses.

BRADLEY SCIENCE MUSEUM in Los Alamos surveys the early history of the development of the atomic bomb and the part played by Los Alamos. Some of the first casings of the atomic bomb are displayed. Other displays explain the various sources of energy other than atomic energy, and there are exhibits on modern weapons research, computers, nuclear accelerators and life science research. Address: Diamond Dr., Los Alamos, NM 87544. Phone: 505/667-4444. Hours: Tues.-Fri. 9-5, Sun.-Mon. 1-5, closed holidays. Free.

FULLER LODGE ART CENTER, in Los Alamos, occupies the west wing of the lodge that served as the dining and recreation hall for the Los Alamos scientists during the war. Before that, it was the dining and recreation hall for the boys school. The center is an art museum featuring works by artist from northern New Mexico. Address: 2132 Central Ave., Los Alamos, NM 87544. Phone: 505/662-9331. Hours: Mon.-Sat. 10-4, Sun. 1-4, closed holidays. Free.

LOS ALAMOS COUNTY HISTORICAL MUSEUM is next door to Fuller Lodge Art Center in a restored log and stone cottage that served as the infirmary for the boys school. The museum records the history of the county from prehistoric times through the development of the atomic bomb. Displays related to the WW II era include photographs of the development and testing of the first atomic device, newspaper articles of the time, military uniforms and other related artifacts. Address: 2130 Central Ave., Los Alamos, NM 87544. Phone: 505/662-6272/4493. Hours: May through Sept. M-Sat. 9:30-4:30, Sun. 1-5. Rest of year M-Sat. 10-4, Sun. 1-4, closed Jan. 1, Easter, Thanksgiving & Dec. 25. Donations requested.

ROSWELL is in the SE part of the state. From 1930 to 1942 Dr. Robert Goddard, the Father of American Rocketry, maintained a small laboratory in Roswell and conducted numerous experiments in rocketry in the desert areas outside the city. Dr. Goddard's work was important in the development of America's wartime and postwar rocket and missile programs.

This mosaic of the American Eagle stands at the former main entrance to the Lordsburg Prisoner of War Camp. It was made by POWs in their spare time.

LT. GEN. DOUGLAS L. McBRIDE MUSEUM is on the campus of the New Mexico Military Institute and honors former members of the Institute and other New Mexicans who have served their country in the military service. On display are uniforms, small arms, medals, flags, photographs, artifacts and memorabilia related to the school and some of the people honored. During WW II some 3000 graduates of the school served in the armed forces and the members of the entire class of 1944 were called to service before they graduated. Museum address: New Mexico Military Institute, W. College Blvd. & N. Main St., Roswell, NM 88201. Phone: 505/624-8007. Hours: Tues.-F 9-3, closed holidays. Free.

ROSWELL ARMY AIR FIELD, 6.5 miles south of town, was established in 1940-41 to meet the needs of the 30,000 Pilot Training Program. It was operated by the Western Flying Training Command to train bombardiers. Later in the war the field also trained co-pilots for B-29 bombers. The air field had a main prisoner of war camp holding about 1200 POWs who worked on the base and in agriculture. After the war the field was turned over to the U.S. Air Force and was known, for a while as Walker Air Force Base. Eventually the field was abandoned by the Air Force and turned over to the community to become Roswell's principal airport. During the war Roswell AAF had the following auxiliary fields:

- Aux. #1, Roswell Air Field #1, near Roswell
- Aux. #3, Roswell Air field #3, 18 miles south of Roswell
- Aux. #8, Artesia Airport, 6.5 miles west of Artesia
- Aux. #9, Roswell Air Field #9, 1.2 miles NW of Roswell

ROSWELL MUSEUM AND ART CENTER near downtown Roswell is the city's main museum and covers many subjects relating to New Mexico, Roswell and the U.S. Southwest. One wing of the museum is devoted to the memory and work of Dr. Robert H. Goddard, who came to the Roswell before and during the war to conduct rocket experiments. Exhibits include Goddard's relocated and restored laboratory that once stood on Mescalero Rd. On display are some of his early rockets, rocket engines, fuel pumps and rocket materials. Outside the museum is one of Goddard's early launch towers which was moved to the museum from its original site. The tower contains a replica of one of his rockets developed by Goddard in 1941-42. Goddard died in 1945 full of plans to return to Roswell and continue his experiments. Museum address: 11th & Main St., Roswell, NM 88201. Phone: 505/624-6744. Hours: M-Sat. 9-5, Sun. & holidays 1-5, closed Thanksgiving and Dec. 25. Free.

Wartime Los Alamos took on the look of an Army camp with too many cars and too many fences. This was the heart of the technical area. To the right is the Gamma Building, one of the main research laboratories.

SANTA FE, the state's capital, is in the north-central New Mexico.

BRUNS GENERAL HOSPITAL was built in Santa Fe by the Federal Government in 1943 to treat war wounded. It was a temporary hospital constructed of wood and asbestos shingles. Bruns had 1575 beds and specialized in general medicine and tuberculosis. In Dec. 1946 it was transferred to the Atomic Energy Commission and Christian Brothers College.

JUSTICE DEPARTMENT INTERNMENT CAMP, SANTA FE: This was one of several camps established in the U.S. early in the war by the Department of Justice for the internment of enemy aliens under the rules of the Geneva Convention. This camp was run by the Department's Immigration and Naturalization Service (INS) and held mainly Japanese aliens. The people of Santa Fe did not relish the idea of having large numbers of Japanese aliens in their midst because of the horrible treatment the men of New Mexico's National Guard had suffered at the hands of Japanese in the Philippines (see Deming, Luna Mimbres Museum above for more details). Fortunately, for the peace of the community, very few of the aliens ever left the camp. The first aliens to arrive at the camp were from the U.S., but later some Peruvian-Japanese and Bolivian-Japanese, who had been expelled by those nations, were sent here under agreements between those countries and the U.S. Government. In early 1943 this camp began receiving Japanese-Americans who had renounced their U.S. citizenship which automatically make them enemy aliens and subject to incarceration in enemy alien camps rather than in relocation camps. Most of these individuals came from the Tule Lake Relocation Camp in California and were very anti-American, pro-Japanese and troublesome. At first they were isolated from the other Japanese internees and closely watched, but later a program was developed whereby two renunciants each were put into barracks with more cooperative Japanese aliens in hopes that the cooperative aliens would exert a moderating influence on the behavior of the renunciants.

When the war ended about half of the renunciants sought legal means to regain their U.S. citizenship, but the other half remained committed and defiant. The former renunciants were allowed to stay on in the U.S. until their status was resolved by the courts, but the hard-core renunciants were hustled off to Japan immediately after Japan's formal surrender in Sept. 1945. The first train-loads of hard-core renunciants left Santa Fe in Nov. 1945 and most of the rest followed in Dec. They were taken to San Francisco and Seattle and put on ships bound for Japan. By Feb. 1946 all of Santa Fe's hard-core renunciants had departed for Japan and in Mar. 1946 the camp was closed. The few Japanese aliens remaining, mostly from Latin America, were sent to Crystal City, TX and then to New Jersey where they were given work (see New Jersey, Bridgeton, for more details).

WHITE SANDS: (See Alamagordo-White Sands Proving Ground)

NEW YORK

The state of New York was America's most populous state during WW II. It had a population of 13,479,000 with more than half living in the New York City area. Just before WW II New York state experienced very hard economic times because of the Great Depression which had began in New York City with the stock market crash of 1929. During those terrible years, however, the state had a young and energetic Governor, Franklin D. Roosevelt, who began at once to take aggressive and, at times, controversial measures to combat the problems. Roosevelt's measures seemed to help . . and he soon caught the nation's attention as a man of action. In 1932 he was nominated by his party for the presidency of the United States and won by a landslide vote. Roosevelt and his supporters considered this as a mandate from the American people to take his New York-tested Depression-fighting policies to Washington and implement them on a national scale. These policies became the nucleus of Roosevelt's famous "New Deal" program.

By the time WW II started New York's economy was better but there were still empty factories and widespread unemployment. New York's 34,506 manufacturing firms and highly skilled work force put the state in an excellent position to manufacture practically any product the Government needed. The defense contracts soon began to flow to New York, and within a relatively short time they turned into a deluge. Business sprang to life, unemployment disappeared and by late 1944 New York state was receiving 10.1% of the nation's total defense outlay which was the second largest in the country after California. Throughout the war the state's manufacturing sector remained very strong producing ships, planes, tanks, motor vehicles, steel, iron, munitions, guns, clothing, boots & shoes, electrical equipment, automotive products, printing & publishing, lumber and much more. New York's mining companies prospered too producing lead, zinc, oil, gypsum, coke, cement, emery, industrial garnets, fibrous talc, slate, salt, stone, sand & gravel. The state's farmers were also busy producing corn, oat, barley, tobacco, potatoes, fruit, hay, cattle, dairy products, poultry and processed food. And, New York's fishermen produced large quantities of sea food.

The coming of war brought new problems, however. First, there was the great fear that New York might be attacked. These fears were not unfounded because all three major Axis nations, Germany, Italy and Japan, had plans to attack the New York City area if the opportunity presented itself. Also German submarines became very active in New York waters early in the war and German saboteurs landed (and were caught) on Long Island less than 7 months after the U.S. entered the war. Furthermore, New York City had tens of thousands of Axis aliens and ethnic nationals whose presents fostered fears of subversion and sabotage. The 1940 national census showed that there were 2,853,000 foreign-born people in the state including 316,800 Germans and 584,000 Italians.

Soon after America went to war there was talk of relocation these people away from the New York area to camps in the interior as was to be the fate the of the ethnic Japanese on the west coast. The relocation of so many people, however, would have been a logistical nightmare, so the Government took a wait-and-see attitude. Even the removal of registered enemy aliens was a problem. There were 1,234,995 of them in New York . . more than twice that of any other state. Most of these people were allowed to remain free although a handful, who were thought to be threats to national security, were taken into custody and incarcerated in internment camps. The war also bought other Axis citizens to New York in the form of Prisoners of war. Some of them wound up in one or the other of New York's 21 POW camps.

The state of New York probably had more famous and important people during the WW II era than any other state. Among them were:

- Franklin E. Roosevelt, President of the United States.
- Eleanor Roosevelt, his wife and First Lady.
- Thomas E. Dewey, Governor of New York and Republican Presidential Candidate during the 1944 and 1948 national elections.
- Henry L. Stimson, Secretary of War under Roosevelt.
- Robert P. Patterson, Secretary of War under Truman.
- Henry Morgenthau, Jr., Secretary of the Treasury.
- Edward R. Stettinius, Jr., Lend-Lease Administrator under Roosevelt and Secretary of State under Truman.
- Robert H. Jackson, Attorney General, Supreme Court Justice and chief U.S. prosecutor at the Nuremberg Trials.
- Frances Perkins, Secretary of Labor.
- James A. Farley, Postmaster General and Roosevelt's Campaign Manager.
- J. Robert Oppenheimer, Director of the Los Alamos, NM Research Laboratory (which developed the atomic bomb).
- Francis J. Spellman, Roman Catholic Archbishop of New York City and Military Vicar to the U.S. Armed Forces.
- Bernard M. Baruch, personal advisor to President Roosevelt and author of the "Baruch Plan" for the control of atomic energy in the postwar years.
- Jeanette Jerome, later Lady Randolph Churchill and mother of Winston Churchill.
- William Joyce, propaganda broadcaster for the Germans known as "Lord Haw Haw".

New York also had 30 Congressional Metal of Honor Winners during WW II, the second highest in the nation[1].

After the war New York, like most states, suffered a brief period of economic and social readjustment, but recovered and prospered well in the postwar years.

ALBANY/SCHENECTADY AREA: This
area is 130 miles north of New York City near the juncture of the Hudson and Mohawk Rivers. Albany is the state's capital. One of the large manufacturers in Schenectady was the

[1] Pennsylvania was first with 35.

American Locomotive Co. which, of course, continued to build locomotives throughout the war as well as M-4 medium tanks and 105 mm mobile howitzers. Schenectady is also the home of the General Electric Corp. which made a wide variety of military products during the war.

SCHENECTADY SERVICE FORCES DEPOT, three miles SW of Schenectady, was built by the Army in 1918 in the village of Rotterdam. The depot was known then as the Schenectady General Reserve Depot and served the Army during the latter months of WW I. Later, it became a supply depot for 55 CCC camps. In 1941 the depot was expanded, acquired its wartime name and was run by the Army's Quartermaster Corps. The depot received, stored and shipped many items, including large numbers of motor vehicles. Most of the depot's items were eventually shipped overseas through the Port of New York. At its peak the depot employed 4000 people. This was a segregated facility so many negroes worked here. Later in the war the depot's name was changed again to Schenectady General Depot and in the postwar years it was changed again to the Schenectady Army Depot. Between Jan. 1948 and Mar. 1949 the depot was a processing station for returning U.S. war dead. The depot expanded again during the Korean War and a federal housing development, Mohawk Manor, was built for depot employees. The depot continued operations for a number of years after the Korean war.

U.S. NAVAL SUPPLY DEPOT, SCOTIA is west of, and adjacent to the town of Scotia, and on the north side of the Mohawk River. Scotia is a northern suburb of Schenectady. The depot was built by the Navy in 1942-43 as a storage and supply depot for naval forces along the U.S. Atlantic coast and in Europe. The depot stored large items such as boilers, turbines and reduction gears and was the home of the Navy's Landing Craft Maintenance and Battle Damage Program. In 1944 the depot also became the home of the Navy's Automotive and Handling Equipment Spare Parts Program. Employment peaked in 1945 at 2342. In 1947 five storehouses were modified to be permanent storage facilities for large machine tools and other large pieces of machinery used in the construction of warships and large guns. During the Korean War the depot became very active again and acquired the Navy's Specification, Forms and Publications Center. The depot remained a Navy facility throughout the Cold War, but saw very little activity.

WATERVLIET ARSENAL is in the town of Watervliet, five miles north of Albany. The Arsenal was built in 1813 as a storage depot for arms and gunpowder, but through the years it became a manufacturing arsenal specializing in large guns. By the beginning of WW II the Arsenal was one of the best equipped gun manufacturers in the country and produced many large guns throughout the war living up to the title it had acquired decades earlier as the "Cannon Headquarters for the U.S. Army". The Arsenal also had an extensive research and

Large guns being manufactured at Watervliet Arsenal during WW II.

development department devoted to the improvement of large guns and their manufacturing processes. In the postwar years the Arsenal remained active and continued producing large guns, missiles and special weapons throughout the Cold War.

Watervliet Arsenal Museum: This fine museum is on the grounds of Watervliet Arsenal in an historic 1859 Arsenal warehouse. The museum relates the history of the Arsenal and there are copies of some of the smaller guns made here, and, models, sections and photos of the larger ones. Some of the Arsenal's manufacturing methods are shown and there is information on how the guns were used. Address: Watervliet Arsenal, (SMCWV-INM), Watervliet, NY 12189-4050. Phone: 518/266-5805/5868. Hours: Tues.-Sat. 10-3, closed federal holidays. Free. Location: off Broadway and SR 32 in the town of Watervliet.

AMAGANSETT, LONG ISLAND:

Amagansett is on the south shore of Long Island 17 miles west of Montauk Point. During the war it was a small fishing village. On the night of June 13/14, 1942, four German saboteurs landed on the beach just east of town from the German submarine U-202. All four men had been residents in the U.S. before the war but had returned to Germany. There, they volunteered to return to America as saboteurs. They were given extensive training in Germany along with four other men who also had lived in the U.S. and had volunteered to return to the U.S. as saboteurs. The 8 men were organized as a team and the latter four were landed by another German submarine near Jacksonville, FL three days later on June 17. Here on Long Island, the four saboteurs came ashore in a small boat, but because of a dense fog, the U-boat commander had deposited them on the wrong beach and only a few yards from East Amagansett Coast Guard Lifesaving Station. As the saboteurs were coming ashore they were discovered by a lone Coastguardsman, 21 year-old Seaman 2nd Class John C. Cullen, who was walking his regular nightly beach patrol. In response to Cullen's questions the leader of the foursome, Georg Dasch, claimed that they were Americans on a very secret mission that would be revealed by the Federal Government in just

a few weeks. But, he insisted, it was imperative that their presence not be reported now[2]. To encourage the Coastguardsman's silence Dasch offered Cullen $100, and then $300. Cullen took the money, said he understood, saluted apologetically and disappeared into the darkness. Cullen, however, was not fooled. He thought the incident very suspicious and reported it at once to his superiors and turned over the money. Meanwhile, the saboteurs changed clothes, buried their equipment and made their way to the coast highway and on to New York City. Coast Guard authorities and others promptly investigated Cullen's report, searched the site and after daylight on the 14th found the saboteur's buried equipment. Meanwhile the saboteurs were well on their way to New York City. Two days later, on June 16, Dasch unexpectedly defected to the Americans. He contacted the FBI and turned himself in. This lead eventually to the arrest of all 8 saboteurs.

BETHPAGE/FARMINGDALE AREA OF LONG ISLAND:

These are adjacent towns in the west-central part of Long Island. Both towns, however, had major aircraft manufacturers. Just east of Farmingdale was a huge Republic Aviation Corp. plant which manufactured the famous P-47 Thunderbolt fighter planes for the AAF. Northeast of Bethpage was the Grumman Aircraft Engineering Corp.

[2]In another version of this account it is reported that the saboteurs claimed to be fishermen whose boat had run aground.

which built F4F Wildcats, TBF Avengers and F6F Hellcats for the Navy.

FARMINGDALE ARMY AIR FIELD was Republic Aircraft Corporation's air field east of Farmingdale. When the U.S. went to war the field was taken over by the 1st AF according to pre-war defense planning and made an operational base for the air defense of the New York area. The air field served this function throughout the war while continuing to be the company's air field. After the war the AAF departed and the air field continued to serve Republic well into the postwar years. During the war Farmingdale AAF had one auxiliary field, Frong's Field at Westhampton Beach.

BRENTWOOD is located near the geographic center of Long Island.

MASON GENERAL HOSPITAL came into being in 1943 in Brentwood when the Federal Government leased the existing Pilgrimage State Hospital and converted it into an Army general hospital to treat war wounded. Mason was a multi-story, all brick hospital that specialized in psychiatry and housed psychotic patients who needed closed ward treatment. Mason was also used as a debarkation hospital. In Dec. 1946 the Army canceled their lease and the hospital was returned to the state.

BUFFALO/NIAGARA FALLS AREA: This was a highly industrialized and strategically located area at the western terminus of the Erie Canal. Some of the major manufacturers in the Buffalo area were Bell Aircraft Co. which made P-39 and P-63 fighter planes; Curtiss-Wright Aircraft Corp. which made P-40 fighter planes, O-52 observation planes and C-46 transports; American Car & Foundry Co. which made 7.2", 155 mm and 240 mm artillery shells; Morrison Steel Products, Inc. which made 250 lb bombs; Buffalo Arms Corp. which made 30 & 50 calibre ammunition and Browning machine guns and American Cyanamid Corp. which made TNT. Niagara Falls, 15 miles NW of Buffalo, had an important manufacturer, the Electro Metallurgical Corp., which cast some of the first uranium ingots for the "Manhattan (Atomic Bomb) Project".

BUFFALO MUNICIPAL AIRPORT was five miles east of town. This was Buffalo's primary airport before and during the war. For several years the Curtiss-Wright Aircraft Corp. had a facility at the airport where they assembled and tested new aircraft. In 1940 the Federal Government built a large new plant at the airport to be operated by Curtiss-Wright for the production of transport planes. The Government

The four German saboteurs who landed on Long Island (left to right): Ernest Peter Burger, George John Dasch, Heinrich Harm Heinck, Richard Quirin. All 8 were quickly caught, tried and 6 were executed. Two, Dasch and Burger, who cooperated with U.S. authorities and testified against the others, were given long prison terms, but released and deported soon after the war.

also enlarged the airport during the war. Both the Army & Navy used the airport and there was a military air freight terminal here. After the war the new Curtiss-Wright plant was acquired by the Westinghouse Electric Corp. In the postwar years the airport evolved into Greater Buffalo International Airport.

FORT NIAGARA is at the mouth of the Niagara River where it flows into Lake Ontario. This site had been a military facility since 1679. By WW II Fort Niagara was old and obsolete but had many well-built and still serviceable buildings. It was therefore used by the Army as a reception center for draftees by the II Corps and later as a replacement center. Still later it had an Army Service Forces Training Center. The fort also served as a main prisoners of war camp holding about 1500 POWs who worked for the military and in the food processing industry. At the end of the war Fort Niagara became an Army separation center. In late 1945 the fort was turned over to the state, but in 1953 it was re-acquired by the Army and used as a headquarters for the anti-aircraft artillery network which was established during that phase of the Cold War for the defense of Niagara Falls and Buffalo. Several years later the Army again departed and the fort became the centerpiece of Fort Niagara State Park. The fort has been restored to its 18th-century atmosphere and there is virtually no reference to its role in WW II.

NAVAL AND SERVICEMAN'S PARK is located on Buffalo's waterfront near the intersection of I-190 and SR 5. It has, as it main attractions, three warships; the cruiser "Little Rock", built in 1944 but too late to see action in WW II and later converted to a guided-missile warship, the destroyer "The Sullivans" built in 1943 and named after the five Sullivan brothers of Waterloo, IA and the WW II submarine "Croaker" which sank the Japanese cruiser "Nagara" and several enemy merchant vessels. All of the vessels are open to the public. Also in the park are aircraft, including a locally produced P-39Q Airacobra fighter plane. Address: 1 Naval Park Cove, Buffalo, NY 14202. Phone: 716/847-1773. Hours: Apr. thru Oct. daily 10-dusk, in Nov. weekends 10-dusk. Admission charged.

NIAGARA FALLS MUNICIPAL AIRPORT was five miles east of the city of Niagara Falls. Before the war it was a local airport and home of Bell Aircraft Corp. When the U.S. went to war the airport was closed to civilian aircraft and was used exclusively by Bell for testing and delivering its newly-built aircraft to the Army & Navy. A small military camp was established at the field for the military personnel known as Camp Bell. After the war the field was re-opened for civilian use and became known as Niagara Falls International Airport.

NIAGARA FALLS ORDNANCE PLANT, was located at 3163 Buffalo Ave. in Niagara Falls. It was built by the Federal Government in 1941 and was operated by the Army Chemical Corps to manufacture impregnite, an explosive. It also was a storage facility for poison gasses. After the war the plant was sold to private interests.

ELMIRA is in western New York south of the Finger Lakes area. Three of the town's larger manufacturers during the war were the Remington Rand Corp. which made bomb

sights and Schweizer Aircraft Corp. which made gliders and Eclipse Machine Div. of Bendix Corp. which made 20 mm aircraft cannons.

ELMIRA HOLDING AND RECONSIGNMENT POINT was a military storage facility built in Elmira in 1942 north of Horseheads and run by the Army's Transportation Corps. Here, everything that the Army's ground forces used was kept in readiness for quick shipment overseas. The Holding Point, as it was known, had 37 miles of railroad tracks and most items were stored on flat-bed railroad cars or in freight cars ready to move out on short notice. There were also several large warehouses. The Elmira Holding Point employed some 1300 civilians and military personnel and, later in the war, had a 400-man Italian Service Unit. After the war the Holding Point was sold to private interests.

VAN ETTEN PRISONER OF WAR CAMP: This was a very unique prisoner of war camp located near the town of Van Etten, 15 miles NE of Elmira. The camp was established in Oct. 1944 in an abandoned and isolated CCC camp and was officially identified as the first camp of its kind for the newly created Intellectual Diversion Program for POWs. This "program", however, was a disguise for a new program just then being implemented to re-educate and train anti-Nazi POWs to serve in future governmental and administrative posts in U.S. occupied Germany. This kind of activity was forbidden by the Geneva Convention so the phrase "Intellectual Diversion" was chosen because it conformed to a legitimate activity for POWs spelled out in Article 17 of the Convention. To those in the know, however, the camp was referred to as the "Idea Factory" or the "Factory". The camp housed about 150 U.S. and German educators and intellectuals, some of them POWs, who were charged with the responsibility of working out the details of the re-education and training program. Within a few months, however, the camp proved to be too small and the program and individuals involved were moved to Ft. Kearny, RI.

FARMINGDALE, LONG ISLAND
(See Bethpage/Farmingdale)

FISHERS ISLAND is located at the eastern end of Long Island Sound and only 8 miles SE of New London, CT.

FORT H.G. WRIGHT is at the western end of Fishers Island. It was built in 1898-99 as a defensive position protecting the entrance to Long Island Sound and was armed with two 12" and two 10" rifles on disappearing carriages. The fort was fully operational throughout WW II and had a small air field. Forts Michie and Terry were subposts. In the late 1950s the Army abandoned the fort and it was sold to private interests.

GENESEO is 28 miles SSW of Rochester.

THE NATIONAL WARPLANE MUSEUM is located at Geneseo Airport SW of town off SR 63. It is dedicated to the restoration and maintenance of flying-condition aircraft of WW II. The museum has over a dozen planes with more being added from time-to-time. Noteworthy among the collec-

tion is a Consolidated PBY-6A Catalina, a Curtiss P-40E, a Boeing B-17G and a Douglas A-26. Visitors may tour the restoration area and watch work in progress. Address: Big Tree Ln., PO Box 159, Geneseo Airport, Geneseo, NY 14454. Phone: 716/243-0690. Hours: M-F 9-5, Sat.-Sun. 10-5. Closed Jan. 1 and Dec. 25. Admission charged.

GENEVA/SENECA FALLS AREA: These towns are located at the northern end of the finger Lakes region.

SENECA ORDNANCE DEPOT was 12 miles south of Seneca Falls and just west of the community of Romulus between Lakes Cayuga and Seneca. The mission of the depot was to store, maintain and ship a wide variety of Army ammunition especially bombs. The depot had a branch prisoner of war camp, holding about 220 POWS who worked in the food industry. Near the end of the war Italian Service Units worked at the depot. The depot survived the war and in 1962 was renamed The Seneca Army Depot. It remained active throughout the Cold War.

U.S. NAVAL TRAINING CENTER, SAMPSON was located on the eastern shore of Lake Seneca about 12 miles SSE of Geneva. This was one of three inland naval training centers[3] built in 1942 to provide boot camp and specialists training for Navy recruits. NTC, Sampson was capable of housing up to 40,000 people and offered training in seamanship, ordnance, aerial gunnery, lookout recognition, chemical warfare and small boat handling. Both sailors and WAVES trained here and by the end of the war some 400,000 individuals had passed through the Center. In 1946 the Navy turned the facility over to the state of New York which used parts of it to build Sampson College and Sampson State Park.

GREAT BEND (See Watertown/Sacketts Harbor/Great Bend Area)

[3]The others were at Farragut, ID and Bainbridge, MD.

President Franklin D. Roosevelt's home at Hyde Park, NY. In July 1944, when he was running for his fourth term, Roosevelt confided in a letter to the Democratic Party Chairman "All that is within me cries out to go back to my home on the Hudson River". It didn't happen. Roosevelt died in office in April 1945.

HYDE PARK is 7 miles north of Poughkeepsie on the east bank of the Hudson River. During the war it was a community of less than 1000 people but known world-wide as the home of President Franklin D. Roosevelt.

HOME OF FRANKLIN D. ROOSEVELT NATIONAL HISTORIC SITE is two miles south of Hyde Park on SR 9. This is a 200 acre estate built in 1826. Franklin's father purchased it in 1867 and re-modeled the main house around 1915. The estate appears today almost exactly as it did when Franklin died in 1945. Included on the grounds are the original stables, icehouse, a walking trail and the Rose Garden which contains the graves of Franklin and his wife, Eleanor. Also buried on the estate is John Roosevelt, their son and Fala, their dog. The estate is open to the public and has a tourist information center, bookstore and provides a shuttle bus to The Eleanor Roosevelt National Historic Site (See below) during Apr. through Oct. Address: Albany Post Rd., Hyde Park, NY 12538. Phone: 914/229-9115. Hours: Apr. thru Oct. daily 9-5, rest of year Thurs.-M 9-5. Closed Jan. 1, Thanksgiving, and Dec. 25. Admission charged.

Franklin D. Roosevelt Library and Museum: This facility is adjacent to the Home of Franklin D. Roosevelt National Historic Site and was America's first presidential library. It was built and dedicated in 1941 while Franklin was still alive. The land was donated by the President. The library contains 45,000 volumes and 16 million pages of manuscripts and the museum displays personal and public artifacts of the President and his family. There are numerous photographs, official documents, personal letters, works of art, gifts from heads of state and family memorabilia. Other exhibits trace the careers of both Franklin and Eleanor. Phone: 914/229-8114. Hours: daily 9-5, closed Jan. 1, Thanksgiving and Dec. 25. Admission charged.

Eleanor Roosevelt National Historic Site: This site is located on SR 9G a few miles from the Home of Franklin E. Roosevelt National Historic Site. It consists of a modest cottage called Val-Kill which was Eleanor's retreat and hideaway from her hectic life as First Lady. After Franklin died, Eleanor lived her until her death in 1962. The cottage is preserved much as it was during her years as a widow. A shuttle bus is available between this site and the Roosevelt Home during Apr. through Oct. Rest of the year the site is accessible by private car, weather permitting. Phone: 914/229-9115. Hours: May. thru Oct. daily 9-5. Rest of year Sat.-Sun. 9-5. Closed Jan. 1, Thanksgiving and Dec. 25. Admission charged.

LAKE PLACID is a resort town in the Adirondack Mountains 32 miles west of Lake Champlain with a number of fine resort hotels. In Sept. 1944 the Army leased several of the best hotels in the area and converted them into one of five redistribution centers[4] for returning service personnel. They were given several weeks of morale-building rest and relaxation before being assigned elsewhere.

MONTAUK POINT is the eastern-most tip of Long Island. It is a popular tourist and fish-

[4]The other areas were Asheville, NC; Miami Beach, FL; Hot Springs, AR and Atlantic City, NJ.

ing area and, because of its strategic location, has had a lighthouse since 1796. The Montauk Lighthouse was operated throughout WW II and postwar records showed that the captains of German submarines used it frequently to get their bearings after having made the long crossing of the North Atlantic from Europe.

CAMP HERO, now Montauk Point State Park, was built in 1941 as a coastal defense position. It was a subinstallation of Fort Totten, and later a sub-post of Fort H.G. Wright. Camp Hero's main battery consisted of two 16" guns and one 6" gun. Late in the war Camp Hero was phased out along with the other U.S. coastal defenses. In 1957 the post was transferred to the Air Force which used it as a radar and air defense station named Montauk Air Force Station. In 1980 the Air Force closed down the radar operations and placed the facility in caretaker status. In 1984 the General Services Administration auctioned off the property except for those parcels in the state park.

FORT TYLER was a small coastal defense position on the tip of Gardiner's Island at the entrance to Gardiner's Bay. It had been a lighthouse reservation up to 1898 when it was transferred to the War Department and converted into a coastal defense position. By WW II the fort had been abandoned for some 20 years. The Navy found it useful, though, as a bombing target for naval aviators in training.

NEW YORK CITY METROPOLITAN

AREA: To many Europeans, the name "New York" was synonymous with "America". It was well known in Europe that this was America's largest city, largest seaport, the home of the Statue of Liberty and the place where their countrymen went when they immigrated to America. To Axis leaders, New York City was target No. 1 in North America and all three major Axis nations, Germany, Italy and Japan, had plans to bomb and even invade the New York City area if the opportunities arose. The Germans built a prototype of a long range bomber that was designed to reach North America and return to Europe. They called it the "New York Bomber" or "America Bomber". The 8 German saboteurs that landed on Long Island (See Amagansett above) and in Florida (See Jacksonville Beach, FL) in June 1942 had plans to attack NYC. These plans called for the destruction of Hell's Gate Bridge over the East River, sabotage of rail lines west of NYC and the poisoning of NYC's water supply with hydrogen cyanide. None of the Axis WW II plans were carried out, however, but German submarines operated close to NYC, enemy spies operated within the city and some es-

Sept. 14-16, 1941: This 114-ship convoy was the largest to date to enter New York Harbor. It took 42 hours to arrive and consisted of British, Norwegian, Dutch and Icelandic ships which had come to pick up Lend Lease war supplies.

caped prisoners of war found refuge here.

New York City and its suburbs comprised one of the most heavily industrialized areas in America and many of America's largest corporations and many military agencies had their headquarters here. Some of the major manufacturers and their products in the NYC area were the U.S. Naval Yard, New York (See below); Consolidated Shipbuilding Corp. which built sub chasers and tugs; Bethlehem Steel Corp. built a variety of ships and did ship repair; Henry B. Nevins, Inc.built mine sweepers and marine motors; Sullivan Dry Dock & Repair Corp. made small naval vessels; Tragesser Copper Works and United Boat Service Corp. made tank lighters; Brewster Aircraft Co. made military aircraft; General Aircraft Corp. and Dade Brothers, Inc. made gliders; Sperry Corp. made aircraft ball turrets and instruments; Technical Development Corp. made gun parts; E.W. Bliss Corp. made torpedoes; Murray Manufacturing Co. made 60 mm and 80 mm shells; Unexcelled Mfg. Corp. made incendiary bombs, flares and signalling devices; American Safety Razor Co. made 37 mm shells and Carl L. Norden, Inc. made bombsights. Another NYC product, the New York Times newspaper, soon became a favorite with German and Italian prisoners of war in U.S. POW camps because of its unbiased reporting and its in-depth reporting on events in Europe.

Even though NYC was a huge metropolis it suffered overcrowding, traffic congestion, increased crime, an under-manned police force, crowded schools, inadequate hotel space and housing shortages. New housing was built constantly during the war but it was never enough. When the war ended NYC's infrastructure was in a sorry state. There were numerous slum areas, the subways were worn out and losing money, crime continued to be high, there was local inflation and persistent areas of overcrowding and congestion.

New York City's harbor was a beehive of activity from the very beginning of the war when British and French merchant ships came to pick up war materials and their warships came to NYC for supplies and repairs. Later, U.S. and other Allied merchant ships flocked to New York to pick up Lend Lease goods and

This monument is the centerpiece of the East Coast Memorial in Battery Park. It depicts an eagle laying a wreath upon the waters.

then returned with raw materials, wounded veterans and prisoners of war. New York Bay became the primary gathering point on the east coast for large convoys.

ARMY PICTORIAL CENTER was located at 35-11 35th Ave. in Long Island City. Before the war this was a large motion picture studio owned by Paramount Pictures. In 1942 the Army took it over, enlarged it, and began making training films and military recordings. A school for combat photographers was also established here. One of the films produced here in 1942, "Prelude to War", won a special Oscar from the Academy of Motion Picture Arts and Sciences. The Center continued in operation after the war and added to its mission the production of television programs. The Center's productions also continued to win Oscars and other awards in the postwar years.

LEO BAECK INSTITUTE, 129 E. 73rd St., New York, NY 10021, is a center dedicated to the remembrance of the Holocaust. The Institute has a museum, a 60,000-volume library, 2000 shelf-feet of archives, an extensive art and photographic collection and produces several publications. Phone: 212/744-6400. Hours: M-F 9-5.

BERNARD BARUCH GRAVE SITE: Baruch, a personal advisor of presidents from Woodrow Wilson to John F. Kennedy and the holder of several important governmental posts, is buried in the Flushing Cemetery in Queens.

BATTERY PARK, at the southern end of Manhattan, has several monuments related to WW II. The largest is the East Coast Memorial which is dedicated to the 4596 men of the U.S. Armed Forces who lost their lives in western Atlantic waters during WW II. The Memorial consists of a short staircase leading into a large open court which containing in its center a monument depicting a spread eagle laying a wreath upon the waters. On either side of the court are a total of 8 stelae containing the names of those lost.

Another monument at Battery Park is the Merchant Mariners Memorial honoring those who served in the American Merchant Marine Service during WW II. The monument depicts the survivors of a sunken ship and was inspired by an actual photograph taken by a German crewman aboard the submarine that sank the U.S. tanker "Muskogee" in the West Indies in 1942. The crewmen depicted were never seen again.

FLOYD BENNET FIELD (See U.S. Naval Air Station, New York)

BROOKLYN ARMY BASE: This was the U.S. Army's main port of embarkation in the NYC area. It was located on the Brooklyn waterfront at 1st Ave. and 58th St. It consisted of a large complex of piers, docks, warehouses, cranes, railroad sidings and other cargo loading equipment which handled the shipment of Army personnel and equipment overseas. During the war more than four million Army personnel shipped out through this facility and its subordinate ports along with everything from heavy tanks to bars of soap. At the end of the war several million men and tons of equipment returned through these same facilities. The Base survived the war and in 1955 was renamed Brooklyn Army Terminal.

BROOKLYN NAVAL YARD (See U.S. Naval Yard, New York)

CIVIL AIR PATROL HEADQUARTERS: The national headquarters of the Civil Air Patrol (CAP) was located at 500 5th Ave., NYC. This organization was founded Dec. 1, 1941, just a week before the attack on Pearl Harbor, by civilian aviators, mechanics, radio operators and other volunteers whose skills and personal equipment might be useful for national defense. Both men and women were eligible for membership. The CAP was under the direction of the Office of Civilian Defense which was headed by New York's Mayor LaGuardia, but provisions were made for close CAP coordination with the Army and Navy. When the U.S. went to war the CAP was pressed into service as one of the volunteer forces aiding the Coast Guard and Navy in patrolling the U.S. coastlines until this duty could be assumed by one of the armed services. Their most important duties were to watch for enemy submarines, vessels in distress and survivors. Some of the CAP's aircraft were armed with depth charges and during the war the CAP was credited with sinking or damaging two submarines. CAP personnel flew over 1/4 million hours on coastal patrols, spotted 173 submarines, reported 91 friendly vessels in distress and contributed to the rescue of 363 people. Postwar German records proved that they were seen as a menace by German submarine captains who almost always submerged and fled the area when encountering a CAP aircraft. The CAP's patrol activities lasted for 18 months and proved to be the CAP's most important contribution to the war effort. In addition to coastal patrols the CAP volunteers acted a air couriers, searched for downed aircraft and flyers and helped train ground observers and search light crews. In Apr. 1943 control of the CAP passed to the Army Air Forces and it became an AAF auxiliary unit. By June 1943 the CAP counted a membership of 75,000 people, and by then 26 of their number had been killed and 90 planes lost. In 1948 the CAP became an auxiliary of the U.S. Air Force and its headquarters were moved to Ellington AFB, TX.

ELLIS ISLAND, in Upper New York Bay, had long been an immigration station through which million of immigrants were processed upon arrival in the U.S. During WW II it was still operating as an immigration station under the direction of the Immigration and Naturalization Service. When, in late 1939, the U.S. Government began interning certain enemy aliens, Ellis Island became one of the temporary internment facilities holding these people. By 1941 there were too many internees to hold in existing facilities, so internment camps were built or acquired in the interior and the internees moved to them. During the rest of the war Ellis Island continued to be a receiving and processing station for enemy aliens prior to their transfer to the camps. After the war Ellis Island processed enemy aliens being deported. In 1954 immigration activities were ended on the island and in 1965 it became a part of the Liberty Island National Historic Site and is now open to the public.

HALLORAN ARMY HOSPITAL was a 5350-bed general hospital located in St. George on Staten Island. It had been a pre-war civilian hospital and was leased by the Federal Government in 1942 to treat war wounded. Halloran specialized in neurology, general and orthopedic surgery and neurosurgery. Later in the war it became a debarkation hospital. Halloran had a main prisoner of war camp holding about 650 German POWs who worked at the hospital. In Dec. 1946 the Army canceled its lease and the hospital was returned to its owners.

FORT HAMILTON is located in Brooklyn on the eastern shore of The Narrows just south of the Verranzano Narrows Bridge. This strategic location has been a military post since 1657 protecting the entrance to Upper New York Bay. Between 1825-31 the U.S. Government built the present-day Fort Hamilton. In the late 1930s most of the fort's obsolete guns were removed and the Fort, with some 100 serviceable buildings, became the home of the Army's 1st Division. When WW II started the 1st Division moved out and the old fort was used as a staging facility for troops being shipped overseas. After the war, when most other forts of this type were being abandoned or sold off, Fort Hamilton was used as a separation center and then retained by the Army for a variety of uses.

In 1974 its historic Officers' Open Mess was declared a National Historic Landmark and when the Verranzano Bridge was built some of the fort's batteries were removed to make way for the bridge. Fort Hamilton served throughout much of the Cold War as headquarters for the Army's New York Area Command and other Regular Army, Army Reserve and National Guard agencies.

Harbor Defense Museum of New York City: This museum is in one of the original caponiers (1825-31) of Fort Hamilton and chronicles the military history of the NYC area from the 17th Century to the present. There is special emphasis on coastal defenses with displays showing coast artillery, machine guns, mines, small arms, uniforms, maps, photographs, drawings and other military artifacts. Address: c/o Fort Hamilton Historical Society, Fort Hamilton, Brooklyn, NY 11252. Phone: 718/630-4349. Hours: M-F 1-4, closed federal holidays. Free.

INTREPID SEA-AIR-SPACE MUSEUM is located on the west side on Manhattan at Pier 86, 46th St. & 12th Ave. The museum has three warships, the WW II-and-postwar-era aircraft carrier "Intrepid", the postwar submarine "Growler" and Viet Nam-era destroyer "Edson". All three ships are open to the public. The "Intrepid", the largest of the ships, was built in 1943 and was in service with the U.S. Navy for 39 years. There are open displays on the flight deck on the "Intrepid" and a collection of aircraft and missiles including several WW II planes. The hangar deck is a large museum containing several Halls, each dedicated to a specific theme. The "Intrepid Hall" focuses on the aircraft carrier's activities during WW II when she saw action in the Pacific. Address: 1 Intrepid Plaza, Pier 86, New York, NY 10036. Phone: 212/245-0072/2533. Hours: Memorial Day thru Labor Day daily 10-5, rest of year W-Sun. 10-5. Last ticket sold 1 hours before closing. Closed Jan. 1, Thanksgiving and Dec. 25. Admission charged.

FORT JAY is on historic Governor's Island 1/2 miles south of the tip of Manhattan. This strategic location has been a miliary post since 1755. Fort Jay was built between 1794-1800. Fort Jay was a popular post with Army per-

LaGuardia Airport soon after completion in 1939.

sonnel and by the 1930s it had earned the nickname as the fort "Across the Street From Broadway". On Dec. 21, 1941, 14 days after the attack on Pearl Harbor, the Army selected Fort Jay as the headquarters for the Eastern Theater of Operations (later redesignated The Eastern Defense Command) under Gen. Hugh A. Drum, Commander of the First Army. Throughout WW II Fort Jay served in this capacity. In 1942 it also served as a reception center. In 1946, when other forts around the country were being abandoned, Fort Jay was retained as the headquarters of the 1st Army. In 1966 the Army turned the post over to the Coast Guard who converted it into a district headquarters and a training center.

FORT LAFAYETTE (See U.S. Naval Magazine, Fort Lafayette, below)

LaGUARDIA AIRPORT is in Queens on the south shore of the East River. It was built as a commercial airport for land planes and sea planes in 1939. At the time, the facility was the largest seaplane base in the world and was known as North Beach Airport. But, it was soon re-

named LaGuardia Airport in honor of NYC's mayor. The airport's main purpose was to relieve congestion at Newark Municipal Airport. Because of its strategic location the Army, Navy and Coast Guard had plans from the beginning to use the airport. When the U.S. went to war the armed forces followed through and established facilities at LaGuardia. None of the armed services took over the airport and commercial activities continue throughout the war. The AAF was, perhaps, the most active at the field designating it as one of their ports of aerial embarkation. After the war LaGuardia became one of the NYC's most important commercial airports.

MANHATTAN ENGINEERING DISTRICT (MED): This rather nondescript title was a cover for one of the most important scientific undertakings of all time . . the development of the atomic bomb. MED was a top secret organization of the Army Engineer Corps whose mission was to design and build the research, development and production facilities needed to bring the atomic bomb into being. The most important components of this project were the huge atomic production facilities at Oak Ridge, TN and Richland, WA, and the research and development laboratory at Los Alamos, NM. It was from this facility on Manhattan that the entire atomic bomb program received its name, "The Manhattan Project". The facility was located in NYC's garment district at 261 5th Ave. Virtually no one in the area knew its true mission and it was heavily guarded throughout the war.

MITCHEL FIELD, two miles NE of Hempstead, LI, had been a military site since the American Revolution. In 1918 it became a training center for Army aviators and several year later was renamed Mitchell Field in honor of a former NYC mayor. By 1939 Mitchel Field had become the headquarters for several Air Corps units. In 1941, after the Air Corps became the Army Air Forces (AAF), the 1st Air Force was organized here and Mitchel Field became its headquarters. On Dec. 8, 1941, one day after the attack on Pearl Harbor, planes from Mitchel Field began long-range air patrols at sea to

Fort Jay on Governor's Island.

Fort Slocum as it appeared shortly after WW II.

guard against possible enemy attacks. At first the planes were few in number and the crews inexperienced flying over water, but with their early-model B-17s and obsolete B-18s the Mitchel crews were able to patrol up to 600 miles out to sea. The air patrols became more proficient and were maintained throughout the war. Between Jan.-Apr. 1942 several Navy planes operated from Mitchel Field doing anti-submarine duties. As the war progressed Mitchel Field became a AAF reception center and a base of operation for the Air Transport Command which used Mitchel as a staging field and an port of aerial embarkation. The field also acquired an AAF Regional Hospital and a debarkation hospital, the Combined Air Defense Training Center, the Tactical Forcast Center and became the arrival point for many wounded service men returning from North Africa and Europe. In Aug. 1942 Wendell Willkie began his famous round-the-world trip from here. The Field had a main prisoner of war camp holding about 250 POWs who worked for the military. On June 22, 1944 Mitchel Field received the first casualties returned to the U.S. from Normandy and its post hospital began to function as a debarkation hospital. After the war the US Air Force took control of the field and named it Mitchel Air Force Base and continued to use it as an air defense facility under the USAF Air Defense Command. In 1961 the Air Force closed the base and its assets were disposed of. Mitchel Field survived as a civilian field for several years, but in 1982 that came to an end and the land was sold for development and many of the buildings became part of Nassau Community College.

Cradle of Aviation Museum: This museum is on the ground of the former Mitchel Field in two of the early hangars. It has a very large collection of aircraft from all eras of aviation including WW II. Most of the aircraft are inside. There is a large display on Charles Lindbergh who began his famous flight to Paris in 1927 from nearby Roosevelt Field. Address: Museum Lane, Mitchel Field, Garden City, NY 11530. Phone: 516/222-1190. Hours: May through Sept. Fri., Sat., & Sun. noon-5. Dona-

tions requested. Location: Off of Charles Lindbergh Rd. south of Nassau Community College.

NEW YORK NAVAL YARD (See U.S. Naval Yard, New York)

NEW YORK PORT OF EMBARKATION (AIR SECTION): The Army's main port of embarkation for the New York City area was in New Jersey, but this facility, located at 58th St. and 1st Ave., served the AAF.

ROOSEVELT FIELD, in Long Island City, was used by Brewster Aircraft Corp. to test its newly built aircraft. It was also used as an assembly field for aircraft awaiting shipment to Britain under the Lend Lease Program.

FORT SLOCUM was on David's Island just off the waterfront of New Rochelle. David's Island was first used by the Army in 1861 for a hospital. In the 1870s Fort Slocum was built as one of NYC's coastal defense. By the beginning of WW II the fort's guns were gone and the old fort was used by the Army for administrative and training purposes. After the war a portion of Fort Slocum was used by the US Air Force as part of the NYC area's defenses under the Air Defense Command. There were also a number Army schools on the post. In the 1960s the fort was closed and sold to private interests.

ALEXANDER de SEVERSKY GRAVE SITE: De Seversky (1894-1974) is buried in Woodlawn Cemetery in the Bronx. He was an emigre from Russia, an aircraft designer and the founder of the Seversky Aircraft Corp. which was the forerunner of Republic Aviation Corp. Seversky was instrumental in the development of early sea planes, amphibians and later, the P-47 fighter plane. He was also a major in the AAF Reserve.

STATUE OF LIBERTY: During the war the island upon which the Statue of Liberty stood was known as Bedloe's Island and the structure upon which the Statue stood was an old coastal defense position known as Fort Wood. Between 1884 and 1886 the Statue of Liberty was built, rising from the center of the fort. In 1933 the Statue of Liberty, Fort Wood and the entire island became a national park. When WW II started the U.S. Navy took control of the park

and put restrictions on visitors to the island. The Coast Guard installed an observation post on the walls of the old fort, and the Statue's flood lights and torch were dimmed, and at times blacked out. Two 200 watt bulbs were left burning in the torch as a warning to aircraft. After the war the island and its structures were returned to the National Park Service and in 1950 the last of the military structures was torn down. The island eventually became known as Liberty Island. The Statue of Liberty is, of course, one of NYC's great tourist attractions. It is accessible by ferries from either the Battery at the tip of Manhattan or from Liberty State Park, NJ.

FORT TILDEN is near Rockaway Point, south of Brooklyn, facing the Atlantic Ocean. Fort Tilden was built in 1917 as a coastal defense position guarding the entrance to Lower New York Bay. Two of the most powerful guns ever made were mounted here. They were 16" rifles which fired a 2100 lb projectile up to 30 miles. When WW II started the guns were still in place and fully operative. The fort, which by then was a sub-post of Fort Hancock, NJ, also had three 3" guns on permanent mounts used for anti-aircraft defense. After the war all of the guns were removed but Fort Tilden continued in use as a missile launch site. Eventually the fort was abandoned by the Army and became a part of Gateway National Recreation Area administered by the National Park Service.

FORT TOTTEN was near the Throgs Neck Bridge on the south shore of the eastern entrance to the East River. Construction of the fort began during the American Civil War but was not completed until 1898. During WW I the fort served as a training and staging camp for ground troops. In 1922 the fort was selected to be a prototype of an up-to-date anti-aircraft installation and the latest anti-aircraft guns were installed. When WW II started this was still the mission of Fort Totten and it became a headquarters for the anti-aircraft section of the Eastern Defense Command coordinating anti-aircraft operations throughout the NYC and New Jersey areas. Fort Totten was retained by the Army after the war as an anti-aircraft defense position and in 1947 acquired the Army's Medical Equipment Development Laboratory. In 1954 the fort received Nike anti-aircraft missiles and served as an anti-aircraft defense position for another 20 years. In the 1980s the Army abandoned the fort and it was given to NYC for use as a park.

THE UNITED NATIONS: The phrase "United Nations" was used throughout the war and referred, at first, to the Allied nations rather than to the structured international organizations that exists today. In those days the League of Nations, which had been established after WW I, still existed but was discredited and in shambles. It was obvious that a new, and hopefully more successful, organization was needed to take its place. Since the concept was promoted by the "United Nations (Allies)" it was only natural that the name should carry over to the new organization. The framework and structure of the "United Nations Organization" (UNO) was established during the war by a series of international conferences and summit

Lockheed Hudson bombers lined up on Floyd Bennett Field in the spring of 1941 awaiting shipment to Britain.

meetings. In Oct. 1945 the Organization was officially born when the required number of member governments ratified its charter. On Dec. 10, 1945 Congress unanimously invited the UNO to establish its permanent home in the U.S. and on Feb. 14, 1946 the General Assembly, then meeting in London, accepted. A search for sites in the U.S. then began. One of the sites considered was an 18-acre area of land covering 6 square blocks on the east side of Manhattan between 42nd St., 48th St. along the East River. This area was occupied at the time by many old low-rise structures of varying degrees of value and importance. The leaders of the UNO expressed interest in the site and John D. Rockefeller, Jr. offered $8.5 million to purchase the land. The offer was accepted, the land purchased and cleared and in 1949 construction of the new UN buildings begun. Today the UNO complex consists of four major buildings, the General Assembly Building, the Secretariat Building, the Library Building and the Conference Building. And, almost every nation on earth is a member.

U.S. MERCHANT MARINE ACADEMY is located on the north shore of Long Island at King's Point near the eastern entrance to the East River. The U.S. Merchant Marine Cadet Corps was created in 1938 by an act of Congress and in 1942 the site at King's Point was selected for its academy. Much of the ground had been the estate of industrialist Walter P. Chrysler. The Academy was built during the war and before war's end was turning out qualified and well-educated Merchant Marine officers. The Academy continued its mission into the postwar years and in 1956 received equal status with the other armed services academies. The grounds of the Academy and several buildings are open to the public daily 9-5 except on federal holidays and during July. Regimental reviews are held on some Saturdays in the spring and fall. For information on the reviews, phone 516/773-5000.

American Merchant Marine Museum: This fine museum is on the grounds of the U.S. Merchant Marine Academy and tells the history of the Academy and the Merchant Marine. On display are ship models, nautical artifacts, paintings, a working model of a marine steam engine, trophies and more. Address: c/o U.S. Merchant Marine Academy, Steamboat Rd., Kings Point, NY 11024. Phone: 516/773-5515. Hours: Tues. & Wed. 11-3:30, Sat. & Sun. 1-4:30. Closed federal holidays and during July. Free.

U.S. NAVAL AIR STATION, NEW YORK (FLOYD BENNETT FIELD): In the glamour and aftermath of Charles Lindbergh's flight to Paris in 1927 the city fathers of NYC decided that they needed a new and modern airport. They selected a spit of barren and swampy land in south Brooklyn at the mouth of Jamaica Bay. The airport was built during 1929-30 on land built up by land fill and was named Floyd Bennett Municipal Airport in honor of the late Floyd Bennett, a pioneer aviator, naval flyer during WW I and Adm. Richard Byrd's co-pilot on his flight to the North Pole. Upon completion the airport was selected by the U.S. Navy as the site of 1 of 8 naval air reserve bases with the mission of providing primary flight training for Navy flyers. In May 1931 the Navy designated their operations at the field as U.S. Naval Air Station, Brooklyn. The Army air mail service also shared the field in the early years but moved to Mitchell Field in 1934. During the 1930s Floyd Bennett Field was the scene of many record-seeking events and was frequently in the news. In 1939 the newer, larger and more modern LaGuardia Airport became NYC's primary airport, so in early 1941 the Navy took control of Floyd Bennett Field and renamed the facility U.S. Naval Air Station, New York. Further development was slow and the field had several non-Navy tenants including a Coast Guard station, an aviation branch of the NYC Police Department, and an Army Air National Guard training unit. One steady activity at the field during 1941 was the partial disassembly of U.S.-made bombers which were flown to the field from the factory, broken down and crated for shipment to Britain under the Lend Lease Program.

After the attack on Pearl Harbor NAS, New York's handful of Navy planes were pressed into patrol duties, while an aggressive expansion program was began enlarging the field and its facilities. During the war

NAS, New York continued its patrol work, functioned as a flight training center for naval reservists, a ferry base, an air transport base, an aerial port of embarkation and an assembly and test center for planes shipped here in pieces for transmittal to the Fleet. The later operation grew to the point where, by 1944, workers at the station could assemble and deliver up to 800 aircraft a month to the Fleet. By Feb. 1945 the station had assembled 20,000 aircraft. As the war ended operations at NAS, New York declined rapidly. The Navy showed little interest in retaining the station so it was returned to commercial use and was again called Floyd Bennett Municipal Airport. By mid-1946 all of the naval operations were gone except for a naval air reserve training center. In 1971 commercial flying ended at the field and in 1974 the field was transferred to the Department of the Interior to become a part of the Gateway National Recreation Area. During the war NAS, New York had one outlying field, Rockaway Air Field, 1 mile WNW of Edgemere, LI.

U.S. NAVAL MAGAZINE, FORT LAFAYETTE was located on a 2.5 acre diamond-shaped island at The Narrows 200 yards off the Brooklyn shore opposite later-built Fort Hamilton. Fort Lafayette was an old Army coastal defense position built in 1812 and originally known as Fort Diamond. In 1868 a fire ravaged the fort leaving only the magazine intact. From then on the fort functioned only as a storage facility for Army supplies and ammunition. In 1898 the fort was transferred to the Navy for the storage of naval supplies and ammunition. During WW II the fort was used as an interim storage facility and transfer point for small and miscellaneous lots of ammunition, mostly small bore, being loaded or unloaded from ships. The fort had a Marine Barracks and was used at times to house naval personnel who

The battleship "Missouri" on its ways at U.S. Naval Ship Yard, New York (see page 178) just before being launched. This was the world's most powerful battleship at the time.

had disembarked at nearby Denyse Wharf. USNM, Fort Lafayette worked closely with U.S. Naval Ammunition Depot, Iona Island 40 miles north near West Point. The Navy retained USNM, Fort Lafayette for a short while after the war, but in 1948 turned it over to the city of New York. In 1960 the old fort was obliterated to make way for the Verranzano-Narrows Bridge.

U.S. NAVAL SHIP YARD, NEW YORK (BROOKLYN NAVY YARD, NEW YORK NAVY YARD): This was the Navy's battleship "factory". Many of the battleships (BB) that took part in both WW I and WW II were built here including the two BBs closely associated with the beginning and end of WW II. The BB "Arizona", which was sunk at Pearl Harbor during the Japanese attack, was built here in 1916 and the BB "Missouri", upon whose deck the Japanese signed the documents of surrender in Sept. 1945, was built here in 1944.

The naval yard began in the late 1700s as a private ship building company which was then purchased by the U.S. Government in 1800. The yard was expanded several time in the early 1800s and by the time of the Civil War was the Union's most important shipyard. Between 1914 and 1944 it became the leading builder of BBs in the U.S. BBs built here that saw action in WW II include the "New York" (BB-34) 1914, "Arizona" (BB-39) 1916, "New Mexico" (BB-40) 1918, "Tennessee" (BB-43) 1920, "North Carolina" (BB-55) 1940, "Iowa" (BB-61) 1942 and "Missouri" (BB-63) 1944[5]. NSY, New York also built cruisers, aircraft carriers, destroyers, Coast Guard cutters, gunboats, barges, lighters, landing ship tanks (LST) and torpedoes. In Dec. 1941, soon after the attack on Pearl Harbor, over 1000 workers at NSY, New York volunteered to go to Hawaii on short notice to help repair the war damage at Pearl Harbor. NSY, New York worked around-the-clock throughout the war and at its peak, in 1944, employed 71,000 people. At that time is was the largest industrial complex in New York state history. This caused a housing shortage in the local area, but not as bad as at other large shipyards around the country. NSY, New York repaired many more ships during the war than

[5]The "Missouri" was christened by Margaret Truman.

it built. Both U.S. and Allies vessels were serviced here. The British Government designated the yard as a British Naval Base because the yard worked on so many British ships. Throughout the war over 5000 ships were repaired here and 250 commercial vessels were converted to war use. The yard had a huge supply department, a Marine Barracks, a materials laboratory, a gyro compass school, a motion picture operators' school, a motion picture exchange, a radio station and a radio laboratory. During the spring of 1945 more than a dozen warships were refitted at NSY, New York to be temporary troop ships which would be used to bring U.S. service personnel home. On their way out they would take prisoners of war back to Europe. Included in this group of ships was the brand new aircraft carrier "Wasp". On Apr. 29, 1945 a new aircraft carrier, then on the ways at NSY, New York, was christened the "Franklin D. Roosevelt". Roosevelt had died 17 days earlier. The new carrier was christened by Mrs. Franklin D. Roosevelt.

At the end of the war the yard had a brief period of cutbacks, but ship production began to rise again with the onset of the Cold War. With aircraft carriers now the primary warship, the yard concentrated on the construction of those types of ships. The yard had another surge of activity during the Korean War refurbishing many WW II ships which were taken out of mothballs and put back into service. After the Korean War the yard resumed construction of aircraft carriers, but in the 1960s it fell on hard times and in 1966 was closed as part of a nation-wide economy move. The yard's assets were acquired by the city of New York and developed into a large industrial center with some of the old facilities being leased back to the Navy.

FORT WADSWORTH is on the eastern tip of Staten Island at The Narrows, the entrance to Upper New York Bay. This site had been a miliary post since 1626. Several forts existed on the site over the years and in 1865 the post was named Fort Wadsworth. In 1919 control of the fort was relinquished by the Coast Artillery and it became a regular Army post. In that year it also acquired an air field, Miller Army Air Field, which adjoins the community of New Dorp four miles to the SW. By the late 1930s

the post had become the home of part of the Army's 1st Division. Soon after the beginning of WW II the 1st Division moved out and the fort was returned to the Coast Artillery, and put under the control of Fort Hancock, NJ. Fort Wadsworth then served as an active part of NYC's defenses throughout the war. In 1944, when the Italian Service Units (ISU) were created, Fort Wadsworth was chosen as their headquarters under Gen. John M. Eager, ISU Commander. And, when the members of the ISU were repatriated at the end of the war they staged here prior to boarding the ships home. Non-cooperative Italians who did not join the ISUs also staged here prior to repatriation, but they left after the ISU members.

The fort was retained after the war and served as an Army training facility for a number of years and home of the 26th Army Band which performed at military functions throughout the NYC area. In 1976 the post was named by the New York Legislature as a "Living National Park Memorial".

NIAGARA FALLS (See Buffalo/Niagara Falls)

ORANGEBURG is 20 miles north of NYC just west of the Hudson River.

CAMP SHANKS, near Orangeburg, operated for only three years but in that time 1,362,6300 troops used it. Camp Shanks was a large staging camp for troops going overseas through the New York ports of embarkation. The camp opened in Jan. 1943 and closed in July 1946. In 1944 Italian Service Units worked here, and the post's hospital became a debarkation hospital near the end of the war. When the war ended in Europe Camp Shanks became a staging area for German prisoners of war being repatriated. On July 23, 1946 the last of the POWs left Camp Shanks and many photographers were on hand to record this momentous event. The last man to walk up the ship's gang plank in New York Harbor was a 22 year old electrician from Heidelberg. In compliance with the photographers' requests he walked up the gang plank 7 times so they could all get enough photographs. After the war the land and assets of Camp Shanks were sold to private developers.

OSWEGO is on Lake Ontario 35 miles NW of Syracuse.

FORT ONTARIO was located on the east bank of the Oswego River where it flows into Lake Ontario. The fort's original purpose was to guard the entrance to the Oswego River from enemy attacks. By the beginning of WW II the old fort was obsolete, but still in the hands of the Army and it had many old and sturdy buildings. The fort was small, but the Army used it during the war as a basic training camp. In mid-1944 the fort was turned over to the War Relocation Administration, the same organization that administered the relocation camps for the ethnic Japanese, and was used to house refugees, mostly Jews, arriving from Europe. The U.S. did not take many European refugees during the war and this was the only location in the U.S. where such refugees were housed. After the war the refugees were returned to Europe. In the postwar years the Army turned the fort over to the state and it became a State Historical Site. In the main building there is a museum with displays that trace the history of

Fort Wadsworth on the eastern tip of Staten Island at The Narrows, the entrance to Upper New York Bay.

German prisoners of war from Camp Shanks board the hospital ship "Francis Y. Slanger" for their return home.

the fort. Address: E. 7th St., Oswego, NY 13126. Phone: 315/343-4711/1342. Hours: Mid-May thru Oct. 31 W-Sat. 10-5, Sun. and holidays 1-5. Admission charged.

OYSTER BAY AREA: This is a beautiful and historic area on the northeastern shore of Long Island. During the war Oyster Bay was a small unincorporated community, but well-known as the home of the late President Theodore Roosevelt. Oyster Bay had some manufacturing firms including the Jakobson Shipyard, Corp. which built mine sweepers, and steel and wooden tugs for the Navy.

OLD ORCHARD MUSEUM: This was the home of Gen. Theodore Roosevelt, Jr. who was the assistant commander of the 1st Div. during the North African operations, and of the 4th Div. during the invasion of Normandy. Roosevelt had also been Governor-General of the Philippines. He died suddenly on July 12, 1944 of a heart attack while on active duty in France. The home was built in 1938 and contains many of the original furnishings and personal belongings of the General. There are exhibits and an audiovisual program relating to the political and family life of the Roosevelt family. Address: Oyster Bay, NY 11771. Phone: 516/922-4447. Hours: daily 9:30-5, closed Jan 1, Martin Luther King, Jr's. Birthday, Thanksgiving and Dec. 25. Admission charged. Location: about three miles east of Oyster Bay near Sagamore Hill National Historic Site.

HENRY L. STIMSON GRAVE SITE: Henry L. Stimson is buried in St. John's Church Memorial Cemetery in Cold Spring Harbor, 13 miles east of Oyster Bay. Stimson, a Republican, served in the Cabinets of three presidents. He was Secretary of War under President Taft, Secretary of State under President Hoover and Secretary of War for a second time under President Franklin Roosevelt. Prior to his Cabinet appointments he was Governor of the Philippines under President Coolidge. In the early 1930s Stimson was an outspoken critic of Japanese expansionism in Manchuria and China. In 1939-40 he became a strong advocate of aid to Britain and partly because of this stand,

President Roosevelt appointed him as Secretary of War in June 1940 soon after the collapse of France. Stimson was also an early advocate of proceeding post-haste with the development of the atomic bomb. And, when the bomb became a reality, he strongly urged President Truman to use it.

PAWLING is 15 miles NW of Danbury, CT and was the home of Thomas E. Dewey, Governor of New York, Republican candidate for President against Franklin Roosevelt[6] in 1944 and against Harry S Truman in 1948.

ARMY AIR FORCES HOSPITAL, PAWLING: This was a former boys preparatory school one mile north of Pawling that was taken over by the AAF and used as a convalescent hospital for AAF personnel and as a personnel distribution center. After the war the hospital was closed.

THOMAS E. DEWEY GRAVE SITE is located in the Pawling Cemetery Mausoleum in Pawling, NY. After his distinguished political career Dewey returned to the practice of law in 1955 and died in 1971.

PLATTSBURGH is on the western shore of Lake Champlain.

PLATTSBURGH BARRACKS, one mile south of Plattsburgh, was built in 1812 as an Army post. It was subsequently occupied and abandoned several times until 1865. From then on, it was occupied continually by various Army units until 1946. Plattsburgh Barracks was a small post but it had many solid old stone buildings, beautiful surroundings and was considered one of the most desirable posts in the Army. During WW II the post was used by the AAF as a convalescent hospital and a personnel redistribution center. In 1946 the post was turned over to the state and used for student housing and a college. In 1955 the US Air Force acquired the post, converted into an air base called Plattsburgh Air Force Base which remained active throughout the Cold War.

PLUM ISLAND is off the eastern tip of Long Island between Long Island Sound and Gardiner's Bay.

[6]Pawling is only 24 miles from Hyde Park, the home of Franklin Roosevelt

FORT TERRY was built on Plum Island in 1898 as a coastal defence position protecting the entrances to both Long Island Sound and Gardiner's Bay. It mounted two 10" rifles and eight 12" mortars. During WW II the fort was armed and manned. It was closed near the end of the war and became a summer training center for the New York National Guard. Later Plum Island, along with the fort, was transferred to the Department of Agriculture which converted the facilities into a laboratory doing research on hoof-and-mouth disease and other animal diseases.

ROME/UTICA AREA: These towns are in the Mohawk River Valley 20 and 25 miles east of Syracuse. Some of the larger companies in the area that did war work were The Savage Arms Corp. of Utica which made Thompson sub-machine guns, gun parts and small caliber ammunition; Remington Arms Co. in Ilion (10 miles SE of Utica) which made Springfield rifles, pistols and small caliber ammunition; Auto Ordnance Co. in Utica which made Thompson sub-machine guns and Remington Rand Corp. which made projectiles.

RHOADS GENERAL HOSPITAL was a 2000-bed temporary hospital of wooden construction built in Utica in 1943 to treat war wounded. It specialized in general medicine and general and orthopedic surgery. In June 1946 the facility was transferred to the state of New York.

ROME ARMY AIR FIELD was two miles ENE of Rome. It was first acquired by the AAF in Feb. 1942 as a facility for the overhauling of aircraft engines and was known as the Rome Air Depot. Between late 1942 and 1948 the facility had a confusing series of name changes, some of which were within months of each other. During the war the field was run by the Air Technical Service Command, but was shared with the Air Transport Command which had a freight terminal here. The field also had a school for aircraft mechanics. On Jan. 29, 1948, just 6 days after having been named Rome Air Force Base, the facility's name was changed one more time to Griffiss Air Force Base in honor of Lt. Col. Townsend E. Griffiss a WW II pilot and native of Buffalo, NY who was accidently shot down by friendly fire over the coast of England after returning from a mission. Griffiss AFB remained active as an Air Force base throughout the Cold War and had no more name changes.

SACKETTS HARBOR (See Watertown/Sacketts Harbor/Great Bend Area)

SCHENECTADY (See Albany/Schenectady Area)

SENECA FALLS (See Geneva/Seneca Falls Area)

SYRACUSE is in the central part of the state midway between Albany and Buffalo. Some of the major manufacturers in Syracuse were the Remington Rand Corp. which made 45 caliber pistols; L.C. Smith & Corona Typewriters, Inc. which made 30 caliber rifles; U.S. Hoffman Machinery Co. which made 155 mm shells and fuzes and the General Electric Corp. which built a new plant here in late 1944 to manufacture America's first jet aircraft engines.

NEW YORK STATE FAIRGROUNDS, near Syracuse, was taken over by the AAF for the duration of the war and used as a specialized air depot.

SYRACUSE ARMY AIR BASE, three miles NNE of town, was the city's local airport before the war. It was taken over by the 1st AF early in 1942 according to pre-war planning and used as a base for combat-ready aircraft defending the eastern seaboard. After the fear of enemy attacks diminished the air field was turned over to the short-lived I Concentration Command. After this command was disbanded the field went to the Air Service Command and was used for training. The Air Technical Service Command and Air Transport Command also had operations at the field. Syracuse AAB had one auxiliary field during the war, Fulton Air Field, 2.5 miles NNE of Fulton, NY. After the war the AAF departed from Syracuse AAB and it was returned to civilian use.

UTICA (See Rome/Utica Area)

WATERTOWN/SACKETTS HARBOR/ GREAT BEND AREA: These communities are in NW New York south of the Thousand Islands area.

MADISON BARRACKS was located on the shore of Lake Ontario in the town of Sacketts Harbor which is 11 miles west of Watertown. The facility was established in 1815 as a post for the regular Army. Madison Barrack was opened and closed several times during the 1800s. During WW I it was used as an Army hospital. During WW II it saw little use and served as a reserve facility for both the Army and Navy. In July 1945 the post was declared surplus and its assets dispose of.

PINE CAMP was just north of the community of Great Bend which is 10 miles east of Watertown. The camp began in 1908 as a training camp for National Guard units from New England. When WW II started it was taken over by the Army and used as a training camp for division-sized units. During the war the 4th Armored, 5th Armored and 45th Infantry Divisions trained here. Early in the war GIs in training here were used as test subjects for a new field ration called "Defense Ham". The tests were successful and the product was adopted by the army and distributed generously to U.S. troops throughout the world. It is better known by its commercial name, "Spam". Pine Camp had a main prisoner of war camp holding about 1000 POWs who worked for the military. In late 1944 Pine Camp became one of several camps where Italian Service Units were trained. Pine Camp had its own air field, Wheeler-Sack Field, one mile NNW of Great Bend which was used in conjunction with the training programs at the camp. Pine Camp remained active after the war and in 1951 the post was renamed Camp Drum in honor of Lt. Gen. Huge Drum, commander of the 1st Army during WW II and later of the New York National Guard. In 1974 the post was made a permanent installation of the Army and renamed Fort Drum. Throughout the postwar years the post was home to many Army units and continued to be a training ground for National Guard and Army Reserve units.

WEST POINT AREA: West Point is 44 miles north of NYC on the Hudson River. It is famous throughout the world as the home of the United States Military Academy.

STEWART FIELD is four miles NW of Newburgh, NY which is 8 miles north of West Point. This was Newburgh's local air field until 1936. In that year it was donated to the U.S. Military Academy to become a training field for the Academy's air cadets. The field therefore came under the administrative control of the Superintendent of the Academy, and from that time on offered basic and advanced flight training to the cadets. The air field was taken over by the US Air Force after the war and served throughout the Cold War. During the war Stewart Field had three auxiliary fields:

- Aux. #1 Montgomery Airport, 2 miles SW of Montgomery
- Aux. #2 Wallkill Air Field, 3 miles NW of Wallkill
- Aux. #3 New Hackensack Airport, .5 mile west of New Hackensack

U.S. MILITARY ACADEMY surrounds the town of West Point and sprawls southwestward for some 10 miles. The heart of the Academy, however, is adjacent to the town. The Academy began as an Army fort during the Revolutionary War. In 1802 it was converted into the Military Academy with the mission to train young men as professional Army officers. The Academy has pursued that mission without interruption to this day. Many of the well-known Army and Army Air Forces officers of WW II gained their education and commissions here. Douglas MacArthur and Simon Bolivar Buckner, Jr. served as Academy Superintendents before the war. All told, some 8800 West Point officers served in various military posts throughout the war. Although they constituted less than 2% of the Army's officers, 83% of the Army's WW II generals, 65% of the Lt. generals and 55% of the major generals (exclusive of medical officers) were West Point graduates. During WW II the normal four-year academic course was reduced to three and as many cadets as possible were admitted and trained. In July 1943 the Academy admitted 1200 plebes, their largest class ever. Cadets had some of their field exercises at existing Army camps around the nation and trained alongside draftees. Some of the lecturers at the Academy where WW II veterans who had returned from the front. In 1945 West Point's summer camp, heretofore known as Camp Popolopen, was renamed Camp Buckner in honor of Gen. Simon Bolivar Buckner, Jr., who was killed on Okinawa. Camp Popolopen had a main prisoner of war camp during the war holding about 300 German POWs who worked at the Academy. Also during the war, a large amount of the nation's silver was stored at West Point. Some of it was sold to industry to be used in electrical equipment because of the copper shortage. The campus of the Academy is open to visitors but many of the academic and administrative buildings are off limits. Visitors are welcome to visit the chapels, Trophy Point, historic Fort Clinton, the West Point Museum and are invited to cadet parades and athletic events. It is suggested that visitors go first to the Visitors Center in Bldg. 618, just inside Thayer Gate. Bus tours are available. The Visitors Center is open daily 9-4:45, closed Jan. 1, Thanksgiving and Dec. 25. Phone: 914/938-2638.

U.S. Military Academy Museum: This excellent museum is on the grounds of the Academy in Olmsted Hall on New South Post. It traces the history of the Academy and has one of the largest collections of military artifacts in the Western Hemisphere. Address: c/o U.S. Military Academy, West Point, NY 10996. Phone: 914/938-2203. Hours: daily 10:30-4:15, closed Jan. 1, Thanksgiving and Dec. 25. Free.

West Point National Cemetery: This cemetery holds the remains of many West Pointers as well as ordinary soldiers. Prominent individuals of the WW II era buried here include: Gen. Lucius Clay, Deputy Chief of Staff and Assistant Chief of Staff in Washington, DC and base section commander at Normandy; Gen. Frank Merrill, Commander of Merrill's Marauders in the China-Burma-India Theater and Gen. Alexander Patch, Army Commander on Guadalcanal and later Commander of the 7th Army in France.

U.S. NAVAL AMMUNITION DEPOT, IONA ISLAND was located on the west bank of the Hudson River 9 miles south of West Point. This was a small Navy depot that was acquired by the Navy in 1900. It served as an assembly facility and a distribution point for ammunition going aboard warships in the New York Harbor area. Ammunition components were brought to NAD, Iona Island from various manufacturers, assembled, inspected and sent on to the ships. This was the depot's main activity in both WW I and WW II. During WW II the depot had a Marine Barracks. In the early postwar years the depot was closed.

WESTHAMPTON BEACH is on the south shore of Long Island 7 miles south of Riverhead.

SUFFOLK COUNTY ARMY AIR FIELD, three miles north of Westhampton Beach, was built by the AAF and turned over to the 1st AF which used it as an operational base protecting Long Island and as a training facility for fighter pilots. At one time during the war Brazilian fighter pilots were trained here. The air field was used for a few years after the war but eventually the AAF departed and the field was turned over to the county and became a general aviation field known as Suffolk County Airport.

YAPHANK is in central Long Island.

CAMP UPTON, five miles NE of Yaphank, was built in 1917 by the Army as a divisional training camp and could house up to 43,000 troops. After WW I the War Department closed the camp but retained the land as a military reservation. In early 1941 the camp was reactivated and served as a reception center for the II Corps and training camp as before. Upton had a main prisoner of war camp holding 500 POWs who worked at the camp. In Sept. 1944 Camp Upton was converted to a convalescent hospital and 8 new masonry buildings were built to accommodate 3500 patients. Eventually the camp was closed and much of the land and building taken over by the Department of Energy which use it to build a new facility called Brookhaven National Laboratories.

NORTH CAROLINA

North Carolina was, believe it or not, one of the major battlegrounds of WW II. The battle field was the state's coastal waters. More Allied ships and more Axis submarines were sunk here than any where else in the Western Hemisphere. The battle reached its height during the first six months of 1942, and then continued intermittently until VE Day. Thousands of people lost their lives off the North Carolina coast and substantial damage was done to the merchant fleets of America and her Allies.

The people of North Carolina, who were only minimally effected by the carnage taking place in their coastal waters, contributed in many ways to the war effort. First and foremost, their state was a large training ground for over two million GIs, Airmen, Sailors and Marines. In the summer of 1941, North Carolina, along with South Carolina, was host to a large-scale Army maneuver that covered thousands of square miles and involved tens of thousands of people.

The construction of new military camps and the expansion of existing ones brought a much needed upsurge in the state's economy which had suffered badly during the Depression. North Carolina was also host to many enemy troops housed in the state's 17 prisoner of war camps.

North Carolina's farmers produced tobacco, cotton, cottonseed oil, corn, hay, peanuts, wheat, soy beans, oats, sweet potatoes, Irish potatoes, truck garden vegetables, poultry, hogs and dairy products. The state had a substantial fishing industry that produced fish, crabs, oysters, shrimp and menhaden. North Carolina's mines gave us mica, feldspar, bromine, gold, phosphates, clays, gravel & stone. During the war state and Federal surveys discovered deposits of tungsten and manganese ores.

North Carolina, while not a large industrial state, had plants and factories that produced ships, aircraft components, munitions, radar components, lumber, poles & pilings, pulp, veneer, furniture, ceramics and clothing. The state's clothing industry supplied the Armed Forces with more clothing than any other state during the war years.

North Carolina, nevertheless, had its share of problems. There was a severe shortage of farm labor, there were housing shortages in some cities and a disastrous hurricane in Aug. 1944 was followed by an epidemic of polio.

North Carolina was a segregated state, but negroes and Indians found ample employment on farms, military bases and in war plants. They also wit-nessed the beginning of the breakdown of the old order that would culminate in the Civil Rights Movement of the next decade. The war brought progressive measures to the state's school system in that the compulsory age of school attendance was raised by the state legislature form 13 to 16. More and better roads were built and several new dams where built which made North Carolina a major producer of hydro-electric power in the postwar years.

ABERDEEN (See Fayetteville/Aberdeen/ Southern Pines)

ASHEVILLE is in the center of a popular touriest area in the western part of the state. In early 1942 the town's famous resort, the Grove Park Inn, was taken over by the Government and used for a very unique purpose. In July 1944 Asheville's four largest hotels, Grove Park Inn, the George Vanderbilt, the Asheville-Biltmore and the Battery Park, were taken over by the Army and used as one of five[1] redistribution center in the U.S. for returning service personnel. They were given several weeks of morale-raising rest and relaxation before being sent on to new assignments. The Air Force took over Lake Lure Inn and Rocky Road Inn at Lake Lure, 25 miles SE of Asheville and used them for the same purpose.

ASHEVILLE-HENDERSON AIRPORT, 11 miles south of town, was the area's local airport and was used by AAF, Navy and Coast Guard during the war. The Army used it as one of three airfields in the country under the command of the Commanding General of the AAF. The airport served as the headquarters for the Army Air Communication System and had an AAF weather wing. The Navy used it

[1]The others were Lake Placid, NY; Miami Beach, FL; Hot Springs, AR and Santa Barbara, CA.

as one of the fields in its air transport system. After the war the airport became known as Asheville Municipal Airport.

GROVE PARK INN, about two miles north of downtown, was one of four luxury hotels[2] leased by the U.S. Government during the first months of the war to house Axis diplomats and their families who needed to be housed temporarily while they awaited exchange for American diplomats from Axis countries. The Greenbrier Hotel in West Virginia and The Homestead in Virginia were leased in Dec. 1941 and soon filled. Grove Park Inn was then leased in Apr. 1942 and housed Italian, Bulgarian and Hungarian diplomats, their families, servants, pets and private possessions. Axis diplomats from Mexico, Cuba and El Salvador were also brought here. Among them were several hundred Japanese diplomats but they were soon sent on to the Greenbrier where most of the other Japanese diplomats were housed. On June 11, 1942 the last of the diplomats left Grove Park Inn to begin their trip home. In Oct. 1942 the Navy took over the Inn and used it as a rest and rehabilitation facility for naval personnel. Grove Park Inn housed mostly naval officers during this time. In the spring of 1944 Manuel L. Quezon, President of the Philippines, and his entourage resided at the hotel for about a month. During that time the hotel was the temporary headquarters of the Philippine Government-in-exile. In July 1944 the Inn, along with three other resort hotels in Asheville, were leased by the Army and designated as a rest and redistribution center for returning combat veterans. The veterans were given a 21-day

[2]The other three luxury hotels were the Homestead in Hot Springs, Virginia; Bedford Springs Hotel at Bedford, PA and the Greenbrier in White Sulphur Springs, West Virginia.

The Grove Park Inn as it appeared at the beginning of the war.

furlough to visit their families and then returned to the Grove Park Inn and the other Asheville resorts for an additional 10-14 days. During this time they were allowed to bring their spouses. Grove Park Inn served the Army until Sept. 1945. It was then renovated at government expense, a condition stipulated in the original lease, and returned to civilian use. The hotel has a portrait gallery showing many of the famous people who have stayed at the hotel over the years. WW II personalities include Franklin and Eleanor Roosevelt and Dwight D. Eisenhower. Address: 290 Macon Ave. Asheville, NC 28804. Phone: 704/252-2711.

MOORE GENERAL HOSPITAL, in Swannanoa, NC east of Asheville on Black Mountain Rd., was built by the Government in 1942 to be a 2605-bed Army hospital. The hospital treated mostly war wounded from Europe and the Mediterranean areas and specialized in general medicine, tropical diseases, general and orthopedic surgery and psychiatry. On June 28, 1944 it received its first wounded from the Normandy invasion which took place only 22 days earlier. The hospital had a branch prisoner of war camp holding about 250 POWs who worked at the hospital. The POW camp later became a 4H camp. In Nov. 1946 the hospital was taken over by the Veterans Administration and was used as a center for the treatment of tuberculosis.

U.S. NAVAL HOSPITAL, KENILWORTH PARK was just south of downtown Asheville on Caldonia Rd. in the Kenilworth section of Asheville. It was originally built as a resort known as the Kenilworth Inn but was later converted into a psychiatric hospital known as Appalachian Hall. In May 1943 it was taken over by the Navy and its resident patients moved elsewhere. The Navy used the facility to treat wounded sailors and Marines and offered a wide variety of medical services. In July 1945 it was renamed U.S. Naval Special Hospital, Kenilworth Park. In Apr. 1946 the Navy returned the facility to its former owners and it again became known as Appalachian Hall.

The entrance to the USS North Carolina Battleship Memorial. The battleship is to the right.

BEAUFORT: (See Cape Lookout/Morehead City/Beaufort area)

CAPE FEAR/WILMINGTON AREA: This is the southern coastal area of North Carolina. Cape Fear is the southern-most of the state's three famous capes and an important landmark to seafarers sailing the U.S. east coast. Wilmington is the largest city in the area 20 miles upriver from the mouth of the Cape Fear River. Wilmington's largest manufacturer was the new North Carolina Shipbuilding Co., a major ship yard, built in 1941 on Wilmington's waterfront. Because of the ship yard and Camp Davis, which was being built 22 miles NE of town, Wilmington was a busy city before the U.S. entered the war. The town was already feeling the pangs of a boom town with housing shortages, a food shortage, overcrowded schools, traffic congestion, etc. When the war came these conditions got a lot worse and stayed bad throughout the war. When the U.S. entered the war the ship yard began working around-the-clock and at its peak employed 21,000 people. It is estimated that Wilmington's population soared from 33,400 before the war to 120,000 by 1943. Federal housing was built to help ease the shortage, but it was unable to keep pace with the demand. There was a branch prisoner of war camp in town bounded by 8th, 10th, Castle and Ann Sts. The POWs worked for the military.

When the war ended, Wilmington's boom rapidly turned to bust. The ship yard, which had built 243 cargo and passenger ships during the war, closed as did Camp Davis. The Brunswick River, however, was selected as one of the sites for mothballed Liberty and Victory ships. Hundreds of ships lined both sides of the river awaiting a buyer or the scrap heap. By 1969 the ships were gone. In 1954 a part of the ship yard reopened as a port terminal. Tourism blossomed in the Wilmington area after the war due in part to the many service personnel and war workers who came to the area and discovered its many attributes.

BLUETHENTHAL FIELD/WILMINGTON ARMY AIR FIELD/CAMP DAVIS ARMY AIR FIELD was three miles NE of downtown Wilmington. It was the area's local pre-war airport and was used by the Army, Navy and Coast Guard during the war. On Dec. 8, 1941, the day after the attack on Pearl Harbor, AAF P-39 fighter planes arrived at the field according to pre-war planning to defend the area and carry out air patrols along the coast. Later B-17s and B-24s flew out of the field performing these missions. Still later, the field was used by the 1st AF for the training of P-40 and P-47 fighter pilots. The AAF eventually took over and expanded the airport renaming it Wilmington Army Air Field. Planes flew from here towing targets for the anti-aircraft gunner trainees at Camp Davis. That portion of the field was designated Camp Davis Army Air Field. After the war the air field was returned to civilian use and became New Hanover International Airport.

FORT CASWELL is an old coastal defense position at the eastern end of Oak Island protecting the mouth of the Cape Fear River. It was built between 1895-1902 but declared surplus after WW I and sold to private interests. At the beginning of WW II the Navy purchased the fort and used it as a submarine tracking station, communications center, training center and a depot. Several of the British trawlers, loaned to the U.S. for anti-submarine patrols, and 6 armed yachts of the "Hooligan Navy" were stationed here. In 1949 the fort was sold to the Baptist State Convention. The fort is open to visitors. Check at the visitor's center for information and passes.

ETHYL CORPORATION SHELLING: The story is told in the Cape Fear/Wilmington area that on July 25, 1943 (other accounts give the date as July 15) a German submarine fired five shells at the Ethyl Corporation plant near Kure Beach, NC. This plant was, at the time, one of only

Fort Caswell as it appeared in the 1990s from one of the old ramparts. Some WW II structures remained after the war, but most of the buildings are older.

The Hatch cover from the German submarine U-85 sunk off Cape Hatteras by the destroyer "Roper" on March 14, 1942. There are four WW II German submarines and one WW II American submarine in North Carolina's waters. Two of the German submarines and the American submarine are accessible to divers.

two such facilities in the nation making the very important "Ethyl" (tetraethyl lead) additive for gasolines which was especially useful in aviation gasoline. The German gunners' aim was off and all five shots overshot the plant and landed in the Cape Fear River. It is also told that the German submarine was sunk the next day by U.S. aircraft. Postwar German documents, however, fail to record this attack, and there are no records of a German submarines having been sunk on July 26, 1943 (or July 16, 1943) along the U.S. east coast. The plant was closed in 1946 and the grounds became part of the buffer zone for the Sunny Point Military Ocean Terminal, a postwar facility.

FORT FISHER is two miles south of Kure Beach on the ocean. It is an old Confederate earthworks fortification that was used by the Army during WW II as a training center for anti-aircraft gunners. Targets would be towed by planes along the coast and the gunners would shoot seaward at the targets. After the war the fort became known as Fort Fisher State Historic Site. A small museum exists at the fort, but there is very little reference to WW II.

USS "NORTH CAROLINA" BATTLESHIP MEMORIAL is located on the west side of the Cape Fear River across from the Wilmington waterfront. The main attraction is, of course, the preserved WW II-era battleship "North Carolina" which saw considerable action in the Pacific. The Memorial is dedicated to the men and women who served in WW II. The ship is open to visitors and every night during the summer months there is light and music display of the ship beginning at 9:00 pm. The Memorial has a large modern Visitors Center which offers many displays related to the ship and its role in WW II. Address: PO Box 417, Wilmington, NC 28402. Phone: 910/762-1829. Hours: daily 8:00-sunset. Admission charged.

CAPE HATTERAS AREA: This is the northernmost and easternmost of North Carolina's three famous capes. It is also the most treacherous for sailors and long before WW II was known as "The Graveyard of the Atlantic". Because of its geographic location, many east coast commercial shipping lanes merge or cross here resulting in an exceptionally heavy congestion of north-south seaborne traffic. The waters off the Cape are shallow in most places and dotted with dangerous shoals. To add to the maze of navigational obstacles, the Gulf Stream passes nearby moving shoreward at times, then seaward at others causing an ever-changing pattern of ocean currents. Finally, the area is subject to occasional hurricanes and severe thunder storms. At the beginning of WW II these facts were well known to Germany's naval commanders. They also knew that U.S. anti-submarine defenses in the area were very weak, so when the U.S. entered the war Cape Hatteras was one of the primary locations along the U.S. east coast where German submarines were sent to operate. Their success in sinking ships was outstanding. Between Jan. and May 1942 German submarines sank or damaged dozens of ships off Cape Hatteras. As American defensive strength grew in the area the presents of U.S. warships off shore and planes overhead was an everyday occurrence. Also in Cape Hatteras waters, the Navy laid one of the largest mine fields in U.S. water consisting of 2635 mines.

The coastal is-

lands and peninsulas that make up the Cape were, during the war, remote, sparsely settled and virtually defenseless. The few people who lived here had front row seats to the most dramatic naval activities along the east coast which, at times, occurred only yards away from their homes.

CAPE HATTERAS NATIONAL SEASHORE MUSEUM OF THE SEA is located at the Visitors Center near Cap Hatteras Lighthouse at the tip of the cape. The museum relates the history of Cape Hatteras and offers many displays and maritime artifacts. The museum's collection spans many decades, but there are several interesting displays related to WW II including the hatch cover of the German submarine U-85 which was salvaged by divers some years ago. The museum is in the former lightkeepers dwelling. Guided tours and lectures are offered. Address: Buxton, NC 27920 Phone: 919/005-4474 Hours: daily 9-5. Free.

BRITISH CEMETERY is located on Cemetery Road in Ocracoke, NC which is near the western end of Ocracoke Island. It consists of four graves of British seamen killed when their ship, the British trawler "HMS Bedfordshire" was torpedoed and sunk by the German submarine U-558 between Cape Hatteras and Cape Lookout on May 1, 1942. Two of the seamen are identified and two are unknown. The bodies of all four were found in the waters off Ocracoke several days after the sinking. The cemetery has been deeded over to the British Government and the British flags flies overhead.

BILLY MITCHELL AIRPORT is located at Frisco, NC about five miles west of the Cape. In 1923 this was a temporary air field built by the citizens of the Cape Hatteras area in response to Brig. Gen. Billy Mitchell's call for an air field from which he could conduct a very important aerial demonstration. Mitchell, an early advocate of military air power, subsequently used the field on Sept. 5, 1923 as his takeoff point to rendezvoused with bombers flying down from Langley Field, VA. Together, they proceeded to bomb and sink two obsolete battleships, the "Virginia" and "New Jersey", which were anchored 20 miles off the coast. This was a demonstration to prove to a

The British Cemetery at Ocracoke, NC contains the graves of four British seamen killed in North Carolina waters during WW II.

Billy Mitchell Airport Frisco, NC.

gathering of high-ranking Army and Navy officers that aircraft could sink large warships. It was one of three such demonstrations Mitchell conducted in the 1920s. Despite the convincing evidence provided by Mitchell and his airmen there was much resistance to his claims within the military, and it was not until the harsh realities of WW II proved him right.

CAPE LOOKOUT/MOREHEAD CITY/ BEAUFORT AREA:
This is North Carolina's third famous cape midway between Cape Hatteras and Cape Fear. Cape Lookout is a National Seashore and a popular tourist area. During WW II, however, it became a critical military location, a place of sanctuary for ships and an area to be defended. Cape Lookout is shaped like a fish hook and the water inside of the hook is known as Lookout Bight. This calm and relatively deep body of water was used as an anchorage for merchant ships during the critical early months of 1942 when German submarines ran rampant along the North Carolina coast. Lookout Bight was protected by an anti-submarine net and a mine field. Beauford Inlet also had a protective mine field. On the Cape itself was a Coast Guard station and an Army coastal defense post consisting of three guns and several barracks. In the postwar years the Coast Guard station and the Army defense post were abandoned and the cape remained uninhabited except by National Seashore personnel and visitors. The foundations for the guns remain but are slowly being eroded by the sea. The area is not easily accessible and visitors should check with local park rangers before attempting the visit the site.

Morehead City and Beaufort were the two largest towns in the Cape Lookout area. Several Coast Guard and Navy anti-submarine patrol vessels operated out of a naval section base at Morehead City as did several of the British trawlers. The base also had a degaussing range. A stone monument at US 70 and 35th St. marks the site of the base. Morehead City's hospital treated many of the survivors from the ships sunk off the coast, and Morehead City's cemetery, as well as other cemeteries in the area, hold the bodies of some of those who were killed. The city has several dive centers that offer diving trips to the sunken WW II ships off shore.

ALICE ROOSEVELT HOFFMAN ESTATE:
This was a large estate on Bogue Bank Island owned by Alice Roosevelt Hoffman, an aunt to Mrs. Theodore Roosevelt, Jr. The estate stretched for 9 miles along the central section of the island and now encompasses parts of the town of Pine Knoll Shore and the Theodore Roosevelt Natural Area. The estate's main house, which was accessible only by a winding dirt road, was located in what is now the 200 block of Oak Leaf Dr. in Pine Knoll Shore. Mrs. Hoffman had lived on the estate for many years and by the time of WW II was old, infirmed and restricted much of the time to a wheelchair. She had few friends and was very reclusive. She was known as the "Queen of Bogue Banks", or at times as "the rich old recluse" and rumors about her had circulated for years. When war started the rumors became uglier prompted, in part, by her continued reclusiveness and her German-sounding name. It was rumored that she had "foreigners" on her payroll, that she was a German spy, that she sent secret radio messages to German submarines off shore about the departure and arrivals of ships and, worst of all, that she refueled German submarines at her private dock. None of these rumors were true and she was quite friendly with those with whom she came in contact. The ocean front area of her land was patrolled by Coastguardsmen, some of whom she befriended. And, from time-to-time, she would have little parties for them with tea and pastries. The Coastguardsmen appreciated her kindness, but her critics claimed it was just a ploy to gain their confidence and pump vital information out of them. The rumors were so intense that for a while soldiers were assigned to watch her house. Mrs. Hoffman continued to live on her estate, maintaining her reclusive life-style, until she died in 1953.

FORT MACON is on the eastern end of Bogue Bank Island and was built in 1834 to protect the entrance to Beaufort Inlet. In 1924 the fort was transferred to the state of North Carolina for use as a park. In Dec. 1941, when the U.S. went to war, the Federal Government leased the fort and converted it into a coastal defense position. The Army stayed until 1945 and in 1946 the fort was returned to the state and was again used as a state park. One of the rooms in the fort has been preserved and furnished at it was during WW II when GIs lived here. Address: PO Box 127, Atlantic Beach, NC 28512. Phone: 919/726-3775.

CHARLOTTE is in the south-central part of the state.

CHARLOTTE ARMY AIR BASE, 5.5 miles west of town, was the city's local airport before the war known as Morris Field. It was taken over by

Bayview Cemetery, Morehead City, NC: The grave of a British gunner who died on one of the many British ships sunk along the North Carolina coast in 1942.

These foundations are the remains of the WW II gun mounts at the tip of Cape Lookout. They are slowly being eroded by the sea.

the 1st AF early in the war and used as a sub-base to Greenville Army Air Base. Combat-ready aircraft were stationed here as part of the America's east coast defenses. In 1946 the AAF departed and the field reverted to it civilian use and eventually became Charlotte-Douglas International Airport.

CHARLOTTE QUARTERMASTER DEPOT was located at 1820 Statesville Rd. in Charlotte. This was a Ford Motor Co. automobile assembly plant before the war that was bought by the Federal Government and converted into a Army quartermaster depot. Five large warehouses were added to the complex and the depot received, stored and shipped a wide variety of items to Army posts in the U.S. and overseas. It is said that the depot handled everything from "soap to fireproof safes". The depot had a branch prisoner of war camp holding about 145 POWs who worked at the depot. After the war the depot was acquired by the Douglas Aircraft Co. and became an assembly plant for missiles. Later, the depot and its warehouses became part of a large industrial complex occupied primarily by the Eckerd (Drugstores) Corp.

DUNN is 22 miles NE of Fayetteville.

THE GENERAL WILLIAM C. LEE AIRBORNE MUSEUM is located at 209 Divine St. in Dunn and is the former home of Gen. Lee who is known as the "Father of the Airborne Infantry". Lee was given the assignment by President Franklin Roosevelt to organize and develop the Army's first airborne (parachute) units. His efforts lead to the development of the Airborne Command which carried out numerous

Fort Macon, at the eastern end of Bogue Bank Island, was over 130 years old but was manned and armed as a coastal defense position during WW II.

airborne assaults and other airborne operations during WW II. The museum features the life of Gen. Lee and focuses on the early development of the Army's airborne units. Address: 209 W. Divine St., Dunn, NC 28334. Phone: 910/892-1947. Hours: M-F 10-4, Sat. 11-4, Sun. 1-4. Admission charged. Divine St. is the first street south of SR 55 (Cumberlain St.).

DURHAM: (See Raleigh/Durham area)

EDENTON is in the NE corner of the state on Albemarle Sound.

U.S. MARINE CORPS AIR STATION, EDENTON was built by the Navy during 1941-42 as a training base for Marine glider troops. The station had facilities for both land planes and seaplanes. In 1943, glider training was faded out and the station was converted into an operational training station for pilots and crews of twin-engine aircraft. The station had one outlying field near Emporia, VA which was used for "bounce drill", simulated landing on aircraft carrier decks. The station suffered from poor water drainage so it was closed in 1946 and put in caretaker status. The station was reopened in 1955 as an auxiliary naval air station, but was closed again in 1959 and its assets sold.

ELIZABETH CITY is in the NE corner of the state on the west bank of the Pasquotank River. The city had several manufacturing firms including a large Consolidated-Vultee Aircraft Corp. plant that made major aircraft components. The city also had one of the largest Coast Guard air stations on the east coast.

U.S. NAVAL AIR STATION (LTA) WEEKSVILLE, ELIZABETH CITY was built in 1941-42 nine miles SE of Elizabeth City near the community of Weeksville. The station was along the northern shore of the Pasquotank River on a peninsula formed by the

river and the Newbegun Creek. Two large blimp hangars were built here which could accommodate up to 6 blimps. The blimps were used to carry out anti-submarine patrols along the U.S. east coast. The first patrols took place in May 1942. In 1943 the station acquired a blimp maintenance and repair facility. The station could also handle seaplanes and served as a transit facility, primarily for PBY's, going to Britain under Lend Lease. In Aug. 1945 the station was reduced to an auxiliary naval air station. In Dec. 1945 it became a storage facility for naval and Marine aircraft, and the last blimps departed in Apr. 1946. The station continued in the blimp business, however, as a fueling station for blimps in transit. In Aug. 1946 the Navy began storing motor vehicles here; trucks, mobile machine shops, mobile cranes, etc. In Aug. 1947 the station became an operational blimp base again with the arrival of four blimps. By then the aircraft storage was slowly fading out. The station conducted blimp tests, LTA training and cross-country

The William C. Lee Airborne Museum in Dunn, NC.

U.S. Naval Air Station (LTA) Weeksville, Elizabeth City no longer exists, but the facility remained in operation as a base for commercial blimps. The WW II blimp hangars also remained in use.

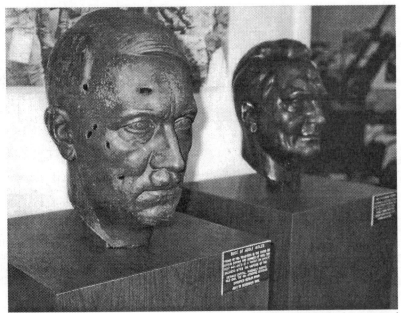

This bullet-riddled bust of Adolph Hitler was found in the ruins of Berlin by troops of the 82nd Airborne Div. The bullet holes are believed to have been made by the Russians during their capture of the city. The bust to the right is that of Hermann Goering. It is also a trophy of WW II but has no bullet holes.

blimp flights. During the Korean War helicopters operated from the station. In 1957, however, during an economy move, NAS(LTA) Weeksville, Elizabeth City was closed and its assets sold to private interests. The station continued to operates in the postwar years as a base for commercial blimps and the WW II hangars remained in use.

FAYETTEVILLE/ABERDEEN/SOUTHERN PINES AREA: This cluster of towns is approximately 50 miles east of Raleigh. During the summer of 1941 large-scale Army maneuvers were carried out in the area. Near the town of Marston, 12 miles SW of Aberdeen, the AAF tested for the first time a system of interlocking steel mats which could be used to quickly build air strips and roads. The tests were successful and the steel mats became known as "Marston Mats". Later in the war the Pinehurst Resort, a golfing resort near Southern Pines, was taken over by the AAF as a rest & relaxation facility for AAF personnel.

FORT BRAGG, 10 miles NW of Fayetteville, was built in 1917-18 as a training camp for Army artillery units and at that time was called Camp Bragg. In 1922 the post became a permanent installation of the Army and given its present name. Ft. Bragg became the home of all the Army's artillery units east of the Mississippi and the training area for the 9th Infantry Division. The fort had its own air field, Pope Field, which operated in conjunction with the ground forces. In 1923 military parachute jumps were first made here from artillery observation balloons. From this beginning, Fort Bragg was chosen, in 1942, to become the home of the Army's new airborne units comprised of parachute and glider units. The post was greatly expanded for its new role and its population shot up from 5400 in 1940 to 67,000 by 1942 and peaked at 157,000. It covered a land area which made it 6 times larger than Washington, DC. Early in WW II Fort Bragg became the reception center for the

4th Army Corps. In 1942 troops under Gen. George Patton staged here prior to their departure for the invasion of North Africa which took place in Nov. 1942. Also in 1942 the 82nd Infantry Div. was reactivated here and reorganized into the Army's first airborne Div. All five WW II airborne divisions - the 82nd, 101st, 11th, 13th and 17th - trained here or at Camp Mackall, 40 miles west. The fort also worked closely with I Troop Carrier Command whose planes delivered the paratroopers and pulled the gliders. Fort Bragg was a segregated camp and one of the nation's first all-negro parachute units, the 555th Parachute Infantry Battalion, training here. The fort also had one of the few all-negro military hospitals in the country. Fort Bragg had one of the first main prisoner of war camps in the nation beginning in late 1942. The POW camp grew to hold some 2000 POWs, most of whom worked for the military. By the time the war ended Fort Bragg, now known as "The Home of the Airborne" and became the postwar home of the 82nd Airborne Div. During the war years the fort was commanded by three outstanding generals, one after the other; Maj. Gen. Omar Bradley (Mar. 1942-June 1942), Maj.

Gen. Matthew B. Ridgeway (June 1942-Aug. 1944) and Maj. Gen. James M. Gavin (Aug. 1944-Mar. 1948). In 1951 the XVIII Airborne Corps was activated here for the Korean War, and in 1952 the fort became the home of the Special Forces (Green Berets). Fort Bragg functioned throughout the Cold War working closely with Fort McPherson, GA and Pope Air Force Base. Together they became one of the largest military complexes in the world.

82nd Airborne Division War Memorial Museum: This museum is on the grounds of Fort Bragg at Ardennes Rd.and Gela St. and is dedicated to those members of the 82nd Airborne Div. who have given their lives for their country. The museum details the history of the 82nd from its days as an infantry division in WW I to the present. Displays include equipment used by parachute and glider troops, U.S. and foreign uniforms, small arms, machine guns, artillery pieces ordnance, field equipment and captured trophies of war. There is also a display called "Barracks Life" showing how GIs lived at Fort Bragg in 1942-43. Address: PO Box 70119, Fort Bragg, NC 28307. Phone: 910/432-5307. Hours: Tues.-Sat. 10-4:30, Sun. 11:30-4. Closed Jan. 1, Dec. 25 and Federal holidays. Free.

U.S. Army John F. Kennedy Special Warfare Museum: This is a second museum on the grounds of Fort Bragg located in the John F. Kennedy Center at Marion and Gruber Rds. The museum focuses on the history of special forces of the U.S. Army from the American Revolution to the present. WW II-related exhibits tell the story of the "Rangers", the OSS and "Merrill's Marauders". Among the very unique weapons in the museum's collection is a glove pistol, an incendiary device designed to be dropped into a gas tank, an inexpensively-made gun called the "Woolworth Gun" designed for very close combat, one-shot guns designed to be concealed in the palm of the hand, sleeve daggers, silencers, mini-cameras and a leaflet bomb. There are also many captured enemy items on display. Address: D-2502, Fort Bragg, NC 28307. Phone: 910/432-4272/1533. Hours: Tues.-Sun. 11:30-4. Free.

Where old Jeeps go to die. Old Jeeps and small trailers, covering about four acres, are stored here at Camp Mackall. Parts are apparently salvaged and used again.

CAMP MACKALL, 40 miles east of Fort Bragg and three miles east of Hoffman, NC, was a subinstallation of Fort Bragg. It was activated in 1940 and became the second largest airborne training center in the nation. It was named after Pvt. John T. Mackall, the first U.S. paratrooper killed in North Africa. Throughout the war activities here were primarily an extension of those at Fort Bragg. The camp had its own main prisoner of war camp holding about 500 POWs who worked at the camp and in agriculture. This was one of the few POW camps in the U.S. that, during 1945, had a secret re-education school sponsored by the Federal Government to teach German POWs, in subtle ways, the principals of democracy. It worked very well here. In the summer of 1945 the POWs formed four political parties within the camp and held an election for there own camp leaders. In 1948 Camp Mackall was deactivated as a training center and converted into a recreation retreat for Army personnel. Very few buildings remained at this facility, but some of them were of WW II vintage.

POPE FIELD was on the northern edge of, and adjacent to, Fort Bragg. It was built in 1919 along with Camp Bragg and served as the camp's air field. At first it was known as Camp Bragg Flying Field but the name was soon changed to Pope Field. Its mission was to provide observation balloons and training of balloon personnel in support of the artillery units at the camp. In 1927 training of bomber crews began here and in 1929 Pope Field became the first U.S. military installation to conduct joint air-ground training. The field was expanded several times in the 1930s and when the 82nd Airborne Division came into being Pope provided the aircraft needed to support the division. The field was under the command of the I Troop Carrier Command, but was shared with the Air Transport Command which had an air freight terminal here. Pope provided services to the various parachute and glider units at Fort Bragg throughout WW II and well into the postwar years. It also continued to serve as a training field for reconnaissance pilots. In 1948 the field was taken over by the US Air Force and renamed Pope Air Force Base but continued to serve the Army as before. Pope AFB was active throughout the Cold War. During WW II Pope Field had two auxiliary air fields; Balloon Field on the grounds of Fort Bragg and Knollwood Field, three miles north of Southern Pines.

GOLDSBORO is 45 miles SE of Raleigh.

SEYMOUR JOHNSON FIELD, 3.5 miles SE of Goldsboro, was built in 1942 to provide an Aviation Cadet Pre-Technical School Training Program for bomber mechanics. The field was first known as Technical School, AAFTTC, Goldsboro. Army transportation troops were also trained here. In Oct. 1942 it was given its wartime name in honor of Navy Lt. Seymour Johnson, a Navy pilot and resident of Goldsboro, who was killed during flight tests in Maryland in 1941. The field also had a school to train AAF officers to operate Provisional Overseas Replacement Centers. There was a branch prisoner of war camp here holding about 400 POWs who worked on the field and in the surrounding forests. Later in the war

the field became a training field for P-47 pilots under the 1st AF. Still later the field was used as a transition center for AAF personnel being transferred from Europe to the Pacific. This was short lived, however, because of the sudden surrender of Japan. The field then became a separation center for the AAF. After the war the field was closed, but was reopened in 1953 by the US Air Force as a training base for jet pilots and renamed Seymour Johnson Air Force Base. The base remained active throughout the Cold War.

GREENSBORO/WINSTON-SALEM/ HIGH POINT AREA:

This cluster of cities is in the north-central part of the state. The textile industry was big in this area and many military uniforms, tents, bolts of camouflage netting, etc. were made here. An important war plants in the area was the Fairchild Aircraft Co. fctory, 1.5 miles east of Burlington, which made military training aircraft.

GREENSBORO-HIGH POINT MUNICIPAL AIRPORT, 8 miles NW of Greensboro, was a civil airport known as Lindley Field. With the coming of the war the AAF, Navy and Marines all used the field. The AAF used it as an aerial debarkation facility for troops going overseas and a re-fueling stop in their air ferry system. Later, the AAF used the field to train fighter and bomber pilots and as a basic training center for new recruits. The Navy used the field as an outlying field to NAS, Atlanta, GA. In the postwar years the facility became a large, modern airport known as Piedmont Triad International Airport and all signs of its service during WW II disappeared.

OVERSEAS REPLACEMENT DEPOT, GREENSBORO was located NE of downtown Greensboro on E. Market St. The facility was built in 1942 and used until early 1944 as a basic training center for new AAF recruits. During that time 87,000 recruits were trained here. In 1944 it became one of 6 Overseas Replacement Depots in the U.S. and the only one in the eastern U.S. All 6 ORDs served as staging facilities for AAF personnel awaiting transfer overseas. At its peak of operation, ORD, Greensboro had 900 buildings, including a large regional hospital, and housed 30,000 people. Personnel stationed here awaiting transfer were treated well and given considerable time off, much of which was spent in Greensboro's night spots. With the end of the war ORD, Greensboro became a separation center. The facility closed in 1946 and many of the buildings and much of the land were turned over to the state and became North Carolina Agricultural & Technical State University. Other parts of the depot were sold off for light industry and

commercial use.

WINSTON-SALEM AIRPORT, three miles NNE of Winston-Salem, was the town's local airport before the war. It was not taken over by the military, but was used by both the AAF and the Navy. The AAF established its Flying Safety Command here and the Navy used it as a fueling stop in the air transport system. In the postwar years the field became known as Smith Reynolds Airport and very few signs remained of it WW II days.

GREENVILLE is in the NE part of the state on the Pamlico River.

GREENVILLE AIRPORT was the community's local airport before the war. Soon after the attack on Pearl Harbor combat-ready AAF planes arrived at the field as part of the AAF's pre-war planning for the defense of the eastern seaboard. When the threat of enemy attacks diminished, the AAF withdrew its planes, but the Navy used the field as an outlying field for both U.S. Marine Corps Air Station, Cherry Point and U.S. Naval Air Station, Atlanta, GA.

HIGH POINT (See Greensboro/Winston-Salem/High Point area)

HOLLEY RIDGE was, before the war, a community of 28 people about midway between Wilmington and Jacksonville.

CAMP DAVIS was built in 1940-41 by the Army just NW of Holley Ridge. It was a training facility for barrage balloon and anti-aircraft units. The first training activity here was that of organizing and training high altitude barrage balloon battalions which were a part of the AAF's anti-aircraft command. When the U.S. went to war in Dec. 1941 virtually all the barrage balloon units at the camp were dispatched at once to critical areas such as the Panama Canal and the U.S. west coast. The camp also had waterfront acreage at the southern end of Topsail Island to use as a firing range for anti-aircraft (AA) gunners and for recreation. The camp had a second firing range at Sears Point near the New River Inlet and a third firing range near Maple Hill, NC 12 miles to the NW. At Topsail Island and Sears Point targets would be towed by aircraft flying just off the coast and the gunners would shoot live ammunition out over the water at the targets. Topsail Island firing range, which is now

This is one of several abandoned roads on the Camp Davis site. It leads to the camp's airstrip which is also abandoned.

Tarawa Terrace is one of several housing areas at Camp Lejeune for Marines and their families.

Topsail Beach, was also used to train searchlight operators. Camp Davis was a segregated camp so negro troops were also trained here in all-negro AA units. The camp had its own air strip, an Officer Candidate School and a branch prisoner of war camp holding about 800 POWs who worked at the camp. Camp Davis grew to be a large training facility with a peak population of 60,000. The area chosen for the camp was swampy and mosquitos and rattlesnakes were a constant problem. To those stationed there it was sometimes referred to as "Swamp Davis". The camp was closed in Oct. 1944 and AA training activities sent elsewhere. It was reopened, however, in the summer of 1945 as an AAF convalescent hospital and redistribution center. The Marine Corps also used parts of the camp for training and as a separation center. Camp Davis was then closed again and its assets sold. Remnants of the camp can be seen along the NW side of U.S. 17 as one passes through Holley Ridge.

In late 1946 the Topsail Beach firing range was acquired by the Navy to test its new top secret ram-jet missiles known as "The Flying Stovepipe". Eight concrete towers were built at that time to house photographic and tracking equipment. The Navy used the range until early 1948 when testing operations were moved to Florida. During that time over 200 missiles were fired from Topsail Beach. The concrete towers remain and have been utilized in very unique ways. Four of them have been incorporated into homes and one of them stands at the entrance to the ocean fishing pier.

JACKSONVILLE is in the SE part of the state 15 miles inland from the mouth of the New River.

CAMP LEJEUNE stretches south from Jacksonville on both sides of the New River all the war to the sea. In the late 1930s the Marine Corps began a search from Maine to Louisiana for a site upon which to build a major Marine base on the east coast. The Jacksonville site was selected. Construction began in early 1941 and at the time the new facility was named U.S. Marine Barracks, New River. In Sept. 1941 the 1st Marine Division took up residence at the camp living in tents. They remained here until

they departed for the South Pacific in 1942. With the entry of the U.S. into the war the construction of permanent facilities at the camp was greatly accelerated and them camp acquired all the necessities of a small city. In Dec. 1942 the name of the camp was given its wartime name in honor of Gen. John H. Lejeune, the 13th Commander of the Marine Corps (1920-29), who had died in 1941. To those who trained here, the camp had yet another name, "Swamp Lagoon" because of the many swamps and marshes within the camp. During the war, Camp Lejeune was a huge training facility with a complex of schools that trained personnel for many of the Corps' needs. There were schools for combat units, paratroopers, artillerymen, amphibious units, engineers, scouts, snipers, medics, radar operators, communications specialists, barrage balloon units, weapon and munitions specialists, motor transport personnel, women Marines, quartermasters, clerks, cooks, bakers and war dogs. Onslow Beach was used extensively for amphibious training, artillery training and anti-aircraft artillery training. One section of the camp, Montford Point, was devoted to the training and housing of negro Marines. This was the only such Marine facility of the east coast for negroes. Montford Point remained a segregated facility until 1948 when President Truman integrated the armed forces. During the war dozens of Marine units were formed at Camp Lejeune and tens of thousands of individuals trained here. When the war ended the camp became a separation center and then settled down to become a peacetime training facility for the Marines and Marine Reserves and a home for many Marine Corps units. Camp Lejeune remained very active throughout the Cold War and continued to grow. The camp's airfield eventually became it own facility known as U.S. Marine Corps Air Station, New River. By the end of the Cold War Camp Lejeune could claim the title as "The World's Most Complete Amphibious Base".

LAURINBURG/MAXTON AREA: These two towns are 7 miles apart in the southern part of the state near the South Carolina state line.

LAURINBURG-MAXTON ARMY AIR BASE was 3.5 miles north of Maxton. It was built in 1942 for the I Troop Carrier Command as a training base for glider crews. Since glider troops were a part of the Army's airborne forces,

this base was closely associated with Fort Bragg, the training camp for parachute units and a major headquarters for airborne units. After the war the air base was converted to civilian use and became a commercial air field known as Laurinburg-Maxton Airport. A monument at the terminal building commemorates the activities that took place here during WW II. During the war the base had two auxiliary fields, Camp Mackall Airfield, 2.5 miles east of Hoffman and Lumberton Municipal Airport 3 miles SW of Lumberton.

MONROE is 20 miles SE of Charlotte near the South Carolina line.

CAMP SUTTON was a small temporary Army camp, comprised mostly of tents, near Monroe used for the training of engineers. It was built in 1942 and named after Frank H. Sutton, a pilot in the Royal Canadian Air Force, who was killed in Libya on Dec. 7, 1941. The camp had a branch prisoner of war camp holding about 600 POWs who worked for the military, in agriculture and in the forests. Some POWs were employed at the Mecklenburg Iron Works in Charlotte. In 1943-44 several Italian Service Units were trained here. Camp Sutton was closed in late 1945 and its assets sold. A state historical marker on Hwy. 74 and a lone smoke stack mark the wartime location of Camp Sutton.

NEW BERN is on the Neuse River and about 45 miles inland from Cape Lookout. The town had a large shipbuilder, the Barbour Boat Works, which built mine sweepers and salvage vessels for the Navy.

CAMP BATTLE was a temporary Army camp located on a former CCC camp site NW of New Bern. It was occupied by a coastal artillery unit whose mission was to protect the bridges over the Neuse and Trent Rivers. The camp was soon abandoned by the Army and in the postwar years became a city park, waste treatment plant and a National Guard post. Location: From SR 43 north/55 west, north of town, take Glenburnie Road. NE 1.2 miles to Oaks Rd. Turn SE on Oaks Rd., proceed .4 miles to Glenburnie Drive. Turn NE on Glenburnie Drive, the camp is at the end of Glenburnie Drive.

U.S. MARINE CORPS AIR STATION, CHERRY POINT is 15 miles SE of New Bern on the south bank of the Neuse River. It was built in 1941 to serve as a Marine air station in cooperation

A park shelter house now rests on the concrete foundation of a WW II building at Camp Battle.

The former Camp Butner Hospital comprised many well-constructed brick buildings which have continued to serve as a state hospital known as John Umstead Hospital.

Other WW II buildings at Camp Butner have been left to decay. Chimneys, such as these, are a common sight at old WW II Army camps. In the foreground is a section of steel Marston Mat probably used during the war as part of a driveway or road.

with the Marine base at Camp Lejeune. Construction was slow because of the swampy conditions, the lack of good roads and railroads in the area and a shortage of labor. By Dec. 1941, though, the station was operational even though the station wasn't commissioned until June 1942. Marine Air Wings operated from Cherry Point carrying out much-needed anti-submarine patrols during the terrible months of early 1942 when so many U.S. and Allied ships were sunk of the North Carolina coast. Navy land and seaplanes also operated from Cherry Point during these months. On July 7, 1942, a Hudson bomber operating out of Cherry Point sank the German sub U-701. A week later, on July 15, 1942, two Marine aircraft from Cherry Point participated in the sinking of the German submarine, U-576, off Diamond Shoals. Training operations at Cherry Point included the training of paratroopers, an aviation ground school and a photographers school. Because of the many swamps on the station there was special emphasis on search

and rescue operations in swampy areas. Cherry Point became the home for all women Marine Reservists assigned to Marine Corps aviation. The station also acquired a major engine overhaul operation and Marine aircraft from all over the nation were flown here for service. During the war the station had 6 auxiliary fields and 11 outlying fields. At its peak the station had 800 planes and 23,520 service personnel on board. At the end of the war Cherry Point served as a separation center. When this activity ended, the station converted to a schedule of peacetime operations and training. Cherry Point remained in operation throughout the Cold War serving the varied needs of the Marine Corps and Marine Corps Reserves.

RALEIGH/DURHAM AREA: These two cities, 20 miles apart, are in the north-central part of the state. Raleigh is the state capital.

CAMP BUTNER was located 10 miles NE of Durham and is now the town of Butner. It was a large camp, built in 1942 as an infantry training and reassignment center and housed up to 35,000 people. The 35th and 78th Infantry Divs. trained here during the war. Camp Butner had a large hospital which treated war wounded and employed many WACs. It also had the largest prisoner of war camp in the state holding about 5000 German and Italian POWs who worked for the military, in agriculture and in the forests. The POW camp had several compounds to separate the various groups of POWs. One compound held hardcore Nazis and

was known as "Little Siberia". Other compounds held foreigners, such as Poles, Czechs, French and Dutch who were captured while serving in the German Army. Some 500 of the foreigners were released to serve in their own national armies. Others were rejected by their governments and remained POWs. Most of the POW branch camps throughout the state were sub-posts of the Butner camp. In Jan. 1945 Butner's post hospital was upgraded to a general hospital and was renamed Camp Butner General Hospital. It specialized in general medicine, trench foot and psychiatry. After the war the state bought the camp and kept the hospital in operation renaming it John Umstead Hospital. Part of the camp was converted into a Federal correctional institute but many other buildings were left to decay.

RALEIGH-DURHAM ARMY AIR BASE was located midway between Raleigh and Durham. The airport was under construction in 1941 when it was taken over by the AAF. The AAF finished the construction and the field was in operation by May 1943. The AAF used the field for training purposes, but allowed one airline, Eastern Airlines, to operate scheduled flights out of the field to serve the civilian needs. Raleigh-Durham AAB had an auxiliary field, Statesboro Field, 4 miles NE of Statesboro, GA. In 1948 Raleigh-Durham AAB reverted to its former owners and evolved into Raleigh-Durham International Airport.

SOUTHERN PINES (See Fayetteville/Aberdeen/Southern Pines Area)
WEEKSVILLE (See Elizabeth City)
WILMINGTON (See Cape Fear/Wilmington Area)
WINSTON-SALEM (See Greensboro/Winston-Salem/High Point Area)

An Army building served as a combination mess hall and civilian air terminal at Raleigh-Durham Army Air Base soon after its completion.

NORTH DAKOTA

North Dakota was one of our bread-basket states during WW II produced large quantities of much-needed food for the war effort. Eighty percent of the state's economy was based on agriculture. In the decade before the war, however, there was considerable suffering in North Dakota due to the double disasters of drought and depression. North Dakota, especially the western part, became a part of the well-known "dust bowl" and was one of several states to lose population during the 1930s. In 1937 the state, with Federal and private financing, began a long term program to build dams, irrigation systems, hydro-electric plants and to prevent soil erosion. "Dry land" farming was introduced and encouraged. When the war came these projects were well along and the state's farmers were able to make significant increases in agricultural production. During WW II North Dakota's farmers broke one agricultural record after the other. The state produced wheat, oaks, corn, barley, rye, potatoes, sugar beets, flax, cattle, hogs, sheep and poultry.

The state had valuable mineral wealth in the form of coal, natural gas, sand & gravel and a wide variety of clays. In 1944 a sizeable new coal field was opened and after the war, in 1951, oil was discovered in the western part of the state near Tioga.

North Dakota ranked last among the 48 states in manufacturing and what manufacturing that existed was devoted primarily to the processing of the state's agricultural products. The state produced milled products, animal feeds, dairy products, meat packing, sugar refining, lumber, publishing & printing.

In 1941 the 3000-acre International Peace Park was opened on the North Dakota/Canadian border. At that time the U.S. was at peace, but Canada was at war. During Feb. & Mar. 1945, the state was on the receiving end of Japanese bombing balloons when two balloon bombs came down harmlessly near Ashley and Grafton. When the war ended the state's economy was in much better shape than when the war started, and North Dakota went on to prosper in the postwar years.

BISMARCK is the capital of North Dakota and is near the geographic center of the state on the Missouri River and I-94.

BISMARCK AIRPORT, four miles SE of downtown, was the area's local airport at the time of the war. It remained a civilian airport throughout the war, but was used by the AAF as a transit field in its ferry system and by the Air Transport Command which operated a military air freight terminal there.

FORT LINCOLN: The location of the WW II-era Fort Lincoln is south of and adjacent to the Bismarck Municipal Airport. Access is by SR 1804. The fort was built in June 1872 to protect the workers on the North Pacific Railroad for the Indians. Thereafter, the post was garrisoned intermittently by the Army as needed. In 1939, when war started in Europe, Fort Lincoln was garrisoned by a small detachment of Army infantrymen. In the spring of 1941 it was selected by the Federal

The entrance to Fort Lincoln as it appeared in the 1990s.

Government to be one of several internment camps for foreign nationals that were to be interned by the U.S. under the terms of the Geneva Convention. This need arose when certain citizens of the warring nations, primarily German and Italian seamen, began falling into American hands. Subsequently, Ft. Lincoln was turned over to the Immigration and Naturalization Service (INS) to serve as a camp for male Germans aliens. The first internees to arrive here were 220 German seamen from the ocean liner "Columbus" which was scuttled by it crew off the coast of New Jersey in Dec. 1939. The German sailors arrived by train on May 31, 1941 in the company of a German Consulate official and were taken directly to the fort. Fort Lincoln was staffed with active and retired INS border guards and local people who had been newly hired and trained. It was here that the Americans got their first experience in handling German prisoners during WW II in which the influence of the Nazi Party was a major factor. There had been no such factor in the POW camps of WW I. The problems experienced here and the lessons learned would effect the future governing, and even the composition, of internment and prisoner of war camps in the U.S.

The internment compound at Fort Lincoln was surrounded by a 10' wire fence which was illuminated with floodlights at night. The accommodations were old, but warm and spacious. The Germans were allowed to chose their own roommates and, not surprisingly, the ardent Nazis tended to congregate together. Soon afterwards they began to impose their will on the others by imposing strict shipboard regimen within the camp. Men were ordered to observe military discipline, wear their uniforms, stand watch and ordinary seamen were instructed to serve officers in the mess hall as was customary aboard ship. The Americans did not interfere with this system, but neither did they encourage it. In a short time it broke down of its own accord and pro-Nazi and non-Nazi factions began to form in the camp. Peace

was maintained, but there was a strong undertone of tension.

All those who wanted to work were offered jobs outside the fort. Some of the jobs involved working on the railroads, and it was soon discovered that this was a another problem. Railroad unions objected to this use of the inexpensive laborers and the pro-Nazis considered the work treasonable and complained to their Swiss representatives. The issue was submitted to the German Government in Berlin, Germany which announced, through the Swiss Representatives, that it had no objections to internees working on American railroads[1]. The Fort Lincoln Nazis were forced to back down and lost a little prestige in the process. The problems with the railroad unions, however, was never really resolved and continued to exist on a nation-wide basis especially when, later in the war, Axis prisoners of war began working on railroads.

On Dec. 20, 1941, after the U.S. entered the war, 110 resident German aliens arrived at the fort, and in Feb. 1942 415 Japanese aliens arrived from the west coast. Suddenly the fort was almost half German and half Japanese. This was to be the fort's peak alien population for a while. With subsequent case reviews conducted by the INS, individuals were soon being released, paroled, deported or transferred and the fort's population began to decline. In June 1942 the 8 German saboteurs, who had landed by submarines in New York & Florida and been captured, were held here briefly before being sent to Washington, DC for trial. By Oct. 1942 the fort's population was down to a mix of about 300 Germans and Japanese. Most were allowed to work on the local harvest that fall. When Chile went to war some of that nation's German aliens were sent here.

In early 1943 German prisoner of war began arriving in the U.S. from North Africa in large numbers and were being incarcerated in existing Army camps. Some of those camps

[1]During the war the Germans used American internees and prisoners of war on their railroads.

had small enemy alien compounds which were subsequently emptied and the internees shipped off to other INS camps. In Mar. 1943 Fort Lincoln got its share ... 1500 new residents. On May 1943 another 1000 arrived. The slow review process began anew and the fort's population began to decline again as individuals left the fort for various reasons.

In Feb. 1945 a third wave of aliens arrived. These were very special individuals who would not be released or paroled and who would be deported because of U.S. law after the war. They were 650 "renunciants", angry young Japanese-Americans, born in the U.S., who had renounced their U.S. citizenship and, in the process, automatically made themselves enemy aliens. These people were the worst of the troublemakers from the entire War Relocation Authority's (WRA) camp system. The WRA was responsible for the relocation and care of the ethnic Japanese removed from the U.S. west coast earlier in the war. The WRA had found it necessary to remove troublemakers from their various camps and assemble them all in one WRA camp at Tule Lake, CA. It was at Tule Lake that some 10,000 individuals renounced their U.S. citizenship. In Jan. 1945, however, a disturbance broke out at Tule Lake and the 650 ring-leaders had been identified and packed off to Fort Lincoln. On Feb. 14 they, and 52 heavily armed INS guards, arrived at Bismarck by train during a severe cold spell. At Ft. Lincoln the "renunciants" were isolated and heavily guarded. The "renunciants" soon organized themselves into small military units (as they had done at Tule Lake), donned their make-shift uniforms and began marching about in military formations ... albeit indoors.

As Japan's fortunes of war declined more and more some of the "renunciants" began to crack. Excessive drinking became a problem[2] and many of these American-born would-be-

---

[2] The internees were allowed to buy beer and wine in their canteen.

warriors-of-the-Emperor began to contemplate their future in a far-away, war-torn and unfamiliar land. Arguments and fights became more frequent and the INS Authorities had to step in and ration the alcohol supply. The hard-core Nazis at the camp, who were also seeing their hopes of victory being dashed, had a similar problem. As soon as the weather permitted the INS Authorities instigated heavily-guarded work projects, both inside and outside the fort to keep the men occupied and their minds off their troubles. Upon learning of Hitler's death in early May 1945 the hard-core Nazis held a ceremony attended by some 200 people. Their leaders gave speeches eulogizing Hitler and lead the group in singing patriotic and Nazi songs. During the summer of 1945 the Germans began to leave for Germany. Their space was taken in July by 600 more "renunciants" sent in from Tule Lake.

In Nov. 1945 the "renunciants" began to move out to west coast ports for their one-way trip to their new homeland. On Feb. 18, 1946 the last batch of "renunciants" left the fort for deportation. Remaining were about 200 former "renunciants" who had changed their minds and hoped to regain their U.S. citizenship in the U.S. courts. The next day the last of the German aliens departed. Some of the Germans departing that day were seaman from the "Columbus". They had spent the entire war at Fort Lincoln. In Mar. 1946 the remaining Japanese were transferred to the INS camp in Santa Fe, NM and Fort Lincoln was closed soon afterwards. The fort was used in the postwar years by state and Federal agencies and in 1963 it became a Job Corps Center. Several years later a job training center for American Indians was established on the site.

IMPORTANT: Do not confuse this site with Fort Lincoln State Park which is 9 miles west and on the other side of the Missouri River.

DEVILS LAKE is 85 miles west of Grand Forks.

CAMP GRAFTON is four miles south of the town of Devils Lake on the north shore of the Lake. Access is via SR 20. The camp was, before the war, the home of North Dakota's National Guard. The Guard was called to Federal service during the war and the camp continued in operation in support of the Guard and the U.S. Army. Camp Grafton remained a small camp was returned to the National Guard after the war.

FARGO is on the eastern border of the state.

BONANZAVILLE, U.S.A., at the western edge of West Fargo, is a reconstructed pioneer village and regional museum. It has an interesting collection of aircraft which include some WW II models. There is also a WW II 60" search light, uniforms, ship models and a collection of captured Japanese weapons and artifacts. In the antique auto collection is a 1936 Rolls-Royce which belonged to King George VI of England, Britain's wartime King. Address: I-94 west & U.S. 10. W. Fargo, ND 58078. Phone: 701/282-2822. Hours: Village and museum open from late May to late Oct. M-F 9-8, S-S 9-5. Museum open rest of year Tues.-F 9:30-4, Village closed. Admission charged.

HECTOR AIRPORT, four miles NNE of downtown Fargo, was the area's local airport before the war. In Feb. 1942 Northwest Airlines was contracted by the Federal Government to open a scheduled military air route from Hector Airport to Fairbanks, AK. The southern terminus of the route was soon moved from Hector Airport to the Minneapolis area because that city had better ground connections with the eastern states. Hector, nevertheless, continued to be used by the Federal Government as a part of its supply route in the construction of the AlCan Highway and the Northwest Staging Route through Canada to Alaska. The airport was not taken over by the AAF and remained a civilian field throughout the war. After the war it became the area's main airport again and retained the name Hector Airport.

OHIO

John W. Bricker was the former Governor of Ohio and Thomas Dewey's Vice presidential running mate in the election of 1944.

During World War II Ohio was one of our great manufacturing states located in the American industrial heartland. The state had several large industrial areas centered around large cities in the northern, central and western parts of the state. Ohio's economy had suffered considerably during the Great Depression and there was considerable unemployment in the state, so the relatively sudden surge of industrial activity brought on by the war was most welcome in the state. Ohio's manufacturing sector picked up steam quickly and the products needed for war began rolling off the assembly lines in large quantities. Ohio eventually became fourth in the nation in the value of wartime industrial contracts. Major items produced in Ohio during the war included

Fleet Admiral Ernest J. King, Chief of Naval Operations, was an Ohioan from Lorain, OH.

ships, airplanes, motor vehicles, steel products, rubber products, glass products, electrical machinery and equipment, machine tools, chemicals, oil refining and munitions. Manufacturing operations did not always run smoothly, however, because of problems involving the shortages of labor and raw materials and intermittent problems with the state's powerful labor unions. In some of the larger cities there were also housing shortages, fuel shortage and the overburdening of city services.

Ohio is also in the "Corn Belt" and a major producer of food. Her main agricultural products were corn, wheat, soybeans, vegetables, sugar beets, tobacco, meat, wool, fresh-water fish, poultry and dairy products. The agricultural sector of her economy also suffered from a shortage of labor which was eased to some degree by the use of prisoners of war and the importation of workers from The Bahamas.

The state's mines and wells produced oil, coal, natural gas, cement, stone, clay and lime.

Prominent individuals from Ohio included Senator Robert A. Taft, son of President William Howard Taft and a leader of the Republican Party for three decades. He was a strong opponent of Franklin Roosevelt's liberal New Deal policies in the 1930s and also opposed many of Roosevelt's moves which drew the nation closer to war. Taft sought the Republican nomination for president in 1940, 1948 and 1952 but was never successful. In 1947 he became co-author of the famous Taft-Hartley Act which put certain controls on big labor unions which had fallen from popular favor across the country because of their aggressive, self-serving and, many believed, unpatriotic behavior during and soon after the war.

Another prominent Ohioan was John W. Bricker, the state's Governor from 1939 to 1945 and Thomas Dewey's Vice Presidential running mate in 1944. Bricker later served as the state's Senator from 1947 to 1959.

Fleet Admiral Ernest J. King, the highest ranking man in the U.S. Navy during WW II, was also an Ohioan. As Chief of Naval Operations and a member of the U.S. Joint Chiefs of Staff he was one of the major planners of American military strategy during the war. He is remembered today as the architect for victory in the Pacific.

Another important military man from the state was Gen. George E. Stratemeyer of Cincinnati. Stratemeyer served as Chief of Air Staff under Gen. Harold "Hap" Arnold before going to the China-Burma-India Theater where he commanded all U.S. air forces there. He later commanded all U.S. air forces in China. Yet another Ohioan of renown was Mildred Gillars who became the German propaganda broadcaster known as "Axis Sally". Gillars was an aspiring actress who was teaching English in Berlin when the war started. She stayed on in Germany to be with her lover, Otto Koischwitz,

Inflated dummy rubber trucks such as this one were designed to confuse the enemy.

an employee of the German Foreign Ministry, and began working for the Germans. She was well known to American GIs all over Europe for her salty language and her playing of the record "Lili Marlene". In 1949 she was convicted of treason by a U.S. court, sent to prison and then paroled in 1961. She returned to Ohio and lived out the remained of her life in Columbus.

The state had 6 prisoner of war camps, and the German saboteurs that were landed in New York and Florida by submarine in June 1942 had targets in Ohio. Their plans called for the sabotage of several of the locks on the Ohio River. The saboteurs were caught, however, before they were able to act.

AKRON is in NE Ohio 25 miles south of Cleveland. America's largest rubber manufacturers were headquartered here; Goodyear Tire & Rubber Co., B.F. Goodrich Rubber Co., General Tire & Rubber Co., Firestone Tire & Rubber Co. and Mohawk Tire & Rubber Co. All of these firms, and dozens of smaller ones, produced a high percentage of the rubber products used in North America and by the U.S. armed forces. Akron was an important center of rubber research and was deeply involved in the all-important development of synthetic rubbers and plastics. This research was extremely successful and the U.S. emerged from the war much less dependent upon the import of natural rubber than before.

The great rubber companies and the many other manufacturers in the Akron area produced non-rubber items as well. These included aircraft parts, tank parts, anti-aircraft guns, artillery shells, wheels, major components for the "Manhattan (Atomic Bomb) Project" and subcontracted metal parts.

RAVENNA ORDNANCE PLANT was east of the town of Ravenna which is 10 miles ENE of Akron. This was a large ordnance plant built in 1940-41 to load many types of Army ordnance from 75 mm shells to two ton bombs. The plant was operated by the Atlas Powder

Co. and employed some 15,000 workers. Later in the war the plant served as a depot and was renamed Portage Depot. The plant remained active well into the postwar years and its name was changed again to Ravenna Arsenal. The facility was huge and extended for some 15 miles along the north side of SR 5 east of Ravenna.

BUCYRUS is a county seat 50 miles north of Columbus.

CAMP MILLARD was a small camp built by the Army's Transportation Corp on the local railroad line near the town of Bucyrus. It was used to train Army railroad battalions whose mission was to operate and service railroad equipment in the U.S. and overseas. In Sept. 1945 the camp was closed and its assets disposed of.

CAMBRIDGE is in SE Ohio at the intersection of I-70 and I-77.

FLETCHER GENERAL HOSPITAL was located 1.5 miles north of Cambridge on SR 21. It was built in 1942-43 by the Army to care for war wounded. It consisted of 125 buildings, mostly of brick construction, and was considered at the time to be the most modern Army hospital in the country for treating wounded veterans. The hospital had a branch prisoner of war camp holding about 200 German POWs who worked at the hospital. In 1946 the hospital was turned over to the state which utilized it as a hospital for the mentally retarded. The hospital has gone by various names since the war. In 1992 most of the remaining WW II wooden buildings were torn down.

CANTON is 20 miles south of Akron. Major manufacturers in the town were the International Harvester Corp. which made 20 mm and 75 mm guns; Hercules Motor Co. which made truck motors and Diebold Safe & Lock Co. which made scout cars, M-3A and M-4 half-track trucks and hard-faced plate. In nearby Alliance, OH the Taylorcraft Aviation Corp. manufactured small military aircraft and aircraft parts.

U.S. NAVAL ORDNANCE PLANT, CANTON was built by the U.S. Navy in 1941-42 as a manufacturing plant to produce medium caliber gun mounts and sub-assemblies for

warships. It was part of a new three-plant complex designed to produce big guns at inland locations which were relatively safe from coastal attacks. This plant, and a similar plant in Centerline, MI, sent their gun mounts and sub assemblies to the naval plant at Louisville, KY to be fitted with guns which were made at that plant.

CINCINNATI AREA: Cincinnati is in the SW corner of the state on the Ohio River. This is Ohio's largest river port and the center of a large industrial region. Major manufacturers in the area were the Wright Aeronautical Corp. in Lockland which made modified aircraft engines for trucks; Cincinnati Milling Mach. Co. which made machine tools; Cincinnati Advertising Products Co. which made bombs and anti-tank mines, King Powder Co. of Kings MIlls, OH which made green and black powder and Fashion Frocks, Inc. which made parachutes.

Note: For WW II sites south of the Ohio River see Kentucky, Covington/Newport Area.

KINGS MILLS ORDNANCE PLANT was built in 1942 by the Federal Government near Kings Mills, OH, to manufacture small arms ammunition. Kings Mills is 15 miles NE of Cincinnati on I-71. The plant was run by the Remington Arms Co. and made primarily 45 calibre ammunition. In 1943 it also began producing 30 calibre ammunition. In 1944 the plant was shut down.

LUNKEN AIRPORT is east of downtown Cincinnati on U.S. 52 at Wilmer Ave. It was Cincinnati's main airport before the war and had been used by the Army Air Corps for some time as an intermediate landing field. Early in the war it was taken over by the short-lived I Concentration Command with the intend that it would become the Command's headquarters as well as one of its staging fields for units going overseas. To this end, the field's runways were lengthened and other ground facilities improved. When the I Concentration Command was disbanded the field was given over to general military use and used by both the AAF and Navy. Both services used it as one of the air fields in their respective air transport systems and the AAF had a Flight Service Center here. The airport became a

commercial field again after the war and retained it name, Lunken Airport.

SHARONVILLE ARMY ENGINEER DEPOT was built by the Federal Government in 1942 as a depot for the Army Corps of Engineers. The site was north of the Wright plant and extended to the Butler County line. The depot stored mainly food, munitions and equipment. The facility was retained by the Army after the war, but in 1974 was sold to the city of Sharonville for use as a bulk mail postal center and for development.

CLEVELAND METROPOLITAN AREA: This large metropolitan area is in northern Ohio on the south shore of Lake Erie. It is, and was during WW II, the state's most populated metropolitan area and its largest industrial center. Major manufacturers here were: Fisher Body Div. of General Motors which made major aircraft components; White Motor Co. made armored cars, heavy trucks, special trucks and half-track trucks; Steel Fabricators, Inc. made minesweepers; American Shipbuilding Co. made small vessels for the Navy; Cleveland Tractor Co. made prime mover tractors for artillery; Yoder Co. made M-1 57 mm guns and 105 mm shells;, Truscon Steel Co. made aircraft engine mounts, anti-aircraft gun mounts and bombs; Addressograph-Multigraph Corp. made automatic pilots, primers and fuzes; Enamel Products Co. made 100 lb bombs; Columbia Axle Co. made a variety of bombs; Electric Vacuum Cleaners, Inc. made bomb parts and fuzes; Bishop & Babcock Mfg. Co. made 105 high explosive and chemical shells; Cleveland Welding Co. made 105 mm shells and Gabriel Co. made 60 mm shells and shell fin assemblies.

CLEVELAND MUNICIPAL AIRPORT, 8.5 miles SW of downtown Cleveland, was the area's new and modern airport and one of the largest civil airports in the country. Adjacent to the airport was the huge Fisher Body plant which had been built by the Federal Government to manufacture major aircraft frame components. Both the AAF and Navy used the airport during the war, but neither took it over. The AAF used is as a part of its air transport system and there was an AAF Flight Service Center and an air freight terminal here. The Navy used it as part of its air transport and air ferry systems. After the war the armed forces left the field and the Fisher Body plant was acquired by private interests. The airport once again became the area's main air facility and became Cleveland Hopkins International Airport.

CRILE GENERAL HOSPITAL was a 1867-bed Army hospital located at 7030 York Rd. in Parma Height, OH, a suburb of Cleveland. It was built in 1943-44 by the Federal Government to treat war wounded and specialized in general and orthopedic surgery, plastic surgery, ophthalmologic surgery and psychiatry. The hospital had a branch prisoner of war camp holding about 250 POWs who worked at the hospital. In 1946 it was transferred to the Veterans Administration.

USS COD: This is the WW II submarine "Cod" preserved and on display on Cleveland's downtown lake front. The vessel, a veteran of 7 wartime patrols, is unaltered since its days

M2 half-track cargo and personnel carriers nearing completion at White Motor Co., Cleveland, OH in 1941.

of service meaning that visitors must enter the vessel through its hatches and down vertical ladders just as its crew did. Veterans of the Navy's submarine service are usually on hand to offer tours and answer questions. Address: 1089 N. Marginal Dr., Cleveland, OH 44114. Phone: 216/566-8770. Hours: May through Labor Day daily 10-5. Admission charged. Location: on the shore of Lake Erie between E. 9th St. and the western end of Burke Lakefront Airport.

COLUMBUS is the capital of Ohio and located near its geographic center. One of the largest manufacturers in town was the Curtiss-Wright Corp. which made SBC Helldivers and other aircraft for the Navy.

COLUMBUS GENERAL DEPOT was 6 miles east of town at 3900 E. Broad St. and just south of Port Columbus Airport. It was built in 1918 and known then as the Columbus Quartermaster Reserve Depot. The depot was retained and used by the Army in the years between the wars. During WW II it was greatly expanded and at its peak employed 10,000 people. The depot received, stored and shipped a wide range of supplies for the Army. It continued in service in the postwar years and was known at various times as the Columbus Army Depot, Columbus General Distribution Depot and Defense Construction Supply Center.

FORT HAYES was an old Army munitions depot, built during the Civil War, in downtown Columbus. Its original name was Columbus Arsenal. In 1875 it was renamed Columbus Barracks and was transferred to the Army's General Recruiting Service. In 1922 it was renamed Fort Hayes. Through the years the post was expanded and during both WW I and WW II was used as a reception center. After WW II it became the headquarters for the XX Army Corps and had an Army Reserve center, a National Guard training center and other Army support services. In the 1960s the post was closed and its assets sold.

LOCKBOURNE ARMY AIR BASE, 9.5 miles SE of Columbus, was a civilian airport before the war. It was taken over in early 1942 by the AAF according to pre-war planning to be a defensive base for the area equipped with combat-ready air units. This need soon passed and the field was turned over to the short-lived I Concentration Command to be used as a staging facility for Army units going overseas. In the summer of 1943, after the I Concentration Command was disbanded, the field was turned over to the Southeast Training Command and was used as a training field for pilot instructors for four-engine bombers, primarily B-17s. During the war the field had an auxiliary field, Kenton County Airport, Covington, KY. After the war the field was taken over by the US Air Force and became a part of the Tactical Air Command. In 1980 the base was assigned to the Air National Guard and was renamed Rickenbacker Air National Guard Base and in the 1990s it was closed.

OHIO STATE FAIRGROUNDS, north of downtown Columbus at 17th St., was taken over by the AAF and used as a specialized air depot for the duration of the war under the Air Technical Service Command.

CAPTAIN EDWARD RICKENBACKER GRAVE SITE: "Captain Eddie" Rickenbacker was a famous air ace of WW I, a winner of the Congressional Medal of Honor from that war and a native of Columbus. During WW II he was a civilian and served as a special observer for Gen. Harold "Hap" Arnold and for Secretary of War Henry Stimson. While returning from a trip to the Soviet Union in Oct. 1942 his plane crashed in the Pacific and he and others spent a harrowing 27 days at sea before being rescued. Rickenbacker is buried at Green Lawn Cemetery in Columbus.

U.S. NAVAL AIR FACILITY, COLUMBUS was 7 miles east of downtown Columbus. This was a new civilian airport built just before the war and known as Port Columbus Airport. It was the site of Curtiss-Wright Corp's. aircraft plant located at 4300 E. 5th St. The airport was used by the AAF as a landing field before the war and during the early months of the war but was not taken over by the AAF. In May 1942 the field was leased by the Navy for use by a naval aircraft delivery unit and given its wartime name. The mission of the facility was to receive new aircraft from manufacturers all over the U.S. and Canada, including the Curtiss-Wright plant, test them, in some cases modify them, and then send them on to naval air units for regular service. The naval delivery unit worked primarily with Seahawks, Helldivers and Corsairs. The Curtiss-Wright plant closed in Dec. 1945 and the naval air facility was placed in caretaker status. In Mar. 1946 the airport was reactivated as a Naval Air Reserve training station for Navy and Marine Corps Air Reserve units. It was also used as a stopover point for Navy and Marine aircraft traveling across country. In June 1959 the facility was disestablished and returned to its civilian owners. It then became an active civilian airport and retained it former name, Port Columbus Airport.

DAYTON is in the SW part of the state and is the center of another of Ohio's several major industrialized area. Dayton was the home of the Wright Brothers and thanks to them and their early work with aircraft had become a cradle of aviation activities. When WW II started, Dayton was a city very much involved with the airplane. Major manufacturers in the Dayton area during the war were Frigidaire Div. of General Motors which made aircraft propellers, machine guns and aircraft engine parts; Waco Aircraft Co. of Troy, OH 15 miles north of Dayton, which made gliders and National Cash Register Co. which made optical bombsight lenses, Sperry compensating gun sights, 37 mm high explosive shells and fuzes.

DAYTON MUNICIPAL AIRPORT, 7 miles north

The North Dayton War Memorial just north of downtown Dayton.

of downtown Dayton, was the city's main airport before the war. Early in the war it was taken over by the AAF, improved, and used as a sub-base to Wright Field. Much of Wright's acceleration service testing was done here. After the war the airport was returned to the city and became Dayton's main airport, the James M. Cox Dayton International Airport.

NORTH DAYTON WAR MEMORIAL is located just north of downtown at the intersection of Keowee St. and Valley Pike. It is an impressive outdoor memorial dedicated to those who served in World War I, World War II, The Korean War and Viet Nam.

PATTERSON FIELD was located 9 miles NE of downtown Dayton. It was first known as Wilbur Wright Field (not to be confused with Wright Field four miles to the SW which was built later) and first occupied in June 1917 by the Army's Signal Corps Aviation School. In Jan. 1918 Fairfield Aviation General Supply Depot was opened adjacent to Wilbur Wright Field to supply that field and other Signal Corps aviation activities in the midwest. During WW I Wilbur Wright Field was used to train aviators, aircraft mechanics and armorers. After WW I Wilbur Wright Field became a storage facility for many of the Air Corps's surplus aircraft and other equipment. In 1924 Wright Field, was built four miles to the SW and in 1931 Wilbur Wright Field was renamed Patterson Field. During WW II Patterson Field and the adjacent depot, which by then had become known as Fairfield Air Depot, remained a separate entity from Wright Field. The Patterson Field/Fairfield Air Depot complex functioned primarily as a supply and distribution facility although it also had aircraft maintenance schools, a weather school, a school for supply personnel, an air freight terminal and an AAF regional hospital. In Feb. 1942 the new 10th Air Force was created under Gen. Lewis H. Brereton and activated at Patterson Field. The 10th AF later served in China. Fairfield Air Depot was a control depot with many sub-depots across the nation. In 1945 Patterson Field/Fairfield Air Depot was merged with Wright Field for administrative purposes. When the US Air Force took over the complex in 1948 it renamed the entire

Above, left: A British-made Nissen Hut, a forerunner to the American Quonset Hut, is on disply at the US Air Force Museum

Left: The US Air Force Museum, Wright-Patterson Air Force Base, Dayton, OH. This is the world's largest air museum.

Above, right: "Bock's Car", the B-29 bomber that dropped the second atomic bomb on Japan thus hastening the end of WW II. Seen above the B-29 is a Japanese "Ohka" flying bomb, a suicide weapon used by the Japanese in the last year of the war.

facility Wright-Patterson Air Force Base.

WRIGHT FIELD, five miles NE of downtown Dayton, was built in 1927 on land donated to the Government by aviation-minded citizens of Dayton. It replaced a smaller air field, McCook Field, which was just north of downtown Dayton near the present-day intersection of SR 4 and I-75. McCook had become a center of aviation research and development since WW I days and the home of the Army Air Corps' Materiel Division. McCook Field, however, could not be expanded so the need for a new field was satisfied by the construction of Wright Field. The Air Corps' Engineering School was established at Wright and produced graduates who, for the most part, went on to work with the Materiel Division. Aeronautical scientists, engineers and other personnel concentrated at Wright Field from its earliest days and by WW II Wright Field was one of the AAF's largest research and development facilities. When the U.S. went to war, in Dec. 1941, there were some 2000 research and development projects already underway at Wright. All during WW II the field was a beehive of activity and was in a state of nearly constant expansion. Many of the nation's most important technological developments related to military aircraft were made here. During the first year of the war the field had more projects than it could handle and many of them were spun off to Eglin Field in Florida. Captured enemy equipment was tested and evaluated here in the field's Captured Enemy Equipment Technical Data

Lab. In the summer of 1944 this Lab acquired fragment of crashed German V-1 "buzzbombs" and set about to make an American copy of the weapon. This was done in just three weeks and the first American-made "buzzbomb" was successfully tested in Aug. 1944. The AAF was so impressed with the weapon that an order for 1000[1] was placed with Republic Aviation Corp. for use against both Germany and Japan. The American version of the V-1 was labelled the JB-2. At the time, a parallel project was underway at Wright to develop a flying bomb of U.S. design, but with the development of the JB-2 this project was downgraded in priority.

In 1945 Wright Field was merged with Patterson Field/Fairfield Air Depot for administrative purposes and in 1948 the entire complex was taken over by the US Air Force and renamed Wright-Patterson Air Force Base. The base soon became the home of the prestigious U.S. Air Force Institute of Technology and the Air Research and Development Command. Throughout the Cold War Wright-Patterson AFB was a very active facility responsible for maintaining America's lead in the ever-changing development of air and space technology.

US. Air Force Museum: This museum, on the grounds of Wright-Patterson Air Force Base, is the oldest and largest air museum in the world. Here, under the guidance of the Air Force, is accumulated one of the world's largest

[1]The order was later increased to 10,000, then cut back to 5,000. By the time the war in the Pacific ended 1391 had been produced, but none had been used yet against the enemy.

collection of military aircraft. On display are some 200 aircraft in the main museum and a Museum Annex which is on the historic Wright Field flight line about a mile from the main museum. A free shuttle bus connects the two locations. The museum has some 1500 other aircraft, most of which are on loan to other museums along with some 10,000 artifacts. Many of the aircraft on display here are one-of-kind models and others are very famous. The museum endeavors to tell the story of aviation from its inception with the Wright Brothers of Dayton to the present. Over 1.5 million visitors pass through the museum each year. World War II models predominate in the collection and almost every well-known aircraft is represented. Among the most outstanding aircraft in the collection is the B-29 bomber, "Bock's Car", which delivered the second atomic bomb to Nagasaki, Japan. A replica of the Nagasaki bomb is on display as well as a replica of the Hiroshima bomb. Other WW II aircraft of importance at the museum include a Messerschmitt Me 262A, the world's first operational jet fighter; a Bell P-59B Aircomet, America's first jet aircraft; President Roosevelt's personal plane, a C-54 named "Sacred Cow"; President Truman's personal plane, a Douglas VC-118 named "Independence" and President Eisenhower's personal plane, a Lockheed VC-121E named "Columbine III".

The museum has a research facility that maintains original prints, manuals and other technical data on historic aircraft. There is also a restoration facility that restores aircraft for the museum. On the grounds outside the museum is a memorial park with memorials, statuary and plaques commemorating various military air units. Nearby is a British-made Nissen Hut typical of the thousands of such huts that housed AAF personnel in Britain during WW II. Missile Mall, in front of the museum, displays several postwar rockets and missiles. Address: Wright-Patterson Air Force Base, OH 45433-6518. Phone: 513/255-3286 or 253-4629. Hours: Daily 9-5. Closed Thanksgiving and Dec. 25. Free. Location: The entrance to the museum is on Springfield Pike 6 miles NE of downtown Dayton. I-70 travelers should exit at SR 4 south towards Dayton 8 miles to the Harshman Rd exit. I-75 travelers should exit at Needmore Rd., east 6 miles.

DENNISON is 27 miles south of Canton.

DENNISON RAILROAD DEPOT MUSEUM is an 1873 railroad depot that served as a WW II Serviceman's Canteen and has been restored to its 1942 appearance. The canteen was known then as "Dreamsville" and was run by the Salvation Army. Free food and other comforts were offered to the GIs passing through. The museum has seven rooms displaying WW II and railroad memorabilia.

FOSTORIA is 30 miles SSE of Toledo. One of the larger firms in town was the S. F. Bowser Co. which made 40 mm projectiles and Mark 1, 2 and 6 projectiles.

FOSTORIA CHEMICAL WARFARE PLANT was built near town by the Federal Government in 1941-42. During the war it produced an ingredient called charcoal whetlerite.

FREMONT is 30 miles south of Toledo. Near downtown Fremont, on the Sandusky River, is Rodger Young Park named in honor of the famous Congressional Medal of Honor winner of WW II and a resident of Fremont. The park is dedicated to all of Sandusky County's service men and women.

LIMA is in NW Ohio on I-75. One of the largest firms in town was the Lima Locomotive Works which, during the war, made M-3 Grant tanks and M-4 Sherman tanks, while continuing to make locomotives and railroad rolling stock.

LIMA TANK DEPOT was built by General Motors for the Federal Government in 1942-43. Its original purpose was to manufacture large guns, but before construction was completed plans were changed and the plant was designated a tank depot. Throughout the war the depot received, stored, maintained and sometimes modified tanks. The depot also handled amphibious landing craft, cargo carriers, self-propelled guns, tank recovery vehicles and ambulances. At its peak, the depot had some 10,000 vehicles in inventory. Activity at the depot began to decline near the end of the war, but this was short-lived because the depot was chosen to be a major storage facility for surplus tanks and other large pieces of equipment. In Aug. 1945 the name of the facility was changed to Lima Ordnance Depot. The depot's floor space was not sufficient to store all the tanks and vehicles that were received so hundreds of low, round metal storage vaults, resembling grain storage bins, were constructed on a parcel of land on St. John's Road, and tanks and vehicles stored there. This facility was referred to as the Lima Tank Farm. During the late 1940s the depot's inventory of tanks steadily declined. In 1950 the last large batch of 300 WW II tanks were sent to the Nationalist Chinese Government on Taiwan after it had been run off the Chinese mainland by the Chinese Communists in 1949. The depot became active again during the Korean War, but from 1959 to 1976 it was mothballed and put on standby basis. Most of the large round steel storage vaults were sold and shipped west to become grain storage bins. In 1976 the depot became a manufacturing facility for new tanks and continued to serve in this capacity until the end of the Cold War.

MARION is 38 miles north of Columbus.

MARION ENGINEER DEPOT (MED) was located east of town in the SW quadrant of the intersection of SR 309 and SR 98. It was immediately south of the Scioto Ordnance Plant. MED was built in 1942 to store and renovate heavy equipment belonging to the Army and was the largest facility of its kind in

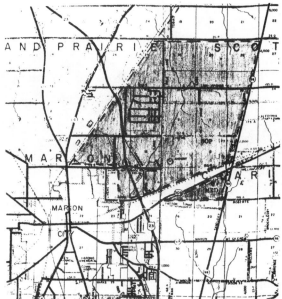

Marion, OH had two large wartime facilities NE of town, the Marion Engineer Depot and the Scioto Ordnance Plant.

the country. MED's main building was two miles long and paralleled SR 309 on the south side. In July 1944 MED's employment peaked at 1487. The depot had a prisoner of war camp holding German POWs who worked at the depot, at nearby Scioto Ordnance Plant and in agriculture. The depot remained active after the war and at various times was known as Marion Holding & Reconsignment Depot and Marion Quartermaster War Aid Depot. In 1961 the facility was disposed of and the buildings and land were sold. In its place emerged three schools, a park, a senior citizens center, a National Guard center and various industrial and commercial enterprises.

SCIOTO ORDNANCE PLANT (SOP) was located NE of, and adjacent to the town of Marion. It had many buildings including its own hospital and dormitories for the workers. Scioto was built in 1942 by the Federal Government to make artillery fuses and boosters under the direction of U.S. Rubber Co. This was the first of what was to be three phases of ordnance manufacturing at the plant during the war. The plant never reached full production in fuses and boosters and in late 1943 Atlas Powder Co. moved in to begin the manufacture of artillery shells. In Jan. 1944 the Permanente Metal Div. of Kaiser Industries set up operations at SOP to manufacture M-76 "goop" bombs and M-74 cluster bombs. In mid-1944 Kilgore Manufacturing Co. joined with Permanente Metals and also produced bombs. In Dec. 1944 there was an accidental explosion in the Kilgore operations which injured 9 workers and Kilgore subsequently pulled out and Ferro-Enamel Co. moved in to finish out the Kilgore contract. Production continued until Aug. 1945 when the Government ordered a halt to all production at SOP. Several months later, however, the plant began production again, this time making 20, 65, 75 mm shells, incendiary bombs and Napalm Barrel Bombs. SOP continued producing various ordnance items for the Army well into the postwar years although some of the building were torn down, some leased to commercial enterprises and

M4A1 Sherman tanks being manufactured at the Lima Locomotive Works in 1942.

The buildings of the former Springfield Engineer Sub Depot are unused and boarded up.

others used for a correctional institute. During the war the plant had a prisoner of war camp with the POWs working at the plant.

PORT CLINTON (See Sandusky/Port Clinton Area)

RAVENNA (See Akron)

SANDUSKY/PORT CLINTON AREA: This area contains several towns on the south shore of Lake Erie midway between Toledo and Cleveland with Sandusky being the largest city.

ERIE PROVING GROUND, 7 miles NW of Port Clinton and just west of Camp Perry, was built in 1918 by the Army to test artillery. The site was selected because many large guns were being manufactured at the time in the Detroit-Toledo-Cleveland areas. In 1920 the post became a storage facility for ordnance materials and was renamed Erie Ordnance Depot. In 1938 the newly-designed M-1 Garand Rifle was publically demonstrated here for the first time. It would go on to become the standard infantry weapon of the U.S. Army during WW II. In 1940 the facility was expanded and an indoor armor plate testing range was built. In Jan. 1941 it regained its original name, Erie Proving Ground. Throughout the war the facility tested and approved sample lots of armor plate being made by the various steel makers around the country as well as mobil artillery guns, gun carriages and mounts and recoil mechanisms. It is estimated that 70% of the armor plate and mobile artillery guns used by the Army during WW II were tested here. The Proving Ground had a large branch prisoner of war camp with the POWs working on the post. In 1946 the facility again became a storage facility and was renamed, for a second time, Erie Ordnance Depot. In the 1950s the depot stored anti-aircraft materials and guided missiles.

CAMP PERRY, five miles west of Port Clinton on SR 2, was a training camp for the Ohio National Guard. It was a small camp yet it had adequate facilities to house and feed up to 10,000 people. It was also in the middle of a tourist area and had its own 3500' beach front on Lake Erie. In late 1942 the Army selected Camp Perry to be a main prisoner of war camp. It eventually held some 2500 POWs, most of whom worked for the military or in the food industry. Most of the branch POW camps throughout Ohio were sub-camps of Camp Perry. After the war the POWs were repatriated and Camp Perry was returned to the Ohio National Guard.

PLUM BROOK DEPOT was built in 1940-41 by the Federal Government three miles south of Sandusky for the purpose of manufacturing TNT and other explosives. The plant continued in operation after the war and in later years became a facility of NASA.

SPRINGFIELD is 20 miles NE of Dayton. Major manufacturers in the town were the Champion Co. which made 20 and 40 mm high explosive shells and Bauer Bros,, Inc. which made 105 mm high explosive shells.

SPRINGFIELD ENGINEER SUB DEPOT was a depot of the Army Engineer Corps located at 1076 Kenton St. During the war it received, stored and shipped a variety of items for the Engineers. The facility was used after the war, but was eventually abandoned and boarded up.

TOLEDO is in NW Ohio at the western end of Lake Erie and was another of the state's wartime industrial centers. One of Toledo's manufacturers made a product that was known around the world and has become synonymous with WW II ... the "Jeep". This versatile little vehicle was developed by the Willys-Overland Motor Co. of Toledo and thousands of them were made here in Willys' plants[2].

Willys also made aircraft fuselage sub-assemblies, artillery gun breech housings, 30 mm and 50 mm bullet cores and 155 mm high explosive chemical artillery shells. Another well-known manufacturer in Toledo was the Packard Motor Car Co. which made Rolls-Royce aircraft engines under license from that British firm. Other manufacturers were the Toledo Shipbuilding Co. which made ice breakers and Acklin Stamping Co. which made 105 mm high explosive shells. The Army Ordnance Corps took over the hugh New York Central Railroad shop in Toledo and used it, under contract with Electric Auto-Lite Co., as a tank depot and a modification facility for various combat vehicles. This operation lasted less than a year and was moved to Lima

ROSSFORD ORDNANCE DEPOT, on South Oregon Road, was built in 1942 by the Federal Government and operated by the International Harvester Corp. as a storage facility for non-combat military vehicles and spare parts, mainly Jeeps. At first it was known as the Toledo Ordnance Depot, but it was given its wartime name in 1943. The depot received new Jeeps, spare parts and automotive tools from the three leading Jeep manufacturers, Willys-Overland, General Motors and Ford, stored and

[2]Jeeps were also made in large numbers by Ford Motor Co. and General Motors in other locations.

HOT FROM THE "LINES" AT WILLYS-OVERLAND..

HELL BENT FOR VICTORY

WILLYS

MOTOR CARS   TRUCKS AND JEEPS

The Willys-Overland Co. told the world in ads that they made the famous "Jeep".

maintained them, and issued them to the various branches of service. At its peak, the depot employed 3500 people. The depot also had a clerical school for parts clerks. As the war ended this facility, in a major realignment, became a master depot and absorbed the inventories of non-combat vehicles from five other depots. By 1947 the depot had some 20,000 vehicles in storage, of which 7000 were Jeeps. The rest were automobiles, busses, small trucks, trailers, etc.

Rossford remained active into the early 1960s and was one of Toledo's largest employers. In the 1950s it became known as Rossford Army Depot. In 1962, however, the depot began to scaled down and eventually closed in 1964. The facility was acquired by the state and converted into a large vocational high school. It later became a two-year college known as Penta Technical Institute and still later became Michael J. Owens State Technical College.

WILMINGTON is 40 miles NE of Cincinnati.
CLINTON COUNTY ARMY AIR FIELD, two miles SE of town, was the community's local airport before the war. It was taken over by the AAF to serve as a sub-base to Wright Field in Dayton. The field was used to test gliders and was an all-weather flying center. The field was retained by the AAF and eventually taken over by the US Air Force and renamed Clinton County Air Force Base. The field was later abandoned by the Air Force and became a commercial airfield.

YOUNGSTOWN AREA is on the NE edge of the state near the Pennsylvania state line and was the center of one of the state's several industrial areas. Major manufacturers in the area were Federal Machine & Welder Co. of nearby Warren, OH which made M-4 medium tanks, Republic Steel Corp. of Niles, OH which made incendiary bombs, Commercial Shearing & Stamping Co. of Youngstown which made 1000 lb anti-personnel bombs, E. W. Bliss Co. which made torpedoes and Mullins Mfg. Corp. of Salem, OH which made 105 mm high explosive shells and 3" cartridge casings.

LORDSTOWN ORDNANCE DEPOT, four miles south of Warren, OH on SR 45, was built in 1942 by the Federal Government to serve as an Army ordnance supply depot. It received, stored and shipped a wide variety of munitions to Army facilities in Ohio and the surrounding states. The depot became a sub-depot of the Rossford Ordnance Depot and was used by the Army well into the postwar years.

OKLAHOMA

Oklahoma was one of several states in the Union that was in desperate economic straits before the war, but emerged from the war in relatively healthy condition. During the 1930s the state's two main commodities, oil and food had been greatly depressed. The price of oil was depressed by an over-supply and food prices were depressed due to the general effects of the Great Depression, plus a series of disastrous droughts that turned western Oklahoma into a part of the famous "Dust Bowl". The state had some manufacturing, but it was mostly related to the oil and food industries such as refining, milling, meat packing and dairy products. There was some mineral wealth in the state, other than oil, in the form of natural gas, coal, lead, zinc, gypsum, asphalt, cement and clay.

In 1939 the beginning of the war in Europe helped stimulate the world-wide need for oil and food which, in turn, helping Oklahoma to some degree. By 1940 soil conservation and dry land methods of farming began to come into practice in the state helping to rejuvenate farming. During 1940-41 oil production began to decline in some of the older pools, but four new pools were discovered keeping that segment of the economy on course. Also in 1941 iron ore was discovered in the Arbuckle Mountains near Sulphur, OK adding a new dimension to the state's economy. With America's entry into the war, demands for oil and food surged and the state's oil interests and farmers responded eagerly. Throughout the war the state's farms produced wheat, corn, cotton, oats, grain sorghums, broom corn, vegetable and fruit.

The Federal Government added considerably to Oklahoma's new prosperity by building several large manufacturing plants and many military facilities in the state. The demand for oil stimulated exploration and all through the war many new oil wells were brought into production. The state suffered from a manpower shortage, as did most farm states, but the presents of 15 prisoner of war camps in the state helped alleviate this problem when the POWs were put to work on the farms.

When peace came, Oklahoma had a robust and growing economy. The demands for oil and food continued in the postwar years and manufacturing had come to the state to stay.

ALTUS is in the SW corner of the state.
ALTUS ARMY AIR FIELD, 3.5 miles NE of town, was built in 1942 as a training field for the 70,000 Pilot Training Program. It was first known as Altus AAF Advanced Flying School but in 1943 was given its wartime name. Altus specialized in the training of pilots of twin-engine bombers and during the war 5377 pilots graduated from here. The air field was closed at the end of the war but reactivated in 1953 as Altus Air Force Base. It then continued in operation throughout the Cold War. During WW II the air field had the following auxiliary fields:

- Aux. #1 Altus Auxiliary Field #1, immediately west of Blair
- Aux. #2 Victory Airport, 1.5 miles north of Victory
- Aux. #3 Olustee Airport, 2.5 miles south of Olustee
- Aux. #4 Altus Auxiliary Field #4, 1 mile south of Headrick
- Altus Training Annex, 2.5 miles NW of El Dorado

ALVA is in the north-central part of the state.
ALVA PRISONER OF WAR CAMP was located on the outskirts of town. This was a main POW camp holding about 4500 POWs. During the summer of 1943 after the Americans realized that they had to separate ardent pro-Nazis and various troublemakers for more cooperative POWs in the various camps across the country, the Alva camp was selected to be one of those to receive pro-Nazi officers. Once this was accomplished, the camp was more heavily guarded than before and those POWs who were allowed to leave the camp for work were permitted to work only on jobs for the military where they could be carefully watched and wouldn't be a threat to civilians. The internal affairs of the camp were controlled by the POWs themselves and, as might be expected, brought strict order to the camp. As the war turned against Germany the most fanatical of the POWs formed a suicide club based on the persistent, but erroneous, rumor that they would be sent to the Soviet Union after the war as slave laborers. Members of the club vowed that upon hearing of the collapse of Germany or the death of Adolph Hitler they would carry out a Japanese-style Banzai attack with whatever weapons they had and attempt to kill as many Americans as possible before being killed themselves. Informants in the camp warned the Americans of the club's existence and the club's leaders were very carefully watched and at time isolated. When VE-Day came nothing happened. After the war the POWs were repatriated to Germany and the camp was closed.

ARDMORE is in the south-central Oklahoma near the Texas state line.
ARDMORE ARMY AIR FIELD, 11 miles NE of town, was built for the I Troop Carrier Command as a training facility, but was transferred to the 3rd AF without the I Troop Carrier Command having occupied the field. The 3rd AF used the field as a training field for combat air crews and for reconnaissance pilots. There was a branch prisoner of war camp holding about 250 POWs who worked for the military. After the war the Ardmore AAF was declared surplus and acquired by private interests.

BOISE CITY is in the western end of the Oklahoma panhandle. This community of 1300 people had the unique distinction of being the only American city in the contiguous 48 states to be bombed during WW II. It happened in July 1943 when an American bomber, on a practice bombing mission out of Dalhart, TX, dropped six 100 lb practice bombs on the city. The bomber crew somehow mistook the town for its intended target, a bombing range 45 miles away. The bombs, each filled with four lbs of explosive, damaged a Baptist Church and a garage. There were no casualties.

CHICKASHA is 30 miles SW of Oklahoma City.
BORDEN GENERAL HOSPITAL was a 1000-bed Army hospital built in Chickasha in 1942-43 to

Hutments at Fort Sill in July 1942.

serve as a speech and hearing therapy center for the Army Medical Corps. It also specialized in general and orthopedic surgery. Borden was located at the west end of Chickasha Ave. The hospital had a branch prisoner of war camp holding about 100 POWs who worked at the hospital. The POWs were housed at the Fairgrounds east of town. In Dec. 1944-Jan. 1945 the hospital was hastily expanded to make room for a surge of new patients as a result of the "Battle of the Bulge". In 1946 the hospital was closed and declared surplus and turned over to the community. Several facilities eventually took over the site including the Grady Memorial Hospital, Chickasha Clinic, Chickasha High School and a sheltered workshop.

CHICKASHA AIRPORT is four miles NW of town. In 1940-41 it had a private flying school that was contracted by the Army Air Corps to give elementary flight training to Air Corps cadets.

CLINTON is 70 miles east of Oklahoma City.
U.S. NAVAL AIR STATION, CLINTON, 17 miles SW of Clinton, was built by the Navy in 1942-43 and served several purposes. It was the headquarters of the Training Task Force Command, it had an aircraft modification center, it tested and developed new equipment, it had an Air Navigation School and a Naval Air Station School. Navy pilots were trained here in single-engine aircraft, twin-engine aircraft and gliders. The modification center was quit active modifying up to 125 planes a month. In the spring of 1944 training operations began to decline as did the other activities, and by Dec. 1945 the station was disestablished. In June 1946 it was officially closed. The station was then acquired by private interests and served as a local airport. During the war the station had outlying fields at Eagle Mountain Lake, Durant, Stillwater, Ada, Hobart, Delhi, Hydro, Fort Worth, TX, Conroe, TX and Traverse City, MI.

ENID is 60 miles north of Oklahoma City.
ENID ARMY AIR FIELD, four miles south of town, was built in 1941-42 to meet the needs of the 30,000 Pilot Training Program and during the war it had four different names: Air Corps Basic Flying School, Enid; Enid Army Flying School; Enid Army Air Field; and AAF Pilot School, Basic, Enid Army Air Field. The field

specialized in training pilots and crews in twin-engine aircraft, primarily B-25s. The air field continued in operation after the war except for a brief period from 1947-48. In 1948 it was taken over by the US Air Force and renamed Enid Air Force Base. In 1949 it was renamed Vance Air Force Base in honor of a WW II Congressional Medal of Honor winner Lt. Col. Leon R. Vance, Jr. who, though severely wounded, saved the crew of his crippled B-24 at great risk to himself. Vance survived the incident only to disappear over the North Atlantic on a flight evacuating him from England to the U.S. Vance AFB served the Air Force throughout the Cold War. During WW II the base had the following auxiliary fields:
- Aux. #1, Drummond Airport, 2.5 miles SW of Drummond
- Aux. #2, Waukomis Airport, 4 miles NE of Waukomis
- Aux. #5, Breckenridge Air Field, 3 miles NE of Breckenridge
- Aux. #6, Carrier Field, 2 miles NE of Carrier
- Aux. #?, Perry Municipal Airport, 6.5 miles north of Perry
- Aux. #?, Enid Municipal Airport, 5.2 miles ESE of Enid

FREDERICK is in the SW corner of the state near the Texas line.
FREDERICK ARMY AIR FIELD, 2.5 miles SE of town, was the local airport before the war. It was taken over by the AAF to meet the needs of the 70,000 Pilot Training Program and used to train crews in twin-engine bombers, primarily B-26s. In 1946 the air field was declared surplus and returned to its former owners and again became the local airport. During the war the air field had the following auxiliary fields:
- Aux. #1, Tipton Airport, 4.5 miles SW of Tipton
- Aux. #2, Davidson Airport, 2.5 miles NW of Davidson
- Aux. #3, Grandfield Airport, 3 miles west of Grandfield
- Aux. #4, Chattanooga Airport, 4 miles SW of Chattanooga
- Aux. #5, Vernon Airport, 5 miles north of Vernon, TX
- Aux. #?, Olney Municipal Airport, 4 miles SW of Olney, TX

LAWTON is 70 miles SW of Oklahoma City.
FORT SILL is just north of the town of Lawton and covers about three times as much area as Lawton. The fort was built in 1870-75 as an Army cavalry post. In 1902 the first artillery unit arrived at the post and Fort Sill has been associated with artillery ever since. The School of Fire for Artillery was established here in 1911 and during WW I evolved into the U.S. Army Field Artillery School, the premier school in the US Army for artillerymen. The post acquired its own air field, Post Field, which used to train air observation personnel working in conjunction with artillery units. Both aircraft and balloons were flown from the field. In the years between the wars much of the Army's work on mobilizing and updating field artillery was done here at Fort Sill. By 1939 Fort Sill was the Army's most important artillery post and had become world renowned for its advancements in artillery fire control and direction techniques. During the war the post was expanded considerably and trained thousands of artillerymen for the Army. Most of the Army's artillery officers in WW II spend some time at Fort Sill in the Field Artillery School. The fort also produced officers in its Officer Candidate School. The fort became a reception center early in the war for the 8th Crops Area and was also the concentration and training camp for the National Guards from Arizona, Colorado, New Mexico and Oklahoma. Fort Sill was a segregated post and had been since its beginning when the famous "Buffalo Soldiers" (elite negro cavalrymen) were posted here during the Indian days. The post had one of the first main prisoner of war camp in the country holding about 1600 Germans who worked mostly for the military. There was also a small internment camp for enemy aliens holding Japanese aliens from Hawaii and later Japanese aliens expelled from Panama, Peru, Bolivia and Nicaragua. In the postwar years the fort continued to lead in the advancement of field artillery and become deeply involved in atomic weapons and missiles. The post was active throughout the Cold War and became a National Historic Landmark.

U.S. Army Field Artillery Museum and Fort Sill Museum: This museum, on the grounds of Fort Sill, preserves the history of the fort from its inception to the present. The museum is housed in some of the fort's original buildings. Inside the museum are display of artillery pieces, aircraft, vehicles, ordnance, small arms, nuclear weapons, rockets & missiles, communication equipment, field equipment, uniforms, documents, flags, photographs and dioramas. Outside the museum is Cannon Walk along which many large and historic field artillery pieces are displayed. Many of the pieces are of WW II vintage. Address: 437 Quanah Rd., Ft. Sill, OK 73503-5100. Phone: 405/351-5123. Hours: daily 8:30-4:30. Closed Jan. 1 & 2 and Dec. 25 & 26. Free. Access to the museum is through the fort's Key Gate. Exit I-44 at the Key Gate interchange and follow the signs to the gate.

Missile Park: This park is also on the ground of Ft. Sill and displays missiles and rockets dating from 1944. Phone: 405/351-5123. Hours: Daily dawn to dusk. Free.

The former headquarters building of the McAlester POW camps is now a VFW post.

McALESTER is 100 miles SE of Oklahoma City.

CAMP McALESTER PRISONER OF WAR CAMP: This was a main prisoner of war camp built in 1942 on the north edge of the then city limits of McAlester. Its first occupants, however, were not prisoners of war, but enemy aliens of several nationalities. When large numbers of POWs began to be received from overseas, the internees at McAlester were sent to other camps and some 3800 German POWs took their place. The POWs worked for the military, in agriculture and on the surrounding ranches. It is claimed locally that their labor was so valuable to the ranchers during the war that they prevented some ranches from going out of business. After becoming experienced ranch hands, some of the POWs participated in local rodeos. The McAlester camp was also used as a staging camp for German POWs that were to be repatriated early for humanitarian reasons. These included sick, wounded, disabled and protected personnel. These POWs were gathered at McAlester and then shipped out to ports of embarkation to be returned to Germany on ships of neutral nations.

After the war the POWs were repatriated and the camp was closed. One of the original camp buildings remained in use as a VFW post and is located on Gene Stipe Blvd.

U.S. NAVAL AMMUNITION DEPOT, McALESTER was located 8 miles south of McAlester on the outskirts of the community of Savanna and was built in 1942. The depot received, stored and shipped a wide variety of naval ammunition ranging from 20 mm shells to 16" projectiles. At its peak, the depot employed some 8000 people. The depot remained active after the war and in 1977 was turned over to the Army and renamed US Army Ammunition Depot. By then it was storing ammunition for all branches of the military service. The facility served throughout the Cold war and part of grounds became a game preserve.

MIAMI is in the NE corner of the state.

MIAMI AIRPORT, two miles NW of town, was the area's local airport before the war. It had a privately-owned flying school known as Spartan Aircraft Co. and was one of several in the nation contracted by the Army Air Corps to give elementary flight training to Air Corps cadets in 1940-41. After the Army's contract ended the

school trained British pilots for a while.

MUSKOGEE is 35 miles SE of Tulsa.

FORT GRUBER, 18 miles SE of Muskogee, was built in 1942 by the Army to serve as a training camp for division-sized units. It was a large camp and during the war the 42nd and 88th Infantry Divisions trained here. The camp had a main prisoner of war camp holding about 5000 POWs who worked for the military and in agriculture. In 1947 the camp was closed and most of it became a game preserve.

HATBOX FIELD, two miles west of downtown Muskogee, was the community's main airport before the war. It had a training school for pilots, Spartan Aviation School, that was contracted by a the Army Air Corps in 1940-41 to give primary flight training to Air Corps cadets. In the postwar years Hatbox Field became the community's secondary airport.

MUSKOGEE ARMY AIR FIELD was built by the Government 5.5 miles south of Muskogee to serve as a training field for pilots and crews of P-38s and B-25s. After the war the city purchased the field and it became the city's main airport known as Davis Field. Some of the WW II buildings were converted into an industrial park.

MUSKOGEE WAR MEMORIAL PARK & USS "BATFISH": This park and museum are four miles NE of downtown Muskogee in the Port of Muskogee area on the Arkansas River. The park is dedicated to Oklahomans of all the branches of the armed forces that have served this country in wartime. In the park is a large museum housing military artifacts and displays from WW I to the present. On the grounds of the museum is the WW II submarine "Batfish" which had a distinguished career during the war and sank 14 Japanese

vessels. Also on display on the museum grounds are large guns, torpedoes and a depth charge. Inside the museum are artillery pieces, vehicles, field equipment, small arms, aircraft and ship models, uniforms, documents, maps, photographs and more. Address: PO Box 253, Muskogee, OK 74401. Phone: 918/682-6294. Hours: Mar. 15 - Oct. 15. M-Sat. 9-5, Sun. 1-5. Closed rest of year. Admission charged. Location: Exit Muskogee Turnpike at the Port of Muskogee Exit and proceed directly to the park.

OKLAHOMA CITY is the capital of Oklahoma and located near the geographic center of the state. One of the major manufacturers in the city was the Douglas Aircraft Co. which modified aircraft and made several models of military aircraft.

AIR SPACE MUSEUM (also known as THE OKLAHOMA AVIATION & SPACE HALL OF FAME & MUSEUM) is located in the Kirkpatrick Center at NE 52nd St. and N. Eastern Ave. This is one of several museums, gardens, and galleries in the Center. The Air Space Museum has a wide variety of aircraft on display from very early models to space-age types. There are only a few WW II items in the museum. They include a replica of a German V-2 rocket, a 10' model of the battleship "Oklahoma", which was one of the ships damaged at Pearl Harbor, and a German-made Bucker Jungmeister bi-plane which was one of the training planes used by the Luftwaffe to train their pilots during WW II. The 45th Infantry Division Museum is just south of the Air Space Museum. Address of the Air Space Museum: 2100 N.E. 52nd St. Oklahoma City, OK 73111. Phone: 405/424-1443/427-5461. Hours: Memorial Day through Labor Day M-Sat. 9-6, Sun. noon-6. Rest of year M-F 9:30-5, Sat. 9:30-6, Sun. noon-6. Closed Thanksgiving and Dec. 25. Admission charged.

THE FORTY-FIFTH INFANTRY DIVISION MUSEUM: This is a fine state-operated museum in Oklahoma City dedicated to the 45th Infantry Div. which, traditionally included the Oklahoma National Guard. The museum collects, preserves and exhibits object and equipment relevant to the history of Oklahoma's citizen soldiers. Displays range from the days of the American Revolution to the present with heavy emphasis on WW II. Of unique interest in the museum is the Bill Mauldin Room which displays more than 200 original drawings by the famous WW II cartoonist. Mauldin was a member of the 45th Div. Another significant display is the Reaves Military Weapons Collection, one of the largest of its kind in the country. Adjacent to the

The 45th Infantry Division Museum in Oklahoma City, OK.

museum is Thunderbird Military Park where vehicles, aircraft, artillery pieces and other equipment are on display. Picnic facilities are available in the park. The Air Space Museum is just north of this museum. Address of the 45th Infantry Museum: 2145 NE 36th St. Oklahoma, City, OK 73111. Phone: 405/424-5313. Hours: Tues.-Fri. 9-5. Sat. 10-5, Sun. 1-5. Free. Location: On the north side of NE 36th St. just west of its intersection with I-35.

MUSTANG AIRPORT is five miles SW of El Reno. It was one of the airports in the country that had a private flying school that was contracted by the Army Air Corps in 1940-41 to give elementary flight training to Air Corps pilots.

FORT RENO was located four miles west of the town of El Reno on the north bank of the Canadian River. The post was established in 1874 after the Cheyenne Uprising to protect a nearby Indian Agency. In 1908 the post became a remount station purchasing and breeding horses and mules for the Army. In 1938 Fort Reno was converted to a depot known as the Reno Quartermaster Depot, and served this mission throughout WW II. Remount operations continued at the fort although the Army's need for horses was rapidly declining. The Coast Guard, though, developed an increasing need for horses for their beach patrols, so many of Fort Reno's horses were assigned to the Coast Guard. Coastguardsmen came to Ft. Reno for training in handling horses and were instructed by Army personnel. Also in 1942 a relocation camp was built at Ft. Reno to hold up to 2500 ethnic Japanese who had been relocated from the U.S. west coast, but the camp went unoccupied. In July 1943 the camp was converted to a main prisoner of war camp for German POWs. The camp held about 1000 POWs who worked for the military. In 1949 the Army abandoned the post and it became the Fort Reno Livestock Research Station.

TINKER FIELD, 8.5 miles SE of downtown Oklahoma City, was built by the Federal Government in 1943 along with Modification Center #17 which was run by the Douglas Aircraft Co. that modified and built aircraft for the armed services. The installation was first known as Midwest Air Depot, then Oklahoma City Air Depot. In Nov. 1943 it was named Tinker Field in honor of Maj. Gen. Clarence Tinker, Commander of the Hawaii-based 7th Air Force who was killed on a raid over Wake Island. The Douglas plant built C-47 and C-54 transports and A-26 bombers, and also modified B-17, B-24 and B-29 bombers. Over half of the C-47s produced during WW II were produced at this plant. In June 1945 a large maintenance center was added and also run by Douglas. This Center reconditioned and modified aircraft, engines and other related equipment coming from overseas and domestic service. When the war ended the manufacture of aircraft ended, but the reconditioning and maintenance operations increased as more and more equipment returned for servicing. The US Air Force took over Tinker Field and the maintenance operation in 1948 renaming the facility Tinker Air Force Base. The base was expanded and by 1950 Tinker AFB was the Air Force's largest maintenance and supply depot. Reconditioning and maintenance operations continued into the postwar years and many

testing operations were added, especially in regards to jet engines. Tinker AFB closed during the 1990s after the end of the Cold War.
WILL ROGERS FIELD, 8 miles SW of downtown Oklahoma City, was the city's municipal airport before the war. Elements of the 3rd AF moved onto the field early in the war but did not take it over and commercial operation continued along with those of the AAF. The 3rd AF used the field for combat crew training, the training of operational and replacement airmen and had a photo reconnaissance school here. A branch prisoner of war camps existed at the field holding about 230 POWs who worked for the military. The Navy used the field as a stop-over stations in its air transport system. At the end of the war the AAF and Navy departed and the field once again became Oklahoma City's municipal airport.

U.S. NAVAL AIR STATION, SHAWNEE was two miles NW of Downtown Shawnee, OK an eastern suburb of Oklahoma City. Before the war it was Shawnee's local airport. During the first year of the war the AAF, Navy and Marines all made use of the field while it continued to operate as a commercial air field. The AAF used the field to train Army air cadets of the War Training Service of the Civil Aeronautics Administration, the Navy used it as an auxiliary field to NATTC, Norman and the Marines used it for glider training. In early 1943 the Navy leased the entire field for the duration of the war on the condition that they provide the community of Shawnee with a new airport to meet the city's needs. This was done with the construction of a new, but smaller, field about 8 miles north of town. At first, the Navy called their new station US Naval Auxiliary Air Facility, Shawnee and it was under the command of NATTC, Norman and used in conjunction with their flight training program. In March 1944, however, the Naval Air Navigation School was transferred here from Hollywood, FL and the facility was upgraded to an air station and became independent of NATTC, Norman. The station acquired about 50 R4D and C-47 aircraft modified to train navigators and the school, when fully operational, graduated about 200 navigators a month. In early 1945 navigation training began

to be scaled down and at the end of March 1945 all navigational training and equipment was moved to NAS, Clinton. In April the station was disestablished and returned to it pre-war owners and again became Shawnee's local airport.
U.S. NAVAL AIR TECHNICAL TRAINING CENTER, NORMAN, was two miles south of downtown Norman, OK, a southern suburb of Oklahoma City. The training center was built by the Navy in 1942 to train aircraft mechanics, metalsmiths, ordnancemen and radarmen. It also offered primary flight training for naval air cadets. The station had 197 buildings including a 600-bed hospital and was first known as U.S. Naval Training School (Aviation Maintenance), Norman. But, in Feb. 1943 the station was given its wartime name. Many of the trainees here were Waves and women Marines. Some British airmen were also trained on the station. Maintenance training concentrated on Navy fighter planes such as Avengers, Wildcats, Hellcats and Corsairs. At the end of the war the station served as a separation center and then, under pressures from state officials and officials of the nearby University of Oklahoma, was closed down so that its facilities could be used to house the thousands of ex-servicemen enrolled at the University and their families. In 1952, during the Korean War, the station was reactivated and used again as a training center for mechanics and other maintenance personnel. This lasted until 1959 when the station was closed again. In the postwar years the station was used as a private air field.

OKMULGEE is 35 miles south of Tulsa on US 75.

GLENNAN GENERAL HOSPITAL was a 1690-bed facility built in Okmulgee by the Federal Government in 1943 to treat prisoners of war. This was one of two such general hospitals in the U.S. serving POWs. The other was at Camp Forrest, TN. In Dec. 1945 Glennan General Hospital was closed and transferred to Oklahoma A & M College.

PRYOR is 26 miles east of Tulsa.

OKLAHOMA ORDNANCE WORKS was built south of Pryor on US 69 by the Federal Government in 1941-42 to produce smokeless powder, TNT, pistol powder, tetryl, nitric and sulphuric acids. The latter products were used

Modification Center #16 under construction at Tulsa Municipal Airport. This plant was run by Douglas Aircraft Co. and produced B-24 bombers.

in explosives. The plant was operated by Du Pont de Nemours & Co. and at its peak employed 10,000 people. The plant had a small branch prisoner of war camp with the POWs working at the plant. In late 1945 the plant was closed and put into caretaker status under the control of National Gypsum Co. In the mid-1960s most of the land and buildings were acquired by the state and converted into an industrial center known as Mid-America Industrial District. About 480 acres were sold to developers who built homes, apartments and a shopping center and 180 acres, along with 24 former staff homes, were sold to the Cherokee Indian Nation.

TONKAWA is in north-central Oklahoma 35 miles NE of Enid.

TONKAWA PRISONER OF WAR CAMP was a main POW camp built by the Federal Government near the town of Tonkawa to house some 1100 German non-commissioned officers (NCO). This was one of several camps built throughout the country for this purpose. After the war the camp's POWs were repatriated and the camp was closed.

TULSA, 90 miles NE of Oklahoma City, was sometime called "The Oil Capital of the World". The city also had a number of manufacturing firms and was an important commerce and transportation center. Tulsa was one of the western cities to prosper greatly during the war along with such cities as Albuquerque, Las Vegas, Phoenix and Denver. During this rapid growth spurt there were considerable problems in the city in housing, inflation, overcrowded schools, traffic congestion and an overloading of city services. Major manufacturers in the city were the Douglas Aircraft Co. which made B-24 bombers and modified other aircraft, Spartan Aircraft Corp which made aircraft and aircraft parts and W. C. Norris Mfg. Co. which made 90 mm shells.

TULSA MUNICIPAL AIRPORT was located 6 miles NE of downtown Tulsa. Early in the war the airport had a privately-owned flying school known as the Spartan School of Aeronautics. The Army Air Corps contracted with the school in 1940-41 to give elementary flight training to Air Corps cadets. In 1940 the Oklahoma Air National Guard set up operations at the airport. This was also the site of the Douglas Aircraft Co. plant which had been built by the Federal Government and was officially known as Modification Center #16. Both the AAF and the Navy used the field sharing the facilities with the commercial interests which continued to operate throughout the war. The AAF had agencies here that worked closely with Douglas testing and accepting the new B-24s as they came off the assembly line. The Air Transport Command also had a miliary air freight terminal here. The Navy used the field as one a stop-over in its air ferry and air transport systems. In the postwar years the airport evolved into the Tulsa International Airport.

STRINGTOWN is in SE Oklahoma on U.S. 65.

STRINGTOWN DETENTION CENTER: This was a former penitentiary that was reactivate during the war for several uses. At various times it held enemy aliens sent to the U.S. by several Latin American countries and Samoans who were German citizens1. Near the end of the war it became a prisoner of war camp for German naval personnel.

¹Samoa had been a German colony up to 1919 when it was taken over by the U.S.

OREGON

Oregon was the only state of the then-forty-eight states to be attacked three ways by the enemy during WW II. Her shore line was shelled by an enemy submarine, her forests were fire-bombed twice by enemy aircraft and she was attacked in 51 separate locations by Japanese balloon bombs which was more than any other state, and the state suffered the only loss of life in the U.S. due to the balloon attacks.

In Sept. 1939, however, when the war started in Europe, Oregon was remote from the war and was affected by it only in that the US military buildup had stimulated Oregon's economy and the draft had taken away some of her men for military service. On December 7, 1941, that attitude changed overnight. Suddenly the US was at war with a well-armed and aggressive enemy that had boldly demonstrated its naval might, at Hawaii, Oregon's nearest neighbor to the west. Many in Oregon believed that it was entirely possible that the naval force that had attacked Hawaii could sail on and attack U.S. west coast. War jitters swept through the state and wild rumors spread (just as they had in California and Washington State) that enemy ships were lurking offshore, that there were secret enemy air fields in the desert and that the local ethnic Japanese were in league with the Japanese Government acting as spies and planning sabotage. These fears were amplified when, in mid-December, Japanese submarines appeared off the west coast and attacked several ships. Actions were taken to strengthen Oregon's defenses and prepare her citizens for air raids and other types of attacks. Oregon's cities created civil defense organization, practiced blackouts and prepared bomb shelters. When the order came to relocate the ethnic Japanese from the west coast

Oregon's leaders and most of her citizens approved of it without question.

Fears of enemy attacks gradually diminished in Oregon, but they never really disappeared. This was with good cause, because many people rightfully believed that the Japanese never lost the capability to attack the west coast, even in the final days of the war.

The state had a powerful senator in Washington, DC, Senator Charles L. McNary. He was Senate Minority Leader and Wendell Willkie's vice-presidential running mate during the 1940 election. Unfortunately, McNary died in 1944.

Oregon was one of the few states in the union that had only a few prisoner of war camps. There were only two main camps and four branch camps.

The state's industry boomed during the war. Her existing ship yards were loaded with work by 1941 and had to be expanded and new ones built. Her lumber industry worked around the clock supplying lumber for the tens of thousands of "temporary" wooded buildings that had to be built all over the country at military facilities, war plants and to house war workers. This great demand for lumber resulted in the depletion of some of the state's best forests during the war. In late 1945 two of Oregon's largest lumber mills had to shut down due to a shortage of logs. This resulted in substantial layoffs and several strikes. Oregon's other products, paper, pulp, meat, grain and mercury were also much in demand, but nothing equalled lumber and ships.

The end of the war brought more unemployment to the state as her ship yards shut down. The cutback was fast and dramatic. At the end of 1945 31,500 people were employed in the ship yards and by the end of 1946 that figure had dropped to 3000.

Oregon's other economic sectors held up well in the early postwar years because there remained strong demands for food and minerals. The lumber industry remained the state's largest employer despite the on-going shortage of logs.

ASTORIA/WARRENTON AREA: This area is in the NW corner of the state at the mouth of the Columbia River. Since the Columbia River is such an important waterway, this area is one of the most militarily strategic parts of the state and has been protected by fortifications for many years on both the Oregon and Washington sides.

Clatsop Beach, which fronts on the ocean west of Warrenton and stretches for miles down the coast, was considered an ideal invasion beach for a potential enemy. During the war temporary gun emplacements existed along the beach and it was heavily patrolled by the Coast Guard.

The mouth of the Columbia River, which had been mined during the Spanish-American War and World War I was mined again during WW II. The mines were controlled by the Army from Fort Columbia on the Washington side of the river.

CAMP CLATSOP¹ was located on the Pacific Ocean four miles south of Warrenton. The main gate of the camp was on U.S. 101. Camp Clatsop was built in 1927 by the state and was used as a summer training ground for the Oregon National Guard. Soon after the outbreak of WW II in Europe the Oregon National Guard was nationalized and the camp was taken over by the Federal Government and

¹Not to be confused with Fort Clatsop National Monument which is associated with Lewis and Clark.

This is one of several coastal defense positions along Camp Clatsop's three-miles of ocean frontage. They were armed and manned during WW II as part of the area's coastal defenses.

This monument on DeLaura Road commemorated the shelling of Fort Stevens, by the Japanese submarine I-25 on the night of June 21/22, 1942.

used as a training facility for infantry units. Fortification along the ocean front were armed and manned as part of the area's coastal defense system. After the war the camp was returned to the Oregon National Guard and in 1959 its named was changed to Camp Rilea.

On the north edge of the camp, on DeLaura Road is a stone monument which tells the story of the shelling of Fort Stevens by a Japanese submarine on June 21, 1942.

COLUMBIA RIVER MARITIME MUSEUM is located on the south bank of the Columbia River just east of downtown Astoria. It houses the finest and most extensive maritime collection in the Northwest and preserves 200 years of river history. Exhibits related to WW II include the actual bridge of the destroyer "Knapp" which was launched in 1943 and served in both WW II and the Korean War. The bridge was donated to the museum when the "Knapp" was scrapped in 1973. Other WW II displays include the periscopes and part of the conning tower of the submarine "Rasher", a WW II torpedo, a large bronze propeller from a Landing Ship Tank

(LST), twin 20 mm anti-aircraft guns, and other artifacts. Address: 1792 Marine Dr. (US 30), Astoria, OR 97103. Phone: 503/325-2323. Hours: daily 9:30-5, closed Thanksgiving and Dec. 25. Admission charged.

FORT STEVENS was located on a peninsula jutting out into the mouth of the Columbia River NW of Warrenton. The fort began in 1865 when earthworks and muzzle-loading cannons were installed to protect the entrance to the Columbia River. These were replaced in the following years with permanent concrete emplacements and 10" and 12" rifles. These later emplacements, some with newer guns, were used throughout WW II by the fort's 2500-man garrison. The fort was responsible for protecting the mines field laid in the mouth of the river and guarding against submarine activities and any enemy threats to land areas. The most outstanding event that happened at the fort during the war was the shelling of the fort by a Japanese submarine on the night of

June 21, 1942 (see below).

In 1947 the Army abandoned the fort and it became a state park known as Fort Stevens Historic Area & Military Museum. Many of the old gun emplacements and buildings remain. World War II-related structures on the fort include Battery Pratt which was modernized just before WW II and Battery Mishler which was covered over at the beginning of the war. Battery Mishler is the only battery of its kind in the US. Other WW II structures include Battery 245 (which was built during the war and armed with two 6" rifles), the WW II rifle range, WW II barracks area (were only foundations remain) and the mine loading building built in 1941.

Fort Stevens Museum is located in the old War Games Building which was used for that purpose during WW II. The building was built in 1911. On display are many artifacts relating to the fort's long history. There are a generous number of WW II displays in the museum including fragments of the shells fire at the fort by the Japanese submarine in June 1942. The Museum offers tours to the underground portions of Battery Mishler and a general tour of the park in an army truck. Address: Fort Stevens State Park, Attn: Historic Area, Hammond, OR 97121. Phone: 503/861-2000. Hours: Memorial Day thru Labor Day weekend, daily 10-6, rest of year W-Sun. 10-4. Free.

The Shelling of Fort Stevens: About midnight June 21/22, 1942 the Japanese submarine I-25, operating on the surface of the water, crept silently toward the Oregon shore with Fort Stevens beyond. The seas were calm, the weather clear and 72 degrees F. I-25's captain, Meiji Tagami, knew the area well. He and his

Battery 245 at Fort Stevens. This was the only new battery built at the fort during WW II.

sub had been here during Dec. 1941 and patrolled the area for several days. He also knew exactly where he was as he approached Fort Stevens because he could navigate by the Cape Disappointment Lighthouse which was shining brightly, the light of the Coast Guard lightship "Relief" anchored at the mouth of the river and he could see the lights from the town of Gearhart to the south. I-25 approached the shore through a small fleet of fishing vessels much to the surprise of the fishermen. The Japanese captain reasoned that where there were fishing boats there would be no US anti-submarine mines. Unknowingly, however, I-25 approached Fort Stevens directly in front of, and within range of, the fort's biggest guns. Tagami's mission was to fire his deck gun on Fort Stevens. A similar attack had been planned when he was here in Dec. 1941 but was called off at the last moment. Tagami positioned I-25 and at the right moment ordered his gun crew to commence firing. The crew began firing shells in rapid order in the general direction of the fort. They had no specific target in view. The first shots alerted everyone on duty at the fort and many civilians nearby. The flashes from I-25's gun could be seen clearly on shore. Unfortunately Fort Stevens' defenses were not fully manned because it was a weekend and the fort was in the midst of a chicken pox epidemic. Those on duty, however, quickly deduced that their attacker was a submarine and sounded the alarm. The fort's base line stations quickly plotted the location of the sub and the AAF radar station at North Head also got a reading on the sub. But the American guns remained silent. Not even the search lights went on. Somehow incoming data to the fort's command post erroneously indicated that the sub was 500 to 1000 yards beyond the range of the fort's guns. The fort's commander therefore ordered that the guns not to fired nor the search lights turned on for fear that they would be seen by the attacker and immediately become targets.

After firing 17 shots I-25 quickly departed on the surface passing again through the fleet of fishing boats and the awe-struck fishermen. I-25's shells did very little damage. They destroyed a baseball diamond backstop and a tree. The worst damage came 16 months later when a nearby rural area had a sudden power failure. It was discovered then that a fragment from one of I-25's shells had torn the insulation from an overhead power line and the metal wire had been eaten through by corrosion.

The attack made national headlines, stimulated a whole host of rumors locally and brought sight-seers and souvenir hunters from miles around. Over the next few weeks several hundred pounds of "genuine Jap shell fragments" were found and sold at healthy prices.

I-25 sailed northward and patrolled the waters off Canada and Alaska before returning to Japan on July 10.

U.S. NAVAL AIR STATION, ASTORIA: This facility consisted of three separate entities: NAS, Tongue Point, a seaplane base; NAS Airport, Astoria, Clatsop County Airport and Moon Island Airport at Hoquiam, WA.

In 1939 Congress approved funds to build a naval air station at Tongue point, a penin-

One of the original three seaplane hangars at Tongue Point. This one is used by the Job Corps as a recreation hall and for classes. Note the seaplane ramp in the foreground.

sula jutting into the Columbia River, but there were many delays. Meanwhile, the Navy, in need of air facilities in the Astoria area, began to use the civilian facilities at Moon Island Airport near Hoquiam, WA. In 1942 the Navy also contracted with Clatsop County Airport in Warrenton to use that facility and build enough new hangars and other buildings in order to put two squadrons of land based aircraft on coastal patrol duty. The Navy called this facility U.S. Naval Air Station Airport, Astoria. Army aircraft also used the airport from time-to-time and the airport remained open for civilian use. In 1943 the mission of NAS Airport, Astoria was expanded somewhat to include a school offering flight training to carrier air support units.

In the spring of 1943 construction got under way at Tongue Point on the naval air station. Some PBY Catalinas soon arrived and began carrying out coastal patrols. By May 1943, as barracks and messing facilities neared completion, the mission of NAS, Tongue Point was temporarily side-tracked and the newly completed facilities used to assist the Kaiser Co. in a critical shipbuilding program which included the construction of 50 carrier escorts and 61 troop transports. As a result, NAS, Tongue Point's facilities were used to house and feed teams of workers flown in to work on the Kaiser program. In the meantime construction on the remaining NAS facilities were temporarily suspended. The station's PBYs also gave their first priority to the needs of the shipbuilding program and served as transport planes. This arrangement lasted until July 1944.

Meanwhile, in May 1944, the three Navy facilities in the area; NAS, Tongue Point (partially completed); NAS Airport, Astoria and Moon Island Airport were organized into one entity and named U.S. Naval Air Station, Astoria. NAS Airport, Astoria then became U.S. Naval Auxiliary Air Station, Astoria and the naval facilities at Moon Island Airport became U.S. Naval Auxiliary Air Station, Moon Island.

In June 1944 the Navy decided to discontinue the use of PBYs at NAS, Astoria in favor of newer PBM Mariners. In support of this

program a maintenance training school for PBM mechanics was established at Tongue Point. In April 1945 anti-submarine patrols were discontinued and NAS, Astoria began to be scaled down. In 1946 the station was placed in caretaker status and the facilities at the two airports were returned to civilian owners.

In the postwar years the Tongue Point facilities were used by the Coast Guard and another part of the complex became a Job Corps Center. The Coast Guard also used some of the facilities at Clatsop County Airport.

BEND is 85 miles east of Eugene. Bend's old airport, SE of town, had a flying school that was contracted by the Army Air Corps in 1940 to give primary flight training to Air Corps cadets.

CAMP ABBOT was on the site of the present-day community of Sunriver, OR 15 miles south of Bend on U.S. 97. During the 1930s a CCC camp existed near the site. The area has heavy snowfalls and frigid temperatures during the winter months and was chosen by the Army in 1942 as a site for a winter warfare Engineer Replacement Training Center. Camp Abbot was then built during 1942-43 with the capacity to house and train up to 10,000 troops at a time. The first troops arrived in Mar. 1943. The units underwent a 17 week training course here in which they learned to work and live in cold mountainous conditions. During the 14 month life of the camp some 90,000 troops passed through.

In June 1944 the camp was abandoned and in the years that followed most of the building were moved, or razed or left to deteriorate. The only WW II building to survive was the officers' club. In the 1960s the planned community of Sunriver was developed on the old camp site and the officers club building was restored and converted into a community centerpiece called the Great Hall. It is open to Sunriver residents and visitors alike. Camp Abbot's sewer sedimentation tanks are in use again by the community and several WW II building foundations can be seen in the area as well as the abutments of a bridge built by the Engineers called Besson Bridge.

The five children and Elsie Mitchell (wedding photo) killed on Gearhart Mountain by the Japanese bombing balloon.

BLY is a small lumbering community in the mountains 40 miles NE of Klamath Falls. It was near here that the Japanese achieved their greatest success from their bombing balloons campaign. One of their balloons killed a woman and five children. These were the only deaths recorded during the war due to the bombing balloons and the only deaths in the contiguous 48 states during the war due to enemy action.

JAPANESE BOMBING BALLOON DEATHS ON GEARHART MOUNTAIN: By May 1945 the Japanese had ended their balloon bombing campaign against North America considering it a failure. But, many downed balloons were scattered throughout the western part of the country and had not yet been discovered by the Americans.

On Saturday, May 5, 1945, the Reverend Archie Mitchell and his pregnant wife, Elsie, took their church's sunday school class on a fishing trip into the forests on the slopes of Gearhart Mountain. The class consisted of five children. They travelled by car down a Forest Service road to reach a good fishing stream known to Rev. Mitchell. Mitchell stopped the car near a path that lead to the stream and let his wife and the children out. Mrs. Mitchell and the children proceeded to walk down the path while Mitchell backed the car down the road several yards and parked it in a clearing. Nearby was a three-man Forest Service work crew working on a road grader that had become stuck. As Mitchell was walking up the road towards the path he heard his wife call to him to come see what they had found. Seconds later there was a loud explosion followed almost immediately by a smaller explosion.

Mitchell and the three workmen ran to the site to find Mrs. Mitchell badly injured, her clothes on fire and four of the five children dead from the mysterious explosions. In the ground in the midst of the dead and injured was a smoking crater 12" deep by 15" wide x 36" long. Also laying about were strange-looking pieces of metal, fabrics and cords. Mitchell beat out the flames of his wife's clothing with his hands but within minutes she was dead. The fifth child also soon died. Mitchell and the workmen, of course, went for help immediately and in the coming days the Army, Navy, FBI and County Sheriff investigated the incident and concluded that the devices that had exploded were the main 15 Kg high explosive anti-personnel bomb and one of the incendiary bombs of a downed Japanese bombing balloon. The consensus of opinion was that Mrs. Mitchell and the children were gathered around the devices when someone pulled or otherwise disturbed the bombs and they went off.

Federal authorities tried to keep the incident a secret, but word of the deaths spread quickly throughout southern Oregon and was picked up by several newspapers. The Federal authorities, then did a complete about face and decided to divulge to the American public the whole truth about the Japanese bombing balloons, which heretofore had been successfully kept secret. The official opinion now was that the public should know so that no more incidents such as this would happen. The Federal Government then began a program warning people that downed Japanese bombing balloons existed in large numbers throughout the western part of the U.S. and if found should not be touched and the authorities notified at once. The program succeeded because balloons

continued to be found and there were no more reports of injuries or deaths.

In June 1946 a second bombing balloon was found on Gearhart Mountain, but no one was injured.

In 1949 the Federal Government paid compensation to the families of those killed on Gearhart Mountain. The Reverend Mitchell was awarded $5000 and the family of each child $3000.

By then, however, the Reverend Mitchell was in Viet Nam. In 1947 he had volunteered to do missionary work there. Mitchell was subsequently caught up in that war and disappeared. No further word was heard of him for several years. In 1973 when all military and civilian prisoners were released by the Viet Cong there was still no word of Rev. Mitchell.

In 1950 the Weyerhaeuser Corp. erected a monument on the Gearhart Mountain site and established a small park. The site is accessible today by car, but not during the winter months. Visitors should inquire locally for directions and road conditions.

For years after the incident the citizens of Bly and the surrounding area harbored ill feeling against all Japanese.

BOARDMAN (See Pendleton/Hermiston/Boardman area)

BROOKINGS/GOLD BEACH/PORT ORFORD AREA: These are three coastal towns on the southern coast of Oregon. Before the war much of the lumber produced in this area was sold to the Japanese. Therefore, Japanese seamen and businessmen knew the area quite well.

Port Orford has one of the best natural harbors on the Oregon coast and Japanese vessels often put in there to pick up lumber. During September 1942 Port Orford's harbor had another Japanese visitor but he didn't come to pick up lumber. During this time a sequence of events happened along this coast that were unique in the history of WW II in North America.

Aug. 1942: In August the Japanese leaders planned to send a task force of aircraft-carrying submarines to the US and Canadian west coast as they had done in December 1941 to raid Allied shipping and bomb U.S. land targets in retaliation for the Doolittle raid on Japan several months earlier. However, the Americans invaded Guadalcanal that month in the South Pacific and the Japanese were forced to commit most of their submarines to that theater. They decided, though, to send at least one sub to the west coast of North America and they picked I-25 for the job. I-25's captain and crew knew the area because they had patrolled Oregon waters in Dec. 1941 and again in June 1942 when they shelled Fort Stevens (see above). Therefore, on August 15 I-25, with her "Glen" seaplane aboard, left Yokusuka Naval Base in Japan for her third patrol to North America. I-25's crew had had plenty of experience sending their plane over enemy territory. Since the start of the war I-25's plane had successfully overflown Sidney and Milbourne, Australia; Hobart, Tasmania; Auckland and Wellington, New Zealand and Suva, Fiji Islands.

I-25's new mission was to cross the Pacific to the Canadian coast, turn south raiding Canadian and US shipping as she went, and then, when off the coast of Oregon, send her plane over the Oregon forests to drop incendiary bombs in hopes of starting forest fires.

Before dawn Sept. 9, 1942: By this time I-25 had completed her patrol of Canadian and U.S. waters and stood off Brookings, OR ready to bomb the Oregon forests. She surfaced off Brookings using the Brooking lighthouse as a reference point and launched her "Glen" seaplane. The "Glen" flew inland about 50 miles and dropped two 170 lb incendiary bombs in a densely forested area known as Wheeler Ridge. The bombs exploded and caused a column of smoke but failed to start the forest on fire. What the Japanese had not counted on was that during this time of year the forest floor was very wet due to seasonal rain and snowfall. The column of smoke was seen by alert forest rangers in a watch tower and subsequently investigated. They had also spotted the small plane circling the area as though the pilot was looking for something, but at first didn't put the two events together. Meanwhile the "Glen" returned to the coast, and using the Brookings Lighthouse as a reference point, rendezvoused safely with I-25. On the return trip the "Glen" pilot had spotted two merchant ships off the Oregon coast and, of course, reported them to the sub's captain who had every intention of going after them once the seaplane was safely aboard. However, minutes after the seaplane was tucked away in its deck hangar a US patrol plane approached, spotted I-25 and moved in for an attack dropping two depth charges. I-25 dived

Forester Fred Flynn holds one of the un-ignited incendiary pellets from the Japanese bombs.

and got away, but her captain suspected that an intensive search would now be launched by the Americans, especially now that (he believed) their forests were burning, so he gave up the idea of attacking the two merchant ships and took I-25 close into shore looking for a place to hide. He soon found a good one . . Port Orford's deep and spacious harbor. I-25 entered the harbor unnoticed, sank to the bottom and stayed there for more than a day while the crew rested and the American searched in vain for her off shore. I-25 had four more incendiary bombs on board and her captain contemplated bombing the U.S. mainland one more, or perhaps two more times.

Meanwhile back on Wheeler Ridge, the source of the smoke column had been discovered and bomb fragments recovered. In time, the Americans put the events together and realized what had happened.

U.S. radio reports of the unsuccessful bombing of the Oregon forest were picked up in Japan and relayed back to I-25 so that her captain and crew knew that the mission had failed. Upon hearing this the crewmen of I-25 vowed to try again.

Sept. 29, 1942: After leaving Port Orford Harbor I-25 patrolled northward along the coast looking for ships but found none. All the while her captain was waiting for good weather conditions to launch his second attack on the Oregon forests. On Sept. 29, the weather turned favorable and I-25 was again off the coast of southern Oregon near Cape Blanco. I-25 then launched their plane again using the Cape Blanco Lighthouse as their point of reference for launching and retrieving the plane. Just as before, the "Glen" was launched before sun rise and flew inland dropping two bombs in a area known as Grassy Knobs east of Port Orford. Both bombs exploded and the plane returned safely to the sub. Upon approaching the sub the pilot noticed that the sub was leaking oil, a condition that was not known aboard. The captain suspected that the damage occurred that morning during the launching of the plane, which was more difficult than usual. The oil leak was bad news because now the sub was leaving a visible trail in the water. Nevertheless, I-25 continued on its patrol moving southward into California waters where she sank two American tankers before departing for home. A combination of the sub's oil leak and bad weather prevented I-25 from attempting a third bombing.

Meanwhile, back at Grassy Knobs, history continued to repeat itself. The two bombs dropped here also failed to start fires because of the wet conditions of the forest. By coincidence a large crew of workmen were assembled at the Grassy Knobs lookout tower remodeling it for winter when the Japanese plane flew over. Some of the men stopped to watch the plane and saw two "flashes falling from the plane" and heard the explosions. Nearby ranchers also saw the plane and heard the explosions. This time the Americans reacted faster in determining what had happened although they were still too slow to pose a threat to the plane or to I-25.

Twenty years later, in May 1962 the pilot of the "Glen" seaplane, Noburo Fujita, was in-

vited to Brookings annual Azalea Festival and welcomed as an international celebrity. His visit to the community he had bombed during the war made national news and President John F. Kennedy sent a message of welcome to Fujita. While at Brookings Fujita was taken in a small plane over the areas that he had bombed in 1942. In response, Fujita gave the mayor of Brookings the Samurai sword he carried with him on the bombing raids. That sword is on display at Brookings City Hall.

CLATSKANIE is in the NW corner of the state 40 miles NW of Portland. As late as 1968 fishermen found the remnants of a Japanese bombing balloon at the edge of the Columbia River near Clatskanie.

BEAVER ARMY TERMINAL was on the Columbia River about 6 miles NE of Clatskanie. It was built in 1942 and used as a shipping terminal for Army ammunition. As was typical for such terminals, it was in a relatively remote area away from a big city. Beaver had 500,000 square feet of storage space plus 20 ammunition igloos. The terminal was put into caretaker status in 1947, but was reactivated in 1952 for the Korean War. It was also used to store and maintain Army boats and vessels. The terminal continued in operation with the same mission after that war and in 1962 was renamed Sharpe Army Depot. The depot was eventually closed and in later years was used as a power generating plant know as the Beaver Generating Co., a subsidiary of Portland General Electric Co.

CORVALLIS is 28 miles SSW of Salem.

CAMP ADAIR was located 8 miles north of Corvallis on SR 99W. Today it is the site of Adair Village. The camp was built in 1942-43 and used as a training camp for division-size infantry units. During the war the 91st, 95th, 70th and 104th Infantry Divisions trained here. Several full-scale European-style villages were built at the camp and used in the training of the infantrymen. The camp had a 2000-bed hospital and a main prisoner of war camp holding several hundred Italian and German POWs who worked primarily for the military. In June 1945 the camp became one of several Army Replacement Depots which received returning units from overseas, mainly for Europe, and retrained and re-equipped them for further duties, primarily in the Pacific. The sudden end to the war brought and end to the replacement depots and Camp Adair was closed in the spring of 1946. The hospital, however, was turned over to the Navy who used it for a short time to treat wounded Navy personnel returning from the Pacific. The Navy then turned the hospital over to Oregon State College which used it for student housing to accommodate the surge of ex-GIs going back to college. After that the hospital was taken over by the Veterans Administration who used it well into the 1950s. Much of Camp Adair's land was re-purchased by the original owners while land west of the highway was converted into a wildlife area. Between 1957 and 1968 the US Air Force utilized the southern portion of the camp and built a missile tracking station and command center. After the Air Force departed, the old base was subdivided and it parts used for several community, religious and

Camp Adair is typical of many old Army camps around the country. There is a scattering of original and postwar buildings and lone-standing chimneys from buildings long gone.

educational purposes. About 150 of the postwar buildings were rehabilitated and made into private homes. This cluster of private dwelling became the incorporated community of Adair Village.

CORVALLIS ARMY AIR BASE was south of town on SR 99W. Construction of the air field for commercial purposes was begun by the city in 1941, but was taken over by the AAF in 1942. The AAF completed construction and renamed the field Lyndon Field Army Air Base. It was used as an operational air support base. In Dec. 1942 it became a satellite field to Gray Field, WA and in Mar. 1943 it became a sub-base to Portland Army Air Base. At this time it was given its wartime name. Observation and weather squadrons operated from the field as part of the west coast air defense system. Due to its proximity to the coast the field was protected with anti-aircraft guns and was heavily camouflaged.

In May 1944 the field was turned over to the Navy and Marines, renamed US Marine Corps Facility, Corvallis and used as a transition training field for Marine air crews from R4D transports to R5C transports. In June 1945 the mission of the field changed again and it became US Naval Auxiliary Air Station, Corvallis and was utilized as a maintenance, servicing and staging field for combat-ready Fleet air units awaiting assignments to aircraft carriers. At the end of the war the Fleet units departed and in Feb. 1946 the Navy returned the field to the Army. A month later the Army returned it to the city of Corvallis and it became Corvallis Municipal Airport. There is a plaque at the airport entrance telling much of the airport's history.

ESTACADA is a small community 15 miles SE of Portland. On Dec. 31, 1944 a local resident discovered a large deflated balloon hanging in a fir tree near a road 7 miles SE of Estacada. He alerted the state police who had the tree cut down and the balloon retrieved. It was taken to the local high school and spread out on the tennis court. The Army was called and in quickly concluded that it was a Japanese bombing balloon. This was the 8th balloon discovered so far and was virtually intact. The construction of the balloon was

carefully analyzed and compared with the balloon found Dec. 11, 1944 near Kalispell, MT, which, like the Estacada balloon, was very much intact. The Estacada balloon was almost identical to the Kalispell balloon which indicated to the Americans that the balloons were being mass produced and that a bombing campaign was underway.

HERMISTON
(See Pendleton/
Hermiston/Boardman area)

KLAMATH FALLS is in SW Oregon 15 miles north of the state line.

U.S. MARINE RECUPERATION BARRACKS, KLAMATH FALLS was located north of town on Campus Dr. The Barracks was built by the Navy in 1943 as a hospital specializing the treatment of Marines who had contracted tropical diseases, mainly malaria and filariasis. Patients suffering from these diseases are usually ambulatory and require treatment for from three to six months. The hospital had some 80 buildings and could house up to 3000 patients. Since physical exercise was part of the treatment the hospital had both an indoor and outdoor pool, numerous athletic activities, horseback riding, volunteer fire fighting, fire spotting patrols and vocational training. Patients who were able, were encouraged to help with the annual potato harvest. After the war the patient load declined and in March 1946 the facility was closed. It was eventually turned over to the state to become a college known as the Oregon Institute of Technology.

U.S. NAVAL AIR STATION, KLAMATH FALLS, four miles SE of town on SR 140, was the town's local airport before the war. In the early part of the war the Navy used the field as a refueling stop for planes travelling between Seattle and various bases in California. The Army also used the field in its ferrying system. In 1943 when the Navy was looking for additional training fields on the west coast they contracted to take over the airport and use it as a training

facility for fighter pilots. At that time it was given its wartime name. NAS, Klamath Falls, which had the best flying weather in Oregon, continued to be a stop-over field for both the Navy and Army. In early 1945 aircraft from NAS, Klamath Falls shot down Japanese bombing balloons on two separate occasions. In Jan. 1946 the station was disestablished and the air field returned to its pre-war owners and became Klamath Falls Municipal Airport.

MADRAS is 40 miles north of Bend in the Cascade Range.

MADRAS ARMY AIR FIELD was two miles NW of town west of U.S. 26 at Cherry Lane. It was built for the 2nd AF in 1942 and used as a training field for bomber crews. After the war the field was turned over to the local community to become its main airport known as Madras Field.

MEDFORD is in the SW corner of the state 25 miles from the California state line. On Jan. 2, 1945 Medford became one of the few towns in North America that was actually bombed by a Japanese bombing balloon. Most of the balloon bombs fell harmlessly and unnoticed in rural areas. On this day, though, about 6:00 pm, resident of South Peach Street heard a strange whistling sound followed by an explosion and some went to investigate. They found a shallow crated about four feet in diameter near a barn and it was generally agreed that it had been caused by a bomb. It was also agreed that no airplane had been heard. Army authorities from Camp White investigated the situation, retrieved bomb fragments and concluded that the crater was caused by a 5 Kg. Type B incendiary bomb known to be carried by the Japanese bombing balloons.

MEDFORD MUNICIPAL AIRPORT, three miles north of town on SR 22, was Medford's local airport before the war. During the war it was used by both the AAF and the Navy while continuing to serve the local civilian aviation needs. The AAF used the airport and their facilities at the airport as an operational base in the defense of the west coast. They named their facilities Medford Army Air Field. The Navy used the field in its air transport system. The field had a branch prisoner of war camp with most of the POWs working on the air field and in agriculture. After the war the military services departed and the air field became Medford-Jackson County Airport.

CAMP WHITE, 8 miles north of Medford on SR

Two of the original WW II hangars remained in use at the former Madras Army Air field.

62, is the site of present-day White City. The camp was built in 1942 and was divided into two sections, one for training division-size units and the other for training special service forces. The camp could accommodate some 38,000 troops. It had many buildings and a large hospital. In Aug. 1942 the 91st Infantry Division was activated and trained here and the 96th Infantry Division trained here later. The camp had a main prisoner of war camp holding about 1200 POWs who worked for the military. In April 1946 the Army vacated the camp and turned the hospital over to the Veterans Administration. Much of the land and most of the buildings went to the county. In the postwar years many of the camp's buildings were converted into civilian residences and the resulting community was named White City.

NORTH BEND is on the south-central coast of Oregon at Coos Bay. On Feb. 22, 1945 a Japanese bombing balloon was shot down over the city by a US fighter plane at 12,000'. Parts of the balloon were later recovered.

U.S. NAVAL AUXILIARY AIR STATION, NORTH BEND was the community's pre-war airport. It was taken over by the Navy an used as an auxiliary field for NAS, Astoria.

NYASA (See Ontario/Vale/Nyasa)

ONTARIO/VALE/NYASA AREA: These three communities are in east-central Oregon in the Snake River Valley. All three were agricultural towns. This area was one of the few in the nation that accepted ethnic Japanese who were forced to relocate from the coastal defense zone. This part of the state was outside the evacuation zone[2] and already had a sizeable ethnic Japanese population. Here they, and the newcomers, lived and worked in relative harmony with their non-Japanese neighbors throughout the war. Before the relocation camp at Tule Lake, CA became a camp for troublemakers and renunciants, ethnic Japanese were trucked to this area from that camp to work in agriculture. Some of the ethnic Japanese who relocated here during the war stayed on after the war.

This area also had two branch prisoner of war camps, one near Nyasa holding about 500 POWs and the other near Vale with about 250

[2]Highway U.S. 97 was the eastern boundary of the zone.

POWs. The POWs from both camps worked in agriculture.

In early 1945 several Japanese bombing balloons came down in the area. Balloons remnants were found near Ontario on Jan. 2, near Vale on Mar. 10, near Ontario again on Mar. 13, near Nyasa on Mar. 29, near Adrian on Mar. 29, near Harper on Apr. 3, near Huntington May 2 and near Harper again on May 25.

PENDLETON/HERMISTON/BOARDMAN AREA: This cluster of towns is in NE Oregon on, or near, the Columbia River and the intersection of I-84 and I-82. This is one of Oregon's farming and ranching areas.

On March 13, 1945 one of the most intact Japanese bombing balloons ever found was discovered near Echo, OR, which is 7 miles SE of Hermiston. This balloon was thoroughly examined at the time by US military authorities at Moffet Field, CA and is now on display in the National Air and Space Museum in Washington, DC.

BOARDMAN BOMBING RANGE, just south of the town of Boardman, was one of three large general purpose bombing and gunnery ranges established in the west by the Federal Government[3]. It was activated in 1940 primarily for the Army Air Corps and encompassed over one million acres. The thinking was that one large bombing range could serve several operational and training facilities in a general area. Boardman and the others did just that during the war, but most training fields acquired their own ranges.

[3]The others were Tonopah, NV and Wendover, UT.

The sign at the entrance to the former Boardman Bombing Range.

Most of the land selected for Boardman was in the public domain, but sizeable portions were owned by ranchers. The ranchers bitterly complained about the Government taking their land and putting them out of business. Eventually a compromise was reached whereby the land was used alternately for grazing and for bombing.

The Boardman Bombing Range was retained by the Government after the war and was utilized throughout the Cold War. It had several names, and in later years became a naval facility known as U.S. Naval Weapons Systems Training Facility, Boardman, Oregon.

PENDLETON FIELD, three miles NW of town, was the area's pre-war airport built in 1934. Soon after the attack on Pearl Harbor one of the AAF's best trained and most experienced bomber units, the 17th Medium Bomb Group, was rushed to Pendleton Field from March Field, CA per a pre-arranged plan for the defense of the west coast. Some of the unit then moved on to McChord Field, WA and flew anti-submarine missions along the coast. Another AAF unit rushed to the field was the 89th Reconnaissance Squadron.

In Jan. 1942 Gen. Jimmy Doolittle arrived at the field seeking volunteers for a very special top-secret mission . . the bombing of Japan. Doolittle specifically chose the 17th Medium Bomb Group as the source for his volunteers because of their training, experience and the fact that the group had B-25s, the only bomber in the American arsenal at the time that could take off from an aircraft carrier. Enough men volunteered from the 17th to fill Doolittle's needs. In early Feb. they and their planes flew off to Eglin Field, FL for the first phase of their training. One of those who volunteered at Pendleton Field was Lt. Ted Lawson who later wrote the best-seller book "Thirty Seconds Over Tokyo".

The 17th Medium Bomb Group eventually left Pendleton and the field was used from then on by the AAF for the training of various bomber and fighter plane unit. Negro paratroopers also trained here and served as reserve fire fighters for forest fires. After the war the field reverted to its civilian use and became Pendleton Municipal Airport.

The present-day Buddhist Temple in Ontario.

The original wartime gate houses stand at the entrance to Pendleton Field. See page 207.

UMATILLA ORDNANCE DEPOT was built 6 miles west of Hermiston in 1942 on 24 square miles of sheep range and sagebrush. Its mission was to receive, store and ship Army ammunition of all types. Umatilla was one of the few ordnance facilities in the US where the Federal Government built a hospital to care for the workers. Throughout the war the depot served Army units throughout the Pacific and western North America. On Mar. 21, 1944 a tragic explosion occurred in one of the igloos taking the lives of 6 people. At the end of the war

President Roosevelt (left) and Henry Kaiser (right) witness the launching of the "Liberty" ship "Joseph N. Teal" which was built in a record 10 days. The ship was christened by the President's daughter Anna Roosevelt Boettinger.

activity at the depot diminished, but the depot was retained by the Government and used throughout the Cold War.

During WW II the Federal Government built a small community called Ordnance, OR SW of the depot to house workers. Ordnance survived the war and is on I-84 eight miles west of the junction of I-84 and I-82.

PORTLAND was, as it is now, Oregon's largest city. Its wartime population was greatly swollen by the rapid influx of war workers who came to take jobs in the area's ship yards and defense plants. Like most wartime boom towns Portland suffered shortages of such things as housing, transportation, food and city services. To meet the housing needs, the National Housing Authority, a Federal agency, built hundreds of barracks, dormitories and houses for the workers.

By far, the greatest wartime manufacturing in Portland was in ships and the Kaiser Shipbuilding Corp. dominated in this endeavor. Kaiser operated three ship yards; The Oregon Shipbuilding Co.; Kaiser Incorporated, Swan Island and Kaiser Incorporated, Vancouver, WA. The complex was run by Henry Kaiser's son Edgar. The Kaisers gained a well-deserved national reputation for the ability of their companies to build "Liberty" ships in record time. And, many of those ships were built here in the Portland area. Kaiser's innovative measures reduced the time it took to build a cargo ship some

approximately two months to a matter of days.

Other ships made by the Kaiser's yards including escort carriers, troop transports, Landing Ship Tanks (LST) and "Victory"[4] ships. Kaiser's Oregon Shipbuilding Co. made the first "Victory" ship in Jan. 1944.

Other shipbuilders in the area were Commercial Iron Works which built a variety of ships for the Navy, Gunderson Brothers Engineering Co. which built tank lighters and Albano-Engine & Machine Works which built patrol craft.

Defense plants in the area included the Pacific Car & Foundry Co. which built M4 Sherman tanks and a new aluminum processing plant built by the government-owned Defense Plant Corporation.

Portland was also a very busy seaport during the war and was the principal port through which Lend Lease materials were shipped to the Soviet Union. In Dec. 1945 Portland was one of the ports used to deport those ethnic Japanese who had renounced their U.S. citizenship during the war.

THE BOMBER COMPLEX: A Preserved B-17G bomber mounted on pylons serve as the main attraction for the business of a former B-17 pilot, Art Lacey, of Milwaukee, OR (a southern suburb of Portland). Lacey's establishment, known as "The Bomber Complex", 13515 SE McLouglin Blvd., consists of a service station, motel and a restaurant called The Bomber Inn.

The B-17G is mounted over the pumps of the service station and one drives under the bomber to fill 'er up.

On the walls of the Bomber Inn are World War II memorabilia and photographs explaining how the B-17G was brought to this location. The Inn's menu is rather unique in that it offers for "Take Off" (breakfast) such selections as "The Bellygunner" and "The Crew Chief". For "Final Approach" (dinner), there's the "Admiral Nimitz" and "Fat Man & Little Boy". Those who are weight conscious can select an entre entitled "The Battle of the Bulge".

OREGON MARITIME CENTER AND MUSEUM in downtown Portland preserved the history of Portland's maritime heritage from the time of Lewis & Clark to the present. There are displays on the famous Kaiser ship yards of WW II and information on the ships they build. The old battleship Oregon is highlighted in the

[4]"Victory" ships were improved version of "Liberty" ships.

The hull of a WW II-era "Liberty" ships has been used in recent years on the Portland waterfront as a floating pier to receive ships bringing automobiles to the U.S. Note the automobile storage lot to he rear. Most of the cars come from Japan.

A B-17G mounted on pylons is the main attraction at the Bomber Complex in Milwaukee, OR.

One of the original WW II hangars remained in use at the former Redmond Army Air Field well into the postwar era.

museum which, during WW II, was obsolete and used as an ammunition barge. After the war it was sold to the Japanese for scrap. One display tells of the States Steam Ship Co. of Portland that used the swastika as its company symbol on its flag and stacks . . until 1940. Address: 113 SW Front Ave., Portland, OR 97204. Phone: 503/224-7724. Hours: Memorial Day thru Labor Day, W-Sun. 11-4, rest of year, F-Sun. 11-4. Admission charged.

OREGON MILITARY MUSEUM is located at Camp Whithycombe, the Oregon National Guard camp near Clackamas, OR, a SE suburb of Portland. The museum traces the military history of Oregon from 1843 to the present. There is a very generous presentation of WW II-era equipment and displays including a PT boat, an M-20 armored command car, an M-3A1 scout car, an M-1 57 mm anti-tank gun, an M-3 105 mm howitzer and several Japanese, German and Soviet pieces of equipment. Address: Camp Whithycombe, Clackamas, OR 97015. Phone: 503/657-6806 Hours: Fri. & Sat. 1-4. Other times by appointment: Free. Location: Exit I-205 at Exit 12A, Market Rd. (Hwys. 212 & 224), proceed east to Clackamas Rd. (102nd Ave.), turn north to Camp Whithycombe's main gate.

PORTLAND ASSEMBLY CENTER FOR ETHNIC JAPANESE: This was the Portland & Pacific International Exposition Center at the Portland Stock Yards in St. Johns. Here ethnic Japanese from Oregon and southern Washington were assembled in early 1942 and processed for their relocation to camps in the interior for the duration of the war. Temporary apartments were build inside the center to hold up to 3800 people at one time. Most of the evacuees went

The evacuees at the Portland Assembly Center were given jobs while they waited to be transferred to the relocation camps. Here young men paint an office desk.

to Minidoka Camp in Idaho with some going to Heart Mtn. WY and Tule Lake, CA. There were no relocation camps in Oregon and this was the state's only assembly center.

The center operated until Sept. 1942 at which time it was turned over to the Portland Port of Embarkation.

PORTLAND ARMY AIR BASE: This was the AAF's facilities at Portland Columbia Airport, Portland's new commercial airport north of downtown on the south shore of the Columbia River. The airport was not taken over by the AAF and continued to accommodate civilian air traffic throughout the war. The AAF used the airport as an operational base, a ferry base and as a part of their air transport service. Portland AAB had a large freight terminal and a debarkation hospital. The Navy also used the field in its air transport and ferry systems.

PORT ORFORD (See Brookings/Gold Beach/Port Orford area)

REDMOND is 15 mile north of Bend.

REDMOND ARMY AIR FIELD, SE of town, was the town's pre-war airport built in 1928. In 1940 it had a flying school that was contracted by the Army Air Corps to give primary flight training to Air Corps cadets. In 1942 the field was taken over by the 2nd AF and used as a training field for the crews of B-17 bombers. Later in the war P-38 fighter planes operated from the field and for a while it was a sub-base of Portland Army Air Base. After the war the AAF departed and the field was returned to the community and became Redmond Municipal Airport, Roberts Field.

TILLAMOOK is in the NW corner of the state near the coast and 60 miles west of Portland. The coastline in the Tillamook area is flat and sandy and was considered one of the more vulnerable beaches in the state for an enemy invasion. Therefore, it was heavily patrolled by the Coast Guard. Horses were the favorite mode of transportation for the Coastguardsmen and were used in relatively large numbers. When the beach patrols were phased out in late 1943 the Federal Government used the Tillamook Fairgrounds as an auction site for most of the surplus horses along the west coast. The horses brought an average of $117 each.

U.S. NAVAL AIR STATION (LTA), TILLAMOOK was three miles SE of town on the east side of U.S. 101. When, in early 1942, the Navy saw the need for a blimp station on the northwest coast of the US Tillamook had exactly what was needed. The site selected for the station was a small valley surrounded by low hills ranging from 700' to 2000'. This created a natural pocket of still air which was secure from the sometimes heavy winds that were common along the northwest coast. It was the only such natural pocket between the Strait of Juan de Fuca and the California border. Therefore, the Navy moved in and began construction of a blimp base which was commissioned in Dec. 1942. The station was equipped with 8 blimps, 7 mobile mooring masts and two large, all-wood, blimp hangars. From 1942 to early 1944 blimps from NAS(LTA), Tillamook patrolled the coastal waters of the northwest. In March 1944 airplanes arrived at the station and also took part in the patrols.

In May 1945 the station was designated to be an aircraft storage facility and slowly began to acquire aircraft. The first aircraft put into storage were 22 F-2 Wildcats. When the war ended more planes arrived for storage and the station put its own blimps into storage. As postwar uses were found for the planes and blimps the station's inventory diminished and by late 1947 the station was decommissioned. It was subsequently turned over to the county and in later years became a small commercial airport and an industrial park. The two blimp hangars are in use and can be easily seen form U.S. 101.

Blimp Hangar Museum: This museum is in Hangar B and tells the story of NAS (LTA), Tillamook for its inception to the present. On display are blimp engines, cabs and propellers as well as precision wind measuring instruments, models of the mooring masts, photographs, documents and other memorabilia. Visitors can go into Hangar B and experience its immense size. Address: 4000 Blimp Blvd., Tillamook, OR 97141. Phone: 503/842-2413. Hours: May 16 through Oct. 31 daily 10-6. Rest of year hours vary. Admission charged.

UMATILLA (See Pendleton/Hermiston/Boardman area)

VALE (See Ontario/Vale/Nyasa area)

WARRENTON (See Astoria/Warrenton area)

Interior of one of the huge blimp hangars at Tillamook during the war.

PENNSYLVANIA

Pennsylvania's contribution to the war effort was many-fold. The state was a great manufacturing state, a food producer, rich in minerals and was heavily populated. In the latter category an unusually large proportion of the state's population, 1/8 of the total, saw service in the armed forces. Of this number 80,000 became war casualties and 20,000 gave their lives. Pennsylvanians won 35 Congressional Medals of Honor which was more than any other state.

In the area of war production, Pennsylvania ranked 7th among all the states, fourth in shipbuilding, third in ordnance production and first in the number of expansion of existing industrial facilities. The state's greatest industrial contribution during the war was, by far, the production of steel. The great steel mills in the Pittsburgh area and elsewhere worked at capacity for most of the war producing steel for every facet of America's war needs. By the end of the war Pennsylvania steel firms alone had produced more steel than Germany and Japan combined. The state also produced 31% of the nation's coal and 30% of its coke. Pennsylvania's 15,000 manufacturing firms turned out ships, aircraft, military vehicles, munitions, machinery, glass, chemicals, petroleum products, textiles, paper and leather. Her oil production was also significant with 81,946 operating wells in the state. Other minerals produced in Pennsylvania included iron ore, natural gas, cement and stone. The state's farms produced grain, hay, tobacco, potatoes, fruit, meat products, dairy products, horses and mules. The state had many of her citizens in positions of responsibility during the war. The most prominent were:

• Francis Biddle, Attorney General
• Frank C. Walker, Postmaster General
• General of the Army George C. Marshall from Uniontown
• General Henry "Hap" Arnold from Gladwyne
• General Carl Spaatz from Boyertown
• General Alexander Patch from Lebanon
• General Joseph T. McNarney from Emporium
• General Jacob L. Devers from York
• Admiral Harold R. Stark from Wilkes-Barre
• Lt. General Lewis H. Brerton from Pittsburgh
• Major General James Gavin from Mount Carmel
• Major General Lyman L. Lemnitzer from Honesdale

When the U.S. went to war the state organized one of the largest civilian volunteer defense organizations in the nation, the Civilian Defense Corps. By the end of the war some 1.6 million people had been mobilized by the Corps.

Pennsylvania was to be one of the targets of the German saboteurs who were landed by submarine on the beaches of Long Island and Florida in June 1942. On their hit list were the Cryolite Metal Works in Philadelphia, the famous Horseshoe Curve of the Pennsylvania Railroad near Altoona and various locks and dams on the Ohio River. None of the attacks were carried out because the saboteurs were caught soon after their arrival. Other Germans and Axis warriors, however, came to Pennsylvania and resided in one or the other of the state's 19 prisoner of war camps.

After the war Pennsylvania's economy made a rather smooth transition to peacetime activities compared to other states. Demands remaining high for steel, manufactured goods and food, and Pennsylvania was able to keep pace with the new demands and prospered.

ALLENTOWN/BETHLEHEM: These two cities are in east-central Pennsylvania. Major industrial firms in the area were the Bethlehem Steel Co. which was headquartered in Bethlehem, PA, and a major producer of steel and armor plate; the Mack Truck Co. of Allentown which made military trucks and power trains for tanks; Consolidated-Vultee Corp. of Allentown which made components for B-24 bombers and other military aircraft; American Armament Corp. of Allentown which made various ordnance items including 1000 lb bombs and Lehigh Foundry, Inc. of Easton, PA which made mortar shells and 105 mm shot.

ALLIED AIR FORCE: This is an air museum at the Queen City Airport two miles south of downtown Allentown. This air field was the site of the Consolidated-Vultee aircraft plant during the war. The museum has a small collection of military and civilian aircraft and the collection is expanding. Address: 1730 Vultee St., Allentown, PA 18103. Phone: 610/791-5122. Hours: May 1 thru Oct. 31 Tues.-Sun. 10-4. Admission charged.

BEAVER FALLS AREA: Beaver Falls is 25 miles NW of Pittsburgh. Three miles to the SW, was a Curtiss-Wright plant making aircraft propellers for the military, and at Rochester, two miles to the SE, the Hydril Corp. made 8"

Gen. George C. Marshall of Uniontown, PA.

high explosive shells, 4.2" chemical warfare shells and 5" shell primers.

AIR HERITAGE MUSEUM AND AIRCRAFT RESTORATION FACILITY is located at Beaver Falls Airport, two miles north on SR 51. The museum displays memorabilia, uniforms, model airplanes, flight suits and other items for WW I and WW II. In an adjacent hangar visitors can watch aircraft undergoing restoration. Address: Beaver Falls Airport, Beaver Falls, PA 15010. Phone: 412/843-2820. Hours: daily noon-5. Donations accepted.

BEDFORD is located in SE Pennsylvania on I-70/76 about 28 miles NE of Cumberland, MD. Just south of town is a popular spa area called Bedford Springs with several fine resort-like hotels. In early 1941 the Navy leased the luxurious 400-room Bedford Springs Hotel as a temporary training facility for radio operators. By the time of the Japanese attack on Pearl Harbor in Dec. 1941 the hotel was vacant so the State Department leased it as one of four such hotels in the country1 to house Japanese diplomats and their families who were awaiting exchange for U.S. diplomats and their families in Japan. The presents of the Japanese at the hotel caused quite an uproar in and around Bedford because of the luxurious treatment the Japanese were receiving. Many local people refused to work at the hotel and other refused to provide services for the hotel because of this feeling. The State Department sent spokesmen into the community to explain that this was accepted treatment of diplomats during wartime according to the Geneva Convention and that American diplomats and their families were receiving similar treatment in Japan. This eased local feelings to some degree, but virtually everyone in Bedford was happy when the Japanese finally left.

BUTLER is 25 miles north of Pittsburgh. The American Bantam Co., a manufacture of small automobiles, played a part in the development of the famous Jeep, but did not manufacture any Jeeps. Rather, they made reconnaissance cars, trailers and aircraft components. The Pullman-Standard Car Mfg. Co. in butler made 155 mm shells in Butler.

DESHONE ARMY HOSPITAL came into being in Butler when the Army took over an unused state-owned tuberculosis

sanatorium in Dec 1942. Deshone was a 1774-bed facility that specialized in general and orthopedic surgery and care of the deaf. In Apr, 1946 the hospital was transferred to the Veterans Administration.

CARLISLE AREA: Carlisle is 18 miles west of Harrisburg.

CARLISLE BARRACKS was one mile north of town on US 11 and during WW II was a relatively small post. The first military post was established here by the British in 1757 and known as the Camp near Carlisle. From 1879 to 1918 the post was the site of the Carlisle Indian Industrial School. From 1920 until the end of WW II the post was the home of the Army's Medical Field Service School. It was at this school that civilian doctors were turned into Army doctors. Dentists, Veterinarians and Medical Corps administrators were also trained here. Carlisle Barracks had an Officers Candidate School during the war and developed field medical equipment, medical text books and medical training programs. In 1946 the Medical Field Service School was transferred to Texas and from 1946 to 1951 Carlisle Barracks housed several other Army schools. In 1951 the post became the home of the U.S. Army War College which remained here throughout the Cold War. In 1963 the post was listed on the registry of National Historic Landmarks.

In Upton Hall, which was built in 1941 and was the main academic building of the Army Medical Field Service School, there exists a magnificent 50' x 8' mural depicting the American soldier in combat during WW II. Both the European and Pacific theaters are depicted in the mural.

Upton Hall, built in 1941, was the main academic building of the Army Medical Field Service School throughout WW II.

General Omar Bradley Museum: This fine museum, dedicated to the memory of WW II General Omar Bradley, was established on the grounds of Carlisle Barracks in 1970. The museum traces the life and career of Bradley and has many photographs, artifacts and personal effects. In the postwar years Bradley rose to become General of the Army and Chairman of the Joint Chiefs of Staff from 1949 to 1953. Address: Carlisle Barracks, PA 17013. Phone: 717/245-3152. Hours: M-F 8-4, closed federal holidays. Free.

Patients at Deshone Army Hospital participating in a one-armed golf match.

Five Hundred pound bombs being stored outside at Letterkenny Ordnance Depot.

This was Dwight and Mamie Eisenhower's home from 1950 until their deaths. It was the only home they ever owned.

The Hessian Powder Magazine Museum: This is a second museum on the grounds of Carlisle Barracks and is housed in a powder magazine built by Hessian soldiers in 1777. There are several rooms in the museum each offering displays and information on the various periods of the post's history. The School Era (20th Century Room) has displays relative to the post's role in WW II. Hours: Late May thru early Sept. Sat.-Sun. 1-4.

CHAMBERSBURG is in the south-central part of Pennsylvania on I-81.

LETTERKENNY ORDNANCE DEPOT was built 6 miles NW of Chambersburg in 1942 to store Army ammunition and bombs prior to their being shipped overseas. Its main entrance was on SR 340. Letterkenny also stored and modernized various pieces of combat vehicles. In 1944 Italian Service Units were employed at the depot to help ease its on-going labor shortage. After the war the depot was made a permanent installation of the Army and continued to store munitions. In 1962 the facility was renamed Letterkenny Army Depot and began storing, repairing and issuing military communications and electronic equipment.

DANVILLE is 42 miles WSW of Wilkes-Barre

on the East Branch of the Susquehanna River. During the war Danville had a large munitions manufacturer, Kennedy Van Saun Mfg. & Engr. Corp. which made 81 mm shells, 60 mm trench mortars and 3" shot. **CHEROKEE ORDNANCE WORKS** was built near Danville early in the war to produce formaldehyde and hexamine. These were ingredients used in the manufacture of the super-explosive RDX.

GETTYSBURG is one of the most famous small towns in the country because of the monumental and decisive battle that took place here during the Civil War. The town also has some WW II history.

EISENHOWER NATIONAL HISTORIC SITE: This was the last home of President Dwight D. Eisenhower from 1950 until his death in 1969. The Eisenhowers purchased this 189-acre working farm in 1950 while Ike was serving as president of Columbia University. They began modifying the main house almost immediately with Mamie supervising the details. The work progressed off and on over five years and upon completion Ike christened the house "Mamie's House". The two farms on either side of the Eisenhower's farm were purchased by a friend, Alton Jones, to add to the Eisenhower's privacy. Ike and Jones went into business together raising purebred Angus cattle. After becoming President Ike visited the farm as much as he could and in 1955, while recuperating from his first heart attack, conducted the nation's business from here. Many famous visitors

came to the farm including Eisenhower's wartime compatriots Winston Churchill and Charles DeGaulle. Upon completing his second presidential term in Jan. 1961 Ike and Mamie retired to the farm permanently. In 1967 the Eisenhowers donated the farm to the U.S. Department of the Interior with the understanding that it would likely become a historic site after their deaths. Ike lived here until he died in 1969 and Mamie lived on in the house until her death in 1979. The farm and buildings are open to the public via shuttle busses from the National Park Visitor Center on SR 134. The house is furnished much as it was when the Eisenhowers lived here in the 1960s and the out-buildings are much the same as when Mrs. Eisenhower died. Address: Gettysburg, PA 17325. Phone: 717/334-1124. Hours: Hours and days of operation may vary, but shuttle busses usually leave at regular intervals from 9-4:15. Reservations are not accepted. Admission charged.

CAMP GEORGE A. SHARPE PRISONER OF WAR CAMP: This was a POW camp established on the Gettysburg battlefield. The camp held about 350 POWs who worked mostly in the surrounding forests. Camp Sharpe operated from Nov. 1943 until late 1945.

GREENVILLE is in NW Pennsylvania 22 miles NE of Youngstown, OH.

CAMP REYNOLDS was built in 1942-43 to be used as a personnel replacement depot. It was first known as Shenengo Personnel Replacement Depot but was later named Camp Reynolds. The camp served as a staging area for Army Service Forces awaiting assignments to Europe and the Caribbean. By the end of 1944 the camp was nearly vacant so it was used as a prisoner of war camp and a salvage center. The POW camp held about 775 prisoners who worked for the military and in the local area. After the war the camp was closed.

HARRISBURG is located in the south-central part of the state and is the state's capitol. The city had a number of war plants including the Harrisburg Steel Corp. which was one of the largest bomb manufacturer in the country. It made bombs up to 500 lbs.

HARRISBURG AIRPORT, four miles SSE of town, is adjacent to the New Cumberland Army Service Depot (below). The airport was used extensively by both the Army and Navy during the war. The Army used it in conjunction with the depot and the Navy had a Photo Reconnaissance Training Detachment at the airport to train pilots in mapping terrain with automatic cameras. The Naval Air Transport Service also used the field. After the war the air field was returned to civilian use and became Capitol City Airport.

FORT INDIANTOWN GAP, 15 miles NE of Harrisburg, was the pre-war home of the Pennsylvania National Guard. The post was slowly built up by the state between 1933 and 1940. The National Guard had no sooner moved in when the Federal Government, in 1941, leased the entire camp and converted it into a large staging camp for the New York Port of Embarkation. The Federal Government increased the number of buildings at the fort from 33 to over 1400. The fort was also a division-sized training camp where several

Soldiers at Camp Reynolds standing at attention.

Main entrance to Indiantown Gap Military Reservation during the war.

units completed their final training. These included the 3rd and 5th Armored Division, the 1st, 5th, 28th, 37th, 77th and 95th Infantry Divisions. The Army Transportation Corps also had a training center here for stevedores. During the war the fort had a main prisoner of war camp holding about 1300 POWs. The POWs worked for the military, in food processing plants and elsewhere. Near the end of the war the fort became a separation center for troops returning from Europe. After Sept. 1946 the fort was returned to the Pennsylvania National Guard, but in Feb. 1951, at the beginning of the Korean War, it was federalized again and served as the home of the Army's 5th Infantry Division until 1953. It was then returned again to the National Guard. Later it became known as Fort Indiantown Gap Military Reservation.

MIDDLETOWN AIR SERVICE COMMAND CONTROL DEPOT: This was an Army depot built in 1917 on the east bank of the Susquehanna River 10 miles south of Harrisburg and just west of Middletown. By 1939 it was one of three Army Air Corps air depots in the country. The depot had its own airfield, Olmstead Field, to the SW along the river. After the creation of the Army Air Forces in 1941 the depot was given its wartime name. As the AAF expanded, so did the Middletown depot acquiring a number of sub-depots and detached facilities. The main depot operated 24 hours a day during the war and inventories some 250,000 parts for military aircraft. The depot also had aircraft maintenance and overhaul facilities and specialized in C-54s, the AAF's largest transport plane. At its peak the depot had some 18,000 employees, nearly half of them women.

One of the more important detached facilities of the depot was the State School of Aeronautics which operated in the State Farm Show Building in Harrisburg. Here, in less than two years, over 12,000 persons were trained for jobs at the depot. When the school closed, the building was used as an engine overhaul facility.

At Olmstead field there was a main prisoner of war camp with some 300 POWs who worked at the depot. The depot remained active for more than a decade after the war but was eventually closed. Much of the land was given to Pennsylvania State University and Olmstead Field became Harrisburg International Airport.

NEW CUMBERLAND ARMY SERVICE FORCES DEPOT was located just east of New Cumberland, PA on the west bank of the Susquehanna River. The depot was built in 1918 and between the wars was used to store material for the Quartermaster Corps, Ordnance Corps, Signal Corps and Medical Corps. In 1940-41 additional barracks were built at the depot to become a reception center for Pennsylvania's draftees. This was a separate entity from the depot and was known as the New Cumberland Reception Center. It functioned from Feb. 1941 to July 1945. During that time about 90% of those drafted in Pennsylvania were processed through this center. The Center also had a special training unit that taught some 13,000 illiterate future GIs how to read and write. In Aug. 1945 the Center was converted to an Army branch disciplinary barracks which functioned until 1959.

The New Cumberland depot expanded during the war and became very active. It continues to stock a wide variety of items for five of the six branches of the Army Service Forces, the four mentioned above plus the Chemical Corps. The depot was adjacent to the Harrisburg Airport (above) and made frequent use of the airport, but did not take it over. Later in the war a main prisoner of war camp was established at the depot holding about 500 POWs who worked at the depot and in the local area. The depot remained in operation throughout the Cold War and became known as the New Cumberland Army Depot.

U.S. ARMY AIR FORCES INTELLIGENCE SCHOOL: This was a top-secret intelligence school established in the old Harrisburg Academy. As the name implies, its mission was to train AAF personnel in the gathering, interpretation of and use of intelligence information. The school's program was modeled after a similar program established by the British Royal Air Force (RAF). The school operated from the summer of 1942 until April 1944.

U.S. NAVAL SUPPLY DEPOT, MECHANICSBURG was located at Mechanicsburg, 8 miles SW of Harrisburg. It was commissioned in 1942 and served as a distribution point for everything from garbage cans to machine tools for the Navy. It was the largest of four such depots in the country and was the only source of mechanical parts of the Navy's destroyer escort ships. The facility had a technical information center which specialized in providing engineering services and information on internal combustion engines, landing craft and destroyer escort machinery.

LANCASTER AREA is about 30 miles south of Harrisburg. During the war Lancaster and many of the surrounding towns had manufacturing firms which received defense contracts. The Hamilton Watch Co. of Lancaster made mechanical timing fuzes for military ordnance; the Armstrong Cork Co., also of Lancaster, made 20 mm, 37 mm and 40 mm shells and casing, 105 mm chemical shells and four-lb incendiary bomb bodies and the Animal Trap Co. of America in Lititz, 8 miles north of Lancaster, made 30 and 50 calibre bullet cores.

MARIETTA HOLDING AND CONSIGNMENT POINT was located at Marietta, 13 miles west of Lancaster. This facility was one of several in the country that stored war materials in and on railroad cars and in warehouses for quick

The New Cumberland Army Service Forces Depot.

transfer to ports of embarkation or end users. The facility was run by the Army's Quartermaster Corps.

MEADVILLE is in the NW corner of the state 32 miles south of Erie, PA on I-79. The Talon Co. of Meadville, a zipper manufacturer, made 75 mm howitzers, M-48 fuses and other artillery gun parts during the war.

KEYSTONE ORDNANCE PLANT, south of town, was built early in the war by the Federal Government to make TNT. This was a large plant and it set production records of TNT greater than any other plant in the U.S. Later in the war the plant was converted to make large artillery shells.

MIDDLETOWN (See Harrisburg Area)

PHILADELPHIA AREA: Philadelphia was, as it is now, Pennsylvania's largest city. The Philadelphia metropolitan area was already heavily industrialized and during the war acquired 1/6 of the total defense work in the country. In the early 1940s the town hosted Republican National Convention for that election year at which Wendell Willkie and Charles L. McNary were nominated as the party's presidential and vice-presidential candidates.

As manufacturing firms geared up for war production and the city's military installations built up for war, the city was inundated with new workers and military people. As a result a housing shortage developed, rents shot up, schools, streets and stores became congested, crime rose and the city's services were stretched to the limit. Before the war ended the city was forced to built a new sewer plant to keep from polluting the Delaware and Schuylkill Rivers. To pay for the wartime needs the City Council imposed a 1.5% tax on all city wage-earners.

Philadelphia's harbor became very busy during the early stages of the war and was one of the main departure points for ships carrying Lend Lease goods to the Soviet Union. As the war progressed Philadelphia's harbor was one of the few ports on the east coast that re-mained open to ships of neutral nations.

When the U.S. went to war, the people of Philadelphia suffered the same fears of enemy attacks as did people in other large cities along the east coast. This was with good cause because the Axis powers had plans to attack the major east coast cities if the opportunities arose. In Dec. 1941, soon after the attack on Pearl Harbor, the 1st Air Force sent several units of fighter planes to Philadelphia's new airport per a pre-arranged plan to defend the city. Philadelphia was subjected to regular blackouts during the early months of the war and a Civilian Defense Corps was formed to direct the evacuation of the city should it become necessary. It was discovered that the city's air raid warning system had serious faults when the city was "bombed" five times without warning by U.S. air crews in training along the east coast using Philadelphia as their objective.

In early 1942 the city became the new home of the Securities and Exchange Commission when it was moved out of Washington, DC to make space available for more essential war agencies.

The city's roster of major manufacturers gives an idea of the many items of war made in the Philadelphia area:
- Philadelphia Navy Yard built warships up to the size of battleships. See detail below.
- Frankford Arsenal made a wide variety of ordnance. See below.
- Dravo Corp. built mine sweepers, patrol boats and tank landing craft.
- Cramp's Shipyard built cruisers, submarines and Navy tugs.
- Sun Shipbuilding & Dry Dock Corp. of Chester built freighters, tankers and cargo ships. Sun was the largest producer of tankers in the world.
- Westinghouse Electric Co. of Lester, PA produced turbines and gears for Victory ships.
- Budd Manufacturing Co. of Philadelphia made cargo planes.
- Brewster Aircraft Corp. of Johnsville built dive bombers.
- Kellett Aircraft Corp. of Upper Darby did important development work on helicopters for the Army.
- P-V Engineering Forum of Sharon Hill built Navy helicopters • Kaiser Cargo Industries, Fleetwings Div., of Bristol built aircraft components.
- Bendix Aviation Corp. produced Gyro Flux Gate Compasses, an important aircraft guidance device and controls for 37 mm anti-aircraft guns.
- G. & A. Aircraft Co. of Hatboro made aircraft components.
- Baldwin Locomotive Works of Eddystone made M-3, M-4 and M-6 tanks and parts.
- General Steel Casting Corp. of Eddystone developed a method for casting upper tank hulls and produced them throughout the war.
- Autocar Co. of Ardmore made half-track vehicles, trucks, scout cars and tractors.
- Roxboro Steel Co. of Philadelphia made 75 mm guns & gunsights.
- Empire Ordnance Corp. of Philadelphia made 75 mm tank and anti-tank guns.
- Dexdale Hosiery Mills of Lansdale made marine engines and beaching units.
- R.F. Sedgley, Inc. of Philadelphia made rifles, rifle barrels • and machine gun parts.
- Roberts & Mander Stove Co. of Hatboro made fragmentation bombs and parachute cases.
- Machined Metal Co. of Conshohock made 75 mm and 90 mm shells and propeller drive shafts.
- Bulova Watch Co. of Philadelphia made detonating fuzes and tank telescopes.
- Wyeth, Inc. of Philadelphia made pharmaceuticals, penicillin and blood plasma.

In 1944, as military needs began to be met, some Philadelphia manufacturers were allowed to resume production of consumer goods. In Aug. 1944 a serious transit strike erupted in Philadelphia and the Army had to be called in to keep the busses and trolleys running. The main issue of the strike, the raising of negroes to operators, was a portent of things to come. By war's end the city's infrastructure was badly in need of repair, so major programs were started to improve city streets, subways, the water system and airports.

All in all, Philadelphia prospered greatly during the war and much of that prosperity carried over into the postwar years after a not unexpected period of readjustment.

CHESTER TANK DEPOT in Chester, PA, 13 miles SW of Philadelphia, was an Army facility that received and modified tanks to comply with recent design changes and to prepare them for shipment overseas. This had been a Ford Motor Co. assembly plant before the war and was run by Ford during the war. The Chester Tank Depot was the largest of three such facilities in the nation[2].

FRANKFORD ARSENAL, 9 miles NE of downtown Philadelphia on the Delaware River, was established by the Federal Government in

A 75 mm recoilless rifle designed at Frankford Arsenal and built by Miller Machinery Co. of Pittsburgh.

[1]The other hotels were the Greenbrier in West Virginia, The Homestead in Virginia and the Grove Park Inn in North Carolina.

[2]The others were located at Lima, OH and Richmond, CA.

1816. Through the years it expanded and by WW II was essentially an ordnance research and engineering center, engaged in projects dealing with fire control, instrument and guidance systems, armaments, pilot ejection catapults, direct fire weapons and chronometers. In the 1930s the arsenal did a lot of experimental work on the manufacturing and production of artillery shells, work that became very necessary in the 1940s. During the war Frankford was the only Government arsenal to manufacture small arms ammunition. It used its manufacturing operation to train workers and supervisors for other small arms plants that were built around the country. Frankford also provided architectural plans and production line layouts for the new plants. Frankford had a training facility for optical workers and by the end of the war had increased the number of experienced optical workers in the country 70 fold. In addition, the arsenal did preliminary work on the production of fragmentary bombs and bomb fuzes. The famous 75 mm recoilless rifle, one of the best tank-killers of the war, was developed at Frankford. The arsenal continued in operation as a research and development center in the postwar years, but in 1977 it was closed. In 1983 about 80 acres of land and 170 buildings were sold to a developer.

FORT MIFFIN is on Mud Island at the mouth of the Schuylkill River near the southern end of the Philadelphia Naval Yard. The fort was built in 1771-77. In the century and a half before WW II it was expanded, abandoned, and reoccupied several times. In 1915 it was designated as a National Historic Landmark. In 1926 the Navy acquired part of the fort to store small amounts of ammunition in support the Philadelphia Navy Yard which adjoined the fort on the east. In WW II the old fort was pressed into service once again as an anti-aircraft battery while continuing to serve as an ammunition storage depot for the Navy. After the war Fort Miffin returned again to being an historic site and was reopened to the public. There is very little evidence, though, of the fort's role in WW II.

PENN'S LANDING is a 37-acre park on the Philadelphia waterfront between Market and Lombard Sts. It marks the spot where William Penn landed in 1682. On display are several historic ships open to the public including the WW II submarine "Becuna". This is a guppy-class submarine, built in 1943, which saw action with Halsey's 7th Fleet in the Pacific. Phone: 215/922-1898. Hours: daily 10-4:30, closed Jan. 1 and Dec. 25. Admission charged and includes admission to Adm. Dewey's flagship "Olympia".

PHILADELPHIA CARGO PORT OF EMBARKATION was located at Pier 98 on the Philadelphia waterfront at Hog Island. It was an Army facility through which thousands of tons of supplies were loaded on cargo ships and sent to the far distant battle fronts. About 10% of all the supplies shipped overseas by the Army went through this POE. So much live ammunition was shipped through the POE that

Ships being serviced by the Philadelphia Navy Yard. Second from left is the cruiser "Wilkes Barre", third from left is the battleship "South Dakota" and to the right of the crane in an unidentified aircraft carrier.

the nearby Philadelphia Municipal Airport was closed for a year and a half because it was feared that a plane crash might touch off some of the stored ammunition and cause a great disaster.

PHILADELPHIA NAVY YARD was located about four miles south of downtown Philadelphia on League Island at the confluence of the Schuylkill and Delaware Rivers. It was moved in this location in 1876 from the its original 1801 site three miles to the north. During WW I the Yard had a sizeable expansion and played a major role in supporting the Navy during that war. Activity at the Yard decreased in the 1920s, but the Yard remained in operation dismantling warships in compliance with the Washington Treaty and repairing, modernizing and maintaining many of the Navy's active warships. During the Depression years of the 1930s the Yard was one of the better employers in the Philadelphia area thanks to the Navy having assigned a long-term program to the yard to modernize five of the Navy's older battleships, the "Arkansas", "Wyoming", "Oklahoma", "Pennsylvania" and "New Mexico". Also, the Roosevelt Administration maintained a policy of countering naval activities of potential enemies such as Germany, Italy and Japan by ordering the production of new ships to keep pace with their naval expansion. This program started modestly with the construction of Coast Guard cutters and small destroyers to keep within the isolationist policies of the times, but culminated in 1937 when the Roosevelt Administration authorized the Philadelphia Navy Yard to built its first new battleship, the "Washington".

When war started in Europe in 1939 the Yard was busy with new construction, but took on yet another role. It had always been looked upon as a destroyer support base and it began to do just that by overhauling and repairing destroyers working the neutrality patrols or being given to Britain. This included the 50 destroyers given to Great Britain in Sept. 1940 in the "Bases for Destroyers" deal. All 50 destroyers had been mothballed at Philadelphia. Between 1939 and 1941 the Yard enjoyed a modest expansion, but after the attack on Pearl Harbor all the stops were pulled and the Yard

embarked on one long expansion program that last throughout the war. In 1942 employment jumped five-fold. During the war the Yard built 53 new ships, including two battleships, the "New Jersey" and "Wisconsin", and three aircraft carriers, the "Princeton", "Antietam" and "Valley Forge". The Yard also repaired 574 ships, converted 41 others and built two large dry docks. The Yard manufactured many of its own boilers, propellers, catapults, life boats and life jackets. At its peak some 45,000 people were employed here.

With the end of hostilities, the Yard, as was expected, cut back drastically. Employment went from 40,000 to 12,000 within a year. Yet, it remained active decommissioning ships, scraping ships and repairing ships for transfer to friendly nations or to new buyers. Again, as before the war, a sizeable mothball fleet was built up in the Delaware River. In Nov. 1945 the name of the Yard was changed, somewhat belatedly, to The Philadelphia Naval Shipyard and Navy Base to reflect its new size and importance. For the next 10 years, though, the Yard made no new ships. It had work, however, doing repairs, conversions and maintenance. In the 1970s and 1980s the Yard fell on hard times, in part, because it was not suited for the construction of nuclear powered ships. The Yard survived another few year, though, until the ax finally fell in the early 1990s and the Yard was closed.

The U.S. Naval Aircraft Factory: This was a separate naval facility at the eastern end of League Island. It was established in 1917 as a research and development center to support the Navy's new air arm. The Factory was the only facility of its type in the Navy. At various times it built prototype aircraft and produced some small production lots of aircraft. The Factory acquired its own air field, Mustin Field, in 1926 and two large hangars. During WW II the Factory continued its many research and development programs, built 156 flying boats and served as a naval auxiliary air station. The Factory also modified aircraft until this operation moved to Johnsville in 1944. In 1953 the Naval Aircraft Factory merged with other naval air-facilities and became a part of the Naval Air Material Center. In 1963 this entity

Uniforms are piled high at the Philadelphia Quartermaster Corps Depot in 1941 as the Army strives to outfit tens of thousands of draftees and new recruits.

The Valley Forge General Hospital during WW II.

was redesignated the Naval Air Engineering Center (NAES) and Mustin Field was shut down to reduce air congestion with nearby Philadelphia International Airport. In 1974 NAES itself was closed and its functions transferred elsewhere.

PHILADELPHIA QUARTERMASTER DEPOT was located at 2800 S. 20th St. in Philadelphia. This was a pre-WW I facility and the central procurement agency for the Army's clothing. The facility primarily bought clothe and made the many articles of clothing required by the Army. In a year's time during the war the depot bought enough clothe to wrap around the world 10 times. The depot also acted as a production laboratory and filled emergency orders. All of the Army's flags were made here and the purchasing department bought all of the Army's medals and band instruments. Like most existing Army facilities, the Philadelphia Quartermaster Depot had a rapid build-up in 1942 going from 3000 employees to 16,000. In late 1945 research and development work on Army clothing was transferred here from the Quartermaster depot at Jeffersonville, IN. After the war, production at the Philadelphia depot dropped significantly, but the depot was kept in operation. By the 1960s the depot had become known as the Defense Supply Agency's Defense Clothing and Textile Center.

PHILADELPHIA SIGNAL DEPOT was located at

The dog training center at the Widener Estate at Elkins Park, PA.

5000 Wissahickon Ave. in Philadelphia and was the largest Signal Corps depot in the country. Its mission was to acquire, store and distribute all types of electronic, mechanical and communications equipment used by the Army's Signal Corps. This was the function it performed during WW II. In 1946 the depot was closed and its assets and some of its people moved to a former Glenn L. Martin Aircraft Co. plant in Baltimore, MD where it became a sub-depot of the Holabird Signal Depot.

SCHUYLKILL ARSENAL was located in downtown Philadelphia at 26th St. and Grays Ferry Ave. on the Schuylkill River. It was an existing building purchased by the Federal Government in 1799 to be a powder magazine. By WW II the post consisted of 8.8 acres and had 16 buildings. Early in the war it had a quartermaster replacement training school, but this move out to Camp Lee, VA in Oct. 1941. Schuylkill was then used by the Army as a school for bakers and cooks. Immediately after the war it was used by the Army Reserve and in 1958 it was closed.

U.S. NAVAL AIR STATION, WILLOW GROVE was located 18 miles north of downtown Philadelphia. It was built in the 1920s to be the company field by the Pitcairn Aviation Co., a leader in the development and construction of safe aircraft and autogiros. The company had close ties with the U.S. Navy because as early as 1931 the Navy utilized several of their autogiros. By the early 1940s it was clear that autogiros would give way to helicopters and the Pitcairn Aviation Co. fell on hard times. In 1941 the Navy was looking for a way to relieve some of the congestion at the Naval Aircraft Factory's Mustin Field so they purchased Pitcairn Air Field. In 1942 Navy student pilots began training at the field in N3N "Yellow Peril" biplanes. In Jan. 1943 the station was given its wartime name and

was expanded. NAS, Willow Grove operated throughout WW II as a training facility specializing in training pilots and crew in ferrying operations, formation flying and anti-submarine warfare. In Dec. 1945 the facility was turned over to the Naval Reserve. During the Korean an Viet Nam Wars the field became very active again as a training field. The station continued in operation throughout the Cold War and served the Naval and Marine Reserves in a wide variety of ways.

Willow Grove Air Park: This is a collection of historic aircraft in an open display area near the main entrance to NAS, Willow Grove. Several WW II aircraft are in the collection including a Messerschmitt ME-26 jet, a Kawanishi N1K1 "Rex", a Nakajima B6N1, and an Arado 196 float plane that operated off the German cruiser Prinz Eugen. Viewing hours: sunrise to sunset. Free.

U.S. NAVAL AIRCRAFT SUPPLY DEPOT was another large depot in Philadelphia that stored parts, tools and equipment for naval aircraft. It was one of only two such depots in the country. Also at the depot was the Naval Aviation Supply Office, the main purchasing organization for naval aircraft parts.

WIDENER ESTATE: This was a Coast Guard dog and horse training facility at Elkins Park, a northern suburb of Philadelphia. It was on the estate of P.A.B. Widener which was well equipped with outbuildings and stables. The dogs and horses trained here were used primarily in the U.S. on beach patrols.

PHOENIXVILLE/VALLEY FORGE AREA: This is the historic Valley Forge area, 20 miles west of Philadelphia. Phoenixville was one of the larger towns in the area and was the eastern terminus of the "Big Inch" oil pipe line. This pipe line, built in 1942-43, began at Longview, TX and was intended to insure a safe and adequate supply of oil products to the east coast. The supply of oil had become very much at risk in early and mid 1942 when German submarine ravaged commercial shipping along the U.S. east coast and in the Gulf of Mexico and sank many oil tankers. The "Big Inch" pipe line was 24" in diameter, 1381 miles long and delivered 300,000 barrels of oil a day.

VALLEY FORGE GENERAL HOSPITAL, five miles west of Valley Forge Historic Park, was a complex of two-story brick buildings built in

1942-43 to treat war sounded. It consisted of 183 acres of land and had over 100 buildings. The hospital specialized in plastic surgery, ophthalmologic surgery, psychiatry and in treating men blinded in the war. It became a research center in the development of the acrylic artificial eye and was noted also for its research work on infectious hepatitis. It had 2509 beds and was intended to be semi-permanent. This was one of only a few Army hospitals in the country that had closed wards for the treatment of severe mental cases. The hospital had a main prisoner of war camp which held about 250 POWs who worked at the hospital. The facility remained an Army hospital after the war and in 1952 changed its focus to diseases of the chest and neuropsychiatric disorders.

PITTSBURGH AREA, in western Pennsylvania, had long been known as America's steel center and was the home of several of America's largest steel firms. Pittsburgh was a booming town before the war as the U.S. built up its armed forces in the wake of developments in Europe and the Far East. By 1941 nearly all of Pittsburgh's major industries had converted to defense work and most of the steel mills were working at their capacity. The city's population swelled somewhat during the war (estimates put it at an increase of 100,000), but this was not as bad as Philadelphia's and other large cities throughout the nation. The city could really have used more people because throughout the war there was a constant labor shortage. Pittsburgh, though, had problems with congested streets, noise, water pollution and especially smoke pollution. These problems got so bad in the early years of the war that the city fathers were forced to take serious measures to correct them. In Dec. 1942 the city had yet another problem when a major flood shut down several important plants. Labor problems, including wild-cat strikes, were a frequent problems especially in the big steel mills.

Pittsburgh's industries were of such importance to the nation's war effort that the AAF extended their extensive east coast volunteer ground observer program inland as far as Pittsburgh to guard against enemy air attacks. The city was also used, unbeknownst to its citizens, as a training ground for OSS agents. Advanced OSS students were sent to Pittsburgh with orders to try to gain entrance to closely guarded war plants, power plants and other vital war facilities. They were given fake identification documents and told to apply for jobs in certain factories. The students were very successful and each success was reported by the OSS to the proper authorities so that security measures could be tightened.

Pittsburgh was also the center of Pennsylvania's coal region and this industry boomed, but it too was plagued with labor shortages and union problems.

Some of the major manufacturers in the Pittsburgh area during the war were:
- United States Steel Corp., the nation's largest steel maker, made a wide variety of steel products.
- Jones & Laughlin Steel Corp. of McKeesport, a major steel producer and manufacturer, made 105 mm shells, 500 & 1000 lb bombs.

- Canonsburg Steel & Irons Works of Canonsburg made projectiles up to 5".
- Alcoa of Pittsburgh made aluminum.
- Dravo Corp. of Pittsburgh made patrol craft for the Navy.
- United Engineering & Foundry Co. of Pittsburgh made howitzers.
- Blaw Knox & Co. of Pittsburgh made 100 lb bombs.
- Mesta Machine Co. of West Homestead made 155 mm guns, barbett carriages, 75 mm gun tube forgings, large ring gear forgings, 36" mortars and drive shafts for ships.
- Westinghouse Electric & Mfg. Co. of Pittsburgh made torpedoes, torpedo tubes and turbine drives for ships.
- Miller Printing Machinery Co. of Pittsburgh made 75 mm recoilless rifles.
- Standard Steel Spring Co. made armor plate and 500 lb anti-personnel bombs.
- National Tube Co. of McKeesport made bombs and 75 mm to 105 mm artillery shells.
- American Cyanamide & Chemical Co. of New Castle, made dynamite and electric blasting caps.
- H.K. Porter Co. of Pittsburgh made locomotives and 8" high explosive shells.
- H.J. Heinz Co. of Pittsburgh made aircraft fuselages & aircraft stabilizers.
- Pressed Steel Car Co. of Pittsburgh made M-3 medium tanks and 75 mm shells.
- Armstrong Cork Co. of Pittsburgh made 75 mm shells.
- Pittsburgh Water Heater Co. of Pittsburgh made bomb fuzes.
- Union Switch & Signal Co. of Swissvale made 45 calibre Colt automatic pistols.
- Aluminum Cooking Utensil Co. of New Kensington made 30 calibre cartridge cases.
- Vitale Fire Works Mfg. Co. of New Castle made 30 cal. cartridges.

In 1944 there was a noticeably business downturn in the city as the nation's war needs began to be met. There was still, however, a labor shortage. When the war ended, there was a further weakening of the economy, but it was short lived. By 1946-47 Pittsburgh's steel mills and factories were humming again as the needs for consumer goods increased.

By late 1945 the city's planners were beginning to get an upper hand on smoke and water pollution and traffic congestion. And, in that year they began a major project to clear away an ugly slum and industrial area on the city's riverfront. What evolved was a large and beautiful park known as the Golden Triangle at the western tip-end of the city where the Allegheny and Monongahela Rivers merge to form the Ohio River. This project became one of the nation's models for urban renewal in the coming years.

CARNEGIE SCIENCE CENTER, near downtown Pittsburgh, is a museum displaying many aspects of science including a working foundry, industrial robots, lasers, cryogenics and electrical equipment. In front of the Center, anchored in the river, is the WW II submarine "Requin". This sub was completed in 1945 and reached Guam just as the war ended so it saw no military action. Address: 1 Allegheny Ave., Pittsburgh, PA 15212. Phone: 412/237-3400. Hours for the "Requin": M-Tues. noon-5, W-F

noon-6, Sat.-Sun. 10-6. Admission and parking charged.

PITTSBURGH-ALLEGHENY COUNTY AIRPORT, 5.3 miles south of the city, was used by both the Army and Navy during the war. Neither, however, took it over and it remained a commercial field serving civilian aircraft. The AAF's Air Transport Command used the field and had a Flight Service Center and air freight terminal here while the Navy's Air Transport Command Service and their Air Ferry Command operated from the field. After the war the air field became the Allegheny County Airport.

SOLDIERS AND SAILORS MEMORIAL HALL, located at 5th & Bigelow Sts. in Pittsburgh, honors Pennsylvania's veterans of all wars including WW II. On display are uniforms, weapons, photographs, documents, flags, medals and a display on black military history. Address: 5th & Bigelow Sts., Pittsburgh, PA 15207. Phone: 412/621-4253. Hours: M-F 9-4, Sat.-Sun. 1-4. Closed Jan. 1, Labor Day, Thanksgiving, and Dec. 25. Free.

POTTSVILLE is 28 miles NNW of Reading on SR 61.

CRESSONA ORDNANCE DEPOT was built south of Pottsville near the community of Cressona at the beginning of the war to store ammunition for the Army. It was also a major repair and maintenance center for ordnance items.

READING is midway between Harrisburg and Philadelphia on I-176.

MID-AMERICA AIR MUSEUM is located at Reading Regional Airport three miles NW of town on SR 183. This is a large air museum with a collection of some 30 aircraft on display. Many of the planes are of WW II vintage including a P-61 Black Widow that was resurrected from the New Guinea jungle. Other WW II aircraft include a Douglas R4D Dakota, PT-13 and PT-19 trainers, a Messerschmitt Bf 108 Taifun, a B-25 Mitchell bomber and an SNJ-4 Texan. Address: Reading Regional Airport, Rd. #9, Box 9381, Reading PA 19605. Phone: 610/372-7333. Hours: daily 9:30-4, closed major holidays. Admission charged.

READING ARMY AIR FIELD, three miles NW of town, was the area's local airport before the war. Early in the war the AAF took it over and used it as a branch of the Middletown Air Technical Service Command. The air field had a branch prisoner of war camp which held about 275 POWs who worked in agriculture. After the war the field was used by the US Air force as part of the Air Defense Command, but it was eventually returned to civilian ownership and became Reading's main airport.

SCRANTON/WILKES-BARRE AREA is in the NE part of the state on I-81 and I-84. One of the major manufacturers in the area was the West Pittston Iron Works of West Pittston which made 75 mm guns and telescoping gun sights, and another was the Murray Corp. which made wings for B-29 bombers.

TOBYHANNA MILITARY RESERVATION is 15 miles SE of Scranton on I-380. This was a pre-war Army facility but was not garrisoned until early 1942. During WW II it was first utilized as a training camp for small AAF units under the control of the Middletown Air Service

The Pennsylvania Ordnance Works was constructed of wooden trusses to save steel. It also saved money.

Command. There was a small main prisoner of war camp here holding about 100 POWs who worked in the local area. In 1943 the camp was converted into an AAF storage depot. After the war it became an Army facility again and was used by the Signal Corps and called Tobyhanna Signal Depot. In 1962 it was renamed the Tobyhanna Army Depot, but still served the Signal Corps as well as the National Guard. The post operated throughout the Cold War and was closed in the 1990s.

STATE COLLEGE is near the center of the state south of I-80.

PENNSYLVANIA MILITARY MUSEUM-28TH DIVISION SHRINE is located on U.S. 322 in Boalsburg, an eastern suburb of State College. It honors Pennsylvania's soldiers from the Revolutionary War to the present and emphasizes the role of the Army's 28th Infantry Division which the Pennsylvania National Guard becomes when mobilized. The WW II era is well represented among the displays and consist of military vehicles, artillery pieces, small arms, uniforms, military equipment, personal documents, maps, paintings and drawings, dioramas, flags, medical equipment and other memorabilia. WW II tanks, half-tracks and personnel carriers are displayed in the museum and on the museum grounds. Address: PO Box 148, Boalsburg, PA 16827. Phone: 814/466-6263. Hours: Tues.-Sat. 9-5, Sun. noon-5, closed Jan. 1, Thanksgiving and Dec. 25. Admission charged.

VALLEY FORGE (See Phoenixville/Valley Forge)

WILKES-BARRE (See Scranton/Wilkes-Barre Area)

WILLIAMSPORT is in the north-central part of the state on the West Branch of the Susquehanna River. Major manufacturers in the area were Aviation Corporation of America which made aircraft engines, Sylvania Electric Co. which made electrical components for the military and Darling Valve & Mfg. Co. which made 105 mm shells.

PENNSYLVANIA ORDNANCE WORKS was built south of Williamsport near the town of Montgomery by the Federal Government early in the war to produce TNT. It later included the manufacture of large artillery shells. In 1944 all production ceased and the facility and was converted into an ammunition storage depot. At that time it was renamed Susquehanna Ordnance Depot. The Army retained the depot after the war and it served as a sub-depot to Letterkenny.

YORK is 21 miles south of Harrisburg. Two of the major war plants in York were York Safe & Lock Co. which made Bofors anti-aircrft guns and gun carriages for the Navy, and Read Machinery Co. which made 105 mm shells and 60 mm mortars

SHRINE OF ST. KOLBE: This is a shrine to a Polish Roman Catholic priest, Maximilian Kolbe, who was killed by the Nazis at Auschwitz and, since the war, has been canonized. It is on the grounds of St. Thomas Catholic Church in New Salem, PA a southwestern suburb of York. Father Kolbe was a Franciscan priest who successfully bargained with the Nazis to take his life and spare the life of a family man who had been sentenced to death. Inscribed on the shrine in both Polish and English is a quotation taken from Father Kolbe's own preaching "Without Sacrifice There Is No Love". Address: St. Thomas Church, Rt. 1 Box 1871, New Salem, PA 15468. Phone: 717/245-6279. Hours: Always visible. Free.

U.S. NAVAL ORDNANCE PLANT, YORK was built in York early in the war and made anti-aircraft guns for the Navy.

Anti-aircraft guns being manufactured at the U.S. Naval Ordnance Plant, York, PA.

RHODE ISLAND

The 713,346 citizens of wartime Rhode Island, America's smallest state, proved to be an industrious lot during the war. They produced a wide variety of war materials and food for the nation and some 93,000 of their number served in the armed forces.

When the war started in Europe Rhode Island's economy was slowly reviving from the Great Depression despite the fact that one of the state's oldest industries, the textile industry, was declining because the textile mills were moving south for cheaper labor and to be closer to the cotton. Fortunately, the state's machine tool and metal working industries were on the increase and compensating for the loss of textile jobs and state revenues. During the war the state produced ships, machine tools, machined metal products, Quonset Huts, aircraft components, barrage balloons, rubber products, textiles and clothing, grain, hay, potatoes, fruit, meat products, dairy products, stone, sand and gravel.

In 1941, before the U.S. went to war, the state legislature created a Council of Defense to devise ways to protect Rhode Island in the event of enemy attacks. With thousands of Rhode Islanders being drafted the legislature, in 1942, looked to the future and passed laws requiring the state, municipalities and construction firms doing business with the state rehire returning veterans after the war. When the war ended, Rhode Island's economy was hard hit. The sudden cancellation of defense contracts, especially in the shipbuilding industry, put many people out of work. And, the textile firms in the state resumed their exodus to the south. Rhode Island did not recover significantly until the 1950s, but from then on the state's fortunes continued to climb thanks, in part, to it strong manufacturing base.

BRISTOL is on the east side of Narragansett Bay. During the war it had one large manufacturer, the Herreshoff Mfg. Co. In peacetime the company made racing and pleasure yachts, but in wartime it made mine sweepers, motor transport vessels and the Navy's first patrol/torpedo (PT) boats.

HERRESHOFF MARINE MUSEUM, in downtown Bristol, displays the products of the Herreshoff Mfg. Co. of Bristol. Displays and exhibits emphasize the company's strong position in the field of yachting, but there are also displays on Navy patrol/torpedo (PT) boats, the first models of which were made for the Navy by Herreshoff. Address: 7 Burnside St., Bristol, RI 02809. Phone: 401/253-5000. Hours: May thru Oct. M-F 1-4, Sat.-Sun. 11-4. Admission charged.

CHARLESTOWN is on the SW coast of the state.

U.S. NAVAL AUXILIARY AIR STATION, CHARLESTOWN was built two miles SW of Charlestown by the Navy in 1942 as an auxiliary air station to NAS, Quonset Point. During the war night-fighter pilots trained here. When the war ended the station faced decommissioning, but was given a reprieve when the Navy Air Navigation Project moved in. This was a project to design, test and develop engineering tests and air navigational electronic aids and traffic control systems. The station also supported air groups being rotated between ground and fleet duties. These activities declined and in May 1950 NAAS, Charleston was downgraded to an outlying field to NAS, Quonset Point.

LITTLE COMPTON/SAKONNET AREA is in the SE corner of the state on a peninsula overlooking the Sakonnet River, which is one of the entrances to Narragansett Bay, and Rhode Island Sound.

FORT CHURCH was built in the 1920s and armed with 8" naval guns removed from a U.S. warship in accordance with the Washington Naval Treaty of 1922. In 1940 a larger and more modern battery, mounting twin 16" guns, was constructed near Little Compton which, together with a similar battery at Point Judith, could command the entire entrance to Narragansett Bay. The new battery was called the West Reservation and the older battery the East Reservation. The West Reservation was a self-supporting battery and could function without the aid of the East Reservation. The West Reservation was camouflaged to look like a farm and the East Reservation was camouflaged to look like a large summer residence. Fort Church had a third entity, the South Reservation, which was armed with 8" guns and had a commanding view of the ocean from high ground. During the war all three batteries were armed and manned. The fort served as a sub-post of Fort Adams. After the war Fort Church was abandoned and in 1954 it was sold to the former land owners and others.

NARRAGANSETT PIER/POINT JUDITH AREA is on the western shore of the entrance to Narragansett Bay.

FORT NATHANIEL GREENE was located on the Narragansett Peninsula at Point Judith. The site was first acquired by the Federal Government in 1934 and called Point Judith Military Reservation. Construction of a modern coastal defense battery, mounting twin 16" guns, was soon begun and was completed in 1940. The new facility was named Fort Nathaniel Greene. Together with a similar battery at Sakonnet, on the eastern shore, its guns protected the entire entrance to Narragansett Bay. The post was manned throughout most of the war and was a sub-post of Fort Adams. For a few years after the war it was used by the Rhode Island National Guard. In 1947, however, the Army declared the fort to be surplus and sold it to the state to be used as a park and for several other purposes. The main battery became the centerpiece of a state park and opened to the public.

FORT KEARNEY was a 25-acre coast artillery post established in 1909 four miles north of Narragansett Pier on S. Ferry Rd. Its guns overlooked the main entrance to Narragansett Bay and Conanicut Island. The fort was reactivated in 1940 as a sub-post to Ft. Adams and was armed and manned for most of the war. In Mar. 1945 a secret program, which had been established by the Army at a former CCC camp near Van Etten, New York several months earlier, moved to Fort Kearney. The program concerned the training of carefully selected German prisoners of war and some aliens for service as administrators and police in the soon-to-be-established U.S. Army Government of Occupation in Germany. The program was officially known as the "Intellectual Diversion Program" to conform to language in the Geneva Convention governing the care of prisoners of war and to disguise its real purpose[1]. At Kearney, the program was expanded and the program, and the fort, became known collectively as "The Factory". The initial phase of the program proved to be very successful and was expanded. Nearby Fts. Getty and Wetherill were then incorporated into the program. Ft. Getty was used to train administrators and Ft. Wetherill trained police. Many of the POWs selected were college graduates or had had experience in business or as civil servants in Germany. All were from western Germany because the Soviets, who would occupy eastern Germany, had demanded that all German POWs be returned to their home areas. Several of the members of the test program were retained as instructors for those who followed. In late 1945 the program was moved from the three forts to Ft. Eustis, VA where all activities was consolidated. Ft. Kearney closed soon afterwards and was declared surplus.

FORT VARNUM was a new small coastal defense position built in 1942-43 on the western shore of Narragansett Bay near Narragansett Pier overlooking the entrance to the Bay. The post was manned and armed during the war. In 1948 the fort was turned over to the state and used as a training facility for the Rhode Island National Guard.

NEWPORT, on the southern coast of Rhode Island near the entrance to Narragansett Bay, was a resort community with many magnificent estates belonging to some of America's richest people. Newport was also a Navy town, with several important naval installations in the area. During the war the community suffered a critical housing shortage and some of the ocean-front mansions were utilized to house service personnel.

FORT ADAMS was on a strategic peninsula on the north shore of Newport jutting into Narragansett Bay and forming the western arm of Newport Harbor. The first guns were mounter on the site in 1683. The post was expanded over the years and saw action in several of America's wars. By WW II Fort Adams was one of the largest coastal forts in the nation and had a mix of old and new coastal defense weapons. It was the command fort for other coastal defenses in the area including Forts Getty, Nathaniel Greene, Church, Wetherill and Kearney. This situation remained intact throughout WW II with the wartime

[1]The Geneva Convention did not cover the treatment of POWs with regard to this subject, but the Americans wanted to keep their actions secret for fear of Germany retaliation against American POWs.

Fort Adams as it now appears.

mission being that of protecting Narragansett Bay. Fort Adams was the site of Rhode Island's only main prisoner of war camp which held about 200 POWs who worked for the military. The fort remained active after the war, but in 1950 it was abandoned by the Army. In 1953 Ft. Adams became an inactive sub-post of the Boston Army Base and in 1958 it was used to house Navy personnel. The old fort was eventually turned over to the state and parts of it turned into a state park and the remainder sold to private interests. The old fort then became the centerpiece of the Fort Adams State Park.

CAMP BURNSIDE was a Civil War-era training camp located on the southern tip of Conanicut Island. The facility had long been abandoned but, during WW II, the Navy acquired the site and used it for a radar station.

FORT GETTY was a 31-acre coastal defense post located five miles west of Fort Adams on the western shore of Conanicut Island and three miles SW of Jamestown. It was built between 1900 and 1909 as one of Narragansett Bay's coastal defenses. After WW I the fort was re-

duced to caretaker status and remained that way until early 1945 when it was used as one of three forts in the area in a program to train former German prisoners of war for service in the U.S. Army's Government of Occupation in Germany. See Ft. Kearney, above, for details on this program and Ft. Getty's use. After WW II Fort Getty was abandoned by the Army, but was used briefly by the Navy in 1954. The Navy withdrew and in 1955 the old fort was sold to the town of Jamestown for recreational purposes.

FORT GREBLE was located about five miles west of Fort Adams and three miles west of Jamestown on Dutch Island. It was build between 1900-1902 to be one of Narragansett Bay's coastal defenses, but was deactivated in 1906. It was used during WW I then closed again. During WW II it was used as a rifle range and then abandoned again by the Army a short time later.

FORT HAMILTON was located on Rose Island about one mile north of Goat Island in Newport Harbor. Construction of Ft. Hamilton was begun in the early 1800s but never completed. Through the years it was used off-and-on by the city of Newport as a quarantine station and one of its buildings was converted into a lighthouse. During WW II anti-aircraft guns were placed at the old fort near the lighthouse.

FORT WETHERILL is on the eastern shore of Conanicut Island two miles south of Jamestown and directly opposite Fort Adams. The first fortifications were built on the site in 1776. Over the years the fort evolved into a major coastal defense position and was utilized in most of America's wars. During WW II it was still armed and manned and served to protect the Newport area. It was a sub-post of Fort Adams. In the spring of 1945 Fort Wetherill became one of three forts in the area in which carefully selected German prisoners of war were secretly trained for service in the U.S. Army's Government of Occupation in Germany. See Fort Kearney, above, for details on this program and the use of Fort Wetherill.

Beginning in 1951 Fort Wetherill was used by the Navy for a few years, but in the mid 1980s it was transferred to the state. It then be-

came a state park.

U.S. NAVAL HOSPITAL, NEWPORT was located in the northern part of Newport directly across from Goat Island. It evolved in the late 1890s from several medical and dental station facilities to become its own entity with the above name. During WW I NH, Newport was expanded, and after the war it continued in operation to serve naval personnel and their dependents. By Dec. 1941 the hospital had 269 beds. During 1942 the facility underwent a major expansion to about 1300 beds and throughout the war it continued to serve the medical and dental needs of the area's naval personnel. This mission continued into the postwar years although at a reduced rate. In 1972 when the Navy's medical facilities all over the country underwent a major reorganization and NH, Newport lost its identity and became a part of the U.S. Naval Regional Medical Center, Newport.

U.S. NAVAL OPERATING BASE, NEWPORT came into being in Apr. 1941 when several of the major naval facilities in the Newport area were merged into one command for improved efficiency and administration. The merged components consisted of the Naval War College, Naval Training Station, Naval Net Depot, Naval Torpedo Station, Naval Fuel Depot, Naval Hospital and the Naval Air Station, Quonset Point. Each component maintained its own mission and commander, but answered administratively to NOB, Newport. As mobilization progressed other activities were placed under NOB, Newport's control; a Marine barracks, Motor Patrol Boat Training Center, tug operations, piloting, logistical services, harbor facilities, security operations, shore protection, housing, recreational facilities and liaison with the Army. Virtually all of NOB, Newport's major components expanded during the war and by 1943-44 the base had 15 major components and a compliment of 162,000 service personnel and civilians. In the latter months of the war activities and personnel at NOB, Newport began do decline, and when the war ended this decline accelerated. In 1946 NOB, Newport was downgraded to a Naval Base to reflect its new peacetime structure. U.S. Naval Base, Newport functioned until 1974 at which time it was disestablished and its surviving major components returned to being separate naval entities.

U.S. NAVAL TORPEDO STATION, NEWPORT was located on Goat Island in Newport Harbor. It was established in 1869 in an old fort on the island, Fort Wolcott, that had its beginning in 1799. NTS, Newport was an experimental facility that specialized in the development of torpedoes and torpedo explosives and equipment. Through the years the station endeavored to keep pace with, and hopefully outpace, torpedo technology being developed by the other navies of the world. The station also became involved in the development of various naval gear. During WW I all experimentation at NAS, Newport ceased and the station's facilities were devoted 100% to the production of torpedoes, depth charges, bombs and mines. The station was greatly enlarged to accomplish this mission. After WW I the station returned to its research and development programs, limited manufacture of torpedoes and torpedo

The sprawling facilities of U.S. Naval Operating Base, Newport. In the foreground is the Naval War College and in the distance is Coasters Island.

storage. In 1931 NAS, Newport was in the forefront of experiments on the launching of torpedoes from aircraft. Activity accelerated in the late 1930s and when the national emergency was declared in May 1941 the station began a major expansion in its capability to manufacture torpedoes. The station continued its research programs especially with regards to homing torpedoes. When the U.S. went to war the station began non-stop, around-the-clock production of torpedoes. Torpedo production peaked in early 1944 as did the station's employment at 12,600 service personnel and workers. For that year NAS, Newport was Rhode Island's largest industrial employer. In 1945 activity began to wind down and, with the end of the war, declined rapidly. Torpedo production stopped and torpedoes began to be returned for storage. During the war the station had produced some 20,000 torpedoes, or 1/3 of the wartime Navy's requirements. In the early postwar years the station returned to research and development, but not to manufacturing. Newer facilities built during the war had taken over that activity. By 1951 R & D operations had declined and in that year the station was formally disestablished and its assets taken over by the Navy's underwater ordnance people. At that time the station became U.S. Naval Underwater Ordnance Station, Newport, an activity that remained throughout the Cold War.

U.S. NAVAL TRAINING STATION, NEWPORT was located on Coasters Island which is just off the northern shore of Newport. The station was established in 1883. By the 1890s the facility had become the Navy's principal naval training station. In the early 1900s several naval service schools were built on Coasters Island and were associated with the training station. During WW I the station was greatly expanded and acquired an air field, Cloyne Field. Through the 1920-30s activities diminished to the point where the station turned out only 700 to 800 recruits per year. In 1937 NTS, Newport acquired 151 acres of land and 60 buildings at Coddington Point on the mainland, and in 1938 the station expanded again as a result of the Naval Expansion Act of 1938. During 1939 the station turned out 4300 recruits. When the war started in Europe the number of recruits jumped to some 16,000 in 1941, and to an all-time high of 25,000 in 1942. The service schools also expanded and turned out about 36,000 graduates during the war.

In Nov. 1943 recruit training operations at NTS, Newport were abruptly halted and much the training personnel assigned to other naval training stations. NTS, Newport was given a new mission, that of training Ships' Pre-Commissioning Details. These were groups of officers and men who would take over the initial operation of a newly-built warship just prior it's commissioning. The service schools remained as before and one more school, the Indoctrination School for Officers, was added.

When the war ended, activities at the pre-commissioning school remained strong because most of the ships under construction were eventually completed and commissioned. As this activity declined, however, the pre-commissioning school was transferred to Norfolk and Miami. In 1946 all activities at NTS, New-

port were cut back drastically. And, in that year, with the disestablishment of NOB, Newport, the training station became its own entity once again. In the late 1940s and early 1950s the station served as a post-demobilization center, a receiving center for naval personnel moving to and from ships of the Atlantic Fleet, naval housing and several schools. For a brief period during the Korean War NTS, Newport again trained recruits. But, in 1952 the order came for recruit training operations to move to Bainbridge, MD and later that year the assets of the training station were absorbed by the Naval Base.

U.S. NAVAL WAR COLLEGE was located on Coasters Island which is off the northern shore of Newport. It was established in the 1880s to provide advanced courses in naval matters for officers of the U.S. Navy in the face of the rapid changes in naval technology that were then occuring. The College, however, wasn't widely accepted in the Navy nor in the U.S. Congress and was often short of funds. Also, attendance was voluntary. The College prodded along, nevertheless, and in 1895 entered a new field, that of naval war planning. This activity brought favorable attention within the Navy and put the College on more solid political and financial ground. When the U.S. became involved in WW I, however, the College's staff was drained away and the College was closed for the duration of the war and did not reopen until 1922. At that time its program of war planning was not resumed and the College's old critics surfaced putting the College again on shaky ground. When WW II began there were efforts to close the College as before, but Adm. Chester Nimitz, a graduate of the College and one of its stronger supporters, saw that it stayed open and that its curriculum was even expanded. By the end of the war the College had proven its worth. In 1946 Adm. Raymond Spruance assumed the presidency of the College and propelled it to new heights. Under his direction a new department was established at the College to study the lessons learned during WW II. This department was known as the "World War II Battle Evaluation Group". From then on, the College was a respected and valued agency of the Navy and continued to function throughout the Cold War.

Naval War College Museum: This museum is located at the Naval Education and Training Center on Coasters Island and traces the history of the War College. It also focuses on the history of naval warfare and the naval history of the Narragansett area. The museum emphasizes the importance of professional implementation of strategic and tactical objectives. On display are artifacts from the American Revolution to the present including a sizeable display on WW II. Address: Coasters Island, Newport, RI 02841-5010. Phone: 401/841-4052/

This is "Belmead," one of the Newport mansions of the rich and famous. It was purchased by the government during the war to house naval personnel from the Naval Training Station. Many of the other mansions were abandoned and in decay at the time.

1317. Hours: June thru Sept. M-F 10-4 and weekends noon-4, rest of year M-F 10-4. Free.

PROVIDENCE is the capital of the state.

HILLGROVE ARMY AIR FIELD was 7 miles south of Providence near the town of Hillgrove. This was a pre-war civilian airport that was taken over by the AAF early in the war and used for a variety of purposes. After the war the AAF departed and the field was returned to its civilian owners and became T. F. Green Airport.

RHODE ISLAND HOLOCAUST MEMORIAL MUSEUM is located near downtown Providence and has displays, artifacts and memorabilia related to the Holocaust of WW II. The museum also has a resource center, a library, a speaker's bureau, educational programs and published a news letter. Address: JCC of Rhode Island, 401 Elmgrove Ave., Providence, RI 02906. Phone: 401/861-8800. Hours: M-Thurs. 8:30 am-10 pm, Fri. 8:30-5.

QUONSET POINT AREA is near the western shore of Narragansett Bay.

U.S. NAVAL ADVANCED BASE DEPOT, QUONSET POINT/U.S. NAVAL CONSTRUCTION BATTALION CENTER, DAVISVILLE: These were two naval facilities that evolved along with the construction of NAS, Quonset Point and, together with NAS, Quonset Point, formed one large inter-related naval complex. The U.S. Naval Advanced Base Depot (ABD) was built in 1941-42 concurrently with NAS, Quonset Point on land north of, and adjacent to it. ABD began on 85 acres of land on the Quidnesset peninsula, but before the war ended it stretched four miles inland. Inasmuch as NAS, Quonset Point was the assembly point for men and supplies going to Argentia, Newfoundland after the British-American "Bases for Destroyer Deal", ABD's first mission was to store, service and ship the equipment, materials and supplies necessary to establish the U.S. base at Argentia. Eventually ABD began shipping supplies to other overseas bases, a function it continued throughout the war. Another and very large part of ABD's activity was the manufacture of the newly designed Quonset Huts, under private contractor direction. During the war 32,000 huts were manufactured at ABD.

British-made Nissen Huts were used as models for the American-made Quonset Huts. This hut is on display at the U.S. Air Force Museum, Dayton, OH and is one of the few Nissen Huts in the country.

While ABD and NAS, Quonset Point were under construction the U.S. Naval Construction Battalion Center (NCBC) was also under construction at nearby Davisville. This was a base for the newly formed naval construction battalions known as "SeaBees". NCBC first became an assembly point for newly trained sailors coming out of boot camp that were destined for the SeaBees. At NCBC the men were processed and sent on to Camp Allen at NOB, Norfolk for specialized SeaBee training. In Aug. 1942 the Navy began training SeaBees here and established a camp for that purpose called Camp Endicott. In 1943 an Advance Base Proving Ground (ABPG) was created within the NCBC complex to test and develop various pieces of equipment the SeaBees used. ABPG specialized in developing pontoons which were used for bridges, dry docks, ferries and barges. In 1944 the Navy's Civil Engineering Training Schools was moved to Camp Endicott from Camp Peary. This school trained SeaBee officers. Also in 1945 Camp Endicott acquired a 6500-acre reservation near East Greenwich, RI where the equipment under development was field-tested.

In the spring of 1945 the training of organized SeaBee battalions ended at NCBC and the training of replacements began. By war's end over 100,000 enlisted men had been trained as SeaBees at NCB. As was typical of such fa-cilities, both ABD and NCB began to be phased down after the war.

In Jan. 1946 ABD was designated as an annex of U.S. Naval Supply Depot, Newport, a facility on the Naval Base, while NCB continued on as its own entity. During the Korean War both facilities became active once more, but then phased down again after that war. In 1974, under the Navy's new base realignment program, both facilities were disestablished except for a residual activity that offered limited training and support to Naval Reserve SeaBee units. Most of the ABD's and NCB's land was acquired by the state or sold for industrial purposes.

U.S. NAVAL AIR STATION, QUONSET POINT was on the south end of the Quidnesset peninsula and built in 1940. From a rather humble beginning NAS, Quonset Point would evolve in the coming years into the largest naval air station on the east coast. This included absorbing, in the process, the assets of an old coastal defense post, Fort Dyer. Seaplanes began operating at the station within a few month and the first land planes and fleet aircraft in Dec. 1940. These aircraft took part in America's Neutrality Patrols of that year.

While the base was under construction naval officials approached civilian construction contractors and asked them to develop a prefabricated, knockdown hut, adaptable for easy shipment and fast re-assembly at distant locations. They offered the British Nissen Hut as a model. Within three months the new huts, christened Quonset Huts, were designed, tested, ap-

proved and put into production at the nearby Naval Construction Battalion Center at Davisville. The first Quonset Huts were shipped overseas in June 1941.

NAS, Quonset Point acquired an Assembly and Repair Department to service naval aircraft and a training school for Reserve officers. Throughout the war aircraft from NAS, Quonset Point participated in anti-submarine patrols, convoy escort, coastal patrols, air and sea rescue and other operational activities. NAS, quonset Point acquired two auxiliary air stations, one on Martha's Vineyard and the other at Charleston, RI. In Jan. 1943 the Commander, Air Fleet, Quonset was established at the station and had operational control over all naval aircraft from Argentia, Newfoundland to Cape May, NJ. Also during 1943 the station acquired a navigation school and a naval training school that prepared officers for administrative and technical positions. In Oct. 1944 the Commander, Naval Air Bases, 1st Naval District, Boston moved onto the station. This command controlled four naval stations, a Coast Guard station, 17 naval auxiliary air stations and several others facilities in northeastern part of the U.S.

The end of the war brought the expected readjustment and realignment at NAS, Quonset Point and activities declined. In 1947, however, the station became the first in the nation to receive operational naval jet aircraft. These planes later became the nucleus of the Navy's first jet carrier squadron. The station was still quite active and an important operational base when the Korean War erupted in 1950. Because of the high state of readiness and activity at NAS, Quonset Point the war had minimal effect on the station. NAS, Quonset Point remained an active base until 1974 when the Navy's Shore Base Realignment Program caused the station to begin a slow phase-down in preparation for eventual decommissioning. The station's physical assets where disposed of to local, state and federal agencies and to the public.

WESTERLY is in the SW corned of the state on the state line.

U.S. NAVAL AUXILIARY AIR STATION, WESTERLY was 2.5 miles SSE of Westerly. It was established by the Navy early in the war as an auxiliary air station to NAS, Quonset Point. NAAS, Westerly was an operational field and its aircraft participated in anti-submarine patrols, coastal patrols, convoy escort and other duties. After the was the station was decommissioned.

WOONSOCKET is 13 miles north of Providence near the state line. One of Woonsocket's largest defense plants was the U.S. Rubber Co. which built barrage balloons and inflatable boats and rafts.

WORLD WAR II MEMORIAL STATE PARK is located on Social St. in Woonsocket and honors Rhode Island citizens who served in WW II. It is the site of many events in the summer and an annual Autumnfest in the fall.

Quonset Huts in Alaska during the war. There are thousands of WW II Quonset Huts scattered throughout the country and still in use.

SOUTH CAROLINA

In the years before World War II the state of South Carolina was beset with many problems. It was primarily a rural state with an economy that was dependent upon agriculture, some mining and some textile-making. South Carolina was a "Deep South" state, rigidly segregated and subject to occasional hurricanes. It had little power in Washington, DC and was of little interest to industrialists. The boll weevil plague of the 1920s had caused havoc with the cotton crop and forced many farmers to switch to new and unfamiliar crops. Despite the boll weevil, however, cotton continued to be the state's second most abundant crop. On the positive side of the ledger the state was experiencing a trickle of new textile mills moving in from New England to be near the cheap cotton and cheap labor, and the New Deal Administration in Washington had blessed the state with several government-funded work projects. The state was also home to several long-standing military facilities and the military felt welcome in the state.

In the late 1930s, with the Depression began to ease and with war clouds brewing in both Europe and the Far East, the fortunes of the state began to improve, albeit slowly. South Carolina could offer the nation and the world tobacco (the state's leading cash crop), cotton, grain, forest products, meat, poultry, vegetables, fish, processed foods, textiles, clothing, furniture, stone, clay, chemicals and small amounts of gold. While other states were getting fat defense contracts to build ships, airplanes and tanks, South Carolina had to wait for the wartime prosperity to trickle down. While she waited a hurricane roared thru the state in Aug. 1940 causing considerable damage and killing more than three dozen people. In that year, though, one of the state's old friends, the U.S. Army, established two large training camps in South Carolina that helped the economy noticeably. One was at Columbia and other at Spartanburg. In the late summer of 1941 the U.S. Army conducted large-scale maneuvers in northern South Carolina and southern North Carolina. This tore up some of the state's real estate, but brought in lots of money. Some 400,000 men participated in the maneuvers which consisted of the "Blue Army" of North Carolina attacking the "Red Army" of South Carolina attempting to take the South Carolina town of Camden. The "Reds" had fewer men, but had two armored divisions. The "Blues" were able to knock out most of the "Red" Army's tanks and take Camden and win the contest. It was later said that these maneuvers were of great value to American forces in North Africa against the Rommel's Afrika Korps which was well equipped with tanks.

When the U.S. went to war the AAF built sevral new air fields in the state while the Navy, which had existing facilities in the Charleston and Beaufort areas, expanded its aviation holdings. Some new manufacturing firms moved into the state during the war and the Army dotted the South Carolina landscape with 20 prisoner of war camps.

In Washington, DC the state's senior senator, James F. Byrnes from Columbia, had risen to prominence and in 1940 was appointed to the Supreme Court. A year later Franklin Roosevelt called him to work in his administration as his special assistant to straighten out certain domestic matters. Byrnes was given a powerful new post as head of the Office of Economic Stability. He subsequently became one of Roosevelt's closest advisors and the press labelled him "the Assistant President". During his long years in Washington Byrnes had befriended a fellow senator from Missouri, Harry S Truman. When Truman became President of the United State in Apr. 1945 he selected Byrnes to be his Secretary of State and one of his closest confidants. Byrnes's influence was very strong in the Truman Administration during the closing months of the war and the early postwar era.

South Carolina's other senator, "Cotton Ed" Smith, was at the other end

The U.S. Army was desperately short of tanks during the maneuvers in North and South Carolina, so trucks were used as substitutes.

South Carolina's Jimmy Byrnes made the cover of Life magazine soon after this appointment as head of the Office of Economic Stability.

of the political spectrum. It was said of him that his main interest was to "keep the negroes down and the price of cotton up".

The state had yet another individual who went down in the history books of WW II. He was Robert H. Best of Sumter who defected to the Germans before the war and became one of their propaganda broadcasters under the name "Guess Who?" In 1944 Best pompously announced his candidacy for President of the United States.

When the war ended, most, but not all, of the state's military installations shut down, but most of the industrial firms stayed on. Soon, other industrial enterprises moved in and the state began to develop a solid industrial base. All in all, South Carolina emerged from WW II in much better shape than she was before the war.

AIKEN is 15 miles NE of Augusta, GA.

AIKEN ARMY AIR FIELD, 6.5 miles NE of town, was the area's local airport before the war. It was taken over by the AAF early in the war and used as a sub-base to Daniel Field in Georgia. The field had a branch prisoner of war camp holding about 300 POWs who worked in the local forests. After the war Aiken Field was returned to its pre-war owners.

BEAUFORT is in the southern part of the state near the coast.

RECRUIT DEPOT, MARINE BARRACKS, PARRIS ISLAND was one of the major Marine training camps of WW II. The Parris Island-Beaufort area has an excellent harbor and has long been an important seaport in both war and peace. As a result, the area has been fortified on and off for over 400 years. The Navy's presents in the area began during the Civil War when Federal troops captured the area and built a naval station near Beaufort called U.S. Naval Station, Port Royal. The station later became a coaling station, then a naval disciplinary barracks. The first marines arrived in 1891 to act as guards. At the beginning of WW I the Marine barracks here was enlarged and used to train Marine recruits. In 1915 the entire base was turned over to the Marines to be used for that purpose. At that time the facility was known as U.S. Marine Barracks, Port Royal. In 1919 MB, Port Royal had a brief period of expansion which included the addition of a "flying field" at which some of the first Marine pilots were trained. Soon after the expansion, the name of the base was changed to Recruit Depot, Marine Barracks, Parris Island because by then the post had taken over most of Parris Island. In the 1920s and 1930s the facility suffered cutbacks typical of other military bases, but continued to turned out new Marines. With the advent of troubles in Europe and the Far East, Marine training at RD,MB, Parris Island increased steadily after 1938 and in 1942 the base was turning out 6800 Marines a month. The station was again expanded and by the end of the war some 240,500 Marines, including Women Marines, had been trained here. During the war the base also acquired an elementary school for illiterate recruits and a school for drill instructors. In 1946 the name of the post was changed again to U.S. Marine Corps Recruit Depot, Parris Island. After WW II there were the typical cutbacks at MCRD, Parris Island, but when the Korean War erupted the base again trained large numbers of Marines. After that war the base continued in operation training Marines throughout the Cold War. In the 1960s and 1970s the base was modernized and most of the WW II structures torn down.

Marine Corps Recruit Depot Museum: This museum is located on the grounds of MCRD, Parris Island and interprets the military and civilian history of Parris Island from the beginning of European occupation to the present. The museum's main emphasis is on the Spanish era and the Spanish settlement of Santa Elena. There are, however, displays and artifacts from WW II including uniforms, small arms, maps, photographs, artillery pieces and ship models. Address: Marine Corps Recruiting Depot, Parris Island, SC 29905-5000. Phone: 803/525-2951. Hours: daily 10-4:30, closed Jan. 1, Thanksgiving and Dec. 25. Free.

U.S. NAVAL AIR STATION, BEAUFORT came into existence during the summer of 1942 when a commercial air field, which was under construction 7 miles north of Beaufort, was taken over by the Navy for use as an operational field for anti-submarine patrols. The commercial field was expanded and the station was ready of occupancy in the summer of 1943. But, by that time the submarine menace had passed so NAS, Beaufort was utilized as a training field where naval pilots were given advanced "shakedown" training. These pilots also carried out coastal and anti-submarine patrols. NAS, Beaufort had two outlying fields; Georgetown Airport, 1 mile NW of Georgetown, and Georgetown County Airport, 4 miles south of Georgetown. When the war ended the Navy turned the field over to local authorities and it became a county airport as it was intended to be before the war. In the mid 1950s the Marine Corps needed additional air facilities again and re-acquired the field. It was

first used as an auxiliary field for Marine Corps Air Station, Cherry Point but eventually became its one separate entity in 1960. It was then called U.S. Marine Corps Air Station, Beaufort and served throughout the Cold War.

CHARLESTON is centrally located on South Carolina's coast and was a very busy seaport during the war. Many coastal and trans-oceanic convoys utilized the port and some formed up here. On Mar. 12, 1942 the first of many U.S. convoys to India left from here. Throughout the war Charleston was the home port for a several hospital ships operating in Europe and the Mediterranean.

CHARLESTON ARMY AIR FIELD was 8 miles NNW of downtown Charleston in North Charleston. It was the area's pre-war airport and was taken over by the 1st AF in 1942 to become a training field for the crews of B-17 and B-24 bombers, fighter pilots and ground crews. Many of those trained here went on to be a part of the famous 8th Air Force. The air field had a main prisoner of war camp and the POWs worked primarily for the military. In 1944 the base was assigned to the AAF's Military Air Transport Service (MATS) and training shifted to that of pilots and crews in C-54 transports. Many of these people went on to the China-Burma-India theater to fly the "Hump". Charleston AAF also served as a terminus for MATS flights to and from Europe and the Near East. In 1944 Italian Service Units worked at the field. The air field was returned to civilian use after the war, but in 1953 it was reactivated by the US Air Force and became Charleston Air Force Base. It then functioned throughout the Cold War and was, for most of that time, an air transport and airlift facility.

CHARLESTON ARMY DEPOT was located three miles east of Charleston Army Air Field at the juncture of the Cooper River and Goose Creek. It was first established by the Army in 1916 as a mule remount station. During WW II it became Charleston Army Depot and worked closely with the Charleston Port of Embarkation as their storage and repair facility for Army-owned marine equipment and harbor craft. In Nov. 1945, when Charleston POE was deactivated, the depot received most of their marine equipment and small craft for storage. The depot was then made a sub-installation of the New York POE. The depot remained in operation throughout the Cold War and had several name changes. Most of that time it stored and serviced the Army's marine equip-

ment and small boats.

CHARLESTON PORT OF EMBARKATION was on the Charleston water front and was one of eight ports of embarkation established by the U.S. Army in 1942 to handle the shipment of Army and AAF personnel and supplies overseas. The POE had a branch prisoner of war camp with about 500 POWs who worked for the Army. The POE functioned throughout the war and was deactivated in Nov. 1945.

THE CITADEL is one of the nation's oldest and most honored state-run miliary schools. It is located just northwest of downtown Charleston on the Ashley River. During the war the Citadel went on an accelerated schedule and turned out as many graduates as possible. Most of them went directly into the armed forces upon graduation. After the war the school returned to its peacetime schedule and in 1954 Gen. Mark Clark became its president.

The Citadel Museum: This museum is on the grounds of the Citadel and traces the history of the school from it founding to the present. There are some displays and exhibits on the school's role in WW II. Address: 25 Elmwood Ave., Charleston, SC 29403. Phone: 800/868-3294 and 803/792-6846. Hours: Sun.-F 2-5, Sat. noon-5, closed holidays. Free. Each Friday afternoon during the school year there is a cadet dress parade at 3:45.

FORT MOULTRIE was located on the southern end of Sullivan's Island. Three Fort Moultries existed on the site beginning in 1674. The third Fort Moultrie, which survived until after WW II, was well-known in history as being the fort that fired the first shots of the American Civil War on nearby Fort Sumter which was controlled by Federal troops. The Fort Moultrie of WW II was quite different, however, from the Fort Moultrie of the Civil War because it had been modified and improved over the years. Nevertheless, it was manned and armed at the beginning of WW II and remained so throughout most of the war. In 1947, after 171 years of service, the fort was deactivated. In 1961 it was taken over by the National Park Service and became a historic site.

PATRIOTS POINT NAVAL & MARITIME MUSEUM is the world's largest naval and maritime museum and is located across the Cooper River from downtown Charleston. Six historic ships are at anchor at the museum and five of them are from WW II; the aircraft carrier "Yorktown", the destroyer "Laffey", the submarine "Clamagore" and the Coast Guard cut-

Fort Sumter as it appeared just before WW II.

ters "Comanche" and "Ingham". Also on display is the postwar nuclear-powered merchant ship "Savannah". All of the ships are open to the public and the battle records of the WW II ships are on display in each ship. A movie on the "Yorktown" is shown regularly in the ship's theater. Other items exhibited at the museum are landing craft, aircraft, missiles, rockets and rocket launchers, artillery pieces, field equipment, ordnance items, mines, small arms, uniforms, ship models, maps and photographs. Address: 40 Patriots Point Rd., Mt. Pleasant, SC 29465. Phone: 803/884-2727. Hours: Apr. thru Sept. daily 9-6, rest of year 9-5, closed Dec. 25. Admission charged.

STARK GENERAL HOSPITAL was located five miles NW of the city. It was a 2400-bed facility built in 1941 of temporary wooden construction to serve as a general hospital for the Army. Later, it also served as a debarkation hospital. Stark specialized in general and orthopedic surgery. There was a branch prisoner of war camp at Stark with about 250 Pows who worked at the hospital. In Oct. 1945 the facility was turned over to the Charleston County Board of Control.

FORT SUMTER, in Charleston Harbor, is one of the most famous old forts in America because it was here, on Apr. 12, 1961, that the American Civil War started. In the 1870s the fort was reconstructed and its walls cut to about half their original height. Consequently, the fort that survived until WW II was considerably different than the fort of Civil War days. By WW II all of the fort's guns were obsolete or had been removed, but the fort was used anyway as a subpost of Fort Moultrie. Ninety mm anti-aircraft guns were mounted in the fort as part of the air defenses for Charleston Harbor. This proved to be Fort Sumter's last hurrah. In 1948 it was disarmed and designated a National Monument. The fort has a small museum which concentrates on the fort's long history and displays some WW II items. Tours of Fort Sumter leave from Charleston City Marina at 17 Lockwood Blvd in Charleston and from Patriots Point Naval and Maritime Museum in Mount Pleasant. Inquire as to times, lengths of tours and costs.

U.S. NAVAL AMMUNITION DEPOT, CHARLESTON was located 10 mile north of downtown Charleston at the juncture of the Cooper River and Goose Creek across from the Charleston Army Depot. It was built in 1941-42 to replace a much smaller WW I-era depot on the east bank of the Cooper River. Throughout the war NAD, Charleston received, stored and supplied naval ammunition to ships at the naval ship yard and to other Navy ships in the Charleston area. After the war NAD, Charleston was placed in maintenance and later become a U.S. Naval Reservation.

U.S. NAVAL SHIPYARD, CHARLESTON was located on both banks of the Cooper River five miles north of downtown Charleston. The main portion of the yard was on the west back. As early as 1812 a small naval facility existed in the city but was eventually closed. In 1901, after years effort by the local citizens re reinterest the Navy in the site, the Federal Government agreed to accept an offer of land from the city of Charleston upon which to build a

Fort Jackson during the early part of WW II.

small naval yard. Additional land was acquired and a small naval yard was built over the next 7 years. The Charleston Naval Shipyard evolved into a important naval facility during WW I and remained active in the years between the wars. The naval yard remained small, however, by the standards of other yards and did mostly repair work, maintenance and fitting out of Navy ships. By the mid-1930s the yard started to get orders for new ships. When WW II started more orders flooded in for new ships and the yard underwent a major expansion. During WW II the Charleston Naval Yard built destroyers, destroyer escorts, destroyer tenders, Coast Guard cutters, several different types of landing craft, tugs, fast troop transports and derricks. All the while yard personnel continued to do repairs, maintenance and fitting out. Within the yard was one of several powerful radio stations in the country that listened to German submarine radio transmissions from the North Atlantic. In July 1943 the yard reached its peak employment of 25,948. With the end of the war the yard had the expected cutbacks and cancellations of orders, but soon the yard became involved in the decommissioning and storing of surplus ships. Six months after the war the yard still had 12,600 employees. In Nov. 1945 the Navy reorganized their facilities in the Charleston area and created a naval base with the naval yard becoming its major entity. The new U.S. Naval Base, Charleston had nine other entities including the soon-to-be-closed U.S. Naval Ammunition Depot. For several years after the war destroyer-sized vessel and smaller were decommissioned at the naval yard and mothballed at the yard and in the Wando River. The naval base, with its naval yard, remained operative throughout most of the Cold War but was closed in the 1990s.

COLUMBIA is near the center of the state and is the state capital.

JAMES F. BYRNES GRAVE SITE: South Carolina's former senator and wartime political figure, James F. Byrnes, is buried in the graveyard of Trinity Episcopal church at 1100 Sumter St., Columbia, SC.

COLUMBIA ARMY AIR BASE was 6 miles SW of downtown Columbia. It was established by the 1st AF early in the war for use as a training field for pilots and crews of B-25 and B-26 bombers. There was also a branch prisoner of war camp here with about 300 POWs who worked on the base. After the war the field was relinquished to the community and became the area's main airport. Four remote air fields served as auxiliaries to Columbia AAB during the war. They were:

- Barnwell Municipal Airport, 2 miles NW of Barnwell. This air field had a branch prisoner of war camp with about 250 POWs who worked in agriculture and the forests.
- Lexington County Airport, near Lexington
- North Municipal Airport, 1.5 miles SE of North
- John's Island Municipal Airport, 7 miles SW of Charleston

COLUMBIA MUNICIPAL AIRPORT was three miles SE of downtown Columbia and was the area's main airport before the war. It was used extensively by the 3rd AF as a training field for reconnaissance and observation pilots while still remaining a commercial field. It also served as an operational base serving Fort Jackson. The airport has two auxiliary fields, one each at Congaree and Walterboro. Walterboro Airport had a branch prisoner of war camp with 350 POWs who worked for the military. The Navy also used Columbia Municipal Airport at times during the war. After the war the military services departed and the field was returned to commercial use. In the postwar years it became known as Owens Field. Congaree Air Field became the permanent home of the South Carolina Air National Guard in 1946 and was later renamed McEntire Air National Guard Air Base.

FORT JACKSON is east of, and adjacent to, the city of Columbia. It was established in 1917 by the Army as a division-size training camp for WW I and known then as Camp Jackson. After that war it was turned over the South

Carolina National Guard. In 1940 the camp was federalized, named Fort Jackson and used initially as a reception center for the 4th Army Corps. Then it once again became a training camp for Army divisions. At various times during WW II nine divisions trained here totalling over half a million men. Divisions trained here included the 8th, 77th and 30th Infantry Divisions. Fort Jackson was a segregated camp and Negro troops also trained here. The fort had one of the state's two main prisoner of war camps holding about 1600 POWs who worked at the fort, in agriculture and in the forests. Every branch prisoner of war camp in the state was a sub-post of Fort Jackson's camp. In the latter part of the war the fort was used to train infantry replacements. During the Korean War Fort Jackson again became a training camp for Army divisions. The fort was retained by the Army and was active throughout the Cold War serving various Army commands.

Fort Jackson Museum: This museum is on the grounds of Fort Jackson and details the history of the fort from its beginning in 1917 to the present. Displays highlight the training of American soldiers. Address: ATZJ-PTM-P, Fort Jackson, SC 29207-5325. Phone: 803/751-7419/7355. Hours: Tues.-F 10-4, Sat.-Sun 1-4, closed federal holidays. Free.

FLORENCE is in the NE part of the state 70 miles east of Columbia.

FLORENCE FIELD was three miles ESE of Florence. It was used by both the AAF and the Navy during the war but was not taken over by either service. The 1st AF used it early in the war to train pilots and crews in troop carrier aircraft and light bombers. The 1st AF's facilities at the field were then transferred to the 3rd AF in 1943 and the field was used as a sub-base to Greenville AAB as an operational

field and in the training of AAF replacements. The Navy used the field as a refueling stop and as one of the fields in its air ferry system. Florence Field had a prisoner of war camp holding about 400 POWs who worked for the military. Florence Field had two auxiliary field during the war, Hartsville Airport, 2 miles NE of Hartsville and Darlington County Airport, 10 miles north of Darlington. After the war the military services departed from Florence Field and it became a civilian airport.

FLORENCE AIR AND MISSILE MUSEUM is located on U.S. 76/301 east of town at the entrance to Florence Field. On display are about 20 aircraft and missiles, most of which are postwar. WW II aircraft on display include a B-29, B-26 and a rare Navy BTD-1 torpedo bomber. Address: PO Box 1326, Florence, SC 29503. Phone: 803/665-5118. Hours: daily 9-6. Closed Jan. 1 and Dec. 25. Admission charged.

GEORGETOWN is 55 miles NE of Charleston near the coast.

HOBCAW BARONY was a 23,000-acre estate outside of Georgetown that belonged to Bernard Baruch, one of the most influential men in the Roosevelt Administration. The plantation house was 226 years old and had 21 rooms. During the month of May 1944 President Roosevelt came here for a quiet, unpublicized four-week vacation, the longest vacation he had had since becoming president in 1933. It was not only a vacation, but a rest cure. Roosevelt was experiencing the beginning stages of congestive heart failure and had been in poor health throughout most of the winter of 1943-44 suffering a bout of flu and a more serious bout of bronchitis that required his hospitalization at Bethesda Hospital in Maryland in Apr. 1944. He recovered from the bronchitis, but the doctors advised him to quit smoking. He didn't. At Hobcaw Barony he really did relax. He slept up to 12 hours a day, sunned himself, went fishing and crabbing in Winyah Bay, drove around the area and just sat on the porch. On one occasion he went deep sea fishing 15 miles off the coast with Coast Guard boats and Navy blimps on guard nearby. When he returned to Washington, DC he was tanned, rested, thinner, looked better and told reporters that he felt good. But, he really wasn't in good health. Within 11 months he was dead at the age of 63.

GREENVILLE is in the NW corner of the state.

GREENVILLE ARMY AIR BASE was located 7.5 miles south of Greenville and 1.25 miles SW of Conestee. It was established by the 3rd AF early in the

war as an operational base, a training base for the crews of medium bombers and for replacement AAF personnel. The base had three auxiliary field; Coronaca Air Field four miles north of Coronaca, Spartanburg Airport 2.5 miles SW of Spartanburg and Morris Field near Charlotte, NC. Coronaca Air Field had a branch prisoner of war camp with 230 POWs who worked in the forests. Greenville AAB survived for a number of years after the war as a US Air Force base and was part of the Tactical Air Command. It eventually was abandoned, though, by the military.

MYRTLE BEACH is a popular beach community on the northern coast of South Carolina along the beach area known as the "Grand Strand", a 60-mile-long stretch of flat sandy beaches. Such beaches were susceptible to enemy landings so the area was heavily patrolled by the Coast Guard both on and off shore.

MYRTLE BEACH ARMY AIR FIELD was three miles SE of town and was the community's pre-war airport. It was taken over in 1940 by the Army Air Corps to be a support base for several nearby bombing and gunnery ranges. The bombing and gunnery ranges were used by several training fields in South and North Carolina. In 1941, when the Army Air Corps became the Army Air Forces, this field was put under the command of the 3rd AF. Myrtle Beach AAF had a branch prisoner of war camp holding about 600 POWs who worked in the forests. In Nov. 1947 the air field was returned to the community and again became Myrtle Beach's primary air port.

ORANGEBURG is 40 miles south of Columbia just off I-26.

ORANGEBURG MUNICIPAL AIRPORT was five miles south of town and was one of the airports that was chosen by the Army Air Corps in 1940 to provide primary flight training for its pilots by civilian flying schools. When the AAF began training its own pilots the school, known as The Hawthorne School of Aeronautics, contracted with the French Government to train French military pilots. Programs with the French lasted well into 1945. Orangeburg Municipal Airport remained a civilian field throughout the war.

SPARTANBURG is in the NW corner of the state on I-26 and I-85.

CAMP CROFT was located six miles SE of Spartanburg and was built new for the Army in 1942. It was a training center for infantry replacements with a capacity of 15,000 troops. Camp Croft was a segregated came so negro troops also trained here. The camp had a branch prisoner of war camp with some 750 POWs who worked at the camp, in agriculture and in the forests. In Nov. 1945 the camp was declared surplus and eventually became a state park.

SUMTER is 40 miles east of Columbia.

SHAW FIELD was 6 miles west of Sumter on U.S. 76/378 and was the area's prewar airport. The field had a flying school which was contracted by the Army Air Crops in 1940 to give Air Corps cadets primary flight training. When the 30,000 Pilot Training Program came into being in 1941 Shaw was taken over by the 1st AF as a part that program. The field was expanded and

President Roosevelt back at his desk after his four-week vacation in South Carolina. Within 11 months he was dead.

specialized in providing basic flight training for AAF pilots for the rest of the war. Shaw Field had a branch prisoner of war camp that held about 400 POWs who worked on the base and in the forests. The field was retained after the war and became the home of several P-61 night-fighter squadrons. In 1948 the US Air Force took over the field and renamed it Shaw Air Force Base. In 1965 the base was modernized and most of the WW II buildings were torn

down. Shaw AFB operated throughout the Cold War and well into the post-Cold War era. During the war Shaw Field had the following auxiliary air fields:

- Aux. #1, Burnt Gin Airport, 1 miles SE of Wedgefield
- Aux. #2, Rembert Airport, 1.5 miles NW of Rembert
- Aux. #3, Monaghan Airport, 5 miles SW of Sumter
- Aux. #4, Sumter Municipal Airport, 2 miles

NW of Sumter

SOUTH CAROLINA NATIONAL GUARD MUSEUM is located in Sumter and honors the men and women who have served in the state's National Guard. The museum has exhibits from the Revolutionary War to the present. This is a large museum with over 500 pieces of military equipment and 8000 documents. WW II displays are numerous. Address: 395 North Pike West, Sumter, SC 29151-1028. Phone: 803/773-4151. Hours: M-F 8-4:30. Free.

SOUTH DAKOTA

The formal dedication ceremony of the Mt. Rushmore Monument was postponed in 1941 due to war conditions. It wasn't carried out until 50 years later when President George Bush officiated at the formal ceremony on July 4, 1991.

World War II proved to be a mixed blessing for South Dakota. Like the other high planes states South Dakota was in bad economic condition when the war started because of having suffered through the double disasters of the Great Depression and the Dust Bowl. In 1940 South Dakota's population was only 642,961 with 75.4% of her people listed as "rural". When the war-induced industrial buildup began in the late 1930s it was of little benefit to South Dakota. Markets did expand, though, for the state's food products which consisted primarily of grain, meat and dairy products. Her minerals also became important; mica, feldspar, bentonite and gold.

When war plants started up all over the country South Dakota became one of the few states in the nation to lose population as people left the state to take high-paying defense jobs elsewhere. The state also lost people to the armed services. Nevertheless, South Dakota's farmers were able to put about a million additional acres of land into grain production during the war. This was due, in part, to the fact that with prosperity the farmers were better able to afford mechanized farm machinery. There was a constant manpower shortage on the farms, though, and prisoners of war, so widely used in agriculture in other states, were of little help to South Dakota because the state had only two small prisoner of war camps.

In 1941 the mammoth artistic undertaking at Mount Rushmore in the Black Hills was completed and tourist began to flock to the state to

see the faces of the four presidents carved into the mountainside. This bit of good fortune, however, was cut short by gas and tire rationing and the end of auto production. Because of the war and the downturn in tourism, the formal dedication of the Mt. Rushmore Monument was postponed and then forgotten altogether ... until 50 years later. On July 4, 1991 President George Bush officiated at the belated formal dedication.

South Dakota received some perks due to the war, however. Several military installations were built in the state and what industry she had was kept busy with defense work. And, compared to the days of the Depression and the Dust Bowl, her citizens were relatively prosperous.

During the winter of 1944-45 the war came to South Dakota in the form of Japanese bombing balloons. Nine bombing balloons were recovered in the state during that time, but they did no damage.

One South Dakota citizen emerged from the war a famous person. He was Joe Foss, the Marine air ace who downed 27 Japanese planes, won the Congressional Medal of Honor, the Silver Star, the Bronze Star and the Purple

Heart. Foss returned to South Dakota after the war, entered politics and became the state's governor between 1955-1959. In 1959 he became nationally prominent as Commissioner of the American Football League. Another South Dakotan, George S. McGovern, was a B-24 pilot during the war and carried out 55 missions over Europe. McGovern became the state's Senator and later was nominated as the Democrat Party's candidate for president. During the war McGovern's plane was named the "Dakota Queen" and he won the Distinguished Flying Cross.

IGLOO/PROVO: These two small towns are in the extreme SW corner of the state two miles apart.

BLACK HILLS ORDNANCE DEPOT was built about three miles north of Igloo and Provo by the Federal Government in 1942 as an Army ammunition storage depot for large bombs and large calibre ammunition. Many Indians were employed in the construction and subsequent operation of the depot. The depot was intended, from its inception, to be a permanent Army installation after the war. The depot was a huge place and the Government built a small town on the depot's grounds consisting of houses, apartments, dormitories, schools, commissaries, utilities, a theater and a hospital to provide for the workers because of the almost total lack of such facilities in the area. An air field was also built. There was a constant labor shortage at the depot which was eased

This is one of the WW II-era buildings in use at the former Pierre Army Air Field.

The South Dakota National Guard Museum in Pierre, SD.

somewhat in 1943 with the arrival of an Italian Service Unit comprised of former prisoners of war. At the end of the war the Army sent tons of unused ammunition here for storage along with some of its large coastal defense guns and railroad guns. Black Hills Ordnance Depot was, indeed, permanent and continued in operation throughout the Cold War. For many of those years it was one of the state's largest employers.

PIERRE is in the center of the state and is the state's capital.

PIERRE ARMY AIR FIELD was located three miles east of town and had been the city's main airport before the war. It was taken over in 1942 by the 2nd AF to become an auxiliary air field to Rapid City Army Air Base. The air field was used to train bomber pilots and crews in B-17s and other aircraft. In Sept. 1943 Pierre AAF was detached from Rapid City AAB and became its own entity. Its training program then changed and it began a gunnery school where air crews received their final gunnery training before being sent overseas. This activity lasted until June 1945 when the air field was de-activated and returned to its civilian owners. It then became Pierre's

This is General Eisenhower's personal B-25 bomber that he used in Europe during the war. It is on permanent display at the South Dakota Air & Space Museum.

main airport once again.

SOUTH DAKOTA NATIONAL GUARD MUSEUM is located near downtown Pierre and traces the history of the state's National Guard. Displays cover time periods from the state's territorial days to the present. The museum's WW II display is sizeable. Address: 303 E. Dakota Ave., Pierre, SD 57501. Phone: 605-224-9991. Hours: M, W, and F 1-5. Free.

RAPID CITY is in the SW part of the state on I-90.

CAMP RAPID was located one mile north of downtown Rapid City on old U.S. 14. It was established in the mid-1920s as the home of South Dakota's National Guard. The Army leased the camp early in the war and used it to train National Guard troops and other Army personnel. In July 1942 it was taken over by the AAF which utilized the camp until Nov. 1943. Camp Rapid was then returned to the state and eventually closed. A new National Guard camp was established west of town on Main St.

RAPID CITY ARMY AIR BASE was located nine miles NE of town. It was built in 1942 for the 3rd AF to be used as a training base for pilots and crews of heavy bombers. The base's first commander was Charles B. "Barney" Oldfield, the famous race driver. Here, B-17s crews received their final training before being sent overseas. Rapid City AAB had two auxiliary field, one each in Pierre, SD and Ainsworth, NE. In 1944 training emphasis shifted to that of the replacement training of B-17 crewmen. During the summer of 1945 training emphasis shifted again to the training of pilots and crews of B-29s. During the war nine different bomber groups trained here. In late 1945 a variety of air units used the base flying P-61s, P-51s, P-38s and B-25s. Rapid City AAB was retained after the war by the AAF, renamed Rapid City Air Base in Sept. 1946 and became an operational base for B-29s. This lasted until 1949 when the new B-36 bombers began replacing the B-29s. When the US Air Force took over the field in 1947 the base was renamed Weaver Air Force Base. This name was not popular so the name was changed to Rapid City Air Force Base. In 1953 the name was changed again to Ellsworth Air Force Base in honor of General Richard E. Ellsworth, a veteran pilot of WW II, who died in an air crash in 1953. Ellsworth was credited with having flown some 400 missions during the war in the China-Burma-India theater. The base operated throughout the Cold War.

South Dakota Air & Space Museum: This museum is adjacent to Ellsworth Air Force Base and relates the history of air and space activities in South Dakota and of Ellsworth AFB. Many artifacts and aircraft are on display including several WW II aircraft. They include a B-29, B-26, C-47, BT-13 and General Dwight Eisenhower's personal B-25 bomber that he used in Europe during the war. The museum has its own restoration facility and it can be toured by visitors. Address: P.O. Box 871, Box Elder, SD 57719. Phone: 605/385-5188. Hours: Mid-May through mid-Sept., daily 8:30-6, rest of year 8:30-4. Closed Jan. 1, Easter, Thanksgiving and Dec. 25. The museum is free, but there is a charge for the base tours.

SIOUX FALLS is in the SE corner of the state on I-29 and I-90.

Many concrete foundations of WW II buildings still exist at the former Sioux Falls Army Air Field. Here, several of them are being used as parking pads for truck trailers.

The Battleship USS South Dakota in Sioux Falls, SD.

SIOUX FALLS ARMY AIR FIELD was located three miles north of town. It was built in 1942 for the 2nd AF as one of eight technical training air fields built during that period. Watertown Field, two miles NW of Watertown, was an auxiliary field. The base had limited air facilities and maintained an average of only 40 aircraft at the field for training purposes. Sioux Falls AAF specialized in the training of radio operator and radio maintenance personnel. AAF radiomen had a secondary mission aboard combat aircraft as gunners, so when the trainees finished their courses here they went to a gunnery school elsewhere in the country. In the summer of 1945 the base served as a redeployment center for men returning from Europe. After the war the field was turned over to the community and it became the city's primary airport and an industrial park. Later it was named Joe Foss Field in honor of South Dakota's famous WW II ace and governor. A plaque honoring Joe Foss is displayed in the airport terminal.

BATTLESHIP "USS SOUTH DAKOTA" MEMORIAL is located ½ mile east of I-29's exit 79 on W. 12th St. This is a park dedicated to the memory of the battleship "USS South Dakota" which saw lots of action during WW II and was one of the war's most decorated ships. The ship is represented by a full-scale outline of its deck area by a low concrete wall. There are simulated gun turrets and a small forecastle which is a museum. In the museum are artifacts from the ship, a scale model, uniforms, flags and other related naval items. The museum also has a small gift shop. A plaque tells of the ship's WW II battles beginning in Oct. 1942 off Santa Cruz and ending with the Japanese surrender in Tokyo Bay. Address: 805 South Kiwanis, Sioux Falls, SD 57104. Phone: 605/339-7059/7060. Hours: Memorial Day weekend through Labor Day daily 10-5. Open by appointment the rest of the year. Free.

STURGIS is in west-central South Dakota on I-90.

FORT MEADE is located 4.5 miles east of town on SR 34. It was an old frontier fort established by the Army in 1878. When WW II started, Fort Meade was the home to the Army's 4th Cavalry. Since Cavalry units were of little value in modern warfare the unit was disbanded in Apr.

1942 and the fort turned into a training camp for a variety of Army units. Crews of M-5 light tanks were trained here, WACs were trained here as truck drivers and near the end of the war a special unit of glider troops trained here

with a special mission to rescue German scientists before the Soviets could get them. Fort Meade had one of the state's two prisoner of war camps holding both German and Italian POWs. The POWs worked in agriculture and on the post. The POWs covered some of the fort's wooden buildings with a stone facade and most of those buildings survived well into the postwar era. In 1944 Fort Meade was turned over to the Veterans Administration who used the old brick and stone buildings as a hospital. Part of the fort was also acquired by the South Dakota National Guard. This arrangement continue for several decades after the war. Fort Meade eventually became a National Historic Site.

Fort Meade Cavalry Museum: This museum is in one of the beautiful old brick buildings at Fort Meade. It interprets the history of the fort from its beginning in 1878 to the present. Most of the displays are devoted to the early days of the fort, but there are exhibits on the fort's role during WW II. Address: Box 134, Ft. Meade, SD 57741. Phone: 605-347-9822. Hours: Memorial Day weekend through Labor Day daily 8-7, rest of year by appointment. Admission charged.

During WW II these were temporary buildings made of all-wood construction. Prisoners of war covered them over with stone and they survive in good condition for many years.

Fort Meade Cavalry Museum is on the grounds of Fort Meade in this beautiful old brick building.

TENNESSEE

The state of Tennessee, like the other states in the Union, suffered the ill effects of the Great Depression and the surge of industrial and military activities in the late 1930s and early 1940s was a welcome stimulus to the economy. The state was a producer of grain, cotton, tobacco, livestock, forest products, coal, phosphate, manganese ore, zinc, ferro-alloys, limestone, chemicals, footwear, rayon, hosiery and allied products. All of these products became important during the war and demand for them grew steadily. During the war the state also began to produce air planes and landing craft. Tennessee had one other important asset to offer the nation at this time ... cheap electricity. This was due to the development of the Tennessee Valley Authority (TVA) program of the 1930s that dammed the Tennessee and other Rivers in many places, created power-generating stations, hugh lakes and, in general, tamed the river. By 1940 the TVA was capable of generating more electricity than any other power system in the country. Cheap and abundant electricity and water were a necessity in the development of the atomic bomb so the state attracted one of the three main facilities established by the "Manhattan Project" in its quest for atomic weapons. That facility eventually became the community of Oak Ridge, TN. The TVA's energy also attracted other new industrial facilities, but not as much as one might expect. Tennessee's industrial surge came after the war in the 1950s-60s.

Various locations in the TVA system, including a huge new aluminum plant near Knoxville, were targets on the hit list of the eight German saboteurs who landed by submarine in Florida and New York in June 1942. The saboteurs, however, were caught before they could carry out their missions.

Tennessee had its share of prisoner of war camps which totalled 10, including one of the largest in the country. In Washington, DC, Cordell Hull, from Pickett County Tennessee, served at Secretary of State throughout most of the war and was a very influential member of the Roosevelt Administration. Jesse Jones, from Robinson County, TN also served in Roosevelt's Cabinet as Secretary of Commerce. In Congress, the state had two young men who would go to become politically prominent in the post-war years; Estes Kefauver and Albert Gore.

BYRDSTOWN is in north-central Tennessee east of Dale Hollow Lake.

CORDELL HULL BIRTHPLACE MUSEUM, off SR 325, 1.5 miles west of SR 42/111, displays artifacts and memorabilia of Cordell Hull, Secretary of State from 1933 to 1944. Hull was born nearby in a log cabin and a replica of that cabin is on display at the museum. On Dec. 7, 1941, it was Cordell Hull who received the Japanese declaration of war on the United States from the Japanese ambassador and special envoy. Hull was instrumental in the creation of the United Nations and won a Nobel Prize in 1945 for his efforts in that respect. The Nobel metal is on display in the museum. Address: Byrdstown, TN 38549. Phone: 615-864-3247.

Hours: Thurs.-M 9-5. Free.

CHATTANOOGA is on the southern edge of the state on the Tennessee River and the Georgia state line. Some of the major war plants in the area were: the Chattanooga Implement & Mfg. Co. which made 60 mm shells; the Wheland Co. which made 90 mm guns, gun parts and 75 mm shells; and the Columbian Iron Works that made 105 mm high explosive shells.

NATIONAL MEDAL OF HONOR MUSEUM is located in downtown Chattanooga and honors those individuals who have won the nation's highest award for valor. The placing of this museum in Chattanooga is most appropriate because the nation's first recipient of the award is buried in nearby Chattanooga National Cemetery. All of the Medal of Honor winners of WW II are mentioned in the museum. Address: 400 Georgia St., Chattanooga, TN 37302. Phone: 423/267-1737. Hours: M-Sat. 9-4:40, closed Jan. 1, Thanksgiving and Dec. 25. Donations requested.

VOLUNTEER ORDNANCE WORKS was built nine mile east of downtown Chattanooga in 1941 by the Federal Government to make the explosives TNT, DNT and oleum. The plant was run by the Hercules Powder Co. Near the end of the war the plant was converted to manufacture large calibre artillery shells. Volunteer Ordnance Works remained in operation long into the post war era and eventually became a military reservation.

CLARKSVILLE is 35 miles NW of Nashville near the Kentucky state line. It is one of the two post towns for Fort Campbell. For details on Ft. Campbell see Hopkinsville, KY.

CROSSVILLE is 60 miles west of Knoxville on I-40.

CROSSVILLE PRISONER OF WAR CAMP was located in a former CCC camp on the south edge of town at the intersection of Taylor's Chapel Rd. and Pomona Rd. The Crossville camp was a main POW camp holding about 1700 POWs, both German and Italian, who had been identified as troublemakers. The town of Crossville was chosen because of its remote location and the surrounding area which was very hilly and heavily forested. These things discouraged escapes. The Germans proved to be more of a problem than the Italians and the two groups were separated from the beginning. Among the Italians prisoners were several generals. When Italy surrendered and changed sides the Italians were removed from the camp to prevent friction between them and the Germans. The camp functioned until late 1945 and then was closed. In the 1950s it became a 4-H camp. Some of the old WW II buildings remained in daily use and a one-room museum exists at the camp preserved some of the POW camp's artifacts. Locally, the camp has long been known as "The Jap Camp" despite the fact that Japanese prisoners were never held here.

DYERSBURG is 60 miles NNE of Memphis on I-155.

DYERSBURG ARMY AIR FIELD was located 11 miles south of Dyersburg just NW of the small community of Halls. It was established early in the war to be a base of operation for the short-lived I Concentration Command. When this command was reorganized the field was transferred to the 3rd AF to be used as a training field for pilots and crews of heavy bombers. After the war the field was abandoned by the AAF.

KINGSPORT is in the NE corner of the state near the state line.

HOLSTON ORDNANCE WORKS was built by the Federal Government in 1943 just west of, and adjacent to, the town of Kingsport. It was run by the Eastman Defense Corp. and it's mission

These are items on display in the one-room museum of the old Crossville Prisoner of War Camp. On the table in the foreground is a scale model of the POW camp. Against the wall are two grave markers of POWs who died and were buried nearby. After the war their bodies were exhumed and returned to Germany and their grave markers were left behind.

was to produce the super-explosive RDX by a newly developed production method. RDX was used in depth charges and "Block Buster" bombs. This was a huge plant that was designed to replace several other plants in the country making RDX by an older and more expensive method. Holston functioned throughout the remainder of the war and into the postwar years. It operated, on and off, throughout the Cold War and retained its original name.

MEMPHIS is in the extreme SW corner of the state on the Mississippi River. Major war plants in the area were the McDonnell Aircraft Corp. which made AT-15 trainer planes, Pidgeon-Thomas Iron Co. which made landing craft and Caine Steel Co. which made 75 mm shells and track link forgings.

CHICKASAW ORDNANCE WORKS was located at Millington, a northern suburb of Memphis. The plant was built in 1940-41 by Du Pont de Nemours & Co. under contract from the British Government to produce smokeless gun powder for the British armed forces. After Lend Lease came into being the plant was taken over by the U.S. Government, but still produced for the British. The plant also produced TNT and DNT.

KENNEDY GENERAL HOSPITAL was a large two-story semi-permanent Army hospital located in Memphis. It was built in 1942-43 to care for war wounded. It had 4387 beds and specialized in neurology, general and orthopedic surgery, thoracic surgery, neurosurgery and psychiatry. The Army operated Kennedy until June 1946 at which time it was turned over to the Veterans Administration.

MEMPHIS ARMY AIR FIELD was the area's pre-war airport, Memphis Municipal Airport, and was located 7 miles SE of downtown Memphis. It was taken over by the AAF's Air Transport Command in 1942 and used as an operational field in the Army's air transport system. During the war the field was enlarged and the runways lengthened. The field had an air freight terminal and a Flight Service Center. After the war the air field was returned to its civilian owners and eventually became Memphis International Airport.

MEMPHIS SERVICE FORCES DEPOT was built in 1942 on Airways Blvd. about three miles SE of downtown Memphis to serve as a general depot for the non-combat commands of the Army. It received, stored and shipped a wide variety of items for the Army's Quartermaster, Engineer, Chemical and Medical Corps. The depot had a main prisoner of war camp holding about 1600 POWs who worked at the depot. The depot was retained by the Army after the war and in the postwar years was renamed Memphis Army Depot and then Defense Depot, Memphis.

MUD ISLAND is just off downtown Memphis in the Mississippi River. At the southern end of the island is a 52-acre park which has many attractions related to the Mississippi River and the history of the area. Also in the park is a pavilion in which the famous B-17 bomber "Memphis Belle" is on permanent display. This plane flew 25 missions over Europe early in the war at a time when only two out of three planes and crews survived trying to reach that

The Memphis Belle, a 25-mission B-17 bomber of WW II, in its permanent home at Mud Island, Memphis, TN.

goal. After accomplishing their 25 missions, the "Memphis Belle" and her crew returned to the U.S. in 1943 and made a nation-wide public relations tour selling war bonds. At that time a movie of the plane's exploits was made and shown throughout the nation. After the tour, the bomber was used for training in Florida and when the war ended it was scheduled to be scraped. A group of private individuals, who recognized the plane's historical significance, saved her from the scrap heap and she became an outdoor display in front of the National Guard Armory in Memphis. In the late 1980s the plane was restored to flying condition and made another nation-wide tour in 1990-91. And, the 1943 movie was updated and shown again. The film is shown also in the "Memphis Belle's" pavilion twice daily. Address: 125 N. Front St., Memphis, TN 38103. Phone: 901/576-7203. Hours: park grounds Memorial Day weekend thru Labor Day daily 10-5, rest of year Tues.-Sun. 10-5. Admission charged.

U.S. NAVAL AIR STATION, MEMPHIS was located one mile east of Millington, TN a northern suburb of Memphis. The site was first utilized during WW I when the War Department leased the land and assigned it to the Army's Signal Corps to be used as a training field for pilots and aircraft mechanics. It was known then as Park Field. After WW I the Army purchased the land and used it as a storage facility of surplus WW I aircraft. Parts of the field were leased to civilian and government agencies which kept the field fairly active in the years between the wars. In 1939 the Navy acquired the field and converted it into one of three new Naval Reserve Aviation Bases (NRAB) for the training of Naval Reserve pilots. Later, regular Navy pilots began to be trained here, and in Sept. 1943 the facility became a commissioned naval air station and was given its wartime name. A week later a large naval aircraft maintenance school began to move in, grew rapidly and came to dominate the air station. Eventually the maintenance school became one of the largest in the country. A short time later the Naval Air Mobile Training Group was established here and consisted of groups of instructors who travelled from air station to air station giving maintenance instructions to resident mechanics on the new types of aircraft coming out. When the war

ended, NAS, Memphis was designated as a permanent air station. The maintenance school was scaled down, but remained in operation and the training of Navy and Marine Reserve pilots resumed. The station expanded, which was very unusual in the early postwar era, and became the headquarters of the Naval Air Technical Training Center (NATTC). This acted as a magnet and within a few years there were 24 different technical schools at the station. NAS. Memphis became one of the Navy's largest and most important training facilities in the postwar era and was referred to as the "Enlisted Man's Annapolis of the Air". The station was operational throughout the Cold War and, for many years, was the largest inland naval station in the world.

U.S. NAVAL HOSPITAL, MEMPHIS was located three miles east of Millington just beyond the naval air station. This was a small general hospital of 100 bed built in 1943 which served the naval personnel of the Memphis area. The hospital was independent of the naval air station. After the war it was made a permanent naval facility and enlarged to 330 beds. NH, Memphis continued in operation throughout the Cold War.

MILAN is 75 miles NE of Memphis.

WOLF CREEK ORDNANCE PLANT AND WOLF CREEK AMMUNITION DEPOT: These were two large ordnance facilities built side-by-side three miles east of Milan. The ordnance plant came first being built in 1941-42 as a shell loading plant for the Army and was run by the Procter & Gamble Defense Corp. The plant loaded 20 mm shells, 60 mm mortar shells, 155 mm fuzes and boosters. Before the plant was finished, construction on the depot began. The mission of the depot was to receive the items produced at the ordnance plant, store them and ship them as required. They both functioned until the war ended and in Nov. 1945 were closed and placed on standby status. When the Korean War started they were eventually utilized again. The two facilities were eventually merged and became known as the Memphis Army Depot and later the Milan Army Ammunition Plant. The facility operated at varying degrees of capacity throughout the Cold War.

NASHVILLE is near the center of the state and is the capital of Tennessee. Major war plants

Women workers at the Consolidated-Vultee Aircraft Corp. assembling aircraft engines.

in the Nashville area were the Consolidated-Vultee Aircraft Corp. which made BT-13 Valiant basic trainers and Vengeance dive bombers for the Navy, Allen Mfg. Co. which made aircraft components and 100 lb bombs and the So Ling Hosiery Mills, Inc. which made aircraft parts and sub-assemblies.

NASHVILLE METROPOLITAN AIRPORT (BERRY FIELD), 6 miles SE of downtown Nashville, was brand new in 1937. During the war both the AAF and the Navy used the field, but neither took it over and it continued to serve as a commercial air field. The AAF used the airport to train pilots and crews of the Ferry Command and the Air Transport Command (ATC) used it as one of the air fields in its military air system. The ATC also operated an air freight terminal here. The Naval Air Ferry Command used the airport as one of the fields in its air ferrying system.

SMYRNA ARMY AIR BASE was one mile north of Smyrna, a SE suburb of Nashville. This was a pre-war civilian air field that was taken over by the AAF early in 1942 for use as a combat-ready operational field for AAF squadrons. The need for an operational field so far inland soon passed and the field was converted to a training field for pilots and crews of four-engine bombers, primarily B-24s. Flight instructors were also trained here. The field had two auxiliary field, Campbell Army Air field, near Clarksville and William Northern Field 2.5 miles NW of Tullahoma. After the war the AAF departed and the field was returned to its civilian use and became Smyrna Airport.

THAYER GENERAL HOSPITAL was a 1867-bed Army general hospital built in Nashville in 1943 to care for war wounded. It specialized in general and orthopedic surgery. In Dec. 1945 Thayer was transferred to the Veterans Administration.

OAK RIDGE was a non-city during the war. It wasn't on the maps, most people never heard of it, it wasn't mentioned in the newspapers. But

yet, it existed and was one of the most important communities in the nation.

When the scientists and engineers of the top-secret "Manhattan (Atomic bomb) Project" got underway in 1941 with the mission to build an atomic bomb it was clear that one or more huge and very specialized industrial complexes would be required to produce the ingredients needed for such a weapon. From the scientific knowledge of the day it was known that the extremely rare natural element uranium, a heavy metal, was the most likely element in which a fission reaction (actual splitting of the uranium atoms) might be accomplished by mechanical means. By splitting an atom an exceptionally large amount of energy is released that would be capable of splitting adjacent atoms and thus causing a chain reaction and a tremendous explosion from a relatively small amount of material. Unfortunately, there are two types of uranium mixed together in uranium ore, U-235 and U-238. U-235 is the more fissionable material and only a small percent of the total mix. U-235 cannot be separated from U-238 chemically so it had to be separated mechanically. It was also known that there was another element in the uranium mix, plutonium-239. This element, which had only been discovered in 1940, was present in very

very small amounts, but it too was believed to be fissionable. More importantly, additional plutonium-239 could be *manufactured* by bombarding U-238 with neutrons in a reactor. Then, Plutonium-239 could be easily separated from the mix by chemical means. Therefore, in searching for an extremely powerful weapon of war it was imperative that both uranium U-235 and plutonium-239 be investigated at the same time for their use in weapons.

There were several ways to mechanically separate U-235 from U-238, but it was not know which way was best. Because of the national emergency the two most promising ways, gaseous diffusion and electromagnetic separation, had to be utilized simultaneously on a large scale. There was no time to build pilot plants. The scientists, and the nation, had to gamble major stakes on what limited knowledge existed. Therefore, two huge separation plants, a reactor to make plutonium and several support facilities had to build somewhere in the country and fast. It was decided that a small reactor would be built first and then a much larger one later, along with a chemical separation plant, in order to produce the significant amounts of plutonium needed to make an atomic weapon. Each of the separation plants and the reactor facility would require their own very specialized equipment which would be massive in size. They would consume large amounts of electric power, generate tremendous amount of heat and require lots of water to deep the equipment from overheating. It was a learn-as-you-go process and there was also a need for absolute secrecy. Hovering over the entire program was the possibility, although remote, that something terrible could go wrong resulting in a pre-mature atomic explosion and/or the release of a deadly cloud of radioactive gas that could devastate a wide area of land and kill or severely injure every living thing in its path. All of these factors pointed to the need for a very large industrial facility that was spread out over a large area where there was a sparse population, a good transportation system and plenty of electric

This is one of the two separation plants at Oak Ridge, TN built in 1942. This plant separated U-235 from the mix of U-235, U-238 and plutonium-239 by the gaseous diffusion method.

The American Museum of Science and Energy, Oak Ridge, TN.

power and water. Tennessee's TVA system offered such areas. After an intensive search the managers of the "Manhattan Project" selected the Bethel Valley in eastern Tennessee 18 miles west of Knoxville. Once selected, the area soon became known to the developers as "Dog Patch" after the mythical hillbilly community in the popular comic strip of the day called "L'il Abner". Land was acquired and during Oct. 1942 the large industrial complex began to rise. Each major facility was located a considerable distance from the other and the overall complex was called Clinton Laboratories after the largest community in the area, Clinton, TN, population 1540. Utilities were brought in, roads and rail lines built and a new and sizeable city built for the workers. When construction was well underway the "Manhattan Project" managers began to question the wisdom of building the large plutonium-producing reactor in this location for safety reasons. It was thus decided to built the big reactor and the chemical separation plant elsewhere. Eventually a site near Richland, WA was selected. Clinton Laboratories then would produce U-235 from their two separation plants and small amounts of plutonium, while Richland, WA would produce larger amounts of plutonium. The products from both locations would be sent to the "wizard's workshop" in Los Alamos, NM where the scientists and engineers would try to make a bomb … or possibly two bombs, one using uranium-235 and one using plutonium. The target date for one or both bombs was late 1944-early 1945.

When the Tennessee complex was completed and the processes got underway, Oak Ridge National Laboratories as it was now called, began to produce as expected. By the end of 1943 useable amounts of U-235 were on their way to Los Alamos as were the first gram-sized quantities of plutonium. By Sept. 1944 Oak Ridge was producing kilogram-lots of U-235 and by July 1945 the scientists at Los Alamos had 50 Kg of enriched uranium-235 which was enough to proceed with the manufacture of several uranium-type atomic bombs even if the plutonium-type bomb failed to materialize. In that month the scientists proved that a plutonium-type bomb could be produced when they successfully detonating the first plu-

tonium device in the New Mexico desert. At that point the U.S. had two types of atomic bombs with which to attack their enemy, and both types were eventually used. The Hiroshima bomb was a uranium bomb and the Nagasaki bomb was a plutonium bomb.

At the end of the war the significance of Oak Ridge, now a city of 75,000 people, was revealed to the public. The complex remained off limits to the public, though, until 1949. At that time it was opened to visitors and incorporated as the city of Oak Ridge, TN. Oak Ridge National Laboratory continued in operation in the post war years producing U-235, plutonium and other related products for military and civilian uses.

Oak Ridge can be toured easily by car and there are a number of well-marked overlooks where visitors can park and view the historic plants mentioned above.

American Museum of Science and Energy: This is a large and excellent museum in Oak Ridge that has many exhibits on the history of Oak Ridge and its on-going contribution to peaceful uses of atomic energy. The founding of Oak Ridge during WW II is told in a permanent exhibit entitled "Oak Ridge Story" on the first floor of the museum. There is a replica of "Little Boy", the uranium bomb, dropped on Hiroshima. Other exhibits tell of the operation of the various facilities at Oak Ridge, the development of various energy sources through the ages and the fundamentals as to how energy is generated from atomic power. The museum also has an energy science lab and offers live demonstrations. Address: 300 S. Tulane, Oak Ridge, TN 37830. Phone: 423/482-7821. Hours: June thru Aug. daily 9-6, rest of year daily 9-5. Closed Jan. 1, Thanksgiving and Dec. 25. Free.

Graphite Reactor: This is the world's oldest nuclear reactor and the first reactor to operate at full power. It was built during WW II and remained in operation until 1963. It is now a National Historic Landmark and open to the public. Phone: 423/574-4160. Hours: M-Sat. 9-4. Free.

PARIS is a county seat in the NW corner of the state.

CAMP TYSON was built in 1942 five miles SW of Paris on U.S. 79. It was an Army training camps for barrage balloon crews and performed this function throughout the war. The training school had been located at Camp Davis, NC at the beginning of the war but was moved to this location. After the war Camp Tyson was closed.

TULLAHOMA is 60 miles SE of Nashville 10 miles SW of I-24.

CAMP FORREST, two miles SE of Tullahoma, was built in 1926 as a training camp for the Tennessee National Guard. In Jan. 1941 the camp was taken over by the Army to be used as a training camp for division-sized units. First, however, it served as a reception center. Then the 33rd Infantry Division, comprised mostly of the Illinois National Guard, moved in for training. Camp Forrest was a segregated camp and negro troops were also trained here. In June 1942 a prisoner of war compound was built and Camp Forrest became host to 36 Japanese prisoners of war. Later 50 more Japanese POWs arrived after the Americans recaptured Wake Island. Also, that summer Japanese aliens from Hawaii were brought to the camp by way of Camp McCoy, WI. In Nov. 1942, after the Allies had invaded North Africa, German POWs began to arrive at the camp. The influx continued until the camp became one of the largest POWs camps in the country. The POW population eventually reached 19,000 at which time the camp was devoted entirely to the incarceration of POWs. In early 1945 Italian Service Units arrived to work at the camp and during the summer of 1945 the German POWs began to be repatriated. Eventually all of the POWs departed and the Army deactivated the camp in June 1946. It then reverted back to the state of Tennessee, but in the early 1950s the US Air Force acquired the camp and established Arnold Air Force Base, named in honor of General Henry "Hap" Arnold who commanded the AAF during WW II. The AFB became the home of Arnold Engineering Development Center (AEDC), one of the Air Forces's major research and development facilities. AEDC functioned throughout the Cold War and worked close with NASA, the Department of Defense, other government agencies and civilian educational.

Camp Forrest Prisoner of War Hospital #2: This was the former station hospital of Camp Forrest. Early in the war it was designated as one of the few Army hospitals in the country to receive and treat Japanese POWs. When German prisoners of war began arriving at Camp Forrest in large numbers the hospital was converted to one of two hospitals in the country devoted exclusively to the treatment of POWs. The other hospital was in Okmulgee, OK. As the POWs patient load dwindled the hospital reverted, in Dec. 1945, to its previous status as post hospital. When Arnold Air Force Base was established in the early 1950s the hospital became a part of that facility.

TEXAS

The state of Texas made a larger contribution to the war effort than did some of the Allied nations. This state, the largest state in the union at the time, provided a wide variety of weapons, ships, food and minerals, including one of the most precious minerals of war ... oil. The state was also a producer of livestock, poultry, grain, cotton, cottonseed oil, peanuts, fruit, non-ferrous metal products, refinery products, oil field machinery, sulphur, helium and iron ore.

In the years just before the war Texas was better off than most states. Her economy had been battered by the Great Depression and two years of drought in 1938 and 1939, but the state enjoyed a steady income from the sale of oil and gas products. In 1939 several large manufactured moved into the state to produce foundry products, clothing, processed food, meat packing and chemicals. Also that year three large power dams were completed on the Colorado River and the state became a producer of cheap and abundant electrical power. By 1940 the economy in some parts of Texas was good, but in others it was still struggling. Also, the shipyards in the Houston area received orders from the Federal Government for 12 new destroyers and the Houston area began to feel the effects of an economic boom. In addition, the armed forces, in 1940 and 1941, began to build new military facilities in the state and enlarge existing ones. During the summer of 1941 the Army carried out large-scale maneuvers in southeastern Texas that also extended across Louisiana and into Mississippi. As the war progressed the state would have the dubious honor of seeing more of its young men and women enlist in the armed services than any other state. This became a contributing factor to the state's growing labor shortage which was relieved, in part, by the importation of laborers from Mexico. Beginning in late 1942 the labor shortage was eased further by the arrival of large numbers of prisoners of war. Eventually Texas had 120 prisoner of war camps, the most of any state.

Throughout WW II Texas was used by the military services as a huge training ground for the armed forces of the U.S. and those of some of our Allies. The Army Air Corps had long known that Texas had ideal flying weather and had established its headquarters and five of its training air field in the San Antonio area. Now, it's successor, the Army Air Forces, and the air arm of the U.S. Navy acquired many more air fields in the state and trained thousands of men and women in all phases of aviation. By war's end a total of 1.25 million service personnel had been trained in Texas.

A number of Texans became prominent during the war including General Dwight Eisenhower, who was born in Denison, TX but grew up in Kansas and always claimed Kansas as his home state. Other prominent Texans included Admiral Chester Nimitz from Fredericksburg, General Clair Chennault from Commerce, General Ira Eaker from Llano, Howard Hughes from Houston and Major Oveta Culp Hobby from Killeen, organizer and first commander of the Women's Auxiliary Army Corps (WAAC), later the Women's Army Corps (WAC). In Washington, DC the state could claim John Nance Garner of Uvalde, Vice President from 1933-1941; Thomas C. Clark of Dallas, Attorney-General; Sam Rayburn from Bonham, the long-time Speaker of the House of Representatives; Senator Tom Connelly from Marlin; Senator Martin Dies from Orange, head of the powerful Dies Committee and Congressman Wright Patman from Texarkana. Also in the House of Representatives was a young man from Austin named Lyndon Johnson. Johnson ran for a Senate seat during a special election in early 1941 but was defeated by a very narrow margin. He would try again for a Senate seat after the war and, at that time, be successful. He would go on from there to become Vice President and eventually President of the United States.

Texas also had the third largest number of Congressional Medal of Honor winners in the nation with 26.[1]

When the war ended, the economy of Texas was stable and growing. Texas had become the nation's third largest producer of aircraft after California and New York, and the aircraft industry had come to stay. Other new industries moved into the state in the early postwar years and the chemical industry became especially strong in the state. Also, in the late 1940s, large reservoirs of oil were discovered in the state's shallow tide waters and the Texans had still more oil to sell.

TEXAS OIL: It has been said that an army marches on its stomach. But, the modern armies of WW II, with their tanks, airplanes and warships, marched on gasoline and diesel fuel. This was born out by the fact that the quest for oil was one of the major objectives of the Axis nations. It was one of the primary reasons Germany thrust into the Balkans in the spring of 1941 to secure the Rumanian oil fields, and again thrust into the southern part of the Soviet Union in 1942 in an attempt to secure the oil fields of the Caucasus. In the Far East, the conquest of the oil fields of Sumatra, Malaya and Borneo were one of Japan's major war aims. When the Axis powers failed in their attempts to secure an adequate supply of oil, or their supplies were cut off by military defeats, the lack of oil helped hasten their defeat.

The Allied Nations had no such problem because they had Texas.

Texas, and the states around Texas, comprised the greatest oil producing region in the

Lyndon Johnson, as a young Congressman from Texas, was a strong supporter of President Roosevelt's New Deal policies and a favorite of the President.

world at the time of WW II and it was thousands of miles from the battle fronts and secure from enemy attacks[2]. Texas and her oil-producing neighbor to the east, Louisiana, also had easy access to the sea and the region's oil was shipped to every corner of the globe to fuel the American War Machine and a large part of the war machines of the Allied nations. In addition to Texas oil, the Allies could count on oil form California, Pennsylvania and other states in the Union is well as a number of foreign sources.

With the spreading wars in Europe and the Far East, and the rebounding of the U.S. and other world economies, the demand for oil rose sharply by 1940. During 1941 oil exploration in Texas was resumed, but no new major oil fields were found stimulating fears that Texas had reached its limit as an oil producing state. Fortunately, this would not be the case. The well drillers hadn't yet looked in all the right places.

When the U.S. went to war the Axis powers made a concerted effort to disrupt the flow of Allied oil around the world by making tankers a primary target of their respective submarine forces. The Germans had some temporary successes in this respect during the first half of 1942 when their submarines devastated the U.S. merchant fleet along the U.S. east coast and in the Gulf of Mexico. Most of the oil that was lost came from Texas. The U.S. rebounded, however, by slowly getting an upper hand on the submarine menace and building more tankers than the submarines could sink. Also, a huge underground oil pipe line was built form Texas to Pennsylvania to supply the U.S. east coast and thereby relieve the tanker fleets of this responsibility.

Texas oil became important in another way during the war . . for synthetic rubbers. Since the main ingredient in synthetic rubber is oil the Federal Government built many of the first

[1]Pennsylvlania was first with 35 and New York was second with 30.

[2]The Japanese did have a plan to bomb the Texas oil fields.

This B-17P is one of the WW II-era planes on display at Dyess Air Park.

synthetic rubber plants in Texas to be close to the source of oil. Rapid successes in the synthetic rubber industry helped solve the Allied nation's critical need for rubber with the result that Texas oil was used around the world in yet another way.

In the struggle for oil during WW II it can truly be said that Texas was our ace in the hole and that her oil was a major contributing factor to the final Allied victory.

ABILENE/SWEETWATER AREA: Abilene is 140 miles west of Ft. Worth and Sweetwater is 40 miles west of Abilene. Both are on I-20.

ABILENE ARMY AIR FIELD was located 7 miles west of downtown Abilene. It was built during 1942 for the 2nd AF and known at first as Tye Field and then, for a short time, as Tye Army Air Base. In Dec. 1942 it was renamed Abilene AAF. Throughout the war it was a training field for fighter pilots and had an auxiliary field, Abilene Air Terminal, three miles ESE of Abilene. After the war the base was inactivated but in 1953 it was taken over by the US Air Force and named Abilene Air Force Base. In Dec. 1956 it was renamed Dyess Air Force Base in honor of Lt. Col. William E. Dyess, a hero of the early Philippines campaign, who was killed in an air crash near Burbank, CA in 1943. Dyess AFB was operational throughout the Cold War.

Dyess Air Park: This is an outdoor display of vintage aircraft near the main gate of Dyess AFB. Most of the planes are postwar, but there are several WW II aircraft in the collection. Phone: 915/696-2196. Hours: daylight hours. Free.

ARLEDGE FIELD, three miles NW of Stamford, which is 35 miles north of Abilene, was one of the civilian air fields used by the Army Air Corps in 1939-40 to train Air Corps cadets. The air field had a private pilot training school which was contracted by the Army Air Corps to give its cadets primary flight training.

AVENGER FIELD, five miles west of Sweetwater, was the town's local airport before the war. The field had a privately-owned flight training school which was contracted by the Army Air Corps is 1939-40 to provide primary flight training for Air Corps cadets. After that program ended, British air cadets were trained here during the summer of 1942. The AAF acquired the field later in 1942 for use as a training field and began training AAF cadets. In Feb. 1943 the field was selected as a training

center for women air ferry pilots known as WASPs (Women's Air Force Service Pilots). This program had begun in San Antonio and soon outgrew its facilities; thus, Avenger Field was acquired. For several months the field was a co-educational flight training field until the male AAF cadets departed. Avenger Field then became the first all-female flight training center in U.S. history. WASPs were not in the AAF. Rather, they were civil servants who trained under military discipline. Between 1942 and 1944 1074 women earned their wings and were trained to fly everything from fighters to bombers. Their primary mission was to delivery new aircraft from the manufacturers to the fighting fronts around the world and thereby relieve male pilots for combat duties. WASPs also flew tow-target planes, planes related to other training missions, cargo planes, weather planes and, at times, served as test pilots. The WASPs were commanded by the well-known pre-war aviatrix, Jacqueline Cochran, and, in time, the air field became known locally as "Cochran's Convent". The WASP Program lasted until Dec. 1944 at which time it was disbanded because enough male AAF pilots had become available to carry out the WASP's missions. After the war Avenger Field returned to being a civil airport once again and eventually grew into a commercial and industrial park. A monument now stands at Avenger Field commemorating the women who comprised the WASP organization. The name of every woman who served as a WASP is listed in the memorial including the 38 WASPs who died while in service.

CAMP BARKELEY was an infantry training center, built in 1941, nine miles SW of Abilene. The first major unit to train at the camp was the 45th Infantry Div. which was comprised of the National Guards of Oklahoma, Arizona, New Mexico and Colorado. Later, armored divisions trained at the camp as did replacements for the Army's Medical Corps. The camp had a prisoner of war compound holding about 700 POWs who worked for the military. In March 1945 the camp was declared surplus and abandoned by the Army.

AMARILLO is near the center of the northern Texas panhandle.

Helium: This is the only place in the world where the lighter-than-air gas, helium, is available in natural form in sufficient quantities to be produced commercially. The main helium producing area is the Cliffside Natural Gas Field near Amarillo. Helium is mixed in with the area's natural gas and can be separated out, compressed, stored and shipped as it comes directly from the fields. This unique geological phenomenon gave the U.S. a virtual worldwide monopoly on helium. Since helium is non-flammable it is safe to handle and ideal for airships such as blimps and barrage balloons. Helium, therefore, became a unique products of war which the U.S. would export only to its friends and Allies. All U.S. blimps and most barrage balloons used helium as did those of our Allies. Other nations, who did not have access to helium, had to resort to using hydrogen which is very flammable and dangerous to handle. Hydrogen-filled balloons are relatively easy to shoot down by setting the gas afire with tracer bullets which carry a burning charge of magnesium. Therefore, Axis balloons, including Japan's bombing balloons, were much more vulnerable to attacks than were Allied balloons.

In 1942 the Federal Government built five plants in the Amarillo area to produce an abundant supply of helium for ourselves and our Allies.

AMARILLO ARMY AIR FIELD was located 8 miles east of downtown Amarillo and was the town's

This sign, located at Avenger Field, commemorates the WASPs of WW II. The flying lady above the sign is "Fifinella" the WASP's mascot designed by the Walt Disney Movie Studios during the war.

pre-war airport known as English Field.

The AAF acquired the field early in the war and used it for several purposes. It was a basic training center for Air Force recruits, a school for aircraft mechanics and flight engineers of B-29 bombers and the Air Transport Command used the field in its air route system and operated an air freight terminal here. The field also had a Regional AAF hospital. The Naval Air Transport Service used the field as a part of its air route system. Amarillo AAF had a prisoner of war camp holding about 225 Italian POWs who worked at the air field. In 1948 the air field was acquired by the US Air Force and became Amarillo Air Force Base. It was used until 1968, at which time it was closed and became Amarillo Municipal Airport once again.

AUSTIN, the state capital, is 75 miles NE of San Antonio on I-35.

BERGSTROM ARMY AIR FIELD, 7 miles SE of downtown Austin, was built in 1942 for the short-lived I Concentration Command. When this command was terminated the field was transferred to the I Troop Carrier Command for use as an operational and training base. The field had a combat crew replacement center, a radio school and an advanced pilot-training school. The facility was first known as Del Valle Army Air Base, but in Mar. 1943 it was given its wartime name in honor of Capt. John A. E. Bergstrom, an AAF administrative officer killed Dec. 8, 1941 during a Japanese bombing attack on Clark Field in the Philippines. Capt. Bergstrom was the first native of Austin to die in WW II. Bergstrom AAF was taken over by the US Air Force in 1948 and renamed Bergstrom Air Force Base. It remained operational throughout the Cold War but was eventually closed in the 1990s. During the war Bergstrom AAF had the following auxiliary air fields:

- Site #7, 5 miles NW of Yoakum
- Site #10, 2.5 miles ENE of Navasota
- Austin Municipal Airport, 3 miles NE of Austin
- Gonzales Fd., 6 miles SSW of Gonzales

CAMP MABRY, 3.5 miles NW of downtown Austin, was built in 1890 for the Texas Volunteer Guard, the fore-runner of the Texas National Guard. The camp was federalized during WW I and used for training purposes. In WW II it was federalized again and used to train Army replacements and serve as a supply center. The AAF also had an intelligence school here. After the war Camp Mabry reverted again to the Texas National Guard.

CAMP SWIFT was 25 miles east of Austin on U.S. 290. It was built in 1942 as an Army training camp for division-sized units. The camp was designed to house 30,000 troops at one time, but was expanded and at its peak housed some 90,000 troops. Camp Swift was a segregated camp so negro troops were also trained here. The camp had a main prisoner of war camp holding about 2200 POWs who worked at the camp and at other jobs in the area. In 1947 the training facilities were closed and part of the land parcelled out to the University of Texas, a housing development, ranchers and a Federal youth center. The remainder of the camp became a military reservation.

BIG SPRING is 35 miles NE of Midland on I-20.

BIG SPRING ARMY AIR FIELD was located three miles SW of town. It was the town's pre-war airport and was taken over by the AAF for the 50,000 Pilot Training Program to be used as a training center for glider pilots, bombardiers and navigators. French and Brazilian bombardiers and navigators also trained here. The air

Sam Rayburn's House in Bonham, TX. Rayburn was Speaker of the House of Representatives longer than any other man. During that time he was third in line in the presidential succession.

field had a branch prisoner of war camp holding about 90 POWs who worked on the base. The Air Transport Command also shared the field and operated an air freight terminal here. After the war the air field was taken over by the US Air Force and renamed Webb Air Force Base in honor of 1st Lt. James L. Webb, a fighter pilot and native of Big Spring, who was killed in WW II. Webb AFB functioned until 1977.

BONHAM is a farming center 60 miles NE of Dallas.

SAM RAYBURN HOUSE MUSEUM is located two miles west of town on U.S. 82. Here Sam Rayburn grew to manhood with his 8 brothers and sisters. Rayburn put himself through college, went into politics and in 1940 became Speaker of the House of Representative. Rayburn then held that office longer than any other man in U.S. history. At the time, the U.S. Constitution specified that the man who held that position was next in line in the presidential succession after the Vice President. Rayburn became very close to President Roosevelt and was one of his strongest and most loyal supporters. When something absolutely had to be done in Congress, the top leaders in the Government went to Sam Rayburn. In this respect he was one of the few political leaders in Washington that knew of the development of the atomic bomb because it was he who steered the $1.6 billion appropriation through Congress needed to finance the top secret "Manhattan Project". All his life Rayburn was a died-in-the-wool Southerner and kept of picture of Robert E. Lee in his office always facing south.

Rayburn's home is now a historic site and is open to the public. It is furnished with much of the original furniture and other items the family used. Rayburn returned to this house at every opportunity to be close to his family and friends. Several important people visited him here including his close friends Lyndon B. Johnson and Harry S Truman. Address: Bonham, TX 75418. Phone: 903/583-5558. Hours: Visitors are conducted through the house on tours which begin on the hour Tues.-F at 10, 11, noon, 3 and 4; Sat. 1, 2, 3, 4 and 5; and Sun. 2, 3, 4 and 5. Closed Jan. 1, Thanks-

This is a prisoner of war funeral procession at Camp Swift for a German POW who died at the camp.

The Sam Rayburn Library in Bonham, TX houses many of Rayburn's personal and public papers and artifacts.

giving and Dec. 25. Free.

SAM RAYBURN GRAVE SITE: Sam Rayburn is buried in his beloved Bonham at the Willow Wild Cemetery near the outskirts of town.

SAM RAYBURN LIBRARY is on U.S. 82 four blocks west of downtown Bonham. It preserves Rayburn's personal and official papers as well as books, documents, records of his speeches and many personal items. The library also has a copy of the Congressional Record beginning with the first meeting of Congress in 1789. Exhibits trace the life of Sam Rayburn from a poor farm boy to one of the most powerful men in American politics. A replica of his Washington office is also on display in the Library. Address: Bonham, TX 75418. Phone: 903/583-2455. Hours: M-F 10-5, Sat. 1-5, Sun 2-5. Closed major holidays. Free.

BRADY is 120 miles NE of San Antonio.

BRADY PRISONER OF WAR CAMP: This was a main prisoner of war camp built in 1943 near the town of Brady. It was one of several in the country not associated with a military installation. The Brady camp held about 1600 POWs who worked in the area. After the war the camp was closed and its assets disposed of.

CURTIS AIR FIELD, about three miles NE of town, was Brady's local airport at the beginning of the war. It had a private flying school known as the Brady Air Corps School which was contracted by the Army Air Corps in 1939-40 to give primary flight training to Air Corps cadets. When the Army Air Corps' successor, the Army Air Forces, took control of all flight training the AAF withdrew from the field and it was not used further by the military for the remainder of the war.

BRECKENRIDGE is 50 miles NE of Abilene on US 180 and US 183.

BRECKENRIDGE AVIATION MUSEUM is located at the local airport NE of town and displays more than a dozen antique aircraft. Most of the planes are of WW II vintage and include an E75 Kaydet, AD-4N Skyraider, FM-2F Wildcat, TBM-3 Avenger, T-33 trainer, P-51D Mustang, B-25 bomber and four Corsairs. Address: Stephens County Airport, Breckenridge, TX 76024. Phone: 817/559-3201. Hours: M-F 8-5.

Free.

BROWNSVILLE/HARLINGEN AREA:
This is a rich agricultural area at the southern tip of Texas on the Mexican border and near the mouth of the Rio Grande River. In the 1930s the Brownsville area had become an important air link with Latin America pioneered by Pan American Airways. It remained so during and after the war until long-range jet aircraft made it geographical location less important. Early in the war a Civil Air Patrol unit was very active in Brownsville patrolling the Texas coastline and offshore waters out of one of the Brownsville airports. No prisoner of war camps were located in this area because it was believed that the close proximity of Mexico would encourage escape attempts.

FORT BROWN is located in Brownsville just east of the International Bridge at 600 International Blvd. It was built as a cavalry post in 1846 just prior to the war with Mexico. Brownsville took its name from the fort. When WW II started it was still an active cavalry post, but when the cavalry was phased out the AAF made use of the fort for a while, but in Sept. 1944 the post was abandoned. In the next few years parts of the fort were deeded to the city of Brownsville, and to two colleges. Several of the fort's old buildings are preserved and in use.

BROWNSVILLE MUNICIPAL AIRPORT, five miles east of town, was used by the AAF during the war and continued also to operate as a commercial air field. The 2nd AF used the air field as a port of aerial embarkation and as an operational fields for tow-target aircraft. The Air Transport Command used the field in its air route system. In the spring of 1944 an operational training unit arrived at the field to train ferry pilots for fighter aircraft. This operation stayed until early 1945 then moved out to Greenwood, MS. After the war the air field became an all-civilian field again and became known as Brownsville/South Padre Island Airport.

CONFEDERATE AIR FORCE FLYING MUSEUM is located at Brownsville/South Padre Island Airport and displays a large number of antique aircraft, many of which belong to members of the Confederate Air Force. A large percentage of the aircraft are of WW II vintage and most are flyable and are actively used. Other displays at the museum include military vehicles, artillery pieces, small arms, field equipment, uniforms, dioramas, documents, photographs, paintings and drawings, flags, medals and more. Address: 955 Minnesota, Brownsville, TX 78520. Phone: 210/541-8585. Hours: M-Sat. 9-5, Sun. noon-4. Admission charged.

HARLINGEN ARMY AIR FIELD, three miles NE of Harlingen, was acquired by the AAF in 1942 for use as a flexible gunnery school. This was the second flexible gunnery school in the nation. The first was at Las Vegas, NV. Throughout the war Harlingen AAF performed this mission. Harlingen AAF had an auxiliary air field, Laguna Madre Airport, 10 miles NE of Los Fresnos. The military stayed on at Harlingen until 1961. After that the field was used as a commercial air field and, for many years, was the home of the Confederate Air Force, a nation-wide organization of antique plane collectors and enthusiasts.

IWO JIMA WAR MEMORIAL is located on the south campus parade deck of the Marine Military Academy at the west end of Harlingen Industrial Air Park. The statue of the famous flag-raising at Iwo Jima is the center piece of the memorial and was used as the model for the bronze memorial later placed at Arlington

A Spitfire, rear, and a Corsair, right, are two of the WW II-era planes on display at the Breckenridge Aviation Museum.

This is a 1950 photo showing sculptor Felix de Weldon, left, and his assistant, Idilio Santini, working on the plaster model of the Iwo Jima statue that now stands in Harlingen, TX.

National Cemetery in Virginia. This model was made of plaster but since has been covered with fiberglass to preserve it. The figures are 32' high and the flag-pole is 78' long. In the museum are artifacts from the battle of Iwo Jima and the histories of the men in the statue. Address: 320 Iwo Jima Blvd., Harlingen, TX 78550. Phone: 210/423-6006. Hours: Memorial daily 8-5. Visitors Center M-Sat. 9:30-4, Sun. 1-4. Donations requested.

MOORE FIELD was located 12 miles NE of Mission, TX, an eastern suburb of McAllen which is 40 miles west of Harlingen. This was a pre-war commercial airport that was taken over by

Visitors at the Coleman Warbird Museum examine a WW II aircraft under restoration.

the AAF to meet the needs of the 30,000 Pilot Training Program. It was used as a training field offering basic and advanced flight training to AAF personnel. These activities were conducted at the field throughout the war. The field was returned to its original owners after the war, but from 1954 to 1961 it was militarized again by the US Air Force and named Moore Air Force Base during that period. During WW II Moore Field had the following auxiliary air fields:

- Aux. #1, Edinburg Field, 10 miles north of Edinburg
- Aux. #2, Mission Auxiliary Field, 21 miles NNW of Mission
- Aux. #3, Rio Grande Field, 5 miles north of La Grulla

FORT RINGGOLD was located at David's Landing just east of Rio Grande City which is 40 miles west of McAllen. This fort was built in 1848 just after the Mexican War to serve as a border defense. It was subsequently abandoned and reoccupied several times in the next 93 years. In Mar. 1941 it was occupied again and garrisoned by a 400-man cavalry unit which patrolled the U.S/Mexican border. In Aug. 1944 the Army abandoned the fort once again and it was declared surplus.

TEXAS AIR MUSEUM is located one miles east of Rio Hondo at the Texas Dusting Service air field. This is a collection of about 100 privately-owned aircraft which are displayed on a rotating basis. Many of the planes are from WW II. One of the outstanding planes in the collection is a Yak-3 which was one of the Soviet Union's main fighter planes during WW II. Other WW II aircraft in the collection include two Focke-Wulf 190 F-8s, an AT-6 Texan and a Fiesler Storch. Address: Farm Rd. 106, PO Box 70, Rio Hondo, TX 78583. Phone: 210/748-2112. Hours: daily 9-4. Donations requested.

BROWNWOOD/COLEMAN: Brownwood is 120 miles SW of Fort Worth. Coleman is 28 miles WNW of Brownwood.

CAMP BOWIE was built two miles south of Brownwood in 1940 and was the first major new WW II construction project in the state. The original camp was designed to be the main training center for the Texas National Guard's 36th Infantry Div. Bowie expanded rapidly. In addition to the 36th Inf. Div. several armored divisions also trained here. The post was used further by the 111th Quartermaster Regiment,

Iowa National Guard's 113th Cavalry, the VIII Army Corps and Headquarters, troops of the 3rd Army and various units of the Medical Service, Field Artillery and the WACs. Bowie was a segregated camp so negro troops also served and trained here. In Aug. 1943 a main prisoner of war camp was established here to hold up to 300 POWs. Most of the POWs worked on the post. In 1946 Camp Bowie was closed and later that year abandoned by the Army. Most of the land was sold off except for 102 acres which was retained by the Texas National Guard.

COLEMAN WARBIRD MUSEUM is located at the Coleman Municipal Airport NE of Coleman. This is an aircraft restoration facility and a privately-owned collection of about a dozen aircraft. WW II aircraft in the collection include a PT-19, BT-13, T-6, A-26 and an AT-11. Address: Airport Rd., Coleman, TX 76834. Phone: 915/625-2780. Hours: M-F 8-6, Sat. 8-noon. Free.

DOUGLAS MacARTHUR ACADEMY OF FREEDOM is located one mile south of downtown Brownwood on the campus of Howard Payne University. This is not a museum, but a part of the Social Science Department of the University. The Academy is named in honor of Gen. MacArthur because his ideals paralleled those of the academic program offered by the Academy which are intended to nurture understandings and study of the spiritual, economic, social and political problems of our contemporary society. MacArthur outlined his personal ideals and principles over a period of years in a series of letters to Dr. Guy D. Newman who was then President of the University. Within the Academy are a number of visual display rooms that explain the Academy's goals and philosophy. These rooms are open to visitors

The Texas Air Museum has a collection of about 100 aircraft, some of them very unique.

The General Douglas MacArthur Academy of Freedom at Howard Payne University, Brownwood, TX.

and tourists. One of the rooms, The MacArthur Gallery, honors General MacArthur and displays some of his personal belongings including his Congressional Medal of Honor and his Distinguished Service Cross. Address: Austin (SR 2524) and S. Coggins Sts., Brownwood, TX 76801-2715. Phone: 210/643-7830 Ext. 406. Hours: Guided tours daily 1:30, 2:30 and 3:30; also M-F at 11 and Sat. at 10 and 11. Free.

BRYAN is a county seat 80 miles NW of Houston.

BRYAN ARMY AIR FIELD, 6 miles WSW of town, was Bryan's pre-war airport when it was taken over by the AAF for the 70,000 Pilot Training Program. Bryan AAF became a school for flight instructors teaching instrument flying. The trainees were both officers and enlisted men. This was the first AAF school in the country to give such specialized training. The program proved to be very successful and similar schools were established elsewhere and known as "Little Bryans". Bryan AAF had two auxiliary fields, Aux. #1, Sommerville Field, 9 miles NNE of Sommerville and Aux. #2 Easterwood Airfield, 2.8 miles SW of College Station. The air field passed to the US Air Force after the war and was named Bryan Air Force Base. In 1959 the base was inactivated and most of the facilities turned over to Texas A & M University.

CHILDRESS is in the SE corner of the Texas Panhandle.

CHILDRESS ARMY AIR FIELD, five miles west of town, was activated by the AAF for the 70,000 Pilot Training Program. Bombardiers and navigator were trained here throughout the war. The air field had a branch prisoner of war camp holding about 100 POWs who worked in the area. After the war the air field was turned over to the community of Childress and became its primary airport. The Childress County Heritage Museum at 210 3rd St. N.W. in Childress has permanent displays on the air field during its war days.

COLEMAN (See Brownwood/Coleman)

CORPUS CHRISTI is in SE Texas on the Gulf of Mexico. It is a major sea port with the deepest harbor in Texas.

CORPUS CHRISTI MUSEUM OF SCIENCE & IN-DUSTRY, in Bayfront Arts and Science Park, contains many exhibits concerning the history of science and industry in south Texas. Included in the exhibits is considerable information on the WW II era. Also on display in the museum are two of the most popular Navy training planes of WW II, a North American SNJ Texan and a Naval Aircraft Factory N3N, nicknamed the "Yellow Peril". Address: 1900 N. Chapparral, Corpus Christi, TX 78401. Phone: 512/883-2862. Hours: Tues.-Sat. 10-5. Sat. 1-5, closed holidays. Admission charged except Sat. 10-noon when admission is free.

U.S. NAVAL AUXILIARY AIR STATION, KINGSVILLE was two miles east of Kingsville and served as an auxiliary air station to NAS, Corpus Christi during WW II. It had an outlying field, Site #11, 3.5 miles south of Kingsville. The air station was retained by the Navy after the war and in 1968 became its own command U.S. Naval Air Station, Kingsville.

U.S. NAVAL AUXILIARY AIR STATION, RODD was located 10 miles south of Corpus Christi and was an auxiliary air field to NAS, Corpus Christi. During WW II it had the following outlying fields:

- OLF #10, 1 mile SSW of Aberdeen
- OLF #11, 13 miles SSE of Aberdeen
- OLF #25, 12 miles ESE of Bishop
- OLF #?, Rockport Airport, 4.5 miles north of Rockport

U.S. NAVAL AUXILIARY AIR STATION, WALDRON was 12 miles SSE of downtown Corpus Christi and served as an auxiliary air field to NAS, Corpus Christi during WW II. The station had an outlying field, OLF #14, 12 miles SSE of Aber-

deen. NAAS, Waldron was retained by the Navy after the war and utilized throughout the Cold War.

U.S. NAVAL AIR STATION, CORPUS CHRISTI was built 12 miles SE of downtown Corpus Christi in 1940-41 on the southern shore of Corpus Christi Bay. The station was commissioned on Mar. 12, 1941. Secretary of the Navy Frank Knox delivered the keynote address and Congressman Lyndon B. Johnson was in attendance. The first aircraft to use the station were PBY Catalina seaplanes which were used for both operational and training purposes. N3N "Yellow Peril" land-based trainers arrived next and primary and advanced flight training began for naval cadets. In late Dec. 1941, after the attack on Pearl Harbor, NAS, Corpus Christi became a supply base for patrol boats, mine sweepers and other craft engaged in coastal patrols. Also at that time the station instigated a "boot" camp for new recruits. Flight training remained the station's main function throughout the war. Air cadets from Brazil, Chile, Columbia, Cuba, Ecuador, Mexico, Peru and Uruguay also trained here in programs using their native languages. One American cadet who trained here later became President of the United State; George Bush. By mid-1943 NAS, Corpus Christi was ranked at the world's largest naval air training center and in that year President Roosevelt visited the station. The Naval Air Transport Service and Naval Air Ferry Command also used the station at times. By war's end NAS, Corpus Christi had trained some 35,000 cadets. When the war ended training operations were scaled back, but the station continued to offer advanced flight training. For a few years in the late 1940s the "Blue Angels" air demonstration team made its home here. The station served the Navy in a variety of ways over the next decades and remained operational throughout the Cold War. During WW II NAS, Corpus Christi had the following outlying air fields:

- OLF Beeville, 5.5 miles SE of Beeville
- OLF Cabaniss, 6 miles SSW of Corpus Christi
- OLF Cuddihy, 7.5 miles SW of Corpus Christi

"USS LEXINGTON" MUSEUM ON THE BAY is located on the Corpus Christi waterfront and has as it centerpiece the WW II aircraft carrier "Lexington". This ship was commissioned in 1943 and saw action from Tarawa to Tokyo. Following WW II the "Lady Lex" continued in

The WW II aircraft carrier "Lexington" is on display on the Corpus Christi waterfront. To the right is the Texas State Aquarium.

operation and served longer than any other aircraft carrier in the history of the U.S. Navy. The "Lexington" is open to the public and has several WW II aircraft on display. Address: 2914 N. Shoreland Blvd., Corpus Christi, TX 78402. Phone: 512/888-4873. Hours: daily 9-5, closed Christmas. Admission charged.

CRYSTAL CITY is a county seat 90 miles SW of San Antonio.

CRYSTAL CITY INTERNMENT CAMP was established early in the war in a camp originally built for migrant workers. The camp was expanded and improved to become a camp for enemy alien families. This camp was run by the Immigration and Naturalization Service and is not to be confused with the relocation camps for ethnic Japanese from the U.S. west coast that were run by the War Relocation Authority. Virtually none of the people sent here were American citizens. The first to arrive at this camp, in early 1942, were 137 Japanese women, mostly wives (some with children) of alien businessmen and merchants. Their husbands soon followed. Additional Japanese alien families, and some German families, arrived from Latin American countries under international agreements whereby the U.S. agreed to take care for such people. Conditions were as comfortable as they could be under the circumstances. The camp consisted of 41 three-room cottages and 118 one-room cottages plus service buildings. The people were well-fed, given adequate medical care, work and considerable liberty to leave the camp. Schools were established in the camp and the children were given traditional educations by teachers of their own national origin. Of the several camps of this type established in the U.S. this was considered to be one of the more desirable. At its peak the camp held about 1000 families. Beginning in 1943 the camp began to experience a baby-boom which continued for the remainder of the camp's existence. The children born here were, of course, American citizens. About that time the camp began to receive former U.S. citizens of Japanese descent who had renounced their American citizenship and, by doing so, had automatically become enemy aliens and could no longer stay in the relocation camps. These people were usually angry young Japanese men, born in America, who wanted to return to Japan and fight for the Emperor. Needless to say, they had to carefully watched. After Germany surrendered the German internees were released or repatriated. In June 1945 the internment camp at Seagoville, TX was closed and the remaining internees sent here. In Aug. 1945, with the end of the war a certainty, the Japanese internees (expect for the renunciants) were given the choice of returning to their former place of residence or to Japan. Within a few months all internees had left the camp and it was then closed and its assets disposed of.

DALHART is in the NW corner of the Texas panhandle.

DALHART ARMY AIR FIELD, 3.5 miles SSW of town, was built in 1942 for the 2nd AF to be a training base for operational crews of very heavy bombers. This usually meant B-17s, B-24s and, in some instances, B-29s and B-32s. On July 5, 1943 a very embarrassing indecent hap-

This is the main B-24 bomber assembly line at the Consolidated-Vultee Aircraft Co., in Ft. Worth.

pened to a crew of one of the B-17s on its way to make a practice bombing run at the bombing and gunnery range. The navigator miscalculated and the plane dropped its 100 lb practice bombs on the town of Boise City, OK. The bombs, which were charged with only four pounds of explosive and 96 pounds of sand, did some damage, but caused no casualties. Soon afterwards a slogan made the rounds at Dalhart AAF which was "Remember the Alamo, remember Pearl Harbor, and for God's sake remember Boise City".

Two auxiliary air fields were attached to the post; Dalhart Field #1, 6.5 miles SW of Dalhart, and Aux. #2, Witt Field, 5.5 miles NE of Dalhart. After the war Dalhart AAF was declared surplus and turned over to the community of Dalhart to serve as its local airport.

DALLAS/FORT WORTH AREA: These two cities comprised the largest metropolitan area in Texas. One of the largest defense contractors in the area was Consolidated-Vultee Corp. of Ft. Worth which made B-24 bombers on an assembly-line basis. At its peak this plant produced 50 B-24s a month.

Later in the war the Consolidated-Vultee plant built B-32 bombers, the "insurance" bomber to the B-29. Another large aircraft manufacturer in the area was the North American Aviation Corp. plant in Dallas which built AT-6 trainers, P-51 Mustang fighters and B-24 air frames. Lockheed Aircraft Co. had a plant in Dallas that did aircraft modifications and Globe Aircraft Co. of Ft. Worth made AT-10 trainers and sub-assemblies for P-38s and B-17s. Other big manufacturers were Guiberson Diesel Engine Co. of Garland which made diesel, and later gasoline engines for tanks; American Manufacturing Co. of Texas at Ft. Worth which made large calibre shells and projectiles and Murray Co. of Dallas which made 90 mm high explosive shells.

ASHBURN GENERAL HOSPITAL was built by the

Government in 1943 in McKinney, TX, 20 miles north of Dallas. Ashburn treated war wounded and specialized in general medicine and arthritis cases. The hospital had a branch prisoner of war camp holding about 230 POWs who worked at the hospital. In Dec. 1945 Ashburn was transferred to the Veterans Administration.

THE DALLAS MEMORIAL CENTER FOR HOLOCAUST STUDIES is located in Dallas and provides a museum, library, resource center and archives related to the Holocaust of WW II. The center publishes a newsletter, provides speakers, gives tours and offers teacher workshops. Address: 7900 Northaven Rd., Dallas, TX 75230. Phone: 214/368-4709. Hours: M, W, F 10-4, Thurs. 10-9 and Sun. noon-4.

FORT WORTH ARMY AIR FIELD, 7 miles WNW of Ft. Worth, was a large pre-war airport known as Tarrant Field. This was the site of the Consolidated-Vultee aircraft plant. In 1942 the field was enlarged and the AAF setup operations at the field to provide transition training for pilots and crew from two-engine bombers into B-24s. When Consolidated began producing B-32 bombers Fort Worth AAF followed suit and provided transition training into those planes. During the war Ft. Worth AAF had two auxiliary fields; Gainesville Army Air Field, 4 miles WNW of Gainesville and Olney Airport, 4 miles WSW of Olney. By war's end the Consolidated-Vultee plant had produced more than 3000 bombers.

Fort Worth AAF was retained after the war and under the US Air Force was renamed Carswell Air Force Base in 1948 in honor of Fort Worth native Major Horace S. Carswell, a Medal of Honor Winner and pilot of a B-24 who was killed in China in 1944. The base functioned throughout the Cold War and was closed in the 1990s.

FORT WORTH QUARTERMASTER DEPOT: This depot, activated in 1940, had two locations. The main depot was located 6 miles south of downtown Ft. Worth at 4900 Hempill St. It had the wartime mission of receiving, storing and supplying a wide variety of items for the Army. The second location was about 20 miles NW of town at Eagle Mountain Field which was used in the air shipment of supplies. The main depot had a branch prisoner of war camp with about 325 POWs who worked at the depot. The depot was retained after the war and by 1947 was primarily a storage facility. Between Oct. 1947 and May 1949 the depot had the somber mission of receiving and processing WW II dead from overseas for reburial in the U.S. In the following decades the depot on Hempill St. became known as the Fort Worth General Depot, Fort Worth Army Depot and Fort Worth Defense Supply Center and handled supplies for the Quartermaster, Signal and Transportation Corps. Eagle Mountain Field was eventually transferred to the Texas Air National Guard.

HENSLEY FIELD/U.S. NAVAL AIR STATION, DALLAS was two miles east of Grand Prairie which is midway between Fort Worth and Dallas. This was a prewar airport, built in 1929, for use as a training field for both Army and Navy air reservists. In 1940 the Federal Government's Defense Plant Corporation built a large aircraft manufacturing plant on the west side of the field which was operated by North American Aviation Corp. The plant made T-6 trainers, and P-51 fighter planes during WW II. At its height the plant employed 39,000 people. The nearby community of Avion was built by the Government to house plant workers.

The AAF utilized its portion of the field as a branch of the San Antonio Air Technical Service Command and the AAF's Air Ferry Command used it as a training field for ferry pilots. The Navy converted its facility into a training center for screening out individuals unsuited for flight training. Hensley was also used as an outlying field by the Navy for the training of pilots in night flying. In 1943 the Navy upgraded their facility to a naval air station naming it U.S. Naval Air Station, Dallas and used it to provide primary flight training to Navy,

This bust of Jimmy Doolittle is on display in the Frontier of Flight Museum.

Marine and Coast Guard cadets. Some Free French airmen also trained here. After the war the AAF used their part of the field to store surplus aircraft and engines and in 1946 the Navy's side was converted into a training facility for Navy and Marine Corps air reservists. The AAF's side of the field was taken over by the US Air Force and became a training center for the Air National Guard. Eventually, the Navy took over the entire field and incorporated the Air Force's facilities into NAS, Dallas which continue to function throughout the Cold War. The aircraft plant remained in operation for many years after the war and continued to be used to build aircraft under various owners. In the 1990's NAS, Dallas was closed.

HICKS FIELD, 12.5 miles NW of Fort Worth near the town of Hicks, had been a WW I air field that closed down immediately after that war. In 1940 it was reopened and became a primary flight training facility for the Army Air Corps. After the creation of the Army Air Forces in the summer of 1941, Hicks Field continued as a training field until near the end of the war. After the war it was abandoned by the AAF and became a civilian airport.

LOVE FIELD was five miles NNW of downtown Dallas. It was a WW I aviation training field known as Love Field Airport. The Lockheed Aircraft Co. plant was here and the field was used by the AAF's Air Technical Service Command and the Air Transport Command which had a air freight terminal at the field. After the war the airport was returned to its civilian use and became

Dallas Love Field Municipal Airport.

Frontier of Flight Museum: This fine museum is on the upper mezzanine of the main terminal at Dallas Love Field Municipal Airport and relates the history of aviation in the Dallas/Fort Worth area as well as the history of Love Field. A sizeable part of the museum's displays are devoted to WW II. Address: Love Field Terminal, LB-34, Dallas, TX 75235. Phone: 214/350-3600/1651. Hours: Tues-Sat. 10-5, Sun. 1-5. Admission charged.

MEACHAM AIRPORT, 5.5 miles NNW of downtown Fort Worth, was a prewar airport. It was used during WW II by the Naval Air Transport Service and the Naval Air Ferry Command but was not taken over by the Navy. After the war the Navy departed and Meacham Airport became a civilian field once again.

SEAGOVILLE INTERNMENT CAMP was located near Seagoville, 15 miles SE of downtown Dallas. This was a "Latins Only" and "Women Only" internment camp run by the U.S. Immigration and Naturalization Service. Under international agreements, the U.S. agreed to take enemy aliens from Latin American countries and care for them for the duration of the war. Most of the women interned here were Japanese citizens who had been expelled from the various Latin American countries. Some of the women had diplomatic status and were eventually exchanged. The internees were well cared for and given considerable liberties inside and outside the camp. The facility was a new federal reformatory for women built in 1940 by the Justice Department. It had dormitories, schools, a hospital and an industrial center. When the war ended the internees were given the option of returning to the Latin American country from which they came or returning to Japan. A very small number returned to Latin America, more returned to Japan and about 300 petitioned the U.S. courts to remain in the U.S. and were eventually allowed to stay.

TERRELL AIRPORT was located just south of Terrell, TX which is 20 miles east of Dallas on I-20. This was a prewar airport which had a flight training school, the Dallas Aviation School, that was contracted by the Army Air Corps in 1939-40 to give primary flight training to Air Corps cadets. After the AAF began training its own cadets British air cadets were trained at the field in both primary and advanced flight training.

Silent Wings Museum: This unique museum is located at the Terrell Municipal Airport and is dedicated to the memory of WW II Airborne personnel and depicts the role of glider pilots, glider-born troops, paratroopers, tow pilots, glider mechanics and other personnel of the Troop Carrier Command. The centerpiece of the museum is a fully restored Waco CG-4A glider, one of only three restored gliders of this type in the U.S. Other displays include several other gliders, a Link Trainer, military vehicles, small arms, dioramas showing glider troops in action, uniforms, photographs, documents, medals and large collections of WW II Stars & Stripes newspapers and Yank magazines. Address: 119 Silent Wings Blvd., Terrell Municipal Airport, Terrell, TX 75160. Phone: 214/563-0402. Hours: Tues.-Sat. 10-5, Sun.

Hensley Field/U.S. Naval Air Station, Dallas as it appeared shortly after the war. In the foreground is the North American Aviation Corp. aircraft plant.

Almost 14,000 Waco CG-4A Gliders were produced during the war by 16 different manufacturers and were the most widely used glider of the war. See previous page.

noon-5, closed Thanksgiving and Dec. 25. Free … donations welcome.

U.S. MARINE CORPS AIR STATION AND NAVAL AIR STATION, EAGLE MOUNTAIN LAKE: This station was 18 miles NW of downtown Ft. Worth. It was built in 1942 to be a multiple training facility for Marine Corps glider forces, a satellite field for NAS, Clinton, OK and a training center for Strategic Tasks Air Group II (STAG II), which did research and training work of a classified nature. The station also served as a ferry stop and service facility for seaplanes flying transcontinental routes because they could land on Eagle Mountain Lake. The Fort Worth Quartermaster Depot also had a facility here. After several Marine glider units had been trained it was concluded that glider forces were not practical for the Marines and the Marine Corps abandoned their facilities at the station in June 1943. STAG II took over those facilities and used them until it completed its work in Mar. 1944. At that time the station was returned to the Marine Corps and became the home of two Marine air groups and a helicopter squadron for the duration of the war. After the war the station was retained by the Marine Corps and was used for a variety of aviation training purposed by both the Marines and the Navy. It also continued to service seaplanes. These operations lasted until Dec. 1946 when the station was disestablished. Later the station was acquired by the Texas National Guard and later became known as Eagle Mountain National Guard Base. During the war the station had an outlying field, Beaumont Airport, 10 miles SSE of Beaumont.

DEL RIO/BRACKETTVILLE AREA: This area is 140 miles west of San Antonio on the Mexican border.

FORT CLARK, located one miles SE of Brackettville, was a old cavalry post built in 1852. By the time of WW II it was still an active cavalry post and it remained so for most of the war. In Feb. 1943 the Army reactivated the 2nd Horse Cavalry here which included the all-negro 9th Cavalry Regiment. The primary mission of the cavalry units at Fort Clark was to patrol the U.S./Mexican border. In June 1944 Fort Clark was declared surplus and eventually closed and its assets sold.

LAUGHLIN FIELD, 7 miles east of Del Rio, was built in 1942 for the 70,000 Pilot Training Program. The air field was named in honor of Lt. Jack T. Laughlin, a B-17 pilot and a local resident, killed in Java in Jan. 1942. Laughlin Field's first mission was to offer advanced flight training to AAF pilots, but in Sept. 1942 this mission was changed to bombardier training. It was changed yet again in Dec. 1942 to transition training of combat crews into B-26 bombers. Laughlin had one auxiliary field, Val Verde County Airport, 3 miles NW of Del Rio. The air field was retained after the war, taken over by the US Air Force and named Laughlin Air Force Base. It continued to be a training facility for many years thereafter.

DENISON is 65 miles north of Dallas on U.S. 75 near the state line.

EISENHOWER BIRTHPLACE STATE HISTORIC SITE: General Dwight D. Eisenhower was born in Denison in 1890. His family lived here because his father worked for the local railroad. Six months after Dwight was born the family moved to Abilene, Kansas. Dwight was the only one of the Eisenhower children to be born in Texas. In his younger days he wasn't quite sure where in Texas he was born for when he entered West Point he gave as his birthplace Tyler, TX. That six months, though, and Eisenhower's outstanding military and political record, were enough to create a State Historic Site. The house has been restored and furnished to its 1890 appearance and is open to the public. Address: 208 E. Day St., Denison, TX 75020 (SE of downtown Denison). Phone: 903/465-8908. Hours: June 1 thru Labor Day daily 8-5, rest of year 10-5. Closed Jan. 1 and Dec. 25. Admission charged.

EISENHOWER STATE RECREATION AREA is a lake-front park five miles NE of Denison and named in honor of Dwight D. Eisenhower. The park offers camping, boating, picnicking, trails and swimming.

PERRIN FIELD, four miles south of Denison, was built in 1941 for the 30,000 Pilot Training Program. It was used as a basic flight training center for AAF personnel. Airmen from Brazil, Mexico and Ecuador were also trained here. The air field had a branch prisoner of war camp holding about 200 POWs who worked at the field and in agriculture. Perrin Field survived the war to become Perrin Air Force Base and a part of the US Air Force's Air Training Command. The field was inactivated in 1972 and its assets disposed of. During the war Perrin Field had the following auxiliary air fields:

* Aux. #1, Gibbons Field, 6.4 miles west of Sherman
* Aux. #2, Gaskin Field, 12.5 miles SW of Sherman
* Aux. #3, Bilbo Airport, 9 miles SW of Galena, OK
* Aux. #4, Burton Field, 1.5 miles east of Amprose
* Aux. #?, Gainesville AAF, 3.5 miles WNW of Gainesville

DESDEMONA is a small community 70 miles south of Fort Worth. On the afternoon of March 23, 1945 a Japanese bombing balloon came drifting slowly to earth just south of town. A local aircraft spotter saw the balloon and reported it to the authorities. A bus load of school children returning home from school also saw the balloon. Fascinated by what they saw, the bus driver and his excited passengers began to follow the drifting balloon. It finally came to earth and snagged on something and began waving gently in the breeze. The bus driver drove as close to the strange object as he could and the children piled out and raced towards the balloon. They began tearing at its various parts with their hands and eventually tore the paper gas bag to pieces. Unknowingly, this was a very dangerous thing to do because the bag

This is the house in which Dwight D. Eisenhower was born in 1890. It is now a state historic Site.

These planes of the civil Air Patrol operated from Biggs Field during WW II and patrolled the U.S.-Mexican border.

was still partially filled with flammable hydrogen and the balloon had a self-destruct device designed to ignite the hydrogen under certain conditions. Fortunately, the hydrogen did not ignite and no one was hurt during the incident. When the authorities learned what had happened they came to Desdemona and collected as many of the pieces of the balloon as they could. They also gathered the children of the local school into an assembly and lectured them on the dangers of approaching and touching strange objects that came down from the sky.

DUMAS is 40 miles north of Amarillo in the Texas panhandle.

CACTUS ORDNANCE PLANT, 12 miles south of Dumas, was built by the Federal Government in 1941 to manufacture, from natural gas, an additive for high octane aviation fuels and ammonia which was used in the manufacture of munitions. The plant was operated for the Government by the Shell Oil Company. The Government built barracks and small houses nearby for the workers. There was a small branch prisoner of war camp holding about 60 Italian POWs who worked in the area. After the war the plant closed, but was eventually bought by the Phillips Petroleum Company to make commercial fertilizer. Phillips operated the plant until 1973. Following that, the site was developed into Schroeter Industrial Park.

EAGLE PASS is 125 miles SW of San Antonio on the Mexican border.

EAGLE PASS ARMY AIR FIELD, 10 miles north of town, was activated for the 50,000 Pilot Training Program and was used as a training field throughout the war. In Sept. 1945 it was closed. Eagle Pass AAF had two auxiliary air fields; Aux. #2, Pinto Field, 35 miles NNW of Eagle Pass and Aux. #3, Eagle Pass Auxiliary Field, 9.5 miles ESE of Eagle Pass.

EL PASO is at the extreme western end of Texas on the Rio Grande River and the Mexican border. The town was one of several western cities that experienced a rapid and permanent population growth during and after WW II. On the early morning of July 16, 1945 some of the citizens of El Paso was a sudden and strange flash of light in the northern sky. No one knew it at the time, but it was the flash from the world's first atomic bomb test at White Sands, NM 130 miles away.

WILLIAM BEAUMONT GENERAL HOSPITAL, ad-

joining Fort Bliss, was built in 1921 to serve all of the Army posts in the southwest. By the time of WW II it had 4000 beds and during the war treated many war wounded. Beaumont specialized in general medicine, orthopedic surgery, plastic surgery, ophthalmologic surgery, deep X-ray therapy and psychiatry. The hospital also had a school for medical technicians. Beaumont remained an Army hospital in the postwar years and was one of the Army's largest hospitals.

BIGGS FIELD is 7 miles NE of El Paso and is surrounded by land belonging to Fort Bliss. This was a pre-war air field that was utilized by the 2nd AF during the war as a training field for combat crews of very heavy bombers. Aircraft of the Civil Air Patrol operated from here and patrolled the U.S.-Mexican border. Biggs Field had a branch prisoner of war camp with about 240 POWs who worked on the air field. Biggs was taken over by the US Air Force after the war, renamed Biggs Air Force Base and became a part of the Tactical Air Command.

FORT BLISS borders El Paso on the north and extends for miles northward into New Mexico. The Fort Bliss of WW II was the 6th Fort Bliss to have been established in the El Paso area since 1848. From 1916 on, this Fort Bliss served as a training center for cavalry and field artillery units of the Army. At the beginning of WW II it was the home of the 1st Cavalry Div. which was still a horse-mounted unit. The Division was dismounted, equipped with tanks, trained

in tank warfare and sent to the Pacific in 1943. During much of that time the fort also served as a reception center for the 8th Army Corps. After the 1st Cavalry Div. moved out, an anti-aircraft artillery school moved in from Fort Davis, NC to take advantage of the fort's vacant facilities and the area's clear and sunny weather. The school was enlarged and Fort Bliss eventually became one of the Army's largest anti-aircraft artillery training centers. Bliss was a segregated camp so negro troops also trained here. Almost every AA artillery unit that served in the war received its early training here. Later in the war the fort trained anti-aircraft artillery replacements. The fort had a main prisoner of war camp with about 1800 POWs who worked for the military. There were several huge artillery ranges that stretched far to the north into New Mexico. Fort Bliss was retained after the war and became a training center for missilemen when missiles replaced artillery guns in anti-aircraft defenses.

Third Cavalry Regiment Museum: This museum is in building 2407 at Fort Bliss and has displays and artifacts which trace the history of the 3rd Armored Cavalry Regiment from its days as a horse-mounted unit through its days as a WW II armored regiment and afterwards. Exhibits include tanks, tracked vehicles, aircraft, machine guns, small arms, field equipment, uniforms, flags, maps, documents and much more. Address: ATZC-DPT-MM (near the Jct. of Forrest and Chaffee Rds.), Fort Bliss, TX 79916-5300. Phone: 915/568-1922. Hours: M-F 9-4:30. Free.

U.S. Army Air-Defense Artillery Museum: This unique museum is located in building 5000 on the grounds of Fort Bliss and is the only museum in the U.S. dedicated exclusively to the preservation of historical equipment and artifacts relating to ground-based air defense weapons. Inside the museum and in an outdoor display area are numerous examples of anti-aircraft weapons from the U.S. as well as other nations. Many of the items on display are from WW II. Address: ATZC-DPTM-M, Building 5000 (at Jct. of Pleasanton Rd. and Robt. E. Lee Blvd.), Fort Bliss, TX, 79916-5300. Phone: 915/568-5412. Hours: daily 9-4:30, closed Jan. 1, Easter, Thanksgiving and Dec. 25. Free.

U.S. Army Museum of the Non-Commissioned Officer: This is yet another museum on the

Part of the outdoor display at the Third Cavalry Museum. From right to left: an M-4A3 Sherman tank, M-2 half-track, M-8 armored car and a postwar vehicle.

An Italian 90/53 M1939 90 mm gun mounted on a Lancia truck. This gun was used by the Italian Army during WW II against both air and ground targets and has many similar characteristics of the German 88 mm gun. See previous page.

grounds of Fort Bliss at Biggs Field. Its exhibits interpret the history of the U.S. Army's non-commissioned officers (NCOs), both male and female, and their roles in war and peace from the American Revolution to the present. The museum's displays are laid out in chronological order with a limited amount of information on WW II. Address: ATSS-S-M (Jct. of Staff Sergeant Sims and Barksdale Sts.), Fort Bliss, TX 79918-5000. Phone: 915/568-8646. Hours: M-F 9-4, Sat.-Sun. noon-4. Free.

EL PASO MUNICIPAL AIRPORT, five miles ENE of downtown El Paso and bordering Fort Bliss on the west, was the area's main commercial airport during the war. It was used by both the AAF and the Navy but remained a commercial airport throughout the war. Both services used it in their air ferrying services, the AAF's Air Transport Command operated an air freight terminal on the field and the Naval Air Transport Service used it in the air route system. In the postwar years it became El Paso International Airport.

WAR EAGLE MUSEUM: This is an excellent air museum in Santa Teresa, NM, a western suburb of El Paso. See Las Cruces Area, NM for details.

FORT WORTH (See Dallas/Fort Worth Area)

FREDERICKSBURG is 60 miles north of San Antonio.

THE ADMIRAL NIMITZ STATE HISTORICAL PARK AND MUSEUM OF THE PACIFIC WAR: This is America's only museum devoted exclusively to the war in the Pacific. It also relates the personal history of Admiral Nimitz who was born in Fredericksburg. The museum is located in the restored steamboat-shaped Nimitz Hotel near downtown Fredericksburg. The hotel was built and owned by Nimitz' grandfather in 1852. Displays are arranged in chronological order beginning with the days when Nimitz was a youth and ending with his death in 1966. Many of the displays are hands-on types and numerous video displays offer the visitor the actual sights and sounds related to particular displays. One can steer a submarine, turn on a search light, touch a knocked-out Japanese tank and a replica of the atomic bomb that was dropped on Nagasaki. Inside the museum is Nimitz' restored motor barge that he used at Pearl Harbor; an original Japanese-made Aichi D3A2 "Val" fighter plane, one of only two known to exist and one of the types of aircraft used by the Japanese to attack Pearl Harbor on Dec. 7, 1941; a collection of captured Japanese

weapons; displays on Nimitz' days at Annapolis Naval Academy and an electronic map of the Pacific war. In another building on the site is the Nimitz Gallery of Combat Art displaying many paintings and other works of art related to the war in the Pacific. Outside, the Historic Walk of the Pacific is lined with relics of war such as a crashed Japanese dive bomber, tanks, artillery pieces and the actual conning tower of the U.S submarine "Pintado" which sank 14 enemy ships during the war. There is also a Garden of Peace donated by the people of Japan. Address: 340 E. Main St., Fredericksburg, TX 78624. Phone: 512/997-4379 and 997-7269. Hours: daily 8-5, closed Dec. 25. Admission charged.

GAINESVILLE is 50 miles north of Fort Worth near the state line.

CAMP HOWZE was built six miles NE of Gainesville in 1942 for use as an Army training camp for division-sized units. The camp held up to 40,000 troops. Camp Howze was intended to be temporary and was built with great speed. Ground was broken in April 1942 and the first units moved in during August. Soon afterwards, the 84th Infantry Division was activated here. Howze had a main prisoner of war camp with about 2800 POWs who worked for the military. In Feb. 1946 the camp was declared surplus and its assets eventually disposed of.

GALVESTON is on the Texas coast 30 miles SE of Houston and 60 miles west of the Louisiana border. During WW II it was Texas' most strategically located city. From here air patrols fanned out to cover the major part of the Gulf of Mexico and Galveston Bay was the departure point of much of the state's oil that was shipped by sea. Large convoys formed up in Galveston Bay loaded with oil and other vital war materials and set sail for distant locations. After the war Galveston Bay became one of the larger mothball anchorages for the surplus ships of WW II.

FORT CROCKETT was located on the coast at the western end of the city's sea wall on Seawall Blvd. This fort was built by the Confederates during the American Civil War and was garrisoned after the end of that war by the U.S. Army until 1900. It was occupied again in 1911 and was still garrisoned at the beginning of WW II. During the war it was used as an anti-aircraft artillery post and the headquarters for coastal defense on the Southern Coastal Frontier. The Army Engineers, Signal Corps and Ordnance Corps also utilized the fort, and it had a main prisoner of war camp holding about 600 POWs who worked for the military. After the war the Army abandoned the fort and in the 1950s it was sold at auction. The city of Galveston purchased part of the fort's grounds for recreational use.

GALVESTON ARMY AIR FIELD, five miles SW of downtown Galveston, was the city's pre-war airport. It was taken over by the 2nd AF and used for operational and training purposes and as a base for target towing aircraft. After the war Galveston AAF was closed and the air field returned to its former owners to again become Galveston's main commercial airport.

LONE STAR FLIGHT MUSEUM is located on the east side of Galveston Municipal Airport and specializes in the collecting of aircraft from the

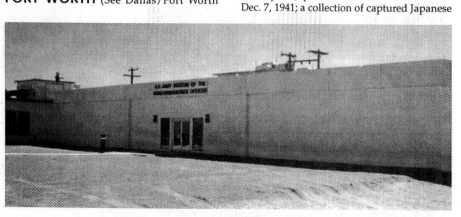

The U.S. Army Museum of the Non-Commissioned Officer, Ft. Bliss, TX.

The Nimitz Hotel in Fredericksburg, TX was built and owned by Adm. Chester Nimitz' grandfather. It is now part of the Admiral Nimitz State Historical Park and Museum of the Pacific War.

1930s and 1940s. Military planes from WW II make up the bulk of the collection. Some of the WW II planes include a T-34, B-17G, PB4Y-2, F6F Hellcat, F7F Tigercat, TBM Avenger, P-38L and a B-25. Address: 2002 Terminal Dr., Galveston, TX 77554. Phone: 409/740-7722. Hours: daily 10-5, closed Jan. 1, Easter, Thanksgiving and Dec. 25. Admission charged.

FORT SAN JACINTO is on the eastern end of Galveston Island overlooking the ship channel into Galveston Bay. The fort was built in 1898-1901 to guard the entrance to the bay. By WW II the fort was still armed and manned and guarded the bay entrance throughout most of the war. It was a sub-post of Fort Crockett. In 1950 it became a U.S. radio compass station, but was eventually abandoned an incorporated into a park.

SEAWOLF PARK is located on the eastern shore of Pelican Island which is across the Port of Galveston Channel from Galveston. The main facilities of the park were once an immigrant quarantine station. In the park are two WW II vessels, the submarine "Cavalla" and the destroyer escort "Stewart". The "Cavalla" saw action in the Pacific and is credited with sinking one of Japan's largest aircraft carriers, the "Shokaku". The "Stewart", which was built in Houston, also saw action during the war and is one of the very few destroyer escorts to survive the war as a memorial. Both ships are open to the public. Address: Seawolf Park, Galveston, TX 77550. Phone: 409/744-5738: Hours: daily 9-5. Admission charged.

FORT TRAVIS was located on Bolivar Point at the western end of the Bolivar Peninsula across the ship channel from Fort San Jacinto. Together they guarded the entrance to Galveston Bay. Fort Travis was built in 1898-99 on the site of a former Confederate Civil War fort. Fort Travis was active during WW II and two new batteries were added; Kimble and #236. Travis was a sub-post of Fort Crockett. After the war Fort Travis was abandoned and became a part of Galveston County Park.

CAMP WALLACE was located 15 miles NW of Galveston near the town of Hitchcock. It was built in 1940-41 as a training camp for Army anti-aircraft units. Later in the war replacements for anti-aircraft units and infantrymen were trained here. Gunnery ranges were available to the camp at the western end of Galveston Island and on San Luis Peninsula, both of which were uninhabited at the time. Camp Wallace was a segregated camp so negro troops also trained here. The camp had a main prisoner of war camp holding about 400 POW who worked at the camp. After the war it was abandoned by the Army but used for a while by the Navy. Eventually Camp Wallace was closed and its assets sold.

U.S. NAVAL AIR STATION (LTA), HITCHCOCK, 1.5 miles SW of Hitchcock, was built in 1942-43 to be one of several blimp stations along the U.S. coast carrying out anti-submarine patrols. NAS, Hitchcock was to have two large blimp hangars, but only one was built. At first six blimps operated out of the station and later another six were added. In July 1943 all of the blimps were safely evacuated from the station as a hurricane passed over the area. By late summer 1944 the need for coastal patrol blimps had diminished and the station was down-graded to a Naval Air Facility and the blimps sent elsewhere. In Jan. 1945 it became a housing facility for an overflow of naval personnel from the naval receiving station in Galveston and its one large hangar was used for storage of aeronautical equipment and materials. Helium was also stored a the station. In May 1947 the station was disestablished and its assets disposed of.

GREENVILLE is 40 miles NE of Dallas on I-30.

MAJORS FIELD, 5.5 miles SSE of Greenville, was acquired by the 2nd AF for the 50,000 Pilot Training Program and was used for training throughout the war. After the war it was abandoned by the AAF to become the area's local airport. Majors Field had the following auxiliary fields during the war:

- Aux. #1, Caddo Mills Airport, 8 miles SW of Greenville
- Aux. #2, Cash Airport, 1 mile SE of Cash
- Aux. #3, South Sulphur Airport, 9.5 miles NNE of Greenville

HARLINGEN (See Brownsville/Harlingen Area)

HEARNE is 55 miles SE of Waco on US 79/190.

CAMP HEARNE PRISONER OF WAR CAMP: This was a large prisoner of war camp built in 1943 near the town of Hearne. It held up to 3000 POWs. Camp Hearne was unique in the POW camp system in that all POW mail was routed thru this location to disguise its origination point and destination. This was done to protect the families of anti-Nazis from reprisals in Germany because anti-Nazis were held in special POW camps and their locations were generally known. In time, it was discovered that pro-Nazis working in the mail program were able to decipher the mail codes and learn the names of some of the anti-Nazis. It was also discovered that they were tabulating a list of those names which they planned to take back to Germany after Germany won the war. When these things were discovered the Germans were removed from the program and replaced by Italian POWs who were much more trustworthy. After the war the camp was abandoned and its assets sold. The camp's headquarters building became an American Legion post and several waist-high concrete models of medieval castles, made by the POWs in their spare time, remain in the area.

HEREFORE is 40 miles SW of Amarillo.

CAMP HEREFORE PRISONER OF WAR CAMP: This was a large main prisoner of war camps for non-cooperative Italian POWs. It held up to 7200 men. The POWs were watched very carefully because there were several escape attempts. Very few of the men were given work outside the camp so most of them had lots of time on their hands which they spent in sports, schooling, reading, music, etc. One POW, Giuseppe Berto, wrote two novels during his time at the camp, "Red is the Sky" and "Works of God". Both were published after the war and Berto won the "Premio Campiello", Italy's equivalent of the Pulitzer Prize. Other POWs at the camp built a small chapel in the cemetery where some of their number were buried. After the war the camp was closed and its assets sold.

The submarine "Cavalla", rear, as seen for the bridge of the destroyer escort "Stewart" in Seawolf Park.

Second Lieutenant Audie Murphy, winner of the Congressional Medal of Honor.

HILLSBORO is 45 miles south of Ft. Worth.

CONFEDERATE RESEARCH CENTER & AUDIE MURPHY GUN MUSEUM is located on the campus of Hill College. The research center, as its name implies, specialized in the American Civil War, but associated with the center is a small museum and research center entitled The Audie Murphy Gun Museum and Weaponry Library. Audie Murphy, a Texan, was America's most decorated soldier during WW II and later became a movie actor. On display are many artifacts associated with Murphy including a piece of the disabled tank destroyer upon which he stood during the exploit that won him the Congressional Medal of Honor. Other displays trace Murphy's life before the war, as a soldier and later as an actor. Museum displays also including captured German and Japanese weapons of WW II. Address: Hill College History Complex, PO Box 619, Hillsboro, TX 76645. Phone: 817/582-2555. Hours: M-F 8-noon and 1-4:30, closed college holidays. Free.

HONDO is 35 miles west of San Antonio.

HONDO ARMY AIR FIELD was built two miles NW of Hondo for the 50,000 Pilot Training Program. It was a training facility for bombardiers and navigators. Late in the war bombardiers, navigators and flight engineers for B-29 bombers trained here. After the war the field was declared surplus and turned over to the local community to become a civilian airport.

HOUSTON AREA: This is a large metropolitan area in SE Texas near the Gulf of Mexico. It was a major seaport and much of the oil from Texas wells was shipped through this port. Several of the important wartime manufacturers in the area were the Brown Shipbuilding Co. which built destroyer escorts, landing craft and patrol boats; San Jacinto

Shipbuilding Co. which built merchant ships and the Houston Shipbuilding Co. which built cargo ships. At nearby Texas City was the world's largest tin smelter which was built during the war, and in Houston the Dickson Gun Plant made large gun barrels for the Navy.

BATTLESHIP "TEXAS" STATE HISTORICAL SITE is located about 18 miles west of downtown Houston at San Jacinto Battleground State Historical Park. The main display is, of course, the battleship "Texas" which is the only battleship on display in the U.S. that took part if both WW I and WW II. The ship was commissioned in 1914 and served the U.S. Navy for 32 years. This ship is open to the public and many artifacts and other displays are on board. Address: 3527 Battleground Rd., La Porte, TX 77571. Phone: 713/479-2411. Hours: W-Sun. 10-5, closed Dec. 25. Admission charged.

BAYTOWN ORDNANCE PLANT was located in Baytown, 20 miles west of downtown Houston. The plant was built by the Federal Government in 1941 to manufacture Toluene, an important ingredient in the explosive TNT. It was located next to an existing Humble Oil refinery and was run by Humble Oil Co. The Toluene made here was manufactured from oil by a new process developed in Germany just prior to the war. After the war the Baytown Ordnance Plant was declared surplus and sold.

ELLINGTON FIELD is 20 miles SE of downtown Houston on Galveston Rd. This was a pre-war airport that had a pilot training school which was contracted by the Army Air Corps in 1939-40 to provide primary flight training to Air Corps cadets. Later in the war the AAF took over the field and operated a reception center here. Later, the field acquired a navigator's training school which moved in from Mather AAB in California. The school trained navigator instructors and offered refresher courses in navigation. Ellington Field also had a sizeable aircraft repair sub-depot. In 1948 the AAF's facilities at the field were taken over by the US Air Force and named Ellington Air Force Base. Also in that year the Civil Air Patrol (CAP) was declared an auxiliary of the Air Force and the CAP headquarters moved here from New York City. In later years the Ellington AFB facility was closed and the air field became a commercial air field.

HOUSTON MUNICIPAL AIRPORT, 9 miles SSE of downtown Houston, was used by the Naval Air Transport Service during the war in its air route system. In late 1942 an experimental program was begun here by the Women's Flying Training Detachment of the AAF to train women

pilots to fly military aircraft in order to become ferry pilots. The program, if successful, would provide female pilots to replace male pilots who were needed for combat duty. Training was done by a private air school, Aviation Enterprises, Ltd. and the program was headed by Jacqueline Cochran a well-known pre-war aviatrix. The program proved to be very successful and soon out-grew its facilities here and was moved to Avenger Field near Sweetwater, TX. There the program was enlarged and renamed the "Women's Air Force Service Pilots" (WASPs).

SAN JACINTO ORDNANCE DEPOT was built in Houston early in the war and was a transshipping depot for Army supplies flowing in and out of the port of Houston. The depot remained active until 1960 at which time it was de-activated and its operations shipped to Red River Arsenal at Texarkana.

U.S. NAVAL AUXILIARY AIR FIELD, CONROE was 3.5 miles NE of Conroe which is 35 miles north of Houston. NAAS, Conroe was acquired by the Navy early in the war to serve as an auxiliary training field for NAS, Clinton, OK. After the war the air field became a commercial airport.

HUNTSVILLE is a county seat 65 miles north of Houston on I-45.

HUNTSVILLE PRISONER OF WAR CAMP was built near Huntsville in 1943. This was a main POW camp for ardent Nazis and held about 2000 POWs. Those who were trustworthy enough to be let out of the camp worked in the forests and with the local Boy Scouts collecting clothes, paper, etc. for recycling. After the war the camp was closed and its assets sold.

KENEDY is 50 miles SE of San Antonio.

KENEDY INTERNMENT CAMP was one of three alien internment camps set up in Texas by the Immigration and Naturalization Service early

The battleship "Texas" saw action in both WW I and WW II. It is now on permanent display in the Houston area.

in the war to receive and house German, Italian and Japanese aliens from Latin America. Kenedy was a camp for men only. It was an abandoned CCC camp that was expanded to hold several thousand internees. The first internees, totalling 525 men, arrived in Apr. 1942 from Peru, Ecuador and Columbia. Later, other aliens arrived from other Latin American countries. In August 1942 a hurricane badly damaged the camp but it was quickly repaired. After the war the internees were discharged or repatriated and the camp was closed.

KILLEEN (See Waco/Temple/Killeen Area)

LAREDO is on the Mexican border 140 miles SW of San Antonio.

LAREDO ARMY AIR FIELD, three miles NE of town, was the city's pre-war airport, Laredo Airdrome. It was taken over by the AAF in 1942 for use as a flexible gunnery school. Both gunners and gunnery instructors were trained here. After the war the AAF departed and the air field became a commercial field once again. However, it was activated again in 1952 by the US Air Force and used as a jet training facility named Laredo Air Force Base. In 1976 Laredo AFB was deactivated and eventually became Laredo International Airport.

FORT McINTOSH was a cavalry post located near downtown Laredo on a high bluff overlooking the Rio Grande River. It was built in 1849 on the site of a former Spanish presidio. Fort McIntosh was garrisoned throughout WW II, but in 1946 it was declared surplus and acquired by the city of Laredo. Most of the facility became a part of Laredo A & I University.

LONGVIEW/MARSHALL AREA: These two cities are in eastern Texas west of Shreveport, LA. Longview was the western terminus of the "Big Inch" oil pipeline built in 1942-43 to supply Texas oil to the U.S. east coast. The Eastern terminus was at Phoenixville, PA. The pipeline was 24" in diameter, 1381 miles long and carried 9 million bbl of oil a month. It was built to reduced the need of supplying oil to the east coast be sea where ships were vulnerable to attacks from enemy submarines.

HARMON GENERAL HOSPITAL was built in Longview in 1942 to treat war wounded. It was a temporary 2218-bed facility constructed of wood and was located south of town on S. Mobberly Ave. Harmon specialized in general medicine, tropical diseases, general and orthopedic surgery, syphilis and psychiatry. There was a branch prisoner of war camp here with about 200 POWs who worked at the hospital. During the war the hospital treated 25,000 patients. In Dec. 1945 it was transferred to the Le Tourneau Foundation and became a part of Le Tourneau College.

LONGHORN ORDNANCE WORKS was located 15 miles NE of Marshall on SR 43. It was built in 1941 by the Federal Government to produce TNT and was run by the Monsanto Chemical Co. By the time TNT production ceased in Aug. 1945, the plant had produced 397 million lbs of the explosive. At that time a second facility was under construction on the grounds of the Longhorn Ordnance Works to produce rocket propellant, but with the end of the war construction was halted. The Longhorn Ordnance Works was placed in standby and in 1951, as a result of the Korean War, was activated again. This time it made pyrotechnic ammunition. Longhorn continued in operation after that war making a variety of munitions and in 1963 was renamed The Longhorn Army Ammunition Plant. The plant functioned throughout most of the Cold War.

LUBBOCK is 105 miles south of Amarillo on I-27.

LUBBOCK FIELD, 10 miles west of town, was built in 1941 for the AAF to meet the needs of the 30,000 Pilot Training Program. Lubbock Field offered primary flight training to cadets and instrument flight training for pilots. Instructors in instrument flight training were also trained here. The air field had a branch prisoner of war camp holding about 230 POWs who worked on the field and in the local area. After the war the air field was retained and used for veterans housing and as a training center for reserves. It was taken over by the US Air Force in 1949 to be used as training center for jet pilots. At that time the field was renamed Reese Air Force Base in honor of 1st Lt. Augustus F. Reese, Jr. a P-38 pilot who was killed in Sardinia during WW II while strafing a train. During the war Lubbock Fd. had the following auxiliary fields:

- Aux. #1, West Field, 22 miles west of Lubbock
- Aux. #2, South Field, 16 miles SW of Lubbock
- Aux. #3, North Field, 23 miles WNW of Lubbock
- Aux. #4, Opdyke Field, 4 miles east of Opdyke
- Aux. #?, Abernathy Field, 5 miles ENE of Abernathy.

SOUTH PLAINS ARMY AIR FIELD, five miles NNE of Lubbock, was the area's local airport when it was activated by the AAF for the 50,000 Pilot Training Program. It was used as a training facility for glider pilots throughout most of the war. At the end of hostilities it was returned to its civilian owners and became Lubbock International Airport. South Plains AAF had two auxiliary air fields during the war; Aux. #1, West Field, 22 miles west of Lubbock and Idalou Air Field, 5.5 miles ENE of Idalou.

MARFA is 165 miles SE of El Paso on US 90.

MARFA ARMY AIR FIELD, 9 miles ESE of town, was known as Marfa Airport before the war. It was activated by the AAF for the 70,000 Pilot Training Program as a training center for the Troop Carrier Command. The Western Flying Training Command also had some training operations at the air field. After the war the air field was returned to its civilian owners. Marfa AAF had the following auxiliary fields:

- Aux. #1, South Field, 15 miles SE of Marfa
- Aux. #3, Ryan Air Field, 16.5 miles WNW of Marfa
- Aux. #4, Marfa Aux. Fd. #4, 4 miles north of marfa
- Aux, #5, Aragon Airport, 8.5 miles WNW of Marfa
- Aux. #7, Marfa Aux. Fd. #7, 2 miles NE of Marfa

FORT D.A. RUSSELL was built on a plateau overlooking the town of Marfa in 1914 to serve as

Gray Ladies take convalescing servicemen for an outing at Harmon General Hospital. The quilted lap robes were made by local women for the patients.

Ellington Field during WW II. In the foreground is the aircraft repair sub-depot.

one of several border patrol forts housing Army cavalry units. At that time it was known as Camp Marfa but by the beginning of WW II the fort had been renamed D.A. Russell. During WW II it was still a cavalry post but was enlarged to also serve as a sub-post for Marfa Army Air Field. Fort D.A. Russell had a main prisoner of war camp with about 180 German POWs who worked for the military. In Dec. 1945 the post was declared inactive and in 1949 was sold to private interests.

MARSHALL (See Longview/Marshall Area)

MATAGORDA ISLAND AND MATAGORDA PENINSULA

MATAGORDA ISLAND AND **MATAGORDA PENINSULA** are two long narrow strips of land along the Texas coast stretching for over 100 miles NE of Corpus Christi. They were uninhabited before and during the war and large areas of both were used as bombing ranges for air crews in training. Throughout the war pilots and crews from a number of air fields utilized the ranges on the island and peninsula and much of the surrounding water. The Matagorda Island range consisted 50,825 acres and was an air-to-air and air-to-ground gunnery range with tow targets available. Matagorda Peninsula had two ranges, a 29,230-acre air-to-air gunnery range on the peninsula and a 704,000-acre air-to-air gunnery range 40 miles to the southeast over water. All three ranges were retained after the war and used well into the postwar years.

McLEAN is 65 miles east of Amarillo on I-40.

CAMP McLEAN PRISONER OF WAR CAMP was located just outside McLean. It was a main POW camp holding about 500 cooperative German POWs who worked in the local area. The camp commander had a very generous release policy and the POWs were often seen in town wandering around on their own. Some of the local citizens objected to this but to no avail. To nearly everyone in McLean the POW camp was referred to as the "Fritz Ritz". After the war the POWs were repatriated, the camp was closed and its assets disposed of.

MEXIA is 40 miles ENE of Waco.

MEXIA PRISONER OF WAR CAMP, near Mexia, was a camp for hard-core Nazis captured in North Africa. It held about 3300 POWs who worked for the military and in agriculture which meant picking cotton in temperatures up to 110 degrees. As was typical of such camps, the internal administration was a carbon copy of Nazi rule in Germany. After the war the camp was closed and its assets disposed of.

MIDLAND/ODESSA AREA

MIDLAND/ODESSA AREA: Midland is 250 miles east of El Paso on I-20. Odessa is 20 miles SW of Midland

MIDLAND AIRPORT (SLOAN FIELD), three miles NW of Midland, was the area's local pre-war airport. It was used by both the AAF and Navy during the war, but was not taken over by either service. The AAF had an air service and maintenance facility at the field and the Air Transport Command utilized the field and operated an air freight terminal here. The AAF and Navy both used the field in their air ferry systems. In 1946 the military operations were withdrawn from the field.

MIDLAND ARMY AIR FIELD was built 9 miles WSW of Midland early in the war for the AAF to meet the needs of the 30,000 Pilot Training

Program. This was a training field for bombardiers and navigators. Bombardier instructors were also trained here. Midland AAF had an auxiliary field, Midland Airport, 3 miles NW of Midland. After the war the air field was declared surplus by the AAF and eventually became Midland's primary airport, Midland International Airport.

Confederate Air Force and American Heritage Airpower Museum: This fine museum is located at Midland International Airport. It is a large air museum and claims to have the most complete collection of flyable WW II aircraft in the world .. some 145 total. It is also the headquarters of the Confederate Air Force, a nation-wide organization of antique aircraft collectors. About 20 of the museum's aircraft are on display at the museum on a rotating basis. The museum has about 70,000 military artifacts and pieces of memorabilia from WW II. There is also an aircraft restoration facility at the museum. Address: Midland International Airport, PO Box 62000, Midland, TX 79711-2000. Phone: 915/563-1000. Hours: M-Sat. 9-5, Sun. and holidays noon-5, closed Dec. 25. Admission charged.

THE PRESIDENTIAL MUSEUM is located near downtown Odessa and has exhibits and educational programs designed to provide a better understanding of the office of the president, election campaigns and the American political process. Included in the exhibits is information about many WW II personalities who had presidential aspirations. They include Franklin Roosevelt, Harry S Truman, John Nance Garner, Henry Wallace, Wendell Willkie, Charles McNary (Willkie's VP running mate), Thomas Dewey, John Bricker (Dewey's VP running mate), Dwight Eisenhower, Richard Nixon, Douglas MacArthur, Robert Taft, Averill Harriman and Paul V. NcNutt. There are numerous displays of campaign materials, presidential artifacts, posters, newspaper clippings, inaugural dresses, First Lady dolls and more. Address: 622 N. Lee St. Odessa, TX 79761. Phone: 915/332-7123. Hours: Tues.-Sat. 10-5, closed holidays. Free.

MINERAL WELLS is a health resort 35 miles west of Fort Worth.

CAMP WOLTERS, three miles east of Mineral Wells, was built in 1925 as a training camp for the Texas National Guard. In 1940 the camp was enlarged and became an Army induction center and a training center for infantry replacements. The camp had a capacity of 25,000 troops. Camp Wolters was a segregated camp so negro troops trained here. It had a main prisoner of war camp with about 600 POWs who worked at the camp and in the local area. In 1946 the post was declared surplus and many of its buildings were sold and relocated. In 1951 the camp was reactivated by the US Air Force, named Wolters Air Force Base, and used to accommodate the Aviation Engineer Force. In 1956 the Army took over the camp again and used it as a training facility for helicopter pilots. After that, Camp Wolters became a permanent Army post and was utilized by various commands throughout the Cold War.

ODESSA (See Midland/Odessa Area)

PALACIOS is 90 miles WSW of Galveston near the Gulf coast.

CAMP CHEMICAL was an operational Army

post established a few days after the attack on Pearl Harbor to protect the vital Dow Chemical Plant A which was close to the Gulf of Mexico and considered vulnerable to attacks from the sea or by saboteurs. Texas National Guardsmen, who had already been called into the Army, manned the post first, but were soon replaced by regular Army troops and a coast artillery units which set up two 6" naval guns on the beach at Quintana. Two 50' watch towers were built on the beach and seven anti-aircraft guns were placed around Plant A and Plant B which was then under construction. The beach in front of the plant was actively patrolled by mounted Coastguardsmen and Coastguardsmen with dogs. Dozens of wartime barracks were built on the site to house workers and soldiers alike. After the war the military services departed from the site and the barracks buildings were torn down.

CAMP HULEN was a pre-war National Guard training camp five miles NW of Palacios. The Army took it over early in the war, enlarged it and used it as a training facility for anti-aircraft units. For the first few months it was a tent camp until wooden barracks could be built for the troops. Camp Hulen had facilities for 14,560 troops. The camp was a segregated facility and negro troops also trained here. The camp had a branch prisoner of war camp with about 200 POWs who worked at the camp. In 1946 the Army returned the camp to the Texas National Guard and it has remained a National Guard camp thereafter.

PAMPA is 50 miles NE of Amarillo in the Texas panhandle.

PAMPA ARMY AIR FIELD was 12.5 miles ENE of Pampa. It was a pre-war air field taken over by the AAF for the 70,000 Pilot Training Program. The air field was used as a training center offering advanced flight training in two-engine bombers. Some Brazilian pilots were trained here. Pampa AAF had two auxiliary fields; Pampa Auxiliary Field #1, 6 miles south of Pampa and Pampa Auxiliary Field # 2, 5.6 miles NNW of Pampa. Pampa AAF was acquired by the US Air Force after the war and renamed Pampa Air Force Base. Several years later, the air field was closed and its assets disposed of.

PARIS is 90 miles NE of Dallas in the NE corner of the state.

CAMP MAXIE was built in 1942 ten miles north of Paris as a training center for infantry divisions. The camp had a capacity of 45,000 troops. There was a main prisoner of war camp here with about 5300 POWs who worked for the military and in the forests. Camp Maxie was closed after the war and its assets disposed of.

PECOS/PYOTE AREA: Pecos is 175 miles east of El Paso on I-20 and Pyote is 21 miles ENE of Pecos, also on I-20.

PECOS ARMY AIR FIELD, two miles SSW of Pecos, was the town's pre-war airport. It was taken over in 1942 by the AAF as a part of the 50,000 Pilot Training Program. Pecos AAF was used throughout the war and was returned to its owners after the end of hostilities. Pecos AAF had the following auxiliary fields:

- Aux. #2, Hermosa Field. 12.2 miles ENE of Pecos

- Aux. #4, Toyah Field, 11.6 miles SSE of Pecos
- Aux. #5, Crystal Airport, 7 miles ENE of Pecos
- Aux. #7, Butte Airport, 4 miles west of Toyah

PYOTE ARMY AIR FIELD was 1.5 miles SW of Pyote. It was built in 1942 for the 2nd AF as a combat training center for crews in very heavy bombers. The Air Transport Command also used the field and operated an air freight terminal here. Pyote AAF had an AAF regional hospital and a branch prisoner of war camp with about 100 POWs who worked on the post. After the war Pyote AAF was used as a storage facility for surplus air craft and, in 1948, was taken over by the US Air Force, renamed Pyote Air Force Base and continued in use as an aircraft storage center under the Air Materiel Command. In 1954 Pyote AFB was closed and its assets sold.

SAN ANGELO is 180 miles NE of San Antonio.

GOODFELLOW FIELD, three miles SE of town, was a pre-war civilian airport that was taken over by the Army Air Corps in 1941 as a primary flight training facility for Air Corps cadets. The field was first named San Angelo Air Corps Basic Flying School, but in 1941 the name was changed to Goodfellow Field in honor of a WW I flyer. Both primary and basic flight training were offered here to Americans, Filipinos, Brazilian, Bolivians and Mexicans. Bombardiers and navigators were also trained as were primary flight instructors. A Federal housing project, Rio Vista, was built adjoining the NW corner of the field to house people employed at the field. Goodfellow was retained after the war and became Goodfellow Air Force Base under the Air Training Command of the US Air Force. During the war Goodfellow had the following auxiliary fields:
- Aux. #1, Oates, Fd., 9.3 miles SE of San Angelo
- Aux. #2, Broome Airport, 10 miles SSE of San Angelo
- Aux. #3, Robbins Fd., 7 miles NNW of San Angelo
- Aux. #4, Lane Fd., 10 miles ESE of San Angelo
- Aux. #5, Pullium Fd., 2 miles NW of Pullium
- Aux. #6, Vancourt Fd., 1.5 miles SW of Vancourt
- Aux. #7, Wall Fd., 3 miles ESE of Wall.

SAN ANGELO ARMY AIR FIELD was built in 1942 eight miles SSW of San Angelo for the 50,000 Pilot Training Program. This was a training field for bombardiers and navigators. After the war the San Angelo AAF was acquired by the city of San Angelo and became its main airport, Mathis Field.

SAN ANTONIO is in south-central Texas.
Years before WW II the Army had selected San Antonio to be the home of the Army's fledgling aviation service which, in the beginning, was under the control of the Army's Signal Corps. In 1917, two air fields were built in the San Antonio area to serve as an aviation cantonment of Fort Sam Houston. They were Kelly and Brooks Fields. The San Antonio area was chosen because of its good flying weather which was so important in those early days of flying. Here the Army Signal Corps trained its pilots, crewmen, maintenance men, administrators and other aviation personnel. As the Army Air Corps gained its own identity and grew in military importance so did these facilities. New facilities were established elsewhere in the country, but they were almost always spinoffs of the San Antonio air fields. In 1928-30 a new and modern air field, Randolph Field, was built in San Antonio confirming and solidifying the fact that San Antonio was the home of the Army Air Corps. Together, the three San Antonio air fields were referred to as the "West Point of the Air".

BROOKE GENERAL HOSPITAL is north of, and adjacent to, Fort Sam Houston. This was a large Army hospital during WW II primarily serving Fort Sam Houston. In 1946 the Army's Medical Service School moved here from Carlisle Barracks, PA and the hospital expanded into a major Army Medical Center and one of the Army's main medical training facilities.

BROOKS FIELD, 6.5 miles SSE of San Antonio, was one of the two original air fields built in the San Antonio area during WW I. Construction began in 1917 and the field opened in Feb. 1918. It was first known as Gosport Field; then Signal Corps Aviation School, Kelly Field #5. In 1918 the field was renamed Brooks Field and retained that name until 1948. In the years between the wars Brooks was home to a balloon and airship school, school of aviation medicine and school for observation squadrons. All the while Air Corps cadets continued to get flight training here including a young man who would become world famous in 1927 .. Charles Lindbergh. In Jan. 1941 Brooks began to offer advanced flight training and the aviation medicine school was enlarged. These were the missions of Brooks Field during WW II. Brooks had one auxiliary air field during the war, San Antonio Municipal Airport, 7.5 miles NNE of San Antonio. Brooks was taken over by the US Air Force in 1948, renamed Brooks Air Force Base and remained operational throughout the Cold War. Its medical facilities became the aerospace medical research center of the Air Force.

Hangar 9-Museum of Flight Medicine: This museum is on the grounds of Brooks AFB in one of the country's few remaining WW I hangars. The museum depicts the history of flight medicine and the history of manned flight. Address: 6570 ABG/MU, Brooks AFB, TX 78235-5000. Phone: 512/536-2203. Hours: M-F 8-4, closed holidays. Free.

CAMP BULLIS is 15 miles NNE of downtown San Antonio on the Leon Springs Military Reservation. It was established in 1917 as a target range and maneuver area for Fort Sam Houston and Camp Travis. Camp Stanley, a WW I infantry training post, was also established here and was later converted to an ammunition storage depot. Both the Regular Army and the National Guard used the facilities at Camp Bullis. In 1922 Camp Bullis was consolidated with Fort Sam Houston and remained a part of Fort Sam Houston throughout WW II. The 2nd, 88th and 95th Infantry Divisions trained here during the war. After the war the facility was utilized by several military agencies; the Army, Texas National Guard, Army Reserves and state and federal law enforcement agencies.

KELLY FIELD, 6 miles SW of San Antonio, was one of the two original Army air fields established in the San Antonio area during WW I. It was first called the Aviation Camp at Fort Sam Houston, then Camp Kelly, then Kelly Field. It remained Kelly Field until 1948. It first served as a Signal Corps office; then an aircraft repair center; a training field for pilots; a school for aircraft mechanics; a school for advanced phases of pursuit and bomber training and, in 1931, Headquarters for the Air Corps' Advanced Flying School. In 1941 Kelly acquired a new gunnery school and a replacement training center. In Nov. 1941 one of the AAF's first reception centers opened here and then merged with the AAF's Classification Center in 1942 to become the San Antonio Aviation Cadet Center. Kelly also absorbed Duncan Field, a WW I air field, which was two miles east of Kelly and had been established by the Army as an aircraft repair depot in 1921. This depot was expanded to become one of four Field Service Sections (Air Depots) in the nation belonging to the AAF's Materials Division. During WW II Kelly acquired a school for navigators, a school for test pilots and a school for airborne artillery observers. The Air Transport Command also used the field and operated an air freight terminal here. In 1948 Kelly Field became Kelly Air Force Base and in the decades that followed was home to a variety of Air Force commands. In the 1990s the facility was closed after the end of the Cold War.

NORMOYLE ORDNANCE DEPOT was located five miles SW of downtown San Antonio on the east side of, and adjacent to Duncan Field (East Kelly Field). This was an old Army depot that stored and maintained ammunition between the wars. Early in WW II it had an ordnance automotive school. In Jan. 1944 Normoyle was transferred to the AAF and became a part of the air depot at Kelly field. Normoyle's personnel and inventory were transferred to the San Antonio Arsenal.

RANDOLPH FIELD is 16 miles ENE of downtown San Antonio. It was built between 1928 and 1930 to be the Army Air Corps' most modern and up-to-date military air field. It was built on the then-new circular field concept[3]. Operations began in the summer of 1931 with a flight training program designed to turn out 300 new Air Corps pilots a year. For the next eight years this was the only place in the country where Air Corps cadets obtained this training. By 1939 Randolph was the largest flight training field in the world, but it wasn't large enough to meet the rapidly expanding needs of the Air Corps and it couldn't be easily expanded because of its circular design. As the need for more training fields became apparent, personnel from Randolph were sent out across the country to locate sites where new training fields might be built and existing air fields utilized. As those sites began to be acquired they became known as "Little Randolphs". In 1939 the Air Corps began the program of contracting civilian flight schools around the nation to provide primary flight training to new Air Corps cadets at commercial airports. The civilian schools would provide mostly primary flight training while the newly acquired Air Corps-operated air fields would provide the remaining two phases of training. In prepara-

EDIT

tion for the civilian training program, many of the civilian instructors were brought to Randolph and given refresher courses and courses in the training of military pilots. In 1940 the Air Corps' training program was divided into three geographical commands, the Eastern Flying Training Command, Gulf (later Central) Flying Training Command and Western Flying Training Command. Randolph became headquarters for the Gulf (Central) Flying Training Command. Randolph also continued its training programs, but began to specialize in very heavy bombers. During 1942, Randolph's last full year of flight training, some 5000 airmen were trained. By 1943 the AAF had enough air fields elsewhere to terminate flight training at Randolph and convert its training facilities into a school for flight instructors. During the remaining war years Randolph turned out some 15,000 flight instructors. Randolph also acquired schools for aviation medicine and air evacuation. In late 1944 Randolph became one of the few air fields around the country to provide transition training for pilots and crews from heavy bombers into the new super-long-range, atomic-bomb-carrying B-29s. Randolph Field remained active after the war and was taken over by the US Air Force in 1948 and renamed Randolph Air Force Base. It continued to be one of the most important military air bases in the country and was home to a number of command headquarters. Randolph AFB served throughout the Cold War and well into the post-Cold War era. During WW II Randolph Field has the following auxiliary field:

- Aux. #2, Cade FD., 9 miles NE of San Antonio
- Aux. #4, Martindale Auxiliary Fd., 7 miles east of San Antonio
- Aux. #5, Clear Springs Airport, 6 miles east of New Braunfels
- Aux. #6, Zuehl Fd., 21 miles NNE of San Antonio
- Aux. #7, Sequin Fd., 3.2 miles east of San Antonio
- Aux. #8, Davenport Fd., 16 miles east of San Antonio

In the desperate month of Apr. 1942 the U.S. Army shows off one of its better assets, its mobility, on the Arthur MacArthur Parade Ground at Fort Sam Houston.

- Aux. #?, Diltz Airport, 4 miles NW of Floresville
- Aux. #?, Rio Medena Airport, 4.5 miles north of Castroville

FORT SAM HOUSTON is three miles NE of downtown San Antonio. The fort began its existence as a quartermasters depot built on donated land in the 1870s. In the 1880s it became a cavalry post known as the Post of San Antonio. In Sept. 1890 it was renamed Fort Sam Houston after Texas's famous political and military hero. The birth of military aviation is said to have occurred here in 1910 when the Signal Corps, after acquiring its first Wright Brothers bi-plane, began using it in Signal Corps operations. Eventually the fort acquired its own air field, Dodd Field. During WW I the fort was greatly expanded and in 1922 absorbed the WW I training post, Camp Travis. It also acquired a large depot, the San Antonio General Depot which grew to considerable size.

Early in WW II the fort became a reception center for the 8th Corps and the concentration and training center for the 2nd Infantry Division. Later, Fort Sam Houston became the training center of the Army's airborne infantry. The fort was a segregated camp so negro troops also served and trained here. During the summer of 1942 some of the Japanese aliens interned form the Hawaiian Islands were held here until internment camps were ready for them. Later that year Fort Sam acquired one of the first main prisoner of war camps in the nation. It eventually held about 3000 POWs who worked primarily for the military. Some of the Army's first POW camp guards were trained here. In late 1944 the fort had vacant barracks which were utilized to house convalescing service personnel in order to provide much-needed space in some of the Army's general hospitals. The fort remained in operation after the war and became the home of several Army commands.

Fort Sam Houston Museum: This museum is on the grounds of Fort Sam Houston and traces the history of the fort from its beginning to the present. There are exhibits on the U.S. 5th Army and the 2nd Infantry Div., the birth of military aviation and famous Americans who served here. The museum has an extensive collection of prisoner of war artifacts from WW II. Address: AFZG-PTM-M, Fort Sam Houston, TX 78234-5000. Phone: 512/221-4886. Hours: W-Sat. 10-4, closed Jan. 1, Thanksgiving and Dec. 25. Free.

This is the administration building of Randolph Field. It was built in the early 1930s and nicknamed the "Taj Mahal". It remained in use throughout the remainder of the 20th Century. The tower is actually a water tank.

Many of the first prisoners of war to arrive at Ft. Sam Houston in late 1942 lived in tents until barracks became available.

U.S. Army Medical Department Museum: This is a second museum at Fort Sam Houston located in building 2264. It is the official museum of the Army's medical department and serves as an educational facility showing the history and development of the Army's medical department and military medical equipment. It also traces the history of the U.S. Army's medical departments from the Civil War to the present. Medical equipment from the U.S., Germany, Japan, the Soviet Union and Viet Nam is on display. Address: HSHA-SMM, Fort Sam Houston, TX 78234-6100. Phone: 512/221-6358. Hours: W-Sun. 10-4, closed federal holidays. Free.

SAN ANTONIO ARSENAL was built in 1858 to provide arms and ammunition to troops guarding the frontier. It was in continuous use up to the late 1970s. During WW II it produced, and stored ammunition for the Army's needs in this region of the country. After the war it was declared surplus and was sold to a chain of retail stores.

SAN ANTONIO AVIATION CADET CENTER was just west of Kelly Field. It was built in 1941 as a part of Kelly Field and was first used as Kelly Field's reception center. In July 1942 it was made its own command and given its wartime name. San Antonio Aviation Cadet Center became a basic training center for recruits and draftees assigned to the AAF and was the largest center of its kind in the country. It also offered office training, chaplain training and cadet pre-flight training. In June 1945 the facility became an AAF personnel distribution center and was renamed the San Antonio District AAF Personnel Distribution Command. AAF personnel returning from overseas were given a period of rest and relaxation here before being assigned to new posts. A rest camp near Hunt, TX, 50 miles NW of San Antonio, was established for this purpose. In July 1946 the facility was converted back into a training center for both men and women of the AAF and named Army Air Forces Military Training Cen-

ter. Later that year, in Oct., the facility was given yet another name; Indoctrination Division, Air Training Command. In July 1947 to was redesignated Lackland (Army) Air Base in honor of Brig. Gen. Frank D. Lackland who had commanded the Advanced Flying School at Kelly Field during the early part of WW II and who had died in 1943. In 1948 the US Air Force took over the facility and named it Lackland Air Force Base. It then remained in operation under that name throughout the Cold War and during most of that time was a training center.

History and Traditions Museum: This museum is on the grounds of Lackland Air Force Base and has a very large collection of vintage aircraft. WW II planes include a B-17G, B-24M, B-25N, B-26, C-47D, P-47N, P-51H and a AT-6C. The museum has other displays including a special display on the Women's Air Force Service Pilots (WASPs) and Air Force Medal of Honor winners. Address: AFMT/LGMH, Lackland AFB, San Antonio, TX 78236-5000. Phone: 512/671-3444/3055. Hours: daily 9-5:45, closed Jan. 1, Easter, Thanksgiving and

Dec. 25. Free.

STINSON FIELD, 6 miles SSE of downtown San Antonio, was a pre-war airport that was used by the AAF, but not taken over by it. The San Antonio Air Technical Service Command had a depot training facility here and the Central Flying Training Command also used the field. After the war the AAF departed and the air field returned to its civilian status.

SAN MARCOS is midway between Austin and San Antonio on I-35.

SAN MARCOS FIELD, five miles east of town, was the town's pre-war airport. It was taken over by the AAF early in the war and used as a training facility for bombardiers and navigators. Chinese and Brazilians were also trained here. During the war San Marcos Field had one auxiliary air field, Castroville Airport, two miles ESE of Castroville. San Marcos Field was inactivated in 1946, but then reactivated in 1953 by the US Air Force and named Gary Air Force Base in honor of 2nd Lt. Edward Gary, a native of San Marcos. The USAF eventually returned the air field to its civilian owners and it became a commercial air field again.

SWEETWATER (See Abilene/Sweetwater Area)

TEMPLE (See Waco/Temple/Killeen Area)

TEXARKANA is in NE Texas on the Texas/Arkansas border.

LONE STAR ORDNANCE PLANT/RED RIVER ARSENAL: These were two facilities built side-by-side in 1941-42 on the south side of US 82 17 miles west of Texarkana. The Lone Star Ordnance Plant manufactured munitions for the Army and Red River Arsenal stored much of that material. The mission of the Lone Star Ordnance changed during the war from one of manufacturing to one of rehabilitating used or damaged ordnance equipment. This included a wide variety of items including tanks and large field guns. During the war Red River Arsenal had a training facility for ordnance personnel. Some 12,000 GIs were trained here form 1941-1945. In Nov. 1945 the two facilities were merged and became the Red River Ordnance Depot. The depot was placed on stand-by status after the war, but reactivated for the Korean War and used for training and storage. In 1962 the facility was renamed the Red River Army Depot and continued in operation for several more years.

M3A3 light tanks being remanufactured at Red River Arsenal during WW II.

TYLER is 90 miles SE of Dallas on I-20.

CAMP FANNIN was located 10 miles NE of Tyler. It was built in 1943 for the Army as a basic training center and a training center for infantry replacements. At its height the camp held 18,680 service personnel. The camp had a main prisoner of war camp holding about 1000 POWs who worked for the military. There was also an Army disciplinary barracks here which help both Americans and prisoners of war convicted of felonies. In 1946 Camp Fannin was declared surplus and disposed of except for the cantonment area.

UVALDE is 70 miles west of San Antonio on US-90.

GARNER FIELD was 2.5 miles ESE of Uvalde. It was one of the many civilian airports in the country that had a private flight training school that was contracted by the Army Air Corps in 1939-40 to provide primary flight training to air cadets. After the program ended the AAF used the air field from time-to-time but did not take it over. Garner Field continued to be the area's local airport in the postwar years.

GARNER MEMORIAL MUSEUM is the former home of Vice President John Nance "Cactus Jack" Garner. Garner was the local Congressman from the Uvalde area who rose to become Speaker of the House of Representatives and then Vice President for two terms (1933-1941) under Franklin D. Roosevelt. Garner actively supported Roosevelt's New Deal in the early years, but then turned against him. He sought the Democrat presidential nomination for himself in 1940, but was unsuccessful. He then actively campaigned against Roosevelt and his third term. Garner eventually returned to Uvalde and is buried in the town cemetery. The museum has displays tracing the private and political life of Garner and has many of his personal artifacts. Address: 333 N. Park St., Uvalde, TX 78802. Phone: 210/278-5018. Hours: M-Sat. 9-noon and 1-5, closed holidays. Admission charged.

VICTORIA is 70 miles NE of Corpus Christi.

ALOE ARMY AIR FIELD was located 5.5 miles WSW of Victoria near the community of Aloe and was a sub-post of Foster Field. It was acti-

vated for the 70,000 Pilot Training Program and used for advanced flight training in single-engine aircraft under the direction of the Central Flying Training Command. Brazilian and Filipino pilots trained here as well as Americans. After the war the air field was declared surplus and abandoned by the AAF. Aloe AAF had the following auxiliary fields:

- Aux. #7, Aloe Aux. Fd. #7, 7.6 NW of Victoria
- Aux. #8, Aloe Aux. Fd. #8, 4.2 miles south of Goliad
- Aux. #9, Aloe Aux. Fd. #9, 15 miles SW of Victoria
- Aux. #10, Aloe Aux. Fd. #10, 7.2 miles ENE of Goliad

FANNIN PRISONER OF WAR CAMP was a main POW camp located near Fannin, TX, 17 miles SW of Victoria. This camp held about 1000 POWs who worked for the military and other employers. After the war the POWs were repatriated, the camp closed and its assets disposed of.

FOSTER FIELD, six miles NE of Victoria, was the area's local airport before the war. It was taken over by the AAF early in the war as a center for advanced flight training in single-engine aircraft. Fixed gunnery instructors were also trained here. Mexican and other Latin American pilots were trained here early in the war, but that program was moved to Napier Fd., Dothan, AL because of local prejudice against Latin Americans. The AAF left the field in 1946 and the facility became the local airport once again; Victoria-Foster Airport. During the war Foster Field had the following auxiliary fields:

- Aux. #2, Foster Aux. Fd. #2, 18 miles NNW of Victoria
- Aux. #4, Nursery Fd., 12.5 miles NNW of Victoria
- Aux. #5, Foster Aux. Fd. #5, 14.5 miles NE of Victoria
- Aux. #6, Foster Aux. Fd. #6, 16.2 miles west of Victoria

WACO/TEMPLE/ KILLEEN AREA:

Waco is about midway between Fort Worth and Austin on I-35. Temple is 30 miles south of Waco and Killeen is 18 miles west of Temple.

This WW II-era Sherman tank is one of several tanks on display at Fort Hood, TX.

BLACKLAND ARMY AIR FIELD, 6 miles NW of Waco, was a civilian airport before the war. It was taken over by the AAF for the 50,000 Pilot Training Program as a sub-base for Waco AAF and used for training purposes. In 1946 the AAF left Blackland AAF and it once again became a civilian air field. During WW II Blackland AAF had the following auxiliary air fields:

- Aux. #1, McGregor Fd., 6.8 miles NE of McGregor
- Aux. #2, Riesel Fd., 6.7 miles WSW of Riesel
- Aux. #?, Temple Fd., 5.5 miles NW of Temple

CAMP HOOD, north of and adjacent to Killeen, was built in 1942 on the site of Fort Gates, an old frontier post dating from 1849. Camp Hood was a huge training camp capable of housing 95,000 troops. The camp specialized in the training of tank destroyer units and was the only facility in the nation training such units. Other Army units also trained here including infantry units. Later in the war Camp Hood concentrated on training replacements for tank destroyer units. Camp Hood had two air fields, Camp Hood Army Air Field and Robert Gray Air Field. It also had a main prisoner of war camp holding about 1700 POWs who worked on the post and in the local area. A branch of the Army disciplinary barracks was located here. After the war, Camp Hood was utilized by the Texas and Oklahoma National Guards and the Army Reserve. In 1970 the facility was designated Fort Hood and became one of the Army's primary training centers for armored units. Fort Hood continued in operation throughout the Cold War.

First Cavalry Division Museum: This museum is on the grounds of Fort Hood and honors the men and women who served in the 1st Cavalry Division, an important Army unit that made its home at Fort Hood after WW II. Displays trace the history of the unit including its participation in WW II. Address: Bldg. 2218, PO Box 5187, Ft. Hood, TX 76544. Phone: 817/287-3626/4198. Hours: M-F 9-3:45, Sat.-Sun. noon-3:45, closed holidays. Free.

2nd Armored Division Museum: This is a second museum on the grounds of Fort Hood honoring the men and women of the 2nd Armored Division which also made it home here in the

The Garner Memorial Museum in Uvalde, TX was the home of John Nance Garner, Vice President of the United States during the early part of WW II.

postwar years. The museum relates the history of the unit from its inception in 1940 to the present. Address: Bldg. 418, PO Box 5009, Fort Hood, TX 76546-5201. Phone: 817/287-3570. Hours: M-F 9-3, Sat.-Sun. noon-3:30 closed Jan. 1, Easter, Thanksgiving and Dec. 25. Free.

McCLOSKEY GENERAL HOSPITAL was built in Temple in 1942 on land donated by the people of Temple to treat war wounded. The main hospital buildings were of semi-permanent construction and the hospital specialized in neurology, amputations, neurosurgery and psychiatry. McCloskey had 3454 beds and a branch prisoner of war camp with about 200 POWs who worked at the hospital and in the local area. In Mar. 1946 the hospital was transferred to the Veterans Administration.

WACO ARMY AIR FIELD was 7 miles NNW of Waco and had been the town's local airport before the war. It was taken over by the AAF for the 30,000 Pilot Training Program and be-

came a training center for AAF flight instructors. Basic flight training instructors, advanced single-engine flight instructors and twin-engine flight instructors were trained here. After the war the AAF returned the air field to its owners and it again became Waco's main airport. During the war Waco AAF had the following auxiliary fields:

- Aux. #3, Cartwright Fd., 1.2 miles ENE of Horn
- Aux. #4, Aguilla Aux. Fd., 1 miles NW of Aguilla
- Aux. #5, Prairie Hill Fd., 1 miles south of Prairie Hill.

WICHITA FALLS is 100 miles NW of Fort Worth near the state line.

SHEPPARD FIELD was five miles north of downtown Wichita Falls. It was the town's prewar airport, Kell Fd., and was taken over in 1941 by the AAF for use as a technical training center. It

was named in honor of Morris E. Sheppard, U.S. Senator from Texas, who had served as Chairman of the Senate Armed Services Committee from 1933 until his death in 1941. Sheppard helped lead the fight for military preparedness before Pearl Harbor. During the war aircraft mechanics, glider maintenance men, cooks and bakers were trained here. In 1943 the field was expanded to accommodate a basic flight training center under the direction of the Central Flying Training Command which began training liaison pilot instructors and helicopter pilot instructors. Sheppard had a regional AAF hospital and two auxiliary fields; Aux. #1, Petrolia Fd., 6.5 miles south of Petrolia and Aux. #2, Electra Airport, 3.4 miles NW of Electra. After the war Sheppard AAF was taken over by the US Air Force in 1948 and renamed Sheppard Air Force Base. It continued to be a training center for a variety of technical command throughout the Cold War.

UTAH

Utah contributed to the successful conclusion of WW II in a variety of ways despite its relatively small wartime population of 550,000 people. The state produced munitions, steel, petroleum products, meat, dairy products, grain, brewing, fruits, sugar beets, vegetables, coal, coke, salt, oil, natural gas, sand, gravel and a very large assortment of ores; gold, silver, copper, lead, zinc, alumite, tungsten, iron, manganese, bismuth, fluorite, arsenic, vanadium, potash and molybdenum. Much of the state's economy was based on mining and agriculture and during the war the shortage of labor was a constant problem despite the fact that the state's population grew by an estimated 13%. To solve the labor problem, many women and imported laborers for Mexico worked on farms, in industry and in the mines. Many of the mines were equipped with automated machinery during the war to save labor. Mining peaked in 1943, but continued strong during the remaining years of the war and into the post war era. In 1952 Utah's mining industry added another commodity ... uranium. The open pit uranium mine near Moab would become one of the nation's largest.

During the 1930s, Utah was in bad economic shape due to the Great Depression and had one of the highest unemployment rates in the nation. In 1939 Utah's economy began to change for the better and improve rapidly. During WW II the value of manufactured products in the state nearly tripled. In 1940-41 major military facilities were constructed in Utah at Ogden, Salt Lake City and Wendover which helped to stimulate the state's economy. In 1942 even more military facilities would be built in the state. Many of the military facilities in northern Utah were depots because it had long been recognized by the U.S. military leaders that this area was strategically located for supplying the U.S. west coast. The main west coast ports of Puget Sound; Portland, OR; San Francisco Bay; Los Angeles and San Diego were all about equidistant from northern Utah,

and there were good rail connections with all of them. Therefore, northern Utah became a storehouse and distribution point for war materials heading west. The state's vast deserts were used extensively for bombing and gunnery ranges during and after the war. In the early months of 1942 when Japanese attacks on the west coast were most feared, Gen. John DeWitt, the commander of the Army's Western Defense Command, made tentative plans to move his headquarters to Salt Lake City it the need arose. It didn't and DeWitt's headquarters stayed in San Francisco, but an Army Corps' headquarters, that could have been used by DeWitt in an emergency, was transferred to Salt Lake City.

During the war Utah had one relocation camp for ethnic Japanese and 11 prisoner of war camps. During the winter of 1944-45 five Japanese bombing balloons came down in the state, none of which did any damage. One of them, however, did give a local sheriff some trying moments.

After the war Utah continued to prosper and grow. Mining continued strong, industry continued to grow and oil production and refining prospered. When the interstate highway system was build in the 1950-60 the state named its main east-west interstate, I-80, in honor of one of the war's great heros ... the Dwight D. Eisenhower Highway.

ABRAHAM is 80 miles SW of Provo.

CENTRAL UTAH RELOCATION CAMP: It was here, in this remote location, that the War Relocation Authority chose to build one of their camps for the ethnic Japanese relocated from the west coast. The camp was built in early 1942 and designed to hold 10,000 people. It was three miles east of Abraham. Most of the people sent here were from the San Francisco Bay area and had been processed at the Tanforan Assembly Center. The camp operated throughout the war and many of the people worked in the local area. The camp was closed in Oct. 1945 and its land and assets disposed of by the Federal Government.

BRIGHAM is now known as Brigham City, 20 miles north of Ogden.

BUSHNELL GENERAL HOSPITAL was a 3377-bed Army hospital built in 1942 near the southern edge of the town. Its mission was to care for war wounded. Bushnell was of two-story brick construction and intended to be a semi-permanent facility. During the war Bushnell specialized in neurology, neurological surgery, amputations, deep X-ray therapy and psychiatry. It had closed wards for psychotic patients. The hospital also had a main prisoner of war camp that first held about Italian 300 POWs and later held German POWs. Both the Italians and Germans worked at the hospital. Bushnell had a 40-bed ward which treated wounded and sick POWs. In June 1946 Bushnell was transferred to the Veterans Administration. Later it became a school for Indians.

DUGWAY, 50 miles SW of Salt Lake City, didn't exist before WW II. This was a part of the Great Salt Lake Desert and the only signs of human life in the area were the Skull Valley Indian Reservation, 10 miles to the north, and Orr's Ranch which appeared on some Utah state maps.

DUGWAY PROVING GROUND surrounded the wartime community that would become Dugway and stretched for 35 miles to the west. It covered 1500 square miles, was the 8th largest Army facility in the nation and was larger than the state of Rhode Island. The site was acquired by the Army's Chemical Corps early in 1942 for use as a testing ground for chemical weapons. Federal housing was built on the eastern edged of the proving ground to house the workers and military personnel and formed the basis for the community of Dugway which was incorporated after the war. Other small, but uninhabited, towns were built on the Dugway Proving Ground and then were bombed with incendiary bombs to test the effectiveness of the bombs. The towns' buildings and simulated gun emplacements

This machine gun, a Browning 50 Cal. Heavy-barrel, was used by all of the U.S. armed forces during WW II.

were also torched by experimental flame throwers. During the war a 4.2" mortar was developed here to lob a huge poison gas-laden shell a considerable distance in the event such weapons had to be used. Fortunately for mankind, they weren't. Dugway had its own air field and a branch prisoner of war camp holding about 100 Italian POWs who worked on the post. After the war Dugway was retained by the Army as a testing ground for chemical, biological and radiological weapons. It remained in operation until well after the end of the Cold War with many of the WW II facilities still in use.

LEHI is 25 miles south of Salt Lake City on Lake Utah.

CAMP WILLIAMS, five miles NW of Lehi, was built in 1914 as a training ground for the Utah National Guard. During WW II the camp became a sub-post of Fort Douglas, was enlarged and used for the training of Army units. In Nov. 1944 the camp was returned to the National Guard.

MOAB is near the east-central edge of the state on US 191 and the Colorado River. In 1942 Moab became one of two sites selected by the War Relocation Authority (WRA) for a "Citizens' Isolation Camp" which was designed to hold troublesome individuals from the Japanese Relocation Camps. The other isolation camp was at Leupp, AZ and both had been former CCC camps.

The need for such camps became evident soon after the ethnic Japanese began moving into the various relocation camps. In each camp a small number of individuals, mostly young Kibei (Nisei men educated in Japan), became uncooperative and caused trouble and needed to be separated from the general camp population. The WRA, working with the Justice Department, established the two isolation camps to hold these individuals. Both camps, run by the Justice Dept., soon filled to capacity

so it was decided to convert the large relocation camp at Tule Lake, CA into a special camp for trouble-makers, dissidents and renunciants. When Tule Lake was ready, the residents of both isolation camps were transferred there and the camps closed.

OGDEN is 25 miles north of Salt Lake City. This was the city in the central Rocky Mountain area best situated to facilitate rail transportation to the west coast. Ogden therefore became a prime location of military depots.

JOHN M. BROWNING FIRE ARMS MUSEUM is located in the restored Ogden Union Station and is one of several museums in the station. The Browning Museum displays a wide selection of military and civilian fire arms with some interesting models from WW II. Of particular interest is a display of the prototypes and first production models of the Browning

Automatic Rifle (BAR) which was used by almost every infantry squad in the U.S. Army during WW II. There is also a 50 Cal. heavy-barrel machine gun that was used by all the services during WW II and a 37 mm cannon of the type used in the nose of P-39 fighter planes. Address: Union Station, 25th & Wall Sts., Ogden, UT 84401. Phone: 801/629-8535. Hours: M-Sat. 10-6, closed Jan. 1, Thanksgiving and Dec. 25. Admission charged.

CLEARFIELD PRISONER OF WAR CAMP: This was a main prisoner of war camp located in Clearfield, a southern suburb of Ogden. The camp held about 500 German POWs who worked for the military. After the war the camp was closed and its assets disposed of.

HILL FIELD, just south of Ogden, began as an Army Air Corps air depot in 1939 named Ogden Air Depot. In Dec. 1939 the post was renamed Hill Field and became the AAF's main air depot and aircraft repair facility in the central Rocky Mountain area. Hill Field had long runways and could handle any airplane in the AAF inventory. An airplane repair shop was completed in Mar. 1942 and an engine repair facility was built in 1944. At its peak during WW II, Hill Field employed 22,000 people. On the post was a main prisoner of war camp holding about 800 Italian POWs who worked for the military. Hill Field had an auxiliary air field, Robert H. Hinckley Airport, 3.5 miles SW of Ogden. In 1948 Hill Field was acquired by the US Air Force and renamed Hill Air Force Base. From 1945 to 1953 it was a major storage facility for surplus WW II aircraft including B-29s. During the Korean War, Hill AFB was a major renovation center for B-29s being used in that war. Some of the B-29s renovated had been stored here. In 1955 Hill AFB absorbed Ogden Arsenal which adjoined the air field. Hill AFB remained active as an air depot and storage facility throughout the Cold War and for many years was Utah's largest employer.

Hill Air Force Base Museum: This fine air museum is on the grounds of Hill Air Force Base and has a large collection of vintage aircraft and displays tracing the history of the base. One of the outstanding aircraft in the collection is a rare Sikorsky R-4B helicopter, the

Hill Air Force Base Museum, Ogden, UT.

first production military helicopter. These helicopters came into use during the closing months of WW II. Other WW II aircraft include a B-29, B-17, P-40, C-47B and PT-17. Address: OO-ALC/XPH Hill Air Force Base, UT 84056. Phone: 801/777-6868. Hours: Jun. thru Sept. Tues.-F 9-7. Sat.-Sun. 9-5:30; rest of year Tues.-F 9-4:30, Sat.-Sun. 9-5:30. Closed Thanksgiving and Dec. 25. Free.

OGDEN ARSENAL, 7 miles south of downtown Ogden, was built soon after WW I and was one of the Army's main storage and repair facilities for munitions in the years between the wars. In 1938 it was designated as an Army Air Corps facility and in 1939 Hill Field was constructed adjacent to the arsenal. During WW II Ogden Arsenal handled much of the ordnance used by Hill Field and other air fields in the west. It also manufactured 100 lb general purpose bombs, 37 mm high explosive shells, primers, fuzes, boosters and loaded various types of ammunition. Ogden Arsenal was unable to expand so some of its operations were shifted to Tooele Ordnance Depot. Ogden Arsenal continued in use after the war and in 1955 was absorbed by Hill Air Force Base.

U.S. NAVAL SUPPLY DEPOT, CLEARFIELD was built in 1943 in Clearfield, a southern suburb of Ogden. This was a general supply facility that backed up Navy supply depots on the west coast. After the war the depot was closed and its assets disposed of.

UTAH SERVICE FORCES DEPOT, 2.5 miles north of downtown Ogden, was built in 1941 on a site that gave it access to the four major railroads that services northern Utah. From here, Army supplies could be sent to virtually any point along the west coast. During WW II it received, stored and shipped a wide variety of items for several branches of the Army and serviced Army posts in 13 states, Alaska and the Pacific. Later in the war the facility became a master depot with other depots under its command. The depot had a main prisoner of war camp holding about 3200 POWs who worked at the depot and at other jobs in the area. In the latter years of the war Italian Service Units worked at the depot.

This is a prewar amphitheater that was formerly a part of Fort Douglas. During WW II USO shows were held here. The amphitheater and the WW II building to the rear now belong to the University of Utah.

The Utah Service Forces Depot continued in operation after the war and functioned throughout the Cold War under several names.

PROVO is 30 miles south of Salt Lake City on the eastern shore of Lake Utah. It was here that in 1940-41 the Defense Plant Corporation, an agency of the Federal Government, built the first steel plant west of the Mississippi River. The plant was known as the Geneva Steel Works. Building steel plants in the west had long been a pet project of President Roosevelt and his fellow New Dealers and the urgency of WW II gave them the opportunity to fulfill this objective. Later in the war another steel plant was built in Fontana, CA in the Los Angeles area. Both plants produced steel during WW II.

SALINA is 90 miles south of Provo.

SALINA PRISONER OF WAR CAMP was a small branch camp housing German POWs who were working on the local farms. This camp was typical of many branch POW camps across the nation established for the POWs who worked in agriculture, the forests, food processing plants and the like. The camp was closed after the war.

SALT LAKE CITY is the capital of Utah.

FORT DOUGLAS, about two miles east of downtown Salt Lake City, was established in 1862 during a period of political unrest with the new Mormon settlers, intermittent raids by Indians on U.S. mail routes and in the middle of the American Civil War. The mission of Camp Douglas, as it was first called, was to establish law and order, enforce U.S. laws, suppress the Indians and secure the loyalty of the Utah Territory for the Union. By the time WW II started the post had been renamed Fort Douglas and was the home of the 38th Infantry Division. During the summer of 1940 the 38th Div. was transferred to Texas and soon afterwards Fort Douglas became an Army reception center. Later it provided housing for AAF personnel stationed at Salt Lake City Airdrome Lease (see below). During the early part of 1942 Fort Douglas was considered by General John DeWitt, Commander of the Army's Western Defense Command, as a location where he might move his headquarters from San Francisco, CA in the event California was invaded. In 1943 IX Corps Headquarters moved here from San Francisco for its own security reasons and to serve as a possible Western Defense Command headquarters, if necessary, for Gen. DeWitt. In late 1943-early 1944 Fort Douglas became a processing center for prisoners of war. POWs arrived here from the east, were processed and then dispersed to various POW camps. The fort also had its own main POW camp with about 250 Italian POWs who worked at the fort. Operations peaked at Fort Douglas in the fall of 1943. The fort was retained by the Army after the war and in 1946 the IX Corps headquarters returned to San Francisco. In 1970 Fort Douglas was placed on the National Register of Historic Places and in 1975 became a National Historic Landmark. In 1979 the Army disposed of most of the fort's land and many of its buildings which went to the University of Utah which bordered the fort on two sides. The remaining facilities were used as military housing and offices for various military agencies including the Utah National Guard, Army Reserves and ROTC. Many of

The Fort Douglas Military Museum is housed in one of the fort's hundred-year-old buildings.

the fort's beautiful old buildings have been preserved and remained in use and in the 1990s the Army closed its last facilities at the fort.

Fort Douglas Military Museum: This is a small museum on the grounds of Fort Douglas that offers displays and information on the history of the fort. Included in the displays are military uniforms dating from 1853. Displays on the WW II era are limited. Phone: 801/588-5188. Hours: Tues.-Sat. 10-noon and 1-4, closed federal holidays. Free.

KEARNS ARMY AIR BASE was located 5.8 miles SSW of downtown Salt Lake City. This was an AAF non-flying ground facility which provided basic training for AAF recruits. It was built early in the war as a temporary facility and had barracks built of wood and covered over with tar paper. The base had a large regional AAF hospital. Kearns functioned throughout the war and operations peaked during 1943. Near the end of the war Kearns AAB became an AAF Personnel Distribution Center for units returning from Europe and scheduled to go to the Pacific. After the war Kearns was declared surplus and disposed of by the AAF.

SALT LAKE CITY AIRDROME LEASE/SALT LAKE CITY ARMY AIR FIELD: Salt Lake City Airdrome Lease was the name first given to Salt Lake City's municipal airport when it was taken over by the Army Air Corps in late 1940. Technically, it was a sub-post of Fort Douglas and AAF personnel from here were housed at Fort Douglas. The airdrome was four miles west of the city and was used by the AAF during the first half of the war as an operational base for heavy bomber units previously stationed at Hamilton Field in the San Francisco Bay area. The bomber units moved out to make room for fighter squadrons which were more useful in air defense than bombers. The air units here, nevertheless, served as support units for those on the west coast and were safe from enemy attacks from the sea. When the threat of enemy attacks along the west coast declined the heavy bombers departed and the AAF converted this facility into an intelligence training center for

enlisted men and renamed it Salt Lake City Army Air Field. The training center soon moved out in late 1944 and the facility was temporarily inactive. It was scheduled to have a Flight Service Center and become an AAF Personnel Distribution Center for units being reassigned from Europe to the Pacific, but this never came about due to the sudden end of the war. After the war the air field was returned to its owners and the AAF facilities were transferred to the Utah Air National Guard. Later, the air field became the Salt Lake City International Airport.

UTAH ORDNANCE PLANT was built by the Federal Government in Salt Lake City early in the war to manufacture small arms ammunition. The plant was run by Remington Arms Co. and specialized in the manufacture of 30 calibre and 50 calibre ammunition and incendiary bombs. The plant became inactive in late 1943 and after the war was sold to private interests.

TOOELE is 25 miles SW of Salt Lake City.

TOOELE ORDNANCE DEPOT, four miles south of town, was built by the Federal Government in 1942 after expansion of the Ogden Arsenal proved to be impossible. This was a huge temporary depot, with two location 15 miles apart, designed to have a useful life of five years. The second location was known as the Deseret Chemical Warfare Depot. Tooele Ordnance Depot was a sub-post of Ogden Arsenal and its mission was to receive, store and ship ammunition and general supplies for the Army. Because of its remote location poison gas was stored at the Deseret Chemical Warfare Depot. The main depot had a training facility for Army ordnancemen and later in the war AAF ordnancemen were also trained here. In 1943 a hospital was built at the depot to care for the depot's personnel. Both the main depot and Deseret Chemical Warfare Depot had main prisoner of war camps. The main depot's camp held about 100 Italian POWs and the Deseret camp about 100 German POWs. All the POWs worked at the depots. Tooele also became one of the few military installations in the nation that accepted ethnic Japanese from the relocation camps as permanent workers. The depot was retained by the Army after the war and would long outlive its intended five years of life. The Army's Engineer Corps used part of the facility immediately after the war while the rest of the depot was charged with receiving, inspecting, repairing, storing and/or disposal of ammunition and general supplies returned from overseas and stateside facilities that were closing or scaling down. In 1955 Tooele Depot received the inventory and operations from Ogden Arsenal when that facility was taken over by the US Air Force. In 1962 the facility was redesignated Tooele Army Depot and served well into the

Cold War era.

TREMONTON is 30 miles north of Ogden. On the morning of Feb. 22, 1945 a rancher called the local sheriff, Warren W. Hyde, to report that a strange balloon had come down on his property. Hyde was one of the few people in the area privy to the secret of the Japanese bombing balloons and suspected that it was such a balloon that was being reported. Hyde phoned the FBI and asked what to do and was told to try to secure the balloon intact, if at all possible, and that help was on the way. Hyde then drove alone to the reported location, spotted the balloon which was on the verge of taking flight again as its gas expanded in the morning sun. Hyde began to chase the balloon on foot trying to catch it and secure it to something solid, but the balloon was trying to rise and was being lurched forward by the winds. It proved very difficult to secure, let along hang on to. At one point Hyde secured a good grip on the balloon but it lifted him aloft and carried him over a ravine. Finally, he was able to secure the balloon to a chokeberry bush. The FBI soon arrived, deflated the balloon, detonated its self-destruction device and carted it away. Sheriff Hyde was later honored for his unique service in a ceremony attended by the Governor and representatives of the Army, Navy and civil defense.

WENDOVER is 110 miles west of Salt Lake City on the Nevada border.

WENDOVER FIELD, one mile south of town, was the area's local airport before the war. In 1940 the Federal Government established four large general bombing and gunnery ranges in the western part of the U.S. for use by the Army Air Corps and the Wendover area was one of the sites chosen[1]. The actual bombing and gunnery range was south and east of Wendover. Its NW was 10 miles south of Wendover and it stretched from there 48 miles to the east and 20 miles to the south. Most of the area was a vast uninhabited salt desert. The air field at Wendover was acquired by the Army Air Corps to support the range. Throughout the war the bombing range and Wendover Field were used by various air training centers in the west.

As the "Manhattan (atomic bomb) Project" began to mature and the B-29 and B-32 long-range bombers, designed to carry the bomb, began rolling off the assembly lines, a remote location was needed in which the bomber air crews could train in utmost secrecy. Wendover Field proved to be such a place. In the late summer of 1944 the leaders of the "Manhattan Project", in cooperation with the AAF, acquired Wendover Field for that purpose. The AAF established a special unit, the 509th Composite Group, whose mission it was to train the 1500 enlisted men and 220 officers of the Group and then deliver the bomb to Japan[2]. Commanding the unit, which consisted of several squadrons of B-29s, was Col. Paul W. Tibbits an experience bomber pilot. The 509th trained at Wendover under such secrecy that those being trained didn't know why they were being

[1]The other three sites were near Tonopah, NV, Boardman, OR and in the Mojave Desert in CA.
[2]In late 1944 the Group also practiced for atomic bombing missions over Germany.

Sheriff Warren W. Hyde of Box Elder County, Utah secured this partially deflated and still armed Japanese bombing balloon unassisted, but not before it lifted him off the ground and took his for a short ride.

This is the B-29 hangar at Wendover Field. It is known as the "Enola Gay" hangar and efforts are underway to preserve it and other structures at Wendover Field as a national monument.

small to service B-29s so one large additional hangar was built for that purpose. By the spring of 1945 the 509th had completed it training and transferred to Tinian Island in the western Pacific. From that island base on Aug. 6, 1945, Col. Tibbits and his air crew delivered the first atomic bomb to Japan and dropped it on the city of Hiroshima. On Aug. 9, 1945, a second atomic bomb was dropped on Nagasaki and on Aug. 11, 1945 Japan surrendered. The mission of the 509th succeeded and it did end the war.

Wendover Field remained a military air field for many years after the end of hostilities and the Wendover Bombing Range continued in operation into the post-Cold War era. All of the original hangars, including the B-29 hangar remain at the field as do about 75 other WW II structures. Efforts are underway to preserve the field and most of these structures as a national monument.

Wendover Welcome Center: This welcome center is across the state line in Nevada near I-80 Exit #1 and has displays on Wendover Field, the 509th Composite Group, uniforms, photos and memorbilia.

trained or how long the training would last. The only hint they were given was that if their mission was successful it could end the war. As part of their training, the B-29 crews flew their planes to distant location such as Batista Air Field in Cuba and back again. This simulated the long flights they would eventually make in the Pacific. Col. Tibbits, himself, piloted one of the B-29s, the "Enola Gay". At Wendover Field the existing hangars were too

VERMONT

The state of Vermont stands out among the other states because of the absence of WW II facilities. The state had no Army air fields, Naval air stations, Naval training facilities, Marine training facilities, prisoner of war camps, internment camps, ordnance plants, supply depots, bombing and gunnery ranges, proving grounds, arsenals, Army general hospitals or major government-built manufacturing plants. Yet the 359,231 residents of the state made a meaningful contribution to the war effort. Vermont had a strong industrial base primarily in quality machine tools, foundry work and metal cutting tools. These much-needed products poured forth from Vermont's factories in great numbers during the war. The upsurge of defense work was most welcome in Vermont because the state had suffered considerably during the Great Depression due to unemployment and business failures. When prosperity returned Vermont produced many important products and was a leader in several. The state was the national leader in the production of asbestos and one of the top leaders in the production of granite, marble, slate, maple syrup and maple sugar. The two latter products became very sought-after commodities when sugar rationing was introduced throughout the nation. Other products from Vermont that contributed to the war effort were grains, potatoes, livestock, dairy products, poultry, fruit, hay, lumber, furniture, textiles, clothing, paper, talc and clay products. In 1942 an old copper deposit was reopened because of the strong demand for that metal.

In 1942 the state set up a Council of Safety based on a similar organization established during colonial days. The mission of the Council was to assist the state's defense industry. Also in 1942 Vermonters gained the honor of leading the nation, per capita, in the collection of scrap metal and scrap rubber.

BURLINGTON is on the NW edge of the state on Lake Champlain.

FORT ETHAN ALLEN was five miles north of Burlington on the north bank of the Winooski River. It was built in 1892 on land once owned by the Revolutionary War hero Ethan Allen and named in his honor. For years it was considered to be one of the Army's most beautiful and desirable posts. Fort Ethan Allen was primarily a cavalry post and a training center for Army artillerymen. By the start of WW II the cavalry was gone, but the artillery center remained and throughout WW II the center trained Army personnel in that specialty. In Mar. 1944 artillery training ended and the post was declared inactive. After the war the fort was used for storage by the Army. In 1952 it was turned over to the US Air Force and converted into an air base named Ethan Allen Air Force Base. In 1960 the Air Force closed the air base and most of its facilities were transferred to the University of Vermont and St. Michael's College.

VIRGINIA

Blackstone Army Air Field retained its wartime name for years after the war. This is its main hangar which dates from WW II. In the foreground is one of many foundations in the area from former WW II buildings.

The state of Virginia was a very busy place during World War II. The state's portion of Chesapeake Bay and Hampton Roads was a beehive of military activity, and the area around the District of Columbia was a beehive of military and political activity. Elsewhere in Virginia soldiers, sailors, Marines, airmen and OSS agents were trained for war in large numbers, and along Virginia's coast submarine warfare was as hot as it was anywhere in the world. Furthermore, the Axis Powers had plans to carry out direct attacks on Virginia if and when the opportunities presented themselves.

The State produced a wide variety of items for war including warships, landing craft, merchant ships, munitions, transportation machinery, electrical equipment, chemicals, furniture, wood products, textiles, clothing, paper, leather, sea food and glass. From virginia's soil came cotton, grain, fruit, tobacco, peanuts, hay, coal, zinc ore, bauxite, copper ore, lead ore, manganese ore, titanium ore, stone, clay and small amounts of oil and natural gas.

The State had 14 prisoner of war camps and the Hampton Roads area was a major port of debarkation for POWs arriving from North Africa and later, Europe. After the war thousands of POWs returned home via the same area.

In Sept. 1944 a damaging hurricane hit the eastern coast of Virginia and before the end of the war the Potomac River and much of Chesapeake Bay were showing signs of serious pollution as a result of the years of hectic production and war-related activities in eastern Virginia, Maryland and the District of Columbia.

Virginia emerged from the war strong and prosperous. Many new industries had moved into the State during the war, especially in the Hampton Roads area, and most of them stayed on. The Military had built numerous facilities throughout the state and many of these too, remained active in the postwar years and throughout the Cold War.

The State was home to several important WW II personalities including Gen. George Marshall from Leesburg; General Alexander Vandergrift, Commandant of the U.S. Marine Corps, from Charlottesville and Senator Harry F. Byrd, the leader of the Southern Democrat faction in the U.S. Senate.

ARLINGTON (See Washington, DC; Virginia Area below)

ALEXANDRIA (See Washington, DC; Virginia Area below)

BLACKSTONE is 40 miles SW of Richmond.

BLACKSTONE ARMY AIR FIELD was 2.5 miles SE of town and was the area's local airport. During the war it served Fort Pickett which was three miles to the east. Blackstone AAF had long runways and could handle large AAF transports. After the war the air field was returned to its civilian owners and for years retained its wartime name. It also became known as Allan C. Perkinson Municipal Airport.

CAMP PICKETT, three miles east of Blackstone, was built in 1942 to be an Army training camp for division-sized units. It could accommodate 75,000 troops. During Sept. and Oct. 1942 units of Gen. George Patton's Task Force A staged here prior to their departure for the invasion of French North Africa. The 79th Infantry Division was the first full division to train here followed by the 3rd Infantry Div. which underwent an amphibious training program that was first used here. Other units that trained here were the 3rd Armored Div., 28th, 31st, 45th, 77th and 78th Infantry Divisions. The camp had a main prisoner of war camp holding about 2700 POWs who worked on the post and in the forests. In late 1944-early 1945 Camp Pickett's station hospital was enlarged and converted into an Army general hospital to treat war wounded. The hospital had 2700 beds and specialized in general medicine, general and orthopedic surgery and psychiatry. In Dec. 1945 the hospital reverted to being the camp's station hospital. Camp Pickett was deactivated in the spring of 1947, reopened in Aug. 1948, but deactivated again in the spring of 1949. It was activated again in 1950 and used as a training camp for the Korean War and then deactivated in 1954. In the fall of 1960 the camp opened again as a training camp for Army Reservists. Soon afterward it was declared a permanent post, renamed Fort Pickett and remained active throughout the Cold War.

BOWLING GREEN is 35 miles north of Richmond.

FORT A.P. HILL, three miles NE of town, was established in 1941 as a maneuver area for the Army's II Corps and for three activated National Guard divisions from the mid-Atlantic states. In the fall of 1942 Fort A.P. Hill was used as a staging area for the headquarter units of Gen. George Patton's Task Force A which departed from Hampton Roads in Oct. for the invasion of French Morocco. In 1944 Fort A.P. Hill became a training center for infantry replacements from nearby Forts Lee, Eustis and Belvoir. Also in 1944 Italian Service Units began working here. The fort remained an active Army post after the war and throughout the Cold War era.

CAPE CHARLES AREA OF THE DELMARVA PENINSULA: This part of Virginia is detached from the rest of Virginia and is bounded by the Atlantic Ocean and Chesapeake Bay.

FORT JOHN CUSTIS was a coastal defense position at the southern end of the peninsula protecting Chesapeake Bay. When construction got under way in 1942 the site was armed with 8" naval guns mounted on railroad cars. As construction progressed twin 16" guns were mounted at the fort. Throughout the war Fort John Custis was a sub-post of Fort Story. After the war Fort John Custis was declared surplus, the guns removed and the fort abandoned.

FISHERMAN'S ISLAND, one mile south of the end of the Delmarva Peninsula, had a small coastal defense position that was manned throughout the war. During the war Fisherman's Island was accessible by water only.

U.S. NAVAL AIR FACILITY AND NAVAL AVIATION ORDNANCE TEST STATION, CHINCOTEAGUE ISLAND: This was a dual-purpose naval facility located on the Delmarva mainland three miles west of Chincoteague. It was first established as an outlying field for NAS, Norfolk but in early 1942 it became an operational naval air base with its own identity. The original

Many WW II buildings remained at Fort Pickett and were in daily use.

This is the engineering model of the 16" guns mounted at Ft. Custis. The model is on display at Ft. Monroe, Hampton, VA.

station was enlarged and became home to carrier fighter, torpedo and composite air squadrons. Later, PB4Ys operated from the field doing coastal patrols. The station had one outlying field, Salisbury Airport, near Salisbury, MD.

In late 1943 the Navy's Bureau of Ordnance moved onto the field and set up a facility to secretly test aviation ordnance and ordnance equipment. These two facilities then functioned side-by-side throughout the remainder of the war. After the war the NAF became a training center of carrier squadrons and the Ordnance Test Station facility began testing missiles. In 1959 the station was transferred to the National Aeronautics and Space Administration (NASA) and remained under their control for the rest of the century. The facility eventually became known as Wallops Island.

CAPE HENRY (See Norfolk/Portsmouth/Virginia Beach area)

DAHLGREN is 35 miles south of Washington, DC on the Potomac River.

U.S. NAVAL SURFACE WEAPONS CENTER, DAHLGREN began in 1918 as an expansion of U.S. Naval Proving Ground, Indian Head, MD and was first used to test naval ordnance. In 1919 it was recognized as a separate command and continued as a test center for naval ordnance. One of its main activities was to test powders manufactured at the Naval Powder Factory in Charles County. MD. In the early 1930s NSWC, Dahlgren acquired its own runway and aircraft for the purpose of testing both aviation ordnance and naval aircraft. During WW II activity increased substantially at NSWC, Dahlgren which continued to serve as a develop and test center throughout the war. Later in the war a part of the "Elsie Project", the Navy's program associated with the development of the atomic bomb, was established here. After the war, activities slumped at Dahlgren, but picked up again during the Korean War, only to slump again after that war. As the Navy became interested in missiles, Dahlgren took on a new mission in that field

and later expanded into space research. Dahlgren continued as an active naval research, development and test facility throughout the Cold War and became known as U.S. Naval Weapons Laboratory, Dahlgren.

FRANKLIN is 40 miles SW of Norfolk.

U.S. NAVAL AUXILIARY AIR STATION, FRANKLIN, two miles NE of Franklin, was the town's prewar airport. It was taken over by the Navy in 1943 to serve as an auxiliary air field for Chambers Field, Norfolk. NAAS, Franklin became a reception and dispersal point for newly built naval aircraft arriving in the Norfolk area. As a part of this function the station also stored and maintained aircraft. Between May 1943 and Nov. 1945 NAAS, Franklin received and dispersed some 5900 aircraft. In Jan. 1946 the station was placed in caretaker status and eventually was returned to its pre-war owners.

FRONT ROYAL is 60 miles west of Washington, DC.

FRONT ROYAL QUARTERMASTER DEPOT: This was a very unique Army facility located three miles from Front Royal. It was the first military training center in the country for dogs. It opened in August 1942 and its mission was to procure, condition and train dogs for the various military services. Many of the dogs used by the Coast Guard beach patrols were trained here. The depot also did some breeding of dogs and training of horses. The dog training program was discontinued during the summer of 1944 but horse training continued. During the

war the depot had a main prisoner of war camp holding about 400 POWs who worked at the depot. After the war the depot continued to train horses and remained active in the early postwar years under the name, Aleshire Quartermaster Depot.

HAMPTON/NEWPORT NEWS/WILLIAMSBURG/YORKTOWN AREA: The cities of Hampton and Newport News form the northern shore of the strategic Hampton Roads waterway. Both are port cities with economies based on transportation, trade, commerce, manufacturing and the military. Williamsburg and Yorktown, just to the north, are two of America's most historic cities and both had military installations during the war. In Newport News was the nation's largest shipbuilders, the Newport News Shipbuilding and Dry Dock Co., located just north of the main Newport News waterfront area. This company built several of the battleships that took part in WW II. They were "Indiana", "Maryland", "Mississippi", "Pennsylvania", "Texas", "West Virginia" and "Kearsarge". The "Maryland", "Pennsylvania" and "West Virginia" were at Pearl Harbor on Dec. 7, 1941 when the Japanese attacked. The "Kearsarge" was an obsolete battleship and in Nov. 1941 was converted into a craneship. Newport News Shipbuilding and Dry Dock Co. also built the aircraft carriers "Yorktown I", which was lost at Midway; "Yorktown II"; "Essex"; "Intrepid"; "Hornet II"; "Franklin"; "Randolph"; "Boxer"; "Ticonderoga"; "Shangri-La" and "Midway". They also built the cruisers "Houston", "Birmingham", "Mobile", "Amsterdam", "Portsmouth", "Vicksburg", "Duluth" and "St. Louis". Destroyers, destroyer escorts, landing craft and other warships also came from this yard. In Oct. 1942 the first LSTs in the nation were produced here, but were not ready for "Operation Torch", the landing in North Africa. The lack of LST's during "Operation Torch " made the landing of large tanks more difficult than would be the case in later invasions. During the latter part of the war Italian Service Units worked at the ship yard to help alleviate the manpower shortage. There are several overlooks along Huntington, Washington and West Avenues from which the ship yard may be viewed.

Needless to say, this area was a boom area during the war and suffered overcrowding,

Men and dogs in training at Front Royal Quartermaster Depot during the war.

housing shortages, inflation, increased crime and severe strains on city services. The Federal Government built several housing developments to help ease the housing shortage. One such development was Stuart Gardens built on the site of a WW I Camp Stuart. A plaque at 16th St. and Roanoke Ave. commemorates the camp and the WW II housing development.

The people of this area didn't know it at the time, but they were on one of the Navy's most ominous lists . . the list of areas most likely to be bombed by the Axis powers if and when they had the capability to do so.

FORT EUSTIS is east of and adjacent to Newport News on the James River. It was built in 1918 as Camp Eustis and used as a training center during WW I. In 1923 it became a permanent post and was renamed Fort Eustis. Some of the Army's biggest coast artillery guns and railroad guns were stored here in the years between the wars. At the beginning of WW II the fort was a training center for balloon observers and field artillery units. In 1941 a coast artillery training school was established here and later in the war replacements were trained for anti-aircraft units. All through the war Fort Eustis served as one of the staging camps in the area for troops going overseas. Fort Eustis had segregated facilities so negro troops also staged here. The fort had a large main prisoner of war camp holding about 4600 German POWs who worked for the military and others. During the summer of 1945 English-speaking anti-Nazi POWs awaiting repatriation to Germany were brought here and given the task of translating Dr. Werner von Braun's notes and papers on Germany's rocket program. These individuals were later given a special commendation by the U.S. Government. Also during the summer of 1945 the Army set up a school at Fort Eustis to train up to 20,000 former German POWs for jobs in the new Army-run occupation government of Germany. This was called the Re-education Program for German POWs. Some Germans, while they were still POWs, had been secretly trained[1] during the

[1]They were secretly trained because it was contrary to the Geneva Convention to subject

This is the U.S. Army Transportation Museum on the grounds of Fort Eustis.

latter days of the war in Rhode Island, but it was soon recognized that many more were needed. Carefully selected German POWs were brought to Fort Eustis from all over the country and given a six-day crash course on the jobs they would perform in the occupation government and on the fundamentals of a democratic society. In Germany they were usually given additional training. Those Americans, and some Germans, who had been involved in the program in Rhode Island were brought to Eustis to work in the program. Eventually 23,147 individuals were graduated from the program and rapidly repatriated to Germany. The last class graduated from the Re-Education Program in Apr. 1946.

In May 1946 Fort Eustis became the headquarters for the Army's Transportation Corps. Other transportation activities were concentrated here and in 1962 the fort was officially designated as the U.S. Army Transportation Center.

U.S. Army Transportation Museum: This fine museum is on the grounds of Fort Eustis and related the history of the Army's transportation service from its beginning to the present. Many pieces of equipment are on display at the museum including trucks, jeeps, aircraft, boats, trains, landing craft, helicopters, wagons and POWs to such training. Besides, the Americans didn't want the Germans to attempt to

several one-of-a-kind experimental vehicles. Many of the vehicles and models in the museum are from WW II. Of particular interest are two rare Jeep prototypes, one made by the Bantam Motor Car Co. and the other by Crosley Motor Cars. There is a large display on the "Red Ball Express", the fast-moving U.S. supply line established by the Army's Transportation Corps across northern France and Germany in late 1944 and early 1945 that kept pace with the rapidly advancing U.S. forces as they drove into Germany. Address: Bldg. 300, Besson Hall, Fort Eustis, VA 23604-5260. Phone: 804/878-1182/1183. Hours: Daily 9-4:40, closed federal holidays and Easter Sunday. Free.

HAMPTON ROADS PORT OF EMBARKATION (POE) was located primarily on the Chesapeake & Ohio Railroad piers on the Newport News waterfront at the end of 25th St. Other piers along the waterfront were also used by the POE. The facility had excellent rail connections inland and POE headquarters was located in the Federal Customs Building at 25th St. and West Ave. Hampton Roads POE was used in both WW I and WW II and was the Army's main port of embarkation in the Hampton Roads area. Throughout the war hundreds of thousands of military personnel and millions of tons of equipment and supplies flowed through this POE. When the war ended the process was reversed. Hampton Roads POE was the third largest in the nation after those at New York and San Francisco. This POE played a direct role in two major invasions in the Mediterranean area. In late Oct. 1942 General Patton's Task Force "A" formed up and departed from the Hampton Roads area and went directly into combat a few weeks later when they invaded French Morocco in North Africa. Task Force "A" was the largest and best-equipped American force ever to leave U.S. soil and go directly into combat. It consisted of 33,737 officers and enlisted men and 28 ships. The troops and equipment loaded at several points in the Hampton Roads area including the Hampton Roads POE. In July 1943 another invasion force under Gen. Troy Middleton formed up in Hampton Roads and departed for the invasion of Sicily. This was known as Task Force "B" and consisted of retaliate and "re-educate" American POWs in their care. After the war the Geneva Convention no longer applied and the re-education program was made public.

Fort Eustis as it looked in the 1990s.

This is the Victory Arch at the entrance to the former Hampton Roads Port of Embarkation.

The James River Reserve Fleet can be seen easily from Fort Eustis. The structure in the foreground is the hull of an old barge used as part of a landfill.

23,776 troops and 37 ships. Throughout the war, ships and convoys departed Hampton Roads for various points in the Mediterranean, Middle East, Persian Gulf and western Europe. Thousands of tons of Lend Lease material also flowed through the Hampton Roads POE.

Hampton Roads POE was one of the main reception points for German and Italian prisoners of war arriving in this country. From Sept. 1942 to May 1945 134,292 POWs arrived at this POE and were dispersed to camps in the interior. The POE had its own main prisoner of war camp with about 600 Italian POWs who worked at the port. When Italy became a co-belligerent most of the Italians were formed into Italian Service Units (ISU) and given more important jobs and more freedom. German POWs where then brought in to take their former jobs. More and more ISUs and German POWs were brought to the POE to work as the war wound down and by Sept. 1945 there were 1300 Italians and 4077 Germans working here. The POE was retained after the war and was later renamed U.S. Army Transportation Terminal, Hampton Roads.

Victory Arch: This stone arch, built in 1962, is located at the entrance to Pier A and straddles 25th St. Bronze plaques commemorate the men and women from the Hampton Roads area that have died in WW I, WW II, The Korean War and Viet Nam War. Also on the arch is a plaque commemorating the Hampton Roads Port of Embarkation. This is the second arch to stand in this location. In early 1919 the first Victory Arch was hastily constructed of wood and plaster to welcome the Doughboys returning from WW I. Through the years it deteriorated and was replaced by the present arch.

CAMP PATRICK HENRY was located on the northern edge of Newport News. The camp was established by the Army's Transportation Corps in 1942 as a staging area for its men and equipment going through the Hampton Road Port of Embarkation (POE). The camp was a sub-post of Fort Eustis, could house 35,000 troops and had a rail shuttle directly to the POE. Other major units staged here too, including the 31st, 45th, 85th, 88th, 91st, 92nd Infantry Divisions, 2nd Cavalry Div. and 10th Mountain Infantry Div. Some foreign troops staged here including Brazilians, British Caribbean, French Caribbean, Greeks, Chinese, Turks, Polish, Canadians and Yugoslavs. The camp had a mockup of a transport ship and as troops waited for sailing orders they were given training in abandoning a ship should it become necessary. When time permitted, some troops were put aboard small vessels and taken to various locations around Chesapeake Bay to practice debarking into landing craft. During the war Camp Patrick Henry had a main prisoner of war camp with about 550 POWs who worked at the camp and the POE. Later, Italian Service Units worked here.

The camp had a large Station hospital which became more and more of a debarkation hospital as wounded soldiers returned from overseas. After the end of hostilities many Italians of the Italian Service Units staged here as they awaited repatriation. By 1946, when the camp was deactivated, some 1.5 million people had passed through Camp Patrick Henry. In 1949 the assets of the camp were sold and some years later an airport, known as Patrick Henry International Airport, was built.

CAMP HILL was located in Newport News north of 64th St. between Jefferson Ave. and the James River. It was built early in the war and was yet another staging camp for troops passing through the Hampton Roads Port of Embarkation (POE). Camp hill was also used as a staging area for military animals. The camp had schools for personnel of the Transportation Corps and for illiterates. The Army bands that played at ship embarkations and debarkations resided here. In late 1943, after Italy surrendered and changed sides, Camp Hill became home for Italian Service Units working at the POE. By war's end some 64,000 troops and 47,000 animals had passed through Camp Hill. After the war Camp Hill was closed and its assets sold.

JAMES RIVER RESERVE FLEET, a mothball fleet, is located off the northern shore of Fort Eustis and can be viewed from Fort Eustis's Harrison Rd. Ships come and go in the mothball fleet, but as late as 1990 there were still 72 WW II "Victory" ships at anchor here. There are waterfront picnic areas all along Harrison Rd.

KECOUGHTAN VETERANS ADMINISTRATION HOSPITAL AND HAMPTON ROADS NATIONAL CEMETERY: These two adjacent facilities are located on the Hampton waterfront between the Hampton River and I-64. During the latter part of the war when many war casualties were being received in the Hampton Roads area the local military hospitals experiences overcrowding. To help relieve the situation this VA hospital made available 500 beds for wounded personnel. Some service personnel who died in the area during the war, both Allied and enemy, were buried in the adjoining Hampton Roads National Cemetery.

LANGLEY FIELD, in northern Hampton on the Back River, marks its beginning from Dec. 1916. It was established as the headquarters and home for the Army's new Flying Corps and Aviation School which were then under the command of the Signal Corps. Two aircraft

This is one of several large concrete foundations that remains at Camp Patrick Henry and was most likely a warehouse.

hangars and one airship hangar were built here. Throughout WW I Army airmen were trained at Langley Field in both airplanes and balloons. The National Advisory Committee for Aeronautics (NACA) was created here with the mission to do "Scientific Research on the Fundamentals of Flight". NACA became one of the most important research and development facilities in the nation in the early years of flying. It worked with, and advised, all of the armed services, government agencies such as the CAA, aircraft manufacturers and private aviation interests.

When the Army Air Corps came into existence, Langley continued on as its general headquarters. In early 1941 the Air Corps headquarters itself moved to Bolling Field in Washington, DC but Langley Field remained an important air facility in the Air Corps' hierarchy.

When the U.S. went to war in Dec. 1941 Langley Field was one of the few air fields in the country that was ready for war. On Dec. 8, 1941 Army bombers from here began regular patrols up to 600 miles out into the Atlantic. Such patrols were normally the responsibility of the Navy, but there weren't enough long-range Navy planes available to fill the need. In early 1942 Langley became an AAF recruit reception center and in Feb. 1942 the Bomber Command of the new 8th Air Force was activated here. When the Americans finally got a handle on combating the German submarine menace along the east coast, Langley Field was one of the main bases for the aviation elements of the hunter-killer forces that became so successful against enemy submarines. During most of the war Langley was home to two aeronautical research laboratories, a radar school, an AAF regional hospital, an air freight terminal and several flight training programs. Langley, of course, remained in operation after the war and in 1947 a modernization program did away with many of the pre-war and WW II buildings. In 1948 Langley was transferred to the US Air Force and was renamed Langley Air Force Base. For several years it was the home of the 9th Air Force. Langley AFB continued in operation throughout the Cold War serving many branches of the Air Force.

MARINERS' MUSEUM is located on the western edge of Mariners' Museum Park in central Newport News. This is an excellent maritime

Some WW II barracks buildings are in use at Fort Monroe.

museum with displays and information on ships and seafarers from ancient times to the present. There are displays on the U.S. Navy during all of America's wars and a considerable amount of information on WW II. There are large and magnificent ship models of many WW II ships including the aircraft carrier "Lexington", the cruiser "Juneau II", the ocean liner "President Coolidge" which was converted into a troop ship and sunk off Espiritu Santo, the Swedish ocean line "Gripsholm" which was involved in various prisoner exchanges and humanitarian mission during the war, the Japanese ocean liner "Fushimi" which was converted to a troop ship and sunk by the U.S. submarine "Tarpon" off the coast of Japan, and many other interesting models. There is an extensive display on how Liberty Ships were built, various marine artifacts, numerous paintings, Photographs and several hands-on exhibits. Address: 100 Marine Dr., Newport News, VA 23606-3759. Phone: 804/595-0368. Hours: M-Sat. 9-5, Sun. noon-5, closed Dec. 25. Admission charged.

FORT MONROE is located at the south end of a long peninsula that juts into Hampton Roads just east of the Hampton Roads Bridge-Tunnel. The present-day Fort Monroe dates from 1818. For many years Ft. Monroe was the home of the Coast Artillery School and headquarters and main defense Station of the harbor defenses of Chesapeake Bay and Hampton Roads. In 1895 Gen. Matthew Ridgeway, the son of a

professional soldier, was born here. During WW II the fort was manned and armed with coastal guns and anti-aircraft guns. The Coast Artillery School functioned throughout the war and an anti-aircraft artillery school and an officer candidate school were added. Underwater naval mines were also stored here. In the latter part of the war the fort's hospital served at times as a debarkation hospital to relieve overcrowding in other hospital. Just north of the fort was an airstrip that belonged to the fort, Walker Army Air Field. In 1946 the artillery school moved to California and the headquarters of the Army Ground Forces moved to Fort Monroe from Washington, DC. Through the postwar years Fort Monroe has been home to several headquarters commands and training schools. Eventually the fort became a National Historic Landmark.

The Casement Museum: This museum is located within the wall of Fort Monroe. The museum traces the long history of the fort and the Army's coast artillery service. The museums has very few displays related to WW II but does have extensive information on coastal artillery guns. Many of these guns were old, and some of them were obsolete, when WW II began, but they were still in place and were used throughout much of the war in coastal forts around the country. After the war most of the guns were scrapped. Address: PO Box 341, Fort Monroe, VA 23651. Phone: 804/727-3391/3973. Hours: Daily 10:30-4:30, closed Jan. 1, Thanksgiving

This is the Mariners' Museum in Newport News.

This is the entrance to the Casement Museum which is within the walls of Fort Monroe.

and Dec. 25. Free.

CAMP PEARY is two miles NE of Williamsburg on the York River. This is a Navy training camp for SeaBees that was established in Nov. 1942 to relieve an overcrowded condition at U.S. Naval Amphibious Training Base, Little Creek. The camp had one of the few prisoner of war camps controlled by the Navy. This camp, a main prisoner of war camp, held about 950 POWs who worked for the Navy. Camp Peary was retained after the war and was utilized throughout the Cold War.

U.S. NAVAL MINE DEPOT, YORKTOWN was located on the York River three miles east of Yorktown. It began in 1917 as a naval coal and oil depot and a storage facility for mines. After WW I the facility became an ammunition depot servicing Navy ships operating in the Hampton Roads and Chesapeake Bay areas while continuing to store mines. In 1928 the depot underwent a large-scale modernization program after the disastrous explosions at the U.S. Naval Ammunition Depot, Lake Denmark, NJ. Because of this program NMD, Yorktown became one of the Navy's most modern ammunition depots. In 1938, as war approached in Europe, activities at NMD, Yorktown picked up considerably and never let down until several years after the war. The depot and its annex at St. Juliens Creek underwent yet another expansion in 1940 as the U.S. Navy built up for the "Two Ocean Navy" program. In 1941 the depot acquired a TNT reclamation facility and a mine assembly plant. When the U.S. went to war activity at NMD, Yorktown soared and in Dec. 1941 an ammunition loading plant was built here. As new mine technology changed during the war NMD, Yorktown was obliged to keep pace. This usually meant new facilities, new techniques and more personnel. The depot acquired a mine warfare school and also stored depth charges, bombs, warheads and their components in large numbers. When the war ended tons of surplus naval ordnance was returned to the depot which remained busy for several years thereafter servicing, repairing, re-storing and/or disposing of naval ordnance. Activity eventually declined at the

On display outside of the War Memorial Museum of Virginia are several pieces of military equipment including this postwar atomic cannon. The museum is to the rear.

depot, but picked up again during the Korean War. By that time the depot was storing and servicing missiles as well as conventional naval ordnance. In 1958 the depot was renamed U.S. Naval Weapons Station, Yorktown and continued to be one of the Navy's main ammunition depots on the east coast.

VIRGINIA AIR AND SPACE CENTER AND HAMPTON ROADS HISTORY CENTER is located near downtown Hampton. This is a new and modern museum with many fine exhibits tracing the history of flight and space travel from it beginning to the present. Emphasis is placed on the early aviation achievements made a Langley Field and on NASA. There are many hands-on exhibits in the three-story center and an IMAX theater. WW II-era items on display include a P-39Q Airacobra fighter plane hanging from the ceiling, the nose section of a B-24D bomber, an exhibit on the Tuskeegee Airmen and an extensive collection of aircraft models. Address: 600 Settlers Landing, Hampton, VA. Phone: 804/727-0800. Hours: M-W 10-5, Thurs.-Sat. 10-7, Sun. noon-7, closed Dec. 25. Admission charged.

WAR MEMORIAL MUSEUM OF VIRGINIA is located in Huntington Park near the eastern terminus of the James River Bridge in Newport News. This museum has some 60,000 military artifacts and tells the stories of America's wars from 1775 to the present. WW II is amply covered in the museum with displays of weapons; American, Italian and Japanese uniforms; posters; the German Nazi Party and Dachau Concentration Camp. Outside the museum are vehicles, artillery pieces and a plaque commemorating the Four Chaplains lost on the SS "Dorchester" off Greenland in 1943. Address: 9285 Warwick Blvd. (US 60), Newport News, VA 23607.

Phone: 804/247-8523. Hours: M-Sat. 9-5, Sun. 1-5, closed Jan. 1, Thanksgiving and Dec. 25. Admission charged.

FORT WOOL is located at the entrance to Hampton Roads on an artificial island about half way across the Hampton Roads Bridge Tunnel. Construction on the fort began in 1819, but because of construction difficulties it was not yet complete by the Civil War. It was serviceable, however, and was used during that war. Construction was resumed after the Civil War and continued off and on throughout its entire life and never has been completed. During WW II the fort was armed and manned as one of the area's coastal defense positions. It mounted 6" and 3" guns and 50 cal. anti-aircraft guns. In 1967 the fort was given to the State of Virginia and opened to the public.

HOT SPRINGS is a resort town and spa in the west-central part of Virginia 45 miles SW of Staunton.

THE HOMESTEAD was the largest and most luxurious hotel in the Hot Springs area in 1941. A few days after the U.S. went to war the Federal Government leased the hotel, and three other remote luxury hotels[2], for the purpose of housing enemy diplomats and their families until they could be exchanged for American diplomats and their families who were being held in enemy hands. This was fortunate timing for the owners of The Homestead because the hotel was closing down for the season and was almost empty. Now the hotel had some long-term guests and received $10.00 a day per person (later dropped to $9.00 a day) from the Government. The few remaining guests were asked to leave by Christmas and on Christmas Eve the first contingent of enemy diplomats arrived consisting of 334 Japanese men, their families, pets, personal belongings, food and alcholic beverages. Virginia was a "dry" State at the time. The FBI handled the transfer and Immigration and Naturalization Service border patrol officers served as guards. Additional enemy diplomats soon arrived, some from Latin American countries, and settled in. The diplomats and their families had the run of the hotel, its grounds and its kitchen where they could prepare their own ethnic foods. Several

[2]The others were the Greenbrier Hotel in White Sulphur Springs, WV; Bedford Springs Hotel in Bedford, PA and the Grove Park Inn in Asheville, NC.

The nose section of the WW II-era B-24 "Old Bessie" is on display at the Virginia Air and Space Center and Hampton Roads History Center.

The luxurious Homestead Hotel in Hot Spring, VA was home to enemy diplomats from Dec. 1941 to the spring 1942 while they awaited repatriation to their home countries.

babies were born here and the Japanese spent a lot of time in the hot baths. The various nationalities were not necessary compatible though, and ethnic slurs, insults, snubs and, at times, screaming arguments occurred. When, in Mar. 1942, the Greenbrier Hotel's Italians were repatriated and vacancies became available there, the Japanese from The Homestead were transferred. Eventually the Greenbrier became an all-Japanese facility. Other transfers occurred including the shipment of Italians and Hungarians to the Grove Park Inn. By spring 1942 all of the diplomats had been repatriated and The Homestead returned to a more normal, although wartime, routine. Returning visitor included Cordell Hull and Gen. & Mrs. George Marshall. From May 18 to June 3, 1943 forty-four nations met at The Homestead to discuss postwar food and agriculture issues and proposed the creation of a United Nations food organization to help better the standards of living of people around the world. A plaque at the hotel commemorates that meeting.

LEXINGTON is 30 miles NW of Staunton.

VIRGINIA MILITARY INSTITUTE, just north of downtown Lexington, was founded in 1839 and, by the middle of the 1800s, had become one of the nation's most prestigious military schools. This four-year State-supported school is sometimes referred to as "The West Point of the South". In 1901, future General-of-the-Army George C. Marshall graduated from VMI

and today the school reveres his memory. During WW II VMI did what most military schools did around the country . . accelerated their academic program and turned out Army officers as fast as possible. Most VMI graduates went directly into military service upon graduation. After the war the school's curriculum returned to normal.

George C. Marshall Museum and Research Library: This is a fine museum and research library on the grounds of VMI and was dedicated in 1964 by Presidents Lyndon Johnson and Dwight Eisenhower. George Marshall rose to be one of the highest ranking officer in the U.S. Army during WW II, was the instigator of the postwar Marshall Plan, President of the American Red Cross, Secretary of Defense, Secretary of State and a Nobel Peace Prize winner. Marshall's outstanding military and political career is outlined by displays and exhibits throughout the museum. Many of Marshall's personal belongings, public papers and artifacts are on display. The museum also has a rare copy of the German Enigma Cipher Machine. Address: Drawer 1600, Lexington, VA, 24450-1600. Phone: 540/463-7103. Hours: Daily 9-5, closed Jan. 1, Thanksgiving and Dec. 25. Free.

The VMI Museum: This is a second museum on the campus of Virginia Military Institute which traces the history of the school and many of the individuals who have been students here. On display are documents, uniforms, medals, student furniture, military equipment, Photographs, paintings, drawings and other artifacts related to the school. Of interest to WW II buffs are letters from Presidents Roosevelt and Truman, personal artifacts of Generals Marshall and Patton and a number of displays on WW II. Address: Jackson Memorial Hall, Virginia Military Institute, Lexington, VA 24450-0304.

The George C. Marshall Museum and Research Library on the grounds of Virginia Military Institute.

Phone: 540/464-7232. Hours: M-Sat. 9-5, Sun. 2-5, closed Jan. 1, Thanksgiving, Dec. 25. Free.

NEW MARKET is in NW Virginia 20 miles NE of Harrisburg on I-81.

NEW MARKET BATTLEFIELD MILITARY MUSEUM, in New Market, highlights the famous Battle of New Market during the American Civil War and the Civil War in general. The museum, however, has additional displays on WW II which include information on Gen. George Patton and Audie Murphy. There is also a video presentation of the "Why We Fight " movie series of WW II. Address: SR 305 North, New Market, VA 22844. Phone: 540/740-8065. Hours: Mar. 15 thru Dec. 15 daily 9-5. Admission charged.

NEWPORT NEWS (See Hampton/Newport News/Williamsburg/Yorktown area)

NORFOLK/PORTSMOUTH/VIRGINIA BEACH AREA: To many people, before, during, and after WW II, the word "Norfolk" was synonymous with "Navy". The strategic location of Norfolk and the surrounding cities dictates that this is a place where the Navy should be. The Norfolk area is centrally located on the U.S. Atlantic coast and guards the entrance to Chesapeake Bay and the various waterways that lead to some of America's most important cities including the nation's capital. Over the years the Navy has acquired many facilities in the area and the Army and Coast Guard are also well represented here.

Several large shipyards existed in the area, the U.S. Naval Shipyard at Portsmouth was, by far, the largest and it built everything from battleships on down. The other ship yards were the Welding Shipyard, Inc. in Norfolk which built tankers and merchant vessels, The Norfolk Shipbuilding & Dry Dock Co. and the St. Helena Shipyard. There were also several war plants in the area. Because of the shipyards and the intense military and industrial activity that went on here during the war the Norfolk area suffered the ills of a wartime boom town. Housing was scarce, schools crowded, city services over-burdened, the crime rate rose and there were shortages of many items and inflation. Several Federal housing developments were built in the area, but they failed to keep pace with the demand. It was only after the war that the Norfolk area began to return to normal.

On Dec. 7, 1941, the day the Japanese attacked Pearl Harbor, all Japanese aliens were rounded up in the Norfolk area. Some, but not all, were subsequently sent to alien internment camps. As in other big cities along the east coast there were fears of enemy attacks which resulted in the need for black outs and other civil defense measures. In some areas around Norfolk barrage balloons were put in place to guard against low-flying enemy aircraft.

The waters off Norfolk in Chesapeake Bay and Hampton Roads were deep and spacious so many large convoys were assembled here during the war and departed for distant locations. The first American convoy of the war left from here on Dec. 13, 1941 for Gibraltar.

CAMP ASHBY was located in the vicinity of U.S. 58 and Thalia Creek in present-day Virginia Beach. This was a small temporary Army train-

The Life-Saving Museum of Virginia is one of only a few such Stations remaining in America.

ing camp that was used during the early part of the war. Later it became a main prisoner of war camp with about 1500 German POWs who worked for the military and in agriculture and elsewhere. Camp Ashby was closed and dismantled after the war and it became a residential section of Virginia Beach.

HAMPTON ROADS NAVAL MUSEUM is located on the second floor of Nauticus, the National Maritime Center, on the Norfolk waterfront. The museum has exhibits on over 200 years of naval history in the Hampton Roads area. There are generous displays covering the WW II era with ship models, Photographs and artifacts. Throughout the National Maritime Center are other exhibits with nautical themes. Address: One Waterside Dr., Suite 248, Norfolk, VA 23510-1607. Phone: 800/ 664-1080 and 804/ 444-8971. Hours: Thurs.-Sun. 10-7, Dec. 22-31 daily 10-7, closed Jan. 1 thru Apr. 7, Thanksgiving and Dec. 25. Admission charged.

LIFE-SAVING MUSEUM OF VIRGINIA is located on the ocean front in Virginia Beach at 24th St. This is one of the few remaining Coast Guard life-saving Stations out of hundreds that dotted the U.S. coastlines for over 50 years up to WW II and for a short time thereafter. Such stations were manned around the clock by Coast Guardsmen ready to take to the sea in small boats in any kind of weather to aid stricken vessels. Life-saving stations such as this one were very active during WW II because of the many ships lost along the U.S. coastline. Hundreds of survivors were rescued by Coastguardsmen operating out of stations like this one. The stations also served as places of residence for Coast Guardsmen on beach patrols. During WW II this station housed Coast Guard beach patrols and their horses. The station has been preserved much as it was during the latter days of its useful life. Inside the museum are extensive displays on WW II including information on the German mine laying operations at the mouth of Chesapeake Bay, the "Hooligan Navy", the British trawlers, beach patrols, aircraft, blimps, ships and German submarines. Address: 24th & Oceanfront, PO Box 24, Virginia Beach, VA 23451. Phone: 804/422-1587. Hours: Tues.-Sat. 10-5, Sun. noon-5 (also Mon. Memorial Day thru Sept, 30 10-5). Closed Thanksgiving and Dec. 25 thru Jan. 1. Admission charged.

THE MacARTHUR MEMORIAL, located in downtown Norfolk in MacArthur Square, is a complex of three buildings consisting of the main memorial building (which was the former Norfolk City Hall), a theater and a gift shop building. The memorial honors General Douglas MacArthur and traces his military and private life. It also serves as his final resting place.

MacArthur was born into a prominent military family and never really had a home town. He adapted Norfolk as such because it was his mother's home town. The main building in the memorial serves as a library and archives and contains many of MacArthur's personal belongings such as his uniforms, corn cob pipes, medals, awards, gifts, papers and Photographs. In the gift shop building is the General's 1950 Chrysler Imperial limousine which he used in Tokyo and New York. Address: MacArthur Square, Norfolk, VA. 23510. Phone: 804/441-2965. Hours: M-Sat. 10-5, Sun. 11-5, closed Jan. 1, Thanksgiving and Dec. 25. Free.

MARY HARDY MacARTHUR MEMORIAL honors the mother of General-of-the-Army Douglas MacArthur. Mary Hardy MacArthur was born in Norfolk and became the wife of Arthur MacArthur, Civil War hero and career soldier. She gave birth to Douglas on Jan. 26, 1880 in Little Rock, AR. The memorial consists of a small park surrounded by a low brick wall with a plaque in front commemorating the memory of Mrs. MacArthur. It is located in the Berkeley district of Norfolk on north Main St. at Bellamy Ave.

NANSEMOND ORDNANCE DEPOT was west of Portsmouth on the eastern bank of the mouth of the Nansemond River. The area has long been known as Pig Point because of a large pig farm that occupied the area for years. In 1918 the Federal Government bought 900 acres at Pig Point and built the Nansemond Ordnance Depot. for use as a transshipping depot for

This is the entrance to the MacArthur Memorial. The statue of the General in the foreground is identical to the one at West Point.

The Mary Hardy MacArthur Memorial in Norfolk honors the mother of General-of-the-Army Douglas MacArthur.

These barracks buildings at Camp Pendleton were constructed during the war to house Army Coastal Artillery personnel and remained in use well into the postwar era.

Army ammunition. The depot was retained after that war and was used again during WW II for the same purpose. Nansemond was retained after WW II and in 1950 transferred to the Marine Corps and used as a supply depot until 1958. It was eventually sold to private interests and later became the Frederick Campus of Tidewater Community College.

FORT NORFOLK was located about 1.4 miles NW of downtown Norfolk on the east bank of the Elizabeth and at the west end of Front St. It was built in the 1790s along with Fort Nelson on the other side of the river to protect the river entrance to Norfolk, Portsmouth and the naval shipyard. Fort Norfolk was used off-and-on over the years and for a long period of time was under the control of the Navy. In 1923 the fort became the headquarters of the Army's Norfolk District and served in that role until

1942. In that year the Army's Engineer Corps took over the fort and used it as their district headquarters. Fort Norfolk served the Engineers throughout the remainder of WW II and well into the postwar era. Many of the fort's old buildings remained in use and the site was eventually put on the State and National Registers of Historic Places.

NORFOLK ARMY AIR FIELD was 6 miles NE of downtown Norfolk and was the city's new main commercial airport when the U.S. went to war in Dec. 1941. Within a few days after the declaration of war, combat-ready P-40 fighter planes of the 1st Air Force arrived at the airport as part of a pre-arranged plan for the defense of the Norfolk area. Because of the strategic location of the area the AAF took over the airport and gave it its wartime name. Norfolk AAF had an intransit air depot. The 1st AF stayed until late 1944 at which time their facilities were declared inactive. After the war, the air field was returned to its owners and soon regained its importance as the area's main airport, Norfolk International Airport.

CAMP PENDLETON, just south of Virginia Beach on General Booth Blvd., was a Virginia National Guard camp before the war. It was taken over by the Army in Sept. 1940 for the duration of the war and was occupied by units and personnel of the Army's Coast Artillery who were serving in the various coastal defenses in the area. After the war the Army returned the camp to the National Guard.

PORTSMOUTH NAVAL YARD MUSEUM is near downtown Portsmouth at the foot of High St. and on the Southern Branch of the Elizabeth River. This fine museum relates the history of the U.S. Naval Shipyard, Norfolk (see below) which is often referred to as the Portsmouth Naval Yard or the Norfolk Naval Yard. The museum has exhibits which trace the history of the U.S. Navy and the ship yard. There are many ship models, naval artifacts, Photographs, paintings, documents, and a scale model of the ship yard as it appeared during WW II. And, there are many other displays in the museum from the WW II era. Address: 2 High St., Portsmouth, VA 23705. Phone: 804/393-8591. Hours: Tues.-Sat. 10-5, Sun. 1-5, closed Jan. 1, Thanksgiving and Dec. 25. Admission charged.

Adjoining the Portsmouth Naval Yard Museum is a second museum, the Portsmouth Lightship Museum. It consists primarily of a Coast Guard light ship "Portsmouth" that operated in the Hampton Roads area from 1915 until after WW II. Admission to the Portsmouth Naval Yard Museum incudes admittance to this museum.

FORT STORY was located on Cape Charles at the entrance to Chesapeake Bay. It was built just before WW I as a coast artillery fort guarding the southern entrance to Chesapeake Bay. It was armed with 16" rifles and three batteries of 6" guns. During WW II the fort also had anti-aircraft guns. In Sept. 1944 the fort was converted into an Army convalescent hospital and remained so until Mar. 1946. During that time is served some 13,000 patients. The fort had a branch prisoner of war camp with the POWs working at the fort. Immediately after the war the Army's Transportation Corps, Sta-

This is one of Fort Story's base end Stations which were used to sight the fort's big guns. The tower is now in the middle of a parking lot south of the fort near 67th St. in Virginia Beach.

The Portsmouth Naval Yard Museum in Portsmouth, VA.

tioned at Fort Eustis in Newport News, began using Fort Story's long water front for amphibious training exercises. In 1948 the Transportation Corps took over the fort and continued to use it for amphibious training well into the postwar years.

U.S. NAVAL AIR STATION, NORFOLK was located east of, and adjacent to, NOB, Norfolk. Before WW I the Navy established an experimental aviation facility on this site which had been used for the 1907 Jamestown Exposition. In 1917, after the U.S. entered, WW I, the government bought 143 acres of the former Exposition land and built an air field to use for the training of Navy pilots and aircraft mechanics. Activity increased and by 1939 the station covered 1140 acres and had some 300 planes on board. Before the U.S. entered the war, planes from here flew patrols deep into the Atlantic enforcing America's neutrality laws. After the Japanese attack on Pearl Harbor the station acquired more land and became the home of four carrier groups. Naval aircraft from here also flew anti-submarine patrols along the coast. NAS, Norfolk acquired five auxiliary air fields located at Fentress, Pungo, Monogram, Creeds and Oceana. In Mar. 1942 the first trans-Atlantic transport squadron of the Naval Air Transport Service (NATS) was formed at NAS, Norfolk using Douglas R4D (DC-3) transports. NATS and the Naval Air Ferry Command had operations at NAS, Norfolk throughout the war. In the postwar years NAS, Norfolk concentrated on aircraft maintenance and became the Navy's main air station in the area for aircraft parts and major aircraft rework projects. Some training continued at the field including the training of reservists. NAS, Norfolk functioned throughout the Cold War and into the post-Cold War era. During WW II NAS, Norfolk had the following outlying fields:

- U.S. Naval Aux. Air Station, Chincoteague, 3.5 miles west of Chincoteague
- U.S. Naval Air Station (LTA), Weeksville, 2 miles NE of Weeksville, NC.
- U.S. Naval Auxiliary Air Station, Manteo, 1.5 miles NW of Manteo, NC.
- Suffock Airport, 4 miles SW of Suffock
- Site #6, 3.5 miles SW of Lively

U.S. NAVAL AMMUNITION DEPOT, ST. JULIENS CREEK is located on the southern edge of Portsmouth and on the west bank of the South Branch of the Elizabeth River. It was established in the 1890s and functioned continuously as a naval ammunition depot from then until after WW II. During WW II it was, of course, very active supplying ammunition to U.S. and Allies warships. NAD, St. Juliens Creek received, stored, loaded, assembled and shipped ammunition. During that time the depot expanded to include a Marine Corps depot and also stored naval fuel.

U.S. NAVAL AMPHIBIOUS TRAINING BASE, LITTLE CREEK is located on the southern shore of Chesapeake Bay between the cities of Norfolk and Virginia Beach. Military activity started here in early 1941 when the Navy set up a temporary facility for the Inshore Patrol which was charged with the protection of sea traffic passing through Lynnhaven Roads, the waters immediately off shore. When the U.S. went to war coastal patrol craft also began using the Little Creek facilities, and over the next three years Little Creek was used for more and more operations. It expanded to include a ship repair center, a training center for SeaBees called Camp Bradford, a training center for armed guards of merchant ships called Camp Shelton, 5650' feet of berthing space and eight new piers. All the while the Station was still considered to be temporary and many of the buildings were built of wood and tarpaper. In the spring of 1943 the SeaBee training operation moved to Camp Peary near Williamsburg and the Navy's amphibious training operations from NOB, Norfolk moved into the vacated Camp Bradford and absorbed Camp Shelton. The amphibious training facilities grew to be the largest organization at the base and trained personnel from all of the armed services. This center was capable of housing and training up to 72,000 troops at a time and by war's end had trained over 200,000 naval personnel and 160,000 Army personnel. NATB, Little Creek also became one of two gathering point on the east coast for newly-built landing craft manufactured in the eastern U.S. prior to their being shipped overseas. A second amphibious training area was located on the Atlantic Ocean south of Virginia Beach at the end of Dam Neck Rd.[3] In August 1945 Little Creek became the home of the Atlantic Fleet's Amphibious Force and the Navy began giving serious consideration to making Little Creek a permanent base. This was eventually done and in the mid-1950s the facilities at the base were completely modernized. After that, the base continued to offer amphibious training to all of the branches of the armed forces and the reserves. Four of the training beaches at the base have been given place-names of WW II amphibious operations; Anzio, Sicily, Normandy, Salerno. Much of the

[3]This facility gained its own identity after the war and has been known in recent years as Fleet Combat Training Center, Atlantic.

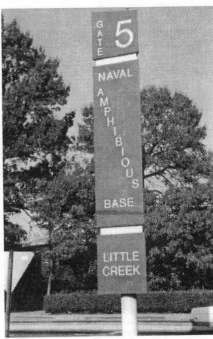

Sign at the entrance to Gate #5.

base can be seen from highway US 60.

U.S. NAVAL AUXILIARY AIR STATION, CREEDS was located three miles NE of Munden near the North Carolina state line. It was bounded by Campbell's Landing Rd., Morris Neck Rd. and Fitztown Rd. NAAS, Creeds was built by the Navy early in the war as an auxiliary field for NAS, Norfolk and was used as a training field for dive bomber pilots. After the war the air field was abandoned. For a while the air field's runways were used as drag strips but later the land was used for farming, forests, residential sites and a small park. The old runways and former ammunition bunkers can be seen from the above-mentioned roads.

U.S. NAVAL AUXILIARY AIR STATION, FENTRESS was located 2.5 miles SE of Fentress. It was established early in the war as an auxiliary air field for NAS, Norfolk. The station was retained after the war and in 1946 became an auxiliary air station to NAS, Oceana. Fentress eventually gained its own identity and became known as U.S. Naval Air Station, Fentress.

U.S. NAVAL AUXILIARY AIR STATION, MONOGRAM was located three miles west of Driver, VA, which is five miles west of Portsmouth. The air field was established early in the war as an auxiliary field for NAS, Norfolk, but it proved to be a disappointment because the field was unusable after a heavy rain. NAAS, Monogram was abandoned after the war.

U.S. NAVAL AUXILIARY AIR STATION, OCEANA was two miles west of downtown Virginia Beach. During WW II this area was swampy and inaccessible wasteland. The Navy, nevertheless, built an outlying air field for NAS, Norfolk in 1940-4. After the attack on Pearl Harbor the station was expanded and used by operational aircraft defending the Norfolk area and doing patrol work at sea. During 1943 the station was expanded again and in Sept. of that year designated an auxiliary air station, still under the control of NAS, Norfolk. By Jan. 1944 a carrier air group of three squadrons was operating from the station. Also that year NAAS,

A part of Creeds Field's runway can be seen in the distance from Campbell's Landing Rd.

The large bronze sign at the main gate of NAS, Oceana implies that the Master Jet Base is a very permanent facility of the Navy. In the rear a flag detail is raising the flag at 8:00 am.

Oceana acquired a Mobile Radar Intercept Training Unit. The station was expanded yet again during the winter of 1944-45 and became home to five more carrier squadrons. By this time there was a generous compliment of the Navy's most modern aircraft operating out of the station which included PB4Y Privateers, SB2C Helldivers, F6F Hellcats, TBF Avengers and F4U Corsairs. When the war ended NAAS, Oceana was one of the very few military facilities in the U.S. to be considered for long-term use and further expansion. With this in mind the station was upgraded to a naval air station and acquired NAAS, Fentress as its own auxiliary air field. In 1950-51 NAS, Oceana was modernized and converted into the Navy's first Master Jet air field and became the home of the Navy's most modern jet aircraft. NAS, Oceana operated well into the post-Cold War era.

U.S. NAVAL AUXILIARY AIR STATION, PUNGO, 7 miles south of downtown Virginia Beach, was a local airport that was taken over by the Navy early in the war for use as a radio station. This was an auxiliary field to NAS, Norfolk, but there was very little air activity here during the war. After the war the station was turned over to the Coast Guard which continued to use the radio facilities and, like the Navy, not the air facilities.

U.S. NAVAL OPERATING BASE, NORFOLK was located on a huge expanse of land in the NW corner of Norfolk and on additional land on the west bank of the Elizabeth River. This was the Navy's largest facility in the Hampton Roads area. NOB, Norfolk began in 1918 when the Navy acquired land north of Norfolk which had been used for the 1907 Jamestown Exposition and built a supply Station, receiving center, training center and an air facility. Some of the abandoned building from the Exposition were utilized at the time. The base expanded rapidly during WW I with first priority being given to recruit training. In June 1918 the headquarters of the 5th Naval District moved onto the base which elevated NOB, Norfolk to a pri-

mary position in the Navy's hierarchy because many naval installations in the Chesapeake Bay area fell under the umbrella of the 5th Naval District. In the 1920s the base functioned at a reduced level, but continued to carry out all of the missions it had acquired during WW I. Also in the years between the wars fleet service schools moved onto the base and the Marine Corps acquired a supply depot here. By 1937 all of NOB, Norfolk's major components were functioning except the submarine facilities which were inactive. The base was one of the largest of its kind in the world and the home of principal elements of the U.S. fleet when it was in the Atlantic. In 1939, before WW II started in Europe, NOB, Norfolk acquired Craney Island on the west bank of the entrance to the Elizabeth River as a fuel storage facility. When the two-ocean Navy came into being NOB, Norfolk became the eastern home of the battleships "California", "Idaho" and "New Mexico" and the carriers "Lexington", "Ranger", "Yorktown" and "Enterprise". As war fears mounted NOB, Norfolk became extremely busy outfitting newly-built ship as well as older ones to meet wartime conditions. Various facilities at the base expanded and by the summer of 1940 NOB, Norfolk was capable of supporting major elements of the Navy in overseas operations. After the U.S. entered the war the base underwent another major expansion. The supply depot, receiving station, training center, Marine barracks and hospital all expanded and the Atlantic Fleet School moved onto the base. New piers and warehouses were built and the WW I-era Norfolk Army Base, a port of embarkation, two miles south of Sewell Point was annexed. NOB, Norfolk also acquired a large expanse of land on the west bank of the York River just north of the Mine Depot as a second fuel storage facility and for additional warehouses. This facility was called Cheatham Annex. NOB, Norfolk also acquired the Cavalier Hotel at Virginia

Beach and converted it into a radar school. In 1942 Camp Allen was built on the southern edge of the base to train SeaBees. Camp Allen was one of the few naval facilities in the country to have a main prisoner of war camp. The POW camp held about 750 POWs who worked for the Navy. In Oct. 1942 a large part of the U.S. armada that carried American troops directly to the invasion of French Morocco was equipped at NOB, Norfolk. At war's end the base began to scale down as did most other military facilities and for a while stored decommissioned aircraft carriers, destroyers and submarines. NOB, Norfolk continued in operation throughout the Cold War and remained one of the Navy's most important facilities on the Atlantic seaboard.

U.S. NAVAL SHIPYARD, NORFOLK is located just south of downtown Portsmouth on the west bank of the Southern Branch of the Elizabeth River. This facility is sometime referred to as the Norfolk Naval Shipyard or the Portsmouth Naval Shipyard. Its beginning can be traced to colonial times when a privately-owned ship yard, known as Gosport Shipyard, was built on the location in 1767. By WW I the yard was known by its present-day name and became extremely busy and was expanded into a giant ship yard for its day. As a result of the Washington Naval Conference of 1920, which limited the size of the world's navies, activity at NS, Norfolk began to decline steadily. Virtually no new ships were built and the yard survived on repair work, maintenance and conversions. Between 1925 and 1934 the yard repaired or modernized the battleships "Texas", "New York", "Nevada", "Arizona", "Mississippi" and "Idaho", all of which would participate in WW II. As the edicts of the Washington Naval Conference crumbled in the early 1930s NS, Norfolk got its first orders in years for new warships. Other orders followed, including an order for a new battleship, the "Alabama". After Pearl Harbor, activity at the yard exploded. Orders for warships poured in, the yard went on around-the-clock operation and the average workweek rose to 56 hours. In Feb. 1943 employment peaked at 43,000 and the yard could have used another 55,000 workers if they could have found them. By the end of the war the yard had built 101 new ships in-

These are radio antennas at Pungo Field erected by the Navy during WW II and later used by the Coast Guard. Part of the field's un-used airstrip can be seen in the foreground.

The newly built aircraft carrier "Lake Champlain" about to be launched at NS, Norfolk.

cluding one battleship, three Essex-class carriers, 10 destroyers escorts, 20 LSTs and 50 LMCs. About 6750 other vessel's were worked on or otherwise serviced and the size of the yard had doubled. Soon after V-J Day a second battleship, the "Kentucky", was launched. Activity, of course, dropped off dramatically after the end of the war, but the yard stayed fairly active, and by 1950 still had over 9000 employees. Activity surged again during the Korean War and then fell back to a relatively steady pace for the remainder of the Cold War.

PETERSBURG is 20 miles south of Richmond.

CAMP LEE was 10 miles NE of downtown Petersburg. The camp was built in 1917 to be a State mobilization camp and later a training center for divisions. After that war the camp's building were demolished and the land was converted into a game preserve. Later, some of the land was incorporated into the National Military Park of Petersburg, a Civil War site. In 1940-41 the War Department constructed a second Camp Lee on the same site to be the new home of the Quartermaster Replacement Training Center (QMARTC), its Officer Candidate School and the Medical Replacement Training Center (MARTC). The QMARTC soon expanded beyond original estimates and the MARTC was transferred to Camp Pickett to give QMARTC more space. Later the QMARTC was redesignated as an Army Service Forces Training Center but retained its original mission of training Quartermaster personnel which it performed throughout WW II. Early in the war Camp Lee served as a reception center for the Army's 3rd Corps Area. This camp had segregated facilities so negro troops were also received and trained here. In Aug. 1944 the Army's Adjutant General's School moved here from Ft. Washington, MD and operated along side the Quartermaster training facilities. Camp Lee had a main prisoner of war camp which held about 820 POWs who worked at Camp Lee and in the forests. By war's end Camp Lee had trained some 300,000 Army personnel. The camp was retained after the war as a quartermaster training center and in 1950 was made a permanent installation of the Army and renamed Fort Lee. Fort Lee functioned throughout the Cold War.

U.S. Army Quartermaster Museum: This is a large Army museum on the grounds of Fort Lee which traces the history of the Quartermaster Corps from its beginning in 1775 to the present. The museum highlights the wide variety of services the QMC performs for the Army which include providing, food, clothing, transportation, petroleum products, aerial supply and mortuary services. Items on display in the museum include field kitchens, items of clothing, motorized and horse-drawn vehicles, flags, dog tags, chaplain's equipment, equipment for dogs and horses, maternity uniforms for women and two of General Dwight Eisenhower's uniforms. Also on display is Gen. Patton's customized Jeep and an exhibit recalling Saturday morning inspection for GIs. Address: A St. & 2nd St., Fort Lee, VA 23801. Phone: 804/734-4203. Hours: Tues.-F 10-5, Sat. & Sun. 11-5, closed Jan. 1, Thanksgiving and Dec. 25. Free.

PORTSMOUTH (See Norfolk/Portsmouth/ Virginia Beach Area)

PULASKI (See Radford/ Pulaski Area)

QUANTICO is 30 miles south of Washington, DC on the Potomac River.

U.S. MARINE CORPS BASE, QUANTICO now surrounds the small community of Quantico and extends for about 30 miles to the northeast. The Marine base came into existence in 1917 as an east coast training center for up to 3500 Marine officers and enlisted men. When the U.S. entered WW I Marines received advanced training here and, upon completion, usually went directly to overseas assignments. In 1918 the leased land was purchased by the Government and MCB, Quantico declared a permanent Marine base. Training then expanded to cover artillery spotters operating from balloons and seaplanes. After WW I MCB, Quantico became a major Marine Corps training facility. Schools opened in auto mechanics, music, typewriting and shorthand. The military failures of the Great War were studied in depth and new technological developments were carefully monitored regarding their importance to the Marine Corps. Research, development and training in amphibious operations soon began to take center stage at MCB, Quantico. Exercises planned here were conducted in Panama, Guantanamo Bay, Cape Cod and Hawaii. As early as 1921 a plan was advanced by Maj. Earl H. Ellis which envisioned that in a war with Japan the Marine Corps might be called upon to hop from island to island across the Pacific in order to reach, and ultimately defeat, Japan. Such a campaign would require numerous amphibious operations. This plan gained wide acceptance in the Marine Corps and was formalized in Marine Corps planning in 1926 as "Operation Orange". Also in the 1920s two combat-ready Marine units, called Marine Expeditionary Forces, were established, one at San Diego, CA and the other here. These units could be called upon on short notice to land on a hostile shore with amphibious operations being very much a part of their quick-response capabilities. Out of the study and training of amphibious operations other areas of need were identified, studied, proposed and tested at Quantico. This included dive bombing operations in support of landings, rapid delivery of large numbers of men and equipment from ship to shore and the use of larger and improved landing craft. In the latter category Quantico Marines began, in the mid-1930s, working with Andrew J. Higgins of New Orleans, a manufacturer of shallow-draft boats and Donald Roebling, a builder of shallow-draft tractor-tread-equipped boats used in the Florida Everglades. Out of these relationships came the famous "Higgins Boats" (LCVP-Landing Craft Vehicle Personnel) and the "Alligator" (LTV-Landing Tracked Vehicle). Both of these pieces of equipment had been developed, tested and were ready when the U.S. entered the war in Dec. 1941. Their existence, and the training the Marine Corps

The U.S. Army Quartermaster Museum, Fort Lee, VA.

A new 155 mm gun is test fired into a tunnel at Radford Ordnance Works. The speed of the projectile can be measured by electronic sensors inside the tunnel.

had acquired in the years before the war, made it possible for the 1st Marine Division to carry out the successful amphibious operations in the Solomon Islands early in the war. Throughout WW II MCB, Quantico was acknowledged at the Marine Corps' primary development and training facility with regards to amphibious operations. The base was enlarged several times and various schools came into being here making MCB, Quantico a primary training center is a number of areas. In 1942 land west of highway US 1 was acquired by MCB, Quantico and named the "Guadalcanal Area" because the terrain was similar to that of the island. This great expanse of land was used for the training of artillerymen and the firing of live ammunition. Aviation training was another high priority at MCB, Quantico and some Marines were given parachute training.

With the end of hostilities, MCB, Quantico became a Marine demobilization center. When that program ended the base resumed its position as a primary research, development and training facility. As helicopters, jets, atomic weapons and the like came along personnel at Quantico were in the forefront of such developments studying their importance and relationship to the U.S. Marine Corps. MCB, Quantico remained very active throughout the Cold War.

U.S. Marine Corps Air-Ground Museum: This excellent museum is located on the grounds of the U.S. Marine Corps Base, Quantico at Brown Field. Restored Marine aircraft and ground equipment are on display in several old hangars whose interiors have been restored to the mid-1930s era. Most of the aircraft are pre-jet models with a generous number of WW II planes on display. This is a large collection of aircraft and includes a Japanese "Baca" suicide aircraft, a Zero and the well-known Marines planes of WW II. Address: Marine Corps Museums Branch Activities, Quantico, VA 22134. Phone: 540/640-2606. Hours: Apr. 1 thru the day before Thanksgiving Tues.-Sat. 10-5, Sun. noon-5. Closed Easter. Free.

RADFORD/PULASKI AREA: These towns are in the western part of Virginia on I-8. Radford is 35 miles west of Roanoke and Pulaski is 14 miles WSW of Radford.

NEW RIVER ORDNANCE PLANT was built 7 miles NE of Pulaski near the community of Dublin by the Federal Government in 1940-41. This was a bag-loader plant that loaded powder in bags for large caliber Army and Navy artillery, primarily 105 mm and 155 mm. The New River Plant was a sub-post of Radford Ordnance Works.

RADFORD ORDNANCE WORKS was a large ordnance plant, with over 8 miles of fencing, built by the Federal Government near Radford in 1940-41. The plant manufactured the explosives DNT, TNT, Double Base, Pentolite, nitroglycerine powder, special powders, rocket propellant and smokeless powder and was run by the Hercules Powder Co. Radford Ordnance did considerable research and development on munitions and also had a branch prisoner of

war camp with about 500 POWs who worked at the plant. The facility was retained after the war and operated intermittently in the postwar years.

RICHMOND is the capital of Virginia. During the early part of the war the Patent Office moved here from Washington, DC to make room for agencies more directly related to the war effort.

McGUIRE GENERAL HOSPITAL was a large Army hospital located in Richmond and had some 1700 beds. The hospital specialized in neurology, neurosurgery and amputations. During the latter part of the war McGuire became a major reception center for wounded service personnel being returned from the European Theater of Operations. McGuire personnel would treat the patients and then disperse them to other hospitals. In Mar. 1946 McGuire was transferred to the Veterans Administration.

RICHMOND ARMY AIR FIELD, 7.5 miles SE of Richmond, was the city's local airport before the war. When the U.S. went to war in Dec. 1941 this field was one of several in the country previously selected to become an AAF operational air field for combat-ready air units of the 1st AF assigned to defend the borders of the nation. During this time the AAF's facilities at the field were named Richmond Army Air Field. The air field had a small main prisoner of war camp with about 150 POWs who worked at the air field. In 1944, after the need to defend American's borders had diminished, Richmond AAF was used as a training facility, but it late 1944 this ended and AAF facilities was declared inactive. After the war the air field once again became a commercial air port and eventually became Richmond International Airport.

Virginia Aviation Museum: This is an interesting air museum on the grounds of Richmond International Airport that displays a collection of about 20 aircraft, most of which are pre-WW II. Other displays include engines, models, air artifacts, Photographs, uniforms and a WW II Norden bombsight. Virginia's Aviation Hall of Fame is located in the museum. Address: 5701 Huntsman Rd., Richmond, VA 23150. Phone: 804/371-0371. Hours: Daily 9:30-5, closed Thanksgiving and Dec. 25. Admission charged.

RICHMOND ARMY SERVICE FORCES DEPOT, 8000 S. Jefferson Davis Hwy. (US 1/301), was built in 1941. and first known as Richmond General Depot. Its mission was to receive, store and ship a wide variety of supplies for the Quartermaster Corps, Army Engineers, Medical Corps and Ordnance Corps. About 5500 people were employed here. In 1943 it was given its wartime name. The depot had one of the largest main prisoner of war camps in the country and at times held up to 2500 POWs. Most of the POWs worked at the depot. Richmond ASF Depot was retained by the Army after the war and continued to serve as a general supply depot. It had various names through the

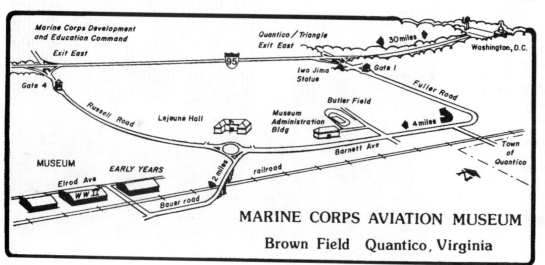

MARINE CORPS AVIATION MUSEUM
Brown Field Quantico, Virginia

McGuire General Hospital during WW II.

years and in the later part of the Cold War was known as the Defense General Supply Center, Richmond.

VIRGINIA WORLD WAR II, KOREAN, VIET NAM

MEMORIAL is located a few blocks east of downtown Richmond on Belvedere St. (US 1) at the north end of the Robert E. Lee Bridge. This impressive memorial honors Virginians who died in these three wars. Their names are contained within the memorial and bronze coffers display various war artifacts. Phone: 804/786-2050. Hours: Daily 8 am - 10 pm. Free.

STAUNTON is in west-central Virginia on I-64 and I-81.

WOODROW WILSON GENERAL HOSPITAL was an Army general hospital built in Staunton in 1942 to treat war wounded. The hospital had 1565 beds and specialized in general medicine, general and orthopedic surgery and syphilis. This was a permanent structure built of brick and in Mar. 1946 it was transferred to August County Commonwealth of Virginia.

VIRGINIA BEACH (See Norfolk/Portsmouth/Virginia Beach Area)

WASHINGTON, DC AREA: This is the area directly across the Potomac River from Washington, DC. During the war this area was a bustling part of Washington, DC and suffered many of the same adverse conditions such as housing shortages, crowded schools, pollution, inflation, high crime rate and severe strains on city facilities. Alexandria was the largest city in the area and had a 1940 population of 33,500. Arlington, while it was well built up and had many residents, was not an incorporated city.

ARLINGTON NATIONAL CEMETERY is directly west of the Lincoln Memorial in DC and accessible via the Arlington Memorial Bridge which spans the Potomac between the District of Columbia and Arlington, VA. Arlington National Cemetery is American's best-known and most prestigious national cemetery and many of America's most famous people are buried here. Federal laws regulates who may be buried at Arlington National Cemetery as well as other national cemetery around the nation. The grounds of the cemetery are beautiful and kept immaculately clean. Many ceremonies are conducted here, some on a daily basis, such as

those at the Tomb of the Unknowns. Other ceremonies are held at the nearby Arlington Memorial Amphitheater.

Within the cemetery are many memorials and monuments. Some of those pertaining to WW II included the U.S. Marine Corps Memorial, American Defenders of Bataan and Corregidor Memorial, Women in Military Service Memorial, the Netherlands Carillon and the SeaBee Memorial. Many of the roads in the cemetery are also named after WW II personalities. Famous WW II personalities buried here include:

- Gen. Creighton Abrams
- Gen. Henry "Hap" Arnold
- Gen. Anthony J. D. Biddle
- Col. "Pappy" Boyington
- Gen. Omar Bradley
- Brigadier Evans F. Carlson, Carlson's Raiders and "Gung Ho" slogan
- Gen. Claire Chennault
- Gen. Benjamin O. Davis
- William J. "Wild Bill" Donovan, Director of the OSS
- Adm. Frank J. Fletcher
- James V. Forrestal, Secretary of the Navy 1944-47
- William F. Friedman, broke the Japanese "Purple Code"
- Adm. William F. "Bull" Halsey. Jr.
- Gen. Lewis B. Hershey
- Adm. Alan G. Kirk
- William F. "Frank" Knox, Secretary of the Navy 1940-44
- Gen. Walter Krueger
- Adm. William D. Leahy
- Lord Lothian, Philip H. Kerr, British Ambassador to U.S. (Apr. 1939-Dec. 1941)
- Gen. George C. Marshall
- Gen. Anthony C. McAuliffe
- Adm. Marc A. Mitchner
- Audie Murphy, Congressional Medal of Honor winner and movie actor
- Adm. Forrest B. Royal
- Gen. Walter C. Short
- Gen. Walter Bedell Smith
- Adm. Harold R. Stark
- Gen. Maxwell Taylor

- Gen. Hoyt Vandenberg
- Gen. Jonathan Wainwright
- Gen. Orde Wingate

Only persons visiting the graves of relatives and the physically handicapped are allowed to drive in the cemetery. Other visitors must park in the parking lot off Memorial Dr. where a fee is charged. Tourmobiles leave the visitors center at regular intervals and offer a narrated tour of the cemetery. Cemetery hours: Apr. thru Sept. 8-7, rest of year 8-5. Phone: 202/554-5100. A fee is charged for the Tourmobile tours.

Marine Corps Memorial, "Iwo Jima Statue": This is the largest cast bronze statue in the world and depicts the famous flag-raising at Iwo Jima during WW II. It is dedicated to all Marines who have given their lives since 1775. The memorial is located near the entrance to Arlington National Cemetery on Marshall Dr. off of US 50. It is open 24 hours a day and free.

FORT BELVOIR was located 10 miles south of Alexandria on US 1. In 1910 the estate of Colonel William Fairfax was purchased by the Federal Government and in 1912 it was transferred to the War Department. During 1918-19 an Army camp, known as Camp Humphry, was built on the property for the training of replace-

Washington, DC as viewed from the entrance to Arlington National Cemetery. In the distance and to the right is the dome of the U.S. Capitol Building and the Washington Monument. Below is the Marine Corps Memorial on the grounds of the cemetery.

Werner von Braun, right, and President John F. Kennedy tour the Marshall Space Travel Center in 1962.

ments for the Army's Engineer Corps. The camp was retained after WW I and became a permanent Army post is 1922 at which time its name was changed to Fort Humphry. In 1935 the name was changed again to Fort Belvoir. The fort became the home of the Engineer Corps and the Engineer School. Throughout WW II some 147,000 Engineer personnel were trained here and in a huge training area in Shenandoah National Park. Fort Belvoir was, from its inception, a segregated camp because negro soldiers were widely used by the Engineer Corps. After WW II Fort Belvoir continued on as the home of the Engineers and acquired several dozen other Army tenant commands.

WERNER von BRAUN GRAVE SITE: Werner von
Braun, the famous German rocket scientist, is buried in Ivy Hill Cemetery in Alexandria. Von Braun headed the project in Germany during WW II that developed the famous V-1 and V-2 rockets. After the war he came to America and was instrumental in the development of America's early rockets and missiles.

FORT HUNT was located 7 mile south of
Alexandria on the west bank of the Potomac River. This was a coastal defense fort built in 1898 as part of the defenses for Washington, DC. In the 1930s the fort was used as a CCC camp. The fort was used during WW II by the OSS and as a an interrogation center for prisoners of war. POWs who were thought to have valuable information, or who wanted to volunteer information, were sent to Fort Hunt for interrogation. While at Fort Hunt the POW's living quarters were electronically "bugged" and reliable German collaborators were mixed in with the POWs in attempts to gain additional information. Many of the Germans submariners captured off the U.S. east coast passed through Fort Hunt for interrogation before being sent on to a permanent POW camp. The POWs were kept in isolation from the general public and driven about in windowless busses and never told where they were. After the war Fort Hunt was abandoned and became a park.

FORT MYER is located in Arlington and adjoins
Arlington National Cemetery on the north and west. The fort was built in 1863 by Union forces as a defense for Washington, DC. during the American Civil War. At that time it was known as Fort Whipple. The fort was retained by the Army after the Civil War, expanded over the years and in 1881 renamed Fort Myer. From 1887 to 1942 the fort was the home of various cavalry units who served not only as defenders of the area but also as ceremonial personnel for the many official functions carried out at Arlington National Cemetery and in the Washington, DC area. From 1919 on, the fort was a training center for elite Army horse units which put on shows and served as ceremonial personnel. Whenever the Army was called upon to provide honor guards and escorts for the President and other high-ranking officials and visitors, personnel from Fort Myer were utilized. When WW II began the 3rd Cavalry Regiment was in residence at Fort Myer, but soon departed to be reorganized and training as an armored unit. The 703rd Military Police Battalion moved in to take their place and perform the necessary military ceremonies. The Army's Band also moved here from the Army War College. Later infantry units moved onto the post. In Feb. 1942 the Army's Provost Marshal General established a school here to train military police. That school eventually moved to Fort Oglethorpe, GA. During WW II many high-ranking Army officers lived at the fort including Gen. George C. Marshall. In the postwar years Fort Myer was home to the elite Army units that protected Washington, DC and performed the military ceremonies. It also became the home of over 100 Army and Department of Defense agencies operating in the Washington, DC area. In recent years it has became a major housing facility for military personnel.

Old Guard Museum: This
museum is on the grounds of Fort Myer and honors the nation's oldest infantry regiment which today serves as the Army's official ceremonial unit and Escort to the President. The regiment was created in 1784 and served during WW II. On display are uniforms, weapons, documents and other artifacts pertaining to the regiment. Address: Bldg. 249, Sherman Ave., Fort Myer, VA 22211. Phone: 703/696-6670. Hours: M-Sat. 9-4, Sun. 1-4. Free.

THE PENTAGON, in the SE
part of Arlington, is known around the world as the headquarters of the armed forces of the United States and is the home of the Department of Defense. This huge military complex was built during WW II due to the rapid expansion of the War Department which simply ran out of space in its existing offices in Washington, DC. The Pentagon was built on land that belonged to Fort Myer and was known as Fort Myer's South Area. At the time construction began the land was being used by the Agriculture Department as a experimental farm. Construction of the Pentagon began in Sept. 1941 and was supervised by Gen. Leslie Groves who would later head the "Manhattan (Atomic Bomb) Project". Construction proceeded around-the-clock and employed up to 13,000 construction workers. The accident rate was high and at times the construction crews got ahead of the architects. To house the Pentagon's future workers a small city was built south of the site called Fairlington. By May 1942 one section of the Pentagon was completed enough to receive the first War Department occupants. By early 1943 the building was completed. It contained 5,100,000 square feet of space, twice that of the Empire State Building in New York City, and was the largest building in the world. Completion of the Pentagon concentrated the War Department's 24,000 employees in one facility where, before, the department had been spread all over the District of Columbia in 17 different locations and several additional outside the District.

Parts of the Pentagon are open to the public and free 1 1/2 hour guided tours leave every 30 minutes from the visitors center. Tour hours M-F 9:30-3:30. Not offered on holidays. Phone: 703/695-1776. The Pentagon also had one of the nation's largest military bookstores.

U.S. NAVAL TORPEDO FACTORY, ALEXANDRIA
was located at 105 N. Union St. in Alexandria on the west bank of the Potomac River. It was built in 1918-19 to produce torpedoes for the Navy. The site was chosen because it had easy water access to the Washington Navy Yard and the Hampton Roads area. A 20,000-yard torpedo test range was constructed at the same time at Piney Point, MD. These facilities were completed after WW I ended so they did not

The Pentagon as it appeared soon after completion.

produce torpedoes for that war. After WW I NTF, Alexandria was used to store, assemble and issue torpedoes to the Navy. The Station also did some specialized manufacturing for the Navy. With the advent of WW II the factory was utilized to its maximum and produced torpedoes throughout the war. With the end of hostilities, torpedo manufacturing ended here and the station was used for several years for records storage. In the 1970s the factory was sold to the city of Alexandria and converted into an art center. It eventually became known as the Torpedo Factory Art Center.

WASHINGTON NATIONAL AIRPORT is located just south of the Pentagon on George Washington Memorial Parkway and the Potomac River. It was built in 1940-41 to replace nearby Washington Hoover Field which, for years, had been inadequate for the area's needs. This airport became the area's main commercial airport during WW II and was considered to be one of the most modern in the world. It had all of the latest air traffic control and safety devices, long well-lighted runways, modern passenger and baggage handling facilities and a parking lot for 8000 cars. It was used regularly by many

of America's top political figures and many foreign dignitaries in their war-related travels and was one of the busiest airports in the nation. The airport was also constructed with an eye for the needs of the military and was used by both the AAF and Navy. The AAF's Air Transport Command had a military air freight terminal here and an Air Flight Service Center while the Navy used the field in its air transport system.

WASHINGTON QUARTERMASTER DEPOT was located on Duke St. in Alexandria about one miles east of I-395. The depot was built in 1819 and for more than a century was known as Washington General Depot. In 1941 it was expanded, assigned to the Army's Quartermaster Corps and given it wartime name. Throughout WW II the depot provided a variety of services for Army personnel in the DC area such as providing travel arrangements, engineer logistics, Army public exhibits, furniture storage, commissary services and recruiting services. The depot was retained after the war and continued to be used as a support facility. In 1950 its name was changed to Cameron Station and in the 1990s it was closed.

WARRENTON is 45 miles SW of Washington DC.

VINT HILLS FARMS, nine miles east of Warrenton on SR 215, had been the estate of the Andrew Low family since 1861. In 1941 the Federal Government purchased the estate and turned it over to the Army's Signal Corps as a training center for Signal Corps personnel. Repair work on Signal Corps equipment was also done here. The estate's original mansion was converted into the officers' club and the post commander lived in a second mansion on the estate built for the family's oldest son in 1890. Vint Hills Farms was retained by the Army after WW II and continued to be a center for electronic and communication-oriented Army commands. In the postwar years it became home to the Army's Electronics Materiel Readiness Activity. In the 1990s, the facility was closed.

WILLIAMSBURG (See Hampton/Newport News/Williamsburg/Yorktown area)

YORKTOWN (See Hampton/Newport News/Williamsburg/Yorktown area)

WASHINGTON

World War II had a major impact on the state of Washington because of its strategic location and its industries. Being located in the northwestern corner of the United State Washington was the gateway to Alaska and to the North Pacific. Her magnificent Puget Sound area provided a strategic and excellent location for the military, especially the Navy, and her well-developed industries of shipbuilding and aircraft manufacturing were of utmost importance to the war effort.

Washington's vast forests provided lumber, paper and pulp, and her farms produced grain, fruits, vegetables and meat. Her mines provided gold, silver, zinc and lead.

During the war Washington became a major manufacturer of aluminum when the Government build four ingot plants and a rolling mill in the state. A large magnesium plant was also built by the Government in Spokane. These plants served the west coast aircraft industry, especially the Boeing Aircraft Co., one of Washington's largest employers and one of the world's largest aircraft manufacturers. Boeing played a primary role in the development of the B-17 bomber and in the B-29 bombers. The Seattle plant built the first three prototype B-29s and the Renton plant built 998 of the 3763 ultimately produced.

Before the war Seattle and Tacoma had been experiencing a population growth of about 10% a year, but when the war started and government orders poured into those areas for ships, planes and other war items, their populations skyrocketed. These cities, and some of the others in the Puget Sound area, suffered a wide range of urban problems in much the same way as other west coast cities. There were severe shortages in housing, city services, consumer goods and an increase in crime and vice, including an epidemic of venereal decease in

1943 at a time when there was an acute shortage of doctors and nurses. The housing shortage in the Puget Sound area was one of the worst in the nation, an ironic twist of fate for a state that had a large lumber industry.

When the Japanese attacked Hawaii in Dec. 1941, there was great fear that Washington cities might be attacked too. Wild rumors spread in the Puget Sound area that a Japanese attack was imminent. These rumors were false but there were, however, Japanese submarines operating off Washington's coast and several ships were attacked. There were also incidents of Japanese subs shelling shore installations in Washington's neighboring state of Oregon, and to the north in the Canadian Province of British Columbia. Washington did come under attack later in the war, though, by Japanese bombing balloons. The balloons did little damage although one balloon managed to shut down the Hanford Engineer Works for a few days. During the balloon attacks, Washington state was chosen by the Army to be the site of the "Sunset Project", an operation designed to detect incoming balloons by radar early enough to notify waiting Army aircraft who would rise and shoot them down. Radar stations were built at several locations along Washington's coast for this purpose. The "Sunset Project" failed, though, because the balloons flew so high and had so little metal in them that radar couldn't detect them.

During the war the state had two main prisoner of war camps and several branch camps. POWs worked in the forests, on farms, in factories and at military camps.

One of Washington's Congressmen, Warren G. Magnuson, went on to the Senate during the war and became a well-known and long-serving public servant after the war. In Seattle a large park at Sand Point is named for him.

President Truman picked a Washington native, Lewis B. Schwellenback, to be his Secretary of Labor. The end of the war brought a period of hard times to Washington. The shipyards, her aircraft industry, the aluminum plants and much of the state's other war industry cut back production drastically. To make matter worse a state-wide loggers strike shut down the lumber industry from Sept. 23 to Dec. 4, 1945. Recovery was slow. Henry Kaiser bought two of the aluminum ingot plants and the rolling mill and put them back into production. The nation's need for lumber and paper revitalized that industry after the strike, and the advent of the Korean War brought many government orders once again to her aircraft industry and ship yards.

ARLINGTON is 35 miles north of Seattle.

U.S. NAVAL AUXILIARY AIR STATION, ARLINGTON: Arlington Airport, three miles SW of town, was built in 1934. When, in 1940, NAS, Seattle needed more training facilities for carrier pilots, Arlington Airport was leased and used as an additional training field. In June 1942, when the Japanese invade the Aleutian Islands of Alaska, the AAF made arrangements with the Navy to use the field as a base for medium bombers to give added protection to the U.S. Northwest. Two new runways were built as were many buildings.

By the summer of 1943 the Japanese threat from the Aleutians had eased, while the need for carrier pilots in the Pacific was on the rise. The AAF thus relinquished the field to the Navy who again used it to train carrier pilots. The training of carrier pilots continued until near the end of the war and gradually phased out. When hostilities ended, the air field was returned to the community of Arlington and became Arlington's Municipal Airport and an industrial park.

Two aircraft carriers, right and left, and a destroyer, center, in the Bremerton mothball fleet anchorage as seen from the highway.

BAINBRIDGE ISLAND, is a large, well populated, island in Puget Sound directly across from Seattle. There was a large ship yard and several important military facilities on the island and nearby. The island also had a sizeable community of ethnic Japanese fisherman. When the war started these people, like ethnic Japanese elsewhere along the west coast, were seen as a threat to the area's security. On Mar. 23, 1942 General DeWitt, the Army's west coast commander, issued "Civilian Exclusion Order No. 1"[1] ordering the evacuation of the ethnic Japanese from Bainbridge Island. Action was swift. They were given 7 days to put their personal affairs in order before being taken away by the Army to the assembly center at Puyallup, WA. From Puyallup they were later sent to relocation camps. After the war many of them returned, and in the postwar years the island became the home of a sizeable ethnic Japanese population once again.

FORT WARD, at the southern end of the island, is an old Army coast artillery fort built in 1900 to protect the entrance to Rich Passage. In 1934 the Army abandoned the fort and in 1938 the Navy acquired it. During the war the Navy used Fort Ward as a radio station and a school for code-breakers. After the war it became a state park.

BANGOR is on the eastern shore of Puget Sound's Hood Channel.

U.S. NAVAL MAGAZINE, BANGOR did not exist for the first three years of the war. In early 1944 the Navy saw the need for a large ammunition magazine in the Puget Sound area to supply its ever-growing Pacific Fleet. Bangor was chosen as the site for the new facility because it

[1]Exclusion Orders were numbered 1 through 108 in the order of their importance to military security and carried out in sequence. Therefore, the ethnic Japanese on Bainbridge Island were considered, at the time, to be the most dangerous community of ethnic Japanese on the west coast other than those who had already been removed from Terminal Island in Los Angeles, CA Harbor under Martial Law.

was out of the way of most of Puget Sound's commercial and military water traffic and away from populated areas. Construction began later that year and was completed by the end of the war.

After the war the base underwent several cutbacks, expansions and name changes as the needs of the Navy changed. In the early 1960s the base was selected as a base for nuclear submarines and the Navy's nuclear missiles because of its relative isolation and remoteness from populated area. The base underwent major changes and in Sept. 1964 was commissioned as a submarine base known as U.S. Naval Submarine Base, Bangor. It then served as one of America's primary nuclear submarine bases throughout the Cold War.

BELLINGHAM is 80 miles north of Seattle on Rosario Strait. The town had a large ship-builder, the North Webster Ship-building Co., and a Boeing aircraft plant.

BELLINGHAM ARMY AIR FIELD, 4.5 miles NW of Bellingham, began as a grass airstrip called Tulip Field. In 1940 a landing strip was paved and United Air Lines began scheduled flights from the field. In 1941 the Federal Government began the construction of two more runways and other facilities making the air field one of the more modern in the area. Ironically, the revitalized airport opened for business on Dec. 7, 1941. Soon afterwards, the AAF took over the airport and used it as an operational base for bombers and fighters protecting the Puget Sound area. In 1947 the field was returned to the city and county, and after a few lean post-war year, began to prosper and eventually evolved into Bellingham International Airport.

BREMERTON is the home of the huge Puget Sound Naval

Shipyard and the northern home port of the U.S. Pacific Fleet. The town owes its existence to the ship yard, which was built first followed by the town that grew up around it.

During the war Bremerton became a small boom town as its ship yard and supporting industry geared up for maximum wartime production. Shortages of housing, schools, city services, food and the like made the quality of life in Bremerton very poor. Conditions did not ease until the war ended.

BREMERTON GROUP, PACIFIC RESERVE FLEET: This is a fleet of mothballed Navy ships in Sinclair Inlet, south of Bremerton, and one of four[2] such mothball fleets in the U.S. Due to the relatively small size of Sinclair Inlet the ships in storage are anchored close together and close to shore. One can easily view the old Navy ships at very close range while driving along state roads 304 and 3. Harbor excursions are available that include tours to the mothballed ships.

USS "Missouri" (BB-63) Battleship: At the time of this writing the famous WW II battleship "Missouri", upon which the surrender of Japan was signed, is at anchor in the mothball anchorage and is open to the public. An effort is underway by local citizens to raise money to make the ship into a permanent attraction. The ship is moored at the west end of the mothball fleet with access via Hwy 16 or through the Kitsap Transit Shuttle. Address: Puget Sound Naval Shipyard, Public Affairs Office, Bremerton, WA 98377. Phone 360/476-7111. Hours: May 20 thru Sept. 4 daily 10-6. Closed for ceremonies Aug. 29-Sept. 2.

BREMERTON NAVAL MUSEUM, in downtown Bremerton, depicts and preserves the history of the Puget Sound Naval Shipyard and, in general, the history of the U.S. Navy. On display are many artifacts from the Shipyard, the

[2]The other mothball fleet anchorages are at Suisun Bay, CA (San Francisco Bay area), Houston/Galveston, TX and the James River, VA.

A ship's propeller being manufactured at the Puget Sound Naval Ship Yard during WW II.

ships it built and serviced, and from the people who worked there. There are ship models, early steam engines, naval weapons, photos, paintings and a full-sized mock up of a ship's bridge. Other displays highlight the battleships "Washington" and "Missouri", and the carrier "Enterprise". Address: 130 Washington Ave., Bremerton, WA 98337. Phone: 360/479-7447. Hours: Tues.-Sat. 10-5, Sun. & holidays 1-5. Donations requested. Location: one block north of the ferry terminal.

U.S. NAVAL SHIPYARD, PUGET SOUND: This huge Navy facility began in 1891 as a modest-sized naval base and drydock to serve the needs of the U.S. Navy in the northwestern part of the U.S. The repair facilities of the base grew steadily and by WW I the ship yard had a drydock large enough to accommodate a battleship.

When WW II started in Europe in 1939 the ship yard was large enough to repair any ship in the U.S. fleet and could build ships as large as heavy cruisers. A steady stream of orders for work boosted the yards workload and payroll. On Dec. 7, 1941 the U.S. battleship "Colorado" was here undergoing repairs and was thus one of America's few undamaged battleships at the beginning of the war. Also in the yard was a British battleship, HMS "Warspite", which had been damaged in the Mediterranean by a German bomb and an Italian torpedo.

The ship yard underwent one expansion after the other during WW II and helped spawn satellite stations, such as the naval magazine at Bangor and the fuel depot at Manchester. Payroll rose steadily and peaked out at 75,000 in 1945. With housing impossible to find in Bremerton, many of the workers commuted by ferry from Seattle, Tacoma and other cities around the Sound.

The principal wartime mission of the yard was to repair battle damaged ships. A total of 344 ships of all types were repaired, overhauled or modernized here during the war including the battleships "Tennessee"[3] "Maryland", "Nevada", "West Virginia", "California", "Pennsylvania", "Washington", "New Jersey", "South Dakota", the carriers "Saratoga", "Enterprise", "Bunker Hill", "Franklin", "Ticonderoga", "Wasp", "Lexington", the cruisers "Nashville", "Wichita", "Minneapolis", "New Orleans", "Pittsburgh", and 68 destroyers. In addition, the yard found time to build 50 new ships. When the war ended in Aug. 1945 there were no drastic cutbacks at the Yard because, thanks to the Japanese Kamikaze attacks during the latter months of the war. The Yard had a large backlog of unrepaired, battle-damaged, ships.

The backlog of damaged warships declined in late 1945 but activity at the mothball anchorage increased. The Korean War saw another spurt of activity at the yard and 16 of the mothballed ships were put back into service. During the Cold War the yard was modernized again to handle the new large ships of the Navy.

CAPE FLATTERY (See Neah Bay)

CHINOOK-ILWACO AREA: This area is in the SW corner of the state at the entrance to the Columbia River. The Ilwaco Airport served

[3]The battleships "Tennessee", "Maryland", "Nevada", "California", and "West Virginia" were all damaged at Pearl Harbor and put back into action before war's end.

This lone WW II hangar survives at Ellensburg AAF but is in need of repairs. Note the poles supporting the back wall.

the military air needs of the area during the war.

FORT CANBY: This is one of two old forts on the Washington side of the river (the other being Fort Columbia). Fort Canby was located at the mouth of the Columbia River on Cape Disappointment and was built in 1864 as a coastal defense guarding the entrance to the river. During WW II the fort was activated as a subpost of Fort Stevens, OR and 8" guns were installed in its old batteries to protect the mine field across the mouth of the River. After the war the guns were removed and in 1950 the Army abandoned the site to the state of Washington for a park. Two batteries remain, McKenzie Head and Battery Harvey Allen. Each can be explored by visitors.

FORT COLUMBIA: This was one of two old forts on the Washington side of the river (the other being Fort Canby, above) and was located about 6 miles up river and from Fort Canby.

Fort Columbia was established in 1896 as a coastal defense guarding the mouth of the river. The fort was a subpost of Fort Stevens, OR and had several batteries, but during WW II only one, Battery Murphy, was activated. It mounted a 6" gun, and controlled the mine field at the entrance to the river. In the first months of the war the Army did not have a mine-layer on the Columbia River so an automobile ferry was acquired to lay the mines. When an Army mine-layer became available, the ferry was retained by the Army as a military ferry for the duration of the war. After the war the mines were removed. In 1950 the fort became a state park. The old batteries remained and 14 of the forts original buildings are in use. The part has an Interpretive Center, museum, youth hostel and theater. The museum has exhibits on the Army's coast artillery corps during WW II. Address: PO Box 236, Chinook, WA 98614. Phone: summer 360/777-8221, winter 360/642-3078. Hours: Apr. 1-Oct. 15, daily 6:30-dusk;, Oct. 16-Mar. 31, Wed.-Sun. 8-dusk. Free.

LONG BEACH ISLAND parallels the Pacific coast, north of the mouth of the Columbia River. At the beginning of the war this long flat beach was seen as one of the most vulnerable beaches in the area for a possible Japanese invasion. Early in 1942 the Wyoming National Guard, which had been federalized and was one of the few mountain units in the U.S. Army, was

rushed to Long Beach Island. There they built defensive positions in the sand and prepared for a possible invasion. By the summer of 1942 Coastguardsmen arrived to patrol the beaches. Eventually the Wyoming National Guard departed, but the Coast Guard stayed on until near the end of the war.

ELLENSBURG is 25 miles north of Yakima.

ELLENSBURG ARMY AIR FIELD, two miles NE of town, began as Ellensburg Airport in the 1930s. In 1943 the AAF took over the airport and the flying school to train fighter pilots. The air field was improved and many buildings were built including a new hangar. A 1500' steel mat runway was built to the northwest of the field for the continued use of the local civilian aviators and crop dusters. Army anti-aircraft units and searchlight units also trained here. Tow planes flew out of Ellensburg towing targets over Yakima Bombing Range for pilots-in-training at other nearby airfield to chase and fire at.

In 1948 the air field was returned to the local community and named Bowers Field: Kittitas County Airport. Ensign Robert K. Bowers was a local man killed during the Japanese attack on Pearl Harbor. Location: The airport is not on any major road or street so visitors should inquire locally for directions.

EPHRATA is in the center of the state. During Feb. and Mar. 1945 there were two Japanese bombing balloon incidents in the area. On Feb. 21 a balloon touched down, dropped three of its sand bags and then sailed off again. On Mar. 10, a balloon was shot down near Ephrata by a military aircraft and much of the balloon was recovered.

EPHRATA ARMY AIR BASE, two miles SE of town off SR 17, began as an emergency landing strip in 1933. In early 1942 it was taken over by the 4th AF and became a training base for pilots and crews of B-17 and B-24 bombers. Many of the barracks buildings at the base were relocated CCC barracks used during the construction of nearby Grand Coulee Dam in the 1930s. In Apr. 1944 the base began training fighter pilots in P-39s, P-63s and P-38s. In Sept. 1945, the base again reverted to training bombers crews, this time in B-24s only. After the war the base was placed on standby by the US Air Force until 1953 when it was turned over to the

The former Ephrata base chapel was moved to town to serve as a local church.

community of Ephrata to become the area's local airport known as the Port of Ephrata.

EVERETT is 30 miles north of Seattle on Possession Sound. The town had a large ship builder, the Everett Pacific Co., which built subchasers and mine sweepers for the U.S. Navy. **PAINE FIELD**, 6.5 miles SW of town, was the area's local airport and known as Snohomish County Airport. When the war started the 4th AF took it over and named it Paine Field. It was used as an operational base by fighter squadrons protecting the Puget Sound area, and as a refueling base for large bombers. In early 1945 Paine Field was one of three air fields in NW Washington assigned to the "Sunset Project" to intercept Japanese bombing balloons. See details of the "Sunset Project" above. On Mar. 13, 1945 remnants of a Japanese bombing balloon were recovered near the field. No damage was caused by the balloon.

After the war the air field was returned to civilian use, but in 1951 the US Air Force returned and used the field again during the Korean War naming it Paine Air Force Base. The Air Force stayed on after the Korean War and Paine became the nation's first Bomarc missile base in the early 1960s.

Later, the field was returned to civilian hands and became Paine Field: Snohomish County Airport. At the north end of the airport is a huge Boeing Co. plant (which offers tours to visitors) and at the south end are the airport operations.

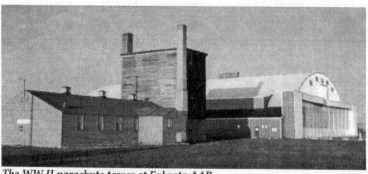

The WW II parachute tower at Ephrata AAB.

Location: The airport is SW of Everett. From I-5 take Exit 189 west on SR 526 three miles to Airport Rd., then south to the airport.

FORKS is in the NW corner of the Olympic Peninsula.

U.S. NAVAL AUXILIARY AIR STATION, QUILLAYUTE, SW of the town of Forks, had been the local airport before the war. It was taken over by the Navy and used as an auxiliary field to NAS, Seattle. In early 1945 it was one of three air fields in NW Washington assigned to the "Sunset Project" to intercept Japanese bombing balloons. See above for details on the "Sunset Project".

HANFORD ENGINEER WORKS (See Richland and the Hanford Engineer Works)

HOQUIAM is a port city on the NW coast of Washington at Grays Harbor.

U.S. NAVAL AUXILIARY AIR STATION, MOON ISLAND, two miles west of town, was Hoquiam's local pre-war airport. It was utilized by the Navy during 1942-43 as a standby and refueling field for planes out of NAAS, Shelton, as a practice landing field for carrier pilots and to aid radio communications with Pacific Beach and NAAS, Shelton. In May 1944 it was designated as an auxiliary air station in its own right under the control of NAS, Astoria, OR. In 1946 NAAS, Moon Island was decommissioned and returned to the community of Hoquiam.

KEYPORT is 12 miles north of Bremerton on Port Orchard Inlet.

U.S. NAVAL TORPEDO STATION, KEYPORT: This facility, first called the Pacific Coast Torpedo Station, was established in 1913/14 with the mission to test, store and repair naval torpedoes. World War I had very little impact. Nevertheless, through the years the station grew steadily and was kept updated. By the early 1940s it was the Navy's primary torpedo station on the west coast and had acquired its wartime name. The station had a powerful radio station, a Marine barracks, a training school for divers and ample torpedo storage, repair and testing facilities including several testing ranges in Port Orchard Inlet.

In 1940 Keyport began a period of very rapid expansion. A new overhaul shop was built, a school on torpedo repair and maintenance was begun, anti-aircraft batteries and barrage balloon stations were built in the area for protection against air attacks, an accelerated apprentice school for toolmakers and machinists was established, housing units were built in nearby Poulsbo and a ferry service begun between Poulsbo and the station to carry workers and service personnel back and forth. The work force at the station sky rocketed and the station operated around the clock throughout WW II. At its peak the station could test and make ready for ship-

ment up to 100 torpedoes a day.

After the war the station had rapid and drastic cutbacks. Activity limped along for several years until the Korean War brought about a mild revitalization. With the advent of nuclear powered submarines, however, the Station became important once again testing, storing and servicing torpedoes. In 1979 a second naval station was established here, the Naval Undersea Warfare Engineering Station. Throughout the Cold War the two stations comprised one of the navy's most important torpedo and underwater warfare facilities on the west coast.

Naval Undersea Museum: This large museum, on the grounds of the Naval Torpedo Station, was established by the Secretary of the Navy to be a repository of documents, records and artifacts relating to the human and technical achievements of undersea history. It is the only facility of its kind in the country.

Items on display relating to WW II include a Japanese "Kaiten" manned torpedo and an MK 24 Mine (FIDO) which was actually the first anti-submarine acoustic homing torpedo developed in the U.S. It was used successfully in the later months of WW II against German submarines. There are displays on the WW II submarine "Croaker", the netlayer "Etlah" and the salvage vessel "Safeguard" which was used during the war to perform deep salvage missions. Also on display is "Alvin", a three-man submersible that located five lost WW II aircraft in the Bermuda Triangle area in 1967 and later surveyed the famous ocean liner "Titanic". Address: Keyport, WA 98345-5000. Phone: 360/396-4148. Hours: Daily 10-4, closed Tues. Free. Location: On SR 308 at the west edge of Keyport city limits.

LA CONNER is 45 miles north of Seattle on Swinomish Slough.

FORT WHITMAN, south of La Conner, was on Goat Island in Skagit Bay at the south entrance to Swinomish Slough. It was an old coastal defense position, with four 6" gun emplacements built in 1911 to protect the south entrance of Swinomish Slough and the east entrance of Deception Pass just to the northwest. As late as 1941 Fort Whitman's only communication with the mainland was by boat and it wasn't until Dec. 9 that the small caretaker staff at the Fort learned of the attack on Pearl Harbor. In Jan. 1942 the Fort was activated and the four open gun positions camouflaged to protect against air attacks. A diesel power generator was installed to provide electricity and a radio station was set up to provide local communications. Three 50 calibre anti-aircraft guns and two mobile 37 mm guns were added to the Fort's defenses. Throughout the war Fort Whitman was a subpost of Fort Worden. Its 6" guns were never fired. In Oct. 1944 the Fort was closed and in 1945 the wooden buildings were demolished. In 1947 the Fort was turned over to the state of Washington to be used, along with the rest of Goat Island, as a wildlife refuge. There is no regular boat service to the island. Anyone wishing to go their would have to make their own arrangements.

MOSES LAKE is 100 miles SW of Spokane.

MOSES LAKE ARMY AIR FIELD, 6 miles NW of town, was built new by the AAF and activated

World War II planes were still operating from a World War II air field in the 1990s. These three PBY amphibians are used to fight forest fires. They, and many like them, were modified after the war to scoop up water into internal tanks while taxiing across a body of water. When the tanks were full, they would take off and water-bomb forest fires.

in Nov. 1942 to train pilots in P-38 fighter planes. Later in the war the base trained B-17 bomber crews. In 1945 the air field was placed on standby and used occasionally by the Boeing Aircraft Co. of Seattle to test new aircraft. In 1948 the air field was reopened by the US Air Force as an operational base by the Air Defense Command with the mission to protect the Hanford Engineer Works and Grand Coulee Dam. Some of the Air Force's best units and newest aircraft was stationed here. In 1950 the name of the air field was changed to Larson Air Force Base in honor of Major Donald A. Larson, a WW II ace from Yakima, WA who was killed over Germany in 1944. Larson was closed in 1966, given to the county and named Grant County Airport. Other parts of the base became a Job Crops center and a community college.

NEAH BAY and the CAPE FLATTERY

AREA: This is one of the most strategic areas in the U.S. It is the entrance to Juan de Fuca Strait which leads eastward to Puget Sound and the Canadian waters of the Strait of Georgia. In the early months of the war it was feared that the Japanese might possibly attempt to mine the waters off Cape Flattery or even establish a beachhead in this remote part of the country from which they could stop the flow of ships in and out of the Juan de Fuca Strait. At the beginning of the war, U.S. military strength in the area was almost non-existent. There existed only a Coast Guard Station on Tatoosh Island near the small coastal community of Neah Bay. There were no coastal defenses here. The nearest big guns were 90 miles to the east in at Port Townsend.

YELLOW BEACH: This long ocean beach extending south from Cape Flattery was considered to be very vulnerable to a Japanese landing. This was especially so because, in the early 1930s, a Japanese mining company had worked the sands of the beach for gold and at that time had landed aircraft on the beach. U.S. Army leaders felt that the Japanese military had excellent knowledge of the beach and the area in general. In Dec. 1941, when the Army rushed what meager forces it had available to defend critical west coast areas, this was one of the places where they were sent. The Army troops, units of the 44th Division, quickly set up defensive positions to repel a possible invasion. After the Japanese defeat at the Battle of

Midway in June 1942, the threat of a west coast invasion diminished and in the following months the Coast Guard arrived and took over from the Army.

LAKE OZETTE: This large lake, south of Yellow Beach (above), is very close to the ocean, and in the early months of the war was seen as an ideal landing place for Japanese seaplanes. When troops of the Army's 44th Division were rushed to the area, they took up positions here too around the lake. When the Coast Guard took over patrolling the area from the Army they put two small boats on the lake and patrolled it daily until near the end of the war.

OLYMPIA, at the southern end of Puget Sound, is the state capital.

OLYMPIA ARMY AIR FIELD, 4.5 miles south of town, was the capital city's local airport before the war. It was utilized, in part, by the AAF and designed as an Army air field. After the war, the AAF departed and the airport again became a civilian airport.

PASCO is in the SE corner of the state at the confluence of the Yakima, Snake and Columbia Rivers.

PASCO ENGINEER DEPOT: During the war the Army Quartermaster Corps built a major supply depot here because of the Pasco's strategic location. The depot is on the north bank of the Columbia River. War material from all over the U.S. was brought here by rail and boat, stored and then shipped out as needed, most

of it going to the Pacific war zones. After the war the depot was retained by the Army for several years and became known as Pasco General Depot. It was then given to the city of Pasco and became a commercial operation. Location: Avenue A and E. Ainsworth.

U.S. NAVAL AIR STATION, PASCO, three miles NW of town, began as a local air strip, built in 1928 by the community of Pasco. Before the war it was used by private planes and the Washington National Guard out of Spokane. It had a flying school and during the winter of 1939-40 Army Air Corps cadets from Portland, OR trained here. In 1942 the U.S. Navy purchased the field and converted it into the U.S. Naval Reserve Air Base, Pasco for primary training of Navy pilots. In time, the station had 16 outlying fields used primarily for landing and take-off practice. The station also had facilities for training aircraft mechanics and other ratings.

On Jan. 1, 1943 the facility was renamed U.S. Naval Air Station, Pasco. Near the end of the war, with the need for pilots diminishing, the station became an operating base for fleet units. One of the outlying fields was equipped with a catapult and arresting gear for carrier pilots to use to simulate take-offs and landings from carriers. When the war ended, activity at the station declined rapidly and in Dec. 1946 the station was decommissioned. It was returned to the city and became known as Tri-Cities Airport. Location: North of Pasco. Exit I-182 at 20th Ave., then proceed north on 20th Ave. to the field. The old military area is on the east side of the field.

PORT ANGELES is on the south shore of Juan de Fuca Strait directly across from Victoria, BC. Two miles NE of town was a Coast Guard Air Station and training facility. During part of the war the U.S. submarine "Tambor", which patrolled areas of the northern Pacific, operated out of this Coast Guard Station.

CAMP HAYDEN, now Salt Creek County Park, was 15 miles west of Port Angeles at Tongue Point. This was a WW II coastal defense position which mounted two 16" guns. Together with similar guns on the Canadian side of Juan de Fuca Strait, Camp Hayden could effectively defend the Strait against penetration by enemy

The Pasco Engineering Depot stretches along E. Ainsworth on both sides of the street as far as the eye can see.

Mounted at Battery Thomas Winsboro are two 3" guns of the type used at the fort before and during the war. This is one of the few places in the U.S. where guns exist in old concrete coastal gun positions.

ships. Construction of the gun positions at Camp Hayden began in 1941 and in early 1945 the guns were mounted and test-fired. The war ended several months later and the guns saw no enemy action. These guns were the first in the country, of their type, to be aimed by computer. They were also the last coastal guns of their type to be mounted in the U.S. After the war the guns were removed and scraped and the facilities turned over to the county. During the Cold War the gun emplacements were designated as a civil defense headquarters in case of an emergency.

PORT ANGELES ARMY AIR FIELD: This air field, just west of town, was home to a squadron of P-38 fighter planes that was a part of the over-

The remains of one of four anti-submarine nets installed in the Puget Sound area during WW II. This view is looking northward across Port Townsend Inlet from Fort Flagler. The concrete block in the foreground was a net anchor block and the pilings in the water held the net upright.

all defensive system of the Puget Sound area. When Japanese bombing balloons began attacking the area the fighters were called upon, from time-to-time, to shoot them down. The Navy also used the field from time to time. The air field later became a local airport.

PORT TOWNSEND is on the western shore of Admiralty Inlet a main entrance to Puget Sound.

FORT FLAGLER was south of Port Townsend at the northern end of Marrowstone Island. The Fort was built between 1897-07, and along with Forts Casey and Worden, served as the main coastal defenses for the entrance to Puget Sound. These three forts were known as "The Devil's Triangle". After WW I Fort Flagler was lightly garrisoned and in 1937 was placed in caretaker status and many of its original buildings removed. In 1940 the Army re-occupied the Fort and used it primarily as a training center for amphibious operations and for Army engineers. A rocky beach on the north shore of the fort served as an anchorage for one of the four anti-submarine nets

installed in the Puget Sound area. This net stretched across Port Townsend Inlet to Port Townsend on the opposite shore. The old beams and anchor blocks that supported the net can be seen from the rocky beach.

The Fort served through the Korean War and in 1953 was turned over to the state to became Fort Flagler State Park. At Battery Thomas Winsboro there are two 3" guns of the type used at the fort before and during the war. This is one of the very few places in the U.S. where guns exist in old concrete coastal gun positions. Address: Fort Flagler State Park, Nordland, WA 98358. Phone: 360/385-1259. Hours: Mid-Apr. thru Sept. 30, daily 6:30-dusk, rest of year, 8-dusk. Free.

FORT TOWNSEND was just south of the town of Port Townsend and was built in 1850 to guard against Indians. It was converted into a state park, known as Old Fort Townsend State Park, long before WW II. During the war a landing field was built on the grounds of the old fort and used by the military.

PORT TOWNSEND AIR FIELD, five miles SW of the town of Port Townsend was the area's local airport. It was used during the war by the AAF. After the war it once again became a local airport.

FORT WORDEN was north of, and adjacent to, the town of Port Townsend. In 1855 a temporary fort was built here named Fort Wilson to guard against Indians. In 1898 the Government chose the site for a major coastal defense position to be called Fort Worden and to be one of the three forts in "The Devil's Triangle" protecting the entrance to Puget Sound. The Fort was completed in 1905 and was occupied continuously by the Army until after WW II[4]. During WW II about half of the gun batteries were activated, the largest being 12". Radar, anti-aircraft batteries, search lights and other facilities were added to the fort. The Navy occupied a part of the Fort and worked with the Army on joint harbor control defenses. The Fort served through the Korean War and in 1953 was closed. In 1957 the state bought the fort and converted some of the buildings into a diagnostic and treatment center. In 1971 the diagnostic and treatment center closed and in 1973 the Fort became Fort Worden State Park. There are a total of 12 gun batteries in the park, an unusually large number compared to similar parks around the country. Address: Fort Worden State Park, PO Box 574, Port Townsend, WA 98368. Phone: 360/385-4730. Hours: Apr. 1 thru mid-Oct. daily 6:30 to dusk, rest of year 8-dusk. Free.

Coast Artillery Museum: This museum is on the grounds of Fort Worden State Park. It's mission is to preserve and pass on to future generations the knowledge and lore of modern coast artillery and to honor the men who served in America's coastal defenses. The museum covers over 50 years of coast artillery history. At the doorway to the museum are two 16" practice projectiles weighing 2340 lbs each. These projectiles, weighing more than a small car, could be hurled 30 miles by 750 lbs of powder. Inside the museum are other projectiles, displays on artillery plotting, a working model of a 12" disappearing gun and a 12" mortar.

The Coast Artillery Museum at Fort Worden State Park, Port Townsend, WA.

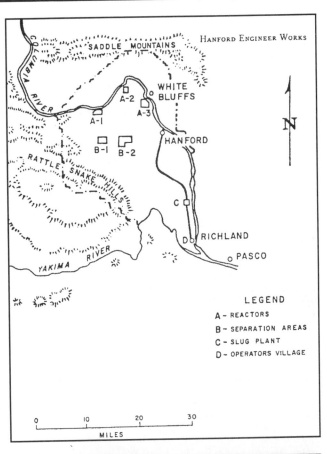

HANFORD ENGINEER WORKS

LEGEND
A – REACTORS
B – SEPARATION AREAS
C – SLUG PLANT
D – OPERATORS VILLAGE

Address: PO Box 574, Port Townsend, WA 98368. Phone: 360/385-2021 or 3295. Hours: Memorial Day thru Labor Day daily 11-5, Presidents' Day (Feb.)-Memorial Day weekends only noon-4, closed rest of year. Free.

RICHLAND and the HANFORD ENGINEER WORKS

Richland, in the SE corner of the state, was an unincorporated farming community of 250 people when the war started. In 1943 the U.S. Government began construction of what was called a super-secret war production plant. One of the first things to happen was the construction of a modest-sized temporary town called Hanford about 40 miles north of Richland, and further to the north work began on a complex of large buildings that was off-limits to everyone except those who were specifically allowed on the construction site.

As the large buildings rose on the horizon north of town, workers began to pour in and take up residence in the temporary town. They had come from all over the country on the promise from Washington's Senator Warren Magnuson that if they accepted a job in this remote part of the country the job would be permanent after the war. This was a promise seldom given to war workers during the war years.

Within 15 months the mystery plant, known only as the Hanford Engineer Works, was in operation producing a product that had no name and was never seen or heard or smelled. Only a handful of the employees knew what was going on. Nevertheless, the plant worked around the clock and there was plenty of overtime for the workers who, by early 1945, numbered 20,000. A thousand guards protecting the plant's great secret and there were hundreds of soldiers stationed at nearby Camp Hanford to protect the plant from an enemy attack. The plant consumed millions of gallons of water from the Columbia River and large high-tension lines provided it with enormous amounts of electricity from the River's dams.

The town of Richland blossomed into a full-sized city of 51,000 people making it Washington's fourth largest city. It had new homes, apartments, schools, shopping centers, a hospital, jail, the world's largest trailer park and a variety of manufacturing enterprises that were suppliers to the mysterious Hanford Works. On Mar. 10, 1945, the plant was suddenly and unexpectedly shut down by the plant's automatic safety equipment. Three days later it began operation again, but the reason for the shut down was as secret as the rest of the business associated with the plant. What the people were not told was that a Japanese bombing balloon, another closely guarded wartime secret, had shut the plant down. The balloon had malfunctioned and drifted across the Yakima Valley about 30 miles west of the plant, struck the main power line bringing electricity from Bonneville Dam to the plant. It was a rainy day and the balloon caused a short circuit that triggered the plant's safety devices. The balloon was removed quickly but it took three days for some of the plant's equipment to become fully operative again.

On Aug. 6, 1945 the people of Richland were as startled as everyone else in the nation to learn that the Americans had a new super weapon called "the atomic bomb" and that it had destroyed the city of Hiroshima in Japan. On Aug. 9 came word that a second atomic bomb had been used to destroy a second Japanese city, Nagasaki. With this, and the sudden end of the war in the Pacific, the secret of the atomic bombs was out and for the first time the people of Richland learned that their mysterious plant had played a very important role in the development of the second bomb. The Hanford plant, from its inception, had converted natural uranium 238, into plutonium 239, the fissionable, or explosive, material used in the Nagasaki bomb[5]. The residents of the area also learned that their plant was the largest of its type in the world.

[5]The first bomb, used against Hiroshima, contained uranium-235, another fissionable material. It did not contain plutonium.

The main gate at the Hanford works during the war.

That was the good news. The bad news was that Oak Ridge, TN had originally been slated as the site where plutonium was to be made, but this was changed because there were fears that a massive nuclear accident might wipe out the nearby city of Knoxville, TN. Therefore, Richland was chosen because a nuclear accident here would wipe out fewer people.

In the months following the end of the war Senator Magnuson's promise came true. The Hanford plant kept on producing plutonium to build up America's arsenal of atomic weapons and for the new peacetime uses that atomic energy promised. The General Electric Co. took over operation of the plant and many of the nuclear power plants and nuclear powered ships built in the 1950s and 60s used plutonium produced at the Hanford plant.

The Hanford Works operated continuously after the war and was expanded many times. The temporary town of Hanford has long been abandoned and most of the buildings are gone. The town site is inside the plant's current security perimeter and off limits to all but authorized personnel.

CAMP HANFORD: This was an Army camp 1.5 miles north of Richland, constructed along with the Hanford Engineer Works, and near its southern entrance, to house the soldiers assigned to the many air defenses around the plant. In 1961 the Army abandoned the camp and turned the facilities over to the Atomic Energy Department. The camp no longer exists.

VISITOR CENTERS: There are two visitor centers near the south entrance of the Hanford Works and about 20 miles north of Richland. One is at Plant #2 and the other at FFTF (Fast Flux Test Facility). Both have displays on their respective operations and the overall Hanford Works. Phone: for the FFTF 509/376-6374, and 509/372-5860 for Plant #2 Visitors Center. Hours for both Visitors Centers: Thurs.-F 11-4, Sat.-Sun. noon-5, closed major holidays. Free: Location: proceed north out of Richland on Stevens Dr. which becomes SR 4 beyond the city limits. Watch for signs for Plant #2 and its Visitor Center on the east side of SR 4. From the entrance to Plant #2, proceed 1/2 mile north on SR 4 to the entrance to FFTF and its Visitors Center. FFTF is on the west side of SR 4.

SEATTLE: Seattle, like every major city along the west coast, became a boom town during WW II because it produced the things needed for war. The Boeing Aircraft Company, one of the nation's major aircraft producers before the war, mushroomed into a gigantic operation with satellite plants not only in Washington, but in other parts of the country. In nearby Renton, WA Boeing built one of the largest aircraft factories in the world to produce B-29 bombers on an assembly line basis[6]. Seattle had several ship yards that expanded to meet the nation's need for ships. A large new alu-

[6]There were two B-29 plants in the country producing B-29s on an assembly line base, Renton, WA and a Boeing-operated plant in Wichita, KS.

minum plant was built to supply the needs of Boeing. The Pacific Car & Foundry Co. of Renton built tanks and special trucks and later expanded into the manufacture of its own armor plate because of the long delay in getting that product from the Chicago area. During the war, Seattle's docks were constantly busy shipping men and material overseas including tons of Lend Lease goods to the Soviet Union. Seattle's dock and water front area was dominated by the military. There was the huge Seattle Army Terminal and the Army's Seattle General Depot, the Seattle Service Forces Depot, the Seattle Quartermaster Depot, the Headquarters of the 13th Naval District, a large Naval hospital, a large Coast Guard Station and a Coast Guard District Headquarters.

It was from Seattle's docks that some of the Japanese aliens, trapped in the U.S. by the war, sailed for Japan aboard neutral ships in exchanges[7] for American citizens who had been trapped in Japan. It was also from Seattle, in Sept. 1945, that several thousand Japanese-Americans, who had renounced their American citizenship, were deported to Japan on the Swedish ship "Gripsholm". A second group left in Nov. 1945 on the U.S. transport "General Randall".

During the war years the city's population soared and there was a serious shortages of housing and the city's services were strained to their limits. After the war, Seattle slowly returned to normal but remained larger in size than it had been before the war, and had a larger and more diversified industrial base.

BOEING FIELD: In the 1920s King County built an airport just south of Seattle on a reclaimed flood plane of the Duwamish River and later named it King County Airport. It had two hangers, one occupied by a variety of civilian tenants and the other by a young aircraft firm called Boeing Aircraft Co. In the next two years the Boeing Aircraft Co. prospered very well and built additional facilities at the airport. In 1930 the field was renamed Boeing Field. During the next decade the company continued to prosper and eventually built a large factory complex along the west side of the field while the other airport operations moved to the east side. During these years Boeing Field served the needs of both the Boeing company and Seattle.

During WW II the need for military aircraft produced by Boeing virtually crowded out the civilian tenants. Therefore, the civil authorities decided to build a new airport about midway between Seattle and Tacoma. In

1944 the Seattle-Tacoma Airport opened and eventually evolved into the Seattle-Tacoma International Airport which eventually became the area's primary commercial airport.

At Boeing Field the Boeing Company took over the east side of the field. The main plant, a huge sprawling complex of building, was considered to be very vulnerable to air attacks so it was elaborately camouflaged to look like a residential area. One of the plant's primary products was the famous B-17 Flying Fortress, which was originally a Boeing design. On the military side of the field there was the training facility for ferry pilots who ferried Boeing's newly manufactured planes to the war zones. The AAF was represented on the field by the Air Technical Service Command and the Air Transport Command. The field served as a port of aerial embarkation and had a large air freight terminal.

After the war Boeing scaled back its operations at Boeing Field and some of the former tenants returned. Later, the air field came to service both the Boeing Aircraft Company and civilian needs and became known as Boeing Field/King County International Airport.

Museum of Flight: This museum is on the east side of Boeing Field/King County International Airport. A part of the museum is in the restored "Red Barn", Boeing's first manufacturing plant dating back to 1917 relocated here from its original site. The Museum traces the aviation history of Washington and the Boeing Aircraft Co. Many of the company's aircraft are on display including Boeing's most famous WW II aircraft, the B-17 Flying Fortress. Altogether, more than 50 aircraft are on display spanning much of the aviation history of the twentieth century. WW II aircraft include a Boeing-Stearman 75 Kaydet (PT-13A), a Bowlus BA-100 Baby Albatross, two Corvair L-13As, a Dornier DO 27, a Douglas DC-3, a Grumman G.36 Wildcat (FM-2), a North American AT-6D Texan and a Vought FG-1D Corsair. Address: 9404 E. Marginal Way South, Seattle, WA 98108. Phone 206/764-5720. Hours: daily 10-5 (Thurs 10-9). Conducted tours available. Closed Dec. 25. Admission charged.

COAST GUARD MUSEUM, NORTHWEST: This is a small museum on Seattle's waterfront. Exhibits cover the history of the Coast Guard from 1812 to the present. On display are ship models, uniforms, lighthouse and buoy lenses, documents, flags, edged weapons, small arms, paintings, drawings, photographs and nautical artifacts. Address: Pier 36, 1519 Alaskan Way South, Seattle, WA 98134. Phone: 206/286-9608. Hours: M-W-F 9-3, Sat.-Sun. 1-5. Free.

CAMP GEORGE JORDAN was an Army camp in the dock area of Seattle at 1st Avenue South and South Spokane St. It opened in Sept. 1942 and was used to house negro soldiers who worked as stevedores at the Seattle Port of Embarkation. The camp operated until 1947 and then was closed. No signs of the camp remain.

FORT LAWTON, three miles NW of downtown Seattle, was built by the Army in the late 1890s as an embarkation point for troops and supplies going to the Pacific and the Far East. Fort Lawton was a large military post with many buildings and in the years before WW II

The Boeing Aircraft Co. plant in Seattle was camouflaged to look like a residential area. Boeing Field is at the top of the photo.

The Visitors Center in Discovery Park is the only remaining building of the Fort Lawton's large WW II hospital.

was used for a variety of purposes. When WW II began it was a training facility for Army engineers. During the war is served as a home for the Army's Transportation Corps, an became a very busy Army embarkation center. Hundreds of buildings were constructed to house and accommodate the troops being embarked. The Fort also had a prisoner of war camp with about 500 POWS who worked at the Fort. By the end of the war over one million American troops had passed through Fort Lawton. After the war the Fort was used as a demobilization center.

Fort Lawton continued in operation after the war and served again as an embarkation center until the end of the Korean War. At that time many of the WW II buildings were torn down and the embarkation activities moved to Fort Lewis. The Fort was then used for air defense activities, as an Army support center and by the Army Reserve. Later, the fort was given to the city for the creation of Discovery Park. A complex of 24 WW II barracks buildings was set aside for use by the Army Reserve and remained in use. Two other areas were retained and were used to house Navy personnel. Officers Row, a row of beautiful turn-of-the-century Victorian houses, remains and is occupied by military personnel.

U.S. NAVAL AIR STATION, SEATTLE: This was a large naval air station that once occupied most of Sand Point peninsula on the western shore of Lake Washington. In later years the site came to be utilized by the U.S. Naval Station, Puget Sound, the National Oceanic and Atmospheric Administration, the University of Washington and Warren G. Magnuson Park.

The air station came into being in the early 1920s when the Government accepted the land at Sand Point as a gift from King County and authorized the construction of an air field for the joint use of the Army and Navy. The field was used for the training of military airmen, by reserve units and at times by the Boeing Company and other commercial aircraft interests. By the late 1920s the Navy had secured control of the field and named it U.S. Naval Air Station, Seattle. During the 1930s Navy and Marine aviators trained here and the station was used as an air link to Alaska. Between 1938

and 1943 the station underwent a series of major expansions. By 1941, hundreds of aviators were in training at the field and there were schools for aviation metalsmiths, machinist mates and radiomen. The Naval Air Transport Command and the Naval Air Ferry Command had operations on station, and it was also used by British and Soviet aircraft in America's Lend Lease program. At times, Boeing used the station as did Pan American Airways.

To house base personnel, two housing developments were built at Cedarville near the station and Kirkland across the lake. During the summer of 1943 when American forces were retaking the Japanese held islands in the Aleutians, the station was a trans-shipping station for men and material going to Alaska. Near the end of the war the station housed naval personnel whose ships were being repaired and/or overhauled in Seattle's various ship yards.

After the war the station remained very active performing a number of mission for the Navy. In 1970, however, the station was scaled

back and large sections of the station given to the city and state. The station had an outlying field during the war, Kitsap County Airport, 7.5 miles SW of Bremerton. In the 1990s the last of the naval facilities at Sand Point were closed.

SHELTON is 15 miles NW of Olympia.
U.S. NAVAL AUXILIARY AIR STATION, SHELTON, 2.5 miles NW of town, had been Sanderson Field before the war, Shelton's local airport. Soon after the war started the Navy took it over to use as an auxiliary air station to NAS, Seattle protecting the Puget Sound area. A blimp tie-down pad was built and for a while blimps operated out of the field. Shelton also provided planes to tow targets for pilots in training at other fields practicing air gunnery. In early 1945 NAAS, Shelton was one of three air fields in NW Washington selected to participate in the "Sunset Project" to intercept Japanese bombing balloons. See above for details on the "Sunset Project". After the war the airport was returned to the community and acquired it prewar name, Sanderson Field. The airport is north of town off U.S. 101.

SPOKANE is in the west central part of the state and was Washington's second largest city. On Feb. 12, 1945 remnants of a Japanese bombing Balloon were recovered near Spokane, the first such remnants found in the state. On Feb. 21, 1945 a second recovery was made which was a part of a cluster of balloons that came down at widely scattered locations in the state.

Spokane prospered during the war and luckily avoided the hectic boom town conditions that prevailed in the Puget Sound area.
FELTS FIELD, NE of downtown Spokane, was Spokane Airport before the war and the city's main airport. It was one of the more modern airports in the country with long runways, up-to-date safety and maintenance facilities and a modern terminal building. It also had a flying school. These features made it ideal for a bomber training base, so in 1942 the AAF took it over to train bomber crews as part of the 30,000 Pilot Training Program. During the war

In Magnuson Park an old ammunition storage igloo challenges a young biker. In the background is Lake Washington which contains about a half dozen WW II airplanes, some of them diveable. A Navy F4U fighter planes was salvaged from the lake in the 1980s and is on display at the Museum of Flight.

The pre-war terminal at Felts Field remains in use at the name "Spokane Airport" from the days when it was Spokane's main airport.

it was known as Felts Field and was a subpost of Geiger Field. After the war the Army departed and the airport became Spokane's secondary airport when Geiger Field became Spokane International Airport.

GEIGER FIELD, 6 miles SW of Spokane, was a small airport known as Sunset Field. In 1941 the 4th AF acquired the field and additional land, renamed it Geiger Field, and built a large air base as a transitional training facility for bomber crews into B-17s. Many of the B-17s came direct from the Boeing factories in the Seattle area. Aviation engineering battalions were also trained here. There was a large AAF supply and repair depot just to the west of the field. The training of B-17 crews continued here until the winter of 1942-43 when unusual weather conditions produced week upon week of fog grounding the planes. After several months of nearly constant fog the B-17s and their crews abandoned the field and were sent elsewhere to complete their training. That winter is remembered as the winter of the "Big

Fog". Later in the war, crews were trained here in C-47 transports.

In 1947 a portion of the field was designated as a municipal airport and commercial airline operations moved here from Felts Field. AAF, and later, US Air Force operations continued at the field until 1960 at which time the military pulled out and the field was designated Spokane International Airport. On the other side of the airport, in the old wartime facilities, a naval facility called the U.S. Naval Air Station, Spokane operated for most of the Cold War. The Navy and the commercial tenants shared the runways.

SPOKANE ARMY AIR FIELD was located 12 miles SW of the city. This base was another product of WW II built on land donated by the local community. The site was chosen by the AAF because of the area's relatively good flying weather and because it was 300 miles inland and relatively safe from enemy air attacks. The air field began operating in Mar. 1942 under the Air Technical Service Command and the Air

Transport Command as a supply and maintenance control depot for Army aircraft operating in the Pacific Northwest and Alaska. The base performed this mission throughout the war and overhauled more than 13,000 aircraft engines on a variety of aircraft. In late 1944 the depot was enlarged so that it could service B-29 bombers. After the war the depot continued to be very active as a supply and maintenance facility and adjusted to meet the needs of the newer aircraft as they came into service. In 1948 the facility was acquired by the US Air Force and was renamed Spokane Air Force Base. In 1950 the name was changed to Fairchild Air Force Base in honor of General Muir S. Fairchild, a native of Washington state, who held several important command positions during WW II and died in 1950 while serving as Vice Chief of Staff of the Air Force. Fairchild AFB continued to be a very active base during the Cold War.

Fairchild Air Force Base Museum: This is an interesting museum on the grounds of Fairchild AFB. It has a small collection of planes including a C-47 transport. The museum is a former WAC barracks and has displays of military artifacts dating back to the Civil War. There is a unique display of old teletype equipment, displays on the history of the 92nd Bomb Group and nearby Fort George Wright, uniforms, flight suits, POW artifacts, U.S. and foreign small arms, rockets and rocket launchers, aircraft models, photographs, paintings, drawings and documents. Address: 92-CSG Bldg. 3511, Fairchild AFB, WA 99011. Phone: 509/247-2100. Hours: M, W, Sat. 10-2; F 6pm-9pm. Donations requested.

FORT GEORGE WRIGHT was four miles NW of Spokane on a high bluff overlooking the Spokane River. This was an old Army post established in 1895 which, for a number of years, was the Army's main post in NE Washington. In 1941 the Army's 4th Infantry Div., which was stationed here, departed for Alaska vacating the fort. The AAF's 2nd AF, which was building several major facilities in the area, badly needed administrative space and occupied the fort for that purpose. In the early years of the war the fort was the headquarters for the 2nd AF. The 2nd AF stayed on throughout the war and the fort became an administrative center for much of the 2nd AF's activities in the western states. There was no air field at the fort, but there was a training camp for Military Police (MPs), a convalescent hospital and a ground school giving a two-week course to Soviet pilots who had been assigned by their government to fly U.S.-made Lend Lease planes from Alaska to the Soviet Union. During this time Fort Wright was a subpost of Spokane AAF. The fort passed to the US Air Force after the war who used it until 1961 at which time it was vacated and sold. With time, the old fort became known as the Fort George Wright Historic District and a cluster of schools came to occupy the site.

SUMAS is a small community on the U.S./Canadian border in the NW corner of the state. On Feb. 21, 1945 a Japanese bombing balloon was seen drifting at about 2000' over the town. The Air Force was alerted and two U.S. fighter planes arrived and shot down the balloon. It

Many remnants of WW II are to be seen at Spokane International Airport including an occasional DC-3 like the one to the left. In the foreground is a foundation from a WW II building and behind are two wooden WW II buildings in use.

The Fort Lewis Military Museum, located on the grounds of historic Fort Lewis, is housed in a beautiful old World War I building, and traces the history of the U.S. Army in the Northwest from 1804.

landed in Canadian territory on the rugged slopes of Vedder Mountain. When it was recovered it had no bombs and there were fears that it carried a biological agent. The balloon was sent to Ottawa for examination and was found to be a conventional bombing balloon that had expended its bombs and did not carry a biological agent.

TACOMA is near the south end of Puget Sound. Tacoma acquired a new aluminum plant during the war and the military was very active in the area. Tacoma suffered some of the problems associated with other wartime boom towns, but they were not as severe as those experienced by her northern neighbor, Seattle.

On Feb. 28, 1945 remnants of a Japanese bombing balloon were found in the Tacoma area and at the nearby community of Vaughn. On Mar. 3, 1945 another balloon was recovered in the suburb of Puyallup. These balloons were unusual in that it was rare for the balloons to come down in, or near, large cities.

FORT LEWIS, about midway between Tacoma and Olympia, was the nation's largest Army installations at time of its creation in 1917. It was known then as Camp Lewis and had a wide variety of terrain from salt water marshes, to towering mountains, forests, fast running streams and lakes. Unlike most WW I camps, Camp Lewis continued in operation after WW I. In 1927 it became a permanent Army post and was given it current name. During WW II Fort Lewis was enlarged and, again, trained soldiers. The 3rd Division of the Regular Army trained here followed by the 41st Division which comprised the National Guards of Idaho, Montana, Oregon, Washington and Wyoming. The 96th Infantry Division also trained here. Large housing developments were built in the area by the Government for the soldiers serving on the base and their dependents. The fort also had its own air field, Gray Field, which was used to train Army pilots in small planes to do reconnaissance and observation missions in support of the ground troops. There was a major medical facility at Fort Lewis, Madigan Army Medical Center,

that was a major debarkation hospital during the war. A large prisoner of war camp was located here holding over 4000 German POWs. Fort Lewis remained in operation throughout the Cold War.

Fort Lewis Military Museum: This is a large and interesting museum on the grounds of Fort Lewis. It is housed in a beautiful old World War I building, one of only two such buildings that remain at the Fort. The museum has four galleries and focuses on the history of the Army in the American Northwest from 1804. On display are small arms, machine guns, field artillery, uniforms, patches, documents, maps, photographs, paintings, drawings, scale models and several dioramas. Outside are amphibious landing craft, tracked vehicles, rockets and rocket launchers, missiles and anti-aircraft guns. Address: Building 4320, Fort Lewis, WA 98498-5000. Phone: 360/967-7206. Hours: W-Sun. noon-4, closed holidays. Free.

Mount Rainier Ordnance Depot: This had been Ft. Lewis's motor transport center, but during the war it was converted into its own entity and given the above name. The depot specialized in the storage and distribution of motorizes vehicles and equipment serving the Puget Sound area.

McCHORD FIELD was 8 miles south of Tacoma. It began in the early 1930s as a local airport known as Pierce County Airport. In 1935 Congress authorized the acquisition of, and expansion of the field, to improved America's defenses in the northwest. The Army Air Corps occupied the airport, and in 1937 renamed it McChord Field. A major building program was completed in 1939. In 1940 combat-ready air units of the 4th AF arrived at the field as a part of the defense planning for the northwest. McChord also became one of the country's largest training bases for bomber crews. This training began in 1940 mostly in B-25 bombers and continued until 1944. McChord also acquired a modification center for P-39 fighters, many of which went to the Soviet Union, via Alaska, under the Lend Lease program. In early June 1942, as a Japanese invasion fleets steamed towards Hawaii and Alaska, bombers of the newly created 8th AF began arriving at McChord from their staging base in New England where they were preparing to

move to the European Theater of Operations (ETO). These planes had hastily been sent to McChord as a reserve force to use against the Japanese if necessary. When the Japanese fleet was defeated at Midway, the bombers of the 8th AF returned to New England and eventually moved to Europe. Operations at McChord returned to normal, but later in the war McChord acquired air transport duties in addition to its other functions.

After the war McChord continued in operation, expanded and became an important air transport facility for planes going to the Pacific and Alaska. The field was taken over by the US Air Force in 1948, renamed McChord Air Force Base and continued in operation throughout the Cold War.

McChord Air Museum: This is a fine, two story, air museum on the grounds of McChord AFB. It relates the history of the airmen and units associated with McChord AFB through the years. There are exhibits on "Enlisted Pilots: 1912-1957", General Doolittle and his Tokyo Raiders, a display on barracks life in the 1940s, a replica of a 1950s briefing room, a gallery of aviation art, the history of the 62nd Military Airlift Wing (which occupied the field in the postwar years), uniforms, scale models, flight equipment and much more. Outside are several aircraft including a B-18 Bolo bomber, B-23 Dragon bomber, C-47 transport, T-33A trainer and a PBY-5A Catalina. Address: PO Box 4205, McChord AFB, WA 98438-5000. Phone: 360/984-2485. Hours: Tues.-Sun. noon-4, closed holidays. Free.

CAMP MURRAY, 12 miles south of Tacoma an American Lake, began in 1903 as training camp

This monument stand in the NE corner of the Western Washington Fairgrounds in Puyallup, WA on the site of the Puyallup Assembly Center. It commemorates the ethnic Japanese who passed through the Center in 1942 on their way to the relocation camps.

for the Washington National Guard. It has served that role ever since. During both WW I and WW II, and again for the Korean War, Washington's National Guard was mobilized here for federal service. Camp Murray owns two islands in American Lake. One is named Guadalcanal Island and the other, Luzon Island. At the entrance to the camp are several monuments to units who have served here and several pieces of postwar military equipment. Location: Exit I-5 at Berkeley St. SW. Camp Murray is just to the west of the exit.

PUYALLUP ASSEMBLY CENTER FOR ETHNIC JAPANESE (CAMP HARMONY): This was a processing center set up by the Army's Wartime Civil Control Administration in early 1942 at the Western Washington Fairgrounds in the suburb of Puyallup to process the ethnic Japanese of western Washington prior to their removal to the relocation camps. The center operated from Apr. 28 to Sept. 12, 1942. At its peak it housed 7390 people. Many who passed through Puyallup were fishermen and their families from Bainbridge Island in Puget Sound. Most were sent to the Tule Lake, CA and Minidoka, ID relocation camps. After the Japanese departed the center was turned over to the Army's 9th Service Command. Today a monument dedicated to the memory of those who passed through the center stands in the NE corner of the fairgrounds near the Meridian St. and 9th Ave. SW entrance.

VANCOUVER is in southern Washington on the north bank of the Columbia River, and is an inland seaport directly across from Portland OR. A large aluminum plant was built in Vancouver and Henry Kaiser, the great ship builder of the war, built two new ship yards in the area, one in Vancouver and the other in Portland, and managed a third. Vancouver, like Portland, became a boom town with many of the associated problems of housing shortages, failure of city services, shortages of consumer goods, crowded schools, and increases in crime and vice. Vancouver emerged from the war a much larger city than before making it Washington's fourth largest city.

VANCOUVER BARRACKS and PEARSON FIELD, now Fort Vancouver National Historic Site, is near downtown Vancouver overlooking the Columbia River. Vancouver Barracks evolved from a British fort protecting a Hudson Bay Company trading post built here in 1829. The U.S. Army took possession of the British fort and in 1853 named it Fort Vancouver. In 1879

it was renamed Vancouver Barracks.

Vancouver Barracks was one of the first Army posts in the country to have its own flying field, Pearson Field. With the acquisition of the field, the Army Air Crops became an integral part of Vancouver Barracks. Pearson Field is claimed to be the oldest operating air field in the U.S. During WW II Vancouver Barrack served as a staging area for troops shipping out through the port of Portland, OR. The post was also used by the Army for a variety of purposes. In 1944 Italian Service Units (ISU) arrived at the Barracks. Some of the men worked on the docks and in the warehouses at Portland, while others worked on the Barracks grounds. Also in 1944 the Army built Barnes General Hospital, a temporary facility constructed of wood, on the grounds of Vancouver Barracks. This 1547-bed hospital treated war wounded and specialized in general medicine and general and orthopedic surgery. In Dec. 1945 Barnes was transferred to the Veterans Administration.

After serving the Army and the AAF in WW II, Vancouver Barracks and Pearson Field were retired from the Army and converted into a National Historic Site, a park-like facility open to the public and serving many community needs of the area. Pearson Field remained an operating air field. Address: Fort Vancouver National Historic Site, 1501 E. Evergreen Blvd., Vancouver, WA 98661. Phone: 360/696-7655. Hours: Fort and Visitors' Center Memorial Day thru Labor Day daily 9-5, rest of year 9-4. Closed Jan. 1, Thanksgiving and Dec. 25. Admission charged.

The George C. Marshall House: This is one of the stately old houses along "Officers' Row" at Vancouver Barracks. It was occupied by a long list of distinguished military officers, but in 1936, recently promoted General George C. Marshall, who was destined to become one of the most famous personalities of WW II, moved into the house with his family. Marshall had been sent to Vancouver Barracks as commander of the Army's 5th Brigade. It was his first major command. General Marshall lived here until 1938. General Marshall went on to be the U.S. Army Chief of Staff during WW II, was promoted to a five-star general in 1944, became Secretary of State in 1947, author of the famous Marshall Plan, Secretary of Defense in 1950-51 and Nobel Peace Prize winner in 1952. The house is restored, decorated in period furnishings

General George C. Marshall.

and open to the public. Address: 1301 Officers' Row, Vancouver, WA 98661. Phone 360/693-3103. Hours: M-F 9-5. Donations requested.

Pearson Air Museum: This museum is on Pearson Field and located in the country's oldest military hanger c. 1904. The museum relates the history of Pearson Field and of Vancouver Barracks. Several aircraft are inside the museum and are rotated with other aircraft in storage. There is a display and monument to the landing of the Soviet aviators in 1937, aviation artifacts, photographs, paintings, documents and a small gift shop. Address: 1105 E. 5th St., Vancouver, WA 98661. Phone: 360/694-7026. Hours: Summer W-Sun noon-5, closed Jan. 1 and Dec. 25. Admission charged.

WALLA WALLA is in the SE corner of the state.

McCAW GENERAL HOSPITAL was built in Walla Walla by the Federal Government in 1943 to treat war wounded. This was a temporary wooden facility with 1502 beds and specialized in neurology, general and orthopedic surgery, neurosurgery and psychiatry. In Nov. 1945 McCaw was transferred to the Veterans Administration.

WALLA WALLA ARMY AIR FIELD, three miles NE of the city, began as a pre-war municipal airport serving the community of Walla Walla. In early 1942 it was one of the first airports in the country to receive combat-ready air units to defend America's shores. The 4th AF took over the airport and converted it into a B-17 and B-24 training base. The air field was enlarged and many buildings were built. In 1947 the air field was returned to the city and county and became Walla Walla Regional Airport and an industrial park. This is one of the best preserved WW II air fields in the country. Over 100 WW II buildings remain, including four original hangars, ammunition bunkers and a rare WW II base hospital. The base hospital is a large rambling collection of wooden, single-story buildings with long covered corridors running from building to building. It is typi-

The U.S. Army Corps of Engineers uses part of the old base hospital which is a rare relic of WW II.

One of several of Fort Casey's big gun positions that dominated the entrance to Puget Sound.

One of two 10" guns on disappearing carriages mounted at Fort Casey. This gun is in the up (firing) position. These guns are from the Philippines and are of 1900s vintage, but some guns of this type were still in use around the country during the early part of WW II.

cal of many such hospitals built at military bases around the country during the war. Most of these hospitals have been removed, and alas, this one, too, is scheduled for removal because of the cost of maintenance and its asbestos content. Location: Northeast of town off U.S. 12.

WHIDBEY ISLAND is a long irregularly shaped island dominating the entrance to Puget Sound. Because of its strategic location military facilities have long been on the island.

FORT CASEY was near the center of the Island on its western shore and just north of the Keystone Ferry to Port Townsend. It was one of the three forts of the "Devil's Triangle" built in the 1890s to defend Admiralty Inlet, the main entrance to Puget Sound. Forts Flagler and Worden in the Port Townsend area, on the west side of Admiralty Inlet, were the other two forts. All had heavy guns capable of doing battle with the largest warships of their day. During WW I Fort Casey was used as a training base for soldiers. In the years between the wars it was inactive, but when WW II started, Fort Casey was reactivated as a subpost of Fort Worden and again used as a training base. Modern guns were mounted in the old batteries, new anti-aircraft batteries were built in the area and Fort Casey once again defended Puget Sound. In 1950 the fort was placed into care-

taker status and in 1956 it was sold to the state to become Fort Casey State Park. Eleven of the old batteries can be visited, two of which have 10" guns from the 1900s mounted on disappearing carriages, one in the up (firing) position and the other in the down (loading) position. Some guns of this type were still in use around the country during the early part of WW II. Fort Casey's original guns were scrapped at various times between 1922 and 1945 for their metal value.

On the park grounds is Admiralty Head Lighthouse, an old lighthouse, that has been converted into a small museum with displays on the history of the Fort. Address: Fort Casey State Park, 1280 S. Fort Casey Rd., Coupeville, WA 98239. Phone: 360/678-4519. Park hours: Apr. 1 - Oct. 30 6:30-dusk; Oct. 16 - Mar. 31 8-dusk.

FORT EBEY was on the north central shore of Whidbey Island facing Juan de Fuca Strait. It was built in 1942 as a fourth coastal defense position to protect the entrance to Puget Sound. Its main batteries consisted of 6" guns mounted in steel turrets, and it had a number of large anti-aircraft batteries. Fort Ebey, like Fort Casey to the south, was a subpost of Fort Worden. Fort Ebey's 6" guns, which could hurl a 105 lb shell 15 miles, were test fired and never fired again. Fort Ebey was deactivated soon after the war and its guns removed. In 1968 the fort was donated to the state, and in 1980 it was converted into Fort Ebey State Park.

U.S. NAVAL AIR STATION, WHIDBEY ISLAND, OAK HARBOR was near the north end of Whidbey Island. It consisted of two facilities during the war, Ault Field just NW of Oak Harbor in Clover Valley, and a seaplane base just to the east of Oak Harbor on Crescent Harbor.

The facility began in 1942 when the Navy saw the need for an air facility in the Pacific Northwest for the rearming and refueling of Navy planes operating in the Puget Sound area. The facility was commission in Sept. 1942 with Ault Field being named in honor of Comdr.

William B. Ault who lost his life in the Battle of the Coral Sea, May 1942. During the war the station performed its intended mission and acquired two Navy schools which trained personnel in aerial rocketry and torpedo overhaul. In 1946 the station was placed on reduced status, but in 1949 it was reactivated and served well into the postwar era. During the WW II the station had two outlying fields, Coupeville Airport, 2 miles SE of Coupeville and Mt. Vernon Airport, 5 miles NW of Mt. Vernon.

YAKIMA is in south central Washington. Yakima was to experience an unusual number of incidents with Japanese bombing balloons during the war, none of which caused any damage. They were as follows (all recoveries of balloon components):

* Mar. 10, 1945; balloon recovered near Toppenish just south of Yakima. On the same day, balloon remnants were recovered at Moxee just west of Yakima.
* Apr. 1, 1945; balloon recovered at Tampico west of Yakima.
* Apr. 19, 1945; balloon recovered at Wapato, SE of Yakima.
* Apr. 30, 1945; second recovery of balloon remnants at Moxee.
* Jun. 21, 1945; second balloon recovered at Tampico.

YAKIMA AIR BASE, three miles SW of town, was Yakima's local airport before the war. It was taken over by the AAF as a training base. Before that, however, the airport had been used to train military pilots who attended Perry Institute, a private school, directly across the street from the airport. Perry Institute had one of the largest privately operated flying schools in the country. Some 5000 airmen trained here on an around-the-clock basis for over two years. After the war the air base was returned to the city and became known as Yakima Air Terminal. Perry Institute continued in operation near the airport and became a large educational facility known as J.M. Perry Institute of Trades, Industries and Agriculture.

YAKIMA ARTILLERY RANGE, also known during the war as East Selah Artillery Range and Yakima Bombing Range, was NE of Yakima east of I-82. At 128,000 acres it is one of the largest military reservations in the country. It operated as a subpost of Fort Lewis early in the war for artillery training and large-scale maneuvers. It was also used for bombing and strafing practice by airmen training at Yakima Air Base. It remained in use after the war and became known as Yakima Firing Center.

Sign at an intersection on the former seaplane base.

WEST VIRGINIA

The U.S. Naval Ordnance Plant, South Charleston as it looked in the 1990s.

The state of West Virginia had been hard-hit economically by the Great Depression so the economic up-turn created by World War II was most welcome in the state. The state's primary mineral product, coal, was much in demand throughout the war to produce the electricity that powered the booming defense plants, ship yards, ordnance plants, military bases and crowded cities. But all was not well in the coal mines because the industry was plagued by constant strikes. The strikes became nasty at times with beatings, shootings, violence and sabotage common occurrences. At one point President Franklin Roosevelt became so concerned about a widespread strike called by John L. Lewis of the United Mine Workers that he threatened to send in troops to work the mines. The United Mine Workers backed down and the miners went back to work.

The other segments of the West Virginia economy didn't have the labor troubles the coal industry had and ran more smoothly during the war. Items coming from West Virginia's factories, farms and soil included steel, glass, pottery, porcelain, chemicals, grain, flour, potatoes, lumber, woodworking, oil, petroleum products, natural gas, cement and stone. Since the state was so mountainous it was not conducive to military flight training so the Army and Navy established no flight training fields in the state. Neither were there any training camps for ground forces built in the state, but West Virginia had three prisoner of war camps. Some of the locks and dams along the Ohio River, the state's western boundary, were targets for sabotage by the German saboteurs who landed on the east coast in June 1942. The saboteurs were captured soon after landing so there were no actual sabotage attempts.

West Virginia emerged from the war with a much more prosperous economy than it had before the war, but the coal industry was still in flux. Labor problems continued in the early postwar years and was a factor in the mine owners spending millions of dollars to automate the mines. Demand for coal also declined as the railroads and other segments of industry moved away from coal-fired steam power to oil, natural gas and diesel power.

In the postwar years Toyky Rose came to West Virginia as a guest of the Federal Government to serve her time in the women's federal prison here.

CHARLESTON, in the SW section of the state, is the state's capital. In 1943 the nation's first large-scale synthetic rubber plant began operating here.

U.S. NAVAL ORDNANCE PLANT, SOUTH CHARLESTON was located near the western edge of South Charleston on McCorkle Ave. (U.S. 60). It was built in 1918 to produce armor plate for battleships and large naval gun forgings. At the time of its construction the plant was known as the U.S. Naval Armor and Projectile Plants, Charleston. The facility was about to go into production when WW I ended and all operations shut down without the plant having produced any armor plate or gun forgings. In 1922 the plant was placed in reserve with all its machinery in place and remained that way until 1939. In that year it was re-activated by the Navy and given its WW II name. The plant then produced armor plant and gun forgings throughout WW II under the dual management of the Carnegie-Illinois Steel Corp. and the General Machinery Ordnance Corp. Each company had a part of the plant under its control. After WW II all production stopped and the plant was used to store surplus machine tools belonging to the government. The inventory of machine tools gradually declined until the Korean War when it was drawn down altogether. In 1953 the plant as declared surplus and sold to the FMC Corp. Later, the facility became known as the Charleston Ordnance Center and has had multiple industrial tenants.

MARTINSBURG is in the state's eastern panhandle 18 miles SW of Hagerstown, MD. **NEWTON D. BAKER GENERAL HOSPITAL** was an Army general hospital built in Martinsburg during 1943-44 to treat war wounded. The hospital was a permanent structure, built of brick, and had 1806 beds. It specialized in neurology, neurosurgery, plastic surgery, ophthalmologic surgery and psychiatry. The hospital had a branch prisoner of war camp with about 250 POWs who worked at the hospital. In June 1946 the hospital was transferred to the Veterans Administration.

MORGANTOWN is in the north-central part of the state.

MORGANTOWN ORDNANCE WORKS was built by the Federal Government in Morgantown in 1941 to produce ammonia from coal. Ammonia was used in the manufacture of several types of explosives. The plant also produced methanol, formaldehyde and hexamine. In late 1942 Morgantown Ordnance Works was one of three plants in the country selected by Gen. Leslie Groves, head of the "Manhattan (atomic bomb) Project", as a backup plant for the manufacture of heavy water which could be used in atomic reactors. This process started at the plant in Feb. 1943 and was run by duPont de Nemours & Co.

POINT PLEASANT is 45 miles NW of Charleston on the Ohio River. For a relatively small town it had several important defense plants which included the Goff-Kirby Co. which made TNT, The General Chemical Co. which also made TNT and the Mariette Manufacturing Co. which made mine planters. There was also a local ship builder that made landing craft for the Navy and the Coast Guard had a supply depot here.

WEST VIRGINIA ORDNANCE WORKS, just north of downtown on Madison Ave., was built by

The Morgantown Ordnance Works during the war.

the Federal Government in 1942 to produce TNT. The plant was operated by duPont de Nemours & Co. and produced TNT throughout the war. In the postwar years the facility was turned over to the Navy and used as a supply depot. It remained in use during the Cold War and became known as Defense Logistics Agency, Defense National Stockpile Zone.

WHITE SULPHUR SPRINGS is a popular health resort located in the SE part of the state on I-64.

THE GREENBRIER HOTEL is the largest and best known hotel in White Sulphur Springs with a reputation for elegant services and accommodations and prices to match. Soon after the attack on Pearl Harbor the State Department leased the hotel for the purpose of housing Axis diplomats and their families in a safe and comfortable facility until they could be exchanged for American diplomats in Axis nations. Three other luxury hotels were also acquired for the purpose[1]. At first a mix of Axis diplomats of different nationalities were sent here, but experience soon revealed that they were not all that compatible and had to be separated. The Greenbrier was thus selected to become an all-Japanese facility. For several months, therefore, The Greenbrier was a small Japanese community with women, children, pets, kids in school, Japanese cooks in the kitchen preparing traditional Japanese food, Japanese taking traditional communal baths in the hot baths, playing tennis and an occasional baby being born . . all under the watchful eyes of the FBI and the guards of the Immigration and Naturalization Service. Both Adm.

[1]The other luxury hotels acquired were the Homestead in Hot Springs, VA; The Bedford Springs Hotel, Bedford, PA and the Grove Park Inn in Asheville, NC.

The Greenbrier Hotel in White Sulphur Springs, WV.

Nomura, the former Ambassador to the U.S., and Special Envoy Saburo Kurusu resided here. These two men had been negotiating with Secretary of State Cordell Hull right up to the time of the Japanese attack on Pearl Harbor and, on Dec. 7, 1941, handed Hull Japan's declaration of war. By the spring of 1942 the diplomats and their families had all left The Greenbrier to be repatriated through neutral nations. In Sept. 1942 the hotel was taken over by the Federal Government again for use as an Army general hospital. It was given the wartime name of Ashford General Hospital and treated war wounded. The Greenbrier's local air strip, two miles SW of town, was also taken over by the Government and named Greenbrier Army Air Field. It served the aviation needs of the hospital. The hotel-turned-hospital had 2025 beds and specialized in general medicine, neurology, neurosurgery and vascular surgery. Ashford also had a center for training military medical officers. The hospital had West Virginia's only main prisoner of war camp which held about 680 POWs who worked at the hospital. By war's end some 20,000 had been treated at Ashford. The hotel remained a hospital until June 1946 at which time Ashford was closed and the hotel returned to its former owners. In the late 1950s a new wing was added to the hotel, but it was considerable more than what it appeared. Beneath the new wing was constructed a large, and very secret, bomb shelter which was large enough to hold the entire Congress of the United States. The Federal Government had a plan at that time that in the event of an atomic attack, The Greenbrier Hotel would become the temporary home of Congress.

WISCONSIN

It is safe to say that nearly every member of the United States armed forces consumed at least two of Wisconsin's products during the war ... milk and cheese. Wisconsin was then, as it is now, America's Dairyland. For years the state lead the nation in the production of dairy products and the war years were no exception. Wisconsin was also a supplier of other important food items and a major manufacturing state. During the war the state produced dairy products, meat, fresh water fish, grain, fruit, tobacco, beer, hay (most of which was consumed locally by the cattle), lumber, paper, pulp, furniture, farm machinery, automobiles, engines, machine tools, construction equipment, electronic appliances, hospital equipment, metal working products, lead, zinc, copper, iron ore, stone, limestone, clay, peat, sand and gravel.

Important WW II personalties associated with Wisconsin included Gen. Hoyt Vandenberg from Milwaukee, Gen. Nathan Twining from Monroe, Adm. Marc A. Mitscher from Hillsboro, General William "Billy" Mitchell from Milwaukee and Richard I. Bong, America's top air ace, from Poplar. Gen. Douglas MacArthur lived in Milwaukee as a boy and Adm. William D. Leahy lived for a while in Ashland.

In 1942 the state legislature made military training compulsory in all state universities and set up a Council of Defense to direct the civil defense activity in the state. By war's end the state could counted 21 prisoner of war camps within its borders. In 1946 Senator LaFollette was defeated at the polls by a newcomer, Joseph McCarthy, a right-wing Republican who would go on to create yet another fascinating chapter in American history.

BARABOO is 30 miles NW of Madison.

BADGER ORDNANCE PLANT was built by the Federal Government in 1942 near Baraboo to make smokeless powder. It was operated by the Hercules Powder Co. The plant was soon

The Wisconsin National Guard Memorial Library and Museum at Camp Williams.

expanded to made TNT, double-base powder, diphenylamine, oleum and rocket propellent. After the war the plant was retained by the government but was inactive most of the early postwar years.

CAMP DOUGLAS is 50 miles east of La Crosse on I-90.

CAMP WILLIAMS, just NE of Camp Douglas, was established in 1888 as a training facility for the Wisconsin National Guard. The Wisconsin National Guard was activated here early in WW II and became part of the 32nd Infantry Div. After the 32nd moved out, the camp was used by the Army for an arctic training school which opened in 1942. The camp had its own air field which was designated Camp Williams Army Air Field. In the postwar years the camp again became the home of the Wisconsin National Guard and the air field became an Air National Guard base known as Volk Field.

Wisconsin National Guard Memorial Library and Museum: This facility is on the grounds of Camp Williams. The Memorial Library has many interesting documents, diaries, scrapbooks, personal histories and films pertaining to the history of the Wisconsin National Guard. The museum has artifacts and displays tracing the history of the Wisconsin National Guard from territorial days to the present. On the museum ground are several vintage airplanes used by the Wisconsin Air National Guard. Ad-

This P-51 Mustang from WW II is mounted on pylons at the entrance to Camp Williams.

dress: Camp Williams-Volk Field, Camp Douglas, WI 54618-5001. Phone: 800/752-6659 and 608/427-1280. Hours: W-Sat. 9-4, Sun. noon-4. Free.

EAU CLAIRE is 80 miles east of Minneapolis-St. Paul on I-94.

EAU CLAIRE ORDNANCE PLANT was an existing vacant plant in Eau Claire when the war started. In the past the plant had made candy and textiles. The U.S. Rubber Co., which had secured a contract from the Federal Government to make small arms ammunition, purchased the plant and converted it to that use. Throughout the war the plant made 30 calibre ammunition.

GREEN BAY is located is at the SW end of Green Bay, an appendage to Lake Michigan.

NATIONAL RAILROAD MUSEUM is located about two miles south of downtown Green Bay on the Fox River. This.is a large railroad museum with about 70 railroad engines and cars dating from 1880. Of interest to WW II buffs is Gen. Dwight Eisenhower's staff train which he used in England during WW II. The train consists of a London & North Eastern Railroad locomotive and several cars. Address: 2285 S. Broadway, Green Bay, WI 54304. Phone: 414/488-4460. Hours: Tues.-Sat. 9-5, Sun.-Mon. noon-5. Closed major holidays. Donations accepted.

KING is a small town 35 miles NW of Oshkosh on SR 22.

THE WISCONSIN VETERANS MUSEUM is located in the F. A. Marden Memorial Center of the Wisconsin Veterans Home. The museum highlights the participation of Wisconsin citizens in WW I and WW II with special emphasis on the history of the 32nd Infantry Division, of which the Wisconsin National Guard was a part. Displays cover the activities of the 32nd when it served under Gen. MacArthur in New Guinea and the Philippines. Also included in the museum are weapons, field equipment, uniforms, captured enemy equipment, photos, drawings, painting and more. Address: SR 22 North, King, WI 54946. Phone: 715/258-5586. Hours:

The Wisconsin Veterans Museum is located in this building, the F.A. Marden Memorial Center in King, WI.

Daily 9-11 and 1-4. Free.

MADISON, south-central Wisconsin, is the capital of the state.

TRUAX FIELD, five miles east of Madison, was the area's local airport before the war and, beginning early in the war, was used from time-to-time by the AAF in its ferrying operations. Early in 1943 the AAF established a school for radio operators of four-engine aircraft here. This was a temporary facility with barracks built of wood and tarpaper. In Wisconsin's cold climate, these barracks proved to be a problem because many of the airmen came down with respiratory diseases. An AAF regional hospital was established at the field partially because of the problem. After the war the AAF abandoned its facilities at Truax Field and departed. The field then served again as a civilian airport.

MANITOWOC is located on Lake Michigan 70 miles north of Milwaukee. During the war it was home to a large shipbuilding firm, the Manitowoc Shipbuilding Co. This company secured a contract from the Navy to build submarines during WW II. The submarines were launched into Manitowoc River, tested in Lake Michigan and then sailed to Chicago. At Chicago the subs were gingerly towed over the many shallow places and under the many bridges that crossed the Sanitary Canal and the upper reaches of the Illinois River. Each submarine was then placed in a floating dry dock and sailed down the Illinois River/Mississippi River route to the Gulf of Mexico. Manitowoc Shipbuilding Co. built and delivered 28 submarines this way during WW II and did it under-budget and ahead of schedule. The Manitowoc Shipbuilding Co. built other vessels for the Navy during the war including landing craft, patrol boats and crawler cranes.

MANITOWOC MARITIME MUSEUM, near downtown Manitowoc, depicts the history of shipbuilding on the Great Lakes and has on permanent display the WW II submarine, "Cobia". The museum has considerable information on the construction of the WW II submarines by the Manitowoc Shipbuilding Co. and there are general exhibits on the activities of the U.S. submarine force throughout WW II. Address: 75 Maritime Dr., Manitowoc, WI 54220. Phone: 414/684-0218. Hours: Memorial Day through Labor Day daily 9-8, rest of year daily 9-5. Closed Jan. 1, Easter, Thanksgiving and Dec. 25. Admission charged.

MILWAUKEE was Wisconsin's largest city during the war the state's most heavily industrialized area. Some of the largest manufacturers in the area were the A.O. Smith Co. which made a bombs, torpedo parts and aircraft landing gears; Allis-Chalmers Corp. which made industrial equipment, Bofors anti-aircraft guns, prime movers for atrillery and sections of Liberty ships; Kearney & Trecker Corp. made truck transmissions; Vilter Manufacturing Co. which made 105 mm howitzers, 3", M-6 and T-12 guns; Pressed Steel Tanks Co. which made bombs; AC Spark Plug Division of General Motors made machine guns; L.F. Mueller Furnace Co. which made tank treads and tank parts and Electrical Connector Manufacturing Co. which made 75 mm high explosive shells.

GENERAL MITCHELL FIELD is 6 miles south of downtown Milwaukee on So. Howell Ave. It was the city's main airport before the war and known then as Milwaukee County Airport. In 1941, after General Billy Mitchell's name had been exonerated by the military, the field was renamed in his honor. Mitchell was a native of Milwaukee. In 1942 the AAF leased part of the field for use as a training center for Air Transport Command pilots and crews. The field had a main prisoner of war camp which held about 800 POWs who worked at the field and in the local area. In Dec. 1944 the AAF's training center ceased operations and was placed on the inactive list. In 1946 the AAF left the field altogether. In the early postwar years some of the AAF's barracks were used to house an overflow from the House of Correction at Franklin, WI and as housing for mental patients. In 1948 full civil control of the field as resumed. In the postwar years the field has retained its wartime name.

GENERAL WILLIAM "BILLY" MITCHELL GRAVE SITE: General "Billy" Mitchell, a native of Milwaukee, is buried in Forest Home Cemetery which is three miles SW of downtown Milwaukee on S. 27th St. Mitchell died before WW II began and had spent much of his military career promoting the theory that aircraft could sink major warships. This theory was very controversial and often criticized during the pre-war years by many of the nation's top naval and Air Corps leaders. In the process of promoting his cause Mitchell was court-martialed and resigned from the service. The events of WW II, however, quickly proved Mitchell right and forced the major navies and air forces of the world to accept his theory and adjust accordingly.

These are just two of the types of bombs made by A.O. Smith Co. of Milwaukee. The bomb on the left if a 22,000 lb semi-armor-piercing bomb and the one on the right is a 2000 lb demolition bomb.

The submarine "Robalo" being launched at the Manitowoc Shipbuilding Co., Manitowoc, WI.

These are some of the WW II aircraft on display at the EAA Aviation Center and Air Museum in Oshkosh.

MILWAUKEE COUNTY WAR MEMORIAL COMPLEX, on the city's waterfront, honors citizens of Milwaukee that have given their lives in American's wars, including WW II. The complex consists of the Charles Allis Art Museum, Milwaukee Art Museum, Performing Arts Center and Villa Terrace.

MILWAUKEE ORDNANCE PLANT was established in Milwaukee by the Federal Government early in the war to make small arms ammunition. The plant was run by the U.S. Rubber Co. and operated until late 1943 at which time production stopped and the plant was placed on standby.

OSHKOSH is in the east-central part of the state on Lake Winnebago.

EXPERIMENTAL AIRCRAFT ASSOCIATION (EAA) AVIATION CENTER AND AIR MUSEUM This is a large, well-known aviation center located at Wittman Field, SE of Oshkosh near the junction of U.S. 41 and SR 44. The museum highlights experimental, sport, recreation and home-built aircraft but has many historic and vintage aircraft on display as well. Most of the WW II aircraft are housed in one hangar called the Eagle Hangar. Planes of WW II include a B-17, Ki-43 Nakajima "Oscar", Mosquito bomber, P-38J, XP-51 Mustang, F8F-2 Bearcat, Me-109 Messerschmitt, A-26C, T-6J, B-25H and more. Other displays include engines, cutaways, propellers, models and photos. Address: Wittman Airfield, Oshkosh, WI 54903-2591. Phone: 414/426-4818. Hours: M-Sat. 8:30-5, Sun. 11-5, closed Jan. 1, Easter, Thanksgiving and Dec. 25. Admission charged.

POPLAR is in the NW corner of the state on U.S. 2.

RICHARD I. BONG MEMORIAL: This memorial honors Richard I. Bong, America's "Ace of Aces", Congressional Medal of Honor winner and native of Poplar. The memorial consists primarily of a P-38 fighter plane of the type Bong flew when he downed 40 enemy aircraft in the Pacific theater of operations. In a one-room museum in an adjoining wing of a school are displays, photographs, personal items, awards, and other memorabilia pertaining to Bong. Bong was killed on Aug. 6, 1945 while testing an experimental P-80 jet. His body was returned to Poplar and he is buried in the local cemetery.

SPARTA is 22 miles ENE of La Crosse on I-90.

CAMP McCOY was 7 miles east of Sparta and was established by the Army in 1909 and at that time was known as Camp Robinson. During WW I the camp was used for the training of artillery units. From 1919 to 1923 it was used as a storage facility and known as Sparta Ordnance Depot. In 1926 the camp was renamed Camp McCoy and in the 1930s the camp served as a CCC facility. In 1941-42 the camp was expanded and used for the training of division-size units. The 32nd Infantry Division, which contained the Wisconsin National Guard, trained here in 1941. At its peak Camp McCoy housed some 35,000 service personnel. During the summer of 1942 enemy aliens from Germany, Italy, Japan and Hungary were held here for several months while they awaited transfer to alien internment camps. Soon after the enemy aliens left the all-Nisei 100th Infantry Battalion, comprised mostly of Japanese-American from Hawaii, arrived at McCoy and underwent training. In late 1942, when large numbers of POWs began arriving in America, Camp McCoy was one of the first Army camps to receive them because camp personnel had had the experience with the enemy aliens and the camp also had available space. McCoy acquired two main prisoner of war camps, one for Germans and one for Japanese. They were side-by-side separated by a road. The German POW camp held about 300 POWs and the Japa-nese camp held about 2500 Japanese POWs making it one of the largest such camps in the U.S. In both cases most of the POWs worked for the military at Camp McCoy. Camp McCoy's station hospital had facilities to care for Japanese POWs and, as a result, received Japanese POWs from other camps in need of medical treatment. At the end of the war Camp McCoy served as an Army separation center and in 1953 it became a training center for Army Reserve units and the Wisconsin National Guard. That became its permanent mission. When the camp is not being used by the military it is usually open to the public for recreational purposes.

WISCONSIN DELLS: This is a beautiful section of the Wisconsin River some 40 miles NW of Madison off I-94. Many tourist attractions have sprung up in the area including two companies that offer rides through the Dells in WW II-era amphibious vehicles called DUKWs (Ducks). The Ducks have been modified to carry passengers in a comfortable manner and are safety-approved by the U.S. Coast Guard. Usually, Duck rides begin at the companies' offices, travel along local roads and into the Wisconsin River. The two companies offering duck rides are:

Dells Duck Tours, two miles south on US 12 and SR 23. Phone: 608/254-6080. Hours: May through Oct. daily 9-6.

Wisconsin Ducks, Inc. 1.5 miles south on US 12 and SR 23. Phone: 608/254-8751. Hours: June through Labor Day daily 8-7, May 1 through early June 9-4, after Labor Day through mid-Oct. 9-4.

The Richard I. Bong Memorial in Poplar, WI.

This is the WW II base hospital at Camp McCoy. During the war it had facilities to care for Japanese POWs and received Japanese POWs from other POW camps. Later the hospital was used for offices.

WYOMING

Wyoming was a pretty good place to be before, during and after World War II. Several decades before WW II the state granted women the right to vote and from then on touted itself as the "Equal Rights" state. In the 1930s oil was discovered in the state, which stimulate the economy for the state's 250,742 residents, and in 1939 Wyoming lead the nation in overall mineral production. Also in the 1930s the Federal Government launched several major construction projects in the state, some of which included the construction of the Alcova, Kortes and Seminoe dams. These projects resulted in jobs, demands for local services, cheap electricity and long-term follow-up irrigation and electrification projects in many areas of the state. In 1940 some 400,000 tourists brought their dollars to Wyoming and visited Yellowstone National Park and many of the state's other sites. During the war Wyoming was secure from enemy attacks, although 12 Japanese bombing balloons did come down in the state. Also during the war the Federal Government built several military installations in the state including 14 prisoner of war camps and one Japanese relocation camp. The residents of these camps proved very useful by working in the state's agricultural sector and in the forests.

After the war, nation-wide demands for Wyoming's products remained strong and tourism experienced a healthy revival. In the 1950s the state's economy was spurred along even further when large deposits of uranium and trona[1] were discovered in the state. The state's main products during the war were oil, natural gas, coal, sulphur, iron ore, bentonite, horses, mules, meat, wool, lumber, grain, potatoes, hay and beet sugar. Despite Wyoming's relatively good fortune, the state's population remained stagnant. When the census of 1950 was taken it was discovered that the state had only 115 more citizens than it had in 1940.

CASPER is in east-central Wyoming on I-25. On Feb. 9, 1945 the remnants of a Japanese bombing balloons were found near Casper, and the remnants of a second balloon was found on Apr. 6, 1945. Neither balloon caused any damage.

CASPER ARMY AIR BASE, 9 miles NW of town, was built in 1942 for the 2nd AF for use as an advanced flight training center for the crews of B-24 bombers. The air field was 5340 ft. above sea level which was quite high for a military training field. Upon completion of their training here the air crews generally went directly overseas to the combat areas. In March 1945 the air field was deactivated and a short time later turned over to the community of Casper to become its local airport.

CHEYENNE, in the SE corner of the state, is the capital of Wyoming.

CHEYENNE AIRPORT, just north of downtown Cheyenne, was the city's pre-war airport. United Air Lines Corp. established an aircraft modification center and a school for technicians

[1] Trona is a source of sodium carbonate widely used by the chemical industry.

here during the war and made modifications on B-17 bombers under contract from the AAF. Many of the planes were modified to become reconnaissance planes or precision bombers. By war's end the center had modified 5500 B-17s and trained some 5000 technicians. The Air Transport Command also used the field from time-to-time.

FORT FRANCIS E. WARREN is located west of, and adjacent to, Cheyenne off I-25. The fort was built in the 1860s to protect railroad construction crews then working in the area. At that time the post was named Fort D.A. Russell. In 1871, after the railroads had been completed, the fort became a quartermaster depot and was called Cheyenne Depot. The facility was later made a permanent Army post and enlarged several times during the next 50 years. In 1930 the fort was renamed Fort Francis E. Warren. By WW II the fort had a target and maneuver area, known as the Pole Mountain Reservation, 30 miles to the west. In 1940 the fort was designated an Army reception center and a replacement training center for Quartermaster Corps personnel, and during the winter of 1940-41 was enlarged once more. Fort Francis E. Warren was a segregated camp so negro troops were also trained here. In Mar. 1942 a Quartermaster Officer Candidate School moved in from Camp Lee, VA. Activity peaked at the fort in Dec. 1942 when its compliment of enlisted men reached 19,251. Training activity then declined rapidly and in July 1943 the training center was deactivated although some Quartermaster training continued until Oct. of that year. Between Mar. 1941 and Sept. 1943 over 122,000 quartermaster personnel had been trained here. Also during 1943 a branch prisoner of war camp was established at the fort for German POWs who worked for the Army. In 1944 the Army began training railroad battalions at the fort because of its easy access to several rail lines. In Nov. of that year Italian Service Units came to the fort to work. In Feb. 1945 the German POW branch camp was enlarged and designated a main prisoner of war camp. In June 1945 Fort Francis E. Warren became a redeployment center for the Army's Transportation Corps receiving men returning from Europe and sending them off to new assignments.

With the end of hostilities, activities at the fort declined and in April 1948 the fort was transferred to the US Air Force. It was then renamed Francis E. Warren Air Force Base and converted into a USAF Aviation Engineering school. In 1975 the post was declared a National Historic Landmark.

Francis E. Warren Air Force Base Museum: This museum in on the grounds of Francis E. Warren Air Force Base in one of the old officers' homes. Exhibits trace the history of the base from its beginning to the present. Displays on the WW II era are limited. Items on display include missiles, rocket launchers, machine guns, small arms, uniforms, unit patches, documents, flags, photos, medals, etc. Address: Bldg. 210, Francis E. Warren AFB, WY 82005-5000. Phone: 307/775-2980: Hours: Sat. & Sun. 1-4. Free.

DOUGLAS is in east-central Wyoming 120 miles north of Cheyenne.

DOUGLAS PRISONER OF WAR CAMP was located one mile west of Douglas. This was a main prisoner of war camp built in the spring of 1943 to hold up to 2500 POWs. The first POWs to use the camp were Italians who arrived in Aug. 1943. The next month Italy surrendered and changed sides and the Italian POWs were then incorporated into the all-volunteer Italian Service Units or moved to other camps. By July 1944 the camp was empty and deactivated. In late Aug., however, it was reopened and received German NCO POWs. These POWs remained until after the end of hostilities and worked in agriculture, on ranches and in the forests. The POWs remained until after the 1945 harvests and then were repatriated to Germany.

GUERNSEY is 80 miles north of Cheyenne on the North Platte River.

CAMP GUERNSEY, near the town of Guernsey, was first used in the early 1930s as a maneuver area for troops stationed at Fort Francis E. Warren. Between 1937 and 1940 the site was converted into a camp for the Wyoming National Guard. The Army used the camp during WW II as a training site for quartermaster troops from Fort Francis E. Warren and, at one time, considered turning it into a branch of the Disciplinary Barracks. The latter, however, never materialized. After the war the Wyoming National Guard took up residence at the camp.

POWELL is in NW Wyoming 60 miles east of

Some of the WW II items on display at the Frances E. Warren Air Force Base Museum.

These are some of the camp's original buildings that remain at the Heart Mountain Relocation Camp site. The building in the distance was the camp's power plant.

These desks, on display at the Homesteader Museum in Powell, were used in the school at the Heart Mountain Relocation Camp.

Yellowstone National Park. On Feb. 22, 1945 remnants of a Japanese bombing balloon were found near the town. The same day, balloon remnants were also found at Kirby, 75 miles to the SE of Powell and at Glendo in the SE part of the state 28 miles SE of Douglas.

HEART MOUNTAIN RELOCATION CAMP: This was one of the relocation camps built in 1942 to house the ethnic Japanese who were evacuated from the U.S. west coast. The camp was 9 miles SW of Powell on US 14 Alt. at the foot of Heart Mountain, a local landmark. The camp was run by the War Relocation Administration (WRA) and opened in Sept. 1942. The camp was built on land that was being converted into irrigated farm land under a Federally funded project known as the Heart Mountain Irrigation Division. Residents arrived at the camp in large numbers during the latter part of 1942 and soon afterwards the camp reached its peak population of 11,100 residents. Most of the residents were from the Los Angeles area. This number steadily declined as residents left the camp for various reasons. In Sept. 1943 903 residents left en masse for Camp Tule, CA after that camp had been designated a facility for troublemakers and renunciants. Over 100 young men left the camp in early 1944 to join the U.S. Army when volunteers were being sought for the 442 Regimental Combat Group[2]. The remaining residents worked in agriculture during the season and in hotels, restaurants, on road gangs and the railroads other times.

In Jan. 1945 the WRA announced that all of the ethnic Japanese could leave all of the camps. That summer most of the residents of Heart Mountain departed and returned to their homes. The last residents left the camp in Nov. 1945 and the camp was soon closed. Several months later the camp's assets were sold and many of the buildings were purchased by local citizens and moved to new locations. There is a network of good roads in the area and the camp site can easily be toured by car. There is a small roadside park on U.S. 14 Alt. with

[2]Twenty of the men from the camp were killed in action.

plaques telling about the camp which is now on the National Register of Historic Places.

HOMESTEADER MUSEUM, in Powell, records local history and has displays on the Heart Mountain Relocation Camp of WW II. Address: 1st & Coulter Ave. (U.S. 14 Alt.), Powell, WY 82435. Phone: 307/754-9481. Hours: May through Aug. Tues.-Sat. 1-5, rest of year 10-12 and 1-5. Free.

SHERIDAN is in the north-central part of the state on I-90.

WYOMING ARMY NATIONAL GUARD ARMORY, just south of Sheridan, has a small museum with displays relating to the Wyoming Army National Guard and its history. Quite a few of the displays concern the Guard's activities during WW II and include uniforms, flags, small arms, captured enemy equipment, photos, drawing and more. Address: 3219 Coffeen Ave. (U.S. 87 South), Sheridan, WY 82801. Phone: 307/672-6442. Hours: Daily 7:30-4:30. Free.

THERMOPOLIS is near the center of the state on U.S. 20 and SR. 120.

At about 6 pm on the evening of Dec. 6, 1944 three people at a coal mine about 15 miles SW of town and a sheep herder in a nearby pasture heard an explosion and looked up to see what they believed to be a parachute descending into a draw several hundred yards from the mine. The sheriff, some local citizens and an Army investigator from Casper Army Air Field investigated the incident and discovered bomb fragments, metal parts and sections of a very large paper bag. These mysterious items were taken to Casper AAF for examination where it was determined that the bomb was not of U.S. manufacture. The items were then send on to the Navy's Technical Air Intelligence Center at U.S. Naval Air Station, Anacostia, Washington,

DC for further analysis, and then on the Naval Research Laboratory. Meanwhile the local people and newspapers speculated on the origin of the bomb. Although no airplane was heard or seen it was believed by most people that the bomb was dropped, perhaps accidentally, from an airplane. Two local newspapers reported on the incident. The mystery of the bomb and the large paper bag remained an enigma for some time until the Naval Research Laboratory had accumulated enough evidence from similar discoveries being made throughout the west to conclude that the items found at Thermopolis were the fragments of a Japanese high explosive shell, and that the metal parts and paper bag were parts of a large Japanese bombing balloons that had carried the bomb to Wyoming from Japan. As it turned out, the discovery of the Japanese bombing balloon remnants at Thermopolis was the fourth such find of its kind in the nation and the reports by the two newspapers were the first published reports of the balloons in the U.S.

This collage of captured enemy flags is on display at the Wyoming Army National Guard Armory in Sheridan.

INDEX

Campbell, Camp, ... 99
Canal Park Visitors Center &
Marine Museum 134
Canby, Fort, ... 275
Cannon Air Force Base 165
Cape Hatteras National Seashore
Museum of the Sea 182
Capehart, Senator Homer, ... 82
Capital Hilton Hotel 52
Capitol City Airport 212
Carlisle Barracks 211
Carlson, Brigidier Evans F., ... 271 (grave site)
Carnegie Science Center 217
Carney, Adm. Robert, ... 89
Carson, Camp 42
Carswell Air Force Base 240
Casement Museum, The, ... 262
Casey, Fort, ... 285
Castle Air Museum 24
Caswell, Fort, ... 181
Cat Island War Dog Center 138
Caven Point Army Base 161
CCC Museum 133
CEC/Seabee Museum 26
Chaffee, Camp 8
Champlin Fighter Museum 6
Chandler, A. B. "Happy", ... 97
Chandler, Douglas, ... 76
Charleston Army Depot 224
Charleston Navy Yard 123
Charleston Port of Embarkation 224
Chemical, Camp, ... 248
Chennault, Col. John S., ... 148
Chennault, Gen. Clair, ... 103, 148, 234, 271 (grave site)
Chester Tank Depot 214
Cheyenne Airport 291
Chicago Municipal Airport 77
Chickasha Airport 198
Chrysler, Walter P., ... 176
Church, Fort, ... 219
Churchill, Winston, ... 46, 64, 68, 89, 141, 164, 169, 212
Churchill Memorial & Library, Winston, ... 141
Citadel, The, ... 224
Citadel Museum, The, ... 224
Civil Air Patrol Headquarters 173
Clairborne, Camp, ... 102
Clark, Camp, ... 144
Clark, Fort, ... 242
Clark, Gen. Mark, ... 78, 89, 102, 224
Clark, Senator Bennet Champ, ... 141
Clark, Thomas C., ... 234
Clark County Heritage Museum 154
Clatsop, Camp, ... 201
Clay Grave Site, Gen. Lucius, ... 179
Cleveland Municipal Airport 192
Clewiston Airport (Riddle Field) 57
Clinch #3, Fort, ... 58
Clinton County Historical Museum 90
Clipper, Camp 12
Coast Artillery Museum 278
Coast Guard Memorial Park 131
Coast Guard Museum, Northwest 280
Cochran, Jacqueline, ... 235, 246
Coleman Warbird Museum 238
Coles, Camp, ... 162
Columbia, Fort, ... 275
Columbia Municipal Airport 225
Columbia River Maritime Museum 202
"Columbus", German Ocean Liner 189
Columbus General Depot 193
Columbus Municipal Airport 82
Combat Air Museum 96
Company of Military Historians, The 48
Confederate Air Force and American Heritage
Airpower Museum 248
Confederate Air Force Flying Museum 237
Confederate Research Center &
Audie Murphy Gun Museum 246
Connelly, Tom, ... 234
Constitution, Fort, ... 158
Cooke, Camp 15
Coolidge, President, ... 178
Corpus Christi Museum of
Science & Industry 239
Coxcomb, Camp 12
Cradle of Aviation Museum 175
Crockett, Fort, ... 244
Croft, Camp, ... 226
Crook, Fort George, ... 152
Crowder, Camp, ... 142
√CRYSTAL CITY TX 168, 240
Cruisers:
"Amsterdam" 259; "Beloxi" 138; "Birmingham" 259; "Duluth" 259; "Helena" 148; "Houston" 259; "Indianapolis" 86; "Juneau I" 91; "Juneau II" 262; "Little Rock" 171; "Minneapolis" 275; "Mobile" 2, 259; "Nagara" (Japanese) 171; "Nashville" 275; "New Orleans" 275; "Pittsburgh" 275; "Portland" 109; "Portsmouth" 259; "St. Louis" 259; "San Francisco" 31, 122; "Savannah" 72; "Tuscaloosa" 109; "Vicksburg" 259; "Vincennes" 89; "Wichita" 109, 275.
Curtis Air Field 237
Curtiss, Glenn, ... 30
Curtiss-Steinburg Field (Parks Airport) 78
Custer, Fort, ... 126
Custis, Fort John, ... 258
Dade, Fort, ... 65
Daggett Municipal Airport 11
Darby, General William O., ... 8
Darby House, The 8
David, Camp, ... 115, 133
Davis, Camp, ... 186
Davis, Elmer, ... 82
Davis, Gen. Benjamin O., (grave site) 271
Dawes, Fort, ... 122
Dayton Municipal Airport 193
De Soto, Fort, ... 65
Dearborn, Fort, ... 158
DeGaulle, Gen. Charles, ... 212
Dekalb-Peachtree Airport 68
Delaware and DuPont, Forts 49
Dells Duck Tours 290
Dennison Railroad Museum 195
Des Moines, Fort, ... 90
Des Moines Municipal Airport 90
Des Plaines, Camp, ... 79
Desert Training Center
(See California/Arizona Maneuver Area)
Destroyers:
"Barry" 54; Evans" 2; "Joseph P. Kennedy, Jr." 124; "Kidd" 103; "Knapp" 202; "Laffey" 224; "Stewart" 245; "Sullivan Brothers" 91, 171; "Ward" 135; "Cassin Young" 122, 123.
Detrick, Fort, ... 114
Devens, Fort, ... 120
Devers, Gen. Jacob L., ... 210
Dewey, Thomas E., ... 169, 178 (grave site), 191, 248
Dewitt, General John, ... 32, 255, 274
Dickson State Park, Johnathon, ... 67
Dies, Senator Martin, ... 234
Dirksen, Everett McKinley, ... 76
Dix, Fort, ... 163
Dix Museum, Fort, ... 163
Dobbins Air Force Base 68
Dodge, Camp, ... 90
Donovan, Wm J. "Wild Bill", ... 71(grave site)
Doolittle, General James, ... 13, 20, 26, 29, 33, 36, 66, 111, 115, 135, 141, 207, 283
Douglas, Donald, ... 29
Douglas, Fort, ... 255
Douglas Aircraft Co. and Clover Field 21
Douglas Military Museum, Fort, ... 256
Dover Air Force Base Historical Center 49
Drum, Fort, ... 179
Drum, Gen. Hugh A., ... 174, 179
Du Pont de Nemours & Co. Powder Plant,
Carneys Point, E.I 159
Dugway Proving Ground 253
Dulles Grave Site, Allen W., ... 113
Dumbarton Oaks 51
Durbin Airport 71
Duvall, Fort, ... 122
Dyess Air Force Base 235
Dyess Air Park 235
Eager, Gen. John M., ... 177
Eaker, Gen. Ira, ... 89, 234
Eaker Air Force Base 8
Eastern California Museum of Inyo County 22
Edison, Camp, ... 162
Edwards, Camp, ... 124
Edwards Air Force Base 24
Eighth Air Force Museum 106
Eisenhower, Gen. (Pres.) Dwight D., ... 21, 43, 44, 52, 53, 64, 89, 92 (grave site), 102, 106, 115, 121, 155, 194, 212, 228, 234, 242, 248, 253, 264, 269, 288,
Eisenhower, Mamie Doud, .. 89, 92 (grave site)
Eisenhower Birthplace, Mamie Doud, ... 89
Eisenhower Birthplace State Historical Site 242
Eisenhower Center, The, ... 92
Eisenhower Highway, Dwight D., ... 253
Eisenhower National Historic Site 212
Eisenhower State Recreation Area 242
El Paso Municipal Airport 244
Elliott, Camp 28
Ellis, Camp, ... 79
Ellis Island 173
Ellsworth Air Force Base 228
Elmira Holding and Reconsignment Point 171
Emory, Fort 28
England Air Force Base 102
Erie Proving Ground 196
Erwin Air Force Auxiliary Field 10
Ethyl Corporation Shelling 181
Eustis, Fort, ... 260
Evans, Camp, ... 162
Evansville Municipal Airport 84
Evansville Shipyard 84
Experimental Aircraft Association Aviation
Center and Air Museum 290
Experimental Aircraft Association Education
Center 60
Fairchild Air Force Base 282
Fairchild Air Force Base Museum 282
Fairfield Air Depot 193
Fannin, Camp, ... 252
Farley, James A., ... 169
Fermi, Enrico, ... 77 (grave site), 78
First Cavalry Division Museum 252
First Division Monument 55
First Division Museum 77
Fisher, Fort, ... 182
Flagler, Fort, ... 278

SPECIAL NOTE

Museums, memorials, monuments, homes, warships and other sites that are open to the public and welcome visitors are highlighted by a tint bar behind the first line of text.